iOS
Apprentice

Third Edition

By Matthijs Hollemans

iOS Apprentice (Third Edition) Updated for Swift 1.2

by Matthijs Hollemans

Copyright ©2015 Razeware LLC.

Notice of Rights

Notice of Liability

Trademarks

ISBN: 978-1-942878-02-5

Table of Contents

Preface

By Ray Wenderlich

"Only the foolish learn from experience — the wise learn from the experience of others."
—*Romanian Proverb*

As an iOS developer and gamer, I like to think of learning iOS development as a massive quest. You start out as a young adventurer with dreams of making your own hit app, and come across many obstacles and challenges along the way. As long as you keep practicing and persisting, you will eventually reach the goal of mastery – the only question is how long your journey will take.

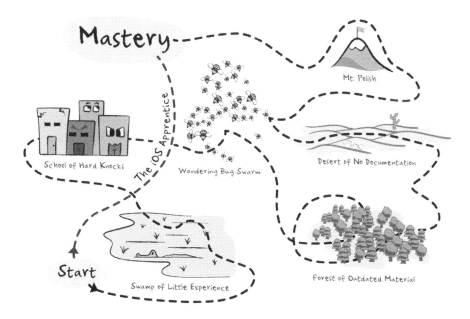

In *The iOS Apprentice*, you get to learn from one of the very best – Matthijs Hollemans. Matthijs has been developing apps and teaching about iOS since the very beginning, and has a knack for making complicated programming topics easy and fun to understand.

In each tutorial, Matthijs teaches you how to make a complete (and practical) iOS app, that is up-to-date with the latest version of Xcode, iOS, and best practices. There's a lot less stumbling around in the dark – Matthijs is there by your side, every step of the way.

The iOS Apprentice is the kind of guide I wish I had when I was first getting started with iOS development. As a practical kind of guy, I love how the series gets you making apps right away – teaching you theory just as you need it. This lets you see results right away, build confidence, and have hands-on practice building something that works. By the time you are done with your apprenticeship, you'll be able to stand on your own two feet and release your own apps to the App Store!

So whether you are a complete beginner to programming or an experienced developer looking to get into the world of iOS development, get ready to learn from Matthijs's wealth of experience, and begin your epic adventure!

— Ray Wenderlich from www.raywenderlich.com

Introduction

In this book you will learn how to make your own iPhone and iPad apps with Apple's new Swift programming language, through a series of four epic-length hands-on tutorials. Everybody likes games, so you'll start with building a simple but fun iPhone game named *Bull's Eye*. It will teach you the basics of iPhone programming, and the other tutorials will build on what you learn there.

Each tutorial in this book describes a new app in full detail, and together they cover everything you need to know to make your own apps. By the end of the book you'll be experienced enough to turn your ideas into real apps that you can sell on the App Store!

Even if you've never programmed before or if you're new to iOS, you should be able to follow along with the step-by-step instructions and understand how these apps are made. Each tutorial has a ton of illustrations to prevent you from getting lost. Not everything might make sense right away, but hang in there and all will become clear in time.

Writing your own iPhone and iPad apps is a lot of fun, but it's also hard work. If you have the imagination and perseverance there is no limit to what you can make these cool devices do. It is my sincere belief that these tutorials can turn you from a complete newbie into an accomplished iOS developer, but you do have to put in the time and effort. By writing these tutorials I've done my part, now it's up to you...

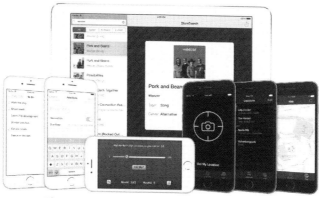

The apps you'll be making in *The iOS Apprentice*

About this book

The iOS Apprentice will help you become an excellent iOS developer, but only if you let it. Here are some tips that will help you get the most out of this book.

Learn through repetition

You're going to make a lot of apps in this book. Even though the apps will start out quite simple, you may find the tutorials hard to follow at first – especially if you've never done any computer programming before – because I will be introducing a lot of new concepts.

It's OK if you don't understand everything right away, as long as you get the general idea. In the subsequent tutorials from this book you'll go over many of these concepts again until they solidify in your mind.

Follow the instructions yourself

It is important that you not just read the instructions but also actually **follow them**. Open Xcode, type in the source code fragments, and run the app in the Simulator. This helps you to see how the app gets built step by step.

Even better, play around with the code. Feel free to modify any part of the app and see what the results are. Experiment and learn! Don't worry about breaking stuff – that's half the fun. You can always find your way back to the beginning.

Don't panic – bugs happen!

You will run into problems, guaranteed. Your programs will have strange bugs that will leave you stumped. Trust me, I've been programming for nearly 30 years and that still happens to me too. We're only humans and our brains have a limited capacity to deal with complex programming problems.

In this course, I will give you tools for your mental toolbox that will allow you to find your way out of any hole you have dug for yourself.

Understanding beats copy-pasting

Too many people attempt to write iPhone apps by blindly copy-pasting code that they find on blogs and other websites, without really knowing what that code does or how it should fit into their program.

There is nothing wrong with looking on the web for solutions – I do it all the time – but I want to give you the instruments and knowledge to understand what you're doing and why. That way you'll learn quicker and write better programs.

This is hands-on practical advice, not just a bunch of dry theory (although we can't avoid *some* theory). You are going to build real apps right from the start and I'll explain how everything works along the way, with lots of pictures that clearly illustrate what is going on. I will do my best to make it clear how everything fits together, why we do things a certain way, and what the alternatives are.

Do the exercises

I will also ask you to do some thinking of your own – yes, there are exercises! It's in your best interest to actually do these exercises. There is a big difference between knowing the path and walking the path... And the only way to learn programming is to do it.

I encourage you to not just do the exercises but also to play with the code you'll be writing. Experiment, make changes, try to add new features. Software is a complex piece of machinery and to find out how it works you sometimes have to put some spokes in the wheels and take the whole thing apart. That's how you learn!

Have fun!

Last but not least, remember to have fun! Step by step you will build up your understanding of programming while making fun apps. By the end of the book you'll have learned the essentials of Swift and the iOS development kit. More importantly, you should have a pretty good idea of how everything goes together and how to think like a programmer.

It is my aim that after these tutorials you will have learned enough to stand on your own two feet as a developer. I am confident that eventually you'll be able to write any iOS app you want as long as you get those basics down. You still may have a lot to learn, but when you're through with *The iOS Apprentice*, you can do without the training wheels.

Introducing the third edition

You are holding a brand new third edition of *The iOS Apprentice*, fully revised for iOS 8 and the new Swift programming language.

It's been four years since I wrote the first edition of this book. That was for iOS version 4.3 – then state-of-the-art, now a relic. Times certainly have changed, and the book has been continually updated to keep up with each new version of Xcode and iOS.

With the introduction of Swift, the choice was obvious: the "apprentice" simply had to be rewritten to take advantage of this new programming language. This is the biggest change to the book yet!

Swift is considered to be easier to learn than the old language, Objective-C, which used to scare off beginners with its strange syntax and quirky nature. Objective-C is not really that bad once you get used to it, but there's no doubt that Swift is a lot nicer.

Apple's own book on Swift is not very beginner-friendly, so it only made sense that we apply the proven formula from *The iOS Apprentice* to Swift in this new edition of the book. Apple believes that Swift lets everyone build amazing apps, and we believe that *The iOS Apprentice* is the best place to get started.

Every single line of text and code in this book was revised and updated for Swift. Entire portions that were relevant only to Objective-C were thrown out, and replaced with explanations of Swift's sparkly new features.

All tutorials were also updated to be compatible with iOS 8, using new APIs where possible.

If you've read the previous Objective-C edition of this book, you'll benefit from going through it again and looking at how the same problems are solved with this wonderful new language. You'll be surprised at how much more expressive Swift is!

Who this book is for

This book is great whether you are completely new to programming, or whether you come from a different programming background and are looking to learn iOS development.

If you're a complete beginner, don't worry – this book doesn't assume you know anything about programming or making apps. Of course, if you do have programming experience, that helps. Swift is a new programming language but in many ways it's similar to other popular languages such as PHP, C#, or Java.

If you've tried iOS development before with the old language, Objective-C, then its low-level nature and strange syntax may have put you off. Well, there's good news: now that we have a modern language in Swift, iOS development has become a lot easier to pick up.

It is not my aim with this book to teach you all the ins and outs of iPhone and iPad development. The iOS SDK (Software Development Kit) is huge and there is no way we can cover everything – but fortunately we don't need to. You just need to master the essential building blocks of Swift and the iOS SDK. Once you understand these fundamentals, you can easily find out by yourself how the other parts of the SDK work and learn the rest on your own terms.

The most important thing I'll be teaching you, is how to think like a programmer. That will help you approach any programming task, whether it's a game, a utility, a web service, or anything else you can imagine.

As a programmer you'll often have to think your way through difficult computational problems and find creative solutions. By methodically analyzing these problems you will be able to solve them, no matter how complex. Once you possess this valuable skill, you can program anything!

iOS 8 and better only

Things move fast in the world of mobile computing. The iPhone 5 is only a few years old but is quickly becoming obsolete. Even iOS version 6, which was released just in 2012, already looks old-fashioned.

The tutorials in this book are aimed exclusively at iOS version 8 and later. Each new release of iOS is such a big departure from previous versions that it just doesn't make sense anymore to keep developing for them.

The majority of iPhone, iPod touch, and iPad users are pretty quick to upgrade to the latest version of iOS anyway, so you don't need to be too worried that you're leaving potential users behind.

Owners of older devices, such as the iPhone 4 or 3GS, may be stuck with iOS version 7.1 or earlier but this is only a tiny portion of the market. The cost of supporting these older iOS versions with your apps is usually greater than the handful of extra customers it brings you.

It's ultimately up to you to decide whether it's worth making your app available to customers with older devices, but my recommendation is that you focus your efforts where they matter most. Apple as a company always relentlessly looks towards the future and if you want to play in Apple's backyard, it's wise to follow their lead. So back to the future it is!

What you need

It's a lot of fun to develop for the iPhone and iPad but like most hobbies (or businesses!) it will cost some money. Of course, once you get good at it and build an awesome app, you'll have the potential to make that money back many times.

You will have to invest in the following:

- **An iPhone, iPad, or iPod touch.** I'm assuming that you have at least one of these. Even though I mostly talk about the iPhone in this book, everything I say applies equally to all of these devices. Aside from small hardware differences, they all use iOS and you program them in exactly the same way. You should be able to run any of the apps you will be developing on your iPad or iPod touch without problems.

- **A Mac computer with an Intel processor.** Any Mac that you've bought in the last few years will do, even a Mac mini or MacBook Air. It needs to have at least OS X 10.10 Yosemite. Xcode, the development environment for iOS apps, is a memory-hungry tool so having at least 4 GB of RAM in your Mac is no luxury. You might be able to get by with less, but do yourself a favor and upgrade your Mac. The more RAM, the better. A smart developer invests in good tools!

- **A paid iOS Developer Program account.** This will cost you $99 per year and it allows you to run your apps on your own iPhone, iPad, or iPod touch while you're developing, and to submit finished apps to the App Store. You can download all the development tools for free if you're a paid member, including beta previews of upcoming versions of iOS.

With some workarounds it is possible to develop iOS apps on Windows or a Linux machine, or a regular PC that has OS X installed (a so-called "Hackintosh"), but you'll save yourself a lot of hassle by just getting a Mac.

If you can't afford to buy the latest model, then consider getting a second-hand Mac from eBay. Just make sure it meets the minimum requirements (Intel CPU, preferably more than 1 GB RAM). Should you happen to buy a machine that has an older version of OS X (10.8 Mountain Lion or earlier), you can upgrade to the latest version of OS X from the online Mac App Store for free or a small fee.

Join the program

To sign up for the Developer Program, go to developer.apple.com/programs/ios and click the **Enroll Now** button.

Tip: Make sure you're on the page for the iOS program. There are also Mac and Safari developer programs and you don't want to sign up for the wrong one!

On the sign-up page you'll need to enter your Apple ID. Your developer program membership will be tied to this account. It's OK to use the same Apple ID that you're already using with iTunes and your iPhone, but if you run a business you might want to create a new Apple ID to keep these things separate.

There are different types of iOS Developer Programs. You'll probably want to go for the regular iOS Developer Program, either as an Individual or as a Company. There is also an Enterprise program but that's for big companies who will be distributing apps within their own organization only. If you're still in school, the University Program may be worth looking into.

You buy the Developer Program membership from the online Apple Store for your particular country. Once your payment is processed you'll receive an activation code that you use to activate your account.

Signing up is usually pretty quick. In the worst case it may take a few weeks, as Apple will check your credit card details and if they find anything out of the ordinary (such as a misspelled name) your application may run into delays. So make sure to enter your credit card details correctly or you'll be in for an agonizing wait.

If you're signing up as a Company then you also need to provide a D-U-N-S Number, which is free but may take some time to request. You cannot register as a Company if you have a single-person business such as a sole proprietorship or DBA ("doing business as"). In that case you need to sign up as an Individual.

You will have to renew your membership every year but if you're serious about developing apps then that $99/year will be worth it.

The free account

If you're strapped for cash, you'll be happy to know that it's possible to develop for iOS without paying a dime. There is a free Apple developer account but this restricts you to running your apps in the Simulator only. You cannot run the apps on any of your devices and, more importantly, you can't submit to the App Store.

If you just want to get your feet wet with iOS development but you're not sure yet whether you'll like it, then stick to the free account for the time being. You can run all the apps from this tutorial in the Simulator just fine, but of course that isn't as cool as seeing them on your own iPhone.

To sign up for the free account, go to developer.apple.com/register/. You can always upgrade to the paid account later.

Xcode

After you sign up, the first order of business is to download and install Xcode and the iOS SDK (Software Development Kit).

Xcode is the main development tool for iOS. It has a text editor where you'll type in your source code and it has a visual tool for designing your app's user interface.

Xcode transforms the source code that you write into an executable app and launches it in the Simulator or on your iPhone. Because no app is bug-free, Xcode also has a debugger that helps you find defects in your code (unfortunately, it won't automatically fix them for you, that's still something you have to do yourself).

You can download Xcode for free from the Mac App Store (http://itunes.apple.com/app/xcode/id497799835?mt=12). This requires at least OS X Yosemite (10.10), so if you're still running OS X Mavericks or even Mountain Lion you'll first have to upgrade to the latest version of OS X (also available for free from the Mac App Store). Get ready for a big download, as the full Xcode package is about 2 GB.

Important: You may already have a version of Xcode on your system that came pre-installed with OS X. That version is hopelessly outdated so don't use it. Apple puts out new releases on a regular basis and you are encouraged to always develop with the latest Xcode and the latest available SDK on the latest version of OS X.

I wrote the latest revision of this book with **Xcode version 6.3** and the **iOS 8.3** SDK on OS X Yosemite (10.10). By the time you're reading this the version numbers have no doubt gone up again. Don't panic if the screenshots don't correspond 100% to what you see on your screen. In most cases the differences will be minor.

Many older books and blog posts (anything before 2010) talk about Xcode 3, which is radically different from Xcode 6. More recent material may mention Xcode versions 4 or 5, which at first glance are similar to Xcode 6 but differ in many of the details. So if you're reading an article and you see a picture of Xcode that looks different from yours, they're talking about an older version. You may still be able to get something out of those articles, as the programming examples are still valid. It's just the tool that is slightly different.

What's ahead: an overview

The *iOS Apprentice* is split into four tutorials, moving from beginning to intermediate topics. In each tutorial you will build a complete app, from scratch! Let's take a look at what's ahead.

Tutorial 1: Getting Started

In the first tutorial in the book, you'll start off by building a game called *Bull's Eye*. In the process, you'll learn how to use Xcode, Interface Builder, and Swift in an easygoing manner.

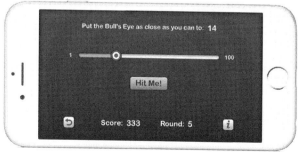

Tutorial 2: Checklists

In the second tutorial, you'll create your own to-do list app. You'll learn about the fundamental design patterns that all iOS apps use, and about table views, navigation controllers and delegates. Now you're making apps for real!

Tutorial 3: MyLocations

In the third tutorial, you'll develop a location-aware app that lets you keep a list of spots that you find interesting. In the process, you'll learn about Core Location, Core Data, Map Kit, and much more!

Tutorial 4: StoreSearch

Mobile apps often need to talk to web services and that's what you'll do in this final tutorial of the book. You'll make a stylish app that lets you search for products on the iTunes store using HTTP requests and JSON.

Let's get started and turn you into a real iOS developer!

Book source code and forums

You can get the source code for the book here:

http://www.raywenderlich.com/store/ios-apprentice/source-code

We've also set up an official forum for the book at raywenderlich.com/forums. This is a great place to ask any questions you have about the book or about making iOS apps in general, or to submit any errata you may find.

We hope to see you on the forums! ☺

PDF Version

We also have a PDF version of this book available, which can be handy if you ever want to copy/paste code or search for a specific term through the book as you're developing.

And speaking of the PDF version, we have some good news!

Since you purchased the physical copy of this book, you are eligible to buy the PDF version at a significant discount if you would like (if you don't have it already). For more details, see this page:

http://www.raywenderlich.com/store/ios-apprentice/upgrade

About the author

 **Matthijs Hollemans** is a mystic who lives at the top of a mountain where he spends all of his days and nights coding up awesome apps.

Actually he lives below sea level in the Netherlands and is pretty down-to-earth, but he does spend too much time in Xcode.

Check out his website at www.matthijshollemans.com.

Tutorial 1: Getting Started

The iPhone may pretend that it's a phone but it's really a pretty advanced computer that also happens to make phone calls.

Like any computer, the iPhone works with ones and zeros. When you write software to run on the iPhone, you somehow have to translate the ideas in your head into those ones and zeros that the computer can understand.

Fortunately, you don't have to write any ones and zeros yourself. That would be a bit too much to ask of the human brain. On the other hand, everyday English is not precise enough to use for programming computers.

You will use an intermediary language, *Swift*, that is a little bit like English so it's reasonably straightforward for us humans to understand, while at the same time it can be easily translated into something the computer can understand as well.

This is the language that the computer speaks:

```
Ltmp96:
    .cfi_def_cfa_register %ebp
    pushl   %esi
    subl    $36, %esp
Ltmp97:
    .cfi_offset %esi, -12
    calll   L7$pb
L7$pb:
    popl    %eax
    movl    16(%ebp), %ecx
    movl    12(%ebp), %edx
    movl    8(%ebp), %esi
    movl    %esi, -8(%ebp)
    movl    %edx, -12(%ebp)
    movl    %ecx, (%esp)
    movl    %eax, -24(%ebp)
    calll   _objc_retain
    movl    %eax, -16(%ebp)
    .loc    1 161 2 prologue_end
```

Actually, what the computer sees is this:

```
00011001010011110100100011001111110010100
00101000100111101011011100111010110110101001
01010001110011111010111011000011100011010
10010000011100010100110100111110011001111
```

The `movl` and `calll` instructions are just there to make things more readable for humans. Well, I don't know about you, but for me it's still hard to make much sense out of it.

It certainly is possible to write programs in that arcane language – that is what people used to do in the old days when computers cost a few million bucks apiece and took up a whole room – but I'd rather write programs that look like this:

```
func handleMusicEvent(command: Int, noteNumber: Int, velocity: Int) {
  if command == NoteOn && velocity != 0 {
    playNote(noteNumber + transpose, velocityCurve[velocity] / 127)

  } else if command == NoteOff || (command == NoteOn && velocity == 0) {
    stopNote(noteNumber + transpose, velocityCurve[velocity] / 127)

  } else if command == ControlChange {
    if noteNumber == 64 {
      damperPedal(velocity)
    }
  }
}
```

The above snippet is from a sound synthesizer program. It looks like something that almost makes sense. Even if you've never programmed before, you can sort of figure out what's going on. It's almost English.

Swift is a hot new language that combines traditional object-oriented programming with aspects of functional programming. Fortunately, Swift has many things in common with other popular programming languages, so if you're already familiar with C#, Python, Ruby, or JavaScript you'll feel right at home with Swift.

Swift is not the only option for making apps. Until recently, iPhone and iPad apps were programmed in Objective-C, which is an object-oriented extension of the tried-and-true C language. Because of its heritage, Objective-C has some rough edges and is not really up to the demands of modern developers. That's why Apple created a new language.

Objective-C will still be around for a while but it's obvious that the future of iOS development is Swift. All the cool kids are using it already.

C++ is another language that adds object-oriented programming to C. It is very powerful but as a beginning programmer you probably want to stay away from it. I only mention it because C++ can also be used to write iOS apps, and there is an unholy marriage of C++ and Objective-C named Objective-C++ that you may come across from time to time.

I could have started *The iOS Apprentice* with an in-depth treatise on the features of Swift but you'd probably fall asleep halfway. So instead I will explain the language as we go along, very briefly at first but more in-depth later.

In the beginning, the general concepts – what is a variable, what is an object, how do you call a method, and so on – are more important than the details. Slowly but surely, all the secrets of the Swift language will be revealed to you.

Are you ready to begin writing your first iOS app?

The Bull's Eye game

In this first lesson you're going to create a game called Bull's Eye.

This is what the game will look like when you're finished:

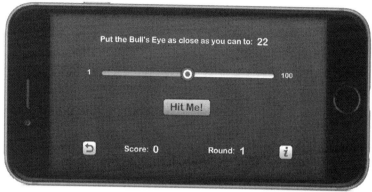

The finished Bull's Eye game

The objective of the game is to put the bull's eye, which is on a slider that goes from 1 to 100, as close to a randomly chosen target value as you can. In the screenshot above, the aim is to put the bull's eye at 44. Because you can't see the current value of the slider, you'll have to "eyeball" it.

When you're confident of your estimate you press the "Hit Me!" button and a popup, also known as an *alert*, will tell you what your score is:

An alert popup shows the score

The closer to the target value you are, the more points you score. After you dismiss the alert popup by pressing the OK button, a new round begins with a new random target. The game repeats until the player presses the "Start Over" button (the curly arrow in the bottom-left corner), which resets the score to 0.

This game probably won't make you an instant millionaire on the App Store, but even future millionaires have to start somewhere!

Making a programming to-do list

Exercise: Now that you've seen what the game will look like and what the gameplay rules are, make a list of all the things that you think you'll need to do in order to build this game. It's OK if you draw a blank, but give it a shot anyway. ■

I'll give you an example:

> *The app needs to put the "Hit Me!" button on the screen and show an alert popup when the user presses it.*

Try to think of other things the app needs to do – no matter if you don't actually know how to accomplish these tasks. The first step is to figure out *what* you need to do; *how* to do these things is not important yet.

Once you know what you want, you can also figure out how to do it, even if you have to ask someone or look it up. But the "what" comes first. (You'd be surprised at how many people start programming without a clear idea of what they're actually trying to achieve. No wonder they get stuck!)

Whenever I start working on a new app, I first make a list of all the different pieces of functionality I think the app will need. This becomes my programming to-do list. Having a list that breaks up a design into several smaller steps is a great way to deal with the complexity of a project.

You may have a cool idea for an app but when you sit down to write the program the whole thing can seem overwhelming. There is so much to do... and where to begin? By cutting up the workload into small steps you make the project less daunting – you can always find a step that is simple and small enough to make a good starting point and take it from there.

It's no big deal if this exercise is giving you difficulty. You're new to all of this! As your understanding grows of how software works, it will become easier to identify the different parts that make up a design, and to split it into manageable pieces.

This is what I came up with. I simply took the gameplay description and cut it into very small chunks:

- Put a button on the screen and label it "Hit Me!"

- When the player presses the Hit Me button the app has to show an alert popup to inform the player how well she did. Somehow you have to calculate the score and put that into this alert.

- Put text on the screen, such as the "Score:" and "Round:" labels. Some of this text changes over time, for example the score, which increases when the player scores points.

- Put a slider on the screen and make it go between the values 1 and 100.

- Read the value of the slider after the user presses the Hit Me button.

- Generate a random number at the start of each round and display it on the screen. This is the target value.

- Compare the value of the slider to that random number and calculate a score based on how far off the player is. You show this score in the alert popup.

- Put the Start Over button on the screen. Make it reset the score and put the player back into the first round.

- Put the app in landscape orientation.

- Make it look pretty. :-)

I might have missed a thing or two, but this looks like a decent list to start with. Even for a game as basic as this, there are already quite a few things you need to do. Making apps is fun but it's definitely a lot of work too!

The one-button app

Let's start at the top of the list and make an extremely simple first version of the game that just displays a single button. When you press the button, the app pops up an alert message. That's all you are going to do for now. Once you have this working, you can build the rest of the game on this foundation.

The app will look like this:

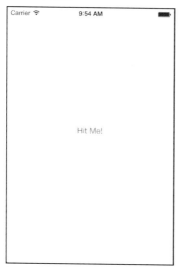 

The app contains a single button (left) that shows an alert when pressed (right)

Time to start coding! I'm assuming you have downloaded and installed the latest version of the SDK and the development tools at this point.

In this tutorial, you'll be working with **Xcode 6.3** or better. Newer versions of Xcode may also work but anything older than version 6.3 is a no-go.

Because Swift is a very new language, it tends to change between versions of Xcode. If your Xcode is too old – or too new! – then not all of the code in this book may work properly. (For this same reason you're advised not to use beta versions of Xcode, only the official one from the Mac App Store.)

➤ Launch Xcode. If you have trouble locating the Xcode application, you can find it in the folder **/Applications/Xcode** or in your Launchpad. Because I use Xcode all the time, I placed its icon in my dock for easy access.

Xcode shows the "Welcome to Xcode" window when it starts:

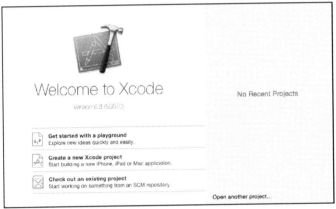

Xcode bids you welcome

Choose **Create a new Xcode project**. The main Xcode window appears with an assistant that lets you choose a template:

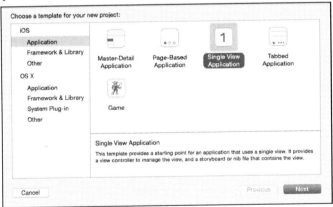

Choosing the template for the new project

There are templates for a variety of application styles. Xcode will make a pre-configured project for you based on the template you choose. The new project will already include many of the source files you need. These templates are handy because they can save you a lot of typing. They are ready-made starting points.

➤ Select **Single View Application** and press **Next**.

This opens a screen where you can enter options for the new app:

Configuring the new project

➤ Fill out these options as follows:

• Product Name: **BullsEye**. If you want to use proper English, you can name the project Bull's Eye instead of BullsEye, but it's best to avoid spaces and other special characters in project names.

• Organization Name: Fill in your own name here or the name of your company.

• Company Identifier: Mine says "com.razeware". That is the identifier I use for my apps and as is customary, it is my domain name written the other way around. You should use your own identifier here. Pick something that is unique to you, either the domain name of your website (but backwards) or simply your own name. You can always change this later.

• Language: **Swift**

• Devices: **iPhone**

• Use Core Data: Leave this unchecked.

Press **Next**. Now Xcode will ask where to save your project:

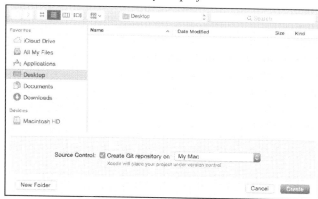

Choosing where to save the project

➤ Choose a location for the project files, for example the Desktop or your Documents folder.

Xcode will automatically make a new folder for the project using the Product Name that you entered in the previous step (in your case BullsEye), so you don't need to make a new folder yourself.

At the bottom of the window there is a checkbox that says, "Create Git repository on My Mac". You can ignore this for now. You'll learn about the Git version control system in one of the next tutorials.

➤ Press **Create** to finish.

Xcode will now create a new project named BullsEye, based on the Single View Application template, in the folder you specified.

When it is done, the screen looks like this:

The main Xcode window at the start of your project

There may be small differences with what you're seeing on your own computer if you're using a version of Xcode newer than 6.3. Rest assured, any differences will only be superficial.

Note: If you don't see a file named ViewController.swift in the list on the left but instead have ViewController.h and ViewController.m, then you picked the wrong language when you made the project (Objective-C). Start over and be sure to choose Swift as the programming language.

➤ Press the **Run** button in the top-left corner:

Press Run to launch the app

Note: If this is the first time you're using Xcode, it may ask you to enable developer mode. Click **Enable** and enter your password to allow Xcode to make these changes.

Xcode will labor for a bit and then it launches your brand new app in the iOS Simulator. The app may not look like much yet – and there is not anything you can do with it either – but this is an important first milestone in your journey.

What an app based on the Single View Application template looks like

If Xcode says "Build Failed" or "Xcode cannot run using the selected device" when you press the Run button, then make sure the picker at the top of the window says **BullsEye > iPhone 6** (or any other number) and not **iOS Device**:

Making Xcode run the app on the Simulator

If your iPhone is currently connected to your Mac with the USB cable, Xcode may have attempted to run the app on your iPhone and that may not work without some additional setting up. At the end of this tutorial I'll show you how to get the app to run on your iPhone so you can show it off to your friends, but for now just stick with the Simulator.

➤ Next to the Run button is the **Stop** button (the square thingy). Press that to exit the app.

You might be tempted to press the home button on the Simulator, just as you would on your iPhone (or choose the **Hardware → Home** menu item), but that won't actually terminate the app. It will disappear from the Simulator's screen but the app stays suspended in the Simulator's memory, just as it would on a real iPhone.

Until you press Stop, Xcode's activity viewer at the top says "Running BullsEye on iPhone 6":

The Xcode activity viewer

It's not really necessary to stop the app, as you can go back to Xcode and make changes to the source code while the app is still running. However, these changes will not become active until you press Run again. That will terminate any running version of the app, build a new version, and launch it in the Simulator.

What happens when you press Run?

Xcode will first *compile* your source code – that is: translate it – from Swift into a machine code that the iPhone (or the Simulator) can understand. Even though the programming language for writing iPhone apps is Swift or Objective-C, the iPhone itself doesn't speak those languages. A translation step is necessary.

The compiler is the part of Xcode that converts your Swift source code into executable binary code. It also gathers all the different components that make up the app – source files, images, storyboard files, and so on – and puts them into the so-called "application bundle".

This entire process is also known as *building* the app. If there are any errors (such as spelling mistakes), the build will fail. If everything goes according to plan, Xcode copies the application bundle to the Simulator or the iPhone and launches the app. All that from a single press of the Run button.

Adding the button

I'm sure you're as little impressed as I am with an app that just displays a dull white screen, so let's add a button to it.

The left-hand side of the Xcode window is named the **Navigator area**. The row of icons at the top determines which navigator is visible. Currently that is the **Project navigator**, which shows the list of files that are in your project.

The organization of these files roughly corresponds to the project folder on your hard disk, but that isn't necessarily always so. You can move files around and put them into new groups to your heart's content. We'll talk more about the different files that your project has later.

> In the **Project navigator**, find the item named **Main.storyboard** and click it once to select it:

The Project navigator lists the files in the project

Like a superhero changing his clothes in a phone booth, the main editing pane now transforms into the **Interface Builder**. This tool lets you drag-and-drop user interface components such as buttons into the app. (OK, bad analogy, but Interface Builder *is* a super tool in my opinion.)

➤ If it's not already blue, click the **Hide or show utilities** button in Xcode's toolbar:

Click this button to show the Utilities pane

These toolbar buttons change the appearance of Xcode. This one in particular opens a new pane on the right side of the Xcode window.

Your Xcode should now look something like this:

Editing Main.storyboard in Interface Builder

This is the *storyboard* for your app. The storyboard contains the designs for all of your app's screens, and shows how the app goes from one screen to another with big pointy arrows. Currently the storyboard contains just a single screen or *scene*.

This initial scene is represented by a square in the middle of the Interface Builder canvas. You may find this odd, considering that iPhones are not actually square.

This is a new feature of iOS 8 called "size classes" or "universal storyboards" that lets you design a single storyboard that caters to the different screen sizes of the various iPhone models. You won't need that for this app, so first you'll turn it off.

➤ In the Utilities pane on the right, select the first tab to open the **File inspector**:

Disabling the Use Size Classes option in the File inspector

➤ Uncheck the **Use Size Classes** option. When Xcode asks for confirmation, click **Disable Size Classes** to continue.

Now Interface Builder shows the dimensions of an actual iPhone device:

The scene is no longer square

The scene has the size of an iPhone 5s (and the 5 and 5c). To keep things simple, you will first design the app for the iPhone 5 screen. Later you'll also make the app fit on the smaller iPhone 4S and the larger iPhone 6 and 6 Plus.

➤ In the Xcode toolbar, select **BullsEye** > **iPhone 5s** to switch simulators:

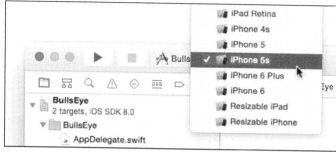

Switching the Simulator to iPhone 5s

Now when you run the app, it will run on the iPhone 5s Simulator, which is slightly smaller than the iPhone 6 (try it out!).

Back to the storyboard:

➤ At the bottom of the Utilities pane you will find the **Object Library** (make sure the third button, the one that looks like a circle, is selected):

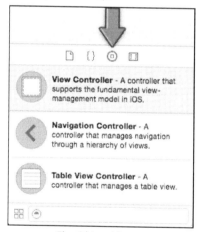

The Object Library

Scroll through the items in the Object Library's list until you see **Button**.

➤ Click on **Button** and drag it into the working area, on top of the white view.

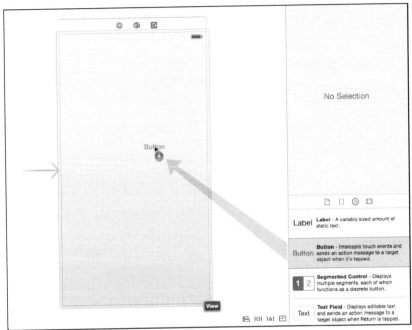

Dragging the button on top of the view

That's how easy it is to add new buttons, just drag & drop. That goes for all other user interface elements too. You'll be doing a lot of this, so take some time to get familiar with the process.

➤ Drag-and-drop a few other controls, such as labels, sliders, and switches, just to get the hang of it.

This should give you some idea of the UI controls that are available in iOS. Notice that the Interface Builder helps you to layout your controls by snapping them to the edges of the view and to other objects. It's a very handy tool!

➤ Double-click the button to edit its title. Call it **Hit Me!**

The button with the new title

As of iOS 7 buttons no longer have borders. If you've used previous versions of iOS then you no doubt have seen the standard "round rect" button, which had a thin gray border with rounded corners. One of the major features of the new flat design style from iOS 7 and 8 is that those borders are now gone, at least for the standard buttons.

When you're done playing with Interface Builder, press the Run button from Xcode's toolbar. The app should now appear in the Simulator, complete with your "Hit Me!" button. However, when you tap the button it doesn't do anything yet. For that you'll have to write some Swift code!

Xcode will autosave

You don't have to save your source code files after you make changes to them because Xcode will automatically save any modified files when you press the Run button. Nevertheless, Xcode isn't the most stable piece of software out there and occasionally it may crash on you before it has had a chance to save your changes, so I still like to press ⌘+S on a regular basis to save my files.

The source code editor

A button that doesn't do anything when tapped is of no use to anyone, so let's make it show an alert popup. In the finished game the alert will display the player's score, but for now we shall limit ourselves to a simple text message (the traditional "Hello, World!").

➤ In the **Project navigator**, click on **ViewController.swift**.

The Interface Builder will disappear and the editor area now contains a bunch of brightly colored text. This is the Swift source code for your app:

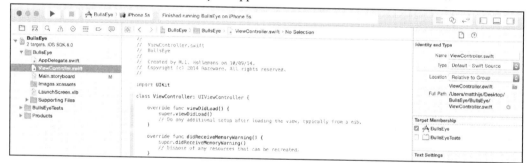

The source code editor

➤ Add the following lines directly above the very last } bracket in the file:

```
@IBAction func showAlert() {
}
```

The source code for **ViewController.swift** should now look like this:

```
//
//  ViewController.swift
//  BullsEye
//
//  Created by <you> on <date>.
//  Copyright (c) <year> <you>. All rights reserved.
//

import UIKit

class ViewController: UIViewController {

  override func viewDidLoad() {
    super.viewDidLoad()
    // Do any additional setup after loading the view, typically from a nib.
  }
```

```
override func didReceiveMemoryWarning() {
  super.didReceiveMemoryWarning()
  // Dispose of any resources that can be recreated.
}

@IBAction func showAlert() {
}
}
```

How do you like your first taste of Swift? Before I can tell you what this all means, I first have to introduce the concept of a view controller.

View controllers

You've edited the **Main.storyboard** file to build the user interface of the app. It's only a button on a white background, but a user interface nonetheless. You also just added source code to **ViewController.swift**.

These two files – the storyboard and the Swift file – together form the design and implementation of a *view controller*. A lot of the work in building iOS apps is making view controllers. The job of a view controller is to manage a single screen from your app.

Take a simple cookbook app, for example. When you launch the cookbook app, its main screen lists the available recipes. Tapping a recipe opens a new screen that shows the recipe in detail with an appetizing photo and cooking instructions. Each of these screens is managed by its own view controller.

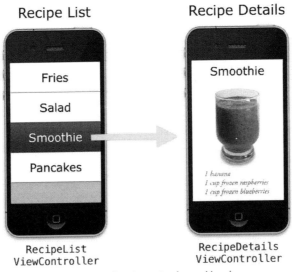

The view controllers in a simple cookbook app

What these two screens do is very different. One is a list of several items; the other presents a detail view of a single item.

That's why you also need two view controllers: one that knows how to deal with lists, and another that can handle images and cooking instructions. One of the design principles of iOS is that each screen in your app gets its own view controller.

Currently Bull's Eye has only one screen (the white one with the button on top) and thus only needs one view controller. That view controller is simply named ViewController and the storyboard and Swift file work together to implement it.

Simply put, the Main.storyboard file contains the design of the view controller's user interface, while ViewController.swift contains its functionality – the logic that makes the user interface work, written in the Swift language.

Because you used the Single View Application template, Xcode automatically created the view controller for you. Later you will add a second screen to the game and you will create your own view controller for that.

Making connections

The line of source code you have just added to ViewController.swift lets Interface Builder know that the controller has a "showAlert" action, which presumably will show an alert popup. You will now connect the button to that action.

➤ Click **Main.storyboard** to go back into Interface Builder.

There should be a pane on the left, the **Outline pane**, that lists all the items in your storyboard. If you do not see that pane, click the small toggle button in the bottom-left corner of the Interface Builder canvas to reveal it.

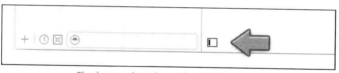

The button that shows the Outline pane

➤ Click the **Hit Me button** once to select it.

With the Hit Me button selected, hold down the **Ctrl** key, click on the button and drag up to the **View Controller** item in the Outline pane. You should see a blue line going from the button up to View Controller.

(Instead of holding down Ctrl, you can also right-click and drag, but don't let go of the mouse button before you start dragging.)

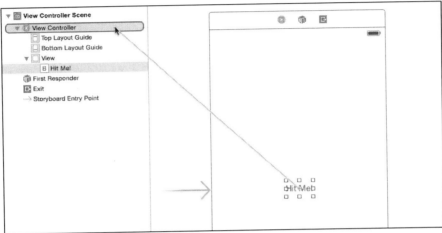

Ctrl-drag from the button to View Controller

Once you're on View Controller, let go of the mouse button and a small menu will appear. It contains two sections, "Action Segue" and "Sent Events", with one or more options below each. You're interested in the **showAlert** option under Sent Events. This is the name of the action that you added earlier in the source code of **ViewController.swift**.

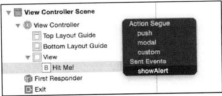

The popup menu with the showAlert action

➤ Click on **showAlert** to select it. This instructs Interface Builder to make a connection between the button and the line `@IBAction func showAlert()`.

From now on, whenever the button is tapped the `showAlert` action will be performed. That is how you make buttons and other controls do things: you define an action in the view controller's Swift file and then you make the connection in Interface Builder.

You can see that the connection was made, by going to the **Connections inspector** in the Utilities pane on the right side of the Xcode window.

➤ Click the small arrow-shaped button at the top of the pane to switch to the Connections inspector:

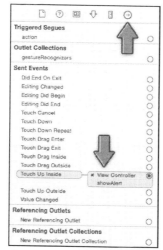

The inspector shows the connections from the button to any other objects

In the Sent Events section, the "Touch Up Inside" event is now connected to the `showAlert` action. You can also see the connection in the Swift file.

➤ Select **ViewController.swift** to edit it.

Notice how to the left of the line with `@IBAction func showAlert()`, there is a solid circle? Click on that circle to reveal what this action is connected to:

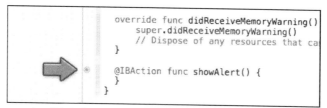

A solid circle means the action is connected to something

Acting on the button

You now have a screen with a button. The button is hooked up to an action named `showAlert` that will be performed when the user taps the button.

Currently, however, the action is empty and nothing will happen (try it out). You need to give the app more instructions.

➤ In **ViewController.swift**, add the following lines to `showAlert`:

```
@IBAction func showAlert() {
  let alert = UIAlertController(title: "Hello, World", message: "This is my first app!",
                           preferredStyle: .Alert)

  let action = UIAlertAction(title: "Awesome", style: .Default, handler: nil)

  alert.addAction(action)

  presentViewController(alert, animated: true, completion: nil)
}
```

These new lines provide the actual functionality of this action.

The commands between the { } brackets tell the iPhone what to do, and they are performed from top to bottom.

The code in showAlert creates an alert with a title "Hello, World", a message "This is my first app!", and a single button labeled "Awesome".

If you're not sure about the distinction between the title and the message: both show text, but the title is slightly bigger and in a bold typeface.

➤ Click the **Run** button from Xcode's toolbar. If you didn't make any typos, your app should launch in the Simulator and you should see the alert box when you tap the button.

Congratulations, you've just written your first iOS app! What you just did may have been mostly gibberish to you, but that shouldn't matter. We take it one small step at a time.

The alert popup in action

You can strike off the first two items from the to-do list already: putting a button on the screen and showing an alert when the user taps the button.

Take a little break, let it all sink in, and come back when you're ready for more! You're only just getting started...

> **Note:** Just in case you get stuck, I have provided the complete Xcode projects for several checkpoints in this tutorial inside the Source Code folder that comes with this tutorial. That way you can compare your version of the app to mine, or – if you really make a mess of things – continue from a version that is known to work.
>
> You can find the project files for the app you've made thus far in the **01 - One Button App** folder.

Problems?

If Xcode gives you a "Build Failed" error message after you press Run, then make sure you typed in everything correctly. Even the smallest mistake will totally confuse Xcode. It can be quite overwhelming to make sense out of the error messages. A small typo at the top of the source code can produce several errors elsewhere in that file.

Typical mistakes are differences in capitalization. The Swift programming language is case-sensitive, which means it sees Alert and alert as two different names. Xcode complains about this with a "<something> undeclared" or "Use of unresolved identifier" error.

When Xcode says things like "Parse Issue" or "Expected <something>" then you probably forgot a curly bracket } or parenthesis) somewhere. Not matching up opening and closing brackets is a common error.

(Tip: If you move the text cursor over a closing bracket, Xcode will highlight the corresponding opening bracket.)

Tiny details like this are very important when you're programming. Even one single misplaced character can prevent the Swift compiler from building your app.

Fortunately, such mistakes are easy to find.

Xcode makes sure you can't miss errors

When Xcode detects an error it switches the pane on the left, where your project files used to be, to the **Issue navigator**. This list shows all the errors and warnings that Xcode has found. (You can go back to the project files with the small buttons at the top.)

Apparently, I forgot a comma somewhere.

Click on the error message and Xcode takes you to the line in the source code with the error. It even suggests what you need to do to resolve it (image on next page):

```
    let action = UIAlertAction(title: "Awesome", style: .Default,   ⊙ Expected ',' separator
        handler: nil)
                                              Issue ⊙ Expected ',' separator
    alert.addAction(action)                   Fix-it  Insert ","

    presentViewController(alert, animated: true, completion: nil)
    }
}
```

Fix-it suggests a solution to the problem

Sometimes it's a bit of a puzzle to figure out what exactly you did wrong when your build fails, but fortunately Xcode lends a helping hand.

Errors and warnings

Xcode makes a distinction between errors (red) and warnings (yellow). Errors are fatal. If you get one, you are not allowed to run the app. Warnings are informative. Xcode just says, "You probably didn't mean to do this, but go ahead anyway."

In my opinion, it is best to treat all warnings as if they were errors. Fix the warning before you continue and only run your app when there are zero errors and zero warnings. That doesn't guarantee the app won't have any bugs, but at least it won't be silly ones.

How does an app work?

It will be good at this point to get some sense of what goes on behind the scenes of an app.

An app is essentially made up of **objects** that can send messages to each other. Many of the objects in your app are provided by iOS, for example the button – a UIButton object – and the alert popup – a UIAlertController object. Some objects you will have to program yourself, such as the view controller.

These objects communicate by passing messages to each other. When the user taps the Hit Me button in the app, for example, that UIButton object sends a message to your view controller. In turn the view controller may message more objects.

On iOS, apps are *event-driven*, which means that the objects listen for certain events to occur and then process them.

As strange as it may sound, an app spends most of its time doing... absolutely nothing. It just sits there waiting for something to happen. When the user taps the screen, the app springs to action for a few milliseconds and then it goes back to sleep again until the next event arrives.

Your part in this scheme is that you write the source code that will be performed when your objects receive the messages for such events.

In the app, the button's Touch Up Inside event is connected to the view controller's showAlert action. So when the button recognizes it has been tapped, it sends the showAlert message to your view controller.

Inside showAlert, the view controller sends another message, addAction, to the UIAlertController object. And to show the alert, the view controller sends the message presentViewController.

Your whole app will be made up of objects that communicate in this fashion.

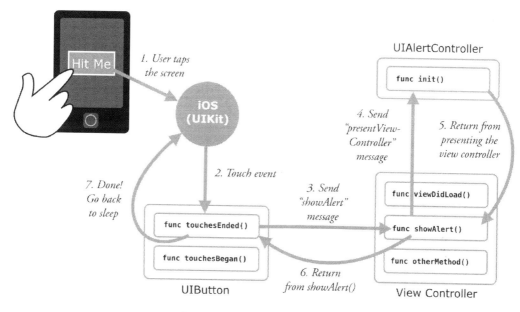

The general flow of events in an app

Maybe you have used PHP or Ruby scripts on your web site. This event-based model is different from how a PHP script works. The PHP script will run from top-to-bottom, executing the statements one-by-one until it reaches the end and then it exits.

Apps, on the other hand, don't exit until the user terminates them (or they crash!). They spend most of their time waiting for input events, then handle those events and go back to sleep.

Input from the user, mostly in the form of touches and taps, is the most important source of events for your app but there are other types of events as well. For example, the operating system will notify your app when the user receives an incoming phone call, when it has to redraw the screen, when a timer has counted down, and many more.

Everything your app does is triggered by some event.

Tackling the to-do list

Now that you have accomplished the first task of putting a button on the screen and making it show an alert, you'll simply go down the list and tick off the other items.

You don't really have to do this in any particular order, although some things make sense to do before others. For example, you cannot read the position of the slider if you don't have a slider yet.

So let's add the rest of the controls – the slider and the text labels – and turn this app into a real game!

When you're done, the app will look like this:

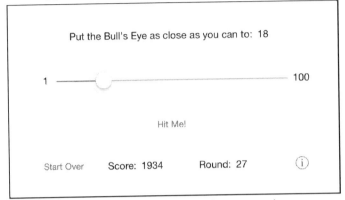

Put the Bull's Eye as close as you can to: 18

1 ———————○————————————————— 100

Hit Me!

Start Over   Score: 1934   Round: 27   ⓘ

The game screen with standard UIKit controls

Hey, wait a minute… that doesn't look nearly as pretty as the game I promised you! The difference is that these are the standard UIKit controls. This is what they look like straight out of the box.

You've probably seen this look before because it is perfectly suitable for regular apps. But because the default look is a little boring for a game, you'll put some special sauce on top later in this lesson.

UIKit and other frameworks

iOS offers a lot of building blocks in the form of frameworks or "kits". The UIKit framework provides the user interface controls such as buttons, labels and navigation bars. It manages the view controllers and generally takes care of anything else that deals with your app's user interface. (That is what UI stands for: User Interface.)

If you had to write all that stuff from scratch, you'd be busy for a while. Instead, you can build your app on top of the system-provided frameworks and take advantage of all the work the Apple engineers have already done for you.

Any object you see whose name starts with UI, such as UIButton, comes from UIKit. When you're writing iOS apps, UIKit is the framework you'll spend most of your time with but there are others as well.

Examples of other frameworks are Foundation, which provides many of the basic building blocks for building apps; Core Graphics for drawing basic shapes such as lines, gradients and images on the screen; AVFoundation for playing sound and video; and many others.

The complete set of frameworks for iOS is known collectively as Cocoa Touch.

Portrait vs. landscape

Notice that the dimensions of the app have changed: the iPhone is tilted on its side and the screen is wider but less tall. This is called *landscape* orientation.

You've no doubt seen landscape apps before on the iPhone. It's a common display orientation for games but many other types of apps work in landscape mode too, usually in addition to the regular "upright" *portrait* orientation.

For instance, many people prefer to write emails with their device flipped over because the wider screen allows for a bigger keyboard and easier typing.

In portrait orientation, the iPhone 5 screen consists of 320 points horizontally and 568 points vertically. For landscape these dimensions are switched.

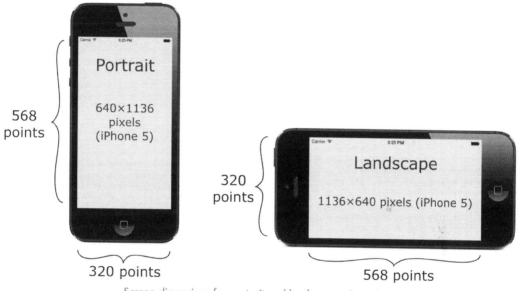

Screen dimensions for portrait and landscape orientation

So what is a *point*?

On older devices – up to the iPhone 3GS and corresponding iPod touch models, as well as the first iPads – one point corresponds to one pixel. As a result, these low-resolution devices don't look very sharp because of their big, chunky pixels.

I'm sure you know what a pixel is. In case you don't, it's the smallest element that a screen is made up of. The display of your iPhone is a big matrix of pixels that each can have their own color, just like a TV screen. Changing the color values of these pixels produces a visible image on the display. The more pixels, the better the image looks.

On the high-resolution Retina display of the iPhone 4 and later models, one point actually corresponds to two pixels horizontally and vertically, so four pixels in total. It packs a lot of pixels in a very small space, making for a much sharper display, which accounts for the popularity of Retina devices.

On the new iPhone 6 Plus it's even crazier: it has a 3x resolution with *nine* pixels for every point. Insane! You need to be eagle-eyed to make out the individual pixels on this fancy Retina HD display. It becomes almost impossible to make out where one pixel ends and the next one begins, that's how miniscule they are.

It's not only the number of pixels that differs between the various iPhone models. Over the years they have received different form factors, from the small 3.5-inch screen in the beginning all the way up to 5.5-inches on the iPhone 6 Plus.

The form factor determines the width and height of the screen in points:

Device	Form factor	Screen dimension in points
iPhone 3GS and older	3.5"	320×480
iPhone 4 and 4S	3.5"	320×480
iPhone 5, 5c and 5s	4"	320×568
iPhone 6	4.7"	375×667
iPhone 6 Plus	5.5"	414×736
iPad (all models)	7.9" and 9.7"	768×1024

In the early days of iOS, there was only one screen size. But those days of "one size fits all" are long gone. Now we have a variety of screen sizes to deal with.

Remember that UIKit works with points instead of pixels, so you only have to worry about the differences between the screen sizes measured in points. The actual number of pixels is only important for graphic designers because images are still measured in pixels.

Developers work in points, designers work in pixels.

The difference between points and pixels can be a little confusing, but if that is the only thing you're confused about right now then I'm doing a pretty good job. ;-)

In this tutorial you'll initially work with just the iPhone 5 screen size of 320×568 points – just to keep things simple. Later on in the tutorial you'll also make the game fit on the other types of iPhones.

Converting the app to landscape

To convert the app from portrait into landscape, you have to do two things:

1. Make the view in **Main.storyboard** landscape instead of portrait.

2. Change the **Supported Device Orientations** settings of the app.

➤ Open **Main.storyboard** in the Interface Builder. Click on the view controller to select it.

Tip: You can also click in the **Outline pane.** This pane shows the view hierarchy of the storyboard. Here you can see that the View Controller contains the main view (which is simply named View), which in turn contains one sub-view at the moment, the button.

Sometimes it is easier to select the item you want from this list, especially if your screen design is getting crowded.

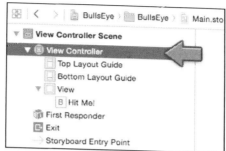

The Outline pane shows the view hierarchy of the storyboard

Remember, if the Outline pane is not visible, click the little icon at the bottom to reveal it:

This button shows or hides the Outline pane

➤ Go to the **Inspector** pane, which is at the other end of the Xcode window, and activate the **Attributes inspector**.

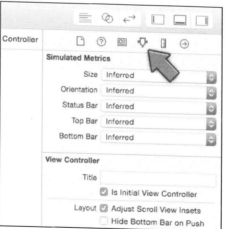

The Attributes inspector for the View Controller

If you haven't already played with this part of Interface Builder: the Inspector area shows various aspects of the item that is currently selected. The Attributes inspector, for example, lets you change the background color of a view or the size of the text on a button. As you become more proficient with Interface Builder, you'll be using all of these inspector panes to configure your views.

To rotate the view controller to landscape, you're looking for the **Orientation** setting in the **Simulated Metrics** section. It is currently set to Inferred, which really means portrait in this case.

➤ Change Orientation to **Landscape**.

This changes the dimensions of the view controller. It also puts the button in an awkward place.

➤ Move the button back to the center of the view because an untidy user interface just won't do in this day and age.

Hit Me!

The view in landscape orientation

That takes care of the view layout.

➤ Run the app on the iPhone 5s Simulator. The screen does not show up as landscape yet, and the button is no longer in the center either.

However, if you rotate the Simulator to landscape, then everything will look as it should.

➤ Choose **Hardware** → **Rotate Left** or **Rotate Right** from the iOS Simulator's menu bar at the top of the screen, or hold ⌘ and press the left or right arrow keys on your keyboard. This will flip the Simulator around.

Notice that in landscape orientation the app no longer shows the iPhone's status bar. This is a new feature of iOS 8, giving apps more room for their user interfaces.

You should do one more thing. There is a configuration option that tells iOS what orientations your app supports. New apps that you make from the template always support both portrait and landscape orientation.

➤ Click the **BullsEye** project icon at the top of the **Project navigator**. The main pane of the Xcode window now reveals a bunch of settings for the project.

➤ Make sure that the **General** tab is selected:

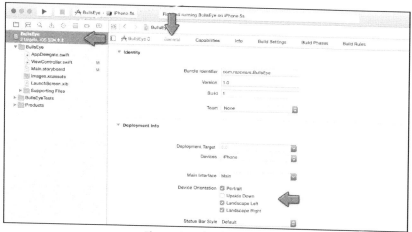

The settings for the project

In the section **Deployment Info,** there is an option for **Device Orientation**.

➤ Check only the **Landscape Left** and **Landscape Right** options and leave the Portrait and Upside Down options unchecked.

Run the app again and it properly launches in the landscape orientation right from the beginning.

The app in landscape orientation

Objects, data and methods

Time for some programming theory. Yes, you cannot escape it.

Swift is a so-called "object-oriented" programming language, which means that most of the stuff you do involves objects of some kind. I already mentioned a few times that an app consists of objects that send messages to each other.

When you write an iOS app, you'll be using objects that are provided for you by the system, such as the UIButton object from UIKit, and you'll be making objects of your own, such as view controllers.

So what exactly *is* an object? Think of an object as a building block of your program.

Programmers like to group related functionality into objects. *This* object takes care of parsing an RSS feed, *that* object knows how to draw an image on the screen, and that object over there can perform a difficult calculation.

Each object takes care of a specific part of the program. In a full-blown app you will have many different types of objects (tens or even hundreds).

Even your small starter app already contains several different objects. The one you have spent the most time with so far is ViewController. The Hit Me button is also an object, as is the alert popup. And the texts that you put on the alert – "Hello, World" and "This is my first app!" – are also objects.

The project also has an object named AppDelegate, even though you're going to ignore that for this lesson (but feel free to look inside its source file if you're curious). These object thingies are everywhere!

An object can have both *data* and *functionality*:

- An example of data is the Hit Me button that you added to the view controller earlier. When you dragged the button into the storyboard, it actually became part of the view controller's data. Data *contains* something. In this case, the view controller contains the button.

- An example of functionality is the showAlert action that you added to respond to taps on that button. Functionality *does* something.

The button itself also has data and functionality. Examples of button data are the text and color of its label, its position on the screen, its width and height, and so on. The button also has functionality: it can recognize that the user taps on it and will trigger an action in response.

The thing that provides functionality to an object is commonly called a *method*. Other programming languages may call this a "procedure" or "subroutine" or "function". You will also see the term function used in Swift; a method is simply a function that belongs to an object.

Your showAlert action is an example of a method. You can tell it's a method because the line says func (short for "function") and the name is followed by parentheses:

All method definitions start with the word func and have parentheses

If you look through the rest of **ViewController.swift** you'll see several other methods, such as viewDidLoad() and didReceiveMemoryWarning().

These currently don't do much; the Xcode template placed them there for your convenience. These specific methods are often used by view controllers, so it's likely that you will need to fill them in at some point.

The concept of methods may still feel a little weird, so here's an example:

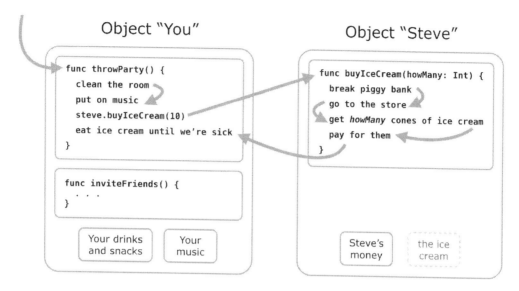

Every party needs ice cream!

You (or at least an object named "You") want to throw a party but you forgot to buy ice cream. Fortunately, you have invited the object named Steve who happens to live next door to a convenience store. It won't be much of a party without ice cream, so at some point during your party preparations you send object Steve a message asking him to bring some ice cream.

The computer now switches to object Steve and executes the commands from his buyIceCream() method, one by one, from top to bottom.

When his method is done, the computer returns to your throwParty() method and continues with that, so you and your friends can eat the ice cream that Steve brought back with him.

The Steve object also has data. Before he goes to the store he has money. At the store he exchanges this money data for other, much more important, data: ice cream! After making that transaction, he brings the ice cream data over to the party (if he eats it all along the way, your program has a bug!).

"Sending a message" sounds more involved than it really is. It's a good way to think conceptually of how objects communicate, but there really aren't any pigeons or mailmen involved. The computer simply jumps from the throwParty() method to the buyIceCream() method and back again.

Often the terms "calling a method" or "invoking a method" are used instead. That means the exact same thing as sending a message: the computer jumps to the method you're calling and returns to where it left off when that method is done.

The important thing to remember is that objects have methods (the steps involved in buying ice cream) and data (the actual ice cream and the money to buy it with).

Objects can look at each other's data (to some extent anyway, Steve may not approve if you peek inside his wallet) and can ask other objects to perform their methods. That's how you get your app to do things.

Adding the rest of the controls

Your app already has a button, but you still need to add the rest of the UI controls. Here is the screen again, this time annotated with the different types of views:

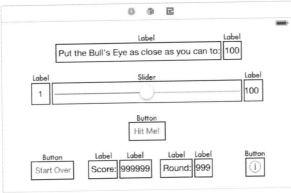

The different views in the game screen

As you can see, I put placeholder values into some of the labels (for example, "999999"). That makes it easier to see how the labels will fit on the screen when they're actually used. The score label could potentially hold a large value, so you'd better make sure the label has room for it.

➤ Try to re-create this screen on your own by dragging the various controls from the Object Library. You can see in the screenshot above how big the items should (roughly) be. It's OK if you're a few points off.

Tip: The (i) button is actually a regular Button, but its **Type** is set to **Info Light** in the **Attributes inspector**:

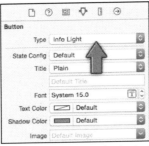

The button type lets you change the look of the button

➤ Set the attributes for the **slider**. Its minimum value should be 1, its maximum 100, and its current value 50.

The slider attributes

When you're done, you should have 12 user interface elements in your view: one slider, three buttons and a whole bunch of labels. Excellent.

➤ Run the app and play with it for a minute. The controls don't really do much yet (except for the button that should still pop up the alert), but you can at least drag the slider around.

You can tick a few more items off the to-do list, all without any programming! That is going to change really soon, because you will have to write Swift code to actually make the controls do anything.

The slider

The next item on your to-do list is: "Read the value of the slider after the user presses the Hit Me button."

If, in your messing around in Interface Builder, you did not accidentally disconnect the button from the showAlert action, you can modify the app to show the slider's value in the alert popup. (If you did disconnect the button, then you should hook it up again first.)

Remember how you added an action to the view controller in order to recognize when the user tapped the button? You can do the same thing for the slider. This action will be performed whenever the user drags the slider's knob.

The steps for adding this action are largely the same as what you did before.

➤ First, go to **ViewController.swift** and the following at the bottom, just before the final closing bracket:

```
@IBAction func sliderMoved(slider: UISlider) {
  println("The value of the slider is now: \(slider.value)")
}
```

➤ Go back to the storyboard and Ctrl-drag from the slider to View Controller in the Outline pane. Let go of the mouse button and select **sliderMoved:** from the popup. Done!

If you now look at the **Connections inspector** for the slider, you'll see that the sliderMoved: action is hooked up to the slider's Value Changed event.

This means the sliderMoved() method will be called every time the slider's value changes, which happens when the user drags the slider to the left or right.

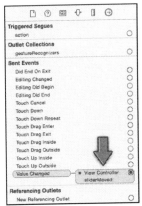

The slider is now hooked up to the view controller

➤ Run the app and drag the slider.

As soon as you start dragging, the Xcode window opens a new pane at the bottom, the so-called **Debug area**, showing a list of messages:

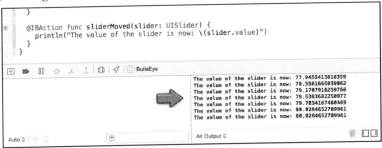

println messages in the Debug area

If you slide the slider all the way to the left, you should see the value go down to 1. All the way to the right, the value should be 100.

The `println()` function is a great help to show you what is going on in the app. Its entire purpose is to write a text message to the Debug area. Here, you used it to verify that you properly hooked up the action to the slider and that you can read its value as the slider is moved.

I often use `println()` to make sure my apps are doing the right thing before I add more functionality. Printing a message to the Debug area is quick and easy.

> **Note:** Did you notice that the `sliderMoved:` action has a colon in its name but `showAlert` does not? That's because the `sliderMoved()` method takes a single parameter, `slider`, while `showAlert()` does not have any parameters. If an action method has a parameter, Interface Builder adds a : to the name. You'll learn more about using parameters soon.

Strings

To put text in your app, you use something called a "string". The strings you have used so far are:

```
"Hello, World"
"This is my first app!"
"Awesome"
"The value of the slider is now: \(slider.value)"
```

The first three were used to make the `UIAlertController`; the last one you used with `println()` above.

Such a chunk of text is called a string because you can visualize the text as a sequence of characters, as if they were beads on a piece of string (sorry, it doesn't have anything to do with underwear):

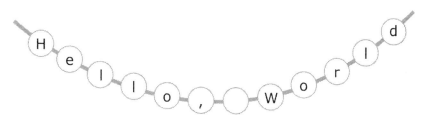

A string of characters

Working with strings is something you need to do all the time when you're writing apps, so over the course of this tutorial series you'll get quite experienced with it.

To create a string, simply put the text in between double quotes. In other languages you can often use single quotes as well, but in Swift they must be double quotes. And they must be plain double quotes, not typographic "sixes and nines".

To summarize:

```
// This is the proper way to make a Swift string:
"I am a good string"

// These are wrong:
'I should have double quotes'
''Two single quotes do not make a double quote''
"My quotes are too fancy"
@"I am an Objective-C string"
```

The `println()` statement used the string, `"The value of the slider is now: \(slider.value)"`.

Anything between the characters `\(…)` inside a string is special. Think of it as a placeholder: `"The value of the slider is now: X"`, where X will be replaced by the value of the slider.

Filling in the blanks is a very common way to build up strings in Swift.

Introducing variables

Printing information with `println()` to the Debug pane is very useful during development of the app, but it's absolutely useless to the user because they can't see any of this.

Let's improve this action method and make it show the value of the slider in the alert popup. So how do you get the slider's value into showAlert()?

When you read the slider's value in sliderMoved(), that piece of data disappears when the action method ends. It would be handy if you could remember this value until the user taps the Hit Me button.

Fortunately, Swift has a building block exactly for this purpose: the *variable*.

➤ Open **ViewController.swift** and add the following at the top, directly below the line that says class ViewController:

```
var currentValue: Int = 0
```

You have now added a variable named currentValue to the view controller object.

The code should look like this (I left out the insides of the methods):

```
import UIKit

class ViewController: UIViewController {
  var currentValue: Int = 0

  override func viewDidLoad() {
    . . .
  }

  override func didReceiveMemoryWarning() {
    . . .
  }

  @IBAction func showAlert() {
    . . .
  }

  @IBAction func sliderMoved(slider: UISlider) {
    . . .
  }
}
```

It is customary to add the variables above the methods, and to indent everything with a tab or two to four spaces. Which one you use is largely a matter of personal preference. I like to use two spaces. (You can configure this in Xcode's preferences panel. From the menu bar choose Xcode → Preferences… → Text Editing and go to the Indentation tab.)

Remember when I said that a view controller, or any object really, could have both data and functionality? The showAlert() and sliderMoved() actions are examples of functionality, while the currentValue variable is part of its data.

A variable allows the app to remember things. Think of a variable as a temporary storage container for a single piece of data. There are containers of all sorts and sizes, just as data comes in all kinds of shapes and sizes.

You don't just put stuff in the container and then forget about it. You will often replace its contents with a new value. When the thing that your app needs to remember changes, you take the old value out of the box and put in the new value.

That's the whole point behind variables: they can *vary*. For example, you will update currentValue with the new position of the slider every time the slider is moved.

The size of the storage container and the sort of values the variable can remember are determined by its *data type*, or just *type*.

You specified the type `Int` for the `currentValue` variable, which means this container can hold whole numbers (also known as "integers") between at least minus two billion and plus two billion. `Int` is one of the most common data types but there are many others and you can even make your own.

Variables are like children's toy blocks:

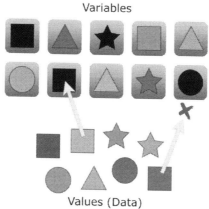

Variables are containers that hold values

The idea is to put the right shape in the right container. The container is the variable and its type determines what "shape" fits. The shapes are the possible values that you can put into the variables.

You can change the contents of each box later. For example, you can take out the blue square and put in a red square, as long as both are squares. But you can't put a square in a round hole: the data type of the value and the data type of the variable have to match.

I said a variable is a *temporary* storage container. How long will it keep its contents? Unlike meat or vegetables, variables won't spoil if you keep them for too long – a variable will hold onto its value indefinitely, until you put a new value into that variable or until you destroy the container altogether.

Each variable has a certain lifetime (also known as its *scope*) that depends on exactly where in your program you defined that variable. In this case, `currentValue` sticks around for just as long as its owner, `ViewController`, does. Their fates are intertwined.

The view controller, and thus `currentValue`, is there for the duration of the app. They don't get destroyed until the app quits. Soon you'll also see variables that live much shorter.

Enough theory, let's make this variable work for us.

➤ Change the contents of the `sliderMoved()` method in **ViewController.swift** to the following:

```
@IBAction func sliderMoved(slider: UISlider) {
  currentValue = lroundf(slider.value)
}
```

You removed the `println()` statement and replaced it with this line:

```
currentValue = lroundf(slider.value)
```

What is going on here?

You've seen `slider.value` before, which is the slider's position at that moment. This is a value between 1 and 100, possibly with digits behind the decimal point. And `currentValue` is the name of the variable you have just created.

To put a new value into a variable, you simply do this:

```
variable = the new value
```

This is known as "assignment". You *assign* the new value to the variable. It puts the shape into the box. Here, you put the value that represents the slider's position into the `currentValue` variable.

Easy enough, but what is the `lroundf` thing? Recall that the slider's value can have numbers behind the decimal point. You've seen this with the `println()` output in the Debug pane as you moved the slider.

However, this game would be really hard if you made the player guess the position of the slider with an accuracy that goes behind the decimal point. That will be nearly impossible to get right!

It is more fair to use whole numbers only. That is why `currentValue` has data type `Int`, because that stores *integers*, a fancy term for whole numbers.

You use the function `lroundf()` to round the decimal number to the nearest whole number and you then store that rounded-off number into `currentValue`.

Functions and methods

You've already seen that methods provide functionality, but *functions* are another way to put functionality into your apps (the name sort of gives it away). Functions and methods are how Swift programs combine multiple lines of code into single, cohesive units.

The difference between the two is that a function doesn't belong to an object while a method does. In other words, a method is exactly like a function – that's why you use the `func` keyword to define them – except that you need to have an object to use the method. But regular functions, or *free functions* as they are sometimes called, can be used anywhere.

Swift provides your programs with a large library of useful functions. The function `lroundf()` is one of them and you'll be using a few others during this lesson as well. `println()` is also a function, by the way. You can tell because the function name is always followed by parentheses that possibly contain one or more parameters.

➤ Now change the `showAlert()` method to the following:

```
@IBAction func showAlert() {
  let message = "The value of the slider is: \(currentValue)"

  let alert = UIAlertController(title: "Hello, World", message: message,
                      preferredStyle: .Alert)
```

```
  let action = UIAlertAction(title: "OK", style: .Default, handler: nil)

  alert.addAction(action)

  presentViewController(alert, animated: true, completion: nil)
}
```

The highlighted parts indicate the changes to this method.

As before, you create and show a `UIAlertController`, except this time its message says: "The value of the slider is: X", where X is replaced by the contents of the `currentValue` variable (a whole number between 1 and 100).

Suppose `currentValue` is 34, which means the slider is about one-third to the left. The new code above will convert the string `"The value of the slider is: \(currentValue)"` into `"The value of the slider is: 34"` and puts that into a new object named `message`.

The old `println()` did something similar, except that it printed the result to the Debug pane. Here, however, you do not wish to print the result but show it in the alert popup. That is why you tell the `UIAlertController` that it should now use this new string as the message to display.

➤ Run the app, drag the slider, and press the button. Now the alert should show the actual value of the slider.

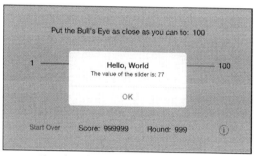

The alert shows the value of the slider

Cool. You have used a variable, `currentValue`, to remember a particular piece of data, the rounded-off position of the slider, so that it can be used elsewhere in the app, in this case in the alert's message text.

If you tap the button again without moving the slider, the alert will still show the same value. The variable keeps its value until you put a new one into it.

Your first bug

There is a small problem with the app, though. Maybe you've noticed it already. Here is how to reproduce the problem:

➤ Press the Stop button in Xcode to completely terminate the app, then press Run again. Without moving the slider, immediately press the Hit Me button.

The alert now says: "The value of the slider is: 0". But the slider's knob is obviously at the center, so you would expect the value to be 50. You've discovered a bug!

Exercise: Think of a reason why the value would be 0 in this particular situation (start the app, don't move the slider, press the button). ∎

Answer: The clue here is that this only happens when you don't move the slider. Of course, without moving the slider the sliderMoved() message is never sent and you never put the slider's value into the currentValue variable.

The default value for the currentValue variable is 0, and that is what you are seeing here.

➤ To fix this bug, change the declaration of currentValue to:

```
var currentValue: Int = 50
```

Now the starting value of currentValue is 50, which should be the same value as the slider's initial position.

➤ Run the app again and verify that the bug is solved.

You can find the project files for the app up to this point under **02 - Slider and Variables** in the tutorial's Source Code folder.

Enough playing around... let's make a game!

You've built the user interface and you know how to find the position of the slider. That already knocks quite a few items off the to-do list.

The big remaining items are generating the random value for the target and calculating how well the player did.

But first, there's still an improvement to make on the slider.

Outlets

You managed to store the value of the slider into a variable and show it on the alert. That's good but you can still improve on it a little.

What if you decide to set the initial value of the slider in the storyboard to something other than 50, say 1 or 100? Then currentValue would be wrong again because the app always assumes it will be 50 at the start. You'd have to remember to also fix the code to give currentValue a new initial value.

Take it from me, those kinds of small things are hard to remember, especially when the project becomes bigger and you have dozens of view controllers to worry about, or when you haven't looked at the code for weeks.

Therefore, to fix this issue once and for all, you're going to do some work inside the viewDidLoad() method in **ViewController.swift**. That method currently looks like this:

```
override func viewDidLoad() {
  super.viewDidLoad()
  // Do any additional setup after loading the view, typically from a nib.
}
```

When you created this project based on Xcode's template, Xcode already put the viewDidLoad() method into the source code. You will now add some code to it.

The `viewDidLoad()` message is sent by UIKit as soon as the view controller loads its user interface from the storyboard file. At this point, the view controller isn't visible yet, so this is a good place to set instance variables to their proper initial values.

➤ Change `viewDidLoad()` to the following:

```
override func viewDidLoad() {
  super.viewDidLoad()
  currentValue = lroundf(slider.value)
}
```

The idea is that you take whatever value is set on the slider in the storyboard (whether it is 50, 1, 100, or anything else) and use that as the initial contents of `currentValue`.

Recall that you need to round off the number, because `currentValue` is an `Int` and integers cannot take digits behind the decimal point.

Unfortunately, Xcode complains about these changes when you press Run. Try it for yourself.

➤ Try to run the app.

Xcode says "Build Failed", followed by something like: "Error: Use of unresolved identifier 'slider'".

That happens because `viewDidLoad()` does not know anything named `slider`.

Then why did this work earlier, in `sliderMoved()`? Let's take a look at that method again:

```
@IBAction func sliderMoved(slider: UISlider) {
  currentValue = lroundf(slider.value)
}
```

Here you do the exact same thing: you round off `slider.value` and put it into `currentValue`. So why does it work here but not in `viewDidLoad()`?

The difference is that `slider` is a so-called *parameter* of the `sliderMoved()` method:

```
@IBAction func sliderMoved(slider: UISlider) {
```

Parameters are the things inside the parentheses following a method's name. In this case there's a single parameter named `slider`, which refers to the `UISlider` object that sent this action message.

Action methods can have a parameter that refers to the UI control that triggered the method. That is convenient when you wish to use that object in the method, just as you did here (the object in question being the `UISlider`).

When the user moves the slider, the `UISlider` object basically says, "Hey view controller, I'm a slider object and I just got moved. By the way, here's my phone number so you can get in touch with me."

The `slider` parameter contains this "phone number" but it is only valid for the duration of this particular method.

In other words, `slider` is *local*; you cannot use it anywhere else.

Locals

When I first introduced variables, I mentioned that each variable has a certain lifetime, known as its *scope*. The scope of a variable depends on where in your program you defined that variable.

There are three possible scope levels in Swift:

1. **Global scope.** These objects exist for the duration of the app and are accessible from anywhere.

2. **Instance scope.** This is for variables such as `currentValue`. These objects are alive for as long as the object that owns them stays alive.

3. **Local scope.** Objects with a local scope, such as the `slider` parameter of `sliderMoved()`, only exist for the duration of that method. As soon as the execution of the program leaves this method, the local objects are no longer accessible.

Let's look at the top part of `showAlert()`:

```
@IBAction func showAlert() {
  let message = "The value of the slider is: \(currentValue)"

  let alert = UIAlertController(title: "Hello, World", message: message,
                          preferredStyle: .Alert)

  let action = UIAlertAction(title: "OK", style: .Default, handler: nil)

  . . .
```

Because the `message`, `alert`, and `action` objects are created inside the method, they are locals. They only come into existence when the `showAlert()` action is performed and cease to exist when the action is done.

As soon as the `showAlert()` method completes, i.e. when there are no more statements for it to execute, the computer destroys the `message`, `alert`, and `action` objects. Their storage space is no longer needed.

The `currentValue` variable, however, lives on forever... or at least for as long as the `ViewController` does (which is until the user terminates the app). This type of variable is named an *instance variable*, because its scope is the same as the scope of the object instance it belongs to.

In other words, you use instance variables if you want to keep a certain value around, from one action event to the next.

The solution is to store a reference to the slider as a new instance variable, just like you did for `currentValue`. Except that this time, the data type of the variable is not `Int`, but `UISlider`. And you're not using a regular instance variable but a special form called an *outlet*.

➤ Add the following line to **ViewController.swift**:

```
@IBOutlet weak var slider: UISlider!
```

It doesn't really matter where this line goes, just as long as it is somewhere inside the brackets for `class ViewController`. I usually put outlets with the other instance variables.

This line tells Interface Builder that you now have a variable named `slider` that can be connected to a `UISlider` object. Just as Interface Builder likes to call methods "actions", it calls these variables outlets. Interface Builder doesn't see any of your other variables, only the ones marked with `@IBOutlet`.

Don't worry about `weak` or the exclamation point for now. Why these are necessary will be explained in the next tutorials. For now just remember that a variable for an outlet needs to be declared as `@IBOutlet weak var` and has an exclamation point at the end. (Sometimes you'll see a question mark instead; all this hocus pocus will be explained in due time.)

➤ Open the storyboard. Hold Ctrl and click on the slider. Don't drag anywhere just yet: let go of the mouse button and a menu pops up that shows all the connections for this slider. (Instead of Ctrl-clicking you can also right-click once.)

This popup menu works exactly the same as the Connections inspector. I just wanted to show you that it exists as an alternative.

➤ Click on the open circle next to **New Referencing Outlet** and drag to **View Controller**:

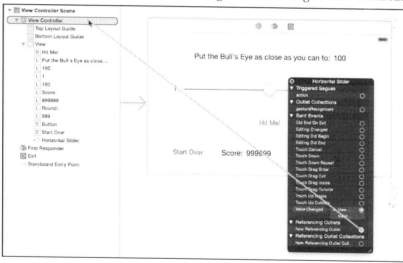

Connecting the slider to the outlet

➤ In the popup that appears, select **slider**.

This is the outlet that you just added to the object. You have successfully connected the slider object from the storyboard to the view controller's `slider` outlet.

Now that you have done all this setup work, you can refer to the slider object from anywhere inside the view controller using the `slider` variable.

With these changes in place, it no longer matters what you choose for the initial value of the slider in Interface Builder. When the app starts, `currentValue` will always correspond to that setting.

➤ Run the app and immediately press the button. It correctly says: "The value of the slider is: 50". Stop the app, go into Interface Builder and change the initial value of the slider to something else, say, 25. Run the app again and press the button. The alert should read 25 now.

Put the slider's starting position back to 50 when you're done playing.

Exercise: Give `currentValue` an initial value of 0 again. It doesn't really matter what its initial value is – it will be overwritten in `viewDidLoad()` anyway – but Swift demands that all variables always have *some* value and 0 is as good as any. ∎

Comments

You've seen green lines that begin with `//` a few times now. These are comments. You can write any text you want after the `//` symbol as the compiler will ignore such lines completely.

```
// I am a comment! You can type anything here.
```

Anything between the `/*` and `*/` markers is considered a comment as well. The difference between `//` and `/* */` is that the former only works on a single line, while the latter can span multiple lines.

```
/*
  I am a comment as well!
  I can span multiple lines.
*/
```

The `/* */` comments are often used to temporarily disable whole sections of the source code, usually when you're trying to hunt down a pesky bug, a practice known as "commenting out".

The best use for comment lines is to explain how your code works. Well-written source code is self-explanatory but sometimes additional clarification is useful. Explain to who? To yourself, mostly. Unless you have the memory of an elephant, you'll probably have forgotten exactly how your code works when you look at it six months later. Use comments to jog your memory.

As you have seen, Xcode automatically adds a comment block with copyright information at the top of the source code files. Personally, I don't care much for these copyright blocks. Feel free to remove those lines if you don't like them either.

Generating the random number

You still have quite a ways to go before the game is playable, so let's get on with the next item on the list: generating a random number and displaying it on the screen.

Random numbers come up a lot when you're making games because often games need to have some element of unpredictability. You can't really get a computer to generate numbers that are truly random and unpredictable, but you can employ a so-called *pseudo-random generator* to spit out numbers that at least appear that way. You'll use my favorite one, the `arc4random_uniform()` function.

A good place to generate this random number is when the game starts.

➤ Add the following line to `viewDidLoad()` in **ViewController.swift**:

```
targetValue = 1 + Int(arc4random_uniform(100))
```

The complete `viewDidLoad()` should now look like this:

```
override func viewDidLoad() {
  super.viewDidLoad()
  currentValue = lroundf(slider.value)
  targetValue = 1 + Int(arc4random_uniform(100))
}
```

What did you do here? First, you're using a new variable, `targetValue`. You haven't actually defined this variable yet, so you'll have to do that in a minute.

If you don't tell the compiler what kind of variable `targetValue` is, then it doesn't know how much storage space to allocate for it, nor can it check if you're using the variable properly everywhere.

You are also calling the function `arc4random_uniform()` to deliver an arbitrary integer (whole number) between 0 and 100.

Actually, the highest number you will get is 99 because `arc4random_uniform()` treats the upper limit as exclusive. It only goes up-to 100, not up-to-and-including. To get a number that is truly in the range 1 - 100, you need to add 1 to the result of `arc4random_uniform()`.

To make this work, you have to add the variable `targetValue` to the view controller; otherwise Xcode will complain that it doesn't know anything about this variable.

➤ Add the new variable to the other variables at the top of **ViewController.swift**:

```
var targetValue: Int = 0
```

Variables in Swift must always have a value, so here you give it the initial value 0. That 0 is never used in the game; it will always be overwritten by the random value in `viewDidLoad()`.

> **Note:** Up until you made this latest change, Xcode may have pointed out that it did not know the `targetValue` variable. That error message should now have disappeared.
>
> Xcode tries to be helpful and it analyzes the program for mistakes as you're typing. Sometimes you may see temporary warnings and error messages that will go away when you complete the changes that you're making.
>
> Don't be too intimidated by these messages; they are only short-lived while the code is in a state of flux.

I hope the reason is clear why you made `targetValue` an instance variable.

You want to calculate the random number in one place – in `viewDidLoad()` – and then remember it until the user taps the button, in `showAlert()`.

➤ Change `showAlert()` to the following:

```
@IBAction func showAlert() {
  let message = "The value of the slider is: \(currentValue)"
            + "\nThe target value is: \(targetValue)"

  let alert = . . .
}
```

Tip: Whenever you see . . . in a source code listing I mean that as shorthand for: this part didn't change. (Don't go replacing what was there with an actual ellipsis!)

You've simply added the random number, which is now stored in `targetValue`, to the message string. This should look familiar to you by now. The `\(targetValue)` placeholder is replaced by the actual random number.

The `\n` character sequence is new. It means that you want to insert a special "new line" character at that point, which will break up the text into two lines so the message is a little easier to read.

➤ Run the app and try it out!

The alert shows the target value on a new line

> **Note:** Earlier you've used the + operator to add two numbers together (just like how it works in math) but here you're also using + to glue different bits of text into one big string.
>
> Swift allows the use of the same operator symbol for different tasks, depending on the data types involved. If you have two integers, + adds them up. But with two strings, + concatenates them into a larger string.
>
> Programming languages often use the same symbols for different purposes, depending on the context. (There are only so many symbols to go around.)

Adding rounds to the game

If you press the Hit Me button a few times, you'll notice that the random number never changes. I'm afraid the game won't be much fun that way.

This happens because you generate the random number in `viewDidLoad()` and never again afterwards. The `viewDidLoad()` method is only called once when the view controller is created during app startup.

The item on the to-do list actually said: "Generate a random number *at the start of each round*". Let's talk about what a round means in terms of this game.

When the game starts, the player has a score of 0 and the round number is 1. You set the slider halfway (to value 50) and calculate a random number. Then you wait for the player to press the Hit Me button. As soon as she does, the round ends.

You calculate the points for this round and add them to the total score. Then you increment the round number and start the next round. You reset the slider to the halfway position again and calculate a new random number. Lather, rinse, repeat.

Whenever you find yourself thinking something along the lines of, "At this point in the app we have to do such and so," then it makes sense to create a new method for it. This method will nicely capture that functionality in a unit of its own.

➤ With that in mind, add the following new method to **ViewController.swift**. It doesn't really matter where you put it, as long as it is inside the brackets of `class ViewController`, so that the compiler knows it belongs to the `ViewController` object.

```
func startNewRound() {
```

```
    targetValue = 1 + Int(arc4random_uniform(100))
    currentValue = 50
    slider.value = Float(currentValue)
}
```

It's not very different from what you did before, except that you moved the logic for setting up a new round into its own method, startNewRound(). The advantage of doing this is that you can use this logic from more than one place.

First you'll call this new method from viewDidLoad() to set up everything for the very first round. Recall that viewDidLoad() happens when the app starts up, so this is a great place to begin the first round.

➤ Change viewDidLoad() to:

```
override func viewDidLoad() {
  super.viewDidLoad()
  startNewRound()
}
```

Note that you've removed the existing statements from viewDidLoad() and replaced them with just the call to startNewRound().

You will also call startNewRound() after the player pressed the Hit Me button, from within showAlert().

➤ Make the following change to showAlert():

```
@IBAction func showAlert() {
  . . .

  presentViewController(alert, animated: true, completion: nil)

  startNewRound()
}
```

Until now, the methods from the view controller have been invoked for you by UIKit when something happened: viewDidLoad() is performed when the app loads, showAlert() is performed when the player taps the button, sliderMoved() when the player drags the slider, and so on. This is the event-driven model we talked about earlier.

It is also possible to call methods by hand, which is what you're doing here. You are sending a message from one method in the object to another method in that same object.

In this case, the view controller sends the startNewRound() message to itself in order to set up the new round. The iPhone will then go to that method and execute its statements one-by-one. When there are no more statements in the method, it returns to the calling method and continues with that – either viewDidLoad() if this is the first time or showAlert() for every round after.

Sometimes you may see method calls written like this:

```
self.startNewRound()
```

That does the exact same thing as just startNewRound() without "self." in front. Recall how I just said that the view controller sends the message to itself? Well, that's exactly what "self" means.

To call a method on an object you'd normally write:

```
receiver.methodName(parameters)
```

The `receiver` is the object you're sending the message to. If you're sending the message to yourself, then the receiver is `self`. But because sending messages to `self` is very common, you can also leave off this special keyword.

To be fair, this isn't exactly the first time you've called methods. `addAction()` is a method on `UIAlertController`, and `presentViewController()` is a method that all view controllers have, including yours.

When you write Swift programs, a lot of what you do is calling methods on objects, because that is how the objects in your app communicate.

I hope you can see the advantage of putting the "new round" logic into its own method. If you didn't, the code for `viewDidLoad()` and `showAlert()` would look like this:

```
override func viewDidLoad() {
  super.viewDidLoad()

  targetValue = 1 + Int(arc4random_uniform(100))
  currentValue = 50
  slider.value = Float(currentValue)
}

@IBAction func showAlert() {
  . . .
  presentViewController(alert, animated: true, completion: nil)

  targetValue = 1 + Int(arc4random_uniform(100))
  currentValue = 50
  slider.value = Float(currentValue)
}
```

Can you see what is going on here? The same functionality is duplicated in two places. Sure, it is only three lines, but often the code you would have to duplicate will be much larger.

And what if you decide to make a change to this logic (as you will shortly)? Then you will have to make this change in two places as well.

You might be able to remember to do so if you recently wrote this code and it is still fresh in memory, but if you have to make that change a few weeks down the road, chances are that you'll only update it in one place and forget about the other.

Code duplication is a big source of bugs, so if you need to do the same thing in two different places consider making a new method for it.

The name of the method also helps to make it clear what it is supposed to be doing. Can you tell at a glance what the following does?

```
targetValue = 1 + Int(arc4random_uniform(100))
currentValue = 50
slider.value = Float(currentValue)
```

You probably have to reason your way through it: "It is calculating a new random number and then resets the position of the slider, so I guess it must be the start of a new round."

Some programmers will use a comment to document what is going on, but in my opinion the following is much clearer:

```
startNewRound()
```

This line practically spells out for you what it will do. And if you want to know the specifics of what goes on in a new round, you can always look up the `startNewRound()` method and look inside.

Well-written source code speaks for itself. I hope I have convinced you of the value of making new methods!

➤ Run the app and verify that it calculates a new random number between 1 and 100 after each tap on the button.

You should also have noticed that after each round the slider resets to the halfway position. That happens because `startNewRound()` sets `currentValue` to 50 and then tells the slider to go to that position. That is the opposite of what you did before (you used to read the slider's position and put it into `currentValue`), but I thought it would work better in the game if you start from the same position in each round.

Exercise: Just for fun, modify the code so that the slider does not reset to the halfway position at the start of a new round. ■

By the way, you may have been wondering what `Float(…)` and `Int(…)` do in these lines:

```
targetValue = 1 + Int(arc4random_uniform(100))
slider.value = Float(currentValue)
```

Swift is a so-called *strongly typed* language, meaning that it is really picky about the shapes that you can put into the boxes. For example, if a variable is an `Int` you cannot put a `Float` into it, and vice versa.

The value of a `UISlider` happens to be a `Float`, which is a number that can have digits after the decimal point – you've seen this when you printed out the value of the slider – but `currentValue` is an `Int`. So this won't work:

```
slider.value = currentValue
```

The compiler considers this an error. Some programming languages are happy to convert the `Int` into a `Float` for you, but Swift wants you to be explicit about such conversions.

When you say `Float(currentValue)`, the compiler takes the integer number that's stored in `currentValue`'s box and puts it into a new `Float` value that it can give to the `UISlider`.

Something similar happens with `arc4random_uniform()`, where the random number gets converted to an `Int` first before it can be placed into `targetValue`.

Because Swift is stricter about this sort of thing than most other programming languages, it is often a source of confusion for newcomers to the language. Unfortunately, Swift's error messages aren't always very clear about what part of the code is wrong or why.

Just remember, if you get an error message saying, "'something' is not convertible to 'something else'" then you're trying to mix incompatible data types. The solution is to explicitly convert one type to the other, as you've been doing here.

Putting the target value into the label

Great, you figured out how to calculate the random number and how to store it in an instance variable, targetValue, so that you can access it later.

Now you are going to show that target number on the screen. Without it, the player won't know what to aim for and that would make the game impossible to win...

When you made the storyboard, you already added a label for the target value (top-right corner). The trick is to put the value from the targetValue variable into this label. To do that, you need to accomplish two things:

1. Create an outlet for the label so you can send it messages

2. Give the label new text to display

This will be very similar to what you did with the slider. Recall that you added an @IBOutlet variable so you could reference the slider anywhere from within the view controller. Using this outlet variable you could ask the slider for its value, through slider.value. You'll do the same thing for the label.

> In **ViewController.swift**, add the following line below the other outlet:

```
@IBOutlet weak var targetLabel: UILabel!
```

> In **Main.storyboard**, click to select the label (the one at the top that says "100").

> Go to the **Connections inspector** and drag from **New Referencing Outlet** to **View Controller**.

Connecting the target value label to its outlet

> Select **targetLabel** from the popup, and the connection is made.

> Now on to the good stuff. Add the following method below startNewRound() in **ViewController.swift**:

```
func updateLabels() {
  targetLabel.text = String(targetValue)
}
```

You're putting this logic into its own method because it's something you might use from different places.

The name of the method makes it clear what it does: it updates the contents of the labels. Currently it's just setting the text of a single label, but later on you will add code to update the other labels as well (total score, round number).

The code inside `updateLabels()` should have no surprises for you, although you may wonder why you cannot simply do:

```
targetLabel.text = targetValue
```

The answer is that you cannot put a value of one data type into a variable of another type. The square peg doesn't fit into the round hole.

The `targetLabel` outlet references a `UILabel` object. The `UILabel` object has a text property, which is a string object. You can only put string values into `text` but the above line tries to put `targetValue` into it, which is an `Int`. That won't fly because an `Int` and a string are two very different kinds of things.

So you have to convert the `Int` into a string, and that is what `String(targetValue)` does. It's similar to what you've seen before with `Float(…)` and `Int(…)`.

Just in case you were wondering, you can also write it as a string with a placeholder like you've done before:

```
targetLabel.text = "\(targetValue)"
```

Which one you like better is a matter of taste. Either approach will work fine.

Notice that `updateLabels()` is a regular method – it is not attached to any UI controls as an action – so it won't do anything until you actually call it. (You can tell because it doesn't say `@IBAction` anywhere.)

The logical place to call `updateLabels()` would be after each call to `startNewRound()`, because that is where you calculate the new target value.

Currently, you send the `startNewRound()` message from two places: `viewDidLoad()` and `showAlert()`, so let's update these methods.

➤ Change `viewDidLoad()` and `showAlert()` to:

```
override func viewDidLoad() {
  super.viewDidLoad()
  startNewRound()
  updateLabels()
}
```

```
@IBAction func showAlert() {
  . . .

  startNewRound()
  updateLabels()
}
```

You should be able to type just the first few letters of the method name, **upd**, and Xcode will complete the rest. Press **Enter** to accept the suggestion.

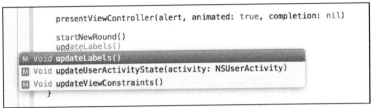

Xcode autocomplete offers suggestions

➤ Run the app and you'll actually see the random value on the screen. That should make it a little easier to aim for.

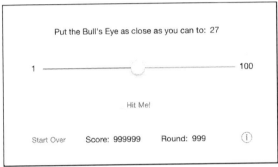

The label in the top-right corner now shows the random value

You can find the project files for the app up to this point under **03 - Outlets** in the tutorial's Source Code folder.

Action methods vs. normal methods

So what is the difference between an action method and a regular method?

Answer: Nothing.

An action method is really just the same as any other method. The only special thing is the `@IBAction` specifier. This allows Interface Builder to see the method so you can connect it to your buttons, sliders, and so on.

Other methods, such as `viewDidLoad()`, do not have the `@IBAction` specifier. This is a good thing because all kinds of mayhem would occur if you hooked such methods up to your buttons.

This is the simple form of an action method:

```
@IBAction func showAlert()
```

You can also ask for a reference to the object that triggered this action, using a parameter:

```
@IBAction func sliderMoved(slider: UISlider)
@IBAction func buttonTapped(button: UIButton)
```

But the following method cannot be used as an action from Interface Builder:

```
func updateLabels()
```

It is not marked as `@IBAction` and as a result Interface Builder can't see it. To use `updateLabels()`, you will have to call it yourself.

Calculating the score

Now that you have both the target value (the random number) and a way to read the slider's position, you can calculate how many points the player scored.

The closer the slider is to the target, the more points for the player.

To calculate the score for this round, you look at how far off the slider's value is from the target:

Calculating the difference between the slider position and the target value

A simple approach to find the distance between the target and the slider is to subtract currentValue from targetValue.

Unfortunately, that gives a negative value if the slider is to the right of the target because now currentValue is greater than targetValue.

You need some way to turn that negative distance into a positive value – or you end up subtracting points from the player's score (unfair!).

Always doing the subtraction the other way around – currentValue minus targetValue – won't solve things because then the difference will be negative if the slider is to the left of the target instead of the right.

Hmm, it looks like we're in trouble here…

Exercise: How would you frame the solution to this problem if I asked you to solve it in natural language? Don't worry about how to express it in computer language for now, just think of it in plain English. ■

I came up with something like this:

> *If the slider's value is greater than the target value,*
> *then the difference is: slider value minus the target value.*
>
> *However, if the target value is greater than the slider value,*
> *then the difference is: target value minus the slider value.*
>
> *Otherwise, both values must be equal,*
> *and the difference is zero.*

This will always lead to a difference that is a positive number, because you always subtract the smaller number from the larger one.

Do the math:

If the slider is at position 60 and the target value is 40, then onscreen the slider is to the right of the target value, and the difference is 60 - 40 = 20.

However, if the slider is at position 10 and the target is 30, then the slider is to the left of the target and has a smaller value. The difference here is 30 - 10 = also 20.

Algorithms

What you've just done is come up with an *algorithm*, which is a fancy term for a series of mechanical steps for solving a computational problem. This is only a very simple algorithm, but it is one nonetheless.

There are many famous algorithms, such as quicksort for sorting a list of items and binary search for quickly searching through such a sorted list. Other people have already invented many algorithms that you can use in your own programs, so that saves you a lot of thinking!

However, in all the programs that you write you'll have to come up with a few algorithms of your own. Some are simple such as the one above; others can be pretty hard and might cause you to throw up your hands in despair. But that's part of the fun of programming.

The academic field of Computer Science concerns itself largely with studying algorithms and finding better ones.

You can describe any algorithm in plain English. It's just a series of steps that you can perform to calculate something. Often you can perform that calculation in your head or on paper, the way you did above. But for more complicated algorithms doing that might take you forever, so at some point you'll have to convert the algorithm to computer code.

The point I'm trying to make is this: if you ever get stuck and you don't know how to make your program calculate something, take a piece of paper and try to write out the steps in English. Set aside the computer for a moment and think the steps through. How you would perform this calculation by hand?

Once you know how to do that, writing the algorithm in computer code should be a piece of cake.

It is possible you came up with a different way to solve this little problem, and I'll show you two alternatives in a minute, but let's convert this one to computer code first:

```
var difference: Int
if currentValue > targetValue {
  difference = currentValue - targetValue
} else if targetValue > currentValue {
  difference = targetValue - currentValue
} else {
  difference = 0
}
```

The "if" construct is new. It allows your code to make decisions and it works much like you would expect from English. Generally, it works like this:

```
if something is true {
  then do this
} else if something else is true {
  then do that instead
} else {
  do something when neither of the above are true
}
```

You put a so-called *logical condition* after the `if` keyword. If that condition turns out to be true, for example `currentValue` is greater than `targetValue`, then the code in the block between the { } brackets is executed.

However, if the condition is not true, then the computer looks at the `else if` condition and evaluates that. There may be more than one `else if`, and it tries them one by one from top to bottom until one proves to be true.

If none of the conditions are found to be valid, then the code in the `else` block is executed.

In the implementation of this little algorithm you first create a local variable named `difference` to hold the result. This will either be a positive whole number or zero, so an `Int` will do:

```
var difference: Int
```

Then you compare the `currentValue` against the `targetValue`. First you determine if `currentValue` is greater than `targetValue`:

```
if currentValue > targetValue {
```

The > is the *greater-than* operator. The condition `currentValue > targetValue` is considered true if the value stored in the `currentValue` variable is at least one higher than the value stored in the `targetValue` variable. In that case, the following line of code is executed:

```
  difference = currentValue – targetValue
```

Here you subtract `targetValue` (the smaller one) from `currentValue` (the larger one) and store the difference in the `difference` variable.

Notice how I chose variable names that clearly describe what kind of data the variable contains. Often you will see code such as this:

```
a = b – c
```

It is not immediately clear what this is supposed to mean, other than that some arithmetic is taking place. The variable names "a", "b" and "c" don't give any clues as to their intended purpose.

Back to the if-statement. If `currentValue` is equal to or less than `targetValue`, the condition is untrue (or *false* in computer-speak) and the program will skip the code block until it reaches the next condition:

```
} else if targetValue > currentValue {
```

The same thing happens here as before, except that now the roles of `targetValue` and `currentValue` are reversed. The computer will only execute the following line when `targetValue` is the greater of the two values:

```
  difference = targetValue – currentValue
```

This time you subtract `currentValue` from `targetValue` (i.e. the other way around) and store the result in the `difference` variable.

There is only one situation you haven't handled yet, and that is when `currentValue` and `targetValue` are equal. If this happens, the player has put the slider exactly on top of the random number, a perfect score. In that case the difference is 0:

```
} else {
  difference = 0
}
```

At this point you've already determined that one value is not greater than the other, nor is it smaller, leaving you only one conclusion to draw: the numbers must be equal.

➤ Let's put this algorithm into action. Add it to the top of showAlert:

```
@IBAction func showAlert() {
  var difference: Int
  if currentValue > targetValue {
    difference = currentValue - targetValue
  } else if targetValue > currentValue {
    difference = targetValue - currentValue
  } else {
    difference = 0
  }

  let message = "The value of the slider is: \(currentValue)"
            + "\nThe target value is: \(targetValue)"
            + "\nThe difference is \(difference)"

  . . .
}
```

Just so you can see that it works, you have added the difference value to the alert message as well.

➤ Run it and see for yourself.

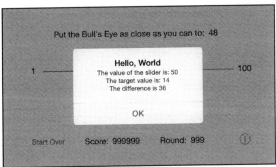

The alert shows the difference between the target and the slider

Alternative ways to calculate the difference

I mentioned earlier that there are other ways to calculate the difference between currentValue and targetValue as a positive number. The above algorithm works well but it is eight lines of code. I think we can come up with a simpler approach that takes up fewer lines.

The new algorithm goes like this:

Subtract the target value from the slider's value.

If the result is a negative number,
then multiply it by –1 to make it a positive number.

Now you're no longer avoiding the negative number, as computers can work just fine with negative numbers, but you simply turn it into a positive number.

Exercise: Convert this algorithm into source code. Hint: the English description of the algorithm contains the words "if" and "then", which is a pretty good indication you'll have to use the if-statement. ∎

You should have arrived at something like this:

```
var difference = currentValue - targetValue
if difference < 0 {
  difference = difference * -1
}
```

This is a pretty straightforward translation of the new algorithm.

You first subtract the two variables and put the result into the `difference` variable.

Notice that you can create the new variable and assign it the result of a calculation, all in one line. You don't need to put it onto two different lines, like so:

```
var difference: Int
difference = currentValue - targetValue
```

Also, in the one-liner version you didn't have to tell the compiler that `difference` takes `Int` values. Because both `currentValue` and `targetValue` are `Int`s, Swift is smart enough to figure out that difference should also be an `Int`.

This feature is called *type inference* and it's one of the big selling points of Swift.

Once you have the subtraction result, you use an if-statement to determine whether `difference` is negative, i.e. less than zero. If it is, you multiply by -1 and put the new result – now a positive number – back into the `difference` variable.

When you write,

```
difference = difference * -1
```

the computer first multiplies `difference`'s value by -1. Then it puts the result of that calculation back into `difference`. In effect, this overwrites `difference`'s old contents (the negative number) with the positive number.

Because this is a common thing to do, there is a handy shortcut:

```
difference *= -1
```

The `*=` operator combines `*` and `=` into a single operation. The end result is the same: the variable's old value is gone and it now contains the result of the multiplication.

You could also have written this algorithm as follows:

```
var difference = currentValue - targetValue
if difference < 0 {
  difference = -difference
}
```

Instead of multiplying by –1, you now use the negation operator to ensure difference's value is always positive. This works because negating a negative number makes it positive again. (Ask a math professor if you don't believe me.)

➤ Give these new algorithms a try. You should replace the old stuff at the top of showAlert() as follows:

```
@IBAction func showAlert() {
  var difference = currentValue - targetValue
  if difference < 0 {
    difference = difference * -1
  }

  let message = . . .
}
```

When you run this new version of the app (try it!), it should work exactly the same as before. The result of the computation does not change, only the technique you used.

The final alternative algorithm I want to show you uses a function.

You've already seen functions a few times before: you used arc4random_uniform() when you made random numbers and lroundf() for rounding off the slider's decimals.

To make sure a number is always positive, you can use the abs() function.

If you took math in school you might remember the term "absolute value", which is the value of a number without regard to its sign.

That's exactly what you need here and the standard library contains a convenient function for it, which allows you to reduce this entire problem to a single line:

```
let difference = abs(targetValue - currentValue)
```

It really doesn't matter whether you subtract currentValue from targetValue or the other way around. If the number is negative, abs() turns it positive. It's a handy function to remember.

➤ Make the change to showAlert() and try it out:

```
@IBAction func showAlert() {
  let difference = abs(targetValue - currentValue)

  let message = . . .
}
```

It doesn't get much simpler than that!

Exercise: Something else has changed... can you spot it? ∎

Answer: You wrote **let** difference instead of **var** difference.

Swift makes a distinction between variables and so-called *constants*. Unlike a variable, the value of a constant cannot change (you probably guessed it from the name).

You can only put something into the box of a constant once but not replace it with something else afterwards.

The keyword var creates a variable while let creates a constant. That means difference is now a constant, not a variable.

In the previous algorithms, the value of `difference` could possibly change. If it was negative, you turned it positive. That required `difference` to be a variable, because only variables can be assigned new values.

Now that you can calculate the whole thing in a single line, `difference` will never have to change once you've given it a value. In that case, it's better to make it a constant with `let`. (Why is that better? It makes your intent clear, which in turn helps the Swift compiler understand your program better.)

By the same token, `message`, `alert`, and `action` are also constants (and have been all along!). Now you know why you declared these objects with `let` instead of `var`. Once they've been given a value, they never need to change.

Constants are very common in Swift. Often you only need to hold onto a value for a very short time. If in that time the value never has to change, it's best to make it a constant (`let`) and not a variable (`var`).

What's the score?

Now that you know how far off the slider is from the target, calculating the player's score for this round is easy.

➤ Change `showAlert()` to:

```
@IBAction func showAlert() {
  let difference = abs(targetValue - currentValue)
  let points = 100 - difference

  let message = "You scored \(points) points"
  . . .
}
```

The maximum score you can get is 100 points if you put the slider right on the target and the difference is zero. The further away from the target you are, the fewer points you earn.

➤ Run the app and score some points!

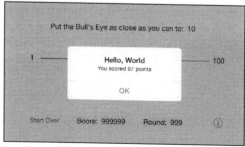

The alert with the player's score for the current round

Exercise: Because the maximum slider position is 100 and the minimum is 1, the biggest difference is 100 - 1 = 99. That means the absolute worst score you can have in a round is 1 point. Explain why this is so. (Eek! It requires math!) ∎

Keeping track of the player's total score

In this game, you want to show the player's total score on the screen. After every round, the app should add the newly scored points to the total and then update the score label.

Because the game needs to keep the total score around for a long time, you will put it in an instance variable.

➤ Add a new score instance variable to **ViewController.swift**:

```
class ViewController: UIViewController {
  var currentValue: Int = 0
  var targetValue: Int = 0
  var score = 0

  . . .
```

Hey, what's that? Unlike for the other two instance variables, you did not state that score is an Int.

If you don't specify a data type, Swift uses *type inference* to figure out what type you meant. Because 0 is a whole number, Swift assumes that score should be an integer, and therefore automatically gives it the type Int. Handy!

In fact, you don't need to specify Int for the other instance variables either:

```
  var currentValue = 0
  var targetValue = 0
```

➤ Make these changes.

Thanks to type inference, you only have to list the name of the data type when you're not giving the variable an initial value. But most of the time, you can safely make Swift guess at the type.

I think type inference is pretty sweet! It will definitely save you some, uh, typing (in more ways than one!).

Now showAlert() can be amended to update this score variable.

➤ Make the following changes:

```
@IBAction func showAlert() {
    let difference = abs(targetValue - currentValue)
    let points = 100 - difference

    score += points

    let message = "You scored \(points) points"

    . . .
}
```

Nothing too shocking here. You just added the following line:

```
score += points
```

This adds the points that the user scored in this round to the total score. You could also have written it like this:

```
score = score + points
```

Personally, I prefer the shorthand += version but either one is okay. Both accomplish exactly the same thing.

Showing the score on the screen

You're going to do exactly the same thing that you did for the target label: hook up the score label to an outlet and put the score value into the label's text property.

Exercise: See if you can do the above without my help. You've already done these things before for the target value label, so you should be able to repeat these steps by yourself for the score label. ■

You should have done the following. You added this line to **ViewController.swift**:

```
@IBOutlet weak var scoreLabel: UILabel!
```

Then you went into the storyboard and connected the label (the one that says 999999) to the new scoreLabel outlet.

Unsure how to connect the outlet? There are several ways to make connections from user interface objects to outlets on the view controller:

• Ctrl-click on the object to get a context-sensitive popup menu. Then drag from New Referencing Outlet to View Controller (you did this with the slider).

• Go to the Connections Inspector for the label. Drag from New Referencing Outlet to View Controller (you did this with the target label).

• Ctrl-drag from View Controller to the label (give this one a try now). Make sure you do it in this order; ctrl-dragging from the label to the view controller won't work.

There is more than one way to ~~skin a cat~~ connect outlets.

Great, that gives you a scoreLabel outlet that you can use to put text into the label. Now where in the code shall you do that? In updateLabels(), of course.

➤ Back in **ViewController.swift**, change updateLabels() to the following:

```
func updateLabels() {
  targetLabel.text = String(targetValue)
  scoreLabel.text = String(score)
}
```

Nothing new here. You convert the score – which is an Int – into a String and then give that string to the label's text property. In response to that, the label will redraw itself with the new score.

➤ Run the app and verify that the points for this round are added to the total score label whenever you tap the button.

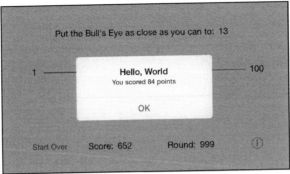

The score label keeps track of the player's total score

One more round...

Speaking of rounds, you also have to increment the round number each time the player starts a new round.

Exercise: Keep track of the current round number (starting at 1) and increment it when a new round starts. Display the current round number in the corresponding label. I may be throwing you into the deep end here, but if you've been able to follow the instructions so far, then you've already seen all the pieces you will need to pull this off. Good luck! ∎

If you guessed that you had to add another instance variable, then you were right. You should have added the following line to the source code:

```
var round = 0
```

It's also OK if you included the name of the data type, even though that is not strictly necessary:

```
var round: Int = 0
```

And also an outlet for the label:

```
@IBOutlet weak var roundLabel: UILabel!
```

As before, you should have connected the label to this outlet in Interface Builder.

Don't forget to make those connections

Forgetting to make the connections in Interface Builder is an often-made mistake, especially by yours truly.

It happens to me all the time that I make the outlet for a button and write the code to deal with taps on that button, but when I run the app it doesn't work. Usually it takes me a few minutes and some head scratching to realize that I forgot to connect the button to the outlet or the action method.

You can tap on the button all you want, but unless that connection exists your code will not respond.

Finally, `updateLabels()` should now look like this:

```
func updateLabels() {
  targetLabel.text = String(targetValue)
  scoreLabel.text = String(score)
  roundLabel.text = String(round)
}
```

Did you also figure out where to increment the round variable?

I'd say the startNewRound() method is a pretty good place. After all, you call this method whenever you start a new round. It makes sense to increment the round counter there.

➤ Change startNewRound() to:

```
func startNewRound() {
  round += 1
  targetValue = 1 + Int(arc4random_uniform(100))
  currentValue = 50
  slider.value = Float(currentValue)
}
```

Note that when you declared the round instance variable, you gave it a default value of 0. Therefore, when the app starts up, round is initially 0. When you call startNewRound() for the very first time, it adds 1 to this initial value and as a result the first round is properly counted as round 1.

➤ Run the app and try it out. The round counter should update whenever you press the Hit Me button.

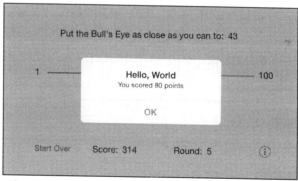

The round label counts how many rounds have been played

You can find the project files for the app up to this point under **04 - Rounds and Score** in the tutorial's Source Code folder. If you get stuck, compare your version of the app with those source files to see if you missed anything.

Polishing the game

You could leave it at this and have a playable game. The gameplay rules are all implemented and the logic doesn't seem to have any big flaws. As far as I can tell, there are no bugs. But there is still some room for improvement.

Obviously, the game is not very pretty yet and you will get to work on that soon. In the mean time, there are a few smaller tweaks you can make.

Unless you already changed it, the title of the alert still says "Hello, World!" You could give it the name of the game, "Bull's Eye", but I have a better idea. What if you change the title depending on how well the player did?

If the player put the slider right on the target, the alert could say: "Perfect!" If the slider is close to the target but not quite there, it could say, "You almost had it!" If the player is way off, the alert could say: "Not even close..." And so on. This gives players a little more feedback on how well they did.

Exercise: Think of a way to accomplish this. Where would you put this logic and how would you program it? Hint: there are an awful lot of "ifs" in the preceding sentences. ∎

The right place for this logic is showAlert(), because that is where you create the UIAlertController. You already make the message text dynamically and now you will do something similar for the title text.

➤ Here is the changed method in its entirety:

```
@IBAction func showAlert() {
  let difference = abs(targetValue - currentValue)
  let points = 100 - difference
  score += points

  var title: String
  if difference == 0 {
    title = "Perfect!"
  } else if difference < 5 {
    title = "You almost had it!"
  } else if difference < 10 {
    title = "Pretty good!"
  } else {
    title = "Not even close..."
  }

  let message = "You scored \(points) points"

  let alert = UIAlertController(title: title, message: message, preferredStyle: .Alert)
  let action = UIAlertAction(title: "OK", style: .Default, handler: nil)
  alert.addAction(action)

  presentViewController(alert, animated: true, completion: nil)

  startNewRound()
  updateLabels()
}
```

You create a new local string variable named title, which will contain the text that goes at the top of the alert. Initially, this title variable doesn't have any value.

To decide which title text to use, you look at the difference between the slider position and the target:

• If it equals 0, then the player was spot-on and you put the text "Perfect!" into title.

• If the difference is less than 5, you use the text "You almost had it!"

• A difference less than 10 is "Pretty good!"

• However, if the difference is 10 or greater, then you consider the player's attempt "Not even close..."

Can you follow the logic here? It's just a bunch of if-statements that consider the different possibilities and choose a string in response.

When you create the `UIAlertController` object, you now give it this `title` variable instead of a fixed text.

Run the app and play the game for a bit. You'll see that the title text changes depending on how well you're doing. That if-statement sure is handy!

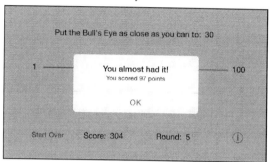

The alert with the new title

Exercise: Give the player an additional 100 bonus points when she has a perfect score.

This will encourage players to really try to place the bull's eye right on the target. Otherwise, there isn't much difference between 100 points for a perfect score and 98 or 95 points if you're close but not quite there.

Now there is an incentive for trying harder – a perfect score is no longer worth just 100 but 200 points. Maybe you can also give the player 50 bonus points for being just one off. ■

➤ Here is how I would have made these changes:

```
@IBAction func showAlert() {
  let difference = abs(targetValue - currentValue)
  var points = 100 - difference

  var title: String
  if difference == 0 {
    title = "Perfect!"
    points += 100
  } else if difference < 5 {
    title = "You almost had it!"
    if difference == 1 {
      points += 50
    }
  } else if difference < 10 {
    title = "Pretty good!"
  } else {
    title = "Not even close..."
  }

  score += points

  . . .
}
```

You should notice a few things:

- In the first `if` you'll see a new statement between its curly brackets. When the difference is equal to zero, you now not only set the title to "Perfect!" but also award an extra 100 points.

- The second `if` has changed too. There is now an `if` inside another `if`. Nothing wrong with that! You want to handle the case where `difference` is 1 in order to give the player bonus points. That happens inside the new if-statement.

    After all, if the difference is more than 0 but less than 5, it could also be 1 (but not necessarily all the time). Therefore, you perform an additional check to see if the difference truly was 1, and if so, add 50 extra points.

- Because these new if-statements add extra points, the `points` object can no longer be a constant; it now needs to be a variable. That's why you changed it from `let` into `var`.

- Finally, the line `score += points` has moved below the `if`s. This is necessary because the app might update the `points` variable inside those if-statements and you want those additional points to count towards the score as well.

If you did it slightly differently, then that's fine too, as long as it works! There is often more than one way to program something, and if the results are the same then each way is equally valid.

➤ Run the app to see if you can score some bonus points!

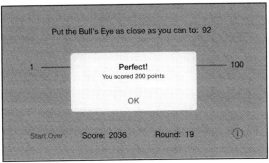

Raking in the points...

I would like to point out one more time the difference between local variables and instance variables. As you should know by now, a local variable only exists for the duration of the method that it is defined in, while an instance variable exists as long as the view controller (the object that owns it) exists. The same thing is true for constants.

In `showAlert()`, there are six locals and you use three instance variables:

```
let difference = abs(targetValue - currentValue)
var points = 100 - difference
var title = . . .
score += points
let message = . . .
let alert = . . .
let action = . . .
```

Exercise: Point out which are the locals and which are the instance variables in the `showAlert()` method. Of the locals, which are variables and which are constants? ∎

Answer: Locals are easy to recognize, because the first time they are used inside a method their name is preceded with `let` or `var`:

```
let difference = . . .
var points = . . .
var title = . . .
let message = . . .
let alert = . . .
let action = . . .
```

This syntax creates a new variable (var) or constant (let). Because these variables and constants are created inside the method, they are locals.

Those six items – `difference`, `points`, `message`, `alert`, and `action` – are restricted to the `showAlert()` method and do not exist outside of it. As soon as the method is done, the locals cease to exist.

You may be wondering how `difference`, for example, can have a different value every time the player taps the Hit Me button, even though it is a constant – after all, aren't constants given a value just once, never to change afterwards?

Here's why: each time a method is invoked, its local variables and constants are created anew. The old values have long been forgotten and you get all new ones.

When `showAlert()` is called, it creates a completely new instance of `difference` that is unrelated to the previous one. That particular constant value is only used until the end of `showAlert()` and then it is forgotten again.

The next time `showAlert()` is called after that, it creates yet another new instance of `difference` (as well as new instances of `points`, `message`, `alert`, and `action`). And so on... There's some serious recycling going on here!

But inside a single invocation of `showAlert()`, `difference` can never change once it has its value. The only local that can change is `points`, because it's a var.

The instance variables, on the other hand, are defined outside of any method. It is common to put them at the top of the file:

```
class ViewController: UIViewController {
  var currentValue = 0
  var targetValue = 0
  var score = 0
  var round = 0
```

As a result, you can use these variables from any method, without the need to declare them again, and they will keep their values.

If you were to do this,

```
@IBAction func showAlert() {
  let difference = abs(targetValue - currentValue)
  var points = 100 - difference

  var score = score + points

  . . .
}
```

then things wouldn't work as you'd expect them to. Because you now put var in front of score, you have made it a new local variable that is only valid inside this method.

In other words, this won't add points to the *instance variable* score but to a new *local variable* that also happens to be named score. The instance variable score never gets changed, even though it has the same name.

Obviously that is not what you want to happen here. Fortunately, the above won't even compile. Swift knows there's something fishy about that line.

> **Note:** To make a distinction between the two types of variables, so that it's always clear at a glance how long they will live, some programmers prefix the names of instance variables with an underscore.
>
> They would name the variable _score instead of just score. Now there is less confusion because names beginning with an underscore won't be mistaken for being locals. This is only a convention. Swift doesn't care one way or the other how you spell your instance variables.
>
> Other programmers use different prefixes, such as "m" (for member) or "f" (for field) for the same purpose. Some even put the underscore *behind* the variable name. Madness!

Waiting for the alert to go away

There is something that bothers me about the game. You may have noticed it too…

As soon as you tap the Hit Me button and the alert pops up, the slider immediately jumps back to its center position, the round number increments, and the target label already gets the new random number.

What happens is that the new round already gets started while you're still watching the results of the last round. That's a little confusing.

It would be better to wait with starting the new round until *after* the player has dismissed the alert popup. Only then is the current round truly over.

Maybe you're wondering why this isn't already happening? After all, in showAlert() you only call startNewRound() after you've shown the alert popup:

```
@IBAction func showAlert() {
  . . .

  let alert = UIAlertController(. . .)
  let action = UIAlertAction(. . .)
  alert.addAction(action)

  // Here you make the alert visible:
  presentViewController(alert, animated: true, completion: nil)

  // Here you start the new round:
  startNewRound()
  updateLabels()
}
```

Contrary to what you may expect, presentViewController(alert, ...) doesn't hold up execution of the rest of the method until the alert popup is dismissed. That's how alerts on other platforms tend to work, but not on iOS.

Instead, `presentViewController()` puts the alert on the screen and immediately returns. The rest of the `showAlert()` method is executed right away, and the new round already starts before the alert popup has even finished animating.

In programmer-speak, alerts work *asynchronously*. Much more about that in a later tutorial, but what it means for you right now is that you don't know in advance when the alert will be done. But you can bet it will be well after `showAlert()` has finished.

So if you can't wait in `showAlert()` until the popup is dismissed, then how do you wait for it to close?

The answer is simple: events! As you've seen, a lot of the programming for iOS involves waiting for specific events to occur – buttons being tapped, sliders being moved, and so on. This is no different. You have to wait for the "alert dismissed" event somehow. In the mean time, you simply do nothing.

Here's how it works:

For each button on the alert, you have to supply a `UIAlertAction` object. This object tells the alert what the text on the button is – "OK" – and what the button looks like (you're using the default style here):

```
let action = UIAlertAction(title: "OK", style: .Default, handler: nil)
```

The third parameter, `handler`, tells the alert what should happen when the button is pressed. This is the "alert dismissed" event you've been looking for.

Currently `handler` is `nil`, which means nothing happens. To change this, you'll need to give the `UIAlertAction` some source code to perform when the button is tapped. When the user finally taps OK, the alert will remove itself from the screen and jump to your code. That's your cue to take it from there.

This is also known as the *callback* pattern. There are several ways this pattern manifests on iOS. Often you'll be asked to create a new method to handle the event. But here you'll use something new: a *closure*.

➤ Change the bottom bit of `showAlert()` to:

```
@IBAction func showAlert() {
  . . .
  let alert = UIAlertController(. . .)

  let action = UIAlertAction(title: "OK", style: .Default, handler: { action in
    self.startNewRound()
    self.updateLabels()
  })

  alert.addAction(action)

  presentViewController(alert, animated: true, completion: nil)
}
```

Two things have happened here:

1. You removed the calls to `startNewRound()` and `updateLabels()` from the bottom of the method.

2. You placed them inside a block of code that you gave to `UIAlertAction`'s `handler` parameter.

Such a block of code is called a closure. You can think of it as a method without a name. This code is not performed right away, only when the OK button is tapped. This closure tells the app to start a new round and update the labels when the alert is dismissed.

➤ Run it and see for yourself. I think the game feels a lot better this way.

Self

You may be wondering why in the handler block you did `self.startNewRound()` instead of just writing `startNewRound()` like before.

The `self` keyword allows the view controller to refer to itself. That shouldn't be too strange a concept. When you say, "I want ice cream," you use the word "I" to refer to yourself. Similarly, objects can talk about (or to) themselves as well.

Normally you don't need to use `self` to send messages to the view controller, even though it is allowed. The exception: inside closures you *do* have to use `self` to refer to the view controller.

This is a rule in Swift. If you forget `self` in a closure, Xcode doesn't want to build your app (try it out). This rule exists because closures can "capture" variables, which comes with surprising side effects. You'll learn more about that in the other tutorials.

Starting over

No, you're not going to throw away the source code and start this project all over! I'm talking about the game's "Start Over" button. This button is supposed to reset the score and put the player back into the first round.

One use of the Start Over button is for playing against another person. The first player does ten rounds, then the score is reset and the second player does ten rounds. The player with the highest score wins.

Exercise: Try to implement this Start Over button on your own. You've already seen how you can make the view controller react to button presses, and you should be able to figure out how to change the `score` and `round` variables. ■

How did you do? If you got stuck, then follow the instructions below.

First, add a method that starts a new game to **ViewController.swift**. I suggest you put it near `startNewRound()` because the two are conceptually related.

➤ Add the new method:

```
func startNewGame() {
  score = 0
  round = 0
  startNewRound()
}
```

This method resets the score and round number, and starts a new round as well.

Notice that you set `round` to 0 here, not to 1. You use 0 because incrementing the value of `round` is the first thing `startNewRound()` does.

If you were to set `round` to 1, then `startNewRound()` would add another 1 to it and the first round would actually be labeled round 2.

So you begin at 0, let `startNewRound()` add one and everything will work out fine.

(It's probably easier to figure this out from the code than from my explanation. This should illustrate why we don't program computers in English.)

You also need an action method to handle taps on the Start Over button.

➤ Add the action method to **ViewController.swift**:

```
@IBAction func startOver() {
  startNewGame()
  updateLabels()
}
```

It doesn't really matter where you place this method, but below the other action methods is a nice place for it.

When the Start Over button is pressed, the `startOver()` action method first calls `startNewGame()` to start a new game (see, if you choose method names that make sense, then reading source code really isn't that hard).

Because `startNewGame()` changes the contents of the instance variables you also call `updateLabels()` to update the text of the score, round and target labels.

Just to make things consistent, in `viewDidLoad()` you should replace the call to `startNewRound()` by `startNewGame()`. Because `score` and `round` are already 0 when the app starts, it won't really make any difference to how the app works but it does make the intention of the source code clearer.

➤ Make this change:

```
override func viewDidLoad() {
  super.viewDidLoad()
  startNewGame()
  updateLabels()
}
```

Finally, you need to connect the Start Over button to the action method.

➤ Open the storyboard and Ctrl-drag from the **Start Over** button to **View Controller**. Let go of the mouse button and pick **startOver** from the popup.

That connects the button's Touch Up Inside event to the action you have just defined.

➤ Run the app and play a few rounds. Press Start Over and the game puts you back at square one.

Tip: If you're losing track of what button or label is connected to what method, you can click on **View Controller** in the storyboard to see all the connections that you have made so far.

You can either right-click on View Controller to get a popup, or simply view the connections in the **Connections inspector**. This shows all the connections that have been made to the view controller.

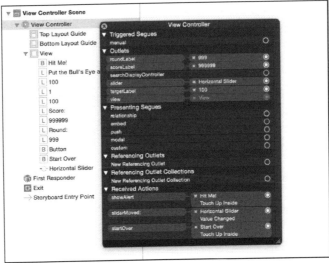

All the connections from View Controller to the other objects

You can find the project files for the current version of the app under 05 - **Polish** in the tutorial's Source Code folder.

Adding the About screen

I hope you're not fed up with this app yet, as there is one more feature that I wish to add to it, an "about" screen that shows some information about the game:

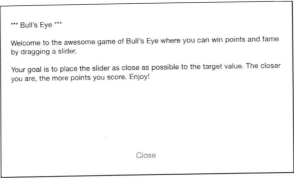

The new About screen

This new screen contains a so-called *text view* with the gameplay rules and a button that lets the player close the screen. You get to the About screen by tapping the **(i)** button on the main game screen.

Most apps have more than one screen, even very simple games, so this is as good a time as any to learn how to add additional screens to your apps.

I have pointed it out a few times already: each screen in your app will have its own view controller. If you think "screen", think "view controller".

Xcode automatically created the main `ViewController` object for you but the view controller for the About screen you'll have to make yourself.

➤ Go to Xcode's **File** menu and choose **New → File...** In the window that pops up, choose the **Cocoa Touch Class** template (if you don't see it then make sure **iOS, Source** is selected on the left):

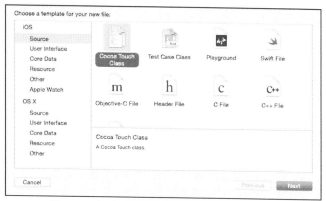

Choosing the file template for Cocoa Touch Class

Click **Next**. Xcode gives you some options to fill out:

The options for the new file

Choose the following:

- Class: AboutViewController

- Subclass of: UIViewController

- Also create XIB file: Leave this box unchecked.

- Language: Swift

Click **Next**. Xcode will ask you where to save this new view controller:

Saving the new file

➤ Choose the **BullsEye** folder (this folder should already be selected).

Also make sure Group says **BullsEye** and that there is a checkmark in front of **BullsEye** in the list of **Targets**.

➤ Click **Create** to finish.

Xcode will make a new file and add it to your project. As you might have guessed, the new file is **AboutViewController.swift**.

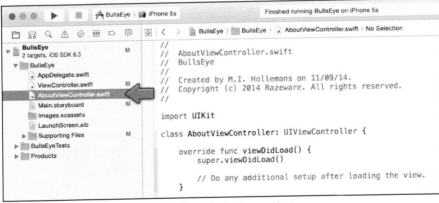

The new file in the Project navigator

To design this new view controller, you need to pay a visit to Interface Builder.

➤ Open **Main.storyboard**. There is no scene representing the About view controller yet, so you'll have to add this first.

➤ From the **Object Library**, choose **View Controller** and drag it into the canvas, to the right of the main View Controller.

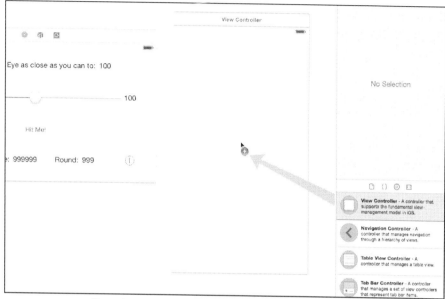

Dragging a new View Controller from the Object Library

This new view controller is totally blank and in portrait orientation.

➤ Click on the round yellow icon in the bar above the view controller to select it and go to the **Attributes inspector**. Under **Simulated Metrics**, set **Orientation** to **Landscape**.

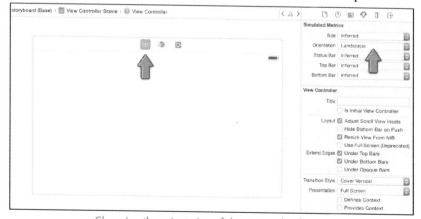

Changing the orientation of the view to landscape

You may need to rearrange the storyboard so that the two view controllers don't overlap. Interface Builder isn't always very neat with where it puts things.

➤ Drag a new **Button** into the screen and give it the title **Close**. Put it somewhere in the bottom center of the view.

➤ Drag a **Text View** into the view and make it cover most of the space above the button.

You can find these components in the Object Library. If you don't feel like scrolling, you can filter the components by typing in the field at the bottom:

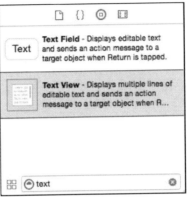

Searching for text components

Note that there is also a Text Field, which is a single-line text component. You're looking for Text View, which can contain multiple lines of text.

After dragging both the text view and the button into the canvas, it should look something like this:

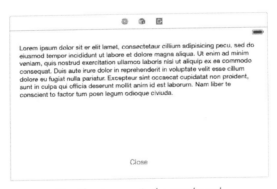

The About screen in the storyboard

➤ Double-click on the text view to make its contents editable. By default, the Text View contains a whole bunch of fake Latin placeholder text (also known as "Lorem Ipsum").

Copy-paste this new text into it:

```
*** Bull's Eye ***

Welcome to the awesome game of Bull's Eye where you can win points and fame by dragging a slider.

Your goal is to place the slider as close as possible to the target value. The closer you are, the more points you score. Enjoy!
```

You can also paste that text into the Attributes inspector for the text view if you find that easier.

➤ Make sure to uncheck the **Editable** box, otherwise the user can actually type into the text view. For this game it should be set to read-only.

The Attributes inspector for the text view

That's the design of the screen finished for now.

So how do you open this new About screen when the user presses the (i) button? Storyboards have a neat trick for this: *segues* (pronounced "seg-way" like the silly scooters). A segue is a transition from one screen to another and they are really easy to add.

➤ Click the **(i) button** in the **View Controller** to select it. Then hold down Ctrl and drag over to the **About** screen.

Ctrl-drag from one view controller to another to make a segue

➤ Let go of the mouse button and a popup appears with several options. Choose **modal**.

Choosing the type of segue to create

Now an arrow will appear between the two screens. This arrow represents the segue.

➤ Click the arrow to select it. Segues also have attributes. In the **Attributes inspector,** choose **Transition, Flip Horizontal.** That is the animation that UIKit will use to move between these screens.

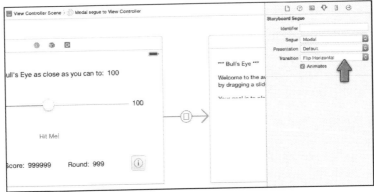

Changing the attributes for the segue

➤ Now you can run the app. Press the (i) button to see the new screen.

The About screen appears with a flip animation

The About screen should appear with a neat animation. Good, that seems to work.

However, there is an obvious shortcoming here: tapping the Close button seems to have no effect. Once the user enters the About screen she can never leave... that doesn't sound like good user interface design to me.

The problem with segues is that they only go one way. To close this screen, you have to hook up some code to the Close button. As a budding iOS developer you already know how to do that: use an action method!

This time you will add the action method to AboutViewController instead of ViewController, because the Close button is part of the About screen, not the main game screen.

➤ Open **AboutViewController.swift** and replace its contents with the following:

```
import UIKit

class AboutViewController: UIViewController {
```

```
@IBAction func close() {
    dismissViewControllerAnimated(true, completion: nil)
  }
}
```

This code inside the `close()` action method tells UIKit to close the About screen with an animation.

If you would have said `dismissViewControllerAnimated(false, ...)`, then there would be no page flip and the main screen would instantly reappear.

From a user experience perspective, it's often better to show transitions from one screen to another with a subtle animation.

That leaves you with one final step, hooking up the Close button's Touch Up Inside event to this new `close` action.

➤ Open the storyboard and Ctrl-drag from the **Close** button to the View Controller. Hmm, strange, the **close** action should be listed in this popup, but it isn't. Instead, this is the same popup you saw when you made the segue:

The "close" action is not listed in the popup

Exercise: Bonus points if you can spot the error. It's a common – and frustrating! – mistake. ∎

The problem is that this scene in the storyboard does not know that it is supposed to represent the `AboutViewController`.

You first added the AboutViewController.Swift source file and then dragged a new view controller into the storyboard, but you haven't told the storyboard that the design for this new view controller, in fact, belongs to `AboutViewController`. (That's why in the outline pane it just says View Controller and not About View Controller.)

➤ Fortunately, this is easily remedied. In Interface Builder, select the new **View Controller** and go to the **Identity inspector** (that's the button to the left of the Attributes inspector).

➤ Under **Custom Class**, type **AboutViewController**.

The Identity inspector for the About screen

Xcode should auto-complete this for you once you've typed the first few characters. If it doesn't, then double-check that you really have selected the View Controller and not one of the views inside it. (The view controller should also have a blue border to indicate it is selected.)

Now you should be able to connect the Close button to the action method.

➤ Ctrl-drag from the **Close** button to **About View Controller** in the outline pane. This should be old hat by now. The popup menu now does have an option for the **close** action. Connect the button to that action.

➤ Run the app again. You should now be able to return from the About screen.

Do you get this warning message in the Debug output pane?

`Unknown class _TtC8BullsEye19AboutViewController in Interface Builder file.`

And does the app crash when you tap the Close button? In that case, something went wrong when you added the `AboutViewController` source files to the project. This is easy enough to fix.

In the Project navigator, select **AboutViewController.swift** and open the **File inspector** (the first of the inspector tabs). Under **Target Membership**, make sure **BullsEye** is selected (but not BullsEyeTests).

Congrats! This completes the game. All the functionality is there and – as far as I can tell – there are no bugs to spoil the fun.

But you have to admit the game still doesn't look very good. If you were to put this on the App Store in its current form, I'm not sure many people would be excited to download it. Fortunately, iOS makes it easy for you to create good-looking apps, so let's give Bull's Eye a makeover.

You can find the project files for the app up to this point under **06 - About Screen** in the tutorial's Source Code folder.

Making it look good

On iOS 8, apps in landscape mode do not display the iPhone status bar, unless you tell them to. That's great for our app. Games require a more immersive experience and the status bar detracts from that.

On iOS 7 and before, the status bar did not automatically disappear in landscape, and earlier editions of this tutorial included lengthy instructions on how to remove the status bar from the app.

Even though that is not required anymore, there are still a few things you can do to improve the way Bull's Eye handles the status bar.

First, you will remove the status bar from the storyboard.

➤ Open **Main.storyboard** and select the **View Controller**. Go to the **Attributes inspector** and under **Simulated Metrics** set **Status Bar** to **None**.

This removes the status bar from the storyboard.

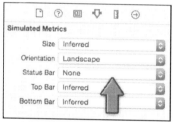

Remove the status bar from the view controller

This setting has no influence on what happens when the app runs. That's why this section is labeled *Simulated* Metrics. Interface Builder merely pretends there is a status bar as a visual design aid, so you can see how your screen design looks with the status bar on top.

Try enabling some of the other simulated options and then run the app; you'll see that it won't make a difference.

The final step to get rid of the status bar forever is to make a change to the app's configuration.

➤ Go to the **Project Settings** screen and under **Deployment Info, Status Bar Style**, check the option **Hide status bar**. This will also hide the status bar during application launch.

Hiding the status bar when the app launches

It's a good idea to hide the status bar while the app is launching. It takes a few seconds for the operating system to load the app into memory and start it up, and during that time the status bar remains visible, unless you hide it using this option.

It's only a small detail but the difference between a mediocre app and a great app is that great apps do all the small details right.

➤ That's it. Run the app and you'll see that the status bar is history.

Info.plist

Most of the options from the Project Settings screen, such as the supported device orientations and whether the status bar is visible during launch, get stored in your app's Info.plist file.

Info.plist is a configuration file inside the application bundle that tells iOS how the app will behave. It also describes certain characteristics of the app that don't really fit anywhere else, such as its version number.

With previous versions of Xcode you often had to edit Info.plist by hand, but with Xcode 6 this is hardly necessary anymore. You can make most of the changes directly from the Project Settings screen.

However, it's good to know that Info.plist exists and what it looks like.

➤ Go to the **Project navigator**. Under the group **Supporting Files** you will find a file named **Info.plist**. Click Info.plist to open it and Xcode's main edit pane will show you its contents.

The Info.plist file is just a list of configuration options and their values. Most of these may not make sense to you, but that's OK – they don't always make sense to me either.

Notice the option **Status bar is initially hidden**. It has the value YES. This is the option that you just changed.

Spicing up the graphics

Getting rid of the status bar is only the first step. We want to go from this:

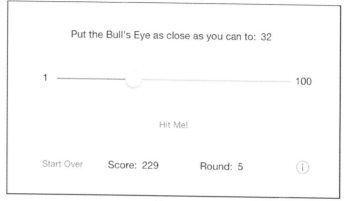

Yawn...

to something that's more like this:

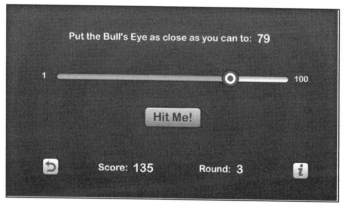

Cool ☺

The actual controls don't change. You'll simply use images to smarten up their look, and you will also adjust the colors and typefaces.

You can put an image in the background, on the buttons, and even on the slider, to customize their appearance. Images should be in PNG format.

If you are artistically challenged, then don't worry, I have provided a set of images for you. But if you do have mad Photoshop skillz, then by all means go ahead and design your own.

The Resources folder that comes with this tutorial contains a subfolder named Images. You will first import these images into the Xcode project.

➤ In the **Project navigator**, find **Images.xcassets** and click on it.

This is the so-called *asset catalog* for the app and it contains all the app's images. Right now, it is empty. Its only contents are placeholders for the app icon, which you'll add soon.

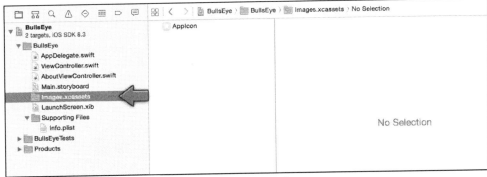

The asset catalog is initially empty

➤ At the bottom of the pane there is a + button. Click it and then select the option **Import…**

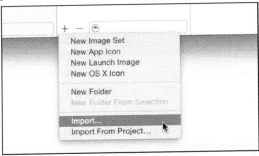

Choose Import to put existing images into the asset catalog

Xcode shows a file picker. Select the **Images** folder from this tutorial's resources and press ⌘+A to select all the files inside this folder.

Choosing the images to import

Click **Open** and Xcode copies all the image files from that folder into the asset catalog:

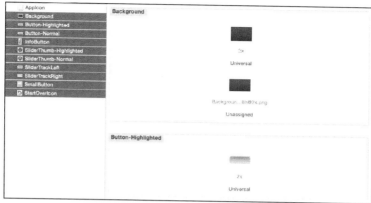

The images are now inside the asset catalog

If Xcode added a folder named Images instead of the individual image files, then try again and this time make sure that you select the files inside the Images folder rather than the folder itself before you click Open.

Try to build the app. If Xcode gives a warning message: "Ambiguous Content: The image set "Background" has an unassigned image", then something was not right with the import.

There are two different versions of the Background image:

- **Background@2x.png**: 640×960 pixels. This image was designed for the 3.5-inch screen of the iPhone 4S. This is the 2x image in the asset catalog.

- **Background-568h@2x.png**: 640×1136 pixels. For devices with a 4-inch screen, notably the iPhone 5, 5c and 5s. Xcode did not know where to put this image and placed it in the "Unassigned" category. This is the image that needs fixing.

➤ In the asset catalog (click on **Images.xcassets**), select the **Background** image set and open the **Attributes inspector**.

➤ Under **Devices**, change from **Universal** to **Device Specific**. De-select **iPad** and **Apple Watch**, and check **Retina 4-inch**.

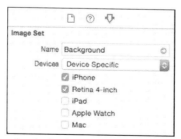

The attributes for the background image in the asset catalog

Now drag from the Unassigned image into the new **Retina 4 2x** slot:

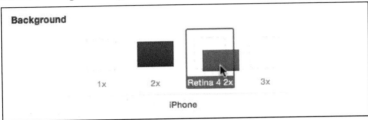

Dragging the image into the empty R4 slot

With this fix in place, the Xcode warning should be gone.

1x, 2x, and 3x displays

Notice that the Background image in the asset catalog has four slots: 1x, 2x, Retina 4 2x, and 3x. Having multiple versions of the same image in varying sizes allows your apps to support the wide variety of iPhone and iPad displays in existence.

1x is for low-resolution screens, the ones with the big, chunky pixels. The only low-resolution devices that can run iOS 8 are the iPad 2 and iPad mini. All iPhone models with 1x screens, such as the 3GS, are too old to bother with.

2x is for high-resolution Retina screens. This covers the iPhone 4S, the iPhone 5, 5c and 5s, the new iPhone 6, and all Retina iPads. Retina images are twice as big as the low-res images, hence the 2x. The images you imported just now are 2x images, except for the extra background image that is slightly larger.

Retina 4 2x images are mostly useful for background images that must cover the entire screen of the iPhone 5, 5c and 5s models, which is larger than the 4S but smaller than the iPhone 6. For some reason the asset catalog allows you to make this exception only for 4-inch screens but not for the iPhone 6's 4.7-inch screen. Most of the time you'll use the regular 2x images anyway.

3x is for the super high-resolution Retina HD screen of the iPhone 6 Plus. If you want your app to have extra sharp images on the top-of-the-line iPhone model, then you can drop them in this slot.

If the app you're making is only for the iPhone and for iOS 8 or higher, then you can leave out the 1x images. For an iPad app – or a universal app that supports both the iPhone and the iPad – you do need to provide 1x images to accommodate the iPad 2 and iPad mini.

Bull's Eye is not a universal app, so 1x images are not necessary. By the way, you can still run Bull's Eye on the iPad, even if the app is not universal. The iPad can run all iPhone apps in a special emulation mode. In that case, the app uses the 2x images.

There is a special naming convention for image files. If the filename ends in **@2x** or **@3x** then that's considered the Retina or Retina HD version. The filename for Retina 4 2x images ends in **-568h@2x**. Low-resolution 1x images have no special name (you don't have to write @1x).

Putting up the wallpaper

Let's begin by changing the drab white background into something more fancy.

➤ Open **Main.storyboard**. Go into the **Object Library** and locate an **Image View**. (Tip: if you type "image" into the search box at the bottom of the Object Library, it will quickly filter out all the other views.)

The Image View control in the Object Library

➤ Drag the image view on top of the existing user interface. It doesn't really matter where you put it, as long as it's inside the Bull's Eye View Controller.

Dragging the Image View into the view controller

➤ With the image view still selected, go to the **Size inspector** (that's the one next to the Attributes inspector) and set X and Y to 0, Width to 568 and Height to 320.

This will make the image view cover the entire screen.

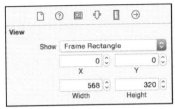

The Size inspector settings for the Image View

> Go to the **Attributes inspector** for the image view. At the top there is an option named **Image**. Click the downward arrow and choose **Background** from the list.

This will put the image from the asset catalog's "Background" group into the image view.

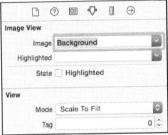

Setting the background image on the Image View

There is only one problem: the image now obscures all the other controls. There is an easy fix for that; you have to move the image view behind the other views.

> In the **Editor** menu in Xcode's menu bar at the top of the screen, choose **Arrange → Send to Back**.

Sometimes Xcode gives you a hard time with this (it still has a few bugs). In that case, pick up the image view in the outline pane and drag it to the top, just below View, to accomplish the same thing.

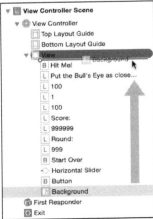

Put the Image View at the top to make it appear behind the other views

Your interface should now look something like this:

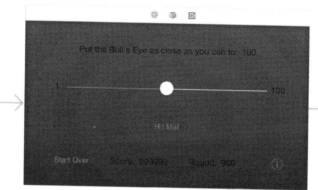

The game with the new background image

> **Note:** Unfortunately, Interface Builder always shows the 3.5-inch version of the background image, making it look stretched out on the wider 4-inch screen that you're designing for. Don't worry, the app will show the proper image when you run it.

> Do the same thing for the **About View Controller**. Add an Image View and give it the same "Background" image.

That takes care of the background. Run the app and marvel at the new graphics.

Changing the labels

Because the background image is quite dark, the black labels have become hard to read. Fortunately, Interface Builder lets you change their color, and while you're at it you might change the font as well.

> Still in the storyboard, select the label at the top, open the **Attributes inspector** and click on the **Color** item.

Setting the text color on the label

This opens the Color Picker. It has several ways to select colors. I prefer the sliders (second tab). If all you see is a gray scale slider, then select RGB Sliders from the select box at the top.

➤ Pick a pure white color, Red: 255, Green: 255, Blue: 255, Opacity: 100%.

➤ Click on the **Shadow** item from the Attributes inspector. This lets you add a subtle shadow to the label. By default this color is transparent (also known as "Clear Color") so you won't see the shadow. Using the Color Picker, choose a pure black color that is half transparent, Red: 0, Green: 0, Blue: 0, Opacity: 50%.

Note: Sometimes when you change the Color or Shadow attributes, the background color of the view also changes. This is a bug in Xcode. Put it back to Clear Color when that happens.

➤ Change the **Shadow Offset** to Horizontal: 0, Vertical: 1. This puts the shadow under the label.

The shadow you've chosen is very subtle. If you're not sure that it's actually visible, then toggle the vertical offset between 1 and 0 a few times. Look closely and you should be able to see the difference. As I said, it's very subtle.

➤ Click on the [T] icon of the **Font** attribute. This opens the Font Picker. By default the System font is selected. That uses whatever is the standard font for the user's device, which currently is Helvetica Neue.

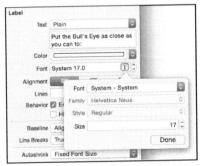

Font picker with the System font

➤ Choose **Font: Custom**. That enables the Family field. Choose **Family: Arial Rounded MT Bold**. Set the **Size** to 16.

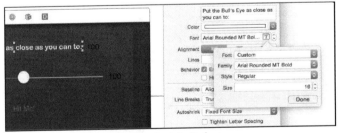

Setting the label's font

➤ The label also has an attribute **Autoshrink**. Make sure this is set to **Fixed Font Size**.

If enabled, Autoshrink will dynamically change the size of the font if the text is larger than will fit into the label. That is useful in certain apps, but not in this one. Instead, you'll change the size of the label to fit the text rather than the other way around.

➤ With the label selected, press ⌘= on your keyboard, or choose **Size to Fit Content** from the **Editor** menu.

The label will now become slightly smaller so that it fits snugly around the text.

(If the Size to Fit Content menu item is disabled, then de-select the label and select it again. Sometimes Xcode gets confused about what is selected. Poor thing.)

You don't have to set these properties for the other labels one by one; that would be a big chore. You can speed up the process by selecting multiple labels and then applying these changes to that entire selection.

➤ Click on the **Score:** label to select it. Hold ⌘ and click on the **Round:** label. Now both labels will be selected. Repeat what you did above for these labels:

• Set Color to pure white, 100% opaque.

• Set Shadow to pure black, 50% opaque.

• Set Shadow Offset to 0 horizontal, 1 vertical.

• Set Font to Arial Rounded MT Bold, size 16.

• Make sure Autoshrink is set to Fixed Font Size.

As you can see, in my storyboard the text no longer fits into the Score and Round labels:

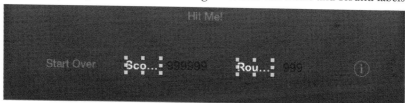

The font is too large to fit all the text in the Score and Round labels

You can either make the labels larger by dragging their handles to resize them manually, or you can use the **Size to Fit Content** option (⌘=). I prefer the latter because it's less work.

Tip: Xcode is smart enough to remember the colors you have used recently. Instead of going into the Color Picker all the time, you can simply choose a color from the Recently Used Colors menu.

Click the tiny arrows and the menu will pop up:

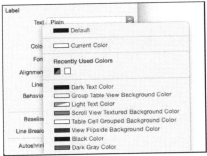

Quick access to recently used colors and several handy presets

Exercise: You still have a few labels to go. Repeat what you just did for the other labels. They should all become white, have the same shadow and have the same font. However, the two labels on either side of the slider (1 and 100) will have font size 14, while the other labels (the ones that will hold the target value, the score and the round number) will have font size 20 so they stand out more. ∎

Because you've changed the sizes of some of the labels, your carefully constructed layout may have been messed up a bit. You may want to clean it up a little.

At this point, my screen looks like this:

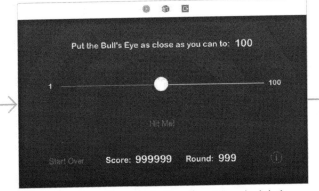

What the storyboard looks like after styling the labels

All right, it's starting to look like something now. By the way, feel free to experiment with the fonts and colors. If you want to make it look completely different, then go right ahead. It's your app!

The buttons

Changing the look of the buttons works very much the same way.

> Select the **Hit Me** button. In the **Size inspector** set its Width to 100 and its Height to 37.

> Center the position of the button on the inner circle of the background image.

> Go to the **Attributes inspector**. Change Type from System to **Custom**.

A "system" button just has a label and no border. By making it a custom button, you can style it any way you wish.

➤ Press the arrow on the **Background** field and choose **Button-Normal** from the list.

➤ Set the **Font** to **Arial Rounded MT Bold**, size 20.

➤ Set the **Text Color** to red: 96, green: 30, blue: 0, opacity: 100%. This is a dark brown color.

➤ Set the **Shadow Color** to pure white, 50% opacity. The shadow offset should be Width 0, Height 1 (for some reason they don't call it horizontal and vertical here).

> **Blending in**
>
> Setting the opacity to anything less than 100% will make the color slightly transparent (with opacity of 0% being fully transparent). Partial transparency makes the color blend in with the background and makes it appear softer.
>
> Try setting the shadow color to 100% opaque pure white and notice the difference.

This finishes the setup for the Hit Me button in its "default" state:

The attributes for the Hit Me button in the default state

Buttons can have more than one state. When you tap a button and hold it down, it should appear "pressed down" to let you know that the button will be activated when you lift your finger. This is known as the *highlighted* state and it is an important visual clue to the user.

➤ With the button still selected, click the **State Config** setting and pick **Highlighted** from the menu. Now the attributes in this section reflect the highlighted state of the button.

➤ In the **Background** field, select **Button-Highlighted**.

➤ Make sure the highlighted **Text Color** is the same color as before (R 96, G 30, B 0, or simply pick it from the Recently Used Colors menu). Change the **Shadow Color** to half-transparent white again.

➤ Check the **Reverses On Highlight** option. This will give the appearance of the label being pressed down when the user taps the button.

You could change the other properties too, but don't get too carried away. The highlight effect should not be too jarring.

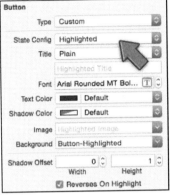

The attributes for the highlighted Hit Me button

To test the highlighted look of the button in Interface Builder you can toggle the **Highlighted** box in the **Control** section, but make sure to turn it off again or the button will initially appear highlighted when the screen is shown.

That's it for the Hit Me button. Styling the Start Over button is very similar, except you will replace its title text by an icon.

➤ Select the **Start Over** button and change the following attributes:

• Set Type to Custom.

• Remove the text "Start Over" from the button.

• For Image choose **StartOverIcon**

• For Background choose **SmallButton**

• Set Width and Height to 32.

You won't set a highlighted state on this button but let UIKit take care of this. If you don't specify a different image for the highlighted state, UIKit will automatically darken the button to indicate that it is pressed.

Make the same changes to the **(i)** button, but this time choose **InfoButton** for the image.

The user interface is almost done. Only the slider is left to do...

The slider

Unfortunately, you can only customize the slider a little bit in Interface Builder. For the more advanced customization that this game needs – putting your own images on the thumb and the track – you have to resort to writing source code.

Everything you have done so far in Interface Builder, you could also have done in code. Setting the color on a button, for example, can be done by sending the `setTitleColor()` message to the button.

However, I find that doing visual design work is much easier and quicker in a visual editor such as Interface Builder than writing the equivalent source code. But for the slider you have no choice.

➤ Go to **ViewController.swift**, and add the following to `viewDidLoad()`:

```
let thumbImageNormal = UIImage(named: "SliderThumb-Normal")
slider.setThumbImage(thumbImageNormal, forState: .Normal)

let thumbImageHighlighted = UIImage(named: "SliderThumb-Highlighted")
slider.setThumbImage(thumbImageHighlighted, forState: .Highlighted)

let insets = UIEdgeInsets(top: 0, left: 14, bottom: 0, right: 14)

if let trackLeftImage = UIImage(named: "SliderTrackLeft") {
  let trackLeftResizable = trackLeftImage.resizableImageWithCapInsets(insets)
  slider.setMinimumTrackImage(trackLeftResizable, forState: .Normal)
}
if let trackRightImage = UIImage(named: "SliderTrackRight") {
  let trackRightResizable = trackRightImage.resizableImageWithCapInsets(insets)
  slider.setMaximumTrackImage(trackRightResizable, forState: .Normal)
}
```

This sets four images on the slider: two for the thumb and two for the track.

The thumb works like a button so it gets an image for the normal, un-pressed state and one for the highlighted state.

The slider uses different images for the track on the left of the thumb (green) and the track to the right of the thumb (gray).

➤ Run the app. You have to admit it looks pretty good now!

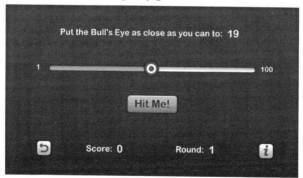

The game with the customized slider graphics

To .png or not to .png

If you recall, the images that you imported into the asset catalog had filenames like **SliderThumb-Normal@2x.png** and so on.

When you create a `UIImage` object, you don't use the original filename but the name that is listed in the asset catalog, **SliderThumb-Normal**.

That means you can leave off the **@2x** bit and the **.png** file extension.

Using a web view for HTML content

The About screen could still use some work.

Exercise: Change the Close button on the About screen to look like the Hit Me button. You should be able to do this by yourself now. Piece of cake! Refer back to the instructions for the Hit Me button if you get stuck. ■

➤ Now select the **text view** and press the **Delete** key on your keyboard. Yep, you're throwing it away.

➤ Put a **Web View** in its place (as always, you can find this view in the Object Library).

A web view, as its name implies, can show web pages. All you have to do is give it a URL to a web site. The web view object is named UIWebView.

For this app you will make it display a static HTML page from the application bundle, so it won't actually have to go onto the web and download anything.

➤ Go to the **Project navigator** and right-click on the **BullsEye** group (the yellow folder). From the menu, choose **Add Files to "BullsEye"**…

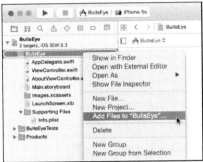

Using the right-click menu to add existing files to the project

➤ In the file picker, select the **BullsEye.html** file from the Resources folder. This is an HTML5 document that contains the gameplay instructions.

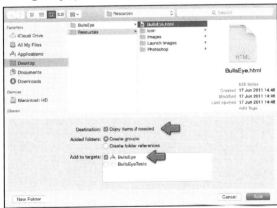

Choosing the file to add

Make sure that **Copy items if needed** is selected and that under **Add to targets**, there is a checkmark in front of **BullsEye** (you can leave BullsEyeTests unchecked).

➤ Press **Add** to add the HTML file to the project.

➤ In **AboutViewController.swift**, add an outlet for the web view:

```
class AboutViewController: UIViewController {

  @IBOutlet weak var webView: UIWebView!

  . . .
}
```

➤ In the storyboard file, connect the UIWebView element to this new outlet. The easiest way to do this is to Ctrl-drag from **About View Controller** to the **Web View**.

(If you do it the other way around, from the Web View to About View Controller, then you'll connect the wrong thing and the web view will stay empty when you run the app.)

➤ In **AboutViewController.swift**, add the viewDidLoad() method:

```
override func viewDidLoad() {
  super.viewDidLoad()

  if let htmlFile = NSBundle.mainBundle().pathForResource("BullsEye", ofType: "html") {
    let htmlData = NSData(contentsOfFile: htmlFile)
    let baseURL = NSURL.fileURLWithPath(NSBundle.mainBundle().bundlePath)
    webView.loadData(htmlData, MIMEType: "text/html", textEncodingName: "UTF-8",
                 baseURL: baseURL)
  }
}
```

This loads the local HTML file into the web view.

The source code may look scary but what goes on is not really that complicated: first it finds the **BullsEye.html** file in the application bundle, then loads it into an NSData object, and finally it asks the web view to show the contents of this data object.

➤ Run the app and press the info button. The About screen should appear with a description of the gameplay rules, this time in the form of an HTML document:

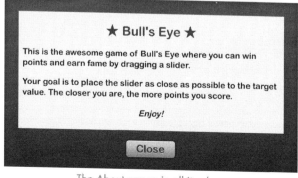

The About screen in all its glory

Supporting the iPhone 4S

So far you have designed the app for the 4-inch screen of the iPhone 5, 5c and 5s, but what about the iPhone 4S? This older model also runs iOS 8 but has a slightly smaller screen, measuring only 3.5 inches.

Both types of screen are equally wide (320 points), but where the 4-inch Retina phones are 568 points tall, the 3.5-inch models have only 480 points. That's a difference of 88 points that your apps have to compensate for somehow.

In this section you'll learn how to do that for Bull's Eye.

➤ Run the app on the **iPhone 4s** Simulator. You can switch between Simulators using the selector at the top of the Xcode window:

Using the scheme selector to switch to the 4-inch Simulator

As you may have expected, a portion of the screen gets cut off:

On the 4-inch Simulator, the app doesn't fill up the entire screen

Obviously, this won't do. You need to make sure the app also works on the smaller screen of the iPhone 4S. Fortunately, UIKit comes with a technology called *Auto Layout* that is designed to make this easy.

➤ Open **Main.storyboard** and select the main **View Controller**.

➤ Click the button with the two overlapping circles in the Xcode toolbar to open the **Assistant editor**.

➤ In the jump bar choose **Preview**. (You may need to click around a bit before this option becomes visible.)

The screen is now split into two. On the left is the storyboard; on the right is a preview pane that shows how the app will look on different iPhone devices.

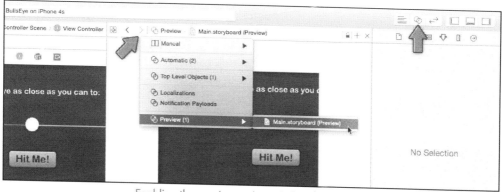

Enabling the preview assistant in Interface Builder

If not everything fits on your screen at once, you can make some room by hiding the navigator and utilities panes with the buttons from the toolbar. You can also collapse Interface Builder's Outline pane. (Or buy an extra 30" monitor!)

The preview assistant currently shows a 4-inch iPhone in portrait. You'll replace this with a 3.5-inch preview so you can see how changes on the storyboard affect the smaller iPhone 4S screen.

➤ Select the iPhone 4-inch preview and press Delete on your keyboard to remove it.

➤ Use the small + button at the bottom to select **iPhone 3.5-inch**.

This adds a preview of the 3.5-inch phone, but again it is in portrait.

➤ Hovering the mouse over the preview makes a rotation icon appear. Click the rotation icon to flip the preview to landscape:

The rotation icon toggles between portrait and landscape

Now the preview pane should look just like the app in the iPhone 4s Simulator, with the right portion of the game cut off.

First, let's fix the background image. You need to make it so that the image is 568 points wide on the 4-inch screen but only 480 points wide on the smaller 3.5-inch screen.

This is where Auto Layout comes to the rescue.

➤ In the storyboard portion of Xcode, select the **Background image view** from the main **View Controller** and click the small **Pin** button at the bottom of the window:

The Pin menu for adding Auto Layout constraints

This menu lets you "pin" a view to its neighboring views.

For the background image view, you want it to always have the same width and height as the view controller itself. The way to do this with Auto Layout is to pin the four sides of the image view to the four sides of the main view.

In other words, the top of the image view will always be in the same spot as the top of the main view. Likewise for the bottom and the left and right sides. Whatever the size of the main view, the image view will follow.

➤ In the **Pin menu**, click the four T-bars at the top so they become solid red. Uncheck **Constrain to margins**. All the spacing fields should be 0.

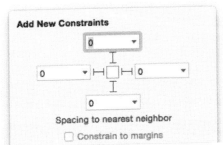

The red bars decide the sides that become pinned down

➤ For **Update Frames** choose **Items of New Constraints**. This will resize the image view to the proper size.

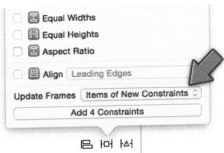

Choosing the correct option for Update Frames

➤ Then click **Add 4 Constraints**.

You won't see much change in the storyboard itself, but in the preview pane the wood grain is no longer stretched out – the circles really are circles, not ovals.

In the Outline pane there is a new item called **Constraints**:

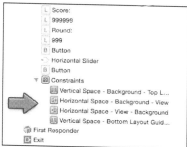

The new Auto Layout constraints appear in the Outline pane

There should be four constraints listed here, two Horizontal Space constraints and two Vertical Space constraints.

Note: Depending on exactly where you view these constraints in Xcode, they may also be called "Trailing Space" and "Leading Space" (for horizontal), and "Top Space" or "Bottom Space" (for vertical).

The way you use Auto Layout is by defining relationships between your different views, the so-called *constraints*. When you run the app, UIKit evaluates these constraints and calculates the final layout of the views. This probably sounds a bit abstract, but you'll see soon enough how it works in practice.

There are different types of constraints. The Horizontal Space and Vertical Space constraints you're using here make sure that the sides of two views stay glued together with a certain amount of spacing between them.

In this case, you set the values of these constraints to 0, which means the views always sit side-by-side, with no extra space to keep them apart. The edges of the image view will always line up with the edges of the application window.

➤ Run the app again on both the 3.5-inch iPhone 4s Simulator and the 4-inch iPhone 5s Simulator.

In both cases, the background should look exactly like their respective images from the Resources folder: **Background@2x.png** for 3.5-inch and **Background-568h@2x.png** for 4-inch.

Let's repeat this for the About screen.

➤ Use the **Pin menu** to add the four constraints to the About screen's background image view. Make sure the four T-bars all have 0 spacing, and that Update Frames says **Items of New Constraints**.

➤ Check the preview pane to verify that it works. The background image should no longer be stretched out.

Of course, the Close button and web view are still completely off.

➤ In the storyboard, drag the **Close** button so that it snaps to the center of the view as well as the bottom guide.

Interface Builder shows a handy guide, the dotted blue line, near the edges of the screen, which is useful for aligning objects. (You may need to move the web view out of the way a bit to make it easier to snap the button.)

The blue lines are guides that help position your UI elements

➤ From the **Pin menu**, select only the T-bar for spacing to the bottom (at 20 points). Also check Width (100) and Height (37).

This means you want the Close button to sit at a distance of 20 points from the bottom of the screen, and give it a certain width and height.

➤ Leave **Update Frames** set to **None**, and click **Add 3 Constraints** to finish.

Pinning the Close button to the bottom

Interface Builder now draws several T-bars around the button:

The Close button has orange constraints

The T-bars represent the constraints, of which the button now has three:

• a Width constraint that says, "This button is always 100 points wide",

• a Height constraint that says, "This button is always 37 points tall", and

• a Vertical Space constraint that keeps the button at 20 points distance from the bottom of the screen.

There is one problem: the T-bars are all supposed to be blue, not orange. Orange indicates that something is wrong with the constraints, usually that there aren't enough of them. (Also notice the dashed orange box off to the side; that's no good either.)

For each view there must always be enough constraints to define both its position and its size. Here, the Close button does have constraints for its size – both width and height – but for its position there is only a constraint in the vertical direction (the Y-coordinate). You also need to add a constraint for its X-coordinate.

For this app, it will look best if the Close button is always centered horizontally.

➤ Click the **Close** button to select it. From the **Align** menu (next to the Pin menu), choose **Horizontal Center in Container** and click **Add 1 Constraint**.

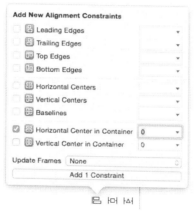

Creating a horizontal centering constraint

Now the constraints all turn blue, meaning that everything is OK:

The constraints on the Close button are valid

➤ Run the app. The Close button should always be perfectly centered, regardless of whether you're on the 3.5-inch or the 4-inch Simulator.

Note: What happens if you don't add any constraints to your views? In that case, Xcode will automatically add constraints when it builds the app. That is why you didn't need to bother with any of this before.

However, these default constraints may not always do what you want. For example, they will not automatically resize your views to accommodate the smaller 3.5-inch screen. If you want that to happen, then it's up to you to add the constraints.

As soon as you add just one constraint to a view, Xcode will no longer add automatic constraints to that view. From then on you're responsible for adding enough other constraints so that UIKit always knows what the position and size of the view will be.

There is one thing left to fix in the About screen and that is the web view.

➤ Select the **web view** and open the **Pin** menu. First, make sure **Constrain to margins** is unchecked, then select all four T-bars and set them to 20 points, except the bottom one which is 8 points:

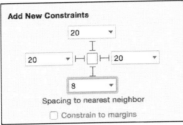

Creating the constraints for the web view

➤ For **Update Frames** select **Items of New Constraints**. Without this setting, Xcode will complain that the size and position of the web view do not correspond with the constraints you're adding. You can always fix that afterwards, but why bother when Xcode can fix it for you?

➤ Click **Add 4 Constraints** to finish.

There are now four constraints on the web view (the blue bars):

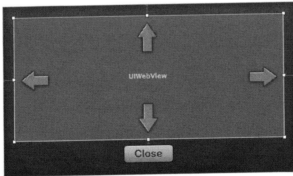

The four constraints on the web view

Three of these connect the web view to the main view, so that it always resizes along with it, and one connects it to the Close button. This is enough to determine the size and position of the web view in any scenario.

➤ Verify in the preview pane that the About screen looks good on the 3.5-inch phone.

Back to the main game screen, which still needs some work to fit on the smaller screen size.

➤ First, clean up the storyboard by dragging all the controls over to the left so that they fit tidily on the 3.5-inch screen. This is where the preview pane comes in real handy!

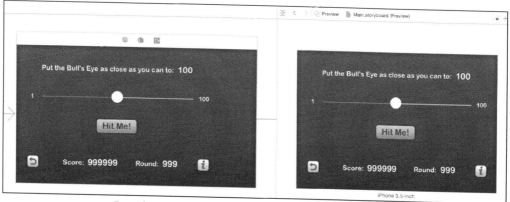

Everything is rearranged to fit on the smaller 3.5-inch screen

Of course, the game looks a bit lopsided now on 4-inch phones. You will fix that by placing all the labels, buttons and the slider into a new "container" view. Using Auto Layout, you'll center that container view in the screen, regardless of how big the screen is.

➤ Select all the labels, buttons, and the slider. You can hold down ⌘ and click them individually but an easier method is to go to the **Outline pane**, click on the first view (the Hit Me button), hold down Shift and click on the last view (in my case the info button):

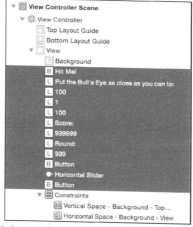

Selecting the views from the Outline pane

You should have selected everything but the background image view.

➤ From Xcode's menu bar, choose **Editor → Embed In → View**. This places the selected views inside a new container view:

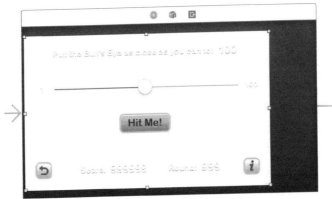

The views are embedded in a new container view

This new view is completely white, which is not what you want eventually, but it does make it easier to add the constraints.

> Select the newly added **container view** and open the **Pin menu**. Put checkboxes in front of **Width** and **Height** in order to make constraints for them. Click **Add 2 Constraints** to finish.

The new constraints will appear as blue T-bars but there is also an orange dotted box. That means there are not enough constraints yet. No problem, you'll add the missing constraints next.

> With the container view still selected, open the **Align menu**. Check the **Horizontal Center in Container** and **Vertical Center in Container** options. For **Update Frames**, select **Items of New Constraints**; then click **Add 2 Constraints** to finish.

All the T-bars should be blue now and the view is perfectly centered.

> Finally, change the **Background** color of the view to **Clear Color** (in other words, 100% transparent).

You now have a layout that works correctly on both the 3.5-inch and 4-inch iPhones! Try it out:

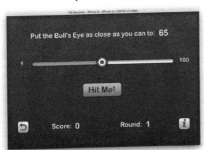

The game running on the 3.5-inch and 4-inch simulators

Auto Layout may take a while to get used to. Adding constraints in order to position UI elements is a little less obvious than just dragging them into place.

But this also buys you a lot of power and flexibility, which you need when you're dealing with devices that have different screen sizes.

You'll learn more about Auto Layout in the other parts of *The iOS Apprentice*.

Supporting the iPhone 6 and 6 Plus

Making the game work on smaller devices is one thing, but what about *larger* devices, such as the new iPhone 6 and 6 Plus?

➤ Try it out! You can open the storyboard and add iPhone 4.7-inch and 5.5-inch previews to the preview pane, or you can run the app in the iPhone 6 and 6 Plus simulators.

What happened? This is what it looks like on the 6 Plus Simulator:

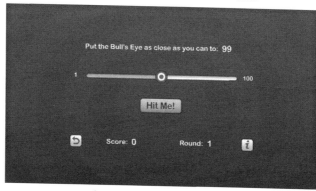

The game on the iPhone 6 Plus

Tip: You can press ⌘-1, ⌘-2, or ⌘-3 to scale the Simulator if it doesn't fit on your screen. That iPhone 6 Plus is a monster!

Well, I guess it's not too bad – but it's not great either. The background image is stretched out again and the app is not taking advantage of all the available space. It would be better if everything were slightly bigger.

There are several ways to tackle this, but we're going to cheat and take the easy way out.

Apps need to opt-in to support the larger screens of the iPhone 6 and 6 Plus.

If an app does *not* opt-in, the iPhone 6/Plus will automatically scale up the app to fill up the extra space. That's great for us, because scaling up is exactly what we want – and with minimal effort.

Apps that do opt-in for iPhone 6 support must provide a so-called *launch screen*.

You've already seen this launch screen in action. Whenever you've run the app, the following "splash screen" briefly popped up:

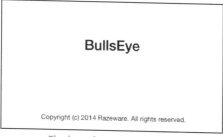

The launch screen in action

Note: Starting up an app usually takes a short while. You can make the transition between tapping the app icon and actually using the app more seamless by using a launch screen. This is a placeholder that is shown while the app is being loaded.

Without this placeholder, the iPhone's screen will simply be blanked out until the app is ready, which isn't very welcoming.

A lot of developers abuse this feature to show a splash screen with a logo, but it's better for the user if you just show a static image of the user interface and not much else. Nobody likes to wait for apps to load and a well-chosen launch screen will give the illusion the app is loading faster than it actually is.

You can use a regular image but you can also use a storyboard file or a XIB file. A XIB, also known as "nib", is like a storyboard except that it can contain the design of only a single screen.

The design for the app's launch screen lives in the file **LaunchScreen.xib**. To get the automatic scaling on the iPhone 6, you need to remove this file.

> In the **Project navigator**, select **LaunchScreen.xib** and press the **Delete** key to remove it. When Xcode asks for confirmation, choose **Move to Trash**.

That alone is not enough. You also need to tell Xcode that it can no longer use this launch screen file.

> Go to the **Project Settings** screen. In the **App Icons and Launch Images** section, make the box for **Launch Screen File** empty:

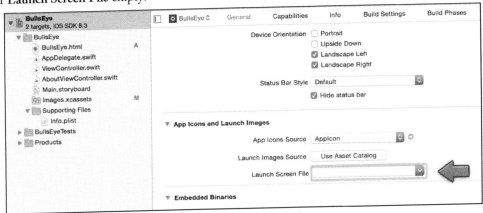

The Launch Screen File field must be empty

> To completely wipe Xcode's memory of this launch screen file, hold down the **Alt/Option** key and choose **Product → Clean Build Folder** from the Xcode menu bar. Confirm by pressing **Clean**.

> Run the app. You should no longer see the launch screen. If you do, choose **iOS Simulator → Reset Contents and Settings** from the Simulator menu bar to start over with a clean slate.

You might be in for a surprise. This is what the app looks like now on the iPhone 6 Simulator:

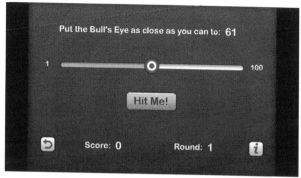

The app is letterboxed on the iPhone 6

There are two black bars on either side of the screen. What you're seeing here is the app in 3.5-inch mode, but scaled up to the iPhone 6's larger screen. Weird!

The solution is to add a 4-inch launch image to the project. This is not a XIB or storyboard file, just a static picture of the wood texture background.

➤ In the **Project navigator**, right-click the **BullsEye** group (the one with the yellow icon) and choose **Add Files to "BullsEye"** from the menu.

➤ Navigate to the **Launch Images** folder from this tutorial's resources and select both the **Default@2x.png** and **Default-568h@2x.png** files.

Make sure **Copy items if needed** is checked and press **Add** to add the files to the project. That's all there is to it!

These two images are identical to the background image but turned sideways (launch images must always be in portrait orientation).

Run the app and notice that the transition into the app looks a lot smoother. It's little details like these that count. And best of all, the app now looks great on the iPhone 6 and 6 Plus!

> **Note:** Simply scaling up the app for the larger phones works well for *Bull's Eye*, but for most apps you'll want to take advantage of all that extra screen space. iOS has several features that help with this – Auto Layout and Size Classes – and you'll learn all about them in the next tutorials.

Crossfade

I can't conclude this tutorial before mentioning Core Animation. This technology makes it very easy to create really sweet animations in your apps, with just a few lines of code. Adding subtle animations (with emphasis on subtle!) can make your app a delight to use.

You will add a simple crossfade after the Start Over button is pressed, so the transition back to round one won't seem so abrupt.

➤ In **ViewController.swift**, add the following line at the top, right below the other import:

```
import QuartzCore
```

The Core Animation technology lives in its own framework, QuartzCore. With the import statement you tell the compiler that you want to use the objects from this framework.

➤ Change the startOver() method to:

```
@IBAction func startOver() {
  startNewGame()
  updateLabels()

  let transition = CATransition()
  transition.type = kCATransitionFade
  transition.duration = 1
  transition.timingFunction = CAMediaTimingFunction(name: kCAMediaTimingFunctionEaseOut)
  view.layer.addAnimation(transition, forKey: nil)
}
```

The calls to startNewGame() and updateLabels() were there before, but the CATransition stuff is new.

I'm not going to go into too much detail here. Suffice to say you're setting up an animation that crossfades from what is currently on the screen to the changes you're making in startNewGame() – reset the slider to center position – and updateLabels() – reset the values of the labels.

➤ Run the app and move the slider so that it is no longer in the center. Press the Start Over button and you should see a subtle crossfade animation.

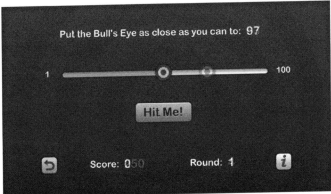

The screen crossfades between the old and new states

The icon

You're almost done with the app but there are still a few loose ends to tie up. You may have noticed that the app has a really boring white icon. That won't do!

➤ Open the asset catalog (**Images.xcassets**) and select **AppIcon**:

The AppIcon group in the asset catalog

This currently has six slots for the different types of icons the app needs.

➤ In Finder, open the **Icon** folder from this tutorial's resources. Drag the **Icon-58.png** file into the **2x** slot for **iPhone Spotlight & Settings 29pt**:

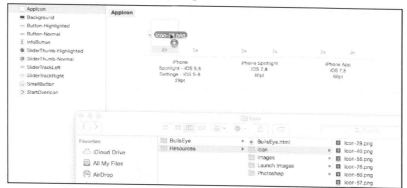

Dragging the icon into the asset catalog

You may be wondering why you're dragging the Icon-58.png file and not Icon-29.png into the slot for 29pt. Remember that this slot says 2x, which means it's for Retina devices and on Retina screens one point counts as two pixels.

➤ Drag the **Icon-87.png** file into the 3x slot next to it. This is for the iPhone 6 Plus with its 3x resolution. Three times 29 is 87. (What, you don't know your times table for 29?)

➤ For **iPhone Spotlight 40pt**, drag the **Icon-80.png** file into the 2x slot and **Icon-120.png** into the 3x slot.

➤ For **iPhone App 60pt**, drag the **Icon-120.png** file into the 2x slot and **Icon-180.png** into the 3x slot.

That's only three icons in two different sizes. Phew!

The other files in the folder are for the iPad. This app does not have an iPad version, but that doesn't prevent iPads from running it. All iPads can run all iPhone apps, but they show up in a smaller frame. To accommodate this, it's nicest if you also supply icons for iPad.

➤ With **AppIcon** still selected, in the **Attributes inspector** check the item **iPad iOS 7.0 and Later Sizes**. This adds six new slots to the AppIcon set.

➤ Drag the icons into the proper slots. Notice that the iPad icons need to be supplied in 1x as well as 2x sizes (but not 3x). You may need to do some mental arithmetic here to figure out which icon goes into which slot!

The full set of icons for this app, including the iPad icons

The **Icon-1024.png** file is not used by the app. This is for submission to the App Store. As part of the app submission, you are required to upload a 1024×1024 pixel version of the icon.

➤ Run the app and close it. You'll see that the icon has changed on the Simulator's springboard. If not, remove the app from the Simulator and try again (sometimes the Simulator keeps using the old icon and re-installing the app will fix this).

The icon on the Simulator's springboard

Display name

One last thing. You named the project **BullsEye** and that is the name that shows up under the icon. However, I'd prefer to spell it "**Bull's Eye**".

There is only limited space under the icon and for apps with longer names you have to get creative to make the name fit. For this game, however, there is enough room to add the space and the apostrophe.

This is a setting that you need to make in the app's Info.plist file.

➤ From the **Project navigator**, under **Supporting Files**, select **Info.plist**.

There is a row near the middle of the list named **Bundle name** that currently has the special value "$(PRODUCT_NAME)". This means Xcode will automatically put the project name, BullsEye, in this field when it adds the Info.plist to the application bundle. This is also the name that appears under the app icon.

You can override this by providing a new entry, **Bundle display name**, and giving that the name you want.

➤ From the Xcode menu bar, choose **Editor** → **Add Item**. (You can also right-click somewhere inside the Info.plist editor and choose Add Row from the menu.)

➤ In the pop-up that appears, choose **Bundle display name**. Give this row the value **Bull's Eye**.

Changing the display name of the app

➤ Run the app and quit it to see the new name under the icon.

The bundle display name setting changes the name under the icon

You can find the project files for the finished app under **07 - Final App** in the tutorial's Source Code folder.

There is also a version named **08 - Final App with Comments** that has a lot of comments to show you what every piece of code does. I also removed anything that was inserted by the Xcode template that isn't actually needed for this game, so that the code is as simple as possible.

Running the game on your device

So far, you've run the app on the Simulator. That's nice and all but probably not why you're learning iOS development. You want to make apps that run on real iPhones! There's hardly a thing more exciting than running an app that *you* made on your own phone.

Don't get me wrong: developing your apps on the Simulator works very well. When developing, I spend most of my time with the Simulator and only test the app on my iPhone every so often.

The Simulator is great, but you do need to run your creations on a real device in order to test them properly.

And, of course, to show the fruits of your labor to other people!

Get with the program

You cannot run apps on your iPhone unless you have a paid iOS Developer Program account. Without this account, your apps will never leave the Simulator.

While it is possible to do a lot of development work on the Simulator, some things it simply cannot do. If your app needs the iPhone's accelerometer, for example, you have no choice but to test that functionality on an actual device. Don't sit there and shake your Mac!

You also need to be a member of the paid Developer Program if you want to put your apps on the iTunes App Store.

Go to developer.apple.com/programs/ios to sign up.

In order to allow Xcode to put an app on your iPhone, the app must be *digitally signed* with your **Development Certificate**. Apps that you want to submit to the App Store must be signed with another certificate, the **Distribution Certificate**.

A *certificate* is an electronic document that identifies you as an iOS application developer and is valid only for a limited amount of time. These certificates are part of your Developer Program account.

In addition to a valid certificate, you also need a so-called **Provisioning Profile** for each app you make. Xcode uses this profile to sign the app for use on your device. The specifics don't really matter, just know that you need a provisioning profile or the app won't go on your device.

Any devices you want to use with Xcode on must be registered with your Developer Program account. There is a limit to how many devices you can register, currently up to 100. This may sound like plenty – you probably don't have a hundred iPhones lying around – but this includes devices of beta testers and anyone else you want to distribute your app to outside of the App Store. Use them sparingly!

(Note: New in iOS 8 is support for the TestFlight beta testing service, which does not require you to register the devices of beta testers with your account.)

Making the certificates and provisioning profiles used to be frustrating and error-prone. Fortunately, those days are over: Xcode 6 makes it really easy.

➤ Connect your iPhone, iPod touch, or iPad to your Mac using the USB cable.

➤ From the Xcode menu bar select **Window** → **Devices** to open Xcode's Devices window.

Mine looks like this (I'm using an iPad mini):

The Xcode Devices window

On the left is a list of devices that can be used for development.

➤ Click on your device name to select it.

If this is the first time you're using the device with Xcode, the Devices window will say something like, "Matthijs's iPad is not paired with your computer." To pair the device with Xcode, you need to unlock the device first (slide to unlock).

After unlocking, an alert will pop up on the device asking you to trust the computer you're trying to pair with. Tap on **Trust** to continue.

Xcode will now refresh the page and let you use the device for development. You may need to unplug the device and plug it back in first.

At this point it's possible to get the error message, "An error was encountered while enabling development on this device." You'll need to unplug the device and reboot it. Make sure to restart Xcode before you reconnect the device. (General tip: If you run into weird problems, restarting Xcode usually fixes it.)

Cool, that is the device sorted.

The next step is setting up the Developer Program account with Xcode. At this point I assume you've already registered and paid for the account and you have your Apple ID and password handy.

➤ Open the **Accounts** pane in the Xcode Preferences window:

The Accounts preferences

➤ Click the + button at the bottom and choose **Add Apple ID**.

Xcode will ask for your Apple ID:

Adding a new Developer Program account to Xcode

➤ Type the username and password for your Developer Program. This is the same login that you use for the iOS Dev Center website.

Xcode verifies your account details and adds them to the accounts window.

➤ Click the **View Details…** button in the bottom-right corner.

This brings up another panel, listing your signing identities (the certificates) and the provisioning profiles. Currently this panel will be empty:

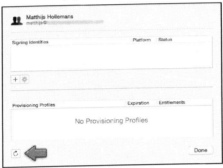

The account details panel

➤ Click the arrow in the bottom-left corner. Xcode now contacts the iOS Dev Center to fetch any certificates and provisioning profiles that you already have.

If this is your first time, you'll get the following message because you do not have a Development Certificate yet:

Xcode could not find a Development Certificate

➤ Click **Request** and wait a few seconds. Great! That wasn't so hard, was it? ☺

While you're waiting, Xcode automatically registers your device with your Developer Program account, creates a new Development Certificate, and downloads and installs the so-called Team Provisioning Profile on your device. (They call it the "team" profile because it will work on all the devices that you have registered with the Developer Program.)

When you're done, close the Accounts window and return to the Devices window.

You can see the profiles that are installed on your device by right-clicking the device name and choosing **Show Provisioning Profiles**:

The provisioning profiles on your device

The Team Provisioning Profile has a so-called *wildcard App ID* (*), which means you can use it for any application you are developing (as long as they don't require any special features such as push notifications).

Thanks to the Team Provisioning Profile you won't have to repeat this procedure for any of the other apps that you will be developing in this series. Xcode knows about the profile now and it will automatically use this profile to sign your apps.

You can also login to the iOS Dev Center website to see what the provisioning profile looks like there. Needless to say, you only have access to this portal if you're in the paid iOS Developer Program.

➤ Go to developer.apple.com/devcenter/ios and log in. Under **iOS Developer Program**, choose **Certificates, Identifiers & Profiles**.

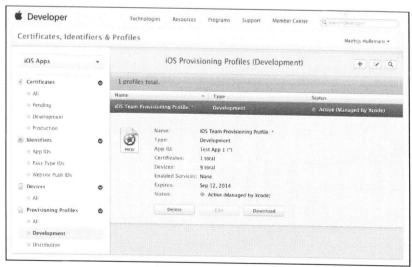

The provisioning website

It's easiest to simply let Xcode handle all the certificate and provisioning profile stuff but you can also manage these things yourself from the iOS Dev Center. You can download the handy **App Distribution Guide** that explains how all of this works in detail.

This concludes the setup. You have added your Developer Program account to Xcode, obtained a Development Certificate, registered your device, and installed a provisioning profile. You're ready to run the app on your phone!

➤ Go back to Xcode's main window and click on the scheme selector in the toolbar to change where you will run the app. The name of your device should be in that list somewhere.

On my system it looks like this:

Changing where the app will be run

➤ Press **Run** to launch the app.

At this point you may get a popup with the question "codesign wants to sign using key … in your keychain". If so, answer with **Always Allow**. This is Xcode trying to use the new Development Certificate you just created but you need to give it permission first.

Does the app work? Awesome! If not, read on...

There are a few things that can go wrong when you try to put the app on your device, especially if you've never done this before, so don't panic if you run into problems.

The device is not connected. Make sure your iPhone, iPod touch, or iPad is connected to your Mac. The device must be listed in Xcode's Devices window and there should not be a yellow warning icon next to the device name.

The device is locked. If your phone locks itself with a passcode after a few minutes, you might get this warning:

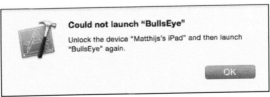

The app won't run if the device is locked

Or you might get a message in the Xcode Debug output pane:

```
error: failed to launch 'BullsEye' -- device locked
```

Simply unlock your phone (type in the 4-digit passcode) and press Run again.

No signing identity found. Your Development Certificate is not found, not valid, or is missing the corresponding private key. When this happens, Xcode will offer to request a new certificate. You can also make the certificate yourself on the iOS Dev Center and add it to Xcode in the Accounts preferences panel.

Code Sign error: a valid provisioning profile matching the application's Identifier 'com.yourname.BullsEye' could not be found. Xcode does not have a valid provisioning profile for signing the app. The installation of the Team Provisioning Profile has apparently failed.

No valid provisioning profile on the device. This really shouldn't happen because Xcode will automatically install the profile onto the device before it runs the app, but you never know.

Xcode could not find a valid private-key/certificate pair for this profile in your keychain. Your development certificate isn't properly installed. This can happen when you moved your certificates to a new computer but forgot to move the corresponding private keys as well.

The first step in solving such problems is to restart Xcode and try again. That's always good advice when Xcode does not do what you want.

If that doesn't help, open the **Preferences** window and go to the **Accounts** tab. Select your account and click the **View Details** button. In the dialog that appears, click the refresh button (the arrow in the bottom-left corner). Xcode will now fetch your data from the iOS Dev Center again.

Alternatively, open the Dev Center website in your browser (tip: it works best on Safari) and download the Provisioning Profile to your computer, then drag it onto the Xcode icon. Click on the Show Provisioning Profiles item under the name of the device and verify that the profile is installed on that device. If necessary, you can click the + button to install the profile manually.

If you want to know how Xcode chooses which profile and certificate to sign your app with, then click on your project name and switch to the **Build Settings** tab. There are a lot of settings in this list, so filter them by typing **code sign** in the search box. (Also make sure **All** is selected, not Basic.)

The screen will look something like this:

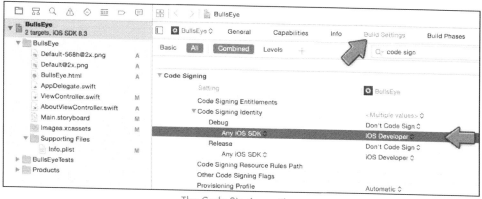

The Code Signing settings

Under **Code Signing Identity** it says **Debug, Any iOS SDK: iPhone Developer**. This is the certificate that Xcode uses to sign the app. If you click on that line, you can choose another certificate. Under **Provisioning Profile** you can change the active profile.

Xcode is actually pretty smart about automatically picking the right provisioning profile for you, but now at least you know where to look.

The end... or the beginning?

This has been a very long lesson – if you're new to programming, you've had to get a lot of new concepts into your head. I hope your brain didn't explode!

At least you should have gotten some insight into what it takes to develop an app.

I don't expect you to understand exactly everything that you did, especially not the parts that involved writing Swift code. It is perfectly fine if you don't, as long as you're enjoying yourself and you sort of get the basic concepts of objects, methods and variables.

If you were able to follow along and do the exercises, you're in good shape!

I encourage you to play around with the code for a bit more. The best way to learn programming is to do it, and that includes making mistakes and messing things up. I hereby grant you full permission to do so! Maybe you can add some cool new features to the game (if you do, let me know).

But for now, pour yourself a drink and put your feet up. You've earned it.

In the Source Code folder for this tutorial you can find the complete source code for the Bull's Eye app, with plenty of added commentary. If you're still unclear about some of what you did, it might be a good idea to look at this cleaned up, commented source code.

If you're interested in how I made the graphics, then take a peek at the Photoshop files in the Resources folder. The wood background texture was made by Atle Mo from subtlepatterns.com.

But that's not all – there's much more ahead! When you're ready, continue on to the next chapter, where you'll make your very own to-do list app.

Tutorial 2: Checklists

To-do list apps are one of the most popular types of app on the App Store, second only to fart apps. Apple even included their own Reminders app as of iOS 5 (but fortunately no built-in fart app).

Building a to-do list app is somewhat of a rite of passage for budding iOS developers, so it makes sense that you create one as well.

Your own to-do list app, **Checklists**, will look like this when you're finished:

The finished Checklists app

The app lets you organize to-do items into lists and then check off these items once you're done with them. You can also set a reminder on a to-do item that will make the iPhone pop up an alert on the due date, even when the app isn't running.

As far as to-do list apps go, Checklists is very basic, but don't let that fool you. Even a simple app such as this already has five different screens and a lot of complexity behind the scenes.

Table views and navigation controllers

This tutorial will introduce you to two of the most commonly used UI (user interface) elements in iOS apps: the table view and the navigation controller.

A **table view** shows a list of things. The three screens above all use a table view. In fact, all of this app's screens are made with table views. This component is extremely versatile and the most important one to master in iOS development.

The **navigation controller** allows you to build a hierarchy of screens that lead from one to another. It adds a navigation bar at the top with a title and a "back" button.

In this app, tapping the name of a checklist – "Groceries", for example – slides in the screen containing the to-do items from that list. The button in the upper-left corner takes you back to the previous screen with a smooth animation. Moving between those screens is the job of the navigation controller.

Navigation controllers and table views are often used together:

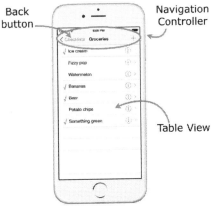

The grey bar at the top is the navigation bar. The list of items is the table view.

Take a look at the apps that come with your iPhone – Calendar, Notes, Contacts, Mail, Settings – and you'll notice that even though they look slightly different, all these apps work in pretty much the same way.

That's because they all use table views and navigation controllers:

These are all table views inside navigation controllers: Notes, Settings, Mail, Calendar, Music

(The Music app also has a *tab bar* at the bottom, something you'll learn about in the next tutorial.)

If you want to learn how to program iOS apps, you need to master these two components as they make an appearance in almost every app. That's exactly what you'll focus on in this tutorial. You'll also learn how to pass data from one screen to another, a very important topic that often puzzles beginners.

When you're done with this lesson, the concepts **view controller**, **table view** and **delegate** will be so familiar to you that you can program them in your sleep (although I hope you'll dream of other things).

This is a very long read with a lot of source code, so take your time to let it all sink in. I encourage you to experiment with the code that you'll be writing. Change stuff and see what it does, even if it breaks the app.

Making mistakes that result in bugs, tearing your hair out in frustration, the light bulb moment when you realize what's wrong, the satisfaction of fixing the bug – they're all essential parts of the learning process.

There's no doubt: playing with the code is the quickest way to learn!

The Checklists app design

Just so you know what you're in for, here is an overview of how the Checklists app will work:

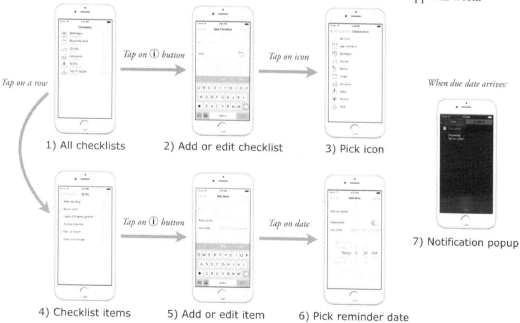

All the screens of the Checklists app

The main screen of the app shows all your checklists (1). You can create multiple lists to organize your to-do items.

A checklist has a name, an icon, and zero or more items. You can edit the name and icon of a checklist in the Add/Edit Checklist screen (2) and (3).

You tap on the checklist's name to view its to-do items (4).

A to-do item has a description, a checkmark to mark the item as done, and an optional due date. You can edit the item in the Add/Edit Item screen (5).

iOS will automatically notify the user of checklist items that have their "remind me" option set (6), even if the app isn't running (7). That's a pretty advanced feature but I think you'll be up for the task.

You can find the full source code of this app in this tutorial's Resources folder, so have a play with it to get a feel for how it works.

Done playing? Then let's get started!

> **Important:** The *iOS Apprentice* tutorials are for Xcode 6.3 and better only. If you're still using Xcode 6.2, or an even older version such as 6.1.1, please update to the latest version of Xcode from the Mac App Store.
>
> But don't get carried away either – often Apple makes beta versions available of upcoming Xcode releases. Please do *not* use an Xcode beta to follow this tutorial. Often the beta versions break things in unexpected ways and you'll only end up confused. Stick to the official versions for now!

Playing with table views

Seeing as table views are so important, you will start out by examining how they work. Making lists has never been this much fun!

Because smart developers split up the workload into small, simple steps, this is what you're going to do in this first section:

1. Put a table view on the app's screen

2. Put data into that table view

3. Allow the user to tap a row in the table to toggle a checkmark on and off

Once you have these basics up and running, you'll keep adding new functionality over the course of this tutorial until you end up with the full-blown app.

➤ Launch Xcode and start a new project. Choose the **Single View Application** template:

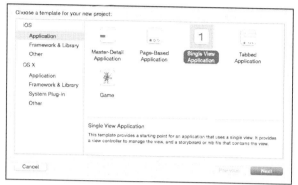

Choosing the Xcode template

Xcode will ask you to fill out a few options:

Choosing the template options

➤ Fill out these options as follows:

• Product Name: **Checklists**

• Organization Name: Your name or the name of your company

• Company Identifier: Use your own identifier here, using reverse domain name notation

• Language: **Swift**

• Devices: iPhone

• Use Core Data: Leave this unchecked.

➤ Press **Next** and choose a location for the project.

You can run the app if you want but at this point it just consists of a white screen.

Checklists will run in portrait orientation only but the project that Xcode just generated also includes the landscape orientation.

➤ Click on the Checklists project item at the top of the project navigator and make sure the **General** tab is selected. Under **Deployment Info, Device Orientation,** make sure that only **Portrait** is selected.

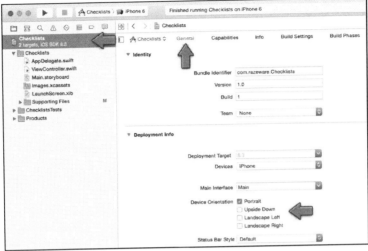

The Device Orientation setting

With the landscape options disabled, rotating the device will no longer have any effect. The app always stays in portrait orientation.

Upside down

There is also an Upside Down orientation but you typically won't use it.

If your app supports Upside Down, users are able to rotate their iPhone so that the Home button is at the top of the screen instead of at the bottom.

That may be confusing, especially when the user receives a phone call: the microphone is at the wrong end with the phone upside down.

iPad apps, on the other hand, are supposed to support all four orientations including upside-down.

Editing the storyboard

Xcode created a basic app that consists of a single view controller. Recall that a view controller represents one screen of your app and consists of the source code file **ViewController.swift** and a user interface design in **Main.storyboard**.

The storyboard contains the designs of all your app's view controllers inside a single document, with arrows showing the flow between them. In storyboard terminology, each view controller is named a *scene*.

You already used a storyboard in Bull's Eye but in this tutorial you will unlock the full power of storyboarding.

➤ Click on **Main.storyboard** to open Interface Builder.

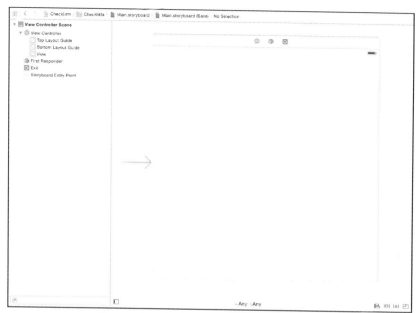

The storyboard editor with the app's only scene

Even though this app is iPhone-only and always in portrait, Interface Builder shows a square canvas.

This is iOS 8's new "size classes" feature. It allows you to design a user interface that is independent of the device's actual dimensions or orientation. You can now create a single storyboard that works across all devices, from iPhone to iPad.

You're not require to use size classes – in Bull's Eye you turned this feature off – but it's good to think about your app's UI in a device independent fashion, so for this tutorial you'll keep the square canvas.

➤ Select **View Controller** and press **Delete** on your keyboard to remove the **View Controller Scene** from the storyboard.

The canvas should now be empty and the outline pane to the left says "No Scenes".

> **Note:** Recall that the outline pane shows the view hierarchy of all the scenes in the storyboard.
>
>
>
> If you cannot see the outline pane, then click the small arrow button at the bottom of the Interface Builder window to toggle its visibility.

You're deleting this scene because you don't want a regular view controller but a so-called **table view controller**. This is a special type of view controller that makes working with table views a little easier.

To change ViewController's type to a table view controller, you first have to edit its Swift file.

➤ Click on **ViewController.swift** to open it in the source code editor and change the following line from this:

```
class ViewController: UIViewController {
```

into this:

```
class ChecklistViewController: UITableViewController {
```

With this change you tell the Swift compiler that your own view controller is now a `UITableViewController` object instead of a regular `UIViewController`.

Remember that everything starting with "UI" is part of UIKit. These pre-fabricated components serve as the building blocks for your own app.

When Xcode made the project, it assumed you wanted the `ViewController` object to be built on top of a basic `UIViewController`, but here you're changing it to use the `UITableViewController` building block instead.

You also renamed `ViewController` to `ChecklistViewController` to give it a more descriptive name. This is your own object – you can tell because its name *doesn't* start with UI.

Over the course of this tutorial you will add data and functionality to the `ChecklistViewController` object to make the app actually do things. You'll also add several new view controllers to the app.

➤ In the Project navigator on the left, click once to select **ViewController.swift,** and then click again to edit its name. (Don't double-click too fast or you'll open the Swift file inside a new source code editor window.)

Change the filename to **ChecklistViewController.swift**:

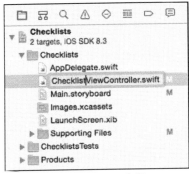

Renaming the Swift file

You may now get a warning: "The document could not be saved. The file has been changed by another application." Click **Save Anyway** to make it go away.

➤ Go back to the storyboard and drag a **Table View Controller** from the Object Library (bottom-right corner) into the canvas:

Dragging a Table View Controller into the storyboard

This adds a new Table View Controller scene to the storyboard.

➤ Go to the **Identity inspector** (the third tab in the inspectors pane on the right of the Xcode window) and under **Custom Class** type **ChecklistViewController** (or choose it using the small arrow).

Tip: When you do this, make sure the actual Table View Controller is selected, not the Table View inside it. There should be a thin blue border around the scene.

Changing the Custom Class of the Table View Controller

The name of the scene in the Scene List on the left should change to "Checklist View Controller Scene". You have successfully changed ChecklistViewController from a regular view controller object into a table view controller.

As its name implies, and as you can see in the storyboard, the view controller contains a Table View object. We'll go into the difference between controllers and views soon, but for now remember that the controller is the whole screen while the table view is the object that actually draws the list.

If there is no big arrow pointing towards your new table view controller, then go to the **Attributes inspector** and check **Is Initial View Controller**.

The arrow points at the initial view controller

The initial view controller is the first screen that your users will see. Without it, iOS won't know which view controller to load from your storyboard when the app starts up and you'll end up staring at a black screen.

➤ Run the app on the Simulator.

You should see an empty list. This is the table view. You can drag the list up and down but it doesn't contain any data yet.

The app now uses a table view controller

By the way, it doesn't really matter which Simulator you use. Table views resize themselves to the dimensions of the device, and the app will work equally well on the small iPhone 4S and the huge iPhone 6 Plus.

Personally, I'm using the iPhone 5s Simulator because that one still fits on my screen, if only barely! (Remember, you can use ⌘1, ⌘2, and ⌘3 to zoom the Simulator window.)

The anatomy of a table view

First, let's talk a bit more about table views. A `UITableView` object displays a list of things.

> **Note:** I'm not sure why it's named a *table*, because a table is commonly thought of as a spreadsheet-type object that has multiple rows and multiple columns, whereas the `UITableView` only has rows. It's more of a list than a table, but I guess we're stuck with the name now. As of iOS 6, UIKit also provides a `UICollectionView` object that works similar to a `UITableView` but allows for multiple columns.

There are two styles of tables: "plain" and "grouped". They work mostly the same but there are a few small differences. The most visible dissimilarity is that rows in the grouped style table are combined into boxes (the groups) on a light gray background.

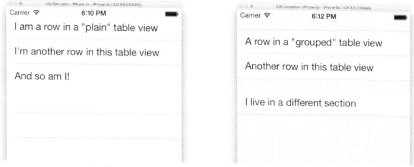

A plain-style table (left) and a grouped table (right)

The plain style is used for rows that all represent something similar, such as contacts in an address book where each row contains the name of one person.

The grouped style is used when each row represents something different, such as the various attributes of one of those contacts. The grouped style table would have a name row, an address row, a phone number row, and so on.

You will use both table styles in the Checklists app.

The data for a table comes in the form of **rows**. In the first version of Checklists, each row will correspond to a to-do item that you can check off when you're done with it.

You can potentially have many rows (tens of thousands) although that kind of design isn't recommended. Most users will find it incredibly annoying to scroll through ten thousand rows to find the one they want, and who can blame them...

Tables display their data in **cells**. A cell is related to a row but it's not exactly the same. A cell is a view that shows a row of data that happens to be visible at that moment. If your table can show 10 rows at a time on the screen, then it only has 10 cells, even though there may be hundreds of rows with actual data.

Whenever a row scrolls off the screen and becomes invisible, its cell will be re-used for a new row that scrolls into the screen.

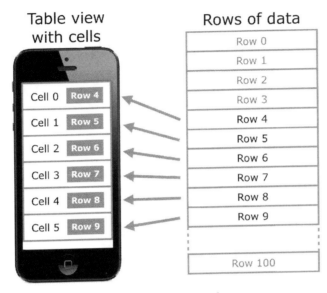

Cells display the contents of rows

Until iOS 5 you had to put in quite a bit of effort to create cells for your tables but these days Xcode has a very handy feature named **prototype cells** that lets you design your cells visually in Interface Builder.

➤ Open the storyboard and click the empty cell to select it.

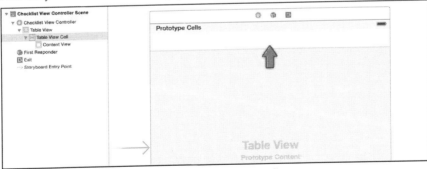

Selecting the prototype cell

Sometimes it can be hard to see exactly what is selected, so keep an eye on the outline pane to make sure you've picked the right thing.

➤ Drag a **Label** from the Object Library into this cell. Make sure the label spans the entire width of the cell (but leave a small margin on the sides).

Adding the label to the prototype cell

Besides the label you will also add a checkmark to the cell's design. The checkmark is provided by something called the **accessory**, which is a built-in subview that appears on the right side of the cell. You can choose from a few standard accessory controls or provide your own.

➤ Select the **Table View Cell** again. Inside the **Attributes inspector** set the **Accessory** field to **Checkmark**:

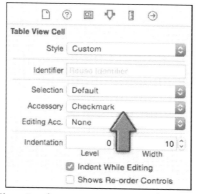

Changing the accessory to get a checkmark

(If you don't see this option, then make sure you selected the Table View Cell, not the Content View or Label below it.)

Your design now looks like this:

The design of the prototype cell: a label and a checkmark

You may want to resize the label a bit so that it doesn't overlap the checkmark.

You also need to set a **reuse identifier** on the cell. This is an internal name that the table view uses to find free cells to reuse when rows scroll off the screen and new rows must become visible.

The table needs to assign cells to those new rows and recycling existing cells is more efficient than creating new cells. This technique is what makes table views scroll smoothly.

Reuse identifiers are also important for when you want to display different types of cells in the same table. For example, one type of cell could have an image and a label and another could have a label and a button. You would give each cell type its own identifier, so the table view can assign the right cell to the right row.

Checklists has only one type of cell but you still need to give it an identifier.

➤ Type **ChecklistItem** into the Table View Cell's **Identifier** field (you can find this in the Attributes inspector).

Giving the table view cell a reuse identifier

➤ Run the app and you'll see... exactly the same as before. The table is still empty.

You only added a cell design to the table, not actual rows. Remember that the cell is just the visual representation of the row, not the actual data. To add data to the table, you have to write some code.

The data source

➤ Head on over to **ChecklistViewController.swift** and add the following methods just before the closing bracket at the bottom of the file:

```
override func tableView(tableView: UITableView, numberOfRowsInSection section: Int) -> Int {
  return 1
}

override func tableView(tableView: UITableView,
                cellForRowAtIndexPath indexPath: NSIndexPath) -> UITableViewCell {

  let cell = tableView.dequeueReusableCellWithIdentifier("ChecklistItem") as! UITableViewCell
  return cell
}
```

These methods look a bit more complicated than the ones you've seen in Bull's Eye, but that's because each takes two parameters and returns a value to the caller. Other than that, they work in the same fashion as the methods you've dealt with before.

These two particular methods are part of UITableView's **data source** protocol.

The data source is the link between your data and the table view. Usually the view controller plays the role of data source and therefore implements these methods.

The table view needs to know how many rows of data it has and how it should display each of those rows. But you can't simply dump that data into the table view's lap and be done with it. You don't say: "Dear table view, here are my 100 rows, now go show them on the screen."

Instead, you say to the table view: "This view controller is now your data source. You can ask it questions about the data anytime you feel like it."

Once it is hooked up to a data source – your view controller – the table view sends a "numberOfRowsInSection" message to find out how many rows there are.

And when the table view needs to draw a particular row on the screen it sends the "cellForRowAtIndexPath" message to ask the data source for a cell.

You see this type of pattern all the time in iOS: one object does something on behalf of another object. In this case, the ChecklistViewController works to provide the data to the table view, but only when the table view asks for it.

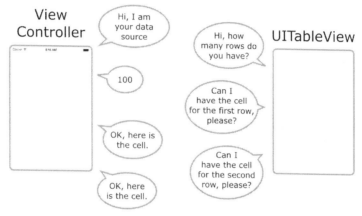

The dating ritual of a data source and a table view

Your implementation of tableView(numberOfRowsInSection) – the first method that you added – returns the value 1. This tells the table view that you just have one row of data.

The return statement is very important in Swift. It allows a method to send data back to its caller. In the case of tableView(numberOfRowsInSection), the caller is the UITableView object and it wants to know how many rows are in the table.

The statements inside a method usually perform some kind of computation using instance variables and any data received through the method's parameters. When the method is done, return says, "Hey, I'm done. Here is the answer I came up with." The return value is often called the *result* of the method.

For tableView(numberOfRowsInSection) the answer is really simple: there is only one row, so return 1.

Now that the table view knows it has one row, it calls the second method you added – tableView(cellForRowAtIndexPath) – to obtain a cell for that row. This method grabs a copy of the prototype cell and gives that back to the table view, again with a return statement.

Inside tableView(cellForRowAtIndexPath) is also where you would normally put the row data into the cell, but the app doesn't have any row data yet.

➤ Run the app and you'll see there is a single cell in the table:

The table now has one row

Notice how the iPhone's status bar partially overlaps the table view. This is new as of iOS 7. On previous versions of iOS the status bar had its own separate area, but now it is simply drawn on top of the view controller.

Later in this tutorial you will fix this small cosmetic problem by placing a navigation bar on top of the table view.

> **Note:** It's possible you're getting the following message in the Xcode debug pane: "Warning once only: Detected a case where constraints ambiguously suggest a height of zero for a table view cell's content view, yadda yadda yadda." I think this is a bug in Xcode or iOS 8.
>
> To make this warning go away, add the following line to `viewDidLoad()`:
>
>   tableView.rowHeight = 44
>
> This forces the rows in the table view to always be 44 points high.

Exercise: Modify the app so now it shows five rows. ∎

That shouldn't have been too hard:

```
override func tableView(tableView: UITableView, numberOfRowsInSection section: Int) -> Int {
  return 5
}
```

If you were tempted to go into the storyboard and duplicate the prototype cell five times, then you were confusing cells with rows.

When you make `tableView(numberOfRowsInSection)` return the number 5, you tell the table view that there will be five rows.

The table view then sends the "`cellForRowAtIndexPath`" message five times, once for each row. Because `tableView(cellForRowAtIndexPath)` currently just returns a copy of the prototype cell, your table view shows five identical rows:

The table now has five identical rows

There are several ways to create cells in `tableView(cellForRowAtIndexPath)`, but by far the easiest approach is what you've done here:

1. add a prototype cell to the table view in the storyboard;

2. set a reuse identifier on the prototype cell;

3. call `tableView.dequeueReusableCellWithIdentifier()`. This makes a new copy of the prototype cell if necessary or recycles an existing cell that is no longer in use.

Once you have a cell, you should fill it up with the data from the corresponding row and give it back to the table view. That's what you'll do in the next section.

Index paths

You've seen that the table view asks the data source for a cell using the `tableView(cellForRowAtIndexPath)` method. So what is an *index-path*?

`NSIndexPath` is simply an object that points to a specific row in the table. It is a combination of a row number and a section number, that's all. When the table view asks the data source for a cell, you can look at the row number inside the `indexPath.row` property to find out for which row this cell is intended.

It is also possible for tables to group rows into sections. In an address book app you might sort contacts by last name. All contacts whose last name starts with "A" are grouped into their own section, all contacts whose last name starts with "B" are in another section, and so on.

To find out to which section a row belongs you'd look at the `indexPath.section` property. The Checklists app has no need for this kind of grouping, so you'll ignore the `section` property of `NSIndexPath` for now.

By the way, the "NS" prefix in `NSIndexPath` means that this object is provided by the Foundation framework. NS stands for NextStep, the operating system from the 1990's that later became Mac OS X and also forms the basis of iOS.

Putting row data into the cells

Currently the rows (or rather the cells) all contain the placeholder text "Label". Let's give each row a different text.

➤ Open the storyboard and select the **Label** inside the table view cell. Go to the **Attributes inspector** and set the **Tag** field to 1000.

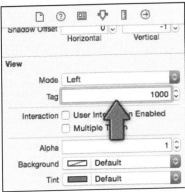

Set the label's tag to 1000

A *tag* is a numeric identifier that you can give to a user interface control in order to easily look it up later. Why the number 1000? No particular reason. It should be something other than 0, as that is the default value for all tags. 1000 is as good a number as any.

Double-check to make sure you set the tag on the *label*, not on the Table View Cell or its Content View. It's a common mistake to set the tag on the wrong view and then the results won't be what you expect!

➤ In **ChecklistViewController.swift**, change tableView(cellForRowAtIndexPath) to the following:

```
override func tableView(tableView: UITableView,
                cellForRowAtIndexPath indexPath: NSIndexPath) -> UITableViewCell {

  let cell = tableView.dequeueReusableCellWithIdentifier("ChecklistItem") as! UITableViewCell

  let label = cell.viewWithTag(1000) as! UILabel

  if indexPath.row == 0 {
    label.text = "Walk the dog"
  } else if indexPath.row == 1 {
    label.text = "Brush my teeth"
  } else if indexPath.row == 2 {
    label.text = "Learn iOS development"
  } else if indexPath.row == 3 {
    label.text = "Soccer practice"
  } else if indexPath.row == 4 {
    label.text = "Eat ice cream"
  }

  return cell
}
```

You've already seen the first line, which gets a copy of the prototype cell – either a new one or a recycled one – and puts it into the local constant named cell:

```
let cell = tableView.dequeueReusableCellWithIdentifier("ChecklistItem") as! UITableViewCell
```

(Recall that this is a constant because it's defined with `let`, not `var`. It is local because it's defined inside a method.)

The first new line in this method is:

```
let label = cell.viewWithTag(1000) as! UILabel
```

Here you ask the table view cell for the view with tag 1000. That is the tag you just set on the label in the storyboard, so this returns a reference to that `UILabel` object.

Using tags is a handy trick to get a reference to a UI element without having to make an `@IBOutlet` variable for it.

Exercise: Why can't you simply add an `@IBOutlet` variable to the view controller and connect the cell's label to that outlet in the storyboard? After all, that's how you created references to the labels in Bull's Eye... so why won't that work here? ∎

Answer: There will be more than one cell in the table and each cell will have its own label. If you connected the label from the prototype cell to an outlet on the view controller, that outlet could only refer to the label from *one* of these cells, not all of them. Since the label belongs to the cell and not to the view controller as a whole, you can't make an outlet for it on the view controller.

Back to the code. The next bit shouldn't give you too much trouble:

```
if indexPath.row == 0 {
  label.text = "Walk the dog"
} else if indexPath.row == 1 {
  label.text = "Brush my teeth"
} else if indexPath.row == 2 {
  label.text = "Learn iOS development"
} else if indexPath.row == 3 {
  label.text = "Soccer practice"
} else if indexPath.row == 4 {
  label.text = "Eat ice cream"
}
```

You have seen this `if` – `else if` – `else` structure before. It simply looks at the value of `indexPath.row`, which contains the row number, and changes the label's text accordingly. The cell for the first row gets the text "Walk the dog", the cell for the second row gets the text "Brush my teeth", and so on.

Note: Computers start counting at 0. If you have a list of 4 items, they are counted as 0, 1, 2 and 3. It may seem a little silly at first, but that's just the way programmers do things.

Therefore, for the first row in the first section, `indexPath.row` is 0 and `indexPath.section` is also 0. The second row has row number 1, the third row is row 2, and so on.

Counting from 0 may take some getting used to, but after a while it becomes natural and you'll start counting at 0 even when you're out for groceries.

➤ Run the app and see that it has five rows, each with its own text:

The rows in the table now have their own text

That is how you write the `tableView(cellForRowAtIndexPath)` method to provide data to the table. You first get a `UITableViewCell` object and then change the contents of that cell based on the row number from `NSIndexPath`.

Just for the fun of it, let's put 100 rows into the table.

➤ Change the code to the following (the highlighted bits indicate the changes):

```
override func tableView(tableView: UITableView, numberOfRowsInSection section: Int) -> Int {
  return 100
}

override func tableView(tableView: UITableView,
                  cellForRowAtIndexPath indexPath: NSIndexPath) -> UITableViewCell {
  let cell = tableView.dequeueReusableCellWithIdentifier("ChecklistItem") as! UITableViewCell

  let label = cell.viewWithTag(1000) as! UILabel

  if indexPath.row % 5 == 0 {
    label.text = "Walk the dog"
  } else if indexPath.row % 5 == 1 {
    label.text = "Brush my teeth"
  } else if indexPath.row % 5 == 2 {
    label.text = "Learn iOS development"
  } else if indexPath.row % 5 == 3 {
    label.text = "Soccer practice"
  } else if indexPath.row % 5 == 4 {
    label.text = "Eat ice cream"
  }

  return cell
}
```

It is mostly the same as before, except that `tableView(numberOfRowsInSection)` returns 100 and `tableView(cellForRowAtIndexPath)` uses a slightly different method to determine which text to display where:

```
if indexPath.row % 5 == 0 {
} else if indexPath.row % 5 == 1 {
} else if indexPath.row % 5 == 2 {
} else if indexPath.row % 5 == 3 {
} else if indexPath.row % 5 == 4 {
}
```

This uses the **remainder operator**, represented by the % sign, to determine what row you're on. (This is also known as the modulo operator.)

The % operator returns the remainder of a division. You may remember this from doing math in school. For example 13 % 4 = 1, because four goes into thirteen 3 times with a remainder of 1. However, 12 % 4 is 0 because there is no remainder.

The first row, as well as the sixth, eleventh, sixteenth and so on, will show the text "Walk the dog". The second, seventh and twelfth row will show "Brush my teeth". The third, eight and thirteenth row will show "Learn iOS development". And so on...

I think you get the picture: every five rows these lines repeat. Rather than typing in all the possibilities all the way up to a hundred, you let the computer calculate this for you (that is what they are good at):

```
First row:      0 % 5 = 0
Second row:     1 % 5 = 1
Third row:      2 % 5 = 2
Fourth row:     3 % 5 = 3
Fifth row:      4 % 5 = 4
Sixth row:      5 % 5 = 0  (same as first row)   *** The sequence
                                                     repeats here
Seventh row:    6 % 5 = 1  (same as second row)
Eighth row:     7 % 5 = 2  (same as third row)
Ninth row:      8 % 5 = 3  (same as fourth row)
Tenth row:      9 % 5 = 4  (same as fifth row)
Eleventh row:  10 % 5 = 0  (same as first row)   *** The sequence
                                                     repeats again
Twelfth row:   11 % 5 = 1  (same as second row)
and so on...
```

If this makes no sense to you at all, then feel free to ignore it. You're just using this trick to quickly get a large table filled up.

➤ Run the app and you should see this:

The table now has 100 rows

Exercise: How many cells do you think this table view uses? ■

Answer: There are 100 rows but only about 14 fit on the screen at a time. If you count the number of visible rows in the screenshot above you'll get up to 13, but it's possible to scroll the table in such a way that the top cell is still visible while a new cell is pulled in from below. So that makes at least 14 cells (a few more on the larger iPhone 6).

If you scroll really fast, then I guess it is possible that the table view needs to make a few more temporary cells, but I'm not sure about that. Is this important to know? Not really. You should let the table view take care of juggling the cells behind the scenes. All you have to do is give the table view a cell when it asks for it and fill it up with the data from the corresponding row.

You'll usually have fewer cells than rows. If the app always made a cell for each row, iOS would run out of memory really fast, especially on large tables. Because not all rows can be visible at once, that would be very wasteful and slow. iOS is a good citizen and recycles cells whenever it can.

Now you know why UITableView makes the distinction between rows – the data, of which you'll usually have lots – and cells – the visible representation of that data on the screen, of which there are only about a dozen.

As the song goes, "Rows and cells, rows and cells, tables all the way. Oh! What fun it is to learn about new things every day."

Strange crashes?

A common question on the iOS Apprentice forums is, "I'm just following along with the tutorial and suddenly my app crashes... What went wrong?"

If that happens to you, then make sure you haven't set a *breakpoint* on your code by accident. A breakpoint is a debugging tool that stops your program at a specific line and jumps into the Xcode debugger. It may appear like a crash, but your program simply paused.

A breakpoint looks like a blue arrow in the left-hand margin:

```
    return 100
}

override func tableView(tableView: UITableView, cellForRowAtIndexPath indexPath:
    NSIndexPath) -> UITableViewCell {

    let cell = tableView.dequeueReusableCellWithIdentifier("ChecklistItem") as!
        UITableViewCell
                                                            Thread 1: breakpoint 1.1
    let label = cell.viewWithTag(1000) as! UILabel
```

If your app crashes and the line at which the error occurred – or the one right before it – has a blue arrow, then you simply hit a breakpoint. Sometimes people click in the margin by mistake and set a breakpoint without realizing it (I've certainly done that!).

To remove the breakpoint, drag it out of the Xcode window.

By the way, the forums are at raywenderlich.com/forums, so drop by if you have any questions.

Tapping on the rows

When you tap a row, the cell colors gray to indicate it is selected. But when you let go, the cell stays selected. You are going to change this so that tapping the row will toggle the checkmark on and off.

A tapped row stays gray

Taps on rows are handled by the table view's **delegate**. Remember I said before that in iOS you often find objects doing something on behalf of other objects? The data source is one example of this, but the table view also depends on another little helper, the table view delegate.

The delegation pattern

The concept of delegation is very common in iOS. An object will often rely on another object to help it out with certain tasks. This *separation of concerns* keeps the system simple, as each object does only what it is good at and lets other objects take care of the rest. The table view offers a great example of this.

Because every app has its own requirements for what its data looks like, the table view must be able to deal with lots of different types of data. Instead of making the table view very complex, or requiring that you modify it to suit your own apps, the UIKit designers have chosen to delegate the duty of filling up the cells to another object, the data source.

The table view doesn't really care who its data source is or what kind of data your app deals with, just that it can send the cellForRowAtIndexPath message and that it will receive a cell in return. This keeps the table view component simple and moves the responsibility for handling the data to where it belongs: in your code.

Likewise, the table view knows how to recognize when the user taps a row, but what it should do in response completely depends on the app. In this app you'll make it toggle the checkmark; another app will likely do something totally different.

Using the delegation system, the table view can simply send a message that a tap occurred and let the delegate sort it out.

Usually components will have just one delegate but the table view splits up its delegate duties into two separate helpers: the UITableViewDataSource for putting rows into the table, and the UITableViewDelegate for handling taps on the rows and several other tasks.

➤ Open the storyboard and **Ctrl-click** on the table view to bring up its connections:

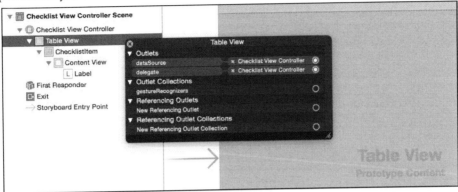

The table's data source and delegate are hooked up to the view controller

You can see that the table view's data source and delegate are both connected to the view controller. That is standard practice for a UITableViewController. (You can also use table views in a basic UIViewController but then you'll have to connect the data source and delegate manually.)

➤ Add the following method to **ChecklistViewController.swift**:

```
override func tableView(tableView: UITableView,
                   didSelectRowAtIndexPath indexPath: NSIndexPath) {

  tableView.deselectRowAtIndexPath(indexPath, animated: true)
}
```

Run the app and tap a row; the cell briefly turns gray and then becomes de-selected again.

➤ Let's make tableView(didSelectRowAtIndexPath) toggle the checkmark, so change it to the following:

```
override func tableView(tableView: UITableView,
                   didSelectRowAtIndexPath indexPath: NSIndexPath) {

  if let cell = tableView.cellForRowAtIndexPath(indexPath) {
    if cell.accessoryType == .None {
      cell.accessoryType = .Checkmark
    } else {
      cell.accessoryType = .None
    }
  }
  tableView.deselectRowAtIndexPath(indexPath, animated: true)
}
```

The checkmark is part of the cell (the accessory, remember?), so you first need to find the UITableViewCell object for the tapped row. You simply ask the table view: what is the cell at this indexPath you've given me?

Because it is theoretically possible that there is no cell at the specified index-path, for example if that row isn't visible, you need to use the special if let statement.

This tells Swift that you only want to perform the rest of the code if there really is a UITableViewCell object. In this app there always will be one – after all, that's what the user just tapped – but Swift doesn't know that.

Once you have the `UITableViewCell` object, you look at the cell's accessory, which you can find with the `accessoryType` property. If it is "none", then you change the accessory to a checkmark; if it was a checkmark, you change it back to none.

> **Note:** To find the cell you call `tableView.cellForRowAtIndexPath()`.
>
> It's important to realize this is *not* the same method as the data source method `tableView(cellForRowAtIndexPath)` that you added earlier.
>
> Despite the similar names they are different methods in different objects, performing different tasks. Tricky, eh?
>
> The purpose of your data source method is to deliver a new (or recycled) cell object to the table view when a row becomes visible. You never call this method yourself; only the `UITableView` may call its data source methods.
>
> The purpose of `tableView.cellForRowAtIndexPath()` is also to return a cell object, but this is an existing cell for a row that is currently being displayed. It won't create any new cells. If there is no cell for that row yet, it will return the special value `nil`, meaning that no cell could be found.
>
> Remember how I said methods should have clear, descriptive names? UIKit is pretty good with its names but this is a case where the same name used in two different places can lead to confusion and despair. Beware this pitfall!

➤ Run the app and try it out. You should be able to toggle the checkmarks on the rows. Sweet!

You can now tap on a row to toggle the checkmark

If the checkmark does not appear or disappear right away but only after you select *another* row, then make sure the method name is not `didDeselectRowAtIndexPath`! Xcode's autocompletion may have fooled you into picking the wrong method name.

Unfortunately, the app has a bug. Here's how to reproduce it:

➤ Tap a row to remove the checkmark. Scroll that row off the screen and scroll back again (try scrolling really fast). The checkmark has reappeared!

In addition, the checkmark seems to spontaneously disappear from other rows. What is going on here?

Again it's the story of cells vs. rows: you have toggled the checkmark on the cell but the cell may be reused for another row when you're scrolling. Whether a checkmark is set or not should be a property of the row, not the cell.

Instead of using the cell's accessory to remember to show a checkmark or not, you need some way to keep track of the checked status for each row. That means it's time to expand the data source and make it use a proper *data model*, which is the topic of the next section.

Phew! That was a lot of new stuff to take in, so I hope you're still with me. If not, then take a break and start at the beginning again. You're being introduced to a whole bunch of new concepts all at once and that can be overwhelming.

But don't fear, it's OK if not everything makes perfect sense yet. As long as you get the gist of what's going on, you're good to continue.

If you want to check your work, you can find the project files for the app up to this point under **01 - Table View** in the tutorial's Source Code folder.

Methods with multiple parameters

Most of the methods you have used in the Bull's Eye tutorial took only one parameter or did not have any parameters at all, but these new table view data source and delegate methods take two:

```
override func tableView(
            tableView: UITableView,                 // parameter 1
            numberOfRowsInSection section: Int) // parameter 2
            -> Int {                                 // return value
    . . .
}
override func tableView(
            tableView: UITableView,                 // parameter 1
            cellForRowAtIndexPath indexPath: NSIndexPath) // parameter 2
            -> UITableViewCell {                     // return value
    . . .
}
override func tableView(
            tableView: UITableView,                  // parameter 1
            didSelectRowAtIndexPath indexPath: NSIndexPath) {  // parameter 2
    . . .
}
```

The first parameter is the UITableView object on whose behalf these methods are invoked. This is done for convenience, so you won't have to make an @IBOutlet in order to send messages back to the table view.

For numberOfRowsInSection the second parameter is the section number. For cellForRowAtIndexPath and didSelectRowAtIndexPath it is the index-path.

Methods are not limited to just two parameters, they can have many. But for practical reasons three is usually more than enough, and you won't see many methods with more than five parameters.

In other programming languages a method with multiple parameters typically looks like this:

```
Int numberOfRowsInSection(UITableView tableView, Int section) {
    . . .
}
```

In Swift we do it a little bit differently, mostly to be compatible with the iOS frameworks, which are all written in the Objective-C programming language.

Let's take a look again at "numberOfRowsInSection":

```
override func tableView(tableView: UITableView,
                    numberOfRowsInSection section: Int) -> Int {
    . . .
}
```

The first parameter looks like this:

```
tableView: UITableView
```

The name of this parameter is "`tableView`". The name is followed by a colon and the parameter's type, `UITableView`.

The second parameter looks like this:

```
numberOfRowsInSection section: Int
```

This one has two names, "`numberOfRowsInSection`" and "`section`".

The first name, `numberOfRowsInSection`, is used when calling the method (this is known as the *external* parameter name). Inside the method itself you use the second name, `section` (the *local* parameter name). The data type of this parameter is `Int`.

This pattern is common in Swift methods: the first parameter of a method only has one name but the other parameters have two. Strange? Yes.

It makes sense if you've ever programmed in Objective-C but no doubt it looks weird if you're coming from another language. Once you get used to it you'll find that this notation is actually quite readable.

The full name of this method is officially `tableView(numberOfRowsInSection)`. If you pronounce that out loud, it actually makes sense. It asks for the number of rows in a particular section of a particular table view.

You don't have to use all the parameters inside the method. Checklists doesn't use table view sections, so you can safely ignore the `section` parameter.

By the way, the return type of the method is at the end, after the -> arrow. If there is no arrow, as in `tableView(didSelectRowAtIndexPath)`, then the method is not supposed to return a value.

Model-View-Controller

No tutorial on programming for iOS can escape an explanation of **Model-View-Controller**, or MVC for short.

MVC is one of the three fundamental design patterns of iOS. You've already seen the other two: *delegation*, making one object do something on behalf of another; and *target-action*, connecting events such as button taps to action methods.

Model-View-Controller roughly means that the objects in your app can be split up into three groups:

- **Model objects.** These objects contain your data and any operations on the data. For example, if you were writing a cookbook app, the model would consist of the recipes. In a game it would be the design of the levels, the score of the player and the positions of the monsters.

The operations that the data model objects perform are sometimes called the *business rules* or the *domain logic*. For the app from this tutorial, the checklists and their to-do items form the data model.

- **View objects.** These objects make up the visual part of the app: images, buttons, labels, text fields, and so on. In a game the views are the visual representation of the game world, such as the monster animations and a frag counter.

  A view can draw itself and responds to user input, but it typically does not handle any application logic. Many views, such as UITableView, can be re-used in many different apps because they are not tied to a specific data model.

- **Controller objects.** The view controller is the object that connects your data model objects to the views. It listens to taps on the views, makes the data model objects do some calculations in response, and updates the views to reflect the new state of your model. The view controller is in charge.

Conceptually, this is how these three building blocks fit together:

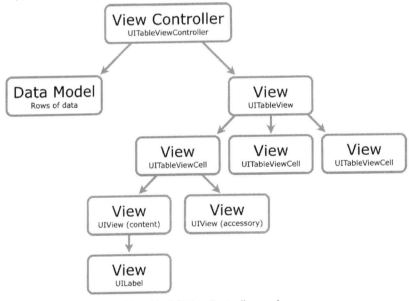

How Model-View-Controller works

The view controller has one main view, accessible through its view property, that contains a bunch of subviews. It is not uncommon for a screen to have dozens of views all at once. The top-level view usually fills the whole screen. You design the layout of the view controller's screen in the storyboard.

In the Checklists app, the main view is the UITableView and its subviews are the table view cells. Each cell also has several subviews of its own, namely the text label and the accessory.

A view controller handles one screen of the app. If your app has more than one screen, each of these is handled by its own view controller and has its own views. Your app flows from one view controller to the other.

You will often need to create your own view controllers but iOS also comes with ready-to-use view controllers, such as the image picker controller for photos, the mail compose controller that lets you write email, and the tweet sheet for sending Twitter messages.

Views vs. view controllers

Remember that a view and a view controller are two different things.

A view is an object that draws something on the screen, such as a button or a label. The view is what you see.

The view controller is what does the work behind the scenes. It is the bridge that sits between your data model and the views.

A lot of beginners give their view controllers names such as `FirstView` and `MainView`. That is very confusing! If something is a view controller, call it "ViewController" and not "View".

I sometimes wish Apple had left the word "view" out of "view controller" and just called it "controller" as that is a lot less misleading.

Creating the data model

So far you've put a bunch of fake data into the table view. The data consists of a text string and a checkmark that can be on or off.

As you saw, you cannot use the cells to remember the data as cells get re-used all the time and their old contents get overwritten.

Table view cells are part of the view. Their purpose is to display the app's data, but that data actually comes from somewhere else: the data model.

Remember this well: the rows are the data, the cells are the views. The table view controller is the thing that ties them together through the act of implementing the table view's data source and delegate methods.

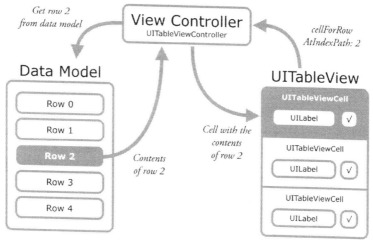

The table view controller (data source) gets the data from the model and puts it into the cells

The data model for this app consists of a list of to-do items. Each of these items will get its own row in the table.

For each to-do item you need to store two pieces of information: the text ("Walk the dog", "Brush my teeth", "Eat ice cream") and whether the checkmark is set or not.

That is two pieces of information per row, so you need two variables for each row.

First I'll show you the cumbersome way to program this. It will work but it isn't very smart. Even though this is not a very good approach, I'd still like you to follow along and copy-paste the code into Xcode and run the app.

You need to understand why this approach is problematic so you'll be able to appreciate the proper solution better.

> In **ChecklistViewController.swift**, add the following instance variables after the `class` `ChecklistViewController` line:

```
class ChecklistViewController: UITableViewController {

  var row0text = "Walk the dog"
  var row1text = "Brush teeth"
  var row2text = "Learn iOS development"
  var row3text = "Soccer practice"
  var row4text = "Eat ice cream"

  . . .
```

These variables are defined outside of any method (they are not "local"), so they can be used by all of the methods from `ChecklistViewController`.

> Change the data source methods into:

```
override func tableView(tableView: UITableView, numberOfRowsInSection section: Int) -> Int {
  return 5
}

override func tableView(tableView: UITableView,
                    cellForRowAtIndexPath indexPath: NSIndexPath) -> UITableViewCell {
  let cell = tableView.dequeueReusableCellWithIdentifier("ChecklistItem") as! UITableViewCell

  let label = cell.viewWithTag(1000) as! UILabel

  if indexPath.row == 0 {
    label.text = row0text
  } else if indexPath.row == 1 {
    label.text = row1text
  } else if indexPath.row == 2 {
    label.text = row2text
  } else if indexPath.row == 3 {
    label.text = row3text
  } else if indexPath.row == 4 {
    label.text = row4text
  }

  return cell
}
```

> Run the app. It still shows the same five rows as before.

What have you done here? For every row you have added an instance variable with the text for that row. Those five instance variables are your data model.

In `tableView(cellForRowAtIndexPath)` you look at `indexPath.row` to figure out which row you're supposed to draw, and put the text from the corresponding instance variable into the cell.

Let's fix the checkmark toggling logic. You no longer want to toggle the checkmark on the cell but on the row. To do this, you add another five new instance variables to keep track of the "checked" state of each of the rows.

➤ Add the following instance variables:

```
var row0checked = false
var row1checked = false
var row2checked = false
var row3checked = false
var row4checked = false
```

These variables have the data type `Bool`. You've seen the data types `Int` (whole numbers), `Float` (numbers with decimals), and `String` (text) before. A `Bool` variable can hold only two possible values: `true` and `false`.

`Bool` is short for "boolean", after Englishman George Boole who long ago invented a type of logic that forms the basis of all modern computing. The fact that computers talk in ones and zeros is largely due to him.

You use `Bool` variables to remember whether something is true (1) or not (0). The names of boolean variables often start with the verb "is" or "has", as in `isHungry` or `hasIceCream`.

The instance variable `row0checked` is `true` if the first row has its checkmark set and `false` if it hasn't. Likewise, `row1checked` reflects whether the second row has a checkmark or not. The same thing goes for the instance variables for the other rows.

> **Note:** How does the compiler know that the type of these variables is `Bool`? You never specified that anywhere.
>
> Swift uses a clever technique called *type inference* to determine the data type of a variable if you don't state it explicitly.
>
> Because you said "`var row0checked = false`", Swift assumes that you intended to make this a `Bool`, as `false` is valid only for `Bool` values.

The delegate method that handles the taps on the rows will now use these new instance variables to determine whether the checkmark for a row needs to be toggled on or off.

➤ Replace `tableView(didSelectRowAtIndexPath)` with the following:

```
override func tableView(tableView: UITableView,
                        didSelectRowAtIndexPath indexPath: NSIndexPath) {

  if let cell = tableView.cellForRowAtIndexPath(indexPath) {
    if indexPath.row == 0 {
      row0checked = !row0checked
      if row0checked {
        cell.accessoryType = .Checkmark
      } else {
        cell.accessoryType = .None
      }
    } else if indexPath.row == 1 {
      row1checked = !row1checked
```

```
        if row1checked {
           cell.accessoryType = .Checkmark
        } else {
           cell.accessoryType = .None
        }
      } else if indexPath.row == 2 {
        row2checked = !row2checked
        if row2checked {
           cell.accessoryType = .Checkmark
        } else {
           cell.accessoryType = .None
        }
      } else if indexPath.row == 3 {
        row3checked = !row3checked
        if row2checked {
           cell.accessoryType = .Checkmark
        } else {
           cell.accessoryType = .None
        }
      } else if indexPath.row == 4 {
        row4checked = !row4checked
        if row4checked {
           cell.accessoryType = .Checkmark
        } else {
           cell.accessoryType = .None
        }
      }
    }
    tableView.deselectRowAtIndexPath(indexPath, animated: true)
}
```

This looks at indexPath.row to find the row that was tapped, and then performs some logic with the corresponding "row checked" instance variable.

Let's look at the first if indexPath.row statement in detail:

```
  if indexPath.row == 0 {
     row0checked = !row0checked
     if row0checked {
        cell.accessoryType = .Checkmark
     } else {
        cell.accessoryType = .None
     }
  } . . .
```

If indexPath.row is 0, the user tapped on the very first row and the corresponding instance variable is row0checked.

You do the following to flip that boolean value around:

```
  row0checked = !row0checked
```

The ! symbol is the **logical not** operator. There are a few other logical operators that work on Bool values, such as **and** and **or**, which you'll encounter soon enough.

What ! does is simple: it reverses the meaning of the value. If row0checked is true, then ! makes it false. Conversely, !false is true.

Think of ! as "not": not yes is no and not no is yes. Yes?

Once you have the new value of row0checked, you can use it to show or hide the checkmark:

```
  if row0checked {
```

```
    cell.accessoryType = .Checkmark
} else {
    cell.accessoryType = .None
}
```

The same logic is used for the other four rows.

In fact, the other rows use the *exact* same logic. The only thing that is different between each of these code blocks is the name of the "row checked" instance variable.

Because the code looks so familiar from one if-statement to the next, we can write this in a better way.

➤ Replace `tableView(didSelectRowAtIndexPath)` with the following:

```
override func tableView(tableView: UITableView,
                 didSelectRowAtIndexPath indexPath: NSIndexPath) {

    if let cell = tableView.cellForRowAtIndexPath(indexPath) {
        var isChecked = false
        if indexPath.row == 0 {
            row0checked = !row0checked
            isChecked = row0checked
        } else if indexPath.row == 1 {
            row1checked = !row1checked
            isChecked = row1checked
        } else if indexPath.row == 2 {
            row2checked = !row2checked
            isChecked = row2checked
        } else if indexPath.row == 3 {
            row3checked = !row3checked
            isChecked = row3checked
        } else if indexPath.row == 4 {
            row4checked = !row4checked
            isChecked = row4checked
        }

        if isChecked {
            cell.accessoryType = .Checkmark
        } else {
            cell.accessoryType = .None
        }
    }
    tableView.deselectRowAtIndexPath(indexPath, animated: true)
}
```

That's a lot shorter!

Notice how the logic that sets the checkmark on the cell has moved to the bottom of the method. There is now only one place where this happens.

To make this possible, you store the value of the "row checked" instance variable into the local variable `isChecked`. This temporary variable is just used to remember whether the selected row needs a checkmark or not.

By using a local variable you were able to remove a lot of duplicated code, which is a good thing. You've taken the logic that all rows had in common and moved it out of their if-statements into a single place.

Code duplication makes programs a lot harder to read. It invites subtle mistakes that cause hard-to-find bugs. Always be on the lookout for opportunities to remove duplicate logic!

Exercise: There is actually a bug in the previous, longer version of this method; did you spot it? ∎

➤ Run the app and observe... that it still doesn't work very well. You have to tap a few times on a row to actually make the checkmark go away.

What's wrong here? Simple: when you declared the rowXchecked variables you set their values to false.

So row0checked and the others think that there is no checkmark on their row, but the table draws one anyway because you enabled the checkmark accessory on the prototype cell.

In other words: the data model (the "row checked" variables) and the views (the checkmarks inside the cells) are out-of-sync.

There are a few ways you could try to fix this: you could set the Bool variables to true to begin with, or you could remove the checkmark from the prototype cell in the storyboard.

Neither is a foolproof solution. What goes wrong here isn't so much that you initialized the "row checked" values wrong or designed the prototype cell wrong, but that you forgot to set the cell's accessoryType property to the right value in tableView(cellForRowAtIndexPath).

When you are asked for a new cell, you always should configure all of its properties. The call to tableView.dequeueReusableCellWithIdentifier() could return a cell that was previously used for a row with a checkmark. If the new row shouldn't have a checkmark, then you have to remove it from the cell at this point (and vice versa).

Let's fix that.

➤ Add the following method to **ChecklistViewController.swift**:

```swift
func configureCheckmarkForCell(cell: UITableViewCell, indexPath: NSIndexPath) {
  var isChecked = false

  if indexPath.row == 0 {
    isChecked = row0checked
  } else if indexPath.row == 1 {
    isChecked = row1checked
  } else if indexPath.row == 2 {
    isChecked = row2checked
  } else if indexPath.row == 3 {
    isChecked = row3checked
  } else if indexPath.row == 4 {
    isChecked = row4checked
  }

  if isChecked {
    cell.accessoryType = .Checkmark
  } else {
    cell.accessoryType = .None
  }
}
```

This new method looks at the cell for a certain row (specified by indexPath) and makes the checkmark visible if the corresponding "row checked" variable is true, or hides it if false. This logic should look very familiar!

You'll call this method from tableView(cellForRowAtIndexPath), just before you return the cell.

➤ Change that method to the following (recall that . . . means that the existing code at that spot doesn't change):

```
override func tableView(tableView: UITableView,
                        cellForRowAtIndexPath indexPath: NSIndexPath) -> UITableViewCell {
  . . .

  configureCheckmarkForCell(cell, indexPath: indexPath)
  return cell
}
```

➤ Run the app again.

Now the app works just fine. Initially all the rows are unchecked. Tapping a row checks it, tapping it again unchecks it. The rows and cells are now always in sync. This code guarantees that each cell always has the value that corresponds to its row.

> **Note:** The new `configureCheckmarkForCell()` method has two parameters, `cell` and `indexPath`. According to Swift conventions, the first parameter does not have its own label. Instead, the name of that parameter is part of the method name:
>
> ```
> configureCheckmarkForCell(someCell, …
> ```
>
> The second parameter has the label `indexPath:`, and you're required to specify that label when you call the method:
>
> ```
> configureCheckmarkForCell(someCell, indexPath: someIndexPath)
> ```
>
> So this won't work:
>
> ```
> configureCheckmarkForCell(someCell, someIndexPath)
> ```
>
> The full name for the method is `configureCheckmarkForCell(indexPath)`. The `indexPath` bit is an integral part of the method name!
>
> It is also possible to give a parameter another label, which is what happens in `tableView(numberOfRowsInSection)` and `tableView(cellForRowAtIndexPath)`.
>
> You could do the same thing in your own method:
>
> ```
> func configureCheckmarkForCell(cell: UITableViewCell,
>                                atIndexPath indexPath: NSIndexPath) {
>   . . .
> }
> ```
>
> Now this method should be called as follows:
>
> ```
> configureCheckmarkForCell(someCell, atIndexPath: someIndexPath)
> ```
>
> And its full name becomes `configureCheckmarkForCell(atIndexPath)`. Adding short prepositions such as "at", "with", or "for" makes the name of the method sound like a proper English phrase. Doesn't it just roll off your tongue?
>
> Inside the method, however, you'd still use `indexPath` – and not the external label `atIndexPath` – to refer to the parameter.
>
> You could also write the method like this:
>
> ```
> func configureCheckmark(#cell: UITableViewCell, indexPath: NSIndexPath) {
>   . . .
> }
> ```
>
> It is supposed to be called as follows. Note that the first parameter now does have a label (that's what the # sign is for):
>
> ```
> configureCheckmark(cell: someCell, indexPath: someIndexPath)
> ```

Its full name is now `configureCheckmark(cell, indexPath)`. You have to admit that doesn't read as nicely as the other options.

Swift allows quite a bit of flexibility in the naming of methods, but standard practice is to put the name of the first parameter into the name of the method, as in `configureCheckmarkForCell(...)`. This naming convention makes it easier for Swift to talk to Objective-C code, which is a good thing as most of the iOS frameworks are written in Objective-C.

Why did you make `configureCheckmarkForCell()` a method of its own anyway? Well, you can use it to simplify `tableView(didSelectRowAtIndexPath)`.

Notice how similar these two methods currently are. That's another case of code duplication that you can get rid of!

You can simplify `didSelectRowAtIndexPath` by letting `configureCheckmarkForCell()` do some of the work.

➤ Replace `tableView(didSelectRowAtIndexPath)` with the following:

```
override func tableView(tableView: UITableView,
                    didSelectRowAtIndexPath indexPath: NSIndexPath) {

  if let cell = tableView.cellForRowAtIndexPath(indexPath) {
    if indexPath.row == 0 {
      row0checked = !row0checked
    } else if indexPath.row == 1 {
      row1checked = !row1checked
    } else if indexPath.row == 2 {
      row2checked = !row2checked
    } else if indexPath.row == 3 {
      row3checked = !row3checked
    } else if indexPath.row == 4 {
      row4checked = !row4checked
    }
    configureCheckmarkForCell(cell, indexPath: indexPath)
  }
  tableView.deselectRowAtIndexPath(indexPath, animated: true)
}
```

This method no longer sets or clears the checkmark from the cell, but only toggles the "checked" state in the data model and then calls `configureCheckmarkForCell()` to update the view.

➤ Run the app again and it should still work.

➤ Change the declarations of the instance variables to the following and run the app again:

```
var row0checked = false
var row1checked = true
var row2checked = true
var row3checked = false
var row4checked = true
```

Now rows 1, 2 and 4 (the second, third and fifth rows) initially have a checkmark while the others don't.

The data model and the table view cells are now always in-sync

The approach that we've taken here to remember which rows are checked or not works just fine, but you'll have to agree that checking each index-path by hand seems like a lot of effort.

For only five rows it's doable, but what if you have 100 rows and they all need to be unique? Should you add another 95 "row text" and "row checked" variables to the view controller, as well as that many additional if-statements? I hope not!

There is a better way: arrays.

Arrays

An **array** is an ordered list of objects. If you think of a variable as a container of one value (or one object) then an array is a container for multiple objects.

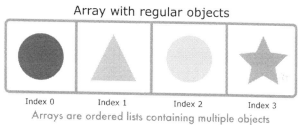

Arrays are ordered lists containing multiple objects

Of course, the array itself is also an object (named Array) that you can put into a variable. And because arrays are objects, arrays can contain other arrays.

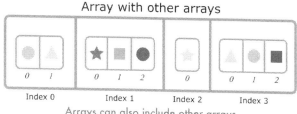

Arrays can also include other arrays

The objects inside an array are indexed by numbers, starting at 0 as usual. To ask the array for the first object, you write array[0]. The second object is at array[1], and so on.

The array is *ordered*, meaning that the order of the objects it contains matters. The object at index 0 always comes before the object at index 1.

> **Note:** Array is a so-called *collection* object. There are several other collection objects and they all organize their objects in a different fashion. Dictionary, for example, contains key-value pairs, just like a real dictionary contains a list of words and a description for each of those words. You'll use some of these other collection types in the later tutorials.

The organization of an array is very similar to the rows from a table – they are both lists of objects in a particular order – so it makes sense to put your data model's rows into an array.

Arrays store one object per index, but your rows currently consist of two separate pieces of data: the text and the checked state. It would be easier if you made a single object for each row, because then the row number from the table simply becomes the index in the array.

Let's combine the text and checkmark state into a new object of your own!

➤ Select the **Checklists** group in the project navigator and right click. Choose **New File...** from the popup menu:

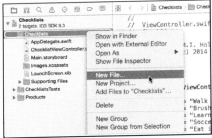

Adding a new file to the project

Under the **Source** section choose **Swift File**:

Choosing the Swift File class template

Click **Next** to continue. Save the new file as **ChecklistItem** (adding the **.swift** file extension is optional):

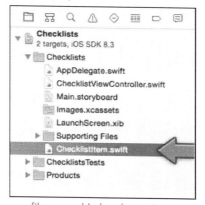

Saving the new Swift file

Press **Create** to add the new file to the project:

The new files are added to the project navigator

➤ Add the following to **ChecklistItem.swift,** below the `import` line:

```
class ChecklistItem {
  var text = ""
  var checked = false
}
```

What you see here is the absolute minimum amount of stuff you need in order to make a new object. The `class` keyword names the object and the two lines with `var` add data items (instance variables) to it.

The `text` property will store the description of the checklist item (the text that will appear in the table view cell's label) and the `checked` property determines whether the cell gets a checkmark or not.

> **Note:** You may be wondering what the difference is between the terms *property* and *instance variable* – we've used both to refer to an object's data items. You'll be glad to hear that these two things mean the same thing.

In Swift terminology, a property is a variable or constant that is used in the context of an object. That's exactly what an instance variable is. So you can use the terms property and instance variable interchangeably.

(In Objective-C, properties and instance variables are closely related but not quite the same thing. In Swift they are the same.)

That's all for now. The `ChecklistItem` object currently only serves to combine the text and the checked flag into one object. Later you'll add more to it.

Before you get around to using an array, let's replace the `String` and `Bool` instance variables in the view controller with these new `ChecklistItem` objects.

➤ In **ChecklistViewController.swift**, remove the old instance variables and replace them with `ChecklistItem` objects:

```swift
class ChecklistViewController: UITableViewController {
  var row0item: ChecklistItem
  var row1item: ChecklistItem
  var row2item: ChecklistItem
  var row3item: ChecklistItem
  var row4item: ChecklistItem
```

This replaces the `rowXtext` and `rowXchecked` instance variables.

Because some methods in the view controller still refer to these old variables, Xcode detects several errors. Before you can run the app again you need to fix these errors, so let's do that now.

➤ Make the following changes to use the new instance variables:

```swift
override func tableView(tableView: UITableView,
                cellForRowAtIndexPath indexPath: NSIndexPath) -> UITableViewCell {

  let cell = tableView.dequeueReusableCellWithIdentifier("ChecklistItem") as! UITableViewCell
  let label = cell.viewWithTag(1000) as! UILabel

  if indexPath.row == 0 {
    label.text = row0item.text
  } else if indexPath.row == 1 {
    label.text = row1item.text
  } else if indexPath.row == 2 {
    label.text = row2item.text
  } else if indexPath.row == 3 {
    label.text = row3item.text
  } else if indexPath.row == 4 {
    label.text = row4item.text
  }

  configureCheckmarkForCell(cell, indexPath: indexPath)
  return cell
}
```

```swift
override func tableView(tableView: UITableView,
                didSelectRowAtIndexPath indexPath: NSIndexPath) {

  if let cell = tableView.cellForRowAtIndexPath(indexPath) {
    if indexPath.row == 0 {
      row0item.checked = !row0item.checked
    } else if indexPath.row == 1 {
```

```
     row1item.checked = !row1item.checked
   } else if indexPath.row == 2 {
     row2item.checked = !row2item.checked
   } else if indexPath.row == 3 {
     row3item.checked = !row3item.checked
   } else if indexPath.row == 4 {
     row4item.checked = !row4item.checked
   }

   configureCheckmarkForCell(cell, indexPath: indexPath)
 }
 tableView.deselectRowAtIndexPath(indexPath, animated: true)
}
```

```
func configureCheckmarkForCell(cell: UITableViewCell, indexPath: NSIndexPath) {
  var isChecked = false

  if indexPath.row == 0 {
    isChecked = row0item.checked
  } else if indexPath.row == 1 {
    isChecked = row1item.checked
  } else if indexPath.row == 2 {
    isChecked = row2item.checked
  } else if indexPath.row == 3 {
    isChecked = row3item.checked
  } else if indexPath.row == 4 {
    isChecked = row4item.checked
  }

  if isChecked {
    cell.accessoryType = .Checkmark
  } else {
    cell.accessoryType = .None
  }
}
```

Instead of using the separate row0text and row0checked variables, you now use row0item.text and row0item.checked. Likewise for the other rows.

That takes care of most of the errors, but not all of them. Xcode complains that "Class ChecklistViewController has no initializers." This was not a problem before, so what has gone wrong?

Previously you gave the "row text" and "row checked" variables a value when you declared them, like so:

```
var row0text = "Walk the dog"
. . .
var row0checked = false
```

With the new ChecklistItem object you can't do that because a ChecklistItem consists of more than one value.

Instead you used a so-called *type annotation* to tell Swift that row0Item is an object of type ChecklistItem:

```
var row0item: ChecklistItem
```

But at this point row0item doesn't have a value yet, it's just an empty container for a ChecklistItem object.

And that's a problem: in Swift programs, all variables should always have a value – the containers can never be empty.

If you can't give the variable a value right away when you declare it, then you have to give it a value inside a so-called *initializer* method.

➤ Add the following to **ChecklistViewController.swift**. This is a special type of method (which is why it doesn't start with the word func). It is customary to place it near the top of the file, just below the instance variables.

```
required init(coder aDecoder: NSCoder) {
  row0item = ChecklistItem()
  row0item.text = "Walk the dog"
  row0item.checked = false

  row1item = ChecklistItem()
  row1item.text = "Brush my teeth"
  row1item.checked = true

  row2item = ChecklistItem()
  row2item.text = "Learn iOS development"
  row2item.checked = true

  row3item = ChecklistItem()
  row3item.text = "Soccer practice"
  row3item.checked = false

  row4item = ChecklistItem()
  row4item.text = "Eat ice cream"
  row4item.checked = true

  super.init(coder: aDecoder)
}
```

Every object in Swift has an init method, or initializer. Some objects even have more than one.

The init method is called by Swift when the object comes into existence.

For the view controller that happens when it is loaded from the storyboard during app startup. At that point, its init(coder) method is called.

That makes init(coder) a great place for putting values into any variables that still need them (soon you'll learn more about what the "coder" parameter is for).

Inside init(coder), you first create a new ChecklistItem object:

```
row0item = ChecklistItem()
```

and then set the properties:

```
row0item.text = "Walk the dog"
row0item.checked = false
```

You repeat this for the other four rows. Each row gets its own ChecklistItem object that you store in its own instance variable.

This is essentially doing the same thing as before, except that this time the text and checked variables are not separate instance variables of the view controller but properties of the ChecklistItem objects.

➤ Run the app just to make sure that everything works again.

Putting the text and checked properties into their own ChecklistItem object already improved the code, but it is still a bit unwieldy.

With the current approach, you need to keep around a ChecklistItem instance variable for each row. That's not ideal, especially not if you want more than just a handful of rows.

Time to put that array into action!

➤ In **ChecklistViewController.swift**, throw away all the instance variables and replace them with a single array variable named items:

```
class ChecklistViewController: UITableViewController {

  var items: [ChecklistItem]
```

This looks similar to how you declared the previous variables but this time there are square brackets around ChecklistItem. Those square brackets indicate that this is going to be an array.

➤ Make the following changes in init(coder):

```
required init(coder aDecoder: NSCoder) {
  items = [ChecklistItem]()

  let row0item = ChecklistItem()
  row0item.text = "Walk the dog"
  row0item.checked = false
  items.append(row0item)

  let row1item = ChecklistItem()
  row1item.text = "Brush my teeth"
  row1item.checked = true
  items.append(row1item)

  let row2item = ChecklistItem()
  row2item.text = "Learn iOS development"
  row2item.checked = true
  items.append(row2item)

  let row3item = ChecklistItem()
  row3item.text = "Soccer practice"
  row3item.checked = false
  items.append(row3item)

  let row4item = ChecklistItem()
  row4item.text = "Eat ice cream"
  row4item.checked = true
  items.append(row4item)

  super.init(coder: aDecoder)
}
```

This is not so different from before, except that you first create – or *instantiate* – the array object:

```
items = [ChecklistItem]()
```

You've seen that the notation [ChecklistItem] means an array of ChecklistItem objects. But that is just the data type of the items variable; it is not the actual array object yet.

To get the array object you have to construct it first. That is what the parentheses () are for: they tell Swift to make the new array object.

The data type is like the brand name of a car. Just saying the words "Porsche 911" out loud doesn't magically get you a new car – you actually have to go to the dealer to buy one. The parentheses () behind the type name are like going to the dealer to buy an object of that type.

The parentheses tell Swift's object factory, "Build me an object of the type array-with-ChecklistItems."

It is important to remember that just declaring that you have a variable does not automatically make the corresponding object for you. The variable is just the container for the object. You still have to instantiate the object and put it into the container.

So until you order an actual array-of-ChecklistItems object from the factory and put that into items, the variable is empty. And empty variables are a big no-no in Swift.

Just to drive this point home:

```
// This declares that items will hold an array of ChecklistItem objects but it does not
// actually create that array. At this point, items does not have a value yet.
var items: [ChecklistItem]

// This instantiates the array. Now items contains a valid array object, but the array
// has no ChecklistItem objects inside it yet.
items = [ChecklistItem]()
```

Each time you make a ChecklistItem object, you also add it into the array:

```
// This instantiates a new ChecklistItem object. Notice the ().
let row0item = ChecklistItem()

row0item.text = "Walk the dog"
row0item.checked = false

// This adds the ChecklistItem object into the items array.
items.append(row0item)
```

Notice that you're also using the parentheses here to create each of the individual ChecklistItem objects.

It's also important that row0item and the others are now local to this method. They are no longer valid instance variable names (because you removed those earlier). That's why you need to use the let keyword; without it, the app won't compile.

At the end of init(coder), the items array contains five ChecklistItem objects. This is your new data model.

Now that you have all your rows in the items array, you can simplify the table view data source and delegate methods once again.

➤ Change these methods:

```
override func tableView(tableView: UITableView,
                    cellForRowAtIndexPath indexPath: NSIndexPath) -> UITableViewCell {
  let cell = tableView.dequeueReusableCellWithIdentifier("ChecklistItem") as! UITableViewCell

  let item = items[indexPath.row]

  let label = cell.viewWithTag(1000) as! UILabel
  label.text = item.text

  configureCheckmarkForCell(cell, indexPath: indexPath)
```

```
    return cell
}
```

```
override func tableView(tableView: UITableView,
                        didSelectRowAtIndexPath indexPath: NSIndexPath) {
  if let cell = tableView.cellForRowAtIndexPath(indexPath) {
    let item = items[indexPath.row]
    item.checked = !item.checked
    configureCheckmarkForCell(cell, indexPath: indexPath)
  }
  tableView.deselectRowAtIndexPath(indexPath, animated: true)
}
```

```
func configureCheckmarkForCell(cell: UITableViewCell, indexPath: NSIndexPath) {
  let item = items[indexPath.row]
  if item.checked {
    cell.accessoryType = .Checkmark
  } else {
    cell.accessoryType = .None
  }
}
```

In each method, you do:

```
let item = items[indexPath.row]
```

This asks the array for the `ChecklistItem` object at the index that corresponds to the row number. Once you have that object, you can simply look at its text and `checked` properties and do whatever you need to do.

If the user were to add 100 to-do items to this list, then none of this code would need to change. It works equally well with five items as with a hundred (or a thousand).

Speaking of the number of items, you can now change `numberOfRowsInSection` to return the number of items in the array, instead of a hard-coded number.

➤ Change the `tableView(numberOfRowsInSection)` method to:

```
override func tableView(tableView: UITableView, numberOfRowsInSection section: Int) -> Int {
  return items.count
}
```

Not only is the code a lot shorter and easier to read, it can now also handle an arbitrary number of rows. That is the power of arrays.

➤ Run the app and see for yourself. It should still do exactly the same as before but its internal structure is much better.

Exercise: Add a few more rows to the table. You should only have to change `init(coder)` for this to work. ∎

Cleaning up the code

There are a few more things you can do to improve the source code.

➤ Replace the `configureCheckmarkForCell()` method with this one:

```
func configureCheckmarkForCell(cell: UITableViewCell,
                               withChecklistItem item: ChecklistItem) {
  if item.checked {
    cell.accessoryType = .Checkmark
  } else {
    cell.accessoryType = .None
  }
}
```

Instead of an index-path, you now directly pass it the `ChecklistItem` object.

> **Note:** This again is an example of a parameter with an extra label, giving it the external name `withChecklistItem`.
>
> It makes the full name of this method `configureCheckmarkForCell(withChecklistItem)` and that's how you will call it from other places in the app. Inside the method itself you use the local name for this parameter, `item`.

Why did you change this method? Previously it received an index-path and then did this to find the corresponding `ChecklistItem`:

```
let item = items[indexPath.row]
```

But in both `cellForRowAtIndexPath` and `didSelectRowAtIndexPath` you already do that as well. So it makes more sense to pass that `ChecklistItem` object directly to the "configure" method instead of making it do the same work twice. Anything that simplifies the code is good.

➤ Also add a new method:

```
func configureTextForCell(cell: UITableViewCell,
                          withChecklistItem item: ChecklistItem) {
  let label = cell.viewWithTag(1000) as! UILabel
  label.text = item.text
}
```

This sets the checklist item's text on the cell's label. Previously you did that in `cellForRowAtIndexPath` but it's clearer to put that in its own method.

➤ Update `tableView(cellForRowAtIndexPath)` so that it calls these new methods:

```
override func tableView(tableView: UITableView,
                   cellForRowAtIndexPath indexPath: NSIndexPath) -> UITableViewCell {
  let cell = tableView.dequeueReusableCellWithIdentifier("ChecklistItem") as! UITableViewCell
  let item = items[indexPath.row]

  configureTextForCell(cell, withChecklistItem: item)
  configureCheckmarkForCell(cell, withChecklistItem: item)

  return cell
}
```

➤ Also update `tableView(didSelectRowAtIndexPath)`:

```
override func tableView(tableView: UITableView,
                        didSelectRowAtIndexPath indexPath: NSIndexPath) {
  if let cell = tableView.cellForRowAtIndexPath(indexPath) {
    let item = items[indexPath.row]
    item.toggleChecked()
    configureCheckmarkForCell(cell, withChecklistItem: item)
  }
  tableView.deselectRowAtIndexPath(indexPath, animated: true)
}
```

This no longer modifies the ChecklistItem's checked property directly but calls a new method named toggleChecked() on the item object.

You still need to add this method to the ChecklistItem object otherwise the app won't run.

➤ Open **ChecklistItem.swift**, and add the following method:

```
func toggleChecked() {
  checked = !checked
}
```

As you can see, the method does exactly what didSelectRowAtIndexPath used to do, except that you've added this bit of functionality to ChecklistItem instead.

A good object-oriented design principle is that you should let objects change their own state as much as possible. Previously, the view controller implemented this toggling behavior but now ChecklistItem knows how to toggle itself on or off.

➤ Run the app, and well, it still should work exactly the same as before – but the code is a lot better. :-)

If you want to check your work, you can find the project files for the current version of the app in the folder **02 - Arrays** in the tutorial's Source Code folder.

Clean up that mess!

So what's the point of making all of these changes if the app still works exactly the same? For one, the code is much cleaner and that helps to avoid bugs. By using an array you've also made the code more flexible. The table view can now handle any number of rows.

You'll find that when you are programming you are constantly restructuring your code to make it better. It's impossible to do the whole thing 100% perfect right from the start.

So you write code until it becomes messy and then you clean it up. After a little while it becomes a big mess again and you clean it up again. The process for cleaning up code is called *refactoring* and it's a cycle that never ends.

There are a lot of programmers who never do clean up their code. The result is what we call "spaghetti code" and it's a horrible mess to maintain.

If you haven't looked at your code for several months but need to add a new feature or fix a bug, you may need some time to read it through to understand again how everything fits together.

It's in your own best interest to write code that is as clean as possible, otherwise untangling that spaghetti mess is no fun.

Adding new items to the checklist

So far your table view contains a handful of fixed rows but the idea behind this app is that users can create their own lists. Therefore, you need to give the user the ability to add to-do items.

In this section you'll expand the app to have a so-called **navigation bar** at the top. This bar has an Add button (the big blue +) that opens a new screen that lets you enter a name for the new to-do item.

When you tap Done, the new item will be added to the list.

The + button in the navigation bar opens the Add Item screen

Presenting a new screen to add items is a common pattern in a lot of apps. Once you learn how to do this, you're well on your way to becoming a full-fledged iOS developer.

What you'll do in this section:

• Add a navigation controller

• Put the Add button into the navigation bar

• Add a fake item to the list when you press the Add button

• Delete items with swipe-to-delete

• Open the Add Item screen that lets the user type the text for the item

As always, we take it in small steps. After you've put the Add button on the screen, you first write the code to add a "fake" item to the list. Instead of writing all of the code for the Add Item screen at once, you simply pretend that some parts of it already exist.

Once you've learned how to add fake items, you can build the Add Item screen for real.

Navigation controllers

First, let's add the navigation bar. You may have seen in the Object Library that there actually is an object named Navigation Bar. You can drag this into your view and put it at the top. However, you won't do that here.

Instead, you will embed the view controller inside a **navigation controller**.

Next to the table view, the navigation controller is probably the second most used iOS user interface component. It is the thing that lets you go from one page to another:

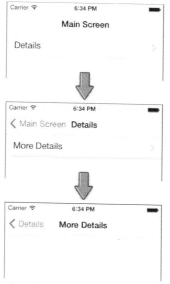

A navigation controller in action

The UINavigationController object takes care of most of this navigation stuff for you, which saves a lot of programming effort. You get a title in the middle of the screen and a "back" button that automatically takes the user back to the previous screen. You can put a button of your own on the right.

Adding a navigation controller is really easy.

➤ Open **Main.storyboard** and select the **Checklist View Controller**.

➤ From the menu bar at the top of the screen, choose **Editor** → **Embed In** → **Navigation Controller**.

Putting the view controller inside a navigation controller

That's it. Interface Builder has now added a new Navigation Controller scene and made a relationship between it and your view controller.

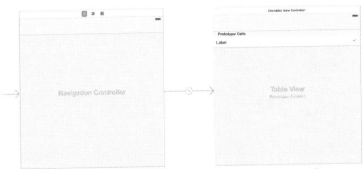

The navigation controller is now linked with your view controller

When the app starts up, the Checklist View Controller is automatically put inside a navigation controller.

➤ Run the app and try it out.

The app now has a navigation bar at the top

The only thing different (visually) is that the app now has a navigation bar at the top. Thanks to this, the status bar no longer overlaps the label from the first cell.

➤ Go back to the storyboard and double-click on the navigation bar inside the Checklist View Controller to make the title editable. Name it **Checklists**.

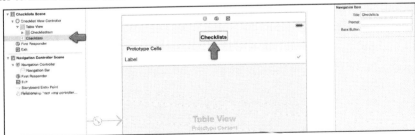

Changing the title in the navigation bar

What you're doing here, is changing a **Navigation Item** object that was automatically added to the view controller when you chose the Embed In command.

The Navigation Item object contains the title and buttons that appear in the navigation bar when this view controller becomes active. Each embedded view controller has its own Navigation Item that it uses to configure what is inside the navigation bar.

When the navigation controller slides a new view controller into the screen, it replaces the contents of the navigation bar with that view controller's Navigation Item.

➤ Go to the Object Library and look for **Bar Button Item**. Drag it into the right-side slot of the navigation bar.

Be sure to use the navigation bar on the Checklist View Controller, not the one from the navigation controller!

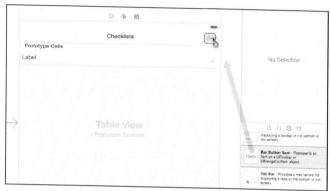

Dragging a Bar Button Item into the navigation bar

By default this new button is named "Item" but for this app you want it to have a big + sign.

➤ In the **Attributes inspector** for the bar button item, choose **Identifier: Add**.

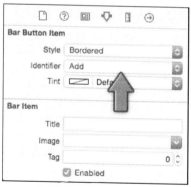

Bar Button Item attributes

If you look through the Identifier list you see a lot of predefined bar button types: Add, Compose, Reply, Camera, and so on. You can use these in your own apps but only for their intended purpose.

You shouldn't use the camera icon on a button that sends an email, for example. Improper use of these icons may lead Apple to reject your app from the App Store and that sucks.

OK, that gives us a button. If you run the app, it should look like this:

The app with the Add button

Of course, pressing the button doesn't actually do anything because you haven't hooked it up to an action yet. In a little while you will create the Add Item screen and show it when the button is tapped. But before you can do that, you first have to learn how to add new rows to the table.

Let's hook up the Add button to an action. You got plenty of exercise on this in the previous tutorial, so this shouldn't be too much of a problem.

➤ Add a new action method to **ChecklistViewController.swift**:

```
@IBAction func addItem() {
}
```

You're leaving this empty for the moment, but it needs to be there so you have something to connect the button to.

➤ Open the storyboard and hook up the Add button to this action. **Ctrl-drag** from the + button to the Checklist View Controller item in the sidebar:

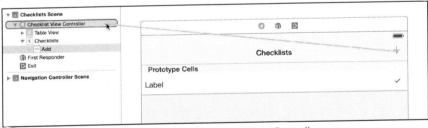

Ctrl-drag from Add button to View Controller

Or, even simpler, Ctrl-drag from the Add button to the yellow circle in the dock area above the scene:

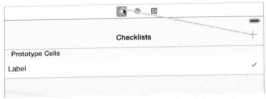

Ctrl-drag from Add button to View Controller (alternative method)

In fact, you can **Ctrl-drag** from the Add button to almost anywhere into the same scene to make the connection (dragging onto the status bar area is a good spot).

➤ After dragging, pick **addItem** from the popup (under **Sent Actions**):

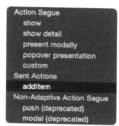

Connecting to the addItem action

Now the connection is made and a tap on the + button will send the "addItem" message to the view controller.

➤ Let's give addItem() something to do. Back in **ChecklistViewController.swift**, fill out the body of that method:

```
@IBAction func addItem() {
  let newRowIndex = items.count

  let item = ChecklistItem()
  item.text = "I am a new row"
  item.checked = false
  items.append(item)

  let indexPath = NSIndexPath(forRow: newRowIndex, inSection: 0)
  let indexPaths = [indexPath]
  tableView.insertRowsAtIndexPaths(indexPaths, withRowAnimation: .Automatic)
}
```

Inside this method you create a new ChecklistItem object and add it to the data model (the items array).

You also have to figure out the row number of this new object and then tell the table view, "I've inserted a row at this index, please update yourself."

Let's take it section by section:

```
let newRowIndex = items.count
```

When you start the app there are 5 items in the array and 5 rows on the screen. Computers start counting at 0, so the existing rows have indexes 0, 1, 2, 3 and 4. To add the new row to the end of the array, the index for that new row must be 5.

In other words, when you're adding a row to the end of a table the index for the new row is always equal to the number of items currently in that table. Let that sink in for a second.

You put the index for the new row in the local newRowIndex. This can be a constant instead of a variable because it never has to change.

The following few lines should look familiar:

```
let item = ChecklistItem()
item.text = "I am a new row"
item.checked = false
items.append(item)
```

You have seen this code before in init(coder). It creates the new ChecklistItem object and adds it to the end of the array.

The data model now consists of 6 ChecklistItem objects inside the items array. Note that at this point newRowIndex is still 5 even though items.count is now 6. That's why you read the item count and stored this value in newRowIndex before you added the new item to the array.

Here it gets tricky:

```
let indexPath = NSIndexPath(forRow: newRowIndex, inSection: 0)
```

Just adding the new ChecklistItem object to the data model (i.e. the array) isn't enough. You also have to tell the table view about this new row so it can add a new cell for that row.

As you know by now, table views use index-paths to identify rows, so first you make an NSIndexPath object that points to the new row, using the row number from the newRowIndex variable. This index-path object now points to row 5 (in section 0).

The next line creates a new, temporary array holding just the one index-path item:

```
let indexPaths = [indexPath]
```

You will use the table view method insertRowsAtIndexPaths(withRowAnimation) to tell it about the new row, but as its name implies this method actually lets you insert multiple rows at the same time.

Instead of a single NSIndexPath object, you need to give it an array of index-paths. Fortunately it is easy to create an array that contains a single index-path object using [indexPath]. The notation [] creates a new Array object that contains the objects between the brackets.

Finally, you tell the table view to insert this new row with a nice animation:

```
tableView.insertRowsAtIndexPaths(indexPaths, withRowAnimation: .Automatic)
```

To recap, you:

1. created a new ChecklistItem object

2. added it to the data model, and

3. inserted a new cell for it in the table view.

➤ Try it out. You can now add many new rows to the table. You can also tap these new rows to turn their checkmarks on and off again. When you scroll the table up and down, the checkmarks stay with the proper rows.

After adding new rows with the + button

The rows are always added to both the table and your data model. When you send the `insertRowsAtIndexPaths` message to the table, you say: "Hey table, my data model has a bunch of new items added to it."

This is important! If you forget to tell the table view about your new items or if you tell the table view there are new items but you don't actually add them to your data model, then your app will crash. These two things always have to be in sync.

Exercise: Give the new items checkmarks by default. ∎

Deleting rows

While you're at it, you might as well give users the ability to delete rows.

A common way to do this in iOS apps is "swipe-to-delete". You swipe your finger over a row and a Delete button slides into the screen. A tap on the Delete button confirms the removal, anywhere else will cancel.

Swipe-to-delete in action

Swipe-to-delete is very easy to implement.

➤ Add the following method to **ChecklistViewController.swift**.

Just to keep things organized, I suggest you put this near the other table view methods.

```
override func tableView(tableView: UITableView,
                        commitEditingStyle editingStyle: UITableViewCellEditingStyle,
                        forRowAtIndexPath indexPath: NSIndexPath) {
  // 1
  items.removeAtIndex(indexPath.row)
  // 2
  let indexPaths = [indexPath]
  tableView.deleteRowsAtIndexPaths(indexPaths, withRowAnimation: .Automatic)
}
```

When the `commitEditingStyle` method is present in your view controller (it comes from the table view data source), the table view will automatically enable swipe-to-delete. All you have to do is:

1. remove the item from the data model, and

2. delete the corresponding row from the table view. This mirrors what you did in `addItem()`. Again you make a temporary array with only one index-path object and then tell the table view to remove the rows with an animation.

➤ Run the app to try it out!

If at any point you got stuck, you can refer to the project files for the app from the **03 - Data Model** folder in the tutorial's Source Code folder.

Destroying objects

By the way, when you do `items.removeAtIndex()`, that not only takes the `ChecklistItem` out of the array but also permanently destroys it.

We'll talk more about this in the next tutorial, but if there are no more references to an object, it is automatically destroyed. As long as a `ChecklistItem` object sits inside an array, that array has a reference to it.

But when you pull that `ChecklistItem` out of the array, the reference goes away and the object is destroyed. Or in computer-speak, it is *deallocated*.

What does it mean for an object to be destroyed? Each object occupies a small section of the computer's memory. When you create an object instance, a chunk of memory is reserved to hold the object's data items.

If the object is deallocated, that memory becomes available again and will eventually be occupied by new objects. After it has been deleted, the object does not exist anymore and you can no longer use it.

On older versions of iOS you had to take care of this memory bookkeeping by hand. Fortunately times have changed for the better. Swift uses a mechanism called Automatic Reference Counting or ARC to manage the lifetime of the objects in your app, freeing you from having to worry about that. I like not having to worry about things!

The Add Item screen

You've learned how to add new rows to the table, but all of these rows get the same text. You will now change the addItem() action to open a new screen that lets the user enter his or her own text for those new ChecklistItems.

The plan for this section:

• Create the Add Item screen using the power of storyboarding

• Add a text field and allow the user to type into it using the on-screen keyboard

• Recognize when the user presses Cancel or Done on the Add Item screen

• Create a new ChecklistItem with the text from the text field

• Add the new ChecklistItem object to the table on the main screen

A new screen means a new view controller, so you begin by adding a new scene to the storyboard.

➤ Go to the Object Library and drag a new **Table View Controller** (not a regular view controller) into the storyboard canvas.

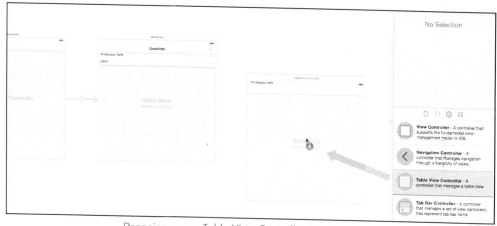

Dragging a new Table View Controller into the canvas

You may need to zoom out to fit everything properly. Right-click on the canvas to get a popup with zoom options, or double-click on an empty spot to zoom to 50%.

➤ With the new view controller in place, zoom back in and select the Add button from the Checklist View Controller. **Ctrl-drag** to the new view controller.

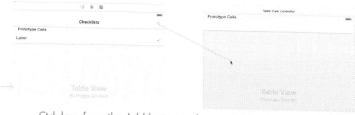

Ctrl-drag from the Add button to the new table view controller

Let go of the mouse and a list of options pops up:

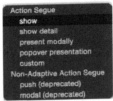

The Action Segue popup

The options in this menu are the different types of connections you can make between the Add button and the new screen.

➤ Choose **show** from the menu.

This type of connection is named a **segue** (if you're not a native English speaker, that is pronounced "seg-way" like the strange scooters that you can stand on).

The segue is represented by the arrow between the two view controllers:

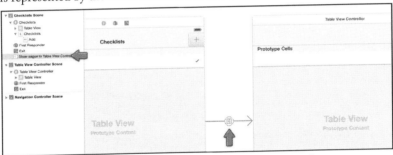

A new segue is added between the two view controllers

➤ Run the app to see what it does.

When you press the Add button, a new empty table slides in from the right. You can press the back button – the one that says "Checklists" – at the top to go back to the previous screen.

The screen that shows up after you press the Add button

You didn't even have to write any code and you have yourself a working navigation controller!

Note that the Add button no longer adds a new row to the table. That connection has been broken and is replaced by the segue. Just in case, you should remove the button's connection with the addItem action.

➤ Select the Add button, go to the **Connections inspector**, and press the small X next to **addItem**.

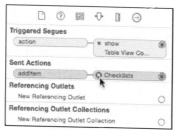

Removing the addItem action from the Add button

Notice that the inspector also shows the connection with the segue that you've just made (under **Triggered Segues**).

So now you have a new table view controller that slides into the screen when you press the Add button. This isn't actually what you want, though. For a screen that lets you add new items, it is better to use a so-called **modal** segue.

➤ Click the arrow between the two view controllers to select the segue.

A segue is an object like any other (remember, everything is an object!) and as such it has attributes that you can change.

➤ In the **Attributes inspector**, choose **Segue**: **Present Modally**.

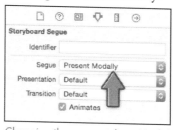

Changing the segue style to Modal

The navigation bar now disappears from the new view controller. This new screen is no longer presented as part of the navigation hierarchy, but as a separate screen that lies on top of the existing one.

➤ Run the app to see the difference.

When you do, you'll notice that you no longer have a way to go back to the previous screen. Eek! Getting stuck is not something users appreciate…

Modal screens usually have a navigation bar with a Cancel button on the left and a Done button on the right. (In some apps the button on the right is called Save or Send.)

Pressing either of these buttons will close the screen, but only Done will save your changes.

The easiest way to add a navigation bar and these two buttons is to wrap the view controller for the Add Item screen into a navigation controller of its own. The steps to do this are the same as before:

➤ Select the table view controller (the new one), choose **Editor** → **Embed In** → **Navigation Controller**.

Now the storyboard looks like this:

Two table view controllers that are both embedded in their own navigation controllers

The new navigation controller has been inserted in between the two table view controllers. The Add button now performs a modal segue to the new navigation controller.

➤ Double-click the navigation bar in the right-most table view controller to edit its title and change it to **Add Item**.

➤ Drag two **Bar Button Items** into the navigation bar, one in the left slot and one in the right slot.

The navigation bar items for the new screen

➤ In the **Attributes inspector** for the left button choose **Identifier: Cancel**.

➤ For the right button choose **Done** for both the **Identifier** and **Style** attributes.

Don't type anything into the button's Title field. The Cancel and Done buttons are built-in button types that automatically use the proper text. If your app runs on an iPhone where the language is set to something other than English, these predefined buttons are automatically translated into the user's language.

➤ Run the app and you'll see that your new screen has Cancel and Done buttons.

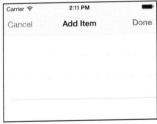

The Cancel and Done buttons in the app

The new buttons look good! But you still need to tell the app what to do when they get tapped…

Making your own view controller object

The Cancel and Done buttons ought to close the Add Item screen and return the app to the main screen, but tapping them has no effect yet.

In the next tutorial you will learn how to perform such a "backwards" segue directly in the storyboard, but here you will do it by writing code – in other words, you have to hook up these buttons to action methods.

Where do you put these action methods? Not in `ChecklistViewController` because that is not the view controller you're dealing with here.

Instead, you have to make a new view controller source code specifically for the Add Item screen and connect it to the scene that you've just designed in Interface Builder.

➤ Right-click on the Checklists group in the project navigator and choose **New File…** Choose the **Cocoa Touch Class** template:

Choosing the Cocoa Touch Class template

➤ In the next step, choose the following options:

• Class: AddItemViewController

• Subclass of: UITableViewController

• Also create XIB file: Uncheck this

• Language: Swift

Choosing the options for the new view controller

Note: Make sure the "Subclass of" field is set to UITableViewController, not just "UIViewController". Also be careful that Xcode didn't rename what you typed into Class to "AddItemTableViewController". It can be sneaky like that…

> Press **Next** and then **Create** to finish.

This adds a new file to the project, **AddItemViewController.swift**. However, it does not make any changes to the storyboard.

> In the storyboard, select the table view controller and go to the **Identity inspector**. Under **Custom Class**, type **AddItemViewController**.

This tells the storyboard that the view controller from this scene is actually your new AddItemViewController object.

Changing the class name of the AddItemViewController

Don't forget this step! Without it, the Add Item screen will simply not work.

Make sure that it is really the view controller that is selected before you change the fields in the Identity inspector (the scene needs to have a blue border). A common mistake is to select the table view and change that.

You will now implement the action methods in **AddItemViewController.swift**.

The Xcode template put a lot of stuff in this file that you don't need. The template assumes you'll fill in this placeholder code before you run the app again. If you try to run the app right now, Xcode will give many warnings.

So let's get rid of that template cruft first.

> In **AddItemViewController.swift**, delete everything inside the class declaration, until you're left with just this:

```
import UIKit

class AddItemViewController: UITableViewController {

}
```

The lines you just deleted included placeholders for the numberOfRowsInSection, cellForRowAtIndexPath and didSelectRowAtIndexPath methods that you've seen before plus a few other data source and delegate methods for the table view. You won't need them for this particular view controller.

Do not skip this step! If you do not remove these methods, the Add Item screen will not work properly.

➤ Add the new `cancel()` and `done()` action methods:

```
@IBAction func cancel() {
  dismissViewControllerAnimated(true, completion: nil)
}

@IBAction func done() {
  dismissViewControllerAnimated(true, completion: nil)
}
```

This tells the "presenting view controller", that is the view controller that presented this modal screen, to close the screen with an animation.

You still need to hook up the Cancel bar button to the `cancel()` action and the Done bar button to the `done()` action.

➤ Open the storyboard and find the Add Item View Controller. **Ctrl-drag** from the bar buttons to anywhere else in the view controller's scene (for example, the status bar) and pick the proper action from the popup menu.

Ctrl-dragging from the bar button to the view controller

➤ Run the app to try it out. The Cancel and Done buttons now return the app to the main screen.

What do you think happens to the `AddItemViewController` object when you dismiss it? After the view controller disappears from the screen, its object is destroyed and the memory it was using is reclaimed by the system.

Every time the user opens the Add Item screen, the app makes a new instance for it. This means a view controller object is only alive for the duration that the user is interacting with it; there is no point in keeping it around afterwards.

Container view controllers

I've been saying that one view controller represents one screen, but here you actually have two view controllers for each screen.

The app's main screen consists of the `ChecklistViewController` inside a navigation controller, and the Add Item screen is composed of the `AddItemViewController` that sits inside its own navigation controller.

The Navigation Controller is a special type of view controller that acts as a container for other view controllers. It comes with a navigation bar and has the ability to easily go from one screen to another. The container essentially "wraps around" these screens.

The Navigation Controller is just the frame that contains the view controllers that do the real work, which are known as the "content" controllers.

Another often-used container is the Tab Bar Controller, which you'll see in the next tutorial.

On the iPad, container view controllers are even more commonplace. View controllers on the iPhone are full-screen but on the iPad they often occupy only a portion of the screen, such as the content of a popover or one of the panes in a split-view.

Static table cells

Let's change the look of the Add Item screen. Currently it is an empty table with a navigation bar on top, but I want it to look like this:

What the Add Item screen will look like when you're done

> Open the storyboard and select the **Table View** object inside the Add Item View Controller.

> In the **Attributes inspector,** change the **Content** setting from Dynamic Prototypes to **Static Cells.**

Changing the table view to static cells

You use static cells when you know beforehand how many sections and rows the table view will have. This is handy for screens that require the user to enter data, such as the one you're building here.

You can design the rows directly in the storyboard. For a table with static cells you don't need to provide a data source, and you can hook up the labels and other controls from the cells directly to outlets on the view controller.

As you can see in the outline pane on the left, the table view now has a Table View Section object hanging under it, and three Table View Cells in that section. (You may need to expand the Table View item first by clicking the arrow next to it.)

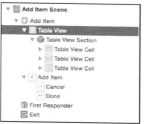

The table view has a section with three static cells

➤ Click on the bottom two cells and delete them (press the **delete** key on your keyboard). You only need one cell for now.

➤ Select the Table View again and in the **Attributes inspector** set its **Style** to **Grouped**. That gives us the look we want.

The table view with grouped style

Next up, you'll add a text field component inside the table view cell that lets the user type text.

➤ Drag a **Text Field** object into the cell and size it up nicely.

➤ In the **Attributes inspector** for the text field, set the **Border Style** to **none** (select the dotted box):

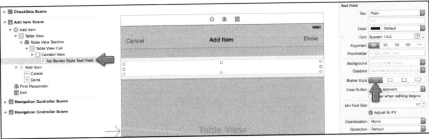

Adding a text field to the table view cell

➤ Run the app and press the + button to open the Add Item screen. Tap on the cell and you'll see the keyboard slide in from the bottom of the screen.

Any time you make a text field active, the keyboard automatically appears. You can type into the text field by tapping on the letters. (On the Simulator, you can simply type using your Mac's keyboard.)

You can now type text into the table view cell

Note: If the keyboard does not appear in the Simulator, press ⌘K or use the **Hardware →
Keyboard → Toggle Software Keyboard** menu option. You can also use your normal Mac
keyboard to type into the text field.

Look what happens when you tap just outside the text field's area, but still in the cell (try tapping in the margins that surround the text field):

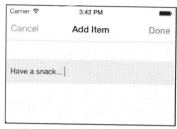

Whoops, that looks a little weird

The row turns gray because you selected it. That's not what you want, so you should disable selections for this row.

➤ In the **AddItemViewController.swift** file, add the following method:

```
override func tableView(tableView: UITableView,
                    willSelectRowAtIndexPath indexPath: NSIndexPath) -> NSIndexPath? {
  return nil
}
```

This is another one of those table view delegate methods. When the user taps in a row, the table view sends the delegate a `willSelectRowAtIndexPath` message that says: "Hi delegate, I am about to select this particular row."

By returning the special value `nil`, the delegate answers: "Sorry, but you're not allowed to!"

Return to sender

You've seen the `return` statement a few times now. You use `return` to send a value from a method back to the method that called it.

Let's take a more detailed look at what it does.

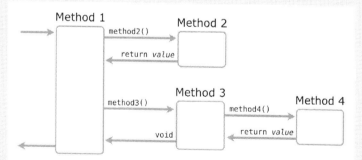

Methods call other methods and receive values in return.

You cannot just return any value. The value you return must be of the data type that is specified after the -> arrow that follows the method name.

For example, `tableView(numberOfRowsInSection)` must return an `Int` value, which is any whole number:

```
   override func tableView(tableView: UITableView,
                          numberOfRowsInSection section: Int) -> Int {
      return 1
   }
```

If instead you were to write,

```
   override func tableView(tableView: UITableView,
                          numberOfRowsInSection section: Int) -> Int {
      return "1"
   }
```

then the compiler would give an error message as "1" is a string, not an Int. To a human reader they look similar and you'd easily understand the intent, but Swift isn't that tolerant. Data types have to match or it just isn't allowed.

Your most recent version of this method looks like this:

```
   override func tableView(tableView: UITableView,
                          numberOfRowsInSection section: Int) -> Int {
      return items.count
   }
```

That is also a valid return statement because the count property from Array also has the type Int.

The tableView(cellForRowAtIndexPath) method is supposed to return a UITableViewCell object:

```
   override func tableView(tableView: UITableView,
                          cellForRowAtIndexPath indexPath: NSIndexPath) -> UITableViewCell {
      let cell = tableView.dequeueReusableCellWithIdentifier("ChecklistItem")
                          as! UITableViewCell
      . . .
      return cell
   }
```

The local constant cell contains a UITableViewCell object, so it's OK to return the value of cell from the method.

The tableView(willSelectRowAtIndexPath) method is supposed to return an NSIndexPath object. However, you can also make it return "nil", which means no object.

```
   override func tableView(tableView: UITableView,
                          willSelectRowAtIndexPath indexPath: NSIndexPath) -> NSIndexPath? {
      return nil
   }
```

That's what the ? behind "-> NSIndexPath?" is for: The question mark tells Swift that you can also return nil from this method. That is only allowed if there is a question mark (or exclamation point) behind the return type.

The special value nil represents "no value" but it's used to mean different things throughout the iOS SDK. Sometimes it means "nothing found" or "don't do anything". Here it means that the row should not be selected.

How do you know what nil means for a certain method? You can find that in the documentation of the method in question.

In the case of willSelectRowAtIndexPath, the iOS documentation says:

"Return Value: An index-path object that confirms or alters the selected row. Return an NSIndexPath object other than indexPath if you want another cell to be selected. Return nil if you don't want the row selected."

This means you can either:

1. Return the same index-path you were given. This confirms that this row can be selected.

2. Return another index-path in order to select another row.

3. Return `nil` to prevent the row from being selected, which is what you did.

So remember, you need to use the `return` statement to exit a method that expects to return something. If you forget, then Xcode will give the following error: "Missing return in a function expect to return".

You've also seen methods that do not return anything:

```
@IBAction func addItem()
```

and:

```
func configureCheckmarkForCell(cell: UITableViewCell,
                    withChecklistItem item: ChecklistItem)
```

These methods do not have an -> arrow. Such a method does not pass a value back to the caller and therefore do not need a `return` statement. (You can still use `return` to exit from such methods but it may not be followed by a value.)

Technically speaking, even methods without a return type *do* return a value, the so-called *empty tuple*. Think of this as a special object that embodies the concept of "nothing". (Don't confuse this with `nil`, which is an actual value.)

You sometimes see this written as:

```
func methodThatDoesNotReturnValue() -> ()
func anotherMethodThatDoesNotReturnValue() -> Void
```

The notation for an empty tuple is (), so in this context the parentheses mean there is no return value. The term `Void` is a synonym for ().

But really, if a method does not return anything it's just as easy to leave out the -> arrow. It's a rule that `@IBAction` methods never return a value.

There is one more thing you need to do to prevent the row from going gray. It's already impossible to select the row, as you've just told the table view you won't allow it.

However, the cell also has a selection color property. Even if you make it impossible for the row to be selected, sometimes UIKit still briefly draws it gray when you tap it. Therefore it is best to also disable this selection color.

➤ In the storyboard, select the table view cell and go to the **Attributes inspector**. Set the **Selection** attribute to **None**.

Now if you run the app, it is impossible to select the row and make it turn gray. Try and prove me wrong! ☺

Reading from the text field

You have a text field in a table view cell that the user can type into, but how do you read the text that the user has typed?

When the user taps Done, you need to get that text and somehow put it into a new `ChecklistItem` and add it to the list of to-do items. This means the `done()` action needs to be able to refer to the text field.

You already know how to refer to controls from within your view controller: use an outlet. When you added outlets in the previous tutorial, I told you to type in the `@IBOutlet` declaration in the source file and make the connection in the storyboard.

I'm going to show you a trick now that will save you some typing. You can let Interface Builder do all of this automatically by Ctrl-dragging from the control in question directly into your source code file.

➤ First, go to the storyboard and then open the **Assistant editor**, using the toolbar button. This button looks like two circles:

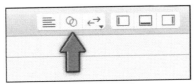

Click the toolbar button to open the Assistant editor

This may make the screen a little crowded – there are now five horizontal panels open. If you're running out of space you might want to close the project navigator and the utilities pane using the other toolbar buttons.

The Assistant editor opens a new pane on the right of the screen. In the Jump Bar (the bar below the toolbar) it should say **Automatic** and the Assistant editor should be displaying the **AddItemViewController.swift** file:

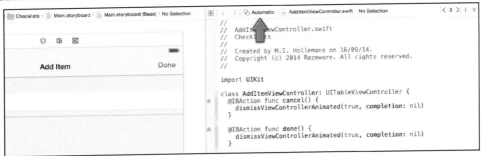

The Assistant editor

"Automatic" means the Assistant editor figures out what other file is related to the one you're currently editing. If you're editing the Storyboard, the related file is the selected view controller's Swift file.

(Sometimes Xcode can be a little dodgy here. If it shows you something other than AddItemViewController.swift, then click in the Jump Bar to select that file.)

➤ With the storyboard and the Swift file side by side, select the text field. Then **Ctrl-drag** from the text field into the Swift file:

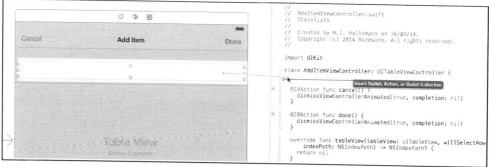

Ctrl-dragging from the text field into the Swift file

When you let go, a popup appears:

The popup that lets you add a new outlet

➤ Choose the following options:

• Connection: Outlet

• Name: **textField**

• Type: UITextField

• Storage: Weak

Note: If "Type" does not say UITextField but UITableViewCell or UIView, then you selected the wrong thing.

Make sure you're Ctrl-dragging from the text field inside the cell, not the cell itself. Granted, it's kinda hard to see, being white on white. If you're having trouble selecting the text field, click it several times in succession.

You can also Ctrl-drag from "No Border Style Text Field" in the outline pane.

➤ Press **Connect** and voila, Xcode has automatically inserted an @IBOutlet for you and connected it to the text field object.

In code it looks like this:

```
@IBOutlet weak var textField: UITextField!
```

Just by dragging you have successfully hooked up the text field object with a new property named textField. How easy was that!

Now you'll modify the done() action to write the contents of this text field to the Xcode debug area, the pane at the bottom of the screen where println() messages show up. This is a quick way to verify that you can actually read what the user typed.

➤ In **AddItemViewController.swift,** change done() to:

```
@IBAction func done() {
  println("Contents of the text field: \(textField.text)")
  dismissViewControllerAnimated(true, completion: nil)
}
```

You can make these changes directly inside the Assistant editor. It's very handy that you can edit the source code and the storyboard side-by-side.

➤ Run the app, press the + button and type something in the text field. When you press Done, the Add Item screen should close and Xcode should open the Debug pane with a message like this:

```
Contents of the text field: Hello, world!
```

Great, so that works. println() should be an old friend by now. It's my faithful debugging companion.

Recall that you can print the value of a variable by placing it inside \(...) in the string. Here you used \(textField.text) to print out the contents of the text field's text property.

Polishing it up

Before you'll write the code to take the text and insert it as a new item into the list, let's improve the design and workings of the Add Item screen a little.

For instance, it would be nice if you didn't have to tap into the text field in order to bring up the keyboard. It would be more convenient if the keyboard automatically appeared once the screen opens.

➤ To accomplish this, add a new method to **AddItemViewController.swift,** viewWillAppear():

```
override func viewWillAppear(animated: Bool) {
  super.viewWillAppear(animated)
  textField.becomeFirstResponder()
}
```

The view controller receives the viewWillAppear() message just before it becomes visible. That is a perfect time to make the text field active. You do this by sending it the becomeFirstResponder() message.

If you've done programming on other platforms, this is often called "giving the control focus". In iOS terminology, the control becomes the *first responder.*

➤ Run the app and go to the Add Item screen; you can start typing right away.

It's often little features like this that make apps a joy to use. Having to tap on the text field before you can start typing gets old really fast. In this fast-paced age, using their mobiles on the go, users don't have the patience for that. Such minor annoyances may be reason enough to switch to a competitor's app. I always put a lot of effort into making my apps as frictionless as possible.

With that in mind, let's style the input field a bit.

➤ Open the storyboard and select the text field. Go to the **Attributes inspector** and set the following attributes:

• Placeholder: Name of the Item

• Font: System 17

• Adjust to Fit: Uncheck this

• Capitalization: Sentences

• Return Key: Done

The text field attributes

There are several options here that let you configure the keyboard that appears when the text field becomes active.

If this were a field that only allowed numbers, for example, you would set the Keyboard to Number Pad. If it were an email address field, you'd set it to E-mail Address. For our purposes, the Default keyboard is appropriate.

You can also change the text that is displayed on the keyboard's Return Key. By default it says "return" but you set it to "Done". This is just the text on the button; it doesn't automatically close the screen. You still have to make the keyboard's Done button trigger the same action as the Done button from the navigation bar.

➤ Make sure the text field is selected and open the **Connections inspector**. Drag from the **Did End on Exit** event to the view controller and pick the **done** action.

If you still have the Assistant editor open, you can drag directly to the source code for the `done()` method:

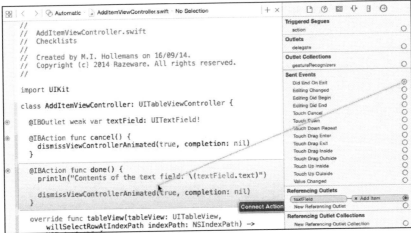

Connecting the text field to the done() action method

To see the connections for the done action, click on the circle in the margin next to the method name. The popup shows that `done()` is now connected to both the bar button and the text field:

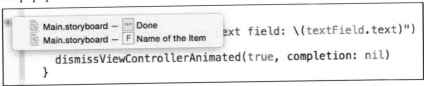

Viewing the connections for the done() method

➤ Run the app. Pressing Done on the keyboard will now close the screen and print the text to the debug area.

The keyboard now has a big blue Done button

It's always good to validate the input from the user to make sure what they're entering is acceptable. For instance, what should happen if the user immediately taps the Done button on the Add Item screen without entering any text?

Adding a to-do item to the list that has no text is not very useful, so in order to prevent this you should disable the Done button when no text has been typed yet.

Of course, you have two Done buttons to take care of, one on the keyboard and one in the navigation bar. Let's start with the Done button from the keyboard as this is the simplest one to fix.

> On the **Attributes inspector** for the text field, check **Auto-enable Return Key**.

That's it. Now when you run the app the Done button on the keyboard automatically is disabled when there is no text in the text field. Try it out!

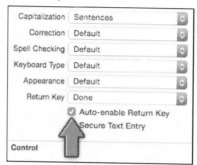

The Auto-enable Return Key option disables the return key when there is no text

For the Done button in the navigation bar you have to do a little more work. You have to check the contents of the text field after every keystroke to see if it is now empty or not. If it is, then you disable the button.

The user can always press Cancel, but Done only works when there is text.

In order to listen to changes to the text field – which may come from taps on the keyboard but also from cut/paste – you need to make the view controller a *delegate* for the text field.

The text field will send events to this delegate to let it know what is going on. The delegate, which will be the AddItemViewController, can then respond to these events and take appropriate actions.

A view controller is allowed to be the delegate for more than one object. The AddItemViewController is already a delegate (and data source) for the UITableView (because it is a UITableViewController). Now it will also become the delegate for the text field object, UITextField.

These are two different delegates and you make the view controller play both roles. Later in this tutorial you'll add even more delegates.

How to become a delegate

Delegates are used everywhere in the iOS SDK, so it's good to remember that it always takes three steps to become someone's delegate.

1) You declare yourself capable of being a delegate. To become the delegate for `UITextField` you need to include `UITextFieldDelegate` in the `class` line for the view controller. This tells the compiler that the view controller can actually handle the notification messages that the text field sends to it.

2) You let the object in question, in this case the `UITextField`, know that the view controller wishes to become its delegate. If you forget to tell the text field that it has a delegate, it will never send you any notifications.

3) Implement the delegate methods. It makes no sense to become a delegate if you're not responding to the messages you're being sent!

Often, delegate methods are optional, so you don't need to implement all of them. For example, `UITextFieldDelegate` actually declares seven different methods but you only care about `textField(shouldChangeCharactersInRange, replacementString)` for this app.

➤ In **AddItemViewController.swift**, add `UITextFieldDelegate` to the class declaration:

```
class AddItemViewController: UITableViewController, UITextFieldDelegate
```

The view controller now says, "I can be a delegate for text field objects."

You also have to let the text field know that you have a delegate for it.

➤ Go to the storyboard and select the text field.

There are several different ways in which you can hook up the text field's delegate outlet to the view controller. I prefer to go to its **Connections inspector** and drag from **delegate** to the view controller's icon in the dock:

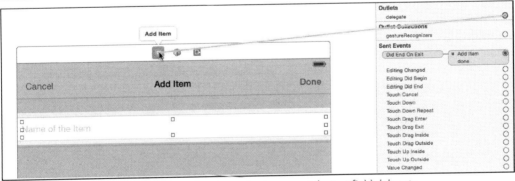

Drag from the Connections inspector to connect the text field delegate

The icon will flash to indicate that the connection was successfully made.

You also have to add an outlet for the Done bar button item, so you can send it messages from within the view controller in order to enable or disable it.

➤ Open the **Assistant editor** and make sure **AddItemViewController.swift** is visible in the assistant pane.

➤ **Ctrl-drag** from the Done bar button into the Swift file and let go. Name the new outlet doneBarButton.

This adds the following property:

```
@IBOutlet weak var doneBarButton: UIBarButtonItem!
```

➤ Add the following to **AddItemViewController.swift**, at the bottom:

```
func textField(textField: UITextField,
            shouldChangeCharactersInRange range: NSRange,
            replacementString string: String) -> Bool {

  let oldText: NSString = textField.text
  let newText: NSString = oldText.stringByReplacingCharactersInRange(range,
                                               withString: string)

  if newText.length > 0 {
    doneBarButton.enabled = true
  } else {
    doneBarButton.enabled = false
  }
  return true
}
```

This is one of the UITextField delegate methods. It is invoked every time the user changes the text, whether by tapping on the keyboard or by cut/paste.

First, you figure out what the new text will be:

```
let oldText: NSString = textField.text
let newText: NSString = oldText.stringByReplacingCharactersInRange(range, withString: string)
```

The textField(shouldChangeCharactersInRange) delegate method doesn't give you the new text, only which part of the text should be replaced (the range) and the text it should be replaced with (the replacement string).

You need to calculate what the new text will be by taking the text field's text and doing the replacement yourself. This gives you a new string object that you store in the newText constant.

NSString vs String

Text strings in Swift are of the data type String. But in the above method you used something called NSString. What is the difference between the two?

NSString is the object that Objective-C programmers use for storing text. To be honest, it is more powerful and often easier to use than Swift's own String.

However, Swift has a trick up its sleeve: String and NSString are "bridged", meaning that you can use NSString in place of String. Here, you want to use NSString's stringByReplacingCharactersInRange(withString) method, so you let Swift know that it should treat the text as an NSString, not as a String.

The notation,

```
    let oldText: NSString = . . .
```

tells Swift that `oldText` should be a constant (because of `let`) of type `NSString`. If you were to leave out the ": `NSString`" bit, Swift would use type inference to determine that it should be a regular Swift `String` instead, which isn't what you want.

By the way, `String` isn't the only thing that is bridged to an Objective-C type. Another example is `Array` and its Objective-C counterpart `NSArray`. Because the iOS frameworks are written in different language than Swift, sometimes these little Objective-C holdovers creep in.

Once you have the new text, you check if it's empty by looking at its length, and enable or disable the Done button accordingly:

```
if newText.length > 0 {
  doneBarButton.enabled = true
} else {
  doneBarButton.enabled = false
}
```

➤ Run the app and type some text into the text field. Now remove that text and you'll see that the Done button in the navigation bar properly gets disabled when the text field becomes empty.

One problem: The Done button is initially enabled when the Add Item screen opens, but there is no text in the text field at that point so it really should be disabled. This is simple enough to fix.

➤ In the storyboard, select the Done bar button and go to the **Attributes inspector**. Uncheck the **Enabled** box.

The Done buttons are now properly disabled when there is no text in the text field:

You cannot press Done if there is no text

There is actually a slightly simpler way to write the above method:

```
func textField(textField: UITextField,
          shouldChangeCharactersInRange range: NSRange,
          replacementString string: String) -> Bool {

  let oldText: NSString = textField.text
  let newText: NSString = oldText.stringByReplacingCharactersInRange(range,
                                                    withString: string)
```

```
    doneBarButton.enabled = (newText.length > 0)
    return true
}
```

You replaced the if-statement by a single line. The if-statement used to do this:

```
if newText.length > 0 {
    // you get here if the length is greater than 0
} else {
    // you get here if the length is equal to 0
}
```

In both cases you check the condition `newText.length > 0`. If that condition is true, i.e. the text length is greater than 0, you set `doneBarButton`'s `enabled` property to `true`. If the condition is false, you set the `enabled` property to `false`.

Notice that these sentences are basically saying: if the condition is `true` then `enabled` becomes `true` but if the condition is `false` then `enabled` becomes `false`. In other words, you always set the `enabled` property to the result of the condition: `true` or `false`.

That makes it possible to skip the `if`, and simply do,

```
doneBarButton.enabled = the result of the condition
```

which in Swift reads as follows:

```
doneBarButton.enabled = (newText.length > 0)
```

The ( ) parentheses are not really necessary. You can also write it like this:

```
doneBarButton.enabled = newText.length > 0
```

However, I find this slightly less readable, so I use the parentheses to make it clear beyond a doubt that `newText.length > 0` is evaluated first and that the assignment takes place after that.

To recap: If `newText.length` is greater than 0, `doneBarButton.enabled` becomes `true`; otherwise it becomes `false`.

You can fit this into a single statement because the *comparison operators* all return true or false depending on the condition. These are Swift's comparison operators:

>   greater than

<   less than

>=   greater than or equal to

<=   less than or equal to

==   equal

!=   not equal

Remember this trick – whenever you see code like this,

```
if some condition {
  something = true
} else {
  something = false
}
```

you can write it simply as:

```
something = (some condition)
```

In practice it doesn't really matter which version you use. I prefer the shorter one; that's what the pros do. Just remember that comparison operators such as == and > always return true or false, so the extra if really isn't necessary.

Adding new ChecklistItems

You now have an Add Item screen with a keyboard that lets the user enter text. The app also properly validates the input so that you'll never end up with text that is empty.

But how do you get this text into a new ChecklistItem object that you can add to the array from the Checklists screen?

Somehow you'll have to make the Add Item screen let the Checklist View Controller know that it is done. This is one of the fundamental tasks that every iOS app needs to do: sending messages from one view controller to another.

Sending a ChecklistItem object to the screen with the items array

Exercise: How would you tackle this problem? The done() method needs to create a new ChecklistItem object with the text from the text field (easy), then add it to the items array and the table view in ChecklistViewController (not so easy). ∎

Maybe you came up with something like this:

```
class AddItemViewController: UITableViewController . . . {

    // This variable refers to the other view controller
    var checklistViewController: ChecklistViewController

    @IBAction func done() {
        // Create the new checklist item object
        let item = ChecklistItem()
        item.text = textField.text

        // Directly call a method from ChecklistViewController
        checklistViewController.addItem(item)
    }
}
```

AddItemViewController has a variable that refers to the ChecklistViewController and done() calls its addItem() method with the new ChecklistItem object.

This will work, but it's not the iOS way. The big downside of this approach is that it shackles these two view controller objects together.

As a general principle, if screen A launches screen B then you don't want screen B to know too much about the screen that invoked it (A). The less B knows of A, the better.

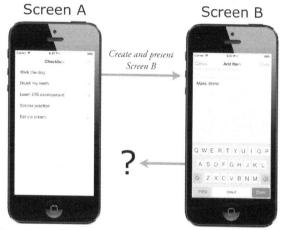

Screen A knows all about screen B, but B knows nothing of A

Giving AddItemViewController a direct reference to ChecklistViewController prevents you from opening the Add Item screen from somewhere else in the app. It can only ever talk back to ChecklistViewController. That's a big disadvantage.

You won't actually need to do this in the Checklists app, but in many apps it's common for one screen to be accessible from multiple places. For example, a login screen that appears after the user has been logged out due to inactivity. Or a details screen that shows more information about a tapped item, no matter where that item is located in the app (you'll see an example of this in the next tutorial).

Therefore, it's best if AddItemViewController doesn't know anything about ChecklistViewController.

But if that's the case, then how can you make the two communicate? The solution is to make your own *delegate*.

You've already seen delegates in a few different places: The table view has a delegate that responds to taps on the rows. The text field has a delegate that you used to validate the length of the text. And the app also has something named the AppDelegate (see the project navigator).

You can't turn a corner in this place without bumping into a delegate...

The delegate pattern is commonly used to handle the situation you find yourself in: Screen A opens screen B. At some point screen B needs to communicate back to screen A, usually when it closes.

The solution is to make screen A the delegate of screen B, so that B can send its messages to A whenever it needs to.

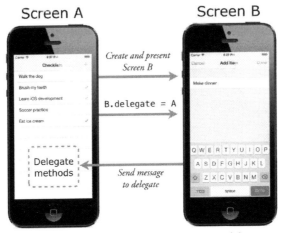

Screen A launches screen B and becomes its delegate

The cool thing about the delegate pattern is that screen B doesn't really know anything about screen A. It just knows that *some* object is its delegate. Other than that, screen B doesn't care who that is.

Just like `UITableView` doesn't really care about your view controller, only that it delivers table view cells when the table view asks for them.

This principle, where screen B is independent of screen A yet can still talk to it, is called *loose coupling* and is considered good software design practice.

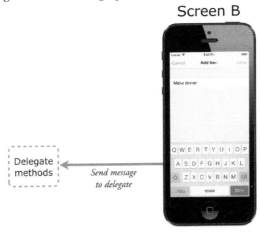

This is what Screen B sees: only the delegate part, not the rest of screen A

You will use the delegate pattern to let the `AddItemViewController` send notifications back to the `ChecklistViewController`, without it having to know anything about this object.

Delegates go hand-in-hand with *protocols*, a prominent feature of the Swift language.

➤ At the top of **AddItemViewController.swift,** add this in between the `import` and `class` lines (it is not part of the `AddItemViewController` object):

```
protocol AddItemViewControllerDelegate: class {
  func addItemViewControllerDidCancel(controller: AddItemViewController)
  func addItemViewController(controller: AddItemViewController,
                     didFinishAddingItem item: ChecklistItem)
}
```

This defines the `AddItemViewControllerDelegate` protocol. You should recognize the lines inside the `protocol { ... }` block as method declarations, but unlike other methods they don't have any source code in them. The protocol just lists the names of the methods.

Think of the delegate protocol as a contract between screen B and any screens that wish to use it.

Protocols

In Swift, a *protocol* doesn't have anything to do with computer networks or meeting royalty. It is simply a name for a group of methods.

A protocol doesn't implement any of the methods it declares. It just says: any object that conforms to this protocol must implement methods X, Y and Z.

The two methods listed in the `AddItemViewControllerDelegate` protocol are:

• `addItemViewControllerDidCancel()`

• `addItemViewController(didFinishAddingItem)`

Delegates often have very long method names!

The first one is for when the user presses Cancel, the second is for when she presses Done. In that case, the `didFinishAddingItem` parameter passes along the new `ChecklistItem` object.

To make the `ChecklistViewController` conform to this protocol, it must provide implementations of these two methods. From then on you can refer to the `ChecklistViewController` using just the protocol name.

If you've programmed in other languages before, you may recognize protocols as being very similar to "interfaces".

Inside `AddItemViewController`, instead of writing the following to refer back to the `ChecklistViewController`,

```
    var delegate: ChecklistViewController
```

you can now write:

```
    var delegate: AddItemViewControllerDelegate
```

The variable `delegate` is nothing more than a reference to *some* object that implements the methods of this protocol. You can send messages to the object from the `delegate` variable, without knowing what kind of object it really is.

Of course, *you* know the object from `delegate` is the `ChecklistViewController` but `AddItemViewController` doesn't need to be aware of that. All it sees is an object that implements its delegate protocol.

If you wanted to, you could make some other object implement the protocol and `AddItemViewController` would be perfectly OK with that. That's the power of delegation: you have removed – or *abstracted* away – the dependency between the `AddItemViewController` and the rest of the app.

It may seem a little overkill for a simple app such as this, but delegates are one of the cornerstones of iOS development. The sooner you master them, the better!

You're not done yet in **AddItemViewController.swift**. The view controller must have a property that it can use to refer to the delegate.

> Add this inside the `class AddItemViewController`, below the outlets:

```
weak var delegate: AddItemViewControllerDelegate?
```

It looks like a regular instance variable declaration, with two differences: `weak` and the question mark.

Delegates are usually declared as being `weak` – not a statement of their moral character but a way to describe the relationship between the view controller and its delegate – and optional (the question mark).

You'll learn more about those things in a moment.

> Replace the `cancel()` and `done()` actions with the following:

```
@IBAction func cancel() {
  delegate?.addItemViewControllerDidCancel(self)
}

@IBAction func done() {
  let item = ChecklistItem()
  item.text = textField.text
  item.checked = false

  delegate?.addItemViewController(self, didFinishAddingItem: item)
}
```

Let's look at the changes you made. When the user taps the Cancel button, you send the `addItemViewControllerDidCancel()` message back to the delegate.

You do something similar for the Done button, except that the message is `addItemViewController(didFinishAddingItem)` and you pass along a new `ChecklistItem` object that has the text string from the text field.

It is customary for the delegate methods to have a reference to their owner as the first (or only) parameter. That's why you pass `self` to both methods – recall that `self` refers to the object itself, in this case `AddItemViewController`. It's also why the method names also start with the term "addItemViewController".

Doing this is not required but still a good idea. For example, it may happen that an object is the delegate or data source for more than one table view. In that case, you need to be able to distinguish between those two table views. To allow for this, the table view delegate methods have a parameter for the `UITableView` object that sent the notification. (Having this reference also saves you from having to make an `@IBOutlet` for the table view.)

> Run the app and try the Cancel and Done buttons. They no longer work!

I hope you're not too surprised… The Add Item screen now depends on a delegate to make it close, but you haven't told the Add Item screen yet who its delegate is.

That means the `delegate` property has no value and the messages aren't being sent to anyone – there is no one listening for them.

Optionals

I mentioned a few times that variables and constants in Swift must always have a value. In other programming languages the special symbol `nil` or `NULL` is often used to indicate that a variable has no value. This is not allowed in Swift for normal variables.

The problem with `nil` and `NULL` is that they are a frequent cause of crashing apps. If an app attempts to use a variable that is `nil` when you don't expect it to be, the app will crash. This is the dreaded "null pointer dereference".

Swift stop this from happening by preventing you from using `nil`.

However, sometimes a variable does need to have "no value". In that case you can make it an *optional*. You mark something as optional in Swift using either a question mark `?` or an exclamation point `!`.

Only variables that are made optional can have the value `nil`.

You've already seen the question mark used with `NSIndexPath?`, the return type of `tableView(willSelectRowAtIndexPath)`. Returning `nil` from this method is a valid response; it means that the table should not select a particular row.

The question mark tells Swift that it's OK for the method to return `nil` instead of an actual `NSIndexPath` object.

The variable that refers to the delegate is usually marked as optional too. You can tell because there is a question mark behind its type:

```
weak var delegate: AddItemViewControllerDelegate?
```

Thanks to the `?` it's perfectly acceptable for `delegate` to be `nil`.

You may be wondering why `delegate` would ever be `nil`. Doesn't that negate the idea of having a delegate in the first place? There are two reasons.

Often delegates are truly optional; a `UITableView` works fine even if you don't implement any of its delegate methods (but you do need to provide at least some of its data source methods).

More importantly, when `AddItemViewController` is loaded from the storyboard and instantiated, it won't know right away who its delegate is. Between the time the view controller is loaded and the delegate is assigned, the variable will be `nil`. And variables that can be `nil` must be optionals.

When `delegate` is `nil`, you don't want `cancel()` or `done()` to send any of the messages. Doing that would crash the app because there is no one to receive the messages.

Swift has a handy shorthand for skipping the work when `delegate` is not set:

```
delegate?.addItemViewControllerDidCancel(self)
```

Here the ? tells Swift not to send the message if delegate is nil. You can read this as, "Is there a delegate? Then send the message." This practice is called *optional chaining* and it's used a lot in Swift.

In this app it should never happen that delegate is nil – it would get users stuck on the Add Item screen again – but Swift doesn't know that. So you'll have to pretend that it can happen anyway and use optional chaining to send messages to the delegate.

Optionals aren't common in other programming languages, so they may take some getting used to. I find that optionals do make programs clearer – most variables never have to be nil, so it's good to prevent them from becoming nil and avoid these potential sources of bugs.

Remember, if you see ? or ! in a Swift program, you're dealing with optionals.

Before you can give AddItemViewController its delegate, you first need to make the ChecklistViewController suitable to be the delegate.

> In **ChecklistViewController.swift**, change the class line to the following:

```
class ChecklistViewController: UITableViewController, AddItemViewControllerDelegate {
```

This tells the compiler that ChecklistViewController now promises to do the things from the AddItemViewControllerDelegate protocol.

If you try to run the app, Xcode gives an error: "Type ChecklistViewController does not conform to protocol AddItemViewControllerDelegate." That is correct: you still need to add the methods that are listed in AddItemViewControllerDelegate.

> Add the implementations of the protocol's methods to ChecklistViewController:

```
func addItemViewControllerDidCancel(controller: AddItemViewController) {
  dismissViewControllerAnimated(true, completion: nil)
}

func addItemViewController(controller: AddItemViewController,
                    didFinishAddingItem item: ChecklistItem) {
  dismissViewControllerAnimated(true, completion: nil)
}
```

Currently these methods simply close the Add Item screen. This is what the AddItemViewController used to do in its cancel() and done() actions. You've simply moved that responsibility to the delegate now.

The code that puts the new ChecklistItem object into the table view is left out for now. You'll add this in a moment, but there's something else you need to do first.

Delegates in five easy steps

In review, these are the steps for setting up the delegate pattern between two objects, where object A is the delegate for object B, and object B will send out the messages:

1. Define a delegate protocol for object B.

2. Give object B an optional delegate variable. This variable should be weak.

3. Make object B send messages to its delegate when something interesting happens, such as the user pressing the Cancel or Done buttons, or when it needs a piece of information.

4. Make object A conform to the delegate protocol. It should put the name of the protocol in its class line and implement the methods from the protocol.

5. Tell object B that object A is now its delegate.

You've done steps 1 to 4, so there is one more thing you need to do (step 5): tell `AddItemViewController` that the `ChecklistViewController` is now its delegate.

The proper place to do that is in the `prepareForSegue(sender)` method.

The `prepareForSegue` method is invoked by UIKit when a segue from one screen to another is about to be performed. Recall that the segue is the arrow between two view controllers in the storyboard.

Using `prepareForSegue` allows you to give data to the new view controller before it will be displayed. Usually you'll do that by setting its properties.

➤ Add this method to **ChecklistViewController.swift**:

```
override func prepareForSegue(segue: UIStoryboardSegue, sender: AnyObject?) {
    // 1
    if segue.identifier == "AddItem" {
        // 2
        let navigationController = segue.destinationViewController as! UINavigationController
        // 3
        let controller = navigationController.topViewController as! AddItemViewController
        // 4
        controller.delegate = self
    }
}
```

This is what `prepareForSegue` does, step-by-step:

1. Because there may be more than one segue per view controller, it's a good idea to give each one a unique identifier and to check for that identifier first to make sure you're handling the correct segue. Swift's == comparison operator does not work on just numbers but also on strings and most other types of objects.

2. The new view controller can be found in `segue.destinationViewController`. The storyboard shows that the segue does not go directly to `AddItemViewController` but to the navigation controller that embeds it. So first you get ahold of this `UINavigationController` object.

3. To find the `AddItemViewController`, you can look at the navigation controller's `topViewController` property. This property refers to the screen that is currently active inside the navigation controller.

4. Once you have a reference to the `AddItemViewController` object, you set its `delegate` property to `self` and the connection is complete. This tells the `AddItemViewController` that from now on, the object known as `self` is its delegate. But what is "self" here? Well, since you are editing **ChecklistViewController.swift**, `self` refers to the `ChecklistViewController`.

Excellent! `ChecklistViewController` is now the delegate of `AddItemViewController`. It took some work, but you're all set now.

➤ Open the storyboard and select the segue between the Checklist View Controller and the Navigation Controller on its right.

➤ In the **Attributes inspector**, type **AddItem** into the **Identifier** field:

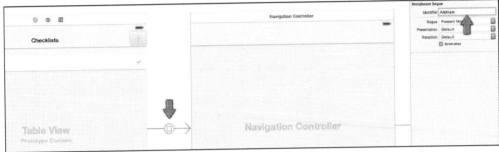

Naming the segue between the Checklists scene and the navigation controller

➤ Run the app to see if it works. (Make sure the storyboard is saved before you press Run, or the app may crash.)

Pressing the + button will perform the segue to the Add Item screen with the Checklists screen set as its delegate.

When you press Cancel or Done, AddItemViewController sends a message to its delegate, ChecklistViewController. Currently the delegate simply closes the Add Item screen, but now this works you can make it do more.

Let's add the new ChecklistItem to the data model and table view. Finally!

➤ Change the implementation of the didFinishAddingItem delegate method in **ChecklistViewController.swift** to the following:

```
func addItemViewController(controller: AddItemViewController,
                           didFinishAddingItem item: ChecklistItem) {
  let newRowIndex = items.count
  items.append(item)

  let indexPath = NSIndexPath(forRow: newRowIndex, inSection: 0)
  let indexPaths = [indexPath]
  tableView.insertRowsAtIndexPaths(indexPaths, withRowAnimation: .Automatic)

  dismissViewControllerAnimated(true, completion: nil)
}
```

This is largely the same as what you did in addItem() before. In fact, I simply copied the contents of addItem() and pasted them into this delegate method. Compare the two methods and see for yourself.

The only difference is that you no longer create the ChecklistItem object here; this happens in the AddItemViewController. You merely have to insert this new object into the items array.

As before, you tell the table view you have a new row for it and then close the Add Items screen.

➤ Remove addItem() from **ChecklistViewController.swift** as you no longer need this method.

Just to make sure, open the storyboard and double-check that the + button is no longer connected to the addItem action. Bad things happen if buttons are connected to methods that no longer exist...

(You can see this in the Connections inspector for the + button, under Sent Actions. Nothing should be connected there. Only the modal segue under Triggered Segues should be present.)

➤ Run the app and you should be able to add your own items to the list!

You can finally add new items to the to-do list

You can find the project files for the app up to this point under **04 - Add Item Screen** in the tutorial's Source Code folder.

Weak

I still owe you an explanation about weak. Relationships between objects can be weak or strong. You use weak relationships to avoid so-called *ownership cycles*.

When object A has a strong reference to object B, and at the same time object B also has a strong reference back to A, then these two objects are involved in a dangerous kind of romance: an ownership cycle.

Normally, an object is destroyed – or *deallocated* – when there are no more strong references to it. But because A and B have strong references to each other, they're keeping each other alive.

The result is a potential *memory leak* where an object that ought to be destroyed isn't, and the memory for its data is never reclaimed. With enough such leaks, iOS will run out of available memory and your app will crash. I told you it was dangerous!

Due to the strong references between them, A owns B but also B owns A:

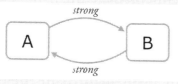

To avoid ownership cycles you can make one of these references weak.

In the case of a view controller and its delegate, screen A usually has a strong reference to screen B, but B only has a weak reference back to its delegate, A.

Because of the weak reference, B no longer owns A:

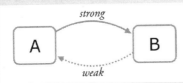

Now there is no ownership cycle.

Such cycles can occur in other situations too but they are most common with delegates. Therefore, delegates are always made weak.

(There is another relationship type, unowned, that is similar to weak and can be used for delegates too. The difference is that weak variables are allowed to become nil again. You may forget this right now.)

@IBOutlets are usually also declared with the weak keyword. This isn't done to avoid an ownership cycle, but to make it clear that the view controller isn't really the owner of the views from the outlets.

In the course of these tutorials you'll learn more about weak, strong, optionals, and the relationships between objects. These are important concepts in Swift, but they may take a while to make sense. Don't lose any sleep over it!

Editing existing checklist items

Adding new items to the list is a great step forward for the app, but there are usually three things an app needs to do with data:

1. adding new items (which you've tackled),

2. deleting items (you allow that with swipe-to-delete), and

3. editing existing items (uhh…).

The latter is useful for when you want to rename an item from your list. We all make typos.

You could make a completely new Edit Item screen but it would work mostly the same as the Add Item screen. The only difference is that it doesn't start out empty but with an existing to-do item.

So instead let's re-use the Add Item screen and make it capable of editing an existing ChecklistItem object.

When the user presses Done you will update the text in that ChecklistItem object. You'll also tell the delegate about it so that it can update the text label of the corresponding table view cell.

Exercise: Which changes would you need to make to the Add Item screen to enable it to edit existing items? ■

Answer:

1. The screen must be renamed to **Edit Item**.

2. You must be able to give it an existing `ChecklistItem` object.

3. You have to place the item's text into the text field.

4. When the user presses Done, you should not add a new item object, but update the existing one.

There is a bit of a user interface problem, though... How will the user actually open the Edit Item screen? In many apps that is done by tapping on the item's row but in the Checklists app that already toggles the checkmark.

To solve this problem, you'll have to revise the UI a little.

When a row is given two functions, the standard approach is to use a **detail disclosure button** for the secondary task:

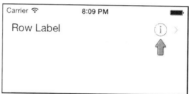

The detail disclosure button

Tapping the row itself will still perform the row's main function, in this case toggling the checkmark. But you'll make it so that tapping the disclosure button will open the Edit Item screen.

> **Note:** An alternative approach is taken by Apple's Reminders app. There the checkmark is on the left and tapping only this left-most section of the row will toggle the checkmark. Tapping anywhere else in the row will bring up the Edit screen for that item.
>
> There are also apps that can toggle the whole screen into "Edit mode" and then let you change the text of an item inline. Which solution you choose depends on what works best for your data.

➤ Go to the table view cell in the storyboard and in the **Attributes inspector** set its **Accessory** to **Detail Disclosure**.

Instead of the checkmark you'll now see a chevron (>) and a blue info button on the right of the cell. This means you'll have to place the checkmark somewhere else.

➤ Drag a new **Label** into the cell and place it on the left of the text label. Give it the following attributes:

• Text: √ (you can type this with **Alt/Option+V**)

• Font: System Bold, size 22

- Tag: 1001

You've given this new label its own tag, so you can easily find it later.

If typing Option-V does not work for you, choose **Edit → Emoji & Symbols** from the Xcode menu bar. Use the search bar to search for "check" – or whatever takes your fancy. (Note that not all of these special symbols may actually work on your iPhone.)

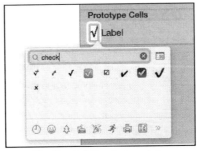

The Emoji & Symbols palette

➤ Resize the text label so that it doesn't overlap the checkmark or the disclosure button. It should be about 490 points wide.

The design of the prototype cell now looks like this:

The new design of the prototype cell

➤ In **ChecklistViewController.swift**, change `configureCheckmarkForCell()` to:

```
func configureCheckmarkForCell(cell: UITableViewCell,
                    withChecklistItem item: ChecklistItem) {
  let label = cell.viewWithTag(1001) as! UILabel
  if item.checked {
    label.text = "√"
  } else {
    label.text = ""
  }
}
```

Instead of setting the cell's `accessoryType` property, this now changes the text in the new label.

➤ Run the app and you'll see that the checkmark has moved to the left. There is also a blue detail disclosure button on the right. Tapping the row still toggles the checkmark, but tapping the blue button doesn't.

The checkmarks are now on the other side of the cell

Next you're going to make the detail disclosure button open the Add/Edit Item screen. This is pretty simple because Interface Builder also allows you to make a segue for a disclosure button.

➤ Open the storyboard. Select the table view cell and **Ctrl-drag** to the Navigation Controller next door to make a segue. From the popup, choose **present modally** from the **Accessory Action** section (not from Selection Segue):

Making a modal segue from the detail disclosure button

There are now two segues going from the Checklists screen to the navigation controller. One is triggered by the + button, the other by the detail disclosure button from the prototype cell.

For the app to make a distinction between the two segues, they must have unique identifiers.

➤ Give this new segue the identifier **EditItem** (in the **Attributes inspector**).

If you run the app now, tapping the blue (i) button will also open the Add Item screen. But the Cancel and Done buttons won't work.

Exercise: Can you explain why not? ∎

Answer: You haven't set the delegate yet. Remember that you set the delegate in `prepareForSegue(sender)`, but only for when the + button is tapped to perform the "AddItem" segue, not for this new "EditItem" segue.

Before you fix the delegate business, you shall make the Add/Edit Item screen capable of editing existing `ChecklistItem` objects.

➤ Add a new property for a `ChecklistItem` object below the other instance variables in **AddItemViewController.swift**:

```
var itemToEdit: ChecklistItem?
```

This variable contains the existing `ChecklistItem` object that the user will be editing. But when adding a new to-do item, `itemToEdit` will be `nil`. That is how the view controller will make the distinction between adding and editing.

Because `itemToEdit` can be `nil`, it needs to be an optional. That explains the question mark.

➤ Add the `viewDidLoad()` method to **AddItemViewController.swift**:

```
override func viewDidLoad() {
  super.viewDidLoad()
  tableView.rowHeight = 44

  if let item = itemToEdit {
    title = "Edit Item"
    textField.text = item.text
  }
}
```

Recall that `viewDidLoad()` is called by UIKit when the view controller is loaded from the storyboard, but before it is shown on the screen. That gives you time to put the user interface in order.

In editing mode, when `itemToEdit` is not `nil`, you change the title in the navigation bar to "Edit Item". You do this by changing the `title` property.

Each view controller has a number of built-in properties and this is one of them. The navigation controller looks for the `title` property and automatically changes the text in the navigation bar.

You also set the text in the text field to the value from the item's `text` property.

> **Note:** You cannot use optionals like you would regular variables. For example, if `viewDidLoad()` would have done the following,
>
>   textField.text = itemToEdit.text
>
> then Xcode would complain with the error message, "ChecklistItem? does not have a member named 'text'".
>
> That's because `itemToEdit` is the optional version of `ChecklistItem`.
>
> In order to use it you first need to *unwrap* the optional. You do that with the following special syntax:
>
>   if let temporaryConstant = optionalVariable {
>   // temporaryConstant now contains the unwrapped value
>   // of the optional variable
>   }
>
> If the optional is not `nil`, then the code inside the if-statement is performed.
>
> There are a few other ways to read the value of an optional, but using `if let` is the safest: if the optional has no value – i.e. it is `nil` – then the code inside the `if let` block is skipped over.
>
> Do you find optionals weird and confusing? Take some comfort in the fact that everyone else does too. This feature of Swift isn't found in many other mainstream languages and most developers do a double take when they first encounter it.
>
> Despite being a little odd, optionals will prevent mistakes with "null pointer dereferences" and help bulletproof your programs against crashes.

The `AddItemViewController` is now capable of recognizing when it needs to edit an item. If the `itemToEdit` property is given a `ChecklistItem` object, then the screen magically changes into the Edit Item screen.

But where do you fill up that `itemToEdit` property? In `prepareForSegue`, of course! That's the ideal place for putting values into the properties of the new screen before it becomes visible.

➤ Change `prepareForSegue` in **ChecklistViewController.swift** to the following:

```
override func prepareForSegue(segue: UIStoryboardSegue, sender: AnyObject?) {
  if segue.identifier == "AddItem" {
    . . .
  } else if segue.identifier == "EditItem" {
    let navigationController = segue.destinationViewController as! UINavigationController
    let controller = navigationController.topViewController as! AddItemViewController
    controller.delegate = self

    if let indexPath = tableView.indexPathForCell(sender as! UITableViewCell) {
      controller.itemToEdit = items[indexPath.row]
    }
  }
}
```

As before, you get the navigation controller from the storyboard, and its embedded `AddItemViewController` using the `topViewController` property. You also set the view controller's `delegate` property so you're notified when the user taps Cancel or Done. Nothing new there.

This is the interesting new bit:

```
if let indexPath = tableView.indexPathForCell(sender as! UITableViewCell) {
  controller.itemToEdit = items[indexPath.row]
}
```

You're in the `prepareForSegue(sender)` method, which has a parameter named `sender`. This parameter contains a reference to the control that triggered the segue, in this case the table view cell whose disclosure button was tapped.

You use that `UITableViewCell` object to find the row number by looking up the corresponding index-path using `tableView.indexPathForCell()`.

The return type of `UITableView`'s `indexPathForCell()` method is `NSIndexPath?`, meaning it can possibly return `nil`. That's why you need to unwrap this optional index-path value with `if let` before you can use it.

Once you have the row number you can obtain the `ChecklistItem` object to edit. You assign this to `AddItemViewController`'s `itemToEdit` property.

Sending data between view controllers

We've talked about screen B (the Add/Edit Item screen) passing data back to screen A (the Checklists screen) through the use of delegates.

But here you're passing a piece of data the other way around – from screen A to screen B – namely, the `ChecklistItem` to edit.

Data transfer between view controllers works two ways:

1. From A to B. When screen A opens screen B, A can give B the data it needs. You simply make a new instance variable in B's view controller. Screen A then puts an object into this property right before it makes screen B visible, usually in `prepareForSegue(sender)`.

2. From B to A. To pass data back from B to A you use a delegate.

This illustration shows how screen A sends data to screen B by putting it into B's properties, and how screen B sends data back to the delegate:

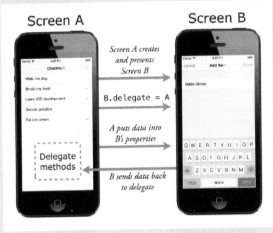

I hope the flow between view controllers is starting to make sense now. You're going to do this sort of thing a few more times in this lesson, just to make sure you get comfortable with it. Making iOS apps is all about creating view controllers and sending messages between them, so we want this to become second nature.

➤ With these steps done, you can now run the app. A tap on the + button opens the Add Item screen as before. But tap the accessory button on an existing row and the screen that opens is named Edit Item. It already contains the to-do item's text:

Editing an item

One small problem: the Done button in the navigation bar is initially disabled. This is because you originally set it to be disabled in the storyboard.

➤ Change `viewDidLoad` in **AddItemViewController.swift** to fix this:

```
override func viewDidLoad() {
  super.viewDidLoad()
  tableView.rowHeight = 44

  if let item = itemToEdit {
    title = "Edit Item"
    textField.text = item.text
    doneBarButton.enabled = true
  }
}
```

You can simply always enable the Done button; when editing an existing item you are guaranteed to pass in a text that is not empty.

The problems don't end here, though. Run the app, tap a row to edit it, and press Done. Instead of changing the text on the existing item, a brand new to-do item with the new text is added to the list.

You didn't write the code yet to update the data model, so the delegate always thinks it needs to add a new row.

To solve this you add a new method to the delegate protocol.

➤ Add the following line to the `protocol` section in **AddItemViewController.swift**:

```
func addItemViewController(controller: AddItemViewController,
                 didFinishEditingItem item: ChecklistItem)
```

The full protocol now looks like this:

```
protocol AddItemViewControllerDelegate: class {
  func addItemViewControllerDidCancel(controller: AddItemViewController)

  func addItemViewController(controller: AddItemViewController,
                   didFinishAddingItem item: ChecklistItem)

  func addItemViewController(controller: AddItemViewController,
                   didFinishEditingItem item: ChecklistItem)
}
```

There is one method that is invoked when the user presses Cancel and two methods for when the user presses Done.

After adding a new item you call `didFinishAddingItem`, but when editing an existing item the new `didFinishEditingItem` method will now be called instead.

By using different methods the delegate (the Checklist View Controller) can make a distinction between those two situations.

➤ In **AddItemViewController.swift**, change the `done()` method to:

```
@IBAction func done() {
  if let item = itemToEdit {
    item.text = textField.text
    delegate?.addItemViewController(self, didFinishEditingItem: item)
  } else {
```

```
    let item = ChecklistItem()
    item.text = textField.text
    item.checked = false
    delegate?.addItemViewController(self, didFinishAddingItem: item)
  }
}
```

First this checks whether the `itemToEdit` property contains an object. You should recognize the `if let` syntax as unwrapping an optional.

If the optional is not `nil`, you put the text from the text field into the existing `ChecklistItem` object and then call the new delegate method. In the case that `itemToEdit` *is* `nil`, the user is adding a new item and you do the stuff you did before (inside the `else` block).

➤ Try to build the app. It won't work.

Xcode says "Build Failed" but there don't seem to be any error messages in **AddItemViewController.swift**. So what went wrong?

You can see all errors and warnings from Xcode in the **Issue navigator**:

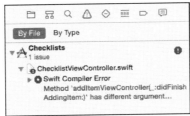

Xcode warns about incomplete implementation

The error is apparently in `ChecklistViewController` because it does not implement a method from the protocol. That is not so strange because you just added the `addItemViewController(didFinishEditingItem)` method to the protocol for the delegate. You did not yet tell the view controller, who plays the role of delegate, what to do with it.

> **Note:** The exact error message in my version of Xcode is "Method … has different argument names from those required by protocol …". That's a bit of a strange error message, wouldn't you say? It doesn't really describe what's wrong, just what Swift is confused about.
>
> As you're writing your own apps you'll probably run into other strange or even undecipherable Swift error messages. This should get better in time. The Swift compiler is very new at the job and still needs to work on its bedside manner.

➤ Add the following to **ChecklistViewController.swift** and the compiler error will be history:

```
func addItemViewController(controller: AddItemViewController,
                 didFinishEditingItem item: ChecklistItem) {
  if let index = find(items, item) {
    let indexPath = NSIndexPath(forRow: index, inSection: 0)
    if let cell = tableView.cellForRowAtIndexPath(indexPath) {
      configureTextForCell(cell, withChecklistItem: item)
    }
  }
  dismissViewControllerAnimated(true, completion: nil)
}
```

The ChecklistItem object already has the new text – it was put there by done() –and it already exists in the table view. But you do need to update the label in its table view cell.

So in this new method you look for the cell that corresponds to the ChecklistItem object and, using the configureTextForCell(withChecklistItem) method you wrote earlier, tell it to refresh its label.

The first statement is the most interesting:

```
if let index = find(items, item) {
```

In order to make the NSIndexPath that you need to retrieve the cell, you first need to find the row number for this ChecklistItem. The row number is the same as the index of the ChecklistItem in the items array, and you can use the find() function to return that index.

Now, it won't happen here, but in theory it's possible that you use find() on an object that is not actually in the array. To account for the possibility, find() does not return a normal value, it returns an optional. If the object is not part of the array, the optional is nil.

That's why you need to use if let here to unwrap the return value of find().

➤ Try to build the app. Whoops, I guess I spoke too soon. Xcode has found another reason to complain: "Type ChecklistItem does not conform to protocol Equatable".

This happens because you can't use find() on just any object, only on objects that are "equatable". find() must be able to somehow compare the object that you're looking for to the objects in the array, to see if they are equal.

Your ChecklistItem object does not have any functionality for that yet. There are a few ways you can fix this, but we'll go for the easy one.

➤ In **ChecklistItem.swift**, change the class line to:

```
class ChecklistItem: NSObject {
```

If you've programmed in Objective-C before, then NSObject will look familiar.

Almost all objects in Objective-C programs are based on NSObject. It's the most basic building block provided by iOS, and it offers a bunch of useful functionality that standard Swift objects don't have.

You can write many Swift programs without having to resort to NSObject, but in times like these it comes in handy.

Building ChecklistItem on top of NSObject is enough to make it satisfy the "equatable" requirement. Later in the tutorial, when you learn about saving the checklist items, you would have had to make it an NSObject anyway, so this is a good solution.

➤ Run the app again and verify that editing items works now. Excellent!

Refactoring the code

At this point you have an app that can add new items and edit existing items using the combined Add/Edit Item screen. Pretty sweet.

Given the recent changes, I don't think the name `AddItemViewController` is appropriate anymore as this screen is now used to both add and edit items.

I propose you rename it to `ItemDetailViewController`.

Now, I've got good news and I've got bad news. Which one do you want to hear first?

The good news is that Xcode has a special menu for refactoring source code, including a tool to rename items. You can find this menu under **Edit → Refactor → Rename...**

The bad news is that in Xcode 6.3 this tool does not work for Swift sources, only for Objective-C. So you can't actually use it. Boohoo!

Just in case you live in the future and your version of Xcode does have a working Refactor menu, here's how you'd do it (if not, skip ahead a page):

➤ Go to **AddItemViewController.swift** and click in the `class` line so that the blinking cursor is on the word `AddItemViewController`. Where you place the cursor is important, so make sure it's in the right spot.

➤ From the Xcode menu bar at the top of the screen choose **Edit → Refactor → Rename...**

Xcode will now ask you for the new name:

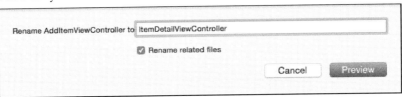

Changing the name of AddItemViewController

➤ Type **ItemDetailViewController** for the new name and check **Rename related files**.

Tip: If Xcode gives the error message "Wait for indexing and try again", then stop the running app first.

➤ Press **Preview**. Xcode opens a screen that shows the files that are about to be changed. Click on a filename to look at the changes that will be made inside of that file.

You'll see that Xcode will simply rename everything from `AddItemViewController` to `ItemDetailViewController`, even inside your storyboard. It's always smart to check what Xcode is going to do... Just. In. Case.

➤ Click **Save** to let Xcode do its thing.

Xcode will now ask if you want to enable automatic snapshots. A snapshot is a copy of your entire project for safekeeping. It is probably a good idea to enable this. If something goes wrong, you can always go back to an earlier snapshot.

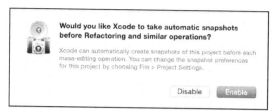

Enable automatic snapshots for simple backups of your project

> Click **Enable** and wait a few seconds for Xcode to complete the operation.

In case you're curious – or you changed your mind! – you can find the snapshots in the **Projects** window (choose **Window → Projects** from the menu bar):

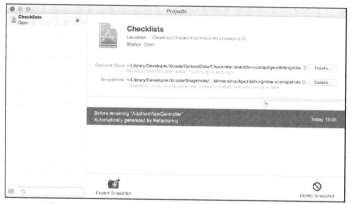

The Projects window lists the snapshots for your project

You can use the **File → Restore Snapshot...** option from the Xcode menu bar to rewrite history. If at some point you wish to make a manual snapshot, use **File → Create Snapshot**.

> Repeat this process to rename the AddItemViewControllerDelegate protocol to ItemDetailViewControllerDelegate. You better get used to those long names!

Note: Resume reading from here if the Refactor menu did not work for you.

For us poor slobs without a working Refactor menu there's only one option: manual labor – you'll have to make these changes by hand. Fortunately, Xcode has a very handy search & replace function.

> Switch to the **Search navigator** (third tab in the navigator pane).

> Click on Find to change it to **Replace**.

> Change Ignoring Case to **Matching Case**.

> Type as the search text: **AddItemViewController**. Important: Make sure the case matches!

> Type in the replacement field: **ItemDetailViewController**.

The search & replace options

> Press **enter** on your keyboard to start the search. This doesn't replace anything yet.

The search navigator shows the files containing matches for the search term. You should see the two Swift source files and Main.storyboard in this list.

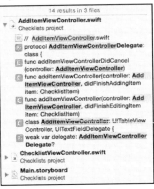

The search results

> Click the **Preview** button. Xcode opens a screen with the files that are about to be changed and the individual changes inside each file:

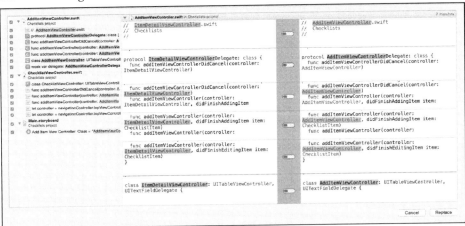

The preview pane shows the changes that Xcode is proposing

Have a look through these files just to make sure Xcode isn't doing anything you'll regret. It should only rename everything that says AddItemViewController to ItemDetailViewController, also inside your storyboard.

➤ Click **Replace** and pray.

Xcode will now ask if you want to enable automatic snapshots. It's a good idea to enable this. If you're going to mess this up, you'll still have a copy of the original. (You can find the snapshots under **Window → Organizer** from the menu bar.)

There's one more thing to fix. Xcode did not automatically rename the source file.

➤ In the project navigator, slowly click **AddItemViewController.swift** twice until the name becomes editable.

Type the new name: **ItemDetailViewController.swift**

Note: The following instructions apply to everyone again.

You're not done yet with these refactorings.

Unfortunately, Xcode isn't able to automatically rename the methods from the delegate protocol for you, so you'll have to do this manually.

➤ Switch to the **Search navigator**

➤ Make sure you're in **Replace** mode (click Find at the top to switch to Replace)

➤ Make sure you're in **Matching Case** mode (if not, click Ignoring Case to switch)

➤ Type for the search text: **addItemViewController**

➤ The as the replacement text: **itemDetailViewController**

➤ Press **enter** to search through the entire project.

Using the Search navigator to find the methods to change

The search results should have only the method names from the delegate protocol, in both ChecklistViewController.swift and ItemDetailViewController.swift.

➤ If you're happy with the proposed changes, click **Replace All**.

I always repeat the search afterwards, ignoring case, to make sure I didn't skip anything by accident.

After these changes, the protocol in **ItemDetailViewController.swift** now has these methods:

```
protocol ItemDetailViewControllerDelegate: class {
  func itemDetailViewControllerDidCancel(controller: ItemDetailViewController)

  func itemDetailViewController(controller: ItemDetailViewController,
                     didFinishAddingItem item: ChecklistItem)

  func itemDetailViewController(controller: ItemDetailViewController,
                     didFinishEditingItem item: ChecklistItem)
}
```

➤ Press ⌘+B to compile the app. If you made all the changes without any mistakes, the app should build without errors.

> **Note:** Getting a "Build Failed" error? Then double-check your spelling.
>
> Swift is case-sensitive, so it considers "itemDetailViewController" and "ItemDetailViewController" to be two completely different words.

Because you made quite a few changes all over the place, it's a good idea to do a *clean* just to make sure Xcode picks up all these changes and that there are no more warnings or compiler errors. You don't have to be paranoid about this, but it's good practice to clean house once in a while.

➤ From Xcode's menu bar choose **Product → Clean**. When the clean is done choose **Product → Build** (or simply press the Run button).

If there are no build issues, run the app again and test the various features just to make sure everything still works! (If the build succeeds but Xcode still shows red error icons in your source file, then close the project and open it again, or restart Xcode. It's the solution that Always Works™.)

If the app crashes for you at this point, double-check that in the storyboard the Custom Class of the view controller now says ItemDetailViewController (see the Identity inspector pane). Xcode sometimes skips this step and then you have to make this change manually.

You can find the project files for the app up to this point under **05 - Edit Items** in the tutorial's Source Code folder.

> **Iterative development**
>
> If you think this approach to development is a little messy, then you're absolutely right.
>
> You started out with one design but as you were developing you found out that things didn't work out so well in practice and that you had to refactor your approach a few times to find a way that works.
>
> Well, this is how software development goes in practice.
>
> You first build a small part of your app and everything looks and works fine. Then you add the next small part on top of that and suddenly everything breaks down. The proper thing to do is to go back and restructure your entire approach so that everything is hunky-dory again... Until the next change you need to make.

Software development is a constant process of refinement. In these tutorials I didn't want to just give you a perfect piece of code and explain how each part works. That's not how software development happens in the real world.

Instead, you're working your way from zero to a full app, exactly the way a pro developer would, including the mistakes and dead ends.

Isn't it possible to create a design up-front – sometimes called a "software architecture design" – that deals with all of these situations, like a blueprint but for software?

I don't believe in such designs. Sure, it's always good to plan ahead. Before writing this tutorial, I made a few quick sketches of how I imagined the app would turn out. That was useful to envision the amount of work, but as usual some of my assumptions and guesses turned out to be wrong and the design stopped being useful about halfway in. And this is only a simple app!

That doesn't mean you shouldn't spend any time on planning and design, just not too much. ;-)

Simply start somewhere and keep going until you get stuck, then backtrack and improve on your approach. This is called *iterative development* and it's usually faster than meticulous up-front planning and provides better results.

Saving and loading the checklist items

Any new to-do items that you add to the list cease to exist when you terminate the app (by pressing the Stop button in Xcode, for example). You can also delete the five default items from the list but they keep reappearing after a new launch. That's not how a real app should behave, of course.

Thanks to the multitasking nature of iOS, an app stays in memory when you close it. The app goes into a suspended state where it does absolutely nothing but will still hang on to its data.

During normal usage, users will never truly terminate the app, just suspend it. However, the app can still be terminated when the iPhone runs out of available working memory, as iOS will terminate any suspended apps in order to free up memory when necessary. And if they really want to, users can kill apps by hand or reset their entire device.

Just keeping the list of items in memory is not good enough because there is no guarantee that the app will remain in memory forever, whether active or suspended.

Instead, you will need to **persist** this data in a file on the iPhone's long-term flash storage. This is no different than saving a file from your word processor on your desktop computer except that iPhone apps should take care of this saving automatically.

The user shouldn't have to press a Save button just to make sure unsaved data is safely placed in long-term storage.

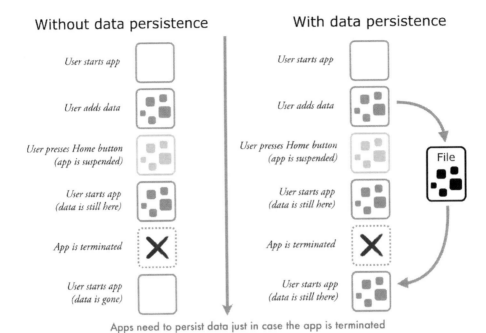

Apps need to persist data just in case the app is terminated

In this section you will:

- Determine where in the file system you can place the file that will remember the to-do list items.

- Save the to-do items to that file whenever the user changes something: adds a new item, toggles a checkmark, et cetera.

- Load the to-do items from that file when the app starts up again after it was terminated.

Let's get crackin'!

The documents directory

iOS apps live in a sheltered environment, also known as the **sandbox**. Each app has its own directory for storing files but cannot access the directories or files of any other apps.

This is a security measure, designed to prevent malicious software such as viruses from doing any damage. If an app can only change its own files, then it cannot break any other part of the system.

Your apps can store files in the so-called "Documents" directory in the app's sandbox.

The contents of the Documents directory are backed up when the user syncs their device with iTunes or iCloud.

When you release a new version of your app and users install the update, the Documents folder is left untouched. Any data the app has saved into this folder stays there even if the app is updated.

In other words, the Documents folder is the perfect place for storing your user's data files.

Let's look at how this works.

➤ Add the following methods to **ChecklistViewController.swift**:

```
func documentsDirectory() -> String {
  let paths = NSSearchPathForDirectoriesInDomains(.DocumentDirectory, .UserDomainMask, true)
                    as! [String]
  return paths[0]
}

func dataFilePath() -> String {
  return documentsDirectory().stringByAppendingPathComponent("Checklists.plist")
}
```

The documentsDirectory() method is something I've added for convenience. There is no standard method you can call to get the full path to the Documents folder, so I rolled my own.

> **Note:** Double check to make sure this says .DocumentDirectory and not .DocumentationDirectory. Xcode's autocomplete can easily trip you up here!

The dataFilePath() method uses documentsDirectory() to construct the full path to the file that will store the checklist items. This file is named **Checklists.plist** and it lives inside the Documents directory.

You use the String method stringByAppendingPathComponent() to build a proper file system path to Checklists.plist. It is possible to call this method directly on the return value of documentsDirectory() because that is also a String.

You could also have written the method like this:

```
func dataFilePath() -> String {
  let directory = documentsDirectory()
  return directory.stringByAppendingPathComponent("Checklists.plist")
}
```

Here you first put the String from documentsDirectory() into a new temporary constant. That's perfectly fine but it's just as easy to combine everything into a single line of code. Both versions of this method do exactly the same thing.

You could also have constructed the full path like this:

```
func dataFilePath() -> String {
  return "\(documentsDirectory())/Checklists.plist"
}
```

This uses string interpolation to add "Checklist.plist" to the Documents directory path, separated by a forward slash. It works, but I advise against doing it this way.

I prefer to use stringByAppendingPathComponent() since that frees me from worrying about whether to use a forward slash or a backward slash, what to do if there already is a slash in the folder name, and many other tiny concerns.

The built-in objects from iOS come with a lot of useful helper methods like these and it's often better to use them instead of reinventing the wheel.

➤ Still in **ChecklistViewController.swift**, add the following two println() statements to the bottom of init(coder), below the call to super.init():

```
required init(coder aDecoder: NSCoder) {
  . . .
  super.init(coder: aDecoder)
```

```
    println("Documents folder is \(documentsDirectory())")
    println("Data file path is \(dataFilePath())")
}
```

➤ Run the app. Xcode's debug area will now show you where your app's Documents directory is actually located.

If I run the app from the Simulator, on my system it says:

```
Documents folder is /Users/matthijs/Library/Developer/CoreSimulator/Devices/078E984C-869F-
4B9D-BA79-521A9ACE6B04/data/Containers/Data/Application/F8B7339F-5E74-4EFD-9CAE-
DDC304F9F03D/Documents

Data file path is /Users/matthijs/Library/Developer/CoreSimulator/Devices/078E984C-869F-4B9D-
BA79-521A9ACE6B04/data/Containers/Data/Application/F8B7339F-5E74-4EFD-9CAE-
DDC304F9F03D/Documents/Checklists.plist
```

If you run it on your iPhone, the path will look somewhat different. Here's what mine says (this is on an iPod touch):

```
Documents folder is /var/mobile/Applications/FDD50B54-9383-4DCC-9C19-C3DEBC1A96FE/Documents

Data file path is /var/mobile/Applications/FDD50B54-9383-4DCC-9C19-
C3DEBC1A96FE/Documents/Checklists.plist
```

The name of the folder that contains the app's Documents folder is "F8B7339F-5E74-4EFD-9CAE-DDC304F9F03D" (on the Simulator) and "FDD50B54-9383-4DCC-9C19-C3DEBC1A96FE" (on the device). There will be a quiz at the end of this section to see if you were able to memorize these folder names (I'm joking!).

The folder name is a random ID that Xcode picks when it installs the app on the Simulator or the device. Anything inside that folder is part of the app's sandbox.

For the rest of this section, run the app on the Simulator instead of a device. That makes it easier to look at the files you'll be writing into the Documents folder. Because the Simulator stores the app's files in a regular folder on your Mac, you can easily examine them from Finder.

➤ Open a new **Finder** window by clicking on the Desktop and typing ⌘+N. Then press ⌘+Shift+G and paste the full path to the Documents folder in the dialog.

The Finder window will go to that folder. Keep this window open so you can see that the Checklists.plist file is actually being created when you get to that part.

The app's directory structure in the Simulator

> **Tip:** The Library folder that contains the Simulator's app directories is hidden from your home directory. Hold down the Alt/Option key and click on Finder's Go menu. This will reveal the Library folder.

You can see several things inside the app's directory:

- The Documents directory where the app will put its data files. Currently the Documents folder is still empty.

- The Library directory has cache files and preferences files. The contents of this directory are managed by the operating system.

- The tmp directory is for temporary files. Sometimes apps need to create files for temporary usage. You don't want these to clutter up your Documents folder, so tmp is a good place to put them. iOS will clear out this folder from time to time.

It is also possible to look inside the Documents directory of apps on your device.

➤ On your iPhone or iPod, go to **Settings** → **General** → **Usage**. Under **Storage** (not iCloud) tap **Manage Storage** and then the name of an app.

You'll now see the contents of its Documents folder:

Viewing the Documents folder on the device

Saving the checklist items

In this section you are going to write code that saves the list of to-do items to the Checklists.plist file when the user adds a new item or edits an existing item. Once you are able to save the items you'll add the code that is required to load this list again when the app starts up.

So what is a **.plist** file?

You've already seen a file named Info.plist in the Bull's Eye lesson. All apps have one, including the Checklists app (see the project navigator for the file named Info.plist, under Supporting Files). Info.plist contains several configuration options that give iOS additional information about the app, such as what name to display under the app's icon on the Springboard.

"plist" stands for Property List and is an XML file format that stores structured data, usually in the form of a list of settings and their values. Property List files are very common in iOS. They are suitable for many types of data storage, and best of all they are simple to use. What's not to like!

To save the checklist items you'll use the NSCoder system, which lets objects store their data in a structured file format.

You actually don't have to care much about that format. In this case it happens to be a .plist file but you're not directly going to mess with that file. All you care about is that the data gets stored in some kind of file in the app's Documents folder, but you'll leave the technical details for NSCoder to deal with.

You have already used NSCoder behind the scenes because that's exactly how storyboards work. When you add a view controller to a storyboard, Xcode uses the NSCoder system to write this object to a file (encoding). Then when your application starts up, it uses NSCoder again to read the objects from the storyboard file (decoding).

The process of converting objects to files and back again is also known as **serialization**. It's a big topic in software engineering.

I like to think of this whole process as freezing objects. You take a living object and freeze it so that it is suspended in time. You store that frozen object into a file on the iPhone's flash drive where it will spend some time in cryostasis. Later you can read that file into memory and defrost the object to bring it back to life again.

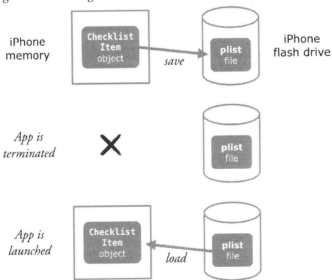

The process of freezing (saving) and unfreezing (loading) objects

> Add the following method to **ChecklistViewController.swift**:

```
func saveChecklistItems() {
  let data = NSMutableData()
  let archiver = NSKeyedArchiver(forWritingWithMutableData: data)
  archiver.encodeObject(items, forKey: "ChecklistItems")
```

```
    archiver.finishEncoding()
    data.writeToFile(dataFilePath(), atomically: true)
}
```

This method takes the contents of the `items` array and in two steps converts this to a block of binary data and then writes this data to a file:

1. `NSKeyedArchiver`, which is a form of `NSCoder` that creates plist files, encodes the array and all the `ChecklistItems` in it into some sort of binary data format that can be written to a file.

2. That data is placed in an `NSMutableData` object, which will write itself to the file specified by `dataFilePath`.

It's not really important that you understand how `NSKeyedArchiver` works internally. The format that it stores the data in isn't of great significance. All you care about is that it allows you to put your objects into a file and read them back later.

You have to call this new `saveChecklistItems()` method whenever the list of items is modified.

Exercise: Where in the source code would you call this method? ■

Answer: Look at where the `items` array is being changed. This happens inside the `ItemDetailViewControllerDelegate` methods. That's where the party's at!

➤ Add a call to `saveChecklistItems()` to the end of these methods inside **ChecklistViewController.swift**:

```
func itemDetailViewController(controller: ItemDetailViewController,
                        didFinishAddingItem item: ChecklistItem) {
  . . .
  saveChecklistItems()
}

func itemDetailViewController(controller: ItemDetailViewController,
                        didFinishEditingItem item: ChecklistItem) {
  . . .
  saveChecklistItems()
}
```

➤ Let's not forget the swipe-to-delete function:

```
override func tableView(tableView: UITableView,
                    commitEditingStyle editingStyle: UITableViewCellEditingStyle,
                    forRowAtIndexPath indexPath: NSIndexPath) {
  . . .
  saveChecklistItems()
}
```

➤ And toggling the checkmark on a row on or off:

```
override func tableView(tableView: UITableView,
                    didSelectRowAtIndexPath indexPath: NSIndexPath) {
  . . .
  saveChecklistItems()
}
```

Just calling `NSKeyedArchiver` on the `items` array is not enough. If you were to run the app now and do something that results in a save, such as tapping a row to flip the checkmark, the app crashes with the following error (try it out):

```
*** Terminating app due to uncaught exception 'NSInvalidArgumentException', reason: '-
[Checklists.ChecklistItem encodeWithCoder:]: unrecognized selector sent to instance
0x7f8d6af3aac0
```

A *selector* is a term Objective-C uses for the name of a method, so this warning means the app tried to call a method named encodeWithCoder() that doesn't actually exist anywhere. (Swift doesn't really use the term selector, but because the iOS frameworks are written in Objective-C you'll still see it being used in the documentation and in error messages.)

The Xcode window has switched to the *debugger* and points out which line caused the crash:

Xcode isn't being very helpful here

The debugger points at the AppDelegate.swift source file as the cause for the crash, but that's a little misleading. If this happened to you too, then you need to enable the Exception Breakpoint.

➤ Switch to the **Breakpoint navigator** and click the + button at the bottom:

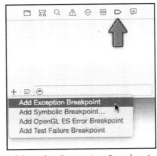

Adding the Exception Breakpoint

Now try it again. Run the app and tap a row to toggle the checkmark. This time Xcode points at the correct line, inside saveChecklistItems():

The app crashes on the code you just added

This line is the culprit:

```
archiver.encodeObject(items, forKey: "ChecklistItems")
```

Apparently the app crashes when trying to encode the items array, or rather the things inside the array.

The "unrecognized selector" crash message means you forgot to implement a certain method. In this case, the missing method appears to be encodeWithCoder() on the ChecklistItem object – that's what the crash message says.

Here is what happened: You asked NSKeyedArchiver to encode the array of items, so it not only has to encode the array itself but also each ChecklistItem object inside that array.

NSKeyedArchiver knows how to encode an Array object but it doesn't know anything about ChecklistItem. So you have to help it out a bit.

➤ Change the class line in **ChecklistItem.swift**:

```
class ChecklistItem: NSObject, NSCoding {
```

You're telling the compiler that ChecklistItem will conform to a new protocol, NSCoding.

The names get confusing: If you want to use the NSCoder system on an object, the object needs to implement the NSCoding protocol.

You've seen that a protocol is just a list of method names. Making an object conform to the protocol means the object should add implementations for the methods from that protocol.

The methods from the NSCoding protocol are:

• func encodeWithCoder(aCoder: NSCoder)

• init(coder aDecoder: NSCoder)

Only two methods, that can't be too bad! The first one is a regular method and it is used for saving – or encoding – the objects.

The other is a special init method. Recall that init methods are used during the creation of new objects, so this one is for loading – or decoding – the objects.

➤ Add the following to **ChecklistItem.swift**:

```
func encodeWithCoder(aCoder: NSCoder) {
  aCoder.encodeObject(text, forKey: "Text")
  aCoder.encodeBool(checked, forKey: "Checked")
}
```

This is the missing method from the unrecognized selector error. When NSKeyedArchiver tries to encode the ChecklistItem object it will send it an encodeWithCoder(coder) message.

Here you simply say: a ChecklistItem has an object named "Text" that contains the value of the instance variable text and a boolean named "Checked" that contains the value of the variable checked.

Just these two lines are enough to make the coder system work, at least for saving the to-do items.

Before you can build and run the app, you need to add some more code. Swift requires that you always implement all the required methods from a protocol and NSCoding has two methods, one for saving and one for loading.

➤ Add the second method to **ChecklistItem.swift**:

```
required init(coder aDecoder: NSCoder) {
  super.init()
}
```

You're not going to use this right away, but it's needed to make the app compile without errors.

> **Note:** This should look familiar. You've already used init(coder) before, to initialize the Checklist View Controller. That's because storyboards also use the NSCoding system to load objects into the app.

Now, init methods are special in Swift. Because you just added init(coder) you also need to add an init() method that takes no parameters. Without this, the app won't build. You'll learn more about why soon.

➤ Also add this method:

```
override init() {
  super.init()
}
```

It doesn't do anything useful, but it keeps the compiler happy.

➤ Run the app again and tap a row to toggle a checkmark. The app didn't crash? Good!

➤ Go to the Finder window that has the app's Documents directory open:

The Documents directory now contains a Checklists.plist file

There is now a **Checklists.plist** file in the Documents folder, which contains the items from the list.

You can look inside this file if you want, but the contents won't make much sense to you. Even though it is XML, this file wasn't intended to be read by humans, only by the NSKeyedArchiver system.

If you're having trouble viewing the XML it may be because the plist file isn't stored as text but as a binary format. Some text editors support this file format and can read it as if it were text (TextWrangler is a good one and is a free download on the Mac App Store).

You can also use Finder's Quick Look feature to view the file. Simply select the file in Finder and press the space bar.

Naturally, you can also open the plist file with Xcode.

➤ Right-click the Checklists.plist file and choose **Open With → Xcode**.

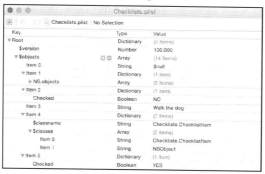

Checklist.plist in Xcode

It still won't make much sense but it's fun to look at anyway.

Expand some of the rows and you'll see this file was made by NSKeyedArchiver and that the names of the ChecklistItems are also in there. But exactly how all these data items fit together, I have no idea.

> **Tip:** NSMutableData, NSKeyedArchiver and NSCoding are objects from the Foundation framework. (You can tell because of the "NS" prefix.)
>
> If you are curious about exactly how these objects or their methods work, you can Alt/Option-click any item in your source code to bring up a popup with a brief description:
>
> ```
> func saveChecklists() {
>     let data = NSMutableData()
>     let archiver = NSKeyedArchiver(forWritingWithMutableData: data)
>     archiver.encodeObject(lists, forKey: "Checklists")
>     archiver.finishEncoding()
>     data.writeToFile(dataFilePath(), atomically: true)
> ```
>
> | Declaration | func finishEncoding() |
> |---|---|
> | Description | Instructs the receiver to construct the final data stream. |
> | | No more values can be encoded after this method is called. You must call this method when finished. |
> | Availability | iOS (8.0 and later) |
> | Declared In | Foundation |
> | Reference | NSKeyedArchiver Class Reference |

I use this all the time to remind myself of how framework objects work. It's good to have a general idea of what objects are available in the frameworks, but no one can remember all the specifics.

So get into the habit of looking up the documentation for any new objects and methods that you encounter. It'll make you learn the iOS frameworks much quicker!

Loading the file

Saving is all well and good but pretty useless by itself, so let's also implement the loading of the Checklists.plist file. It's very straightforward – you're basically going to do the same thing you just did but in reverse.

You've already added an empty init(coder) to **ChecklistItem.swift**. This is the method for unfreezing the objects from the file.

➤ Make the following changes to init(coder):

```
required init(coder aDecoder: NSCoder) {
  text = aDecoder.decodeObjectForKey("Text") as! String
  checked = aDecoder.decodeBoolForKey("Checked")
  super.init()
}
```

Inside init(coder) you do the opposite from encodeWithCoder(). You take objects from the NSCoder's decoder object and put their values inside your own properties. That's all it takes!

What you stored earlier under the "Text" key now goes back into the text instance variable. Likewise for checked and the boolean "Checked" value.

Initializers

Methods named "init" are special in Swift. They are only used when you're creating new objects to make those new objects ready for use.

Think of it as having bought new clothes. The clothes are in your possession (the memory for the object is allocated) but they're still in the bag. You need to go change and put the new clothes on (initialization) before you're ready to go out and party.

When you write the following to create a new object,

```
let item = ChecklistItem()
```

Swift first allocates a chunk of memory big enough to hold the new object and then calls ChecklistItem's init() method with no parameters.

Loading the Checklists.plist file will be done by an NSKeyedUnarchiver object (you'll add this code in a minute). That unarchiver does the following behind the scenes to create the ChecklistItem objects:

```
let item = ChecklistItem(coder: someDecoderObject)
```

This also allocates memory for the new ChecklistItem but it calls init(coder) instead of the regular init().

It is pretty common for objects to have more than one init method. Which one is used depends on the circumstances.

In the case of ChecklistItem, you use init() for creating ChecklistItem objects when the user presses the + button, and you use init(coder) to restore ChecklistItems that were saved to disk.

The implementations of these init methods, whether they're just called init() or init(coder) or something else, always follow the same series of steps. When you write your own init methods, you need to stick to those steps as well.

This is the standard way to write an init method:

```
init() {
  // Put values into your instance variables and constants.
  super.init()

  // Other initialization code, such as calling methods, goes here.
}
```

Note that unlike other methods, init does not have the func keyword.

(Sometimes you'll see it written as override init or required init. That is necessary when you're adding the init method to an object that is a subclass of some other object. Much more about that later.)

Inside the init method, you first need to make sure that all your instance variables and constants have a value. Recall that in Swift all variables must always have a value, except for optionals.

When you declare an instance variable or constant you can give it an initial value, like so:

```
var checked = false
```

It's also possible to write just the variable name and its type, but not give the variable a value yet:

```
var checked: Bool
```

In that case, you have to give this variable a value inside your init method:

```
init() {
  checked = false
  super.init()
}
```

You must use either one of these approaches; if you don't give the variable a value at all, Swift considers this an error. The only exception is optionals, they do not need to have a value (in which case they are nil).

Once you've given all your instance variables and constants values, you call super.init() to initialize this object's superclass. If you haven't done any object-oriented programming at all, you may not know what a *superclass* is. That's fine; we'll completely ignore this topic until the next tutorial.

Just remember that sometimes objects need to send messages to something called super and if you forget to do this, bad things are likely to happen.

After calling super.init(), you can do additional initialization, such as calling the object's own methods. You're not allowed to do that before the call to super.init() because Swift has no guarantee that your object's variables all have proper values until then.

You don't always need to provide an init method. If your init method doesn't need to do anything – if there are no instance variables to fill in – then you can leave it out completely and the compiler will provide one for you.

When you first made ChecklistItem, it didn't have an init() method either. But now that you've added init(coder) you also have to provide an init() that doesn't take any parameters.

Swift's rules for initializers can be a bit complicated, but fortunately the compiler will remind you when you forget to provide an init method.

The implementation of ChecklistItem is now complete. It can bring back to life objects that were serialized (frozen) into the plist file. But you still have to write the code that will actually load this plist. That happens in ChecklistViewController.

A table view controller, like many objects, has more than one init method. There is:

- init(coder), for view controllers that are automatically loaded from a storyboard

- init(nibName, bundle), for view controllers that you manually want to load from a nib (a nib is like a storyboard but only contains a single view controller)

- init(style), for table view controllers that you manually want to create without using a storyboard or nib

This view controller comes from a storyboard, so you'll put the plist loading code into its init(coder). Yup, that's actually the same method you've just implemented in ChecklistItem.

The UITableViewController object gets loaded and unfrozen from the storyboard file using the same NSCoder system that you used for your own files. If it's good enough for storyboards then it's certainly good enough for us!

➤ In **ChecklistViewController.swift**, replace init(coder) with:

```
required init(coder aDecoder: NSCoder) {
  items = [ChecklistItem]()
  super.init(coder: aDecoder)
  loadChecklistItems()
}
```

This follows the pattern for init methods:

1. First you make sure the instance variable items has a proper value (a new array).

2. Then you call super's version of init(). This time you call super.init(coder) to ensure the rest of the view controller is properly unfrozen from the storyboard.

3. Finally, you can call other methods. Here you call a new method to do the real work of loading the plist file.

Note: init(coder) also has method parameters with different external and internal labels. The label coder is part of the method name, but inside the method this parameter is called aDecoder.

When you call super.init, you use the label coder to refer to the parameter of super's init method, and the object from aDecoder as that parameter's value.

➤ Also add the loadChecklistItems() method:

```
func loadChecklistItems() {
  // 1
  let path = dataFilePath()
  // 2
  if NSFileManager.defaultManager().fileExistsAtPath(path) {
    // 3
    if let data = NSData(contentsOfFile: path) {
      let unarchiver = NSKeyedUnarchiver(forReadingWithData: data)
      items = unarchiver.decodeObjectForKey("ChecklistItems") as! [ChecklistItem]
      unarchiver.finishDecoding()
    }
  }
}
```

Let's go through this step-by-step:

1. First you put the results of [self dataFilePath] in a temporary constant named path. You use the pathname more than once in this method so having it available in a local instead of calling dataFilePath() several times over is a small optimization.

2. Then you check whether the file actually exists and decide what happens based on that. If there is no Checklists.plist then there are obviously no ChecklistItem objects to load. This is what happens when the app is started up for the very first time. In that case, you'll skip the rest of this method.

3. When the app does find a Checklists.plist file, you'll load the entire array and its contents from the file. This is essentially the reverse of saveChecklistItems().

   First you load the contents of the file into an NSData object. Because this may fail, you put it in an if let statement. Then you create an NSKeyedUnarchiver object (note: this is an *un*archiver) and ask it to decode that data into the items array. This populates the array with exact copies of the ChecklistItem objects that were frozen into this file.

> **Note:** Double-check that both methods loadChecklistItems() and saveChecklistItems() use the same key name "ChecklistItems" for encoding and decoding the array. If you make a typo here, then the app won't work as expected.
>
> Normally Xcode is very good at pointing out typos but it's not smart enough to realize that the key name in the load and save methods must be the same. That's up to you, the human.

➤ Run the app and make some changes to the to-do items. Press Stop to terminate the app. Start it again and notice that your changes are still there.

➤ Stop the app again. Go to the Finder window with the Documents folder and remove the Checklists.plist file. Run the app once more. You should now have an empty screen.

➤ Add an item and notice that the Checklists.plist file re-appears.

Awesome! You've written an app that not only lets you add and edit data, but that also persists the data between sessions. These techniques form the basis of many, many apps.

Being able to use a navigation controller, show modal edit screens, and pass data around through delegates are essential iOS development skills.

You can find the project files for the app up to this point under **06 - Saving and Loading** in the tutorial's Source Code folder.

Using FileMerge to compare files

You can compare your own work with my version of the app using the FileMerge tool. Open this tool from the Xcode menu bar, under **Xcode → Open Developer Tool → FileMerge**.

You give FileMerge two files or two folders to compare:

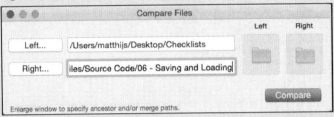

After working hard for a few seconds or so, FileMerge tells you what is different:

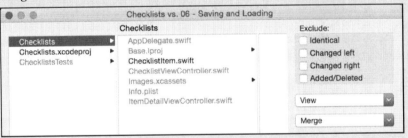

Double-click on a filename from the list to view the differences between the two files:

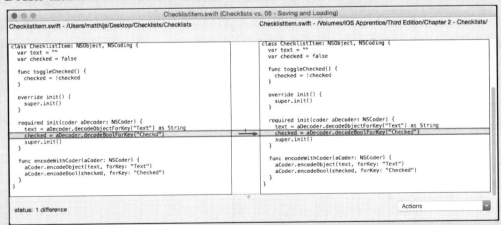

FileMerge is a wonderful tool for spotting the differences between two files or even entire folders. I use it all the time!

If something from the tutorials doesn't work as it should, then do a "diff" – that's what you're supposed to call it – between your own files and the ones from the Source Code folder to see if you can find any anomalies.

This is a good time to take a break, put your feet up, and daydream about all the cool apps you'll soon be writing.

It's also smart to go back and repeat those parts you're still a bit fuzzy about. Don't rush through these tutorials – there are no prizes for finishing first. Rather than going fast, take your time to truly understand what you've been doing.

As always, feel free to change the app and experiment. Breaking things is allowed – even encouraged – here at iOS Apprentice Academy!

Just to make sure you truly get everything you've done so far, next up you'll expand the app with new features that more or less repeat what you just did.

But I'll also throw in a few twists to keep it interesting…

Multiple checklists

The app is named Checklists for a reason: it allows you to keep more than one list of to-do items. So far the app has only supported a single list but now you'll give it the capability to handle multiple checklists.

The steps for this section are:

• Add a new screen that shows all the checklists.

• Create a screen that lets users add/edit checklists.

• Show the to-do items that belong to a particular checklist when you tap the name of that list.

• Save all the checklists to a file and load them in again.

Two new screens means two new view controllers:

1. AllListsViewController shows all the user's lists, and

2. ListDetailViewController allows adding a new list and editing the name and icon of an existing list.

You will first add the AllListsViewController. This becomes the new main screen of the app.

When you're done this is what it will look like:

The new main screen of the app

This screen is very similar to what you created before. It's a table view controller that shows a list of Checklist objects (not ChecklistItem objects).

From now on, I will refer to this screen as the "All Lists" screen and to the screen that shows the to-do items from a single checklist as the "Checklist" screen.

➤ Right-click the Checklists group in the project navigator and choose **New File**. Under **Source** choose the **Cocoa Touch Class** template.

➤ Name the new file **AllListsViewController**, subclass of **UITableViewController**. Make sure the other options are unchecked and the language is **Swift**.

The default template for this file needs some work before you can run the app. As a first step, you'll put some fake data in the table view just to get it up and running.

I always like to take as small a step as possible and then run the app to see if it's working. Once everything works, you can expand on what you have and put in the real data.

➤ In **AllListsViewController.swift**, remove the numberOfSectionsInTableView() method.

➤ Change the tableView(numberOfRowsInSection) method to:

```
override func tableView(tableView: UITableView, numberOfRowsInSection section: Int) -> Int {
  return 3
}
```

➤ Add the tableView(cellForRowAtIndexPath) method:

```
override func tableView(tableView: UITableView,
                  cellForRowAtIndexPath indexPath: NSIndexPath) -> UITableViewCell {

  let cellIdentifier = "Cell"
  var cell: UITableViewCell! = tableView.dequeueReusableCellWithIdentifier(cellIdentifier)
                                  as? UITableViewCell

  if cell == nil {
    cell = UITableViewCell(style: .Default, reuseIdentifier: cellIdentifier)
  }

  cell.textLabel!.text = "List \(indexPath.row)"
  return cell
}
```

In ChecklistViewController the table view used prototype cells that you designed in Interface Builder. Just for the fun of it, in AllListsViewController you are taking a different approach and create the cells in code instead.

Later on I'll explain in more detail how this works, but for now recognize that you're using dequeueReusableCellWithIdentifier() as before. If there is no cell to reuse, you construct a new one with UITableViewCell(style, reuseIdentifier).

You also put some text into the cells, just so there is something to see.

➤ Remove all the commented-out cruft from **AllListsViewController.swift**. Xcode puts it there to be helpful, but it also makes a mess of things.

The final step is to add this new view controller to the storyboard.

➤ Open the storyboard and drag a new **Table View Controller** onto the canvas. Put it somewhere near the first navigation controller.

➤ **Ctrl-drag** from the very first navigation controller to this new table view controller:

Ctrl-drag from the navigation controller to the new table view controller

From the popup menu choose **Relationship Segue - root view controller**:

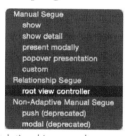

Relationships are also segues

This will break the connection that existed between the navigation controller and the Checklist View Controller so that "Checklists" is no longer the app's main screen.

➤ Select the new table view controller and set its **Class** in the **Identity inspector** to **AllListsViewController**.

➤ Double-click the view controller's navigation bar and change its title to **Checklists**.

This makes Xcode rename the view controller in the outline pane from All Lists View Controller to just Checklists, which is a bit confusing because there's a Checklists view controller already. You'll fix that in a minute.

You may want to reorganize your storyboard at this point to make everything look neat again. The new table view controller goes in between the other scenes.

As I mentioned, you're not going to use prototype cells for this table view. It would be perfectly fine if you did, and as an exercise you could rewrite the code to use prototype cells later, but I want to show you another way of making table view cells.

➤ Delete the empty prototype cell from the All Lists View Controller. (Simply select the Table View Cell and press **delete** on your keyboard.)

> **Ctrl-drag** from the yellow circle icon at the top of All Lists View Controller into the Checklist View Controller and create a **show** segue.

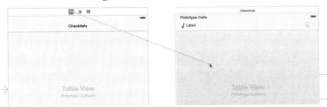

Ctrl-dragging from the All Lists scene to the Checklist scene

This adds a push transition from the All Lists screen to the Checklist screen. It also puts the navigation bar back on the Checklist scene.

> Double-click the navigation bar to change its title to **(Name of the Checklist)**. This is just placeholder text. It helps tell the view controllers apart in the outline pane.

> **Note:** The outline pane doesn't show the name of the view controller object but the text from the navigation item. Very confusing, Xcode!
>
> When I refer to the All Lists View Controller, it's the plural "Checklists Scene" in the outline pane.
>
> The Checklist View Controller that shows a single list of to-do items is now found under "(Name of the Checklist) Scene".

Note that the new segue isn't attached to any button or table view cell.

There is nothing on the All Lists screen that you can tap or otherwise interact with in order to trigger this segue. That means you have to perform it programmatically.

> Click on the new segue to select it, go to the **Attributes inspector** and give it the identifier **ShowChecklist**.

The **Segue** style should be **Show (e.g. Push)** because you're pushing the Checklist View Controller onto the navigation stack when performing this segue.

> In **AllListsViewController.swift**, add the `tableView(didSelectRowAtIndexPath)` method:

```
override func tableView(tableView: UITableView,
                didSelectRowAtIndexPath indexPath: NSIndexPath) {
  performSegueWithIdentifier("ShowChecklist", sender: nil)
}
```

Recall that this table view delegate method is invoked when you tap a row.

Previously, a tap on a row would automatically perform the segue because you hooked up the segue to the prototype cell. However, the table view for this screen isn't using prototype cells and therefore you have to perform the segue manually.

That's simple enough: just call `performSegueWithIdentifier()` with the name of the segue and things will start moving.

> Run the app. It now looks like this:

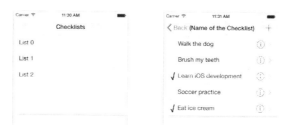

The first version of the All Lists screen (left). Tapping a row opens the Checklist screen (right).

Tap a row and the familiar `ChecklistViewController` slides into the screen.

You can tap the "Back" button in the top-left to go back to the main list. Now you're truly using the power of the navigation controller!

> **Note:** If the app crashes for you at this point, then make sure the
> `tableView(cellForRowAtIndexPath)` method in **AllListsViewController.swift** says this:
>
> ```
> var cell: UITableViewCell! = tableView.dequeueReusableCellWithIdentifier(cellIdentifier)
> ```
>
> Instead of this:
>
> ```
> var cell: UITableViewCell! = tableView.dequeueReusableCellWithIdentifier(
>                                        cellIdentifier, forIndexPath: indexPath)
> ```
>
> Xcode's autocomplete makes it really easy to mistakenly select the second one, but that is not the method you want to use here!

Putting lists into the All Lists screen

You're going to duplicate most of the functionality from the Checklist View Controller for this new All Lists screen.

There will be a + button at the top that lets users add new checklists, they can do swipe-to-delete, and they can tap the disclosure button to edit the name of the checklist.

Of course, you'll also save the array of `Checklist` objects to the Checklists.plist file.

Because you've already seen how this works, we'll go through the steps a bit quicker this time. You begin by creating a data model object that represents a checklist.

➤ Add a new file to the project based on the **Cocoa Touch Class** template. Name it **Checklist** and make it a subclass of **NSObject**.

This adds the file Checklist.swift to the project.

Just like `ChecklistItem`, you're building `Checklist` on top of `NSObject`. This is a requirement for using the `NSCoder` system to load and save these objects.

➤ Give **Checklist.swift** a `name` property:

```
import UIKit

class Checklist: NSObject {
  var name = ""
}
```

Next, you'll give `AllListsViewController` an array that will store these new `Checklist` objects.

➤ Add a new instance variable to **AllListsViewController.swift**:

```
var lists: [Checklist]
```

This is an array that will hold the `Checklist` objects.

> **Note:** You can also write the above as follows:
>
> ```
> var lists: Array<Checklist>
> ```
>
> The version with the square brackets is what's known as *syntactic sugar* for the complete notation, which is `Array<type-of-the-objects-to-put-in-the-array>`.
>
> You will see both forms used in Swift programs and they do exactly the same thing. Because arrays are used a lot, the designers of Swift included the handy shorthand with the square brackets.

As a first step you will fill this new array with test data, which you'll do from the `init(coder)` method. Remember that this method is automatically invoked by UIKit as it loads the view controller from the storyboard.

➤ Still in **AllListsViewController.swift**, add the `init(coder)` method:

```
required init(coder aDecoder: NSCoder) {
    // 1
    lists = [Checklist]()
    // 2
    super.init(coder: aDecoder)
    // 3
    var list = Checklist()
    list.name = "Birthdays"
    lists.append(list)
    // 4
    list = Checklist()
    list.name = "Groceries"
    lists.append(list)

    list = Checklist()
    list.name = "Cool Apps"
    lists.append(list)

    list = Checklist()
    list.name = "To Do"
    lists.append(list)
}
```

You've seen something very much like it a while ago when you added the fake test data to `ChecklistViewController`. Here is what it does step-by-step:

1. Give the `lists` variable a value. You can also write this as `lists = Array<Checklist>()` – that does the exact same thing. I just like the square brackets better.

2. Call `super`'s version of `init(coder)`. Without this, the view controller won't be properly loaded from the storyboard. But don't worry too much about forgetting to call `super`; if you don't, Xcode gives an error message.

3. Create a new `Checklist` object, give it a name, and add it to the array.

4. Here you create three more `Checklist` objects. Because you declared the local variable `list` as `var` instead of `let`, you can re-use it.

Notice how you're performing the same two steps for every new `Checklist` object you're creating:

```
list = Checklist()
list.name = "Name of the checklist"
```

It seems likely that every `Checklist` you'll ever make will also have a name. You can make this a requirement by writing your own `init` method that takes the name as a parameter. Then you can simply write:

```
list = Checklist(name: "Name of the checklist")
```

➤ Go to **Checklist.swift** and add the new `init` method:

```
init(name: String) {
  self.name = name
  super.init()
}
```

This initializer takes one parameter, `name`, and places it into the instance variable, which is also called `name`.

Because both the parameter and the instance variable are called `name`, you use `self.name` to refer to the instance variable.

If you tried to do this,

```
init(name: String) {
  name = name
  super.init()
}
```

then Swift wouldn't understand that the first `name` referred to the instance variable.

To disambiguate, you use `self`. Recall that `self` refers to the object that you're in, so `self.name` means the `name` variable of the current `Checklist` object.

➤ Go back to **AllListsViewController.swift** and change `init(coder)` to use this new initializer:

```
required init(coder aDecoder: NSCoder) {
  lists = [Checklist]()

  super.init(coder: aDecoder)

  var list = Checklist(name: "Birthdays")
  lists.append(list)

  list = Checklist(name: "Groceries")
  lists.append(list)

  list = Checklist(name: "Cool Apps")
  lists.append(list)

  list = Checklist(name: "To Do")
  lists.append(list)
}
```

That's a bit shorter and it guarantees that new `Checklist` objects will now always have their `name` property filled in.

Note that you don't write:

```
var list = Checklist.init(name: "Birthdays")
```

Even though the method is named `init`, it's not a regular method. Initializers are only used to construct new objects and you always write that as:

```
var object = ObjectName(parameter1: value1, parameter2: value2, . . .)
```

Depending on the parameters that you specified, Swift will locate the corresponding `init` method and call that.

Clear? Great! Let's continue building the All Lists screen.

➤ Change the `tableView(numberOfRowsInSection)` method to return the number of objects in the new array:

```
override func tableView(tableView: UITableView, numberOfRowsInSection section: Int) -> Int {
  return lists.count
}
```

➤ Finally, change `tableView(cellForRowAtIndexPath)` to create the cells for the rows:

```
override func tableView(tableView: UITableView,
                     cellForRowAtIndexPath indexPath: NSIndexPath) -> UITableViewCell {
  let cellIdentifier = "Cell"
  var cell: UITableViewCell! = tableView.dequeueReusableCellWithIdentifier(cellIdentifier)
                                 as? UITableViewCell

  if cell == nil {
    cell = UITableViewCell(style: .Default, reuseIdentifier: cellIdentifier)
  }

  let checklist = lists[indexPath.row]
  cell.textLabel!.text = checklist.name
  cell.accessoryType = .DetailDisclosureButton

  return cell
}
```

➤ Run the app. It looks like this:

The table view shows Checklist objects

It has a table view with cells representing `Checklist` objects. The rest of the screen doesn't do much yet, but it's a start.

The many ways to make table view cells

This `tableView(cellForRowAtIndexPath)` method does a lot more than the one from `ChecklistViewController`. There you just did the following to obtain a new table view cell:

```
let cell = tableView.dequeueReusableCellWithIdentifier("ChecklistItem")
                      as! UITableViewCell
```

But here you have a whole chunk of code to accomplish the same:

```
let cellIdentifier = "Cell"
var cell: UITableViewCell! = tableView.dequeueReusableCellWithIdentifier(cellIdentifier)
                                as? UITableViewCell

if cell == nil {
  cell = UITableViewCell(style: .Default, reuseIdentifier: cellIdentifier)
}
```

The call to `dequeueReusableCellWithIdentifier()` is still there, except that previously the storyboard had a prototype cell with that identifier and now it doesn't.

If the table view cannot find a cell to re-use (and it won't until it has enough cells to fill the entire visible area), this method will return `nil` and you have to create your own cell by hand.

There are four ways that you can make table view cells:

1. Using prototype cells. This is the simplest and quickest way. You did this in `ChecklistViewController`.

2. Using static cells. You did this for the Add/Edit Item screen. Static cells are limited to screens where you know in advance which cells you'll have. The big advantage with static cells is that you don't need to provide any of the data source methods (`cellForRowAtIndexPath` and so on).

3. Using a *nib* file. A nib (also known as a XIB) is like a mini storyboard that only contains a single customized `UITableViewCell` object. This is very similar to using prototype cells, except that you can do it outside of a storyboard.

4. By hand, what you did above. This is how you were supposed to do it in the bad old days before iOS 5. Chances are you'll run across code examples that do it this way, especially from older articles and books. It's a bit more work but also offers you the most flexibility.

When you create a cell by hand you specify a certain **cell style**, which gives you a cell with a preconfigured layout that already has labels and an image view.

For the All Lists View Controller you're using the "Default" style. Later in this tutorial you'll switch it to "Subtitle", which gives the cell a second, smaller label below the main label.

Using standard cell styles means you don't have to design your own cell layout. For many apps these standard layouts are sufficient so that saves you some work.

Prototype cells and static cells can also use these standard cell styles. The default style for a prototype or static cell is "Custom", which requires you to use your own labels, but you can change that to one of the built-in styles with Interface Builder.

And finally, a warning: Sometimes I see code that creates a new cell for every row rather than trying to reuse cells. Don't do that! Always ask the table view first whether it has a cell available that can be recycled, using `dequeueReusableCellWithIdentifier()`.

Creating a new cell for each row will cause your app to slow down, as object creation is slower than simply re-using an existing object. Creating all these new objects also takes up more memory, which is a precious commodity on mobile devices. For the best performance, reuse those cells!

Viewing the checklists

The data model consists of the `lists` array from `AllListsViewController` and the `items` array from `ChecklistViewController`, and the `Checklist` and `ChecklistItem` objects that they respectively contain.

You may have noticed that when you tap the name of a checklist, the Checklist screen slides into view but it currently always shows the same to-do items, regardless of which row you tap on.

Each checklist should really have its own list of to-do items. You'll work on that later in this tutorial, as this requires a significant change to the data model.

As a start, let's set the title of the screen to reflect the chosen checklist.

➤ Add a new instance variable to **ChecklistViewController.swift**:

```
var checklist: Checklist!
```

I'll explain why the exclamation mark is necessary in a moment.

➤ Change the `viewDidLoad()` method in **ChecklistViewController.swift** to:

```
override func viewDidLoad() {
  super.viewDidLoad()
  tableView.rowHeight = 44
  title = checklist.name
}
```

This changes the title of the screen, which is shown in the navigation bar, to the name of the `Checklist` object.

You give this `Checklist` object to the `ChecklistViewController` when the segue is performed.

➤ In **AllListsViewController.swift**, update `tableView(didSelectRowAtIndexPath)` to the following:

```
override func tableView(tableView: UITableView,
                  didSelectRowAtIndexPath indexPath: NSIndexPath) {
  let checklist = lists[indexPath.row]
  performSegueWithIdentifier("ShowChecklist", sender: checklist)
}
```

As before, you use `performSegueWithIdentifier()` to start the segue. This method has a `sender` parameter that you previously set to `nil`. Now you'll use it to send along the `Checklist` object from the row that the user tapped on.

You can put anything you want into `sender`. If the segue is performed by the storyboard (rather than manually like you do here) then `sender` will refer to the control that triggered it, for example the `UIBarButtonItem` object for the Add button or the `UITableViewCell` for a row in the table.

But because you start this particular segue by hand, you can put into `sender` whatever is most convenient.

Putting the Checklist object into the sender parameter doesn't give this object to the ChecklistViewController yet. That happens in prepareForSegue(sender), which you still need to write.

➤ Add the prepareForSegue(sender) method to **AllListsViewController.swift**:

```
override func prepareForSegue(segue: UIStoryboardSegue, sender: AnyObject?) {
  if segue.identifier == "ShowChecklist" {
    let controller = segue.destinationViewController as! ChecklistViewController
    controller.checklist = sender as! Checklist
  }
}
```

You've seen this method before. prepareForSegue(sender) is called by the storyboard right before the segue happens. Here you get a chance to set the properties of the new view controller before it will become visible.

> **Note:** The segue's destinationViewController is the ChecklistViewController, not a UINavigationController. That is different from before.
>
> The segue to the Add/Edit Item screen was to a modally presented view controller that was embedded inside a navigation controller.
>
> This time the push segue is directly to the Checklist view controller.
>
> Look in the storyboard and you'll see there is no navigation controller between the All Lists screen and the Checklist screen. The segue goes directly from one to the other.

Inside prepareForSegue(sender), you need to give the ChecklistViewController the Checklist object from the row that the user tapped. That's why you put that object in the sender parameter earlier.

(You could have temporarily stored the Checklist object in an instance variable instead but passing it along in the sender parameter is much easier.)

All of this happens a short time after ChecklistViewController is instantiated but just before ChecklistViewController's view is loaded. That means its viewDidLoad() method (the one that you just added) is called *after* prepareForSegue().

At this point, the view controller's checklist property is filled in with the Checklist object from sender, and viewDidLoad() can set the title of the screen accordingly.

This sequence of events (see also the figure on the next page) is why the checklist property is declared as Checklist! with an exclamation point. That allows its value to be temporarily nil until viewDidLoad() happens.

nil is normally not an allowed value for variables in Swift but by using the ! you override that.

Does this sound an awful lot like optionals? The exclamation point turns checklist into a special kind of optional. It's very similar to optionals with a question mark, but you don't have to write if let to unwrap it.

Such *implicitly unwrapped* optionals should be used sparingly and with care, as they do not have any of the anti-crash protection that normal optionals do.

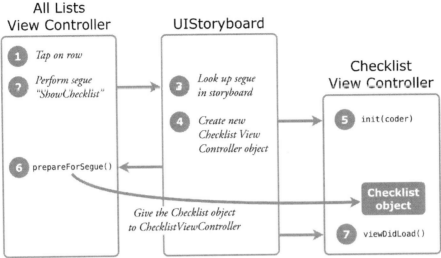

The steps involved in performing a segue▸ Run the app and notice that when you tap the row for a checklist, the next screen properly takes over the title.

The name of the chosen checklist now appears in the navigation bar

Note that giving the Checklist object to the ChecklistViewController does not make a copy of it.

You only pass the view controller a *reference* to that object – any changes the user makes to that Checklist object are also seen by AllListsViewController.

Both view controllers have access to the exact same Checklist object. You'll use that to your advantage later in order to add new ChecklistItems to the Checklist.

Type Casts

In prepareForSegue you do this:

```
override func prepareForSegue(segue: UIStoryboardSegue, sender: AnyObject?) {
    . . .
    controller.checklist = sender as! Checklist
    . . .
}
```

What is that "as! Checklist" thing?

If you've been paying attention – of course you have! – then you've seen this "as something" used quite a few times now. This is known as a *type cast*.

A type cast tells Swift to interpret a value as having a different data type.

(It's the opposite of what happens to certain actors in the movies. For them typecasting results in always playing the same character; in Swift, a type cast actually changes the character of an object.)

Here, sender has type AnyObject?, meaning that it can be any sort of object: a UIBarButtonItem, a UITableViewCell, or in this case a Checklist. Thanks to the question mark it can even be nil.

But the checklist property always expects a proper Checklist object – it wouldn't know what to do with a UITableViewCell... Hence, Swift demands that you only put Checklist objects into the checklist property.

By writing "sender as! Checklist", you tell Swift that it can safely treat sender as a Checklist object.

Another example of a typecast is:

```
let controller = segue.destinationViewController as! ChecklistViewController
```

The segue's destinationViewController property refers to the view controller on the receiving end of the segue. But obviously the engineers at Apple could not predict beforehand that we would call it ChecklistViewController.

So you have to cast it from its generic type (AnyObject) to the specific type used in this app (ChecklistViewController) before you can access any of its properties.

One final example, from loadChecklistItems():

```
items = unarchiver.decodeObjectForKey("ChecklistItems") as! [ChecklistItem]
```

The NSKeyedUnarchiver object decodes the object frozen under the key "ChecklistItems" into an array, but you still need to tell Swift that this really is an array containing ChecklistItem objects.

Without this type cast, Swift considers it an array of AnyObject items, which is incompatible with the data type of the items array.

Note that there is also as? with a question mark. This is for casting optionals.

You've used as? in AllListsViewController's cellForRowAtIndexPath, because dequeueReusableCellWithIdentifier() can return nil if there is no cell object to reuse. That code was:

```
var cell: UITableViewCell! = tableView.dequeueReusableCellWithIdentifier(cellIdentifier)
                        as? UITableViewCell
```

In the case of prototype cells you know this method will never return nil, so in ChecklistViewController you were able to use the non-optional cast "as! UITableViewCell".

But the All Lists screen doesn't have prototype cells. When you're making the cells by hand, nil is an expected response. You need to cast with "as? UITableViewCell", allowing the cell variable to become nil.

Don't worry if this goes over your head right now. You'll see plenty more examples of type casting in action.

The main reason you need all these type casts is interoperability with the Objective-C based frameworks. Swift is less forgiving about types than Objective-C and requires you to be much more explicit (about types; it's not encouraging you to swear more).

Adding and editing checklists

Let's quickly add the Add Checklist / Edit Checklist screen. This is going to be yet another `UITableViewController`, with static cells, and you'll present it modally from the `AllListsViewController`.

If the previous sentence made perfect sense to you, then you're getting the hang of this!

➤ Add a new file to the project, a `UITableViewController` subclass named **ListDetailViewController**.

➤ Replace the contents of **ListDetailViewController.swift** with:

```
import UIKit

protocol ListDetailViewControllerDelegate: class {
  func listDetailViewControllerDidCancel(controller: ListDetailViewController)

  func listDetailViewController(controller: ListDetailViewController,
                        didFinishAddingChecklist checklist: Checklist)

  func listDetailViewController(controller: ListDetailViewController,
                        didFinishEditingChecklist checklist: Checklist)
}

class ListDetailViewController: UITableViewController, UITextFieldDelegate {
  @IBOutlet weak var textField: UITextField!
  @IBOutlet weak var doneBarButton: UIBarButtonItem!

  weak var delegate: ListDetailViewControllerDelegate?

  var checklistToEdit: Checklist?
}
```

I simply took the contents of **ItemDetailViewController.swift** and changed the names. Also, instead of a property for a `ChecklistItem` you're now dealing with a `Checklist`.

➤ Add the `viewDidLoad()` method:

```
override func viewDidLoad() {
  super.viewDidLoad()
  tableView.rowHeight = 44

  if let checklist = checklistToEdit {
    title = "Edit Checklist"
    textField.text = checklist.name
    doneBarButton.enabled = true
  }
}
```

This changes the title of the screen if the user is editing an existing checklist, and it puts the checklist's name into the text field already.

➤ Also add the `viewWillAppear()` method to pop up the keyboard:

```
override func viewWillAppear(animated: Bool) {
  super.viewWillAppear(animated)
  textField.becomeFirstResponder()
}
```

➤ Add the action methods for the Cancel and Done buttons:

```
@IBAction func cancel() {
  delegate?.listDetailViewControllerDidCancel(self)
}

@IBAction func done() {
  if let checklist = checklistToEdit {
    checklist.name = textField.text
    delegate?.listDetailViewController(self, didFinishEditingChecklist: checklist)
  } else {
    let checklist = Checklist(name: textField.text)
    delegate?.listDetailViewController(self, didFinishAddingChecklist: checklist)
  }
}
```

This should look familiar as well. It's essentially the same as what the Add/Edit Item screen does.

To create the new Checklist object in done(), you use its init(name) method and pass the contents of textField.text into the name parameter.

You cannot write this the way you did for ChecklistItems:

```
let checklist = Checklist()
checklist.name = textField.text
```

Because Checklist does not have an init() method that takes no parameters, writing Checklist() results in a compiler error. It only has an init(name) method, and you must always use that initializer to create new Checklist objects.

➤ Also make sure the user cannot select the table cell with the text field:

```
override func tableView(tableView: UITableView,
                  willSelectRowAtIndexPath indexPath: NSIndexPath) -> NSIndexPath? {
  return nil
}
```

➤ And finally, add the text field delegate method that enables or disables the Done button depending on whether the text field is empty or not.

```
func textField(textField: UITextField, shouldChangeCharactersInRange range: NSRange,
            replacementString string: String) -> Bool {
  let oldText: NSString = textField.text
  let newText: NSString = oldText.stringByReplacingCharactersInRange(range,
                                                      withString: string)
  doneBarButton.enabled = (newText.length > 0)
  return true
}
```

Again, this is what you did in ItemDetailViewController but now for Checklist objects instead of ChecklistItem objects.

Let's make the user interface for this new view controller in Interface Builder.

➤ Open the storyboard. Drag a new **Navigation Controller** from the Object Library into the canvas and move it below the other view controllers.

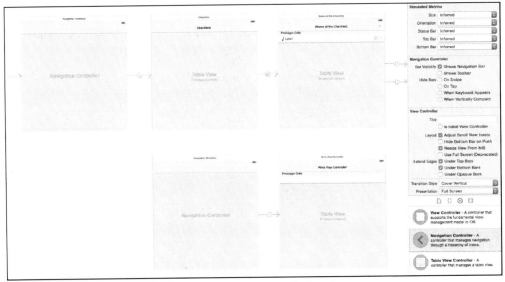

Dragging a new navigation controller into the canvas

Interface Builder already assumes that you want to put a table view controller inside the navigation controller, so that saves you some work.

➤ Select the new Table View Controller (the one named "Root View Controller") and go to the **Identity inspector**. Change its class to **ListDetailViewController**.

➤ Change the navigation bar title from "Root View Controller" to **Add Checklist**.

➤ Add **Cancel** and **Done** bar button items and hook them up to the action methods in the view controller. Also connect the Done button to the **doneBarButton** outlet and uncheck its **Enabled** option.

➤ Change the table view to **Static Cells**, style **Grouped**. You only need one cell, so remove the bottom two.

➤ Drop a new **Text Field** into the cell. Here are the configuration options:

- Border Style: none
- Font size: 17
- Placeholder text: **Name of the List**
- Adjust to Fit: disabled
- Capitalization: Sentences
- Return Key: Done
- Auto-enable Return key: check

➤ Ctrl-drag from the view controller to the Text Field and connect it to the **textField** outlet.

➤ Then Ctrl-drag the other way around, from the Text Field back to the view controller, and choose **delegate** under **Outlets**. Now the view controller is the delegate for the text field.

➤ Connect the text field's **Did End on Exit** event to the **done** action on the view controller.

This completes the steps for converting this view controller to the Add / Edit Checklist screen:

The finished design of the ListDetailViewController

➤ Go to the **All Lists View Controller** (the one titled "Checklists") and drag a **Bar Button Item** into its navigation bar. Change it into an **Add** button.

➤ **Ctrl-drag** from this new bar button to the navigation controller below to add a new **present modally** segue.

➤ Click on the new segue and name it **AddChecklist**.

Your storyboard should now look like this:

The full storyboard: 3 navigation controllers, 4 table view controllers

Almost there. You still have to make the AllListsViewController the delegate for the ListDetailViewController and then you're done. Again, it's very similar to what you did before.

➤ Declare the All Lists view controller to conform to the delegate protocol by adding ListDetailViewControllerDelegate to its class line.

You do this in **AllListsViewController.swift**:

```
class AllListsViewController: UITableViewController, ListDetailViewControllerDelegate {
```

➤ Also in **AllListsViewController.swift**, first extend prepareForSegue to:

```
override func prepareForSegue(segue: UIStoryboardSegue, sender: AnyObject?) {
  if segue.identifier == "ShowChecklist" {
    . . .
  } else if segue.identifier == "AddChecklist" {
    let navigationController = segue.destinationViewController as! UINavigationController
    let controller = navigationController.topViewController as! ListDetailViewController
    controller.delegate = self
    controller.checklistToEdit = nil
  }
}
```

The first if doesn't change. You've added a second if for the new "AddChecklist" segue that you just defined in the storyboard.

As before, you look for the view controller inside the navigation controller (which is the ListDetailViewController) and set its delegate property to self.

> At the bottom of the **AllListsViewController.swift**, implement the following delegate methods.

```
func listDetailViewControllerDidCancel(controller: ListDetailViewController) {
  dismissViewControllerAnimated(true, completion: nil)
}

func listDetailViewController(controller: ListDetailViewController,
                    didFinishAddingChecklist checklist: Checklist) {
  let newRowIndex = lists.count
  lists.append(checklist)

  let indexPath = NSIndexPath(forRow: newRowIndex, inSection: 0)
  let indexPaths = [indexPath]
  tableView.insertRowsAtIndexPaths(indexPaths, withRowAnimation: .Automatic)

  dismissViewControllerAnimated(true, completion: nil)
}

func listDetailViewController(controller: ListDetailViewController,
                    didFinishEditingChecklist checklist: Checklist) {
  if let index = find(lists, checklist) {
    let indexPath = NSIndexPath(forRow: index, inSection: 0)
    if let cell = tableView.cellForRowAtIndexPath(indexPath) {
      cell.textLabel!.text = checklist.name
    }
  }
  dismissViewControllerAnimated(true, completion: nil)
}
```

These methods are called when the user presses Cancel or Done inside the new Add/Edit Checklist screen.

None of this code should surprise you. It's exactly what you did before but now for the ListDetailViewController and Checklist objects.

> Also add the table view data source method that allows the user to delete checklists:

```
override func tableView(tableView: UITableView,
                  commitEditingStyle editingStyle: UITableViewCellEditingStyle,
                  forRowAtIndexPath indexPath: NSIndexPath) {
  lists.removeAtIndex(indexPath.row)

  let indexPaths = [indexPath]
  tableView.deleteRowsAtIndexPaths(indexPaths, withRowAnimation: .Automatic)
```

```
}
```

➤ Run the app. Now you can add new checklists and delete them again:

Adding new lists

> **Note:** If the app crashes, then go back and make sure you made all the connections properly in Interface Builder. It's really easy to miss just one tiny thing, but even the tiniest of mistakes can bring the app down in flames…

You can't edit the names of existing lists yet. That requires one last addition to the code.

To bring up the Edit Checklist screen, the user taps the blue accessory button. In the ChecklistViewController that triggered a segue. You could use a segue here too, but I want to show you another way.

This time you're not going to use a segue at all, but load the new view controller by hand from the storyboard. Just because you can.

➤ Add the tableView(accessoryButtonTappedForRowWithIndexPath) method to **AllListsViewController.swift**.

This method comes from the table view delegate protocol and the name is hopefully obvious enough to guess what it does.

```
override func tableView(tableView: UITableView,
                    accessoryButtonTappedForRowWithIndexPath indexPath: NSIndexPath) {
  let navigationController = storyboard!.instantiateViewControllerWithIdentifier(
                          "ListNavigationController") as! UINavigationController

  let controller = navigationController.topViewController as! ListDetailViewController
  controller.delegate = self

  let checklist = lists[indexPath.row]
  controller.checklistToEdit = checklist

  presentViewController(navigationController, animated: true, completion: nil)
}
```

Inside this method you create the view controller object for the Add/Edit Checklist screen and show it ("present" it) on the screen. This is roughly equivalent to what a segue would do behind the scenes. The view controller is embedded in a storyboard and you have to ask the storyboard object to load it.

Where did you get that storyboard object? As it happens, each view controller has a `storyboard` property that refers to the storyboard the view controller was loaded from. You can use that property to do all kinds of things with the storyboard, such as instantiating other view controllers.

The `storyboard` property is optional because view controllers are not always loaded from a storyboard. But this one is, which is why you can use `!` to *force unwrap* the optional. It's like using if `let`, but because you can safely assume `storyboard` will not be `nil` in this app you don't have to unwrap it inside an if-statement.

The call to `instantiateViewControllerWithIdentifier()` takes an identifier string, `"ListNavigationController"`. That is how you ask the storyboard to create the new view controller. In your case, this will be the navigation controller that contains the `ListDetailViewController`.

You could instantiate the `ListDetailViewController` directly, but it was designed to work inside the navigation controller so that wouldn't make much sense – it would no longer have a title bar or Cancel and Done buttons.

You still have to set this identifier on the navigation controller; otherwise the storyboard cannot find it.

➤ Open the storyboard and select the navigation controller that points to List Detail View Controller. Go to the **Identity inspector** and type **ListNavigationController** into the field **Storyboard ID**:

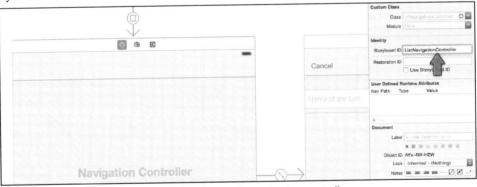

Setting an identifier on the navigation controller

➤ That should do the trick. Run the app and tap some detail disclosure buttons.

(If the app crashes, make sure the storyboard is saved before you press Run.)

Exercise: Set the **ListNavigationController** identifier on the List Detail View Controller instead and see what happens when you run the app. Can you explain this? If you can, kudos! ∎

You can find the project files for the app up to this point under **07 - Lists** in the tutorial's Source Code folder.

Are you still with me?

If at this point your eyes are glazing over and you feel like giving up: don't.

Learning new things is hard and programming doubly so. Set the tutorial aside, sleep on it, and come back in a few days.

Chances are that in the mean time you'll have an a-ha! moment where the thing that didn't make any sense suddenly becomes clear as day.

If you have specific questions, join us on the forums. I usually check in a few times a day to help people out and so do many members of our community. Don't be embarrassed to ask for help! http://raywenderlich.com/forums/

Putting to-do items into the checklists

Everything you've done in the previous section is all well and good, but checklists don't actually contain any to-do items yet.

So far, the list of to-do items and the actual checklists have been separate from each other.

Let's change the data model to look like this:

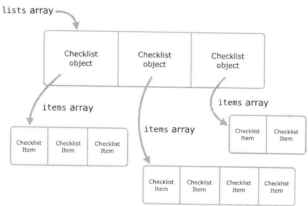

Each Checklist object has an array of ChecklistItem objects

There will still be a `lists` array that contains the `Checklist` objects, but each of these `Checklists` will have its own array of `ChecklistItem` objects.

➤ Add a new property to **Checklist.swift**:

```
class Checklist: NSObject {
  var name = ""
  var items = [ChecklistItem]()

  . . .
```

This creates a new, empty, array that can hold `ChecklistItem` objects and assigns it to the `items` instance variable.

This is slightly different from what you did before. There you declared the array and initialized it in two different steps:

```
var items: [ChecklistItem]

required init(coder aDecoder: NSCoder) {
  items = [ChecklistItem]()
  . . .
}
```

But it's just as easy to do it in a single line, which keeps everything nice and compact.

If you're a stickler for completeness, you can also write it as follows:

```
var items: [ChecklistItem] = [ChecklistItem]()
```

I don't like this way of declaring variables because it violates the DRY principle – Don't Repeat Yourself. Fortunately, thanks to Swift's type inference, you can save yourself some keystrokes.

Regardless of the way you choose to write it, the Checklist object now contains the array of ChecklistItem objects. Initially, that array is empty.

Earlier you fixed prepareForSegue(sender) in **AllListsViewController.swift** so that tapping a row makes the app segue into the ChecklistViewController, passing along the Checklist object that belongs to that row.

Currently ChecklistViewController still gets the ChecklistItem objects from its own private items array. You will change that so it reads from the items array inside the Checklist object instead.

➤ Remove the items instance variable from **ChecklistViewController.swift**.

➤ Then make the following changes in this source file:

```
override func tableView(tableView: UITableView, numberOfRowsInSection section: Int) -> Int {
  return checklist.items.count
}
```

```
override func tableView(tableView: UITableView,
                cellForRowAtIndexPath indexPath: NSIndexPath) -> UITableViewCell {

  . . .
  let item = checklist.items[indexPath.row]
  . . .
}
```

```
override func tableView(tableView: UITableView,
                didSelectRowAtIndexPath indexPath: NSIndexPath) {

  . . .
  let item = checklist.items[indexPath.row]
  . . .
}
```

```
override func tableView(tableView: UITableView,
                commitEditingStyle editingStyle: UITableViewCellEditingStyle,
                forRowAtIndexPath indexPath: NSIndexPath) {
  checklist.items.removeAtIndex(indexPath.row)
  . . .
}
```

```
func itemDetailViewController(controller: ItemDetailViewController,
                          didFinishAddingItem item: ChecklistItem) {
  let newRowIndex = checklist.items.count
  checklist.items.append(item)
  . . .
}
```

```
func itemDetailViewController(controller: ItemDetailViewController,
                          didFinishEditingItem item: ChecklistItem) {
  if let index = find(checklist.items, item) {
    . . .
}
```

```
override func prepareForSegue(segue: UIStoryboardSegue, sender: AnyObject?) {
    . . .
    controller.itemToEdit = checklist.items[indexPath.row]
    . . .
}
```

Anywhere it said items you have changed it to say checklist.items instead.

➤ Delete the following methods from **ChecklistViewController.swift**:

- func documentsDirectory()
- func dataFilePath()
- func saveChecklistItems()
- func loadChecklistItems()
- init(coder)

You recently added these methods to load and save the checklist items from a file. That is no longer the responsibility of this view controller, though. It is better for the app's design if you make the Checklist object do that. Loading and saving data model objects really belongs in the data model itself, rather than in a controller.

But before you get to that, let's first test whether these changes were successful. Xcode is complaining about 5 or so errors because you still call the method saveChecklistItems() at several places in the code. You should remove those lines as you will soon be saving the items in a different place.

➤ Remove the lines that call saveChecklistItems().

➤ Press ⌘+B to make sure the app builds without errors.

Fake it 'til you make it

Let's add some fake data into the various Checklist objects so that you can test whether this new design actually works. In AllListsViewController's init(coder) method you already put fake Checklist objects into the lists array. It's time to add something new to this method.

➤ Add the following to the bottom of **AllListsViewController.swift**'s `init(coder)`:

```
for list in lists {
  let item = ChecklistItem()
  item.text = "Item for \(list.name)"
  list.items.append(item)
}
```

This introduces something you haven't seen before in these tutorials: the `for-in` statement. Like `if`, this is a special language construct.

Programming language constructs

For the sake of review, let's go over the programming language stuff you've already seen. Most modern programming languages offer at least the following basic building blocks:

• The ability to remember values by storing things into variables. Some variables are simple, such as `Int` and `Bool`. Others can store objects (`UIButton`, `ChecklistItem`) or even collections of objects (`Array`).

• The ability to read values from variables and use them for basic arithmetic (multiply, add) and comparisons (greater than, not equals, etc.).

• The ability to make decisions. You've already seen the `if`-statement, but there is also a `switch` statement that is shorthand for `if` with many `else if`s.

• The ability to group functionality into units such as methods and functions. You can call those methods and receive back a result value that you can then use in further computations.

• The ability to bundle functionality (methods) and data (variables) together into objects.

• The ability to repeat a set of statements more than once. This is what the `for-in` statement does. There are other ways to perform repetitions as well: `while` and `do/while`. Endlessly repeating things is what computers are good at.

Everything else is built on top of these building blocks. You've seen most of these already, but repetitions (or **loops** in programmer slang) are new.

If you grok the concepts from this list, you're well on your way to becoming a software developer.

Let's go through that `for` loop line-by-line:

```
for list in lists {
  . . .
}
```

This means the following: for every `Checklist` object in the `lists` array, perform the statements that are in between the curly braces.

The first time through the loop, the temporary `list` variable will hold a reference to the Birthdays checklist, as that is the first `Checklist` object that you created and added to the `lists` array.

Inside the loop you do:

```
let item = ChecklistItem()
item.text = "Item for \(list.name)"
```

```
list.items.append(item)
```

This should be familiar. You first create a new `ChecklistItem` object. Then you set its `text` property to "Item for Birthdays" because the `\(…)` placeholder gets replaced with the name of the `Checklist` object (`list.name`, which is "Birthdays").

Finally, you add this new `ChecklistItem` to the Birthdays `Checklist` object, or rather, to its `items` array.

That concludes the first pass through this loop. Now the `for`-statement will look at the `lists` array again and sees that there are three more `Checklist` objects in that list. So it puts the next one, Groceries, into the `list` variable and the process repeats.

This time the text is "Item for Groceries", which is put into its own `ChecklistItem` object that goes into the `items` array of the Groceries `Checklist` object.

After that, the loop adds a new `ChecklistItem` with the text "Item for Cool Apps" to the Cool Apps checklist, and "Item for To Do" to the To Do checklist.

Then there are no more objects left to look at in the `lists` array and the loop ends.

Using loops will often save you a lot of time. You could have written this code as follows:

```
var item = ChecklistItem()
item.text = "Item for Birthdays"
lists[0].items.append(item)

item = ChecklistItem()
item.text = "Item for Groceries"
lists[1].items.append(item)

item = ChecklistItem()
item.text = "Item for Cool Apps"
lists[2].items.append(item)

item = ChecklistItem()
item.text = "Item for To Do"
lists[3].items.append(item)
```

That's very repetitive, which is a good sign it's better to use a loop. And what if you had 100 `Checklist` objects? Would you be willing to copy-paste that code a hundred times? I'd rather use a loop.

Most of the time you won't even know in advance how many objects you'll have, so it's impossible to write it all out by hand. By using a loop you don't need to worry about that. The loop will work just as well for three items as for three hundred.

As you can imagine, loops and arrays work quite well together.

➤ Run the app. You'll see that each checklist now has its own set of items.

Play with it for a minute, remove items, add items, and verify that each list indeed is completely separate from the others.

Each Checklist now has its own items

Let's put the load/save code back in. This time you'll make AllListsViewController do the loading and saving.

> Add the following to **AllListsViewController.swift**:

```
func documentsDirectory() -> String {
  let paths = NSSearchPathForDirectoriesInDomains(.DocumentDirectory, .UserDomainMask, true)
                as! [String]
  return paths[0]
}

func dataFilePath() -> String {
  return documentsDirectory().stringByAppendingPathComponent("Checklists.plist")
}

func saveChecklists() {
  let data = NSMutableData()
  let archiver = NSKeyedArchiver(forWritingWithMutableData: data)
  archiver.encodeObject(lists, forKey: "Checklists")
  archiver.finishEncoding()
  data.writeToFile(dataFilePath(), atomically: true)
}

func loadChecklists() {
  let path = dataFilePath()
  if NSFileManager.defaultManager().fileExistsAtPath(path) {
    if let data = NSData(contentsOfFile: path) {
      let unarchiver = NSKeyedUnarchiver(forReadingWithData: data)
      lists = unarchiver.decodeObjectForKey("Checklists") as! [Checklist]
      unarchiver.finishDecoding()
    }
  }
}
```

This is mostly identical to what you had before in ChecklistViewController, except that you load and save the lists array instead of the items array. The differences are highlighted.

> Change init(coder) to:

```
required init(coder aDecoder: NSCoder) {
  lists = [Checklist]()
  super.init(coder: aDecoder)
  loadChecklists()
}
```

This gets rid of the test data you put there earlier and makes the loadChecklists() method do all the work.

You also have to make the Checklist object compliant with NSCoding.

> Add the NSCoding protocol in **Checklist.swift**:

```
class Checklist: NSObject, NSCoding {
```

Remember that the NSCoding protocol requires that you add two methods, init(coder) and encodeWithCoder().

➤ Add those methods to **Checklist.swift**:

```
required init(coder aDecoder: NSCoder) {
  name = aDecoder.decodeObjectForKey("Name") as! String
  items = aDecoder.decodeObjectForKey("Items") as! [ChecklistItem]
  super.init()
}
```

```
func encodeWithCoder(aCoder: NSCoder) {
  aCoder.encodeObject(name, forKey: "Name")
  aCoder.encodeObject(items, forKey: "Items")
}
```

This loads and saves the Checklist's name and items properties.

➤ Before you run the app, remove the old **Checklists.plist** file from the Simulator's Documents folder.

If you don't, the app might crash because the internal format of the file no longer corresponds to the data you're loading and saving.

Weird crashes

When I first wrote this tutorial, I didn't think to remove the Checklists.plist file before running the app. That was a mistake, but the app appeared to work fine... until I added a new checklist. At that point the app aborted with a strange error message from UITableView that made no sense at all.

I started to wonder whether I tested the code properly. But then I thought of the old file, removed it and ran the app again. It worked perfectly. Just to make sure it was the fault of that file, I put a copy of the old file back and ran the app again. Sure enough, when I tried to add a new checklist it crashed.

The explanation for this kind of error is that somehow the code managed to load the old file, even though its format no longer corresponded to the new data model. This put the table view into a bad state. Any subsequent operations on the table view caused app to crash.

You'll run into this type of bug every so often, where the crash isn't directly caused by what you're doing but by something that went wrong earlier on. These kinds of bugs can be tricky to solve, because you can't fix them until you find the true cause.

There is a big section devoted to debugging techniques in a later tutorial because it's inevitable that you'll introduce bugs in your code. Knowing how to find and eradicate them is an essential skill that any programmer should master – if only to save you a lot of time and aggravation!

➤ Run the app and add a checklist and a few to-do items.

➤ Exit the app (with the Stop button) and run it again. You'll see that the list is empty again. All your to-do items are gone.

You can add all the checklists and items you want, but nothing gets saved anymore. What's going on here?

Doing saves differently

Previously, you saved the data whenever the user changed something: adding a new item, deleting an item, or toggling a checkmark. That all used to happen in ChecklistViewController.

However, you moved the saving logic into AllListsViewController. How do you make sure changes to the to-do items get saved now? The AllListsViewController doesn't know when a checkmark is toggled on or off.

You could give ChecklistViewController a reference to the AllListsViewController and have it call its saveChecklists() method whenever the user changes something, but that introduces a so-called *child–parent dependency* and you've been trying hard to avoid those (ownership cycles, remember?).

> **Note:** The terms *parent* and *child* are common in software development.
>
> A parent is an object higher up in some hierarchy; a child is an object lower in the hierarchy.
>
> In this case, the "hierarchy" represents the navigation flow between the different screens of the app.
>
> The All Lists screen is the parent of the Checklist screen, because All Lists was "born" first and creates a new ChecklistViewController "baby" every time the user performs the segue.
>
> Likewise, All Lists is also the parent of the List Detail screen. The Item Detail screen, however, is the child of the Checklist view controller.
>
>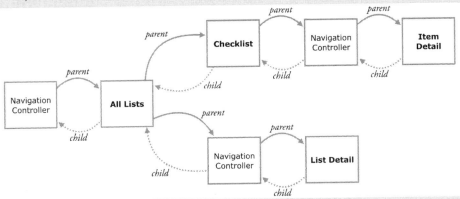
>
> Generally speaking, it's OK if the parent knows everything about its children, but not the other way around (just like in real life, every parent has horrible secrets they don't want their kids to know about – or so I've been told).
>
> As a result, you don't want parent objects to be dependent on their child objects, but the other way around is fine. So the ChecklistViewController asking the AllListsViewController to do things is a big no-no.

You may think: ah, I could use a delegate for this. True – and if you thought that indeed I'm very proud – but instead we'll rethink our saving strategy.

Is it really necessary to save changes all the time? While the app is running, the data model sits in working memory and is always up-to-date.

The only time you have to load anything from the file (the long-term storage memory) is when the app started, but never afterwards. From then on you always make the changes to the objects in the working memory.

But when changes are made, the file becomes out-of-date. That is why you save those changes – to keep the file in sync with what is in memory.

The reason you save to a file is that you can restore the data model in working memory after the app gets terminated. But until that happens, the data in the short-term working memory will do just fine.

You just need to make sure that you save the data to the file just before the app gets terminated. In other words, the only time you save is when you actually need to keep the data safe.

Not only is this more efficient, especially if you have a lot of data, it also is simpler to program. You no longer need to worry about saving every time the user makes a change to the data, only right before the app terminates.

There are three situations in which an app can terminate:

1. While the user is running the app. This doesn't happen very often anymore, but earlier versions of iOS did not support multitasking apps. Receiving an incoming phone call, for example, would kill the currently running app. On iOS 4 and later the app will simply be suspended in the background when that happens.

   There are still situations where iOS may forcefully terminate a running app, for example if the app becomes unresponsive or runs out of memory.

2. When the app is suspended in the background. Most of the time iOS keeps these apps around for a long time. Their data is frozen in memory and no computations are taking place. (When you resume a suspended app, it literally continues from where it left off.)

   Sometimes the OS needs to make room for an app that requires a lot of working memory – often a game – and then it simply kills the suspended apps and wipes them from memory. The apps are not notified of this.

3. The app crashes. There are ways to detect crashes but handling them can be very tricky. Trying to deal with the crash may actually make things worse. The best way to avoid crashes is to make no programming mistakes! :-)

Fortunately for us, iOS will inform the app about significant changes such as, "you are about to be terminated", and, "you are about to be suspended".

You can listen for these events and save your data at that point. That will ensure the on-file representation of the data model is always up-to-date when the app does terminate.

The ideal place for handling these notifications is inside the **application delegate**. You haven't spent much time with this object before, but every app has one. As its name implies, it is the delegate object for notifications that concern the app as a whole.

This is where you receive the "app will terminate" and "app will be suspended" notifications.

In fact, if you look inside **AppDelegate.swift**, you'll see the methods:

```
func applicationDidEnterBackground(application: UIApplication)
```

and:

```
func applicationWillTerminate(application: UIApplication)
```

There are a few others, but these are the ones you need. (The Xcode template put helpful comments inside these methods, so you know what to do with them.)

Now the trick is, how do you call `AllListsViewController`'s `saveChecklists()` method from these delegate methods? The app delegate does not know anything about `AllListsViewController` yet.

You have to use some trickery to find the All Lists View Controller from within the app delegate.

➤ Add this new method to **AppDelegate.swift**:

```
func saveData() {
    let navigationController = window!.rootViewController as! UINavigationController
    let controller = navigationController.viewControllers[0] as! AllListsViewController
    controller.saveChecklists()
}
```

The `saveData()` method looks at the `window` property to find the `UIWindow` object that contains the storyboard.

`UIWindow` is the top-level container for all your app's views. There is only one `UIWindow` object in your app (unlike desktop apps, which usually have multiple windows).

Exercise: Can you explain why you wrote `window!` with an exclamation point? ■

Unwrapping optionals

At the top of AppDelegate.swift you can see that `window` is declared as an optional:

```
var window: UIWindow?
```

To *unwrap* an optional you normally use the `if let` syntax:

```
if let w = window {
    // if window is not nil, w is the real UIWindow object
    let navigationController = w.rootViewController
}
```

As a shorthand you've seen that you can use *optional chaining*:

```
let navigationController = window?.rootViewController
```

If `window` is nil, then the app won't even bother to look at the rest of the statement and `navigationController` will also be nil.

For apps that use a storyboard (as most of them do), you're guaranteed that `window` is never nil, even though it is an optional. UIKit promises that it will put a valid reference to the app's `UIWindow` object inside `window` when the app starts up.

(So why is it an optional? There is a brief moment between when the app is launched and the storyboard is loaded where the `window` property does not have a valid value yet.)

If you're sure an optional will not be nil, you don't have to use if let but you can *force unwrap* by adding an exclamation point:

```
let navigationController = window!.rootViewController
```

That's exactly what you're doing in the saveData() method.

Normally you don't need to do anything with your UIWindow, but in cases such as this you have to ask it for its rootViewController.

This is the very first view controller from the storyboard, the navigation controller all the way over on the left.

You can see this in Interface Builder because this navigation controller has the big arrow pointing at it (in the Attributes inspector it also has the **Is Initial View Controller** box checked; in the outline pane the arrow is called the Storyboard Entry Point).

This is the one:

The left-most navigation controller is the window's root view controller

Once you have the navigation controller, you can find the AllListsViewController. After all, that's the view controller that is embedded in the navigation controller.

Unfortunately, the UINavigationController does not have a "rootViewController" property of its own, so you have to look into its viewControllers array to find the bottom one:

```
let controller = navigationController.viewControllers[0] as! AllListsViewController
```

As usual, a type cast is necessary because the viewControllers array does not know anything about the types of our own view controllers. Once you have a reference to AllListsViewController you can call its saveChecklists() method.

It's a bit of work to dig through the window and navigation controller to find the view controller you need, but that's life as an iOS developer.

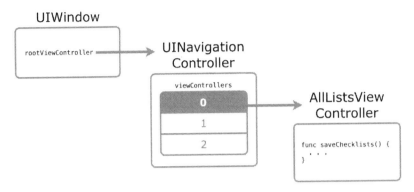

From the root view controller to the AllListsViewController

By the way, the `UINavigationController` does have a `topViewController` property but you cannot use it here: the "top" view controller is the screen that is currently displaying, which may very well be the `ChecklistViewController` if the user is looking at the to-do list. You don't want to send the `saveChecklists()` message to that screen – it has no method to handle that message and the app will crash!

➤ Change the `applicationDidEnterBackground()` and `applicationWillTerminate()` methods to call `saveData()`:

```
func applicationDidEnterBackground(application: UIApplication!) {
  saveData()
}

func applicationWillTerminate(application: UIApplication!) {
  saveData()
}
```

➤ Run the app, add some checklists, add items to those lists, and set some checkmarks.

➤ Then press the **Home button** on the simulator to make the app go to the background. (If your simulator does not show a home button, then press **Shift+⌘+H** or pick **Hardware → Home** from the menu bar.)

Look inside the app's Documents folder using Finder. There is a new Checklists.plist file here.

➤ Press Stop in Xcode to terminate the app. Run the app again and your data should still be there. Awesome!

Xcode's Stop button

Important note: When you press Xcode's Stop button, the application delegate will not receive the `applicationWillTerminate()` notification. Xcode kills the app without mercy.

Therefore, to test the saving behavior, always tap the Home button to make the app go into the background before you press Stop. If you don't press Home first, you'll lose your data. *Caveat developer.*

Improving the data model

The above code works but you can still do a little better. You have made data model objects for `Checklist` and `ChecklistItem`, but there is still code in `AllListsViewController` for loading and saving the Checklists.plist file. That really belongs in the data model as well.

I prefer to create a top-level `DataModel` object for many of my apps. For this app, `DataModel` will contain the array of `Checklist` objects. You can move the code for loading and saving into this new `DataModel` object.

➤ Add a new file to the project using the **Swift File** template. Save it as **DataModel.swift** (you don't need to make this a subclass of anything).

➤ Change **DataModel.swift** to the following:

```
import Foundation

class DataModel {
  var lists = [Checklist]()
}
```

This defines the new `DataModel` object and gives it a `lists` property.

Unlike `Checklist` and `ChecklistItem`, `DataModel` does not need to be built on top of `NSObject`. It also does not need to conform to the `NSCoding` protocol.

`DataModel` will be taking over the responsibilities for loading and saving the to-do lists from `AllListsViewController`.

➤ Cut the following methods out of **AllListsViewController.swift** and paste them into **DataModel.swift**:

- `func documentsDirectory()`
- `func dataFilePath()`
- `func saveChecklists()`
- `func loadChecklists()`

➤ Add an `init()` method to **DataModel.swift**:

```
init() {
  loadChecklists()
}
```

This makes sure that, as soon as the `DataModel` object is created, it will attempt to load Checklists.plist.

The declaration of `lists` already includes an initial value, so you don't need to do anything with it inside this `init`. Also, you don't have to call `super.init()` because `DataModel` does not have a superclass (it is not built on `NSObject`).

Switch to **AllListsViewController.swift** and make the following changes:

➤ Remove the `lists` instance variable.

➤ Remove the `init(coder)` method.

➤ Add a new instance variable:

```
var dataModel: DataModel!
```

The ! is necessary because dataModel will temporarily be nil when the app starts up. It doesn't have to be a true optional – with ? – because once dataModel is given a value, it will never become nil again.

➤ You should already have removed the documentsDirectory(), dataFilePath(), saveChecklists() and loadChecklists() methods.

Xcode still finds a number of errors in **AllListsViewController.swift**. You can no longer reference the lists variable directly, because it no longer exists. Instead, you'll have to ask the DataModel for its lists property.

➤ Everywhere the code for AllListsViewController says lists, replace this with dataModel.lists. You need to do this in the following methods:

- tableView(numberOfRowsInSection)
- tableView(cellForRowAtIndexPath)
- tableView(didSelectRowAtIndexPath)
- tableView(commitEditingStyle, forRowAtIndexPath)
- tableView(accessoryButtonTappedForRowWithIndexPath)
- listDetailViewController(didFinishAddingChecklist)
- listDetailViewController(didFinishEditingChecklist)

Phew, that's a big list! Fortunately, the change is very simple.

To recap, you created a new DataModel object that owns the array of Checklist objects and knows how to load and save the checklists and their items.

Instead of its own array, the AllListsViewController now uses this DataModel object, which it accesses through the dataModel property.

But where does this DataModel object get created? There is no place in the code that currently does dataModel = DataModel().

The best place for this is in the app delegate. You can consider the app delegate to be the top-level object in your app. Therefore it makes sense to make it the "owner" of the data model.

The app delegate then gives this DataModel object to any view controllers that need to use it.

➤ In **AppDelegate.swift**, add a new property:

```
let dataModel = DataModel()
```

This creates the DataModel object and puts it in dataModel.

Even though AllListsViewController also has an instance variable named dataModel, these two things are totally separate from each other.

Here you're only putting the DataModel object into AppDelegate's dataModel property.

➤ Simplify the saveData() method to just this:

```
func saveData() {
  dataModel.saveChecklists()
}
```

If you run the app now, it will crash at once because AllListsViewController's own reference to DataModel is still nil. I told you those nils were no-gooders!

The best place to share the `DataModel` instance with `AllListsViewController` is in the `application(didFinishLaunchingWithOptions)` method, which gets called as soon as the app starts up.

➤ Change that method to:

```
func application(application: UIApplication,
          didFinishLaunchingWithOptions launchOptions: [NSObject : AnyObject]?) -> Bool {

  let navigationController = window!.rootViewController as! UINavigationController
  let controller = navigationController.viewControllers[0] as! AllListsViewController
  controller.dataModel = dataModel

  return true
}
```

This finds the `AllListsViewController` by looking in the storyboard (as before) and then sets its `dataModel` property.

➤ Do a clean build (**Product → Clean**) and run the app. Verify that everything still works. Great!

You can find the project files for the app up to this point under **08 - Improved Data Model** in the tutorial's Source Code folder.

"I'm still confused about var and let!"

If `var` makes a variable and `let` makes a constant, then why were you able to do this in AppDelegate.swift:

```
let dataModel = DataModel()
```

You'd think that when something is constant it cannot change, right?

Then how come the app lets you add new `Checklist` objects to `DataModel` – obviously the `DataModel` object *can* be changed...

Here's the trick: Swift makes a distinction between so-called **value types** and **reference types**, and `let` works a bit differently for both.

An example of a value type is `Int`. Once you create a constant of type `Int` you can never change it afterwards:

```
let i = 100
i = 200       // not allowed
i += 1        // not allowed

var j = 100
j = 200       // allowed
j += 1        // allowed
```

The same goes for other value types such as `Float`, `String`, and even `Array`. They are called value types because the variable or constant directly stores their value.

When you assign the contents of one variable to another, the value is copied into the new variable:

```
var s = "hello"
var u = s       // u has its own copy of "hello"
s += " there"   // s and u are now different
```

But objects that you define with the keyword class (such as DataModel) are reference types. The variable or constant does not contain the actual object, only a reference to the object.

```
var d = DataModel()
var e = d                // e refers to the same object as d
d.lists.removeAtIndex(0) // this also changes e
```

You can also write this using let and it would do the exact same thing:

```
let d = DataModel()
let e = d                // e refers to the same object as d
d.lists.removeAtIndex(0) // this also changes e
```

So what is the difference between var and let for reference types?

When you use let it is not the object that is constant but the *reference* to the object. That means you cannot do this:

```
let d = DataModel()
d = someOtherDataModel   // error: cannot change the reference
```

The constant d can never point to another object, but the object itself can still change.

It's OK if you have trouble wrapping your head around this. The distinction between value types and reference types is an important idea in software development, but also takes a while to understand.

My suggestion is that you use let whenever you can and change to var when the compiler complains. Note that optionals always need to be var, because being an optional implies that it can change its value.

Using NSUserDefaults to remember stuff

You now have an app that lets you create checklists and add to-do items to those lists. All of this data is saved to long-term storage so even if the app gets terminated, nothing is lost.

There are some user interface improvements you can make, though.

Imagine the user is on the Birthdays checklist and presses the Home button to switch to another app. The Checklists app is now suspended. It is possible that at some point the app gets terminated and is removed from memory.

When the user reopens the app some time later it no longer is on Birthdays but on the main screen. Because it was terminated the app didn't simply resume where it left off, but got launched anew.

You might be able to get away with this, as apps don't get terminated often (unless your users play a lot of games that eat up memory) but little things like this matter in iOS apps.

Fortunately, it's fairly easy to remember whether the user has opened a checklist and to switch to it when the app starts up.

You could store this information in the Checklists.plist file, but especially for simple settings such as this there is the NSUserDefaults object

NSUserDefaults works like a dictionary, which is a collection object for storing key-value pairs. You've already seen the array collection, which stores an ordered list of objects. The dictionary is another very common collection that looks like this:

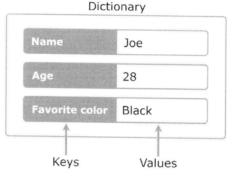

A dictionary is a collection of key-value pairs

Dictionaries in Swift are handled by the Dictionary object (who would've guessed).

You can put objects into the dictionary under a reference key and then retrieve it later using that key. This is, in fact, how Info.plist works.

The Info.plist file is read into a dictionary and then iOS uses the various keys (on the left hand) to obtain the values (on the right hand). Keys are usually strings but values can be any type of object.

To be fair, NSUserDefaults isn't a true dictionary, but it acts like one.

When you insert new values into NSUserDefaults, they are saved somewhere in your app's sandbox so these values persist even after the app terminates.

You don't want to store huge amounts of data inside NSUserDefaults, but it's ideal for small things like settings – and for remembering what screen the app was on when it closed.

This is what you are going to do:

1. On the segue from the main screen (AllListsViewController) to the checklist screen (ChecklistViewController), you write the row index of the selected checklist into NSUserDefaults. This is how you'll remember which checklist was selected.

   You could have saved the name of the checklist instead of the row index, but what would happen if two checklists have the same name? Unlikely, but not impossible. Using the row index guarantees that you'll always select the proper one.

2. When the user presses the back button to return to the main screen, you have to remove this value from NSUserDefaults again. It is common to set a value such as this to -1 to mean "no value".

   Why -1? You start counting rows at 0, so you can't use 0. Positive numbers are also out of the question, unless you use a huge number such as 1000000 – it's very unlikely the user will make that many checklists. -1 is not a valid row index; and because it's a negative value it looks weird, making it easy to spot during debugging.

(If you're wondering why you're not using an optional for this – good question! – the answer is that NSUserDefaults cannot handle optionals. Sad face.)

3. If the app starts up and the value from NSUserDefaults isn't -1, the user was previously viewing the contents of a checklist and you have to manually perform a segue to the ChecklistViewController for the corresponding row.

Phew, it's more work to explain this in English than writing the actual code. ;-)

Let's start with the segue from the main screen. Recall that this segue is triggered from code rather than from the storyboard.

➤ In **AllListsViewController.swift**, change tableView(didSelectRowAtIndexPath) to the following:

```
override func tableView(tableView: UITableView,
                 didSelectRowAtIndexPath indexPath: NSIndexPath) {
  NSUserDefaults.standardUserDefaults().setInteger(indexPath.row, forKey: "ChecklistIndex")

  let checklist = dataModel.lists[indexPath.row]
  performSegueWithIdentifier("ShowChecklist", sender: checklist)
}
```

In addition to what this method did before, you now store the index of the selected row into NSUserDefaults under the key "ChecklistIndex".

To recognize whether the user presses the back button on the navigation bar, you have to set a delegate for the navigation controller. Being the delegate means that the navigation controller tells you when it pushes or pops view controllers on the navigation stack. The logical place for this delegate is the AllListsViewController.

➤ Add the delegate protocol to the class line in **AllListsViewController.swift** (all on one line):

```
class AllListsViewController: UITableViewController, ListDetailViewControllerDelegate,
    UINavigationControllerDelegate {
```

As you can see, a view controller can be a delegate for many other objects at once.

AllListsViewController is now the delegate for both the ListDetailViewController and the UINavigationController, but also implicitly for the UITableView (because it is a table view controller).

➤ Add the delegate method to the bottom of **AllListsViewController.swift**:

```
func navigationController(navigationController: UINavigationController,
              willShowViewController viewController: UIViewController, animated: Bool) {
  if viewController === self {
    NSUserDefaults.standardUserDefaults().setInteger(-1, forKey: "ChecklistIndex")
  }
}
```

This method is called whenever the navigation controller will slide to a new screen.

If the back button was pressed, the new view controller is AllListsViewController itself and you set the "ChecklistIndex" value in NSUserDefaults to -1, meaning that no checklist is currently selected.

Equal or identical

To determine whether the `AllListsViewController` is the newly activated view controller, you wrote:

```
if viewController === self
```

Yep, it's not a typo, that's three equals signs in a row.

Previously to compare objects you used only two equals signs:

```
if segue.identifier == "AddItem" {
```

You may be wondering what the difference is between these two operators. It's subtle but important question about identity. (Who said programmers couldn't be philosophical?)

If you use ==, you're checking whether two variables have the same value.

With === you're checking whether two variables refer to the exact same object.

Imagine two people who are both called Joe. They're different people who just happen to have the same name.

If we'd compare them with `joe1 === joe2` then the result would be false, as they're not the same person.

But `joe1.name == joe2.name` would be true.

On the other hand, if I'm telling you an amusing (or embarrassing!) story about Joe and this story seems awfully familiar to you, then maybe we happen to know this same Joe.

In that case, `joe1 === joe2` would be true as well.

By the way, the above code would have worked just fine if you had written,

```
if viewController == self
```

with just two equals signs. For objects such as view controllers, equality is tested by comparing the references, just like === would do. But technically speaking, === is more correct here than ==.

The only thing that remains is to check at startup which checklist you need to show and then perform the segue manually. You'll do that in `viewDidAppear()`.

➤ Add the `viewDidAppear()` method to **AllListsViewController.swift**:

```
override func viewDidAppear(animated: Bool) {
  super.viewDidAppear(animated)

  navigationController?.delegate = self

  let index = NSUserDefaults.standardUserDefaults().integerForKey("ChecklistIndex")
  if index != -1 {
    let checklist = dataModel.lists[index]
    performSegueWithIdentifier("ShowChecklist", sender: checklist)
  }
}
```

UIKit automatically calls this method after the view controller has become visible.

First, the view controller makes itself the delegate for the navigation controller.

Every view controller has a built-in navigationController property. To access it you use the notation navigationController?.delegate because it is optional. (You could also have written navigationController! instead of ?. The difference between the two is that ! will crash the app if this view controller would ever be shown outside of a UINavigationController and ? won't.)

Then it checks NSUserDefaults to see whether it has to perform the segue.

If the value of the "ChecklistIndex" setting is not -1, then the user was previously viewing a checklist and the app should segue to that screen. As before, you place the Checklist object into the sender parameter of performSegueWithIdentifier().

The != operator means: not equal. It is the opposite of the == operator. If you're mathematically-inclined, with some imagination != looks like ≠. (Some languages use <> for not equal but that won't work in Swift.)

> **Note:** It may not be immediately obvious what's going on here.
>
> viewDidAppear() isn't just called when the app starts up but also every time the navigation controller slides the main screen back into view.
>
> Checking whether to restore the checklist screen needs to happen only once when the app starts, so why did you put this logic in viewDidAppear() if it gets called more than once?
>
> Here's the reason:
>
> The very first time AllListsViewController's screen becomes visible you don't want the "willShowViewController" delegate method to be called yet, as that would always overwrite the old value of "ChecklistIndex" with -1, before you've had a chance to restore the old screen.
>
> By waiting to register AllListsViewController as the navigation controller delegate until it is visible, you avoid this problem. viewDidAppear() is the ideal place for that, so it makes sense to do it from that method.
>
> However, as mentioned, viewDidAppear() also gets called after the user presses the back button to return to the All Lists screen. That shouldn't have any unwanted side effects, such as triggering the segue again.
>
> As it happens, the navigation controller will also call willShowViewController when the back button is pressed, but this happens before viewDidAppear(). The delegate method always sets the value of "ChecklistIndex" back to -1, and as a result viewDidAppear() does not trigger a segue again. And so it all works out…
>
> There are other ways to solve this particular issue but this approach is simple, so I like it.
>
> Is all of this going way over your head? Don't fret about it. To get a better idea of what is going on, sprinkle println() statements over the various methods to see in which order they get called. Change things around to see what the effect is. Jumping into the code and playing with it is the quickest way to learn!

> Run the app and go to a checklist screen. Press the simulator's Home button (Shift+⌘+H), followed by Stop to quit the app.

Tip: You need to press the Home button because NSUserDefaults may not immediately save its settings to disk and therefore you may lose your changes if you kill the app from within Xcode.

➤ Run the app again and you'll notice that Xcode immediately switches to the screen where you were last at. Cool, huh!

> **Note:** If it doesn't work as expected, then double-check that all the lines with NSUserDefaults use the same key name, "ChecklistIndex". If one of them is misspelled, NSUserDefaults is reading from and writing to different items.

Defensive programming

➤ Now do the following: Stop the app and reset the Simulator using the menu item **iOS Simulator → Reset Contents and Settings**.

(Just holding down the app icon until it starts to wiggle and then deleting it is not enough; you need to reset the entire Simulator.)

Then run the app again from within Xcode and watch it crash:

```
fatal error: Cannot index empty buffer
```

The app crashes in viewDidAppear() on the line:

```
let checklist = dataModel.lists[index]
```

What's going on here? Apparently the value of the index constant is not -1, because the code entered the if-statement.

As it turns out index is 0, even though there should be nothing in NSUserDefaults yet because this is a fresh install of the app. The app didn't write anything in the "ChecklistIndex" key yet.

Here's the thing: NSUserDefaults's integerForKey() method returns 0 if it cannot find the value for the key you specify, but in this app 0 is a valid row index.

At this point the app doesn't have any checklists yet, so index 0 does not exist in the lists array. That is why the app crashes.

What you would like instead, is that NSUserDefaults returns -1 if the "ChecklistIndex" key isn't set, because to this app -1 means: show the main screen instead of a specific checklist.

Fortunately, NSUserDefaults will let you set default values for the default values. Yep, you read that correctly.

Let's do that in the DataModel object.

➤ Add the following method inside **DataModel.swift**:

```
func registerDefaults() {
  let dictionary = [ "ChecklistIndex": -1 ]
  NSUserDefaults.standardUserDefaults().registerDefaults(dictionary)
}
```

This creates a new Dictionary instance and adds the value -1 for the key "ChecklistIndex".

The square bracket notation is not only used to make arrays but also dictionaries. The difference is that for a dictionary it always looks like,

```
[ key1: value1, key2: value2, . . . ]
```

while an array is just:

```
[value1, value2, value3, . . . ]
```

NSUserDefaults will use the values from this dictionary if you ask it for a key but it cannot find anything under that key.

➤ Change **DataModel.swift**'s init() to call this new method:

```
init() {
  loadChecklists()
  registerDefaults()
}
```

➤ Run the app again and now it should no longer crash.

Why did you do this in DataModel? Well, I don't really like to sprinkle all of these calls to NSUserDefaults throughout the code. In fact, let's move all of the NSUserDefaults stuff into DataModel.

➤ Add the following to **DataModel.swift**:

```
var indexOfSelectedChecklist: Int {
  get {
    return NSUserDefaults.standardUserDefaults().integerForKey("ChecklistIndex")
  }
  set {
    NSUserDefaults.standardUserDefaults().setInteger(newValue, forKey: "ChecklistIndex")
  }
}
```

This does something you haven't seen before. It appears to declare a new instance variable, indexOfSelectedChecklist, of type Int, but what are these get { } and set { } blocks? This is an example of a *computed property*.

There isn't any storage allocated for this property (so it's not really a variable). Instead, when the app tries to read the value of indexOfSelectedChecklist, the code in the get block is performed. And when the app tries to put a new value into indexOfSelectedChecklist, the set block is performed.

From now on you can simply use indexOfSelectedChecklist and it will automatically update NSUserDefaults.

You're doing this so the rest of the code won't have to worry about NSUserDefaults anymore. The other objects just have to use the indexOfSelectedChecklist property on DataModel.

Hiding implementation details is an important object-oriented programming principle.

If you decide later that you want to store these settings somewhere else, for example in a database or in iCloud, then you only have to change this in one place, in DataModel. The rest of the code will be oblivious to these changes and that's a good thing.

➤ Update the code in **AllListsViewController.swift** to use this new computed property:

```
override func viewDidAppear(animated: Bool) {
  super.viewDidAppear(animated)

  navigationController?.delegate = self
```

```
  let index = dataModel.indexOfSelectedChecklist
  if index != -1 {
    let checklist = dataModel.lists[index]
    performSegueWithIdentifier("ShowChecklist", sender: checklist)
  }
}
```

```
override func tableView(tableView: UITableView,
                        didSelectRowAtIndexPath indexPath: NSIndexPath) {
  dataModel.indexOfSelectedChecklist = indexPath.row

  let checklist = dataModel.lists[indexPath.row]
  performSegueWithIdentifier("ShowChecklist", sender: checklist)
}
```

```
func navigationController(navigationController: UINavigationController,
              willShowViewController viewController: UIViewController, animated: Bool) {
  if viewController === self {
    dataModel.indexOfSelectedChecklist = -1
  }
}
```

The intent of the code is now much clearer. AllListsViewController no longer has to worry about the "how" – storing values in NSUserDefaults – and can simply focus on the "what" – changing the index of the selected checklist.

➤ Run the app again and make sure everything still works.

It's pretty nice that the app now remembers what screen you were on, but this new feature has also introduced a subtle bug in the app. Here's how to reproduce it:

➤ Start the app and add a new checklist. Also add a new to-do item to this list. Now kill the app from within Xcode.

Because you did not press the Home button, the new checklist and its item were not saved to Checklists.plist.

However, there is a (small) chance that NSUserDefaults did save its changes to disk and now thinks this new list is selected. That's a problem because that list doesn't exist anymore (it never made it into Checklists.plist).

NSUserDefaults will save its changes at indeterminate times so it could have saved before you terminated the app.

➤ Run the app again and – if you're lucky? – it will crash with:

```
fatal error: Cannot index empty buffer
```

If you can't get this error to happen, add the following line to the set block of indexOfSelectedChecklist and try again (this forces NSUserDefaults to save its changes every time indexOfSelectedChecklist changes):

```
set {
  NSUserDefaults.standardUserDefaults().setInteger(newValue, forKey: "ChecklistIndex")
  NSUserDefaults.standardUserDefaults().synchronize()
}
```

302 *The iOS Apprentice (Third Edition)*

The reason for the crash is that NSUserDefaults and the contents of Checklists.plist are out-of-sync.

NSUserDefaults thinks the app needs to select a checklist that doesn't actually exist. Every time you run the app it will now crash. Yikes!

This situation shouldn't really happen during regular usage because you used the Xcode Stop button to kill the app. Under normal circumstances the user would press the Home button at some point and as the app goes into the background it will save both Checklists.plist and NSUserDefaults and everything is in sync again.

However, the OS can always decide to terminate the app and then this situation could occur.

Even though there's only a small chance that this can go wrong in practice, you should really protect the app against it. These are the kinds of bug reports you don't want to get because often you have no idea what the user did to make it happen.

This is where the practice of *defensive programming* becomes important. Your code should always check for such boundary cases and be able to gracefully handle them even if they are unlikely to occur.

In our case, you can easily fix AllListsViewController's viewDidAppear() method to deal with this situation.

➤ Change viewDidAppear() to:

```
override func viewDidAppear(animated: Bool) {
  super.viewDidAppear(animated)

  navigationController?.delegate = self

  let index = dataModel.indexOfSelectedChecklist
  if index >= 0 && index < dataModel.lists.count {
    let checklist = dataModel.lists[index]
    performSegueWithIdentifier("ShowChecklist", sender: checklist)
  }
}
```

Instead of just checking for index != -1, you now do a more precise check to determine whether index is valid.

It should be between 0 and the number of checklists in the data model. If not, then you simply don't segue.

This prevents dataModel.lists[index] from asking for an object at an index that doesn't exist.

You haven't seen the && operator before. This symbol means "logical and". It is used as follows:

```
if something && somethingElse {
  // do stuff
}
```

This reads: if something is true **and** something else is also true, then do stuff.

In viewDidAppear() you only perform the segue when index is 0 or greater *and also* less than the number of checklists, which means it's only valid if it lies in between those two values.

With this defensive check in place, you're guaranteed that the app will not try to segue to a checklist that doesn't exist, even if the data is out-of-sync.

> **Note:** The app won't bother to remember whether the user had the Add/Edit Checklist or Add/Edit Item screen open.
>
> These kinds of modal screens are supposed to be temporary. You open them to make a few changes and then close them again. If the app goes to the background and is terminated, then it's no big deal if the modal screen disappears.
>
> At least that is true for this app. If you have an app that allows the user to make many complicated edits in a modal screen, you may want to persist those changes when the app closes so the user won't lose all his work in case the app is killed.
>
> In this tutorial you used NSUserDefaults to remember which screen was open, but iOS actually has a dedicated API for this kind of thing, State Preservation and Restoration. You can read more about this in our book *iOS 6 by Tutorials*.

The first-run experience

Let's use NSUserDefaults for something else. It would be nice if the first time you ran the app it created a default checklist for you, simply named "List", and switched the screen to that list. This enables you to start adding to-do items right away.

That's how the standard Notes app works too: you can start typing a note right after launching the app for the very first time, but you can also go one level back in the navigation hierarchy to see a list of all notes.

To pull this off, you need to keep track in NSUserDefaults whether this is the first time the user runs the app. If it is, you create a new Checklist object.

You can perform all of this logic inside DataModel. It's a good idea to add a new default setting to the registerDefaults() method. The key for this value is "FirstTime".

➤ Change the registerDefaults() method in **DataModel.swift**:

```
func registerDefaults() {
  let dictionary = [ "ChecklistIndex": -1, "FirstTime": true ]
  NSUserDefaults.standardUserDefaults().registerDefaults(dictionary)
}
```

The "FirstTime" setting can be a boolean value because it's either true (this is the first time) or false (this is any other than the first time).

The value of "FirstTime" needs to be true if this is the first launch of the app after a fresh install.

➤ Still in **DataModel.swift**, add a new handleFirstTime() method:

```
func handleFirstTime() {
  let userDefaults = NSUserDefaults.standardUserDefaults()
  let firstTime = userDefaults.boolForKey("FirstTime")
  if firstTime {
    let checklist = Checklist(name: "List")
    lists.append(checklist)
    indexOfSelectedChecklist = 0
    userDefaults.setBool(false, forKey: "FirstTime")
  }
}
```

Here you check NSUserDefaults for the value of the "FirstTime" key. If the value for "FirstTime" is true, then this is the first time the app is being run. In that case, you create a new Checklist object and add it to the array.

You also set indexOfSelectedChecklist to 0, the index of this newly added Checklist object, to make sure the app will automatically segue to the new checklist in AllListsViewController's viewDidAppear().

Finally, you set the value of "FirstTime" to false, so this code won't be executed again the next time the app starts up.

> Call this new method from DataModel's init():

```
init() {
  loadChecklists()
  registerDefaults()
  handleFirstTime()
}
```

> Reset the Simulator to remove the app and its associated data, and run the app again from Xcode.

Because it's the first time you run the app (at least from the app's perspective) after a fresh install, it will automatically create a new checklist named List and switch to it.

You can find the project for the app up to this point under **09 - NSUserDefaults** in the tutorial's Source Code folder.

Improving the user experience

There are a few small features I'd like to add, just to polish the app a little more. After all, you're building a real app here – if you want to make top-notch apps, you have to pay attention to those details.

Showing the number of to-do items remaining

In the main screen, for each checklist the app will show the number of to-do items that do not have checkmarks yet:

Each checklist shows how many items are still left to-do

First, you need a way to count these items.

> Add the following method to **Checklist.swift**:

```
func countUncheckedItems() -> Int {
  var count = 0
  for item in items {
    if !item.checked {
      count += 1
    }
  }
  return count
}
```

With this method you can ask any Checklist object how many of its ChecklistItem objects do not yet have their checkmark set. The method returns this count as an Int value.

You use a for in to loop through the ChecklistItem objects from the items array. If an item object has its checked property set to false, you increment the local variable count by 1.

Remember that the ! operator negates the result. So if item.checked is true, then !item.checked will make it false. You should read it as "if not item.checked".

When the loop is over and you've looked at all the objects, you return the total value of the count to the caller.

Exercise: What would happen if you used let instead of var to make the count variable? ∎

Answer: When count is a constant, Swift won't let you change its value, so the line that does += 1 gives an error message.

➤ Go to **AllListsViewController.swift** and change cellForRowAtIndexPath to:

```
override func tableView(tableView: UITableView,
                        cellForRowAtIndexPath indexPath: NSIndexPath) -> UITableViewCell {

  let cellIdentifier = "Cell"
  var cell: UITableViewCell! = tableView.dequeueReusableCellWithIdentifier(cellIdentifier)
                                   as? UITableViewCell
  if cell == nil {
    cell = UITableViewCell(style: .Subtitle, reuseIdentifier: cellIdentifier)
  }

  let checklist = dataModel.lists[indexPath.row]
  cell.textLabel!.text = checklist.name
  cell.accessoryType = .DetailDisclosureButton

  cell.detailTextLabel!.text = "\(checklist.countUncheckedItems()) Remaining"

  return cell
}
```

Most of the code stays the same, except you now use .Subtitle for the cell style instead of .Default. The "subtitle" cell style adds a second, smaller label below the main label. You can use the cell's detailTextLabel property to access this subtitle label.

You call the countUncheckedItems() method on the Checklist object and put the count into a new string that you place into the detailTextLabel. Notice that you can even call methods inside interpolated strings. Sweet!

> **Note:** To put text into the cell's labels, you wrote:
>
> ```
> cell.textLabel!.text = someString
> cell.detailTextLabel!.text = anotherString
> ```

The ! is necessary because `textLabel` and `detailTextLabel` are optionals.

The `textLabel` property is only present on table view cells that use one of the built-in cell styles; it is `nil` on custom cell designs. Likewise, not all of the cell styles have a detail label, and `detailTextLabel` will be `nil` in those cases.

Here you're using the "Subtitle" cell style, which is guaranteed to have both labels. Because these optionals will never be `nil` for a "Subtitle" cell, you can use ! to *force unwrap* them. This turns the optional into an actual object that you can use.

Be careful with this, though… using ! on an optional that *is* `nil` will crash your app immediately.

You could also have written it as:

```
if let label = cell.textLabel {
   label.text = someString
}

if let label = cell.detailTextLabel {
   label.text = anotherString
}
```

That is safer – no chance of crashing here – but also a bit more cumbersome. Writing ! is just more convenient in this case.

> Run the app. For each checklist it will now show how many items still remain to be done.

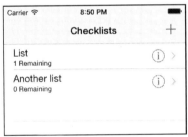

The cells now have a subtitle label

One problem: The to-do count never changes. If you toggle a checkmark on or off, or add new items, the "to do" count remains the same. That's because you create these table view cells once and never update their labels.

Exercise: Think of all the situations that will cause this "still to do" count to change. ■

Answer:

• The user toggles a checkmark on an item. When the checkmark is set, the count goes down. When the checkmark gets removed, the count goes up again.

• The user adds a new item. New items don't have their checkmark set, so adding a new item should increment the count.

• The user deletes an item. The count should go down but only if that item had no checkmark.

These changes all happen in the `ChecklistViewController` but the "still to do" label is shown in the `AllListsViewController`.

So how do you let the All Lists View Controller know about this?

If you thought, use a delegate, then you're starting to get the hang of this. You could make a new "ChecklistViewControllerDelegate" protocol that sends messages when the following things happen:

- the user toggles a checkmark on an item
- the user adds a new item
- the user deletes an item

But what would this delegate – which would be AllListsViewController – do in return? It would simply set a new text on the cell's detailTextLabel in all cases.

This approach sounds good, only you're going to cheat and not use a delegate at all. There is a simpler solution and a smart programmer always picks the simplest way to solve a problem.

➤ Go to **AllListsViewController.swift** and add the viewWillAppear() method to do the following:

```
override func viewWillAppear(animated: Bool) {
  super.viewWillAppear(animated)
  tableView.reloadData()
}
```

Don't confuse this method with viewDidAppear(). The difference is in the verb: *will* versus *did*. viewWillAppear() is called before viewDidAppear(), when the view is about to become visible but the animation hasn't started yet.

The iOS API often does this: there is a "will" method that is invoked before something happens and a "did" method that is invoked after that something happened. Sometimes you need to do things before, sometimes after, and having two methods gives you the ability to choose whichever situation works best for you.

> **API** (a-pee-eye) stands for Application Programming Interface. When people say "the iOS API" they mean all the frameworks, objects, protocols and functions that are provided by iOS that you as a programmer can use to write apps.
>
> The iOS API consists of everything from UIKit, Foundation, Core Graphics, and so on. Likewise, when people talk about "the Facebook API" or "the Google API", they mean the services that these companies provide that allow you to write apps for those platforms.

Here, viewWillAppear() tells the table view to reload its entire contents. That will cause tableView(cellForRowAtIndexPath) to be called again for every visible row.

When you tap the back button on the ChecklistViewController's navigation bar, the AllListsViewController screen will slide back into view. Just before that happens, viewWillAppear() is called. Thanks to the call to tableView.reloadData() the app will update all of the table cells, including the detailTextLabels.

Reloading all of the cells may seem like overkill but in this situation you can easily get away with it. It's unlikely the All Lists screen will contain many rows (say, less than 100) so reloading them is quite fast. And it saves you some work of having to make yet another delegate.

Sometimes a delegate is the best solution; sometimes you can simply reload the entire table.

➤ Run the app and test that it works!

Exercise. Change the label to read "All Done!" when there are no more to-do items left to check. ∎

Answer: Change the relevant code in `tableView(cellForRowAtIndexPath)` to:

```
let count = checklist.countUncheckedItems()
if count == 0 {
  cell.detailTextLabel!.text = "All Done!"
} else {
  cell.detailTextLabel!.text = "\(count) Remaining"
}
```

You put the count into a local constant because you refer to it twice. Calculating the count once and storing it into a temporary constant is more optimal than doing the calculation twice.

Exercise: Now update the label to say "No Items" when the list is empty. ∎

Answer:

```
let count = checklist.countUncheckedItems()
if checklist.items.count == 0 {
  cell.detailTextLabel!.text = "(No Items)"
} else if count == 0 {
  cell.detailTextLabel!.text = "All Done!"
} else {
  cell.detailTextLabel!.text = "\(count) Remaining"
}
```

Just looking at the result of `countUncheckedItems()` is not enough. If this returns 0, you don't know whether that means all items are checked off or if the list has no items at all. You also need to look at the total number of items in the checklist, with `checklist.items.count`.

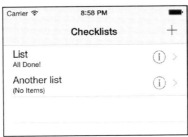

The text in the detail label changes depending on how many items are checked off

Little details like these matter – they make your app more fun to use. Ask yourself, what would make you feel better about having done your chores, the rather bland message "0 Remaining" or the joyous exclamation "All Done!"

A short diversion into Functional Programming

Swift is primarily an object-oriented language, but there is another style of writing software that has become quite popular in recent years: *functional programming*.

The term "functional" means that programs can be expressed purely in terms of mathematical functions that transform data.

Unlike the methods and functions in Swift, these mathematical functions are not allowed to have "side effects" – for any given inputs, a function should always produce the same output. Methods are much less strict.

Even though Swift is not a purely functional language, it does let you use certain functional programming techniques in your apps. They can really make your code a lot shorter.

For example, let's look at `countUncheckedItems()` again:

```
func countUncheckedItems() -> Int {
  var count = 0
  for item in items {
    if !item.checked {
      count += 1
    }
  }
  return count
}
```

That's quite a bit of code for something that's fairly simple. You can actually write this in a single line of code:

```
func countUncheckedItems() -> Int {
  return reduce(items, 0) { cnt, item in cnt + (item.checked ? 0 : 1) }
}
```

`reduce()` is a function that takes an array, looks at each item, and performs the code in the { } block.

Initially, the `cnt` variable contains the value 0, but after each item it is incremented by either 0 or 1, depending on whether the item was checked.

When `reduce()` is done, its return value is the total count of unchecked items.

You don't have to remember any of this for now, but it's pretty cool to see that Swift allows you to express this kind of algorithm very succinctly.

Sorting the lists

Another thing you often need to do with lists is sort them in some particular order.

Let's sort the list of checklists by name. Currently when you add a new checklist it is always appended to the end of the list, regardless of alphabetical order.

Before we figure out how to sort an array, let's think about when you need to perform this sort:

• When a new checklist is added

• When a checklist is renamed

There is no need to re-sort when a checklist is deleted because that doesn't have any impact on the order of the other objects.

Currently you handle these two situations in `AllListsViewController`'s implementation of `didFinishAddingChecklist` and `didFinishEditingChecklist`.

➤ Change these methods to the following:

```
func listDetailViewController(controller: ListDetailViewController,
                    didFinishAddingChecklist checklist: Checklist) {
```

```
    dataModel.lists.append(checklist)
    dataModel.sortChecklists()
    tableView.reloadData()
    dismissViewControllerAnimated(true, completion: nil)
}

func listDetailViewController(controller: ListDetailViewController,
                    didFinishEditingChecklist checklist: Checklist) {
    dataModel.sortChecklists()
    tableView.reloadData()
    dismissViewControllerAnimated(true, completion: nil)
}
```

You were able to remove a whole bunch of stuff from both methods because you now always do reloadData() on the table view.

It is no longer necessary to insert the new row manually, or to update the cell's textLabel. Instead you simply call tableView.reloadData() to refresh the entire table's contents.

Again, you can get away with this because the table will only hold a handful of rows. If this table held hundreds of rows, a more advanced approach might be necessary. (You could figure out where the new or renamed Checklist object should be inserted and just update that row.)

The sortChecklists() method on DataModel is new and you still need to add it. But before that, we need to have a short discussion about how sorting works.

When you sort a list of items, the app will compare the items one-by-one to figure out what the proper order is. But what does it mean to compare two Checklist objects?

In our app we obviously want to sort them by name, but we need some way to tell the app that's what we mean.

> Add the following method to **DataModel.swift**:

```
func sortChecklists() {
  lists.sort({ checklist1, checklist2 in return
            checklist1.name.localizedStandardCompare(checklist2.name) ==
                              NSComparisonResult.OrderedAscending })
}
```

Here you tell the lists array that the Checklists it contains should be sorted using some formula.

That formula is provided in the shape of a *closure*. You can tell by the { } brackets around the sorting code; they are what makes it into a closure:

```
lists.sort({ /* the sorting code goes here */ })
```

You've briefly seen closures in the Bull's Eye tutorial. They wrap a piece of source code into an anonymous, inline method.

The purpose of the closure is to determine whether one Checklist object comes before another, based on our rules for sorting.

The sort algorithm will repeatedly ask one Checklist object from the list how it compares to the other Checklist objects using the formula from the closure, and then shuffle them around until the array is sorted.

This allows sort() to sort the contents of the array in any order you desire. If you wanted to sort on other criteria all you'd have to do is change the logic inside the closure.

The actual sorting formula is this:

```
checklist1.name.localizedStandardCompare(checklist2.name) ==
                         NSComparisonResult.OrderedAscending
```

To compare these two `Checklist` objects, you're only looking at their names.

The `localizedStandardCompare()` method compares the two `name` strings while ignoring lowercase vs. uppercase (so "a" and "A" are considered equal) and taking into consideration the rules of the current *locale*.

A locale is an object that knows about country and language-specific rules. Sorting in German may be different than sorting in English, for example.

That's all you have to do to sort the array: call `sort()` and give it a closure with the logic that compares two `Checklist` objects.

➤ Just to make sure the existing lists are also sorted in the right order, you should also call `sortChecklists()` when the plist file is loaded:

```
func loadChecklists() {
  let path = dataFilePath()
  if NSFileManager.defaultManager().fileExistsAtPath(path) {
    if let data = NSData(contentsOfFile: path) {
      . . .
      sortChecklists()
    }
  }
}
```

➤ Run the app and add some new checklists. Change their names and notice that the list is always sorted alphabetically.

New checklists are always sorted alphabetically

Adding icons to the checklists

Because true iOS developers can't get enough of view controllers and delegates, let's add a new property to the `Checklist` object that lets you choose an icon. We're really going to cement these principles in your mind.

When you're done, the Add/Edit Checklist screen will look like this:

You can assign an icon to a checklist

You are going to add a row to the Add/Edit Checklist screen that opens a new screen for picking an icon.

This icon picker is a new view controller. You won't show it modally this time but push it on the navigation stack so it slides into the screen.

The Resources folder for this tutorial contains a folder named **Checklist Icons** with a selection of PNG images that depict different categories.

The various checklist icon images

> Add the images from this folder to the asset catalog. Select **Image.xcassets** in the project navigator, click the + button at the bottom and choose **Import…**

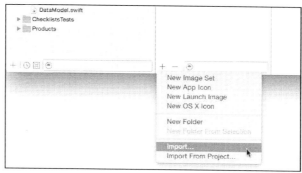

Choosing the option to import new images into the asset catalog

Navigate to the **Checklist Icons** folder and select all the files inside:

Selecting the image files to import

Note: Make sure to select the actual image files, not just the folder.

Click **Open** to import the images. The asset catalog should now look like this:

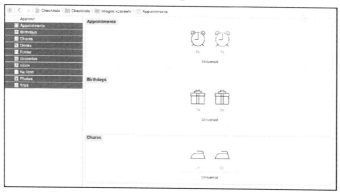

The asset catalog after importing the checklist icons

Each image comes with a 2x version for Retina devices and a 3x version for the iPhone 6 Plus with its incredible Retina HD screen.

As I pointed out in the previous tutorial, you don't need low-resolution 1x graphics, unless your app is universal or iPad-only, or if you want to support iOS versions before 8.0. All iPhones and iPod touch devices that can run iOS 8 have Retina 2x or 3x screens.

➤ Add the following property to **Checklist.swift**:

```
var iconName: String
```

The iconName variable holds the filename of the icon image.

➤ Extend init(coder) and encodeWithCoder() to respectively load and save this icon name in the Checklists.plist file:

```
required init(coder aDecoder: NSCoder) {
  name = aDecoder.decodeObjectForKey("Name") as! String
  items = aDecoder.decodeObjectForKey("Items") as! [ChecklistItem]
  iconName = aDecoder.decodeObjectForKey("IconName") as! String
  super.init()
}

func encodeWithCoder(aCoder: NSCoder) {
  aCoder.encodeObject(name, forKey: "Name")
  aCoder.encodeObject(items, forKey: "Items")
  aCoder.encodeObject(iconName, forKey: "IconName")
}
```

Just in case you feel like extending this app with new features of your own, remember that this is something you need to do for every new property that you add to this object. Otherwise it won't get saved to the plist file.

Xcode now complains about the init(name) method. Apparently it doesn't like that "Property self.iconName is not initialized at super.init call".

That means iconName doesn't have a value yet if the Checklist object is initialized with init(name) instead of init(coder). And as you know by now, all variables that are not optionals must always have a value.

➤ Update init(name) to the following:

```
init(name: String) {
  self.name = name
  iconName = "Appointments"
  super.init()
}
```

This will give all new checklists the "Appointments" icon.

At this point you just want to see that you can make an icon – any icon – show up in the table view. When that works you can worry about letting the user pick their own icons.

➤ Change tableView(cellForRowAtIndexPath) in **AllListsViewController.swift** to put the icon into the table view cell:

```
override func tableView(tableView: UITableView,
                   cellForRowAtIndexPath indexPath: NSIndexPath) -> UITableViewCell {
  . . .

  cell.imageView!.image = UIImage(named: checklist.iconName)
  return cell
}
```

Cells using the standard .Subtitle cell style come with a built-in UIImageView on the left. You can simply give it the image and it will automatically appear. Easy peasy.

➤ Before running the app, remove the Checklists.plist file or reset the Simulator, because you've modified the file format again (you added the "IconName" field in init(coder) and encodeWithCoder). You don't want any weird crashes...

➤ Run the app and now each checklist should have an alarm clock icon in front of its name.

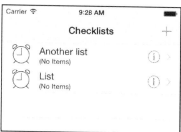

The checklists have an icon

Satisfied that this works, you can now change Checklist's init(name) to give each Checklist object an icon named "No Icon" by default.

➤ In **Checklist.swift**, in init(name) change the line that sets iconName to:

```
iconName = "No Icon"
```

The "No Icon" image is a fully transparent PNG image with the same dimensions as the other icons. Using a transparent image is necessary to make all the checklists line up properly, even if they have no icon.

If you were to set iconName to an empty string instead, the image view in the table view cell would remain empty and the text would align with the left margin of the screen. That looks bad when other cells do have icons:

Using an empty image to properly align the text labels (right)

Let's create the icon picker screen.

➤ Add a new Swift file to the project. Name it **IconPickerViewController**.

➤ Replace the contents of **IconPickerViewController.swift** with:

```
import UIKit

protocol IconPickerViewControllerDelegate: class {
  func iconPicker(picker: IconPickerViewController, didPickIcon iconName: String)
}

class IconPickerViewController: UITableViewController {
  weak var delegate: IconPickerViewControllerDelegate?
}
```

This defines the `IconPickerViewController` object, which is a table view controller, and a delegate protocol that it uses to communicate with other objects in the app.

➤ Add a constant (inside the `class` brackets) to hold the array of icons:

```
let icons = [
    "No Icon",
    "Appointments",
    "Birthdays",
    "Chores",
    "Drinks",
    "Folder",
    "Groceries",
    "Inbox",
    "Photos",
    "Trips"]
```

This is an array that contains a list of icon names. These strings are both the text you will show on the screen and the name of the PNG file inside the asset catalog. The `icons` array is the data model for this table view. Note that it is a non-mutable array (it is defined with `let` and arrays are "value" types), because the user cannot add or delete icons.

This new view controller is a `UITableViewController`, so you have to implement the data source methods for the table view.

➤ Add the following methods to the source file:

```
override func tableView(tableView: UITableView, numberOfRowsInSection section: Int) -> Int {
  return icons.count
}
```

This simply returns the number of icons in the array.

```
override func tableView(tableView: UITableView,
                cellForRowAtIndexPath indexPath: NSIndexPath) -> UITableViewCell {

  let cell = tableView.dequeueReusableCellWithIdentifier("IconCell") as! UITableViewCell

  let iconName = icons[indexPath.row]
  cell.textLabel!.text = iconName
  cell.imageView!.image = UIImage(named: iconName)

  return cell
}
```

Here you obtain a table view cell and give it text and an image. You will design this cell in the storyboard momentarily.

It will be a prototype cell with the cell style "Default" (or "Basic" as it is called in Interface Builder). Cells with this style already contain a text label and an image view, which is very convenient.

➤ Open the storyboard. Drag a new **Table View Controller** from the Object Library and place it next to the List Detail View Controller (the one that says "Add Checklist").

➤ In the **Identity inspector**, change the class of this new table view controller to **IconPickerViewController**.

➤ Select the prototype cell and set its **Style** to **Basic** and its (re-use) **Identifier** to **IconCell**.

That takes care of the design for the icon picker. Now you need to have some place to call it from. To do this, you will add a new row to the Add/Edit Checklist screen.

➤ Go to the **List Detail View Controller** and add a new section to the table view. You can do this by changing the **Sections** field in the **Attributes inspector** for the table view from 1 to 2. This will duplicate the existing section.

➤ Delete the Text Field from the new cell; you don't need it.

➤ Add a **Label** to this cell and name it **Icon**.

➤ Set the cell's **Accessory** to **Disclosure Indicator**. That adds a gray chevron.

➤ Add an **Image View** to the right of the cell. Make it 36 × 36 points big. (Tip: use the Size inspector for this.)

➤ Use the **Assistant Editor** to add an outlet property for this image view to **ListDetailViewController.swift** and name it **iconImageView**.

Now that you've finished the designs for both screens, you can connect them with a segue.

➤ **Ctrl-drag** from the "Icon" table view cell to the Icon Picker View Controller and add a segue (pick **Selection Segue – show**). (Make sure you're dragging from the Table View Cell, not its Content View or any of the other subviews.)

➤ Give the segue the identifier **PickIcon**.

➤ Thanks to the segue, the new view controller has been given a navigation bar. Double-click that navigation bar and change its title to **Choose Icon**.

> **Note:** If Xcode won't let you change the navigation title, then drag a Navigation Item from the Object Library into the view controller.

This part of the storyboard should now look like this:

The Icon Picker view controller in the storyboard

➤ In **ListDetailViewController.swift,** change the willSelectRowAtIndexPath table view delegate method to:

```
override func tableView(tableView: UITableView,
                        willSelectRowAtIndexPath indexPath: NSIndexPath) -> NSIndexPath? {
  if indexPath.section == 1 {
    return indexPath
  } else {
    return nil
  }
}
```

This is necessary otherwise you cannot tap the "Icon" cell to trigger the segue.

Previously this method always returned nil, which meant tapping on rows was not possible. Now, however, you want to allow the user to tap the Icon cell, so this method should return the index-path for that cell.

Because the Icon cell is the only row in the second section, you only have to check indexPath.section. There is no need to check the row number too. Users still can't select the cell with the text field (from section 0).

> Run the app and verify that there is now an Icon row in the Add/Edit Checklist screen. Tapping it will open the Choose Icon screen and show a list of icons.

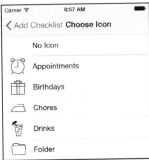

The icon picker screen

You can press the back button to go back but selecting an icon doesn't do anything yet. It just colors the row gray but doesn't put the icon into the checklist.

To make this work, you have to hook up the icon picker to the Add/Edit Checklist screen through its own delegate protocol.

> First, add an instance variable in **ListDetailViewController.swift**:

```
var iconName = "Folder"
```

You use this variable to keep track of the chosen icon name.

Even though the Checklist object now has an iconName property, you cannot keep track of the chosen icon in the Checklist object for the simple reason that you may not always have a Checklist object, i.e. when the user is adding a new checklist.

So you'll store the icon name in a temporary variable and copy that into the Checklist's iconName property at the right time.

You should initialize the iconName variable with something reasonable. Let's go with the folder icon. This is only necessary for new Checklists, which get the Folder icon by default.

> Update viewDidLoad() to the following:

```
override func viewDidLoad() {
  super.viewDidLoad()
  tableView.rowHeight = 44

  if let checklist = checklistToEdit {
    title = "Edit Checklist"
    textField.text = checklist.name
```

```
    doneBarButton.enabled = true
    iconName = checklist.iconName
  }

  iconImageView.image = UIImage(named: iconName)
}
```

This has two new lines: If the `checklistToEdit` optional is not `nil`, then you copy the `Checklist` object's icon name into the `iconName` instance variable. You also load the icon's image file into a new `UIImage` object and set it on the `iconImageView` so it shows up in the Icon row.

Earlier you hooked up the Add/Edit Checklist screen to `IconPickerViewController` with a push segue named "PickIcon". You still need to implement `prepareForSegue(sender)` in order to tell the `IconPickerViewController` that this screen is now its delegate.

➤ Add the following method to **ListDetailViewController.swift**:

```
override func prepareForSegue(segue: UIStoryboardSegue, sender: AnyObject?) {
  if segue.identifier == "PickIcon" {
    let controller = segue.destinationViewController as! IconPickerViewController
    controller.delegate = self
  }
}
```

This should have no big surprises for you.

Of course, Xcode has found something to complain about: it does not like that you wrote "`controller.delegate = self`", because (and I quote),

Type 'ListDetailViewController' does not conform to protocol 'IconPickerViewControllerDelegate'

Exercise: What did we forget? ∎

Answer: You haven't made the view controller conform to the delegate protocol yet, so Swift won't let `ListDetailViewController` become the delegate of the icon picker!

➤ Add the name of that protocol to the class line:

```
class ListDetailViewController: UITableViewController, UITextFieldDelegate,
                       IconPickerViewControllerDelegate {
```

➤ And add the implementation of the method from that protocol somewhere inside the `ListDetailViewController` class:

```
func iconPicker(picker: IconPickerViewController, didPickIcon iconName: String) {
  self.iconName = iconName
  iconImageView.image = UIImage(named: iconName)
  navigationController?.popViewControllerAnimated(true)
}
```

This puts the name of the chosen icon into the `iconName` variable to remember it, and also updates the image view with the new image.

You don't call `dismissViewController()` here but `popViewControllerAnimated()` because the Icon Picker is on the navigation stack.

When creating the segue you used the segue style "show" instead of "present modally", which pushes the new view controller on the navigation stack. To return you need to "pop" it off again.

Recall that `navigationController` is an optional property of the view controller, so you need to use ? (or !) to access the actual `UINavigationController` object.

> **Note:** You've seen `self` used to refer to the object itself. Here you've written:
>
>   self.iconName = iconName
>
> The reason is that `iconName` can refer to two different things here: 1) the second parameter from the delegate method, and 2) the instance variable.
>
> To remove the ambiguity, you prefix the instance variable with "`self.`", so it's clear to the compiler which of the two `iconName`s you intended to use.

➤ Change the `done()` action so that it puts the chosen icon name into the `Checklist` object when the user closes the screen:

```
@IBAction func done() {
  if let checklist = checklistToEdit {
    checklist.name = textField.text
    checklist.iconName = iconName
    delegate?.listDetailViewController(self, didFinishEditingChecklist: checklist)
  } else {
    let checklist = Checklist(name: textField.text)
    checklist.iconName = iconName
    delegate?.listDetailViewController(self, didFinishAddingChecklist: checklist)
  }
}
```

Finally, you must change `IconPickerViewController` to actually call the delegate method when a row is tapped.

➤ Add the following method to the bottom of **IconPickerViewController.swift**:

```
override func tableView(tableView: UITableView,
                        didSelectRowAtIndexPath indexPath: NSIndexPath) {
  if let delegate = delegate {
    let iconName = icons[indexPath.row]
    delegate.iconPicker(self, didPickIcon: iconName)
  }
}
```

And that's it. You can now set icons on the `Checklist` objects.

To recap, you:

• added a new view controller object,

• designed its user interface in the storyboard editor, and

• hooked it up to the Add/Edit Checklist screen using a segue and a delegate.

Those are the basic steps you need to take with any new screen that you add.

➤ Run the app to try it out!

The chosen icon does not appear in the Icon row

Hmm, there seems to be a small problem. After picking an icon it doesn't actually appear in the Icon row.

Exercise: Can you figure this one out? Hint: It doesn't have anything to do with the source code. ■

Answer: When you designed this screen in Interface Builder, you placed the icon's Image View right next to the disclosure indicator:

The design of the Icon cell

However, the storyboard doesn't use the same dimensions as the iPhone screen – it's much wider.

You've been designing on a square canvas that is independent of the screen sizes of the actual devices. The dimensions of this square fall somewhere in between the sizes of iPhones and iPads. Bigger than the iPhone, smaller than the iPad.

Designing for the square allows you to have a resizable user interface that works on both the iPhone and iPad – that's why they're called "universal" storyboards.

When the app is run on an actual device, the view controller is resized to fit that screen. On the iPhone it becomes narrower.

And that's where the problem is: the position of the UIImageView object does not get adjusted for the new screen size. The image view is still there, you just can't see it – it's about 200 points or so off-screen to the right.

What you want to happen instead is that the image view stays glued to the right edge of the screen, always at the same distance from the disclosure indicator. When the view controller shrinks to fit the iPhone screen, the image view should move along with it.

The solution is to add Auto Layout constraints to the image view that tell the app what the relationship is between the image view and the edges of the screen.

➤ Select the **Image View**. Bring up the **Pin menu** using the icon at the bottom of the canvas.

➤ First, uncheck **Constrain to margins**.

➤ Activate the T-bars at the **top** and the **right** so they turn red.

➤ Put checkmarks in front of **Width** and **Height**.

➤ For Update Frames choose **Items of New Constraints**.

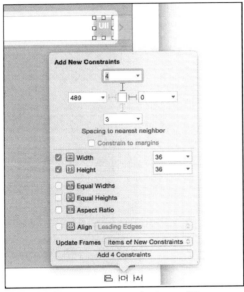

Adding constraints to the Image View

➤ Finally, click **Add 4 Constraints** to finish.

The image view should now look like this:

The Image View with the constraints

Make sure the bars representing the constraints are blue. If they are orange you may have forgotten something in the Pin menu. (Either try again or use the **Editor → Resolve Auto Layout Issues** menu item.)

The most important constraint is the one on the right. This tells UIKit that the right-hand side of the image view should always stick to the right-hand edge of the table view cell's content view.

In other words, no matter how wide or narrow the screen is, the image view will always have the same location relative to the disclosure indicator.

The other three constraints – top, width, and height – were necessary only because all views must always have enough constraints to determine their position and size.

If you don't specify any constraints of your own, Interface Builder will come up with reasonable default constraints. But as soon as you add just one custom constraint, you'll have to add the others too.

➤ Run the app again. Now the icon does properly appear:

The image view is visible

There's still a small improvement to make. In done(), you currently do this:

```
let checklist = Checklist(name: textField.text)
checklist.iconName = iconName
```

Setting the icon name can be considered part of the initialization of Checklist too, so it would be nice if you could write:

```
let checklist = Checklist(name: textField.text, iconName: iconName)
```

➤ Make this change. In **ListDetailViewController.swift**'s done() method, replace the code that creates the new Checklist object with the above.

To make this work, you have to add a new init method to **Checklist.swift** that takes two parameters: name and iconName.

➤ Add the new init method to **Checklist.swift**:

```
init(name: String, iconName: String) {
  self.name = name
  self.iconName = iconName
  super.init()
}
```

Checklist now has three init methods:

- init(name) for when you just have a name
- init(name, iconName) for when you also have an icon name
- init(coder) for loading the objects from the plist file

Note that at this point init(name) and init(name, iconName) do almost the same things. For comparison, here is init(name) again:

```
init(name: String) {
  self.name = name
  iconName = "No Icon"
  super.init()
}
```

Both initializers assign values to self.name and iconName, and call super.init().

The only difference is that init(name) does not have to use the notation "self.iconName" because there iconName can only mean one thing.

You can improve on this by making init(name) call init(name, iconName) with "No Icon" as the value for the iconName parameter.

➤ Replace init(name) with:

```
convenience init(name: String) {
  self.init(name: name, iconName: "No Icon")
}
```

Instead of super.init() it now calls self.init(name, iconName).

Because it farms out its work to another init method, init(name) is known as a *convenience initializer*.

It does the same thing as init(name, iconName) but saves you from having to type iconName: "No Icon" whenever you want to use it.

init(name, iconName) has become the so-called *designated initializer* for Checklist. It is the primary way to create new Checklist objects, while init(name) exists only for the convenience of lazy developers… such as you and me. :-)

➤ Build the app to verify it still works.

Exercise: Give ChecklistItem an init(text) method that is used instead of the parameter-less init(). Or how about an init(text, checked) method? ∎

Making the app look good

You're going to keep it simple in this tutorial as far as fancying up the graphics goes. The standard look of navigation controllers and table views is perfectly adequate, although a little bland. In the next tutorials you'll see how you can customize the look of these UI elements.

Even though this app uses the stock visuals, there is a simple trick to give the app its own personality: changing the **tint color**.

The tint color is what UIKit uses to indicate that things can be interacted with, such as buttons. The default tint color is a medium blue.

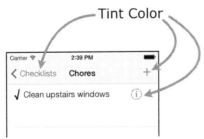

The buttons all use the same tint color

Changing the tint color is pretty easy.

➤ Open the storyboard and go to the **File inspector** (the first tab).

➤ Click **Global Tint** to open the color picker and choose Red: 4, Green: 169, Blue: 235. That makes the tint color a lighter shade of blue.

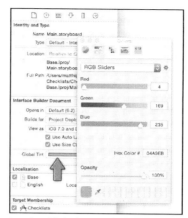

Changing the Global Tint color for the storyboard

Tip: If the color picker only shows a black & white bar, then click the box that says Gray Scale Slider and change it to RGB Sliders.

It would also look nice if the checkmark wasn't black but used the tint color too.

➤ To make that happen, add the following line to `configureCheckmarkForCell()` in **ChecklistViewController.swift**:

```
label.textColor = view.tintColor
```

➤ Run the app. It already looks a lot more interesting:

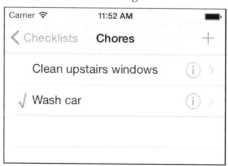

The tint color makes the app less plain looking

No app is complete without an icon. The Resources folder for this tutorial contains a folder named **Icon** with the app icon image in various sizes. Notice that it uses the same blue as the tint color.

➤ Add these icons to the asset catalog (**Images.xcassets**). Recall that icons go into the **AppIcon** section. Simply drag them from the Finder into the slots.

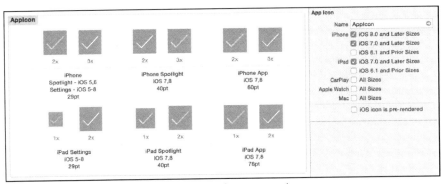

The app icons in the asset catalog

Apps should also have a launch image or launch file. By showing a static picture of the app's UI it will give the illusion the app is loading faster than it really is. It's all smoke and mirrors.

The Xcode template includes the file **LaunchScreen.xib** that is used as the launch file. With some effort you could make this look like the initial screen of the app, but there's an easier solution.

➤ Click **Checklists** at the top of the project navigator to open the **Project Settings** screen.

➤ In the **General** tab, scroll down to the **App Icons and Launch Images** section.

➤ In the **Launch Screen File** box, press the arrow and select **Main.storyboard**.

Changing the launch screen file

This tells the app you'll be using the design from the storyboard as the launch file.

Upon startup, the app finds the initial view controller and converts it into a static launch image. For this app that is the All Lists View Controller inside a navigation controller.

➤ Delete **LaunchScreen.xib** from the project.

➤ From the **Product** menu choose **Clean**. It's also a good idea to delete the app from the Simulator just so it no longer has any copies of the old launch file lying around.

➤ Run the app. Just before the real UI appears you should briefly see the following launch screen:

The empty launch screen

The launch screen simply has a navigation bar and an empty table view. This gives the illusion the app's UI has already been loaded but that the data hasn't been filled in yet.

Using a proper launch screen makes the app look more professional – and faster!

For many apps you can simply use the main storyboard as the launch file, making it a no-brainer to add. Besides, you need a launch file to support the larger screens of the new iPhone 6 and 6 Plus models.

Supporting all iPhone models

The app should run without major problems on all current iPhone models, from the smallest (iPhone 4S) to the largest (iPhone 6 Plus). Table view controllers are very flexible and will automatically resize to fit the screen, no matter how large or small. Give it a try in the different Simulators!

Well, I said no *major* problems. But there are still a few tweaks you can make here and there.

For example, on the 3.5 and 4-inch models, the text may run off the page when you're entering the name of a new checklist or to-do item:

The text field goes beyond the edge of the screen

This is due to the `UITextField` not automatically resizing with the view controller as it shrinks to the available space. The solution, again, is Auto Layout constraints.

➤ Open the storyboard and go to the Add Checklist screen. Select the **Text Field**.

➤ In the **Pin menu,** activate the **top, left,** and **right** T-bars so they become red.

➤ Uncheck **Constrain to margins.**

➤ Put a checkmark in front of **Height** (it should be 30 points high).

➤ For Update Frames choose **Items of New Constraints.**

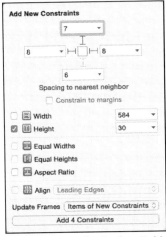

The pin settings for the Text Field

These options will make the text field stick to the sides of the table view cell.

➤ Repeat this procedure for the text field from the Add Item screen.

➤ Run the app and the text should start scrolling when you get to the edge:

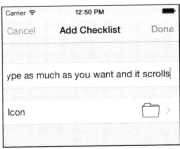

Type to your heart's content

Let's say you enter a very long text. What happens to that text when it gets shown in the other table view?

There is no problem on the All Lists screen:

Built-in cell styles automatically resize

This table view uses the built-in "Subtitle" cell style, which automatically resizes to fit the width of the screen. It also truncates the text with ... when it becomes too large.

For the to-do items list, however, the picture doesn't look so rosy:

The text doesn't fit

The label overlaps the disclosure button on the right and runs off the screen. That's unacceptable.

Because this is a custom prototype cell design, you'll have to add some constraints to prevent this from happening.

➤ In the storyboard, go to the Checklist screen and select the label inside the prototype cell.

➤ First use **Editor → Size to Fit Content** to give the label its ideal size. That makes it a lot smaller, but that's OK. Without doing this first you may run into issues on the next steps.

You want to pin the label to the right edge of the content view so it sticks to the disclosure button. Let's make that constraint first.

➤ Open the **Pin menu** and uncheck **Constrain to margins**.

➤ Activate the T-bar on the **right**. Give it the value 0 so there is no spacing between the label and the disclosure button.

➤ As always, set Update Frames to **Items of New Constraints**. Click **Add 1 Constraint** to add the new constraint.

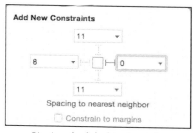

Pinning the label to the right

Whoops, that messes up the label:

The label doesn't have enough constraints yet

Remember that you always need to specify enough constraints to determine the position and size of a view. Here you only added a constraint for the right edge of the label, which is not enough.

No panic! This sort of thing is common while you're adding constraints. To fix it you simply have to add the missing ones.

> With the label still selected, open the **Align menu** (next to Pin). Check **Vertical Center in Container**. Update Frames should be **Items of New Constraints**.

![Add New Alignment Constraints dialog with Vertical Center in Container checked, value 0, Update Frames set to Items of New Constraints, Add 1 Constraint button]

Centering the label vertically

Now everything turns blue again. The label has a valid position, both X and Y.

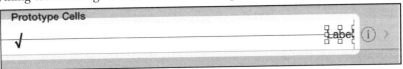

All blue bars but still in the wrong place

Note: Even though you didn't specify any constraints for the label's size, the bars are all blue. How come they are not still orange?

Without size constraints the label uses its contents – the text and the font – to calculate how big needs to be. This is called the *intrinsic content size*.

UI components with an intrinsic size, such as UILabel, don't need to have Width or Height constraints, but this is only valid if you've used Size to Fit Content to reset the label to its intrinsic size first.

Unfortunately, the label is now right aligned. That's not what you wanted… the label should be on the left and just as wide as the cell's content view.

The easiest way to make this happen is to add a new constraint on the left to glue the label to the left edge of the screen as well.

➤ Select the label again. From the **Editor** menu, choose **Pin** → **Leading Space to Superview**.

This adds a very big blue bar for the new constraint, but doesn't actually move the label yet.

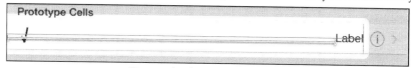

The new leading space constraint

➤ Select the blue bar. In the **Size inspector**, change **Constant** to 40.

That's better:

Making the leading space constraint smaller

The label is now pinned to both edges of the table view cell's content view, so it will get stretched to however wide the table view cell is.

➤ Run the app and the label should properly truncate:

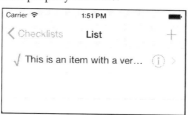

The label now longer runs off the screen

Just in case you're still getting the "Detected a case where constraints ambiguously suggest a height of zero for a table view cell's content view" message in the debug pane, here's how to fix it:

➤ Add the following line to viewDidLoad():

```
tableView.rowHeight = 44
```

Do this in ListDetailViewController.swift, ItemDetailViewController.swift, and ChecklistViewController.swift.

Now the table view cell's height is calculated from the height of the checkmark and the extra spacing above and below. The error message should be gone after this.

You can find the project for the app up to this point under **10 - UI Improvements** in the tutorial's Source Code folder.

Extra feature: local notifications

I hope you're still with me! We have discussed in great detail view controllers, navigation controllers, storyboards, segues, table views and cells, and the data model.

These are all essential topics to master if you want to build iOS apps because almost every app uses these building blocks.

In this section you're going to expand the app to add a new feature: **local notifications**. A local notification allows the app to schedule a reminder to the user that will be displayed even when the app is not running.

You will add a "due date" field to the ChecklistItem object and then remind the user about this deadline with a local notification.

If this sounds like fun, then keep reading. :-)

The steps for this section are as follows:

- Try out a local notification just to see how it works.

- Allow the user to pick a due date for to-do items.

- Create a date picker control.

- Schedule local notifications for the to-do items, and update them when the user changes the due date.

Before you wonder about how to integrate this in the app, let's just schedule a local notification and see what happens.

By the way, local notifications are different from *push* notifications. Push allows your app to receive messages about external events, such as your favorite team winning the World Series.

Local notifications are more similar to an alarm clock: you set a specific time and then it "beeps".

As of iOS 8, an app is only allowed to show local notifications after it has asked the user for permission. If the user denies permission, then any local notifications for your app simply won't appear. You only need to ask for permission once, so let's do that first.

➤ Open **AppDelegate.swift** and add the following code to the method application(didFinishLaunchingWithOptions), just before the return true line:

```
let notificationSettings = UIUserNotificationSettings(forTypes: .Alert | .Sound,
                                   categories: nil)
UIApplication.sharedApplication().registerUserNotificationSettings(notificationSettings)
```

Recall that application(didFinishLaunchingWithOptions) is called when the app starts up. It is the *entry point* for the app – the first place in the code where you can do something after the app launches.

Because you're just playing with these local notifications now, this is a good place to ask for permission.

You tell iOS that the app wishes to send notifications of type "alert" with a sound effect. Later you'll put this code into a more appropriate place.

Things that start with a dot

Throughout the app you've seen things like `.None`, `.Checkmark`, and `.Default` – and now `.Alert` and `.Sound`. These are *enumeration* symbols.

An enumeration, or enum for short, is a data type that consists of a list of possible symbols and their values.

For example, the `UIUserNotificationType` enum contains the symbols:

```
.None
.Badge
.Sound
.Alert
```

You can combine these names (with the | operator) to define what sort of notifications the app will show to the user. Here you've chosen the combination of an alert and a sound effect.

It's easy to spot when an enum is being used because of the dot in front of the symbol name. This is actually shorthand notation; you could also have written it like this:

```
let notificationSettings = UIUserNotificationSettings(
    forTypes: UIUserNotificationType.Alert | UIUserNotificationType.Sound, categories: nil)
```

Fortunately, Swift is smart enough to realize that `.Alert` and `.Sound` are from `UIUserNotificationType`, so you can save yourself some keystrokes.

➤ Run the app. You should immediately get a popup asking for permission:

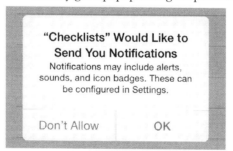

The permission dialog

Tap **OK**. The next time you run the app you won't be asked again; iOS remembers what you chose.

(If you tapped Don't Allow – naughty! – then you can always reset the Simulator to get the permissions dialog again. You can also change the notification options in the Settings app.)

➤ Stop the app and add the following code to `didFinishLaunchingWithOptions`:

```
let date = NSDate(timeIntervalSinceNow: 10)

let localNotification = UILocalNotification()
localNotification.fireDate = date
localNotification.timeZone = NSTimeZone.defaultTimeZone()
localNotification.alertBody = "I am a local notification!"
localNotification.soundName = UILocalNotificationDefaultSoundName

UIApplication.sharedApplication().scheduleLocalNotification(localNotification)
```

This creates a new local notification. It will fire exactly 10 seconds after the app has started.

A local notification is scheduled in the future using an NSDate object, which specifies a certain date and time. You use the timeIntervalSinceNow initializer to create an NSDate object that points at a time 10 seconds into the future.

When you create the UILocalNotification object you give it the NSDate object as its "fire date". You also set the time zone, so the system automatically adjusts the fire date when the device travels across different time zones (for you frequent flyers).

Local notifications can appear in different ways. Here you set a text so that an alert message will be shown when the notification fires. You also set a sound.

Finally, you tell the UIApplication object to schedule the notification.

A word on UIApplication

You haven't used this object before, but every app has one and it deals with application-wide functionality.

You won't directly use UIApplication a lot, except for special features such as local notifications.

The app also provides a delegate object for UIApplication to handle messages concerning the app as a whole, such as applicationDidEnterBackground() and application(didFinishLaunchingWithOptions) that you've seen earlier.

In this app, the delegate for UIApplication is the – aptly named – AppDelegate object. Because every app needs one, the Xcode project templates always include an app delegate object ready-to-go.

➤ Add the following method to **AppDelegate.swift**:

```
func application(application: UIApplication,
                 didReceiveLocalNotification notification: UILocalNotification) {
  println("didReceiveLocalNotification \(notification)")
}
```

This method will be invoked when the local notification is posted and the app is still running or in a suspended state in the background.

You won't do anything here except log a message to the debug pane. For some apps it makes sense to react to the notification, for example to show a message to the user or to refresh the screen.

➤ Run the app. Immediately after it has started, press the Home button (or the **Hardware** → **Home** menu item on the Simulator).

Wait 10 seconds… I know, it seems like an eternity! After an agonizing 10 seconds a message should pop up in Notification Center:

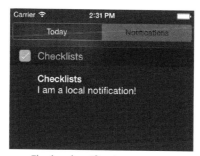

The local notification message

> Tap the notification to go back to the app.

As the app opens, the debug area shows that didReceiveLocalNotification() is called with the notification object. It displays something like this:

```
didReceiveLocalNotification <UIConcreteLocalNotification: 0x7fbabb513720>{fire date = Friday,
July 18, 2014 at 12:12:24 PM Central European Summer Time, time zone = Europe/Amsterdam
(GMT+2) offset 7200 (Daylight), repeat interval = 0, repeat count =
UILocalNotificationInfiniteRepeatCount, next fire date = (null), user info = (null)}
```

Why did I want you to press the Home button? iOS will only show an alert with the notification message if the app is not currently active.

> Stop the app and run it again. Now don't press Home and just wait.

After 10 seconds you should see the "didReceiveLocalNotification" log message in the debug area but no alert is shown. (The notification does show up in Notification Center, though.)

When your app is active and in the foreground, it is supposed to handle any fired notifications in its own manner.

All right, now you know that it works, you should restore **AppDelegate.swift** to its former state because you don't really want to schedule a new notification every time the user starts the app.

> Remove all the local notification code from didFinishLaunchingWithOptions and change it back to the way it was.

You can keep the didReceiveLocalNotification() method, as it will come in handy when debugging the local notifications.

Extending the data model

Let's think about how the app will handle these notifications. Each ChecklistItem will get a due date field (an NSDate object) and a Bool that says whether the user wants to be reminded of this item or not.

Users might not want to be reminded of everything, so you shouldn't schedule local notifications for those items. Such a Bool is often called a *flag*. Let's name it shouldRemind.

You will add settings for these two new fields to the Add/Edit Item screen and make it look like this:

The Add/Edit Item screen now has Remind Me and Due Date fields

The due date field will require some sort of date picker control. iOS comes with a cool date picker view that you'll add into the table view.

First, let's figure out how and when to schedule the notifications. I can think of the following situations:

• When the user adds a new ChecklistItem object that has the shouldRemind flag set, you must schedule a new notification.

• When the user changes the due date on an existing ChecklistItem, the old notification should be cancelled (if there is one) and a new one scheduled in its place (if shouldRemind is still set).

• When the user toggles the shouldRemind flag from on to off, the existing notification should be cancelled. The other way around, from off to on, should schedule a new notification.

• When the user deletes a ChecklistItem, its notification should be cancelled if it had one.

• When the user deletes an entire Checklist, all the notifications for those items should be cancelled.

This list makes it obvious that you don't need just a way to schedule new notifications but also a way to cancel them.

You should probably also check that you don't create notifications for to-do items whose due dates are in the past. I'm sure iOS is smart enough to ignore those notifications, but let's be good citizens anyway.

UIApplication has a method cancelLocalNotification() that allows you to cancel a notification that was previously scheduled. That method takes a UILocalNotification object. Somehow you must associate the ChecklistItem object with a UILocalNotification in order to cancel that notification.

It is tempting to put the UILocalNotification object in ChecklistItem, so you always know what it is, but imagine what happens when the app goes to the background. You save the ChecklistItem object to the Checklists.plist file – but what about the UILocalNotification object?

As it happens, the UILocalNotification conforms to the NSCoding protocol so you could serialize it along with the ChecklistItem object into the plist file. However, that is asking for trouble.

These UILocalNotification objects are owned by the operating system, not by your app. When the app starts again, it is very well possible that iOS uses different objects to represent the same notifications. You cannot unfreeze these objects from the plist file and expect iOS to recognize them.

So let's not store the UILocalNotification objects directly.

What will work better is to give the UILocalNotification a reference to the associated ChecklistItem. Each local notification has a dictionary named userInfo that you can use to store your own values.

You will not use this dictionary to store the ChecklistItem object itself, for the same reason as above: when the app closes and later starts again, it will get new ChecklistItem objects. Even though they look and behave exactly the same as the old ChecklistItems (because you froze and unfroze them), they are likely to be placed elsewhere in memory and the references inside the UILocalNotifications will be broken.

Instead of direct references, you will use a numeric identifier. You will give each ChecklistItem object a unique numeric ID. Assigning numeric IDs to objects is a common approach when creating data models – it is very similar to giving records in a relational database a numeric primary key, if you're familiar with that sort of thing.

You'll save this item ID in the Checklists.plist file and also store it in the userInfo dictionary of the UILocalNotification. Then you can easily find the notification when you have the ChecklistItem object, or the ChecklistItem object when you have the notification.

This will work even after the app has terminated and all the original objects have long been destroyed.

➤ Make these changes to **ChecklistItem.swift**:

```
var dueDate = NSDate()
var shouldRemind = false
var itemID: Int
```

Note that you called it itemID and not simply "id". The reason is that id is a special keyword in Objective-C, and this could cause trouble if you ever wanted to mix your Swift code with Objective-C code.

The dueDate and shouldRemind variables have initial values, but itemID does not. That's why you had to specify the type of itemID – it's an Int – but not for the other two variables.

Swift is smart enough to infer that dueDate cannot be anything but an NSDate, and that shouldRemind should be a Bool.

You have to extend init(coder) and encodeWithCoder() in order to be able to load and save these new properties along with the ChecklistItem objects.

➤ Change these methods in **ChecklistItem.swift**:

```
required init(coder aDecoder: NSCoder) {
  text = aDecoder.decodeObjectForKey("Text") as! String
  checked = aDecoder.decodeBoolForKey("Checked")
  dueDate = aDecoder.decodeObjectForKey("DueDate") as! NSDate
  shouldRemind = aDecoder.decodeBoolForKey("ShouldRemind")
  itemID = aDecoder.decodeIntegerForKey("ItemID")
  super.init()
}
```

```
func encodeWithCoder(aCoder: NSCoder) {
  aCoder.encodeObject(text, forKey: "Text")
  aCoder.encodeBool(checked, forKey: "Checked")
  aCoder.encodeObject(dueDate, forKey: "DueDate")
  aCoder.encodeBool(shouldRemind, forKey: "ShouldRemind")
  aCoder.encodeInteger(itemID, forKey: "ItemID")
}
```

For dueDate you call decodeObjectForKey() and encodeObject(), but for shouldRemind it is decode/encodeBool() and for itemID it is decode/encodeInteger(). Why do you need different methods to encode and decode these things?

This is necessary because the NSCoder system is written in Objective-C and that language makes a distinction between *primitive types* and objects.

In Objective-C, Int, Float, and Bool are primitive types. Everything else, such as String and NSDate, is an object. That is different from Swift, which basically treats everything as an object. But because you're talking to an Objective-C framework here, you need to play by the rules of Objective-C.

Great, that takes care of saving and loading existing objects.

Xcode has spotted one remaining error: init() still needs to give itemID a value. That makes sense: you also have to assign an ID to new ChecklistItem objects, which happens in init().

➤ Make the following changes to init():

```
override init() {
  itemID = DataModel.nextChecklistItemID()
  super.init()
}
```

This asks the DataModel object for a new item ID whenever the app creates a new ChecklistItem object.

Now let's add this new nextChecklistItemID() method to DataModel. As you can guess from its name this method will return a new, unique ID every time you call it.

➤ Hop on over to **DataModel.swift** and add this new method:

```
class func nextChecklistItemID() -> Int {
  let userDefaults = NSUserDefaults.standardUserDefaults()
  let itemID = userDefaults.integerForKey("ChecklistItemID")
  userDefaults.setInteger(itemID + 1, forKey: "ChecklistItemID")
  userDefaults.synchronize()
  return itemID
}
```

You're using your old friend NSUserDefaults again.

This method gets the current "ChecklistItemID" value from NSUserDefaults, adds one to it, and writes it back to NSUserDefaults. It returns the previous value to the caller.

The method also does userDefaults.synchronize() to force NSUserDefaults to write these changes to disk immediately, so they won't get lost if you kill the app from Xcode before it had a chance to save.

This is important because you never want two or more ChecklistItems to get the same ID.

➤ Add a default value for "ChecklistItemID" to the registerDefaults() method (note the added comma after the "FirstTime" item):

```
func registerDefaults() {
  let dictionary = [ "ChecklistIndex": -1, "FirstTime": true, "ChecklistItemID": 0 ]
  NSUserDefaults.standardUserDefaults().registerDefaults(dictionary)
}
```

The first time nextChecklistItemID() is called it will return the ID 0. The second time it is called it will return the ID 1, the third time it will return the ID 2, and so on. The number is incremented by one each time. You can call this method a few billion times before you run out of unique IDs.

Class methods vs. instance methods

If you are wondering why you wrote,

```
class func nextChecklistItemID()
```

and not just:

```
func nextChecklistItemID()
```

then I'm glad you're paying attention. :-)

Adding the class keyword means that you can call this method without having a reference to the DataModel object.

Remember, you did,

```
itemID = DataModel.nextChecklistItemID()
```

instead of:

```
itemID = dataModel.nextChecklistItemID()
```

This is because ChecklistItem objects do not have a dataModel property with a reference to the DataModel object. You could certainly give them such a reference, but I decided that using a **class method** was easier.

The declaration of a class method begins with class func. This kind of method applies to the class as a whole.

So far you've been using **instance methods**. They just have the word func (without class) and work only on a specific instance of that class.

We haven't discussed the difference between classes and instances before, and you'll get into that in more detail in the next tutorial. For now, just remember that a method starting with class func allows you to call methods on an object even when you don't have a reference to that object.

I had to make a trade-off: is it worth giving each ChecklistItem object a reference to the DataModel object, or can I get away with a simple class method? To keep things simple, I chose the latter.

It's very well possible that, if you were to develop this app further, it would make more sense to give ChecklistItem a dataModel property instead.

For a quick test to see if assigning these IDs works, you can put them inside the text that is shown in the ChecklistItem cell label. This is just a temporary thing for testing purposes, as users couldn't care less about the internal identifier of these objects.

➤ In **ChecklistViewController.swift**, change the configureTextForCell method to:

```
func configureTextForCell(cell: UITableViewCell, withChecklistItem item: ChecklistItem) {
  let label = cell.viewWithTag(1000) as! UILabel

  //label.text = item.text

  label.text = "\(item.itemID): \(item.text)"
}
```

I have commented out the original line because you want to put that back later. The new one uses \(...) to add the to-do item's itemID property into the text.

➤ Before you run the app, make sure to reset the Simulator first.

You have changed the format of the Checklists.plist file again and reading an incompatible file may cause weird crashes.

➤ Run the app and add some checklist items. Each new item should get a unique identifier. Press Home (to make sure everything is saved properly) and stop the app.

Run the app again and add some new items; the IDs for these new items should start counting at where they left off.

The items with their IDs. Note that the item with ID 3 was deleted in this example.

OK, that takes care of the IDs. Now lets add the "due date" and "should remind" fields to the Add/Edit Item screen.

(Keep configureTextForCell() the way it is for the time being; that will come in handy with testing the notifications.)

➤ Add the following outlets to **ItemDetailViewController.swift**:

```
@IBOutlet weak var shouldRemindSwitch: UISwitch!
@IBOutlet weak var dueDateLabel: UILabel!
```

➤ Open the storyboard and select the Table View in the Item Detail View Controller (the one that says "Add Item").

➤ Add a new section to the table. The easiest way to do this is to increment the **Sections** field in the **Attributes inspector**. This duplicates the existing section and cell.

➤ Remove the Text Field from the new cell. Drag a new **Table View Cell** from the Object Library and drop it below this one, so that the second section has two rows.

You will now design the new cells to look as follows:

The new design of the Add/Edit Item screen

➤ Add a **Label** to the first cell and give it the text **Remind Me**. Set the font to **System**, size **16**.

➤ Also drag a **Switch** control into the cell. Hook it up to the shouldRemindSwitch outlet on the view controller. In the Attributes inspector, set its **State** to **Off** so it is no longer green.

➤ Pin the Switch to the top and right edges of the table view cell. This makes sure the control will be visible regardless of the width of the device's screen.

➤ The third cell has two labels: Due Date on the left and the label that will hold the actual chosen date on the right. You don't have to add these labels yourself: simply set the **Style** of the cell to **Right Detail** and rename Title to **Due Date**.

➤ The label on the right should be hooked up to the dueDateLabel outlet. (You may need to click it a few times before it is selected and you can make the connection.)

You may need to shift the Remind Me label and the switch around a bit to align them nicely with the labels from the "due date" cell. Tip: select the "Due Date" and "Detail" labels and look in the Size inspector what their margins are (should be 15 points from the edges). Let's write the code for this.

➤ Add a new dueDate instance variable to **ItemDetailViewController.swift**:

```
var dueDate = NSDate()
```

For a new ChecklistItem item, the due date is right now, or NSDate(). That might not make much sense because by the time you have completed the rest of the fields and pressed Done, that due date will be past. But you do have to suggest something here. An alternative default value could be this time tomorrow, or ten minutes from now, but in most cases the user will have to pick their own due date anyway.

➤ Change `viewDidLoad()` to the following:

```
override func viewDidLoad() {
  super.viewDidLoad()
  tableView.rowHeight = 44

  if let item = itemToEdit {
    title = "Edit Item"
    textField.text = item.text
    doneBarButton.enabled = true
    shouldRemindSwitch.on = item.shouldRemind
    dueDate = item.dueDate
  }

  updateDueDateLabel()
}
```

If there already is an existing `ChecklistItem` object, you set the switch control to on or off, depending on the value of the object's `shouldRemind` property. If the user is adding a new item, the switch is initially off (you did that in the storyboard). You also get the due date from the `ChecklistItem`.

➤ The `updateDueDateLabel()` method is new. Add it to the file:

```
func updateDueDateLabel() {
  let formatter = NSDateFormatter()
  formatter.dateStyle = .MediumStyle
  formatter.timeStyle = .ShortStyle
  dueDateLabel.text = formatter.stringFromDate(dueDate)
}
```

To convert the `NSDate` value to text, you use the `NSDateFormatter` object.

The way it works is very straightforward: you give it a style for the date component and a separate style for the time component, and then ask it to format the `NSDate` object.

You can play with different styles here but space in the label is limited so you can't fit in the full month name, for example.

The cool thing about `NSDateFormatter` is that it takes the current locale into consideration so the time will look good to the user no matter where she is on the globe.

➤ The last thing to change in this file is the `done()` action. Change it to:

```
@IBAction func done() {
  if let item = itemToEdit {
    item.text = textField.text
    item.shouldRemind = shouldRemindSwitch.on
    item.dueDate = dueDate
    delegate?.itemDetailViewController(self, didFinishEditingItem: item)
  } else {
    let item = ChecklistItem()
    item.text = textField.text
    item.checked = false
    item.shouldRemind = shouldRemindSwitch.on
    item.dueDate = dueDate
    delegate?.itemDetailViewController(self, didFinishAddingItem: item)
  }
}
```

Here you put the value of the switch control and the `dueDate` instance variable back into the `ChecklistItem` object when the user presses the Done button.

> **Note:** Maybe you're wondering why you're using an instance variable for the `dueDate` but not for `shouldRemind`.
>
> You don't need one for `shouldRemind` because it's easy to get the state of the switch control: you just look at its on property, which is either `true` or `false`.
>
> However, it is hard to read the chosen date back out of the `dueDateLabel` because the label stores text (a `String`), not an `NSDate`. So it's easier to keep track of the chosen date separately in an `NSDate` instance variable.

➤ Run the app and change the position of the switch control. The app will remember this setting when you terminate it (but be sure to press the Home button first).

The due date row doesn't really do anything yet, however. In order to make that work, you first have to create a date picker.

The date picker

The date picker is not a new view controller. Tapping the Due Date row will insert a new `UIDatePicker` component directly into the table view, just like in the built-in Calendar app.

The UIDatePicker component

➤ Add a new instance variable to **ItemDetailViewController.swift**, to keep track of whether the date picker is currently visible:

```
var datePickerVisible = false
```

➤ Add the `showDatePicker()` method:

```
func showDatePicker() {
  datePickerVisible = true

  let indexPathDatePicker = NSIndexPath(forRow: 2, inSection: 1)

  tableView.insertRowsAtIndexPaths([indexPathDatePicker], withRowAnimation: .Fade)
}
```

This sets the new instance variable to `true`, and tells the table view to insert a new row below the Due Date cell. This new row will contain the `UIDatePicker` component.

The question is: where does the cell for this new row come from? Normally you would implement the `tableView(cellForRowAtIndexPath)` method, but remember that this screen uses a table view with static cells.

Such a table view does not have a data source and therefore does not use `cellForRowAtIndexPath`. If you look in **ItemDetailViewController.swift** you won't find that method anywhere.

However, with a bit of trickery you can override the data source for a static table view and provide your own methods.

➤ Add the `tableView(cellForRowAtIndexPath)` method:

```
override func tableView(tableView: UITableView,
                        cellForRowAtIndexPath indexPath: NSIndexPath) -> UITableViewCell {
  // 1
  if indexPath.section == 1 && indexPath.row == 2 {
    // 2
    var cell: UITableViewCell! =
        tableView.dequeueReusableCellWithIdentifier("DatePickerCell") as? UITableViewCell
    if cell == nil {
      cell = UITableViewCell(style: .Default, reuseIdentifier: "DatePickerCell")
      cell.selectionStyle = .None

      // 3
      let datePicker = UIDatePicker(frame: CGRect(x: 0, y: 0, width: 320, height: 216))
      datePicker.tag = 100
      cell.contentView.addSubview(datePicker)
      // 4
      datePicker.addTarget(self, action: Selector("dateChanged:"),
                        forControlEvents: .ValueChanged)
    }
    return cell

  // 5
  } else {
    return super.tableView(tableView, cellForRowAtIndexPath: indexPath)
  }
}
```

Here is what this method does, step-by-step:

1. Check whether this is the index-path for the row with the date picker. If not, jump to step 5.

2. Ask the table view whether it already has the date picker cell. If not, then create a new one. The selection style is `.None` because you don't want to show a selected state for this cell when the user taps it.

3. Create a new `UIDatePicker` component. It has a tag (100) so you can easily find this date picker later.

4. Tell the date picker to call the method `dateChanged()` whenever the user picks a new date. You have seen how to connect action methods from Interface Builder; this is how you do it from code.

   You put the name of the method inside a string. The : after the name signifies that `dateChanged()` takes a single parameter, which will be a reference to the `UIDatePicker`.

   The `Selector()` thingie tells Swift that this isn't a normal string but the name of a method. Now the `UIDatePicker`'s Value Changed event triggers the `dateChanged()` method (you'll add this method soon).

5. For any index-paths that are not the date picker cell, call through to `super` (which is `UITableViewController`). This is the trick that makes sure the other static cells still work.

➤ You also need to override `tableView(numberOfRowsInSection)`:

```
override func tableView(tableView: UITableView, numberOfRowsInSection section: Int) -> Int {
  if section == 1 && datePickerVisible {
    return 3
  } else {
    return super.tableView(tableView, numberOfRowsInSection: section)
  }
}
```

If the date picker is visible, then section 1 has three rows. If the date picker isn't visible, you can simply pass through to the original data source.

➤ Likewise, you also need to provide the `tableView(heightForRowAtIndexPath)` method:

```
override func tableView(tableView: UITableView,
                    heightForRowAtIndexPath indexPath: NSIndexPath) -> CGFloat {
  if indexPath.section == 1 && indexPath.row == 2 {
    return 217
  } else {
    return super.tableView(tableView, heightForRowAtIndexPath: indexPath)
  }
}
```

So far the cells in your table views all had the same height (44 points), but this is not a hard requirement. By providing the `heightForRowAtIndexPath` method you can give each cell its own height.

The `UIDatePicker` component is 216 points tall, plus 1 point for the separator line, makes for a total row height of 217 points.

The date picker is only made visible after the user taps the Due Date cell, which happens in `tableView(didSelectRowAtIndexPath)`.

➤ Add that method:

```
override func tableView(tableView: UITableView,
                    didSelectRowAtIndexPath indexPath: NSIndexPath) {
  tableView.deselectRowAtIndexPath(indexPath, animated: true)
  textField.resignFirstResponder()

  if indexPath.section == 1 && indexPath.row == 1 {
    showDatePicker()
  }
}
```

This calls `showDatePicker()` when the index-path indicates that the Due Date row was tapped. It also hides the on-screen keyboard if that was visible.

At this point you have most of the pieces in place, but the Due Date row isn't actually tap-able yet. That's because **ItemDetailViewController.swift** already has a `willSelectRowAtIndexPath` method that always returns `nil`, causing taps on all rows to be ignored.

➤ Change `tableView(willSelectRowAtIndexPath)` to:

```
override func tableView(tableView: UITableView,
                    willSelectRowAtIndexPath indexPath: NSIndexPath) -> NSIndexPath? {
  if indexPath.section == 1 && indexPath.row == 1 {
```

```
    return indexPath
  } else {
    return nil
  }
}
```

Now the Due Date row responds to taps, but the other rows don't.

➤ Run the app to try it out. Add a new checklist item and tap the Due Date row.

Whoops. The app crashes. After some investigating I found that when you override the data source for a static table view cell, you also need to provide the delegate method `indentationLevelForRowAtIndexPath`.

That's not a method you'd typically use, but because you're messing with the data source for a static table view you need to override it. I told you this was a little tricky.

➤ Add the `tableView(indentationLevelForRowAtIndexPath)` method:

```
override func tableView(tableView: UITableView,
                var indentationLevelForRowAtIndexPath indexPath: NSIndexPath) -> Int {
  if indexPath.section == 1 && indexPath.row == 2 {
    indexPath = NSIndexPath(forRow: 0, inSection: indexPath.section)
  }
  return super.tableView(tableView, indentationLevelForRowAtIndexPath: indexPath)
}
```

The reason the app crashed on this method was that the standard data source doesn't know anything about the cell at row 2 in section 1 (the one with the date picker), because that cell isn't part of the table view's design in the storyboard.

So after inserting the new date picker cell the data source gets confused and it crashes the app. To fix this, you have to trick the data source into believing there really are three rows in that section when the date picker is visible.

Note: I snuck something new in here too. Notice how the second parameter of the method has the word var in front of it? As far as the method is concerned, its parameters are constants.

By declaring it var, the parameter acts as a local variable and you can assign it new values. Here that saves you from having to make a separate local variable to keep track of the new index path.

➤ Run the app again. This time the date picker cell shows up where it should:

The date picker appears in a new cell

However, as soon as you interact with the date picker, the app crashes again.

That's because `UIDatePicker` attempts to call the `dateChanged()` method whenever its value changes (the Value Changed event), but you haven't added that method yet.

➤ Add the `dateChanged()` method to **ItemDetailViewController.swift**:

```
func dateChanged(datePicker: UIDatePicker) {
  dueDate = datePicker.date
  updateDueDateLabel()
}
```

This is pretty simple. It updates the `dueDate` instance variable with the new date and then updates the text on the Due Date label.

➤ Run the app to try it out. When you turn the wheels on the date picker, the text in the Due Date row updates too. Cool.

However, when you edit an existing to-do item, the date picker does not show the date from that item. It always starts on the current time.

➤ Add the following lines to the bottom of `showDatePicker()`:

```
if let pickerCell = tableView.cellForRowAtIndexPath(indexPathDatePicker) {
  let datePicker = pickerCell.viewWithTag(100) as! UIDatePicker
  datePicker.setDate(dueDate, animated: false)
}
```

This locates the `UIDatePicker` component in the new cell, and gives it the proper date.

➤ Verify that this works. Click on the (i) button from an existing to-do item, preferably one you made a while ago, and make sure that the date picker shows the same date and time as the Due Date label.

Speaking of the date label, it would be nice if this becomes highlighted when the date picker is active. You can use the tint color for this (that's also what the built-in Calendar app does).

➤ Change showDatePicker() one last time:

```
func showDatePicker() {
  datePickerVisible = true

  let indexPathDateRow = NSIndexPath(forRow: 1, inSection: 1)
  let indexPathDatePicker = NSIndexPath(forRow: 2, inSection: 1)

  if let dateCell = tableView.cellForRowAtIndexPath(indexPathDateRow) {
    dateCell.detailTextLabel!.textColor = dateCell.detailTextLabel!.tintColor
  }

  tableView.beginUpdates()
  tableView.insertRowsAtIndexPaths([indexPathDatePicker], withRowAnimation: .Fade)
  tableView.reloadRowsAtIndexPaths([indexPathDateRow], withRowAnimation: .None)
  tableView.endUpdates()

  if let pickerCell = tableView.cellForRowAtIndexPath(indexPathDatePicker) {
    let datePicker = pickerCell.viewWithTag(100) as! UIDatePicker
    datePicker.setDate(dueDate, animated: false)
  }
}
```

This sets the textColor of the detailTextLabel to the tint color. It also tells the table view to reload the Due Date row. Without that, the separator lines between the cells don't update properly.

Because you're doing two operations on the table view at the same time – inserting a new row and reloading another – you need to put this in between calls to beginUpdates() and endUpdates(), so that the table view can animate everything at the same time.

➤ Run the app. The date now appears in blue:

The date label appears in the tint color while the date picker is visible

When the user taps the Due Date row again, the date picker should disappear. If you try that right now the app will crash – what did you expect! – which obviously won't win it many favorable reviews.

➤ Add the new hideDatePicker() method:

```
func hideDatePicker() {
  if datePickerVisible {
    datePickerVisible = false

    let indexPathDateRow = NSIndexPath(forRow: 1, inSection: 1)
    let indexPathDatePicker = NSIndexPath(forRow: 2, inSection: 1)

    if let cell = tableView.cellForRowAtIndexPath(indexPathDateRow) {
      cell.detailTextLabel!.textColor = UIColor(white: 0, alpha: 0.5)
    }

    tableView.beginUpdates()
    tableView.reloadRowsAtIndexPaths([indexPathDateRow], withRowAnimation: .None)
    tableView.deleteRowsAtIndexPaths([indexPathDatePicker], withRowAnimation: .Fade)
    tableView.endUpdates()
  }
}
```

This does the opposite of `showDatePicker()`. It deletes the date picker cell from the table view and restores the color of the date label to medium gray.

➤ Change `tableView(didSelectRowAtIndexPath)` to toggle between the visible and hidden states:

```
override func tableView(tableView: UITableView,
                    didSelectRowAtIndexPath indexPath: NSIndexPath) {
  tableView.deselectRowAtIndexPath(indexPath, animated: true)
  textField.resignFirstResponder()

  if indexPath.section == 1 && indexPath.row == 1 {
    if !datePickerVisible {
      showDatePicker()
    } else {
      hideDatePicker()
    }
  }
}
```

There is another situation where it's a good idea to hide the date picker: when the user taps inside the text field.

It won't look very nice if the keyboard partially overlaps the date picker, so you might as well hide it. The view controller is already the delegate for the text field, making this easy.

➤ Add the `textFieldDidBeginEditing()` method:

```
func textFieldDidBeginEditing(textField: UITextField) {
  hideDatePicker()
}
```

And with that you have a cool inline date picker!

➤ Run the app and verify that hiding the date picker works, also when you activate the text field.

Scheduling the local notifications

One of the principles of object-oriented programming is that objects can do as much as possible themselves. Therefore, it makes sense that the `ChecklistItem` object can schedule its own notifications.

➤ Add the following method to **ChecklistItem.swift**:

```
func scheduleNotification() {
  if shouldRemind && dueDate.compare(NSDate()) != NSComparisonResult.OrderedAscending {
    println("We should schedule a notification!")
  }
}
```

This compares the due date on the item with the current date. You can always get the current time by making a new NSDate object with NSDate().

The statement dueDate.compare(NSDate()) compares the two dates and returns one of the following enum values:

- NSComparisonResult.OrderedAscending: dueDate comes before the current date and time. In other words, it is in the past.

- NSComparisonResult.OrderedSame: dueDate is exactly equal to the current date and time (Good luck trying to get this one! You'd have to time it down to the second.)

- NSComparisonResult.OrderedDescending: dueDate represents a time after the current date and time, so it lies in the future.

If the due date is in the past, the println() will not be performed.

Note the use of the && "and" operator. You only print the text when the Remind Me switch is set to "on" *and* the due date is in the future.

You will call this method when the user presses the Done button after adding or editing a to-do item.

➤ Change the done() action in **ItemDetailViewController.swift**:

```
@IBAction func done() {
  if let item = itemToEdit {
    item.text = textField.text
    item.shouldRemind = shouldRemindSwitch.on
    item.dueDate = dueDate
    item.scheduleNotification()
    delegate?.itemDetailViewController(self, didFinishEditingItem: item)
  } else {
    let item = ChecklistItem()
    item.text = textField.text
    item.checked = false
    item.shouldRemind = shouldRemindSwitch.on
    item.dueDate = dueDate
    item.scheduleNotification()
    delegate?.itemDetailViewController(self, didFinishAddingItem: item)
  }
}
```

Only the lines with item.scheduleNotification() are new.

➤ Run the app and try it out. Add a new item, set the switch to ON but don't change the due date. Press Done.

There should be no message in the debug area because the due date has already passed (it is several seconds in the past by the time you press Done).

➤ Add another item, set the switch to ON, and choose a due date in the future.

When you press Done now, there should be a println in the debug area ("We should schedule a notification!").

Now that you've verified the method is called in the proper place, let's actually schedule a new `UILocalNotification` object. First consider the case of a new to-do item being added.

➤ In **ChecklistItem.swift**, change `scheduleNotification()` to:

```
func scheduleNotification() {
  if shouldRemind && dueDate.compare(NSDate()) != NSComparisonResult.OrderedAscending {
    let localNotification = UILocalNotification()
    localNotification.fireDate = dueDate
    localNotification.timeZone = NSTimeZone.defaultTimeZone()
    localNotification.alertBody = text
    localNotification.soundName = UILocalNotificationDefaultSoundName
    localNotification.userInfo = ["ItemID": itemID]

    UIApplication.sharedApplication().scheduleLocalNotification(localNotification)

    println("Scheduled notification \(localNotification) for itemID \(itemID)")
  }
}
```

You've seen this code before when you tried out local notifications for the first time.

You create a `UILocalNotification` object and give it the `ChecklistItem`'s `dueDate` and `text`. You also add a `userInfo` dictionary with the item's ID as the only contents. That is how you'll be able to find this notification later in case you need to cancel it.

Xcode is less impressed with this new code and gives a bunch of error messages.

What is wrong here? `UILocalNotification` is an object provided by UIKit – you can tell by the "UI" in its name. However, `ChecklistItem` hasn't used any other UIKit code until now.

The only framework objects it has used, `NSCoder` and `NSDate`, came from another framework, Foundation.

➤ To tell `ChecklistItem` about UIKit, you need to add the following line to the top of the file, below the other import:

```
import UIKit
```

Now the errors disappear like snow in the sun.

There's another small problem, though. If you've reset the Simulator recently (and you probably have with the most recent data model changes) then the app no longer has permission to send local notifications.

➤ Try it out. Run the app, add a new checklist item, set the due date a minute into the future, and press Done.

The debug pane should print out an error:

```
Attempting to schedule a local notification <UIConcreteLocalNotification: 0x7f900640dfd0>{
  . . .
} with an alert but haven't received permission from the user to display alerts
```

You can't assume the app has permission anymore.

When you were just messing around at this beginning of this section, you placed the permission code in the `AppDelegate` and ran it immediately upon launch. That's not recommended.

Don't you just hate those apps that prompt you for ten different things before you've even had a chance to properly look at them? Let's be a bit more user friendly with our own app!

➤ Add the following method to **ItemDetailViewController.swift**:

```
@IBAction func shouldRemindToggled(switchControl: UISwitch) {
  textField.resignFirstResponder()

  if switchControl.on {
    let notificationSettings = UIUserNotificationSettings(forTypes: .Alert | .Sound,
                                                   categories: nil)
    UIApplication.sharedApplication().registerUserNotificationSettings(notificationSettings)
  }
}
```

When the switch is toggled to ON, this prompts the user for permission to send local notifications. Once the user has given permission, the app won't put up a prompt again.

➤ Open the storyboard and connect the **shouldRemindToggled:** action to the switch control.

➤ Test it out. Run the app, add a new checklist item, set the due date a minute into the future, press Done and tap the Home button on the Simulator.

Wait one minute (patience…) and the notification should appear. Pretty cool!

The local notification in Notification Center

> **Note:** The date picker doesn't show you seconds but they still are there (just watch the println output). If you set the due date to 10:16 PM when it's currently 10:15:54 PM, you'll have to wait until exactly 10:16:54 for the event to fire. It would probably be a better user experience if you always set the seconds to 0, but that's a topic for another day.

That takes care of the case where you're adding a new notification. There are two situations left: 1) the user edits an existing item, and 2) the user deletes an item. Let's do editing first.

When the user edits an item, the following situations can occur:

• Remind Me was switched off and is now switched on. You have to schedule a new notification.

• Remind Me was switched on and is now switched off. You have to cancel the existing notification.

• Remind Me stays switched on but the due date changes. You have to cancel the existing notification and schedule a new one.

• Remind Me stays switched on but the due date doesn't change. You don't have to do anything.

• Remind Me stays switched off. Here you also don't have to do anything.

Of course, in all those situations you'll only schedule the notification if the due date is in the future.

Phew, that's quite a list. It's always a good idea to take stock of all possible scenarios before you start programming because this gives you a clear picture of everything you need to tackle.

It may seem like you need to write a lot of logic here to deal with all these situations, but actually it turns out to be quite simple. First you'll look if there is an existing notification for this to-do item. If there is, you simply cancel it. Then you determine whether the item should have a notification and if so, you schedule a new one.

That should take care of all the above situations, even if sometimes you simply could have left the existing notification alone. The algorithm is crude, but effective.

➤ Add the following to the top of `scheduleNotification()` in **ChecklistItem.swift**:

```
func scheduleNotification() {
  let existingNotification = notificationForThisItem()
  if let notification = existingNotification {
    println("Found an existing notification \(notification)")
    UIApplication.sharedApplication().cancelLocalNotification(notification)
  }
  . . .
```

This calls a new method `notificationForThisItem()`, which you'll add in a second.

If that method returns a valid `UILocalNotification` object (i.e. not `nil`), then you dump some debug info using `println()` and ask the `UIApplication` object to cancel this notification.

➤ Add the new `notificationForThisItem()` method:

```
func notificationForThisItem() -> UILocalNotification? {
  let allNotifications = UIApplication.sharedApplication().scheduledLocalNotifications
                           as! [UILocalNotification]
  for notification in allNotifications {
    if let number = notification.userInfo?["ItemID"] as? NSNumber {
      if number.integerValue == itemID {
        return notification
      }
    }
  }
  return nil
}
```

This asks `UIApplication` for a list of all scheduled notifications. Then it loops through that list and looks at each notification one-by-one.

The notification should have an "ItemID" value inside the `userInfo` dictionary. If that value exists and equals the `itemID` property, then you've found a notification that belongs to this `ChecklistItem`.

If none of the local notifications match, or if there aren't any to begin with, the method returns `nil`.

This is a common pattern that you'll see in a lot of code. Something returns an array of items and you loop through the array to find the first item that matches what you're looking for, in this case the item ID. Once you've found it, you can exit the loop.

> **Note:** The itemID property is an Int, but due to the Objective-C heritage of the frameworks it is actually stored as an object of type NSNumber object inside the notification's userInfo dictionary.
>
> Using .integerValue on the NSNumber turns it back into an Int again.
>
> It's possible that the UILocalNotification object does not have a userInfo dictionary – it's an optional – which is why you write notification.userInfo? with a question mark to access it (optional chaining).
>
> Likewise, there is no guarantee the dictionary actually contains a value under the "ItemID" key or that this value is an NSNumber, so you need to use an optional type cast with as? to retrieve the NSNumber object and if let to check the result for nil.
>
> Of course, for the notifications that *you* scheduled these conditions are always true, but Swift cannot make such assumptions. Therefore you have to build those assumptions into your source code using if let and as?.

➤ Run the app and try it out. Add a to-do item with a due date a few days into the future. A new notification will be scheduled.

➤ Edit the item and change the due date. The old notification will be removed and a new one scheduled for the new date.

You can tell that this happens from the println() output.

➤ Edit the to-do item again but now set the switch to OFF. The old notification will be removed and no new notification will be scheduled.

➤ Edit again and don't change anything; no new notification will be scheduled because the switch is still off. This should also work if you terminate the app in between.

There is one last case to handle: deletion of the ChecklistItem object. This can happen in two ways:

1. the user can delete an individual item using swipe-to-delete

2. the user can delete an entire checklist in which case all its ChecklistItem objects are also deleted.

An object is notified when it is about to be deleted using the deinit message. You can simply implement this method, look if there is a scheduled notification for this item and then cancel it.

➤ Add the following to the bottom of **ChecklistItem.swift**:

```
deinit {
  let existingNotification = notificationForThisItem()
  if let notification = existingNotification {
    println("Removing existing notification \(notification)")
    UIApplication.sharedApplication().cancelLocalNotification(notification)
  }
}
```

That's all you have to do. The special deinit method will be invoked when you delete an individual ChecklistItem but also when you delete a whole Checklist (because then all its ChecklistItems will be destroyed as well, as the array they are in is deallocated).

➤ Run the app and try it out. First schedule some notifications far into the future (so they won't be fired when you're testing) and then remove that to-do item or its entire checklist. You should now see the "Removing existing notification" message in the debug area.

Once you're convinced everything works, you can remove the `println()` statements. They are only temporary for debugging purposes. You probably don't want to leave them in the final app. (They won't hurt any, but the end user can't see those messages anyway.)

➤ Also remove the item ID from the label in the `ChecklistViewController` – that was only used for debugging.

You can find the final project files for the Checklists app under **11 - Local Notifications** in the tutorial's Source Code folder.

That's a wrap!

Things should be starting to make sense by now. I've thrown you into the deep end by writing an entire app from scratch, and we've touched on a number of advanced topics already, but hopefully you were able to follow along quite well with what I'm doing.

If not, then sleep on it for a bit and keep tinkering with the code. Programming requires its own way of thinking and you won't learn that overnight. Don't be afraid to do this tutorial again from the start – it will make more sense the second time around!

This lesson focused mainly on UIKit and its most important controls and patterns. In the next lesson we'll take a few steps back to talk more about the Swift language itself and of course you'll build another cool app.

Here is the final storyboard for **Checklists**:

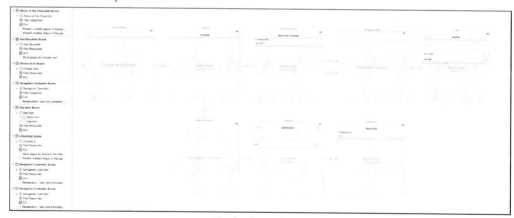

The final storyboard

I had trouble fitting that on my screen!

Take a well deserved break, and when you're ready continue on to the next tutorial, where you'll make an app that knows its place! ☺

Haven't had enough yet? Here are some challenges to sink your teeth into:

Exercise: Put the due date in a label on the table view cells under the text of the to-do item. ■

Exercise: Sort the to-do items list based on the due date. This is similar to what you did with the list of Checklists except that now you're sorting ChecklistItem objects and you'll be comparing NSDate objects instead of strings. (NSDate does not have a localizedStandardCompare method but it does have a regular compare). ■

Tutorial 3: MyLocations

In this tutorial you will look at some of the more alluring technologies from the iOS SDK and you'll dive a lot deeper into the Swift language.

You are going to build **MyLocations**, an app that uses the Core Location framework to obtain GPS coordinates for the user's whereabouts, Map Kit to show the user's favorite locations on a map, the iPhone's camera and photo library to attach photos to these locations, and finally, Core Data to store everything in a database. Phew, that's a lot of stuff!

The finished app looks like this:

The MyLocations app

MyLocations lets you keep a list of spots that you find interesting. Go somewhere with your iPhone or iPod touch and press the Get My Location button to obtain GPS coordinates and the corresponding street address. Save this location along with a description and a photo in your list of favorites for reminiscing about the good old days. Think of this app as a "location album" instead of a photo album.

To make the workload easier to handle, you'll split up the project into smaller chunks:

1. You will first figure out how to obtain GPS coordinates from the Core Location framework and how to convert these coordinates into an address, a process known as **reverse geocoding**.

Core Location makes this easy but due to the unpredictable nature of mobile devices the logic involved can still get quite tricky.

2. Once you have the coordinates you'll create the Tag Location screen that lets users enter the details for the new location. This is a table view controller with static cells, very similar to what you've done in the previous tutorial.

3. You'll store the location data into a Core Data store. In the previous tutorial you saved the app's data into a .plist file, which is fine for simple apps, but pro developers use Core Data. It's not as scary as it sounds!

4. Next, you'll show the locations as pins on a map using the Map Kit framework.

5. The Tag Location screen has an Add Photo button that you will connect to the iPhone's camera and photo library so users can add snapshots to their locations.

6. Finally, you'll make the app look good with custom graphics. You will also add sound effects and some animations into the mix.

But before you get to all that, first some theory. There is still a lot more to learn about Swift and object-oriented programming!

Swift review

In the past tutorials I've shown you a fair bit of the Swift programming language already, but not quite everything. I've glossed over some of the details and told you a few small lies just so you wouldn't drown in new information.

Previously it was good enough if you could more-or-less follow along with what we were doing, but now is the time to fill in the gaps in the theory.

First, let's do a little refresher on what we've talked about so far.

Variables, constants, and types

A **variable** is a temporary container for a specific type of value:

```
var count: Int
var shouldRemind: Bool
var text: String
var list: [ChecklistItem]
```

The **data type**, or just **type**, of a variable determines what kind of values it can contain. Some variables hold simple values such as Int and Bool, others hold more complex objects such as String and Array.

The basic types you've used so far are: Int for whole numbers, Float for decimals, and Bool for boolean values (true and false).

There are a few other fundamental types as well:

• Double. Similar to a Float but with more precision. You will use Doubles later in this tutorial for storing latitude and longitude data.

• Character. Holds just a single character. A String is a collection of Characters.

- UInt. A variation on Int that you may encounter occasionally. The U stands for "unsigned", meaning the type can hold positive values only. It's called unsigned because it cannot have a negative sign (-) in front of the number. UInt can fit numbers between 0 and plus 4 billion but no negative numbers. On a 64-bit device, the upper limit of UInt is even higher, a little over 18 quintillion.

- Int8, UInt8, Int16, UInt16, Int32, UInt32, Int64, UInt64. These are all variations on Int. The difference is in how many bytes they have available to store their values. The more bytes, the bigger the values can be. In practice you almost always use Int, which uses 4 bytes for storage (a fact that you may immediately forget) and can fit whole numbers ranging from minus 2 billion to plus 2 billion. On a 64-bit device, Int uses 8 bytes and can store positive and negative numbers up to about 19 decimal digits. Those are big numbers!

- CGFloat. This isn't really a Swift type, but a type defined by the iOS SDK. It's a decimal point number like Float and Double. For historical reasons, this is used throughout UIKit for floating-point values. (The "CG" prefix stands for the Core Graphics framework.)

Swift is very strict about types, more so than many other languages. If the type of a variable is Int, you cannot put a Float value into it. The other way around also won't work: an Int doesn't go into a Float.

Even though both types represent numbers of some sort, Swift won't automatically convert between different number types. You always need to convert the values explicitly.

For example:

```
var i = 10
var f: Float
f = i        // error
f = Float(i) // OK
```

You don't always need to specify the type when you create a new variable. If you give the variable an initial value, Swift uses **type inference** to determine the type:

```
var i = 10             // Int
var d = 3.14           // Double
var b = true           // Bool
var s = "Hello, world" // String
```

The integer value 10, the floating-point value 3.14, the boolean true and the string "Hello, world" are named **literal constants** or just **literals**.

Note that using the value 3.14 in the example above leads Swift to conclude that you want to use a Double here. If you intended to use a Float instead, you'd have to write:

```
var f: Float = 3.14
```

The ": Float" bit is called a **type annotation**. You use it to override the guess made by Swift's type inference mechanism, which may not always be what you intended.

Likewise, if you wanted the variable i to be a Double instead of an Int, you'd write:

```
var i: Double = 10
```

Or a little shorter, by giving the value 10 a decimal point:

```
var i = 10.0
```

These simple literals such as `10`, `3.14`, or `"Hello world"`, are useful only for creating variables of the basic types – `Int`, `Float`, `String`, and so on. To use more complex types, you'll need to **instantiate** an object first.

When you write the following,

```
var item: ChecklistItem
```

it only tells Swift you want to store a `ChecklistItem` object into the `item` variable, but it does not create that `ChecklistItem` object yet. For that you need to write:

```
item = ChecklistItem()
```

This first reserves memory for the object's data, followed by a call to `init()` to properly make the object ready for use. Reserving memory is also called **allocation**; filling up the object with its initial values is **initialization**.

The whole process is known as **instantiating** the object – you're making an object **instance**. The instance is the block of memory that holds the values of the object's variables (that's why they are called "instance" variables, get it?).

Of course, you can combine the above into a single line:

```
var item = ChecklistItem()
```

Here you left out the "`: ChecklistItem`" type annotation because Swift is smart enough to realize that the type of `item` should be `ChecklistItem`.

However, you can't leave out the `()` parentheses – this is how Swift knows that you want to make a new `ChecklistItem` instance.

Some objects allow you to pass parameters to their `init` method. For example:

```
var item = ChecklistItem(text: "Charge my iPhone", checked: false)
```

This calls the corresponding `init(text, checked)` method to prepare the newly allocated `ChecklistItem` object for usage.

You've seen two types of variables: **local variables**, whose existence is limited to the method they are declared in, and **instance variables** (also known as "ivars") that belong to the whole object and therefore can be used from within any method.

The lifetime of a variable is called its **scope**. The scope of a local variable is smaller than that of an instance variable. Once the method ends, any local variables are destroyed.

```
class MyObject {
  var count = 0      // an instance variable

  func myMethod() {
    var temp: Int    // a local variable
    temp = count     // OK to use the instance variable here
  }

  // the local variable "temp" doesn't exist outside of the method
}
```

If you have a local variable with the same name as an instance variable, then it is said to **shadow** (or **hide**) that instance variable. You should avoid these situations as they can lead to subtle bugs where you may not be using the variable that you think you are:

```
class MyObject {
  var count = 7      // an instance variable

  func myMethod() {
    var count = 42    // local variable "shadows" instance variable
    println(count)    // prints 42
  }
}
```

Some developers place an underscore in front of their instance variable names to avoid this problem: _count instead of count. An alternative is to use the keyword self whenever you use an instance variable:

```
  func myMethod() {
    var count = 42
    println(self.count)    // prints 7
  }
```

Variables are not the only thing than can hold values. A variable is a container for a value that is allowed to *change* over the course of the app being run.

For example, in a note-taking app the user can change the text of the note, so you'd place that text into a String variable. Every time the user edits the text, the variable is updated.

Often you'll just want to store the result of a calculation or a method call into a temporary container, after which this value will never change. In that case, it is better to make this container a **constant** than a variable.

The following values never need to change once they've been set:

```
let pi = 3.141592
let difference = abs(targetValue - currentValue)
let message = "You scored \(points) points"
let image = UIImage(named: "SayCheese")
```

If a constant is local to a method, it's allowed to give the constant a new value the next time the method is called. The value from the previous method invocation has been destroyed when that method ended, and the next time the app enters that method you're creating a new constant with a new value (but with the same name). Of course, for the duration of that method call the constant's value must remain the same.

Tip: My suggestion is to use let for everything. That is the right solution 90% of the time. When you've got it wrong, the Swift compiler will warn that you're trying to change a constant. Only then you change it to a var. This ensures you're not making things variable that don't need to be.

When working with basic values such as integers and strings – so called **value types** – a constant created with let cannot be changed once it has been given a value:

```
let pi = 3.141592
pi = 3                 // not allowed
```

However, with objects that are **reference types**, it is only the reference that is constant. The object itself can still be changed:

```
let item = ChecklistItem()
item.text = "Do the laundry"
item.checked = false
item.dueDate = yesterday
```

But this is not allowed:

```
let anotherItem = ChecklistItem()
item = anotherItem    // cannot change the reference
```

So how do you know what is a reference type and what is a value type?

Objects defined with class are reference types, while objects defined with struct or enum are value types. In practice this means most of the objects from the iOS SDK are reference types but things that are built into the Swift language, such as Int, String, and Array, are value types. (More about this important difference later.)

A variable stores only a single value. To keep track of multiple objects you can use a so-called **collection** object. Naturally, I'm talking about arrays (Array) and dictionaries (Dictionary), both of which you've seen in the previous tutorial.

An **array** stores a list of objects. The objects it contains are ordered sequentially and you retrieve them by index.

```
// an array of ChecklistItem objects:
var items: Array<ChecklistItem>

// using shorthand notation:
var items: [ChecklistItem]

// making an instance of the array:
items = [ChecklistItem]()

// accessing an object from the array:
let item = items[3]
```

You can write an array as Array<Type> or [Type]. The first one is the "official" name, the second is "syntactic sugar" that is a bit easier to read. (Unlike other languages, you don't write Type[]. The type name goes inside the brackets.)

A **dictionary** stores key-value pairs. One object, usually a string, is the key that retrieves another object.

```
// a dictionary that stores (String, Int) pairs; a list of people's names and their ages:
var ages: Dictionary<String, Int>

// using shorthand notation:
var ages: [String: Int]

// making an instance of the dictionary:
ages = [String: Int]()

// accessing an object from the dictionary:
var age = dict["Jony Ive"]
```

The notation for retrieving an object from a dictionary looks very similar to reading from an array – both use the [ ] brackets. For indexing an array you always use a positive integer but for a dictionary you typically use a string.

There are other sorts of collections as well but array and dictionary are the most common ones.

Array and Dictionary are so-called **generics**, meaning that they are independent of the type of thing you want to store inside these collections.

You can have an Array of Int objects, but also an Array of String objects – or an Array of any kind of object, really (even an array of other arrays).

That's why before you can use Array you have to specify the type of object to store inside the array. In other words, you cannot write this:

```
var items: Array    // error: should be Array<TypeName>
var items: []        // error: should be [TypeName]
```

There should always be the name of a type inside the [] brackets or following the word Array in < > brackets.

For Dictionary, you need to supply two type names, one for the type of the keys and one for the type of the values. (If you're coming from Objective-C, be aware that the < > mean something completely different there.)

Swift requires that all variables and constants have a value. You can either specify a value when you declare the variable or constant, or by assigning a value inside an init method.

Sometimes it's useful to have a variable that can have no value, in which case you need to declare it as an **optional**:

```
var checklistToEdit: Checklist?
```

You cannot use this variable directly; you must always test whether it has a value or not. This is called **binding** or **unwrapping** the optional:

```
if let checklist = checklistToEdit {
  // "checklist" now contains the real object
} else {
  // the optional was nil
}
```

The age variable from the dictionary example is actually an optional, because there is no guarantee that the dictionary contains the key "Jony Ive". Therefore, type of age is Int? instead of just Int. Before you can use a value from a dictionary, you need to unwrap it first using if let:

```
if let age = dict["Jony Ive"] {
  // use the value of age
}
```

If you are 100% sure that the dictionary contains the key you can also use **force unwrapping** to read the corresponding value:

```
var age = dict["Jony Ive"]!
```

With the ! you tell Swift, "This value will not be nil. I'll stake my reputation on it!" Of course, if you're wrong and the value *is* nil, the app will crash and your reputation is down the drain. Be careful with force unwrapping!

A slightly safer alternative to force unwrapping is **optional chaining**. For example, the following will crash the app if the navigationController property is nil:

```
navigationController!.delegate = self
```

But this won't:

```
navigationController?.delegate = self
```

Anything after the ? will simply be ignored if navigationController does not have a value. It's equivalent to writing:

```
if navigationController != nil {
  navigationController!.delegate = self
}
```

It is also possible to declare an optional using an exclamation point instead of a question mark. This makes it an **implicitly unwrapped** optional:

```
var dataModel: DataModel!
```

Such a value is potentially unsafe because you can use it as a regular variable without having to unwrap it first. If this variable has the value nil when you don't expect it – and don't they always – your app will crash.

Optionals exist to guard against such crashes, and using ! undermines the safety of using optionals. However, sometimes using implicitly unwrapped optionals is more convenient than using pure optionals. Use them when you cannot give the variable an initial value at the time of declaration, nor in init().

But once you've given it a value, you really ought not to make it nil again. If the value can become nil again, it's better to use a true optional with a question mark.

Sometimes you'll see the exclamation point in the APIs from the iOS frameworks. For example, here is something you'll encounter later on in this tutorial:

```
func mapView(mapView: MKMapView!, viewForAnnotation annotation: MKAnnotation!)
        -> MKAnnotationView!
```

In theory this means that the mapView and annotation parameters can be nil and that the return value of this method can either be an MKAnnotationView object or nil. In practice, the parameters will never be nil but the return value might be.

The exclamation points are only there because this API was written in Objective-C and imported into Swift. Objective-C does not have the concept of an optional and so the Swift compiler must assume the worst.

This method should really read like this:

```
func mapView(mapView: MKMapView, viewForAnnotation annotation: MKAnnotation)
        -> MKAnnotationView?
```

It's still allowed to return nil, so the return type is a true optional.

For most of the iOS API these exclamation points have been removed already, but this hasn't been done everywhere yet. Until then, if you see a ! in a method from the iOS frameworks, refer to the framework documentation to determine which values are really allowed to be nil and which ones you can safely assume will never be nil.

Methods and functions

You've learned that objects, the basic building blocks of all apps, have both data and functionality. The instance variables and constants provide the data, **methods** provide the functionality.

When you call a method, the app jumps to that section of the code and executes all the statements in the method one-by-one. As the end of the method is reached, the app jumps back to where it left off:

```
let result = performUselessCalculation(314)
println(result)

. . .

func performUselessCalculation(a: Int) -> Int {
  var b = Int(arc4random_uniform(100))
  var c = a / 2
  return (a + b) * c
}
```

Methods often return a value to the caller, usually the result of a computation or looking up something in a collection. The data type of the result value is written behind the -> arrow. In the example above, it is Int. If there is no -> arrow, the method does not return a value (also known as "void").

Methods are **functions** that belong to an object, but there are also standalone functions such as println() and arc4random_uniform().

Functions serve the same purpose as methods – they bundle functionality into small re-usable units – but live outside of any objects. Such functions are also called *free* functions.

These are examples of methods:

```
// Method that doesn't have any parameters, doesn't return a value.
override func viewDidLoad()

// Method that has one parameter, slider. It doesn't return a value. The keyword @IBAction
// means that this method can be connected to a control in Interface Builder.
@IBAction func sliderMoved(slider: UISlider)

// Method that has one parameter, otherChecklist. It returns a Bool value (true or false).
func isOrderedBefore(otherChecklist: Checklist) -> Bool

// Method that doesn't have any parameters.
Returns an optional value (because of the question mark)
func notificationForThisItem() -> UILocalNotification?

// Method with two parameters, cell and item, no return value.
// Note that the second parameter has an extra label, withChecklistItem.
func configureCheckmarkForCell(cell: UITableViewCell,
                      withChecklistItem item: ChecklistItem)

// Method with two parameters, tableView and section. Returns an Int value.
override func tableView(tableView: UITableView,
                      numberOfRowsInSection section: Int) -> Int

// Method with two parameters, tableView and indexPath.
// Returns an optional NSIndexPath object (may also return nil).
override func tableView(tableView: UITableView,
      willSelectRowAtIndexPath indexPath: NSIndexPath) -> NSIndexPath?
```

To call a method on an object, you write `object.method(parameters)`. For example:

```
// Calling a method on the lists object:
lists.append(checklist)

// Calling a method with more than one parameter:
tableView.insertRowsAtIndexPaths(indexPaths, withRowAnimation: .Fade)
```

You can think of calling a method as *sending a message* from one object to another: "Hey `lists`, I'm sending you the `append` message for this `checklist` object."

The object whose method you're calling is known as the *receiver* of the message.

It is very common to call a method from the same object. Here, `loadChecklists()` calls the `sortChecklists()` method. Both are members of the `DataModel` object.

```
class DataModel {
  func loadChecklists() {
    . . .
    sortChecklists()  // this method also lives in DataModel
  }

  func sortChecklists() {
    . . .
  }
}
```

Sometimes this is written as:

```
  func loadChecklists() {
    . . .
    self.sortChecklists()
  }
```

The `self` keyword makes it clear that the `DataModel` object itself is the receiver of this message.

> **Note:** In these tutorials I leave out the `self` keyword for method calls, because it's not necessary to have it. Objective-C developers are very attached to `self`, so you'll probably see it used a lot in Swift too. No doubt it will be the topic of heated debate in developer circles, but in the end the app doesn't really care whether you use `self` or not.

Inside a method you can also use `self` to get a reference to the object itself:

```
@IBAction func cancel() {
  delegate?.itemDetailViewControllerDidCancel(self)
}
```

Here `cancel()` sends a reference to the object (i.e. `self`) along to the delegate, so the delegate knows who sent this `itemDetailViewControllerDidCancel()` message.

Also note the use of **optional chaining** here. The `delegate` property is an optional, so it can be `nil`. Using the question mark before the method call will ensure nothing bad happens if `delegate` is not set.

Often methods have one or more **parameters**, so you can make them work on data that comes from different sources. A method that is limited to a fixed set of data is not very useful or reusable. Consider `addValuesFromArray()`, a method that has no parameters:

```
class MyObject {
  var numbers = [Int]()

  func addValuesFromArray() -> Int {
    var total = 0
    for number in numbers {
      total += number
    }
    return total
  }
}
```

Here, numbers is an instance variable. The addValuesFromArray() method is tied closely to that instance variable, and is useless without it.

Suppose you add a second array to the app that you also want to apply this calculation to. One approach is to copy-paste the above method and change the name of the variable to that of the new array. That certainly works but it's not smart programming!

It is better to give the method a parameter that allows you to pass in the array object that you wish to examine, so the method becomes independent from any instance variables:

```
func addValuesFromArray(array: [Int]) -> Int {
  var total = 0
  for number in array {
    total += number
  }
  return total
}
```

Now you can call this method with any [Int] or Array<Int> object as its parameter.

This doesn't mean methods should never use instance variables, but if you can make a method more general by giving it a parameter then that is usually a good idea.

If a method has more than one parameter, the additional parameters usually have an **external label**. These labels become part of the method name. For example:

```
func downloadImageForSearchResult(searchResult: SearchResult,
                        withTimeout timeout: NSTimeInterval,
                        andPlaceOnButton button: UIButton) {
  . . .
}
```

This method has three parameters: searchResult, timeout, and button. Those are the parameter names you'd use in the code inside the method.

The full name for the method is downloadImageForSearchResult(withTimeout, andPlaceOnButton). This uses the external labels. Method names in Swift are often very long!

To call this method, you'd use the external labels:

```
downloadImageForSearchResult(result, withTimeout: 10, andPlaceOnButton: imageButton)
```

Note that the first parameter, searchResult, doesn't have a label but is embedded in the first part of the method name: downloadImageFor**SearchResult**. That is only a convention; there is no hard and fast requirement that you do this.

You can also write it as:

```
func downloadImage(#searchResult: SearchResult,      // note the #
                timeout: NSTimeInterval,              // no external label
                placeOnButton button: UIButton) {
   . . .
}
```

Now you call it as follows:

```
downloadImage(searchResult: result, timeout: 10, placeOnButton: button)
```

Regular functions usually follow this pattern, but you don't see it very often with methods. Swift is pretty flexible with how it lets you name your methods, but it's smart to stick to the established conventions.

Inside a method you can do the following things:

- Create local variables and constants.

- Do simple arithmetic with mathematical operators such as +, −, *, /, and %.

- Put new values into variables (both local and instance variables).

- Call other methods.

- Make decisions with the `if` or `switch` statements.

- Perform repetitions with the `for` or `while` statements.

- Return a value to the caller.

Let's look at the `if` and `for` statements in more detail.

Making decisions

The if-statement looks like this:

```
if count == 0 {
  text = "No Items"
} else if count == 1 {
  text = "1 Item"
} else {
  text = "\(count) Items"
}
```

The expression after `if` is called the **condition**. If a condition is true then the statements in the following { } block are executed. The `else` section gets performed if none of the conditions are true.

You use **comparison operators** to perform comparisons between two values:

==	equal to
!=	not equal
>	greater than
>=	greater than or equal
<	less than
<=	less than or equal

You can use **logical** operators to combine two expressions:

a && b is true if both a *and* b are true

a || b is true when either a *or* b is true (or both)

There is also the logical **not** operator, !, that turns true into false, and false into true.

You can group expressions with ( ) parentheses:

```
if ((this && that) || (such && so)) && !other {
    // statements
}
```

This reads as:

```
if ((this and that) or (such and so)) and not other {
    // statements
}
```

Or if you want to see clearly in which order these operations are performed:

```
if (
        (this and that)
            or
        (such and so)
    )
    and
        (not other)
```

Of course, the more complicated you make it, the harder it is to remember exactly what you're doing!

When you use the == operator, the contents of the objects are compared. This only returns true if a and b have the same value:

```
let a = "Hello, world"
let b = "Hello," + " world"
println(a == b)              // prints true
```

This is different from Objective-C, where == is only true if the two objects are the exact same instance in memory. In Swift, however, == compares the values of the objects, not whether they actually occupy the same spot in memory. (If you need to do that use ===, the identity operator.)

Swift has another very powerful construct in the language for making decisions, the switch statement:

```
switch condition {
  case value1:
    // statements

  case value2:
    // statements

  case value3:
    // statements

  default:
    // statements
}
```

It works the same way as an if statement with a bunch of else ifs. The following is equivalent:

```
if condition == value1 {
  // statements
} else if condition == value2 {
  // statements
} else if condition == value3 {
  // statements
} else {
  // statements
}
```

In such a situation, the `switch` statement would be more convenient to use. Swift's version of switch is more much powerful than the one in Objective-C. For example, you can match on ranges and other patterns:

```
switch difference {
  case 0:
    title = "Perfect!"
  case 1..<5:
    title = "You almost had it!"
  case 5..<10:
    title = "Pretty good!"
  default:
    title = "Not even close..."
}
```

The `..<` is the **half-open range** operator. It creates a range between the two numbers, but the top number is exclusive. So the half-open range `1..<5` is the same as the **closed range** `1...4`. You'll see the `switch` statement in action a little later in this tutorial.

Note that `if` and `return` can be used to return early from a method:

```
func divide(a: Int, by b: Int) -> Int {
  if b == 0 {
    println("You really shouldn't divide by zero")
    return 0
  }
  return a / b
}
```

This can even be done for methods that don't return a value:

```
func performDifficultCalculation(list: [Double]) {
  if list.count < 2 {
    println("Too few items in list")
    return
  }
  // perform the very difficult calculation here
}
```

In this case, `return` simply means: "We're done with the method". Any statements following the `return` are skipped and execution immediately returns to the caller.

You could also have written it like this:

```
func performDifficultCalculation(list: [Double]) {
  if list.count < 2 {
    println("Too few items in list")
  } else {
    // perform the very difficult calculation here
  }
}
```

Whichever you use is up to personal preference. If there are only two cases such as in the above example, I prefer to use an else but the early return will work just as well.

Sometimes you see code like this:

```
func someMethod() {
  if condition1 {
    if condition2 {
      if condition3 {
        // statements
      } else {
        // statements
      }
    } else {
      // statements
    }
  } else {
    // statements
  }
}
```

This can become very hard to read, so I like to restructure that kind of code as follows:

```
func someMethod() {
  if !condition1 {
    // statements
    return;
  }
  if !condition2 {
    // statements
    return;
  }
  if !condition3 {
    // statements
    return;
  }
  // statements
}
```

Both do exactly the same thing, but I find the second one much easier to understand. As you become more experienced, you'll start to develop your own taste for what looks good and what is readable code.

Loops

You've seen the for-in statement for looping through an array:

```
for item in items {
  if !item.checked {
    count += 1
  }
}
```

This performs the statements inside the for block once for each object from the items array. This type of for-loop can be used only with certain collection objects such as Array and Dictionary.

There is a more general purpose version of the for-statement that looks like this:

```
for var i = start; i < end; ++i {
  // statements
}
```

You should read the section with the semicolons as:

```
start condition; end condition; increment
```

For example, when you see,

```
for var i = 0; i < 5; ++i {
  println(i)
}
```

it means you have a for-loop,

- that has a **loop counter** named i starting at 0,

- that keeps repeating for as long as i is smaller than 5 (i.e. the loop ends as soon as i becomes equal to 5),

- and increments i by 1 at the end of each **iteration** (one pass through the loop); the notation ++i means the same as i += 1.

When you run this code, it will print to the Debug area:

```
0
1
2
3
4
```

You can also write a simple loop like this with a half-open or closed range. This outputs the same as above:

```
for i in 0...4 {   // or 0..<5
  println(i)
}
```

But the for-condition-increment loop is still useful. For example, if you wanted to show just the even numbers, you could change the for loop to:

```
for var i = 0; i < 5; i += 2 {
  println(i)
}
```

Note that the scope of the variable i is limited to just this for-statement. You can't use it outside this statement, so its lifetime is even shorter than a local variable.

By the way, you can also write this loop as:

```
for i in stride(from: 0, to: 5, by: 2) {
  println(i)
}
```

The stride() function creates a special object that represents the range 0 to 5 in increments of 2. There's lots of ways to make for loops!

To write the loop through the ChecklistItems array using the general purpose form of the for statement, you'd do something like this:

```
for var i = 0; i < items.count; ++i {
  let item = items[i]
  if !item.checked {
    count += 1
  }
}
```

This is slightly more cumbersome than "`for item in items`", which is why you'll see `for-in` used most of the time.

(Note that `items.count` and `count` in this example are two different things with the same name. The first `count` is a property on the `items` array that returns the number of elements in that array; the second `count` is a local variable that contains the number of unchecked to-do items counted so far.)

The for-statement is not the only way to perform loops. Another very useful looping construct is the `while`-statement:

```
while something is true {
  // statements
}
```

The while-loop keeps repeating the statements until its condition becomes false. You can also write it as follows:

```
do {
  // statements
} while something is true
```

In the latter case, the condition is evaluated after the statements have been executed at least once.

You can rewrite the `ChecklistItems` loop as follows using a `while` statement:

```
var i = 0
while i < items.count {
  let item = items[i]
  if !item.checked {
    count += 1
  }
  i += 1
}
```

Most of these looping constructs are really the same, they just look different. Each of them lets you repeat a bunch of statements until some ending condition is met.

There really is no significant difference between using a `for`, `while` or `do - while` loop, except that one may be easier to read than the others, depending on what you're trying to do.

Just like you can prematurely exit from a method using the `return` statement, you can exit a loop at any time using the `break` statement:

```
var found = false
for item in array {
  if item == searchText {
    found = true
    break
  }
}
```

This example loops through the array until it finds an item that is equal to the value of searchText (presumably both are strings). Then it sets the variable found to true and jumps out of the loop using break. You've found what you were looking for, so it makes no sense to look at the other objects in that array (for all you know there could be hundreds).

There is also a continue statement that is somewhat the opposite of break. It doesn't exit the loop but immediately skips to the next iteration. You use continue to say, "I'm done with the current item, let's look at the next one."

Loops can often be replaced by *functional programming* constructs such as map, filter, or reduce. These are functions that operate on a collection, perform some code for each item, and return a new collection with the results.

For example, using filter on an array will only retain items if they satisfy a certain condition. To get a list of all the unchecked ChecklistItem objects, you'd write:

```
var uncheckedItems = items.filter { item in !item.checked }
```

That's a lot simpler than writing a loop. Functional programming is an advanced topic so we won't spend too much time on it here.

Objects

Objects are what it's all about. They combine data with functionality into coherent, reusable units – that is, if you write them properly!

The data is made up of the object's instance variables and constants. We often refer to these as the object's **properties**. The functionality is provided by the object's methods.

In your Swift programs you will use existing objects, such as String, Array, NSDate, UITableView, and you'll also make your own.

To define a new object, you need a **MyObject.swift** file that contains a class section:

```
class MyObject {
  var text: String
  var count = 0
  let maximum = 100

  init() {
    text = "Hello, world"
  }

  func doSomething() {
    // statements
  }
}
```

Inside the brackets for the class, you add properties (the instance variables and constants) and methods.

There are two types of properties:

- **stored properties** are the usual instance variables and constants

- **computed properties** don't store a value but perform logic when you read or write their values

This is an example of a computed property:

```
var indexOfSelectedChecklist: Int {
  get {
    return NSUserDefaults.standardUserDefaults().integerForKey("ChecklistIndex")
  }
  set {
    NSUserDefaults.standardUserDefaults().setInteger(newValue, forKey: "ChecklistIndex")
  }
}
```

The `indexOfSelectedChecklist` property does not store a value like a normal variable would. Instead, every time someone uses this property it performs the code from the `get` or `set` block. The alternative would be to write separate `setIndexOfSelectedChecklist()` and `getIndexOfSelectedChecklist()` methods, but that doesn't read as nicely.

The keyword `@IBOutlet` means that a property can refer to a user interface element in Interface Builder, such as a label or button. Such properties are usually declared `weak` and optional. Similarly, the keyword `@IBAction` is used for methods that will be performed when the user interacts with the app.

There are three types of methods:

- instance methods
- class methods
- init methods

You know that a method is a function that belongs to an object. To call such a method you first need to have an instance of the object:

```
var myInstance = MyObject()    // create the object instance
. . .
myInstance.doSomething()       // call the method
```

You can also make **class methods**, which can be used without an instance. In fact, they are often used as "factory" methods, to create new instances:

```
class MyObject {
  . . .
  class func makeObjectWithCount(count: Int) -> MyObject {
    let m = MyObject()
    m.count = count
    return m
  }
}

var myInstance = MyObject.makeObjectWithCount(40)
```

Init methods, or **initializers**, are used during the creation of new object instances. Instead of the above factory method you might as well use a custom `init` method:

```
class MyObject {
  . . .
  init(count: Int) {
    self.count = count
  }
}

var myInstance = MyObject(count: 40)
```

The main purpose of an init method is to fill in the object's instance variables. Any instance variables or constants that do not have a value yet must be given one in the init method.

Swift does not allow variables or constants to have no value (except for optionals), and init is your last chance to make this happen.

Objects can have more than one init method; which one you use depends on the circumstances.

A UITableViewController, for example, can be initialized either with init(coder) when automatically loaded from a storyboard, with init(nibName, bundle) when manually loaded from a nib file, or with init(style) when constructed without a storyboard or nib. Sometimes you use one, sometimes the other.

You can also provide a deinit method that gets called when the object is no longer in use, just before it gets destroyed.

By the way, class isn't the only way to define an object in Swift. It also supports other types of objects such as structs and enums. You'll learn more about these later, so I won't give away the whole plot here (no spoilers!).

Protocols

Besides objects you can also define **protocols**. A protocol is simply a list of method names (and possibly properties as well):

```
protocol MyProtocol {
  func someMethod(value: Int)
  func anotherMethod() -> String
}
```

A protocol is like a job ad. It lists all the things that a candidate for a certain position in your company should be able to do.

But the ad itself doesn't do the job – it's just words printed in the careers section of the newspaper – so you need to hire an actual employee who can get the job done. That would be an object.

Objects need to indicate that they conform to a protocol:

```
class MyObject: MyProtocol {
  . . .
}
```

This object now has to provide an implementation for the methods listed in the protocol. (If not, it's fired!)

From then on you can refer to this object as a MyObject (because that is its class name) but also as a MyProtocol object:

```
var m1: MyObject = MyObject()
var m2: MyProtocol = MyObject()
```

To any part of the code using the m2 variable, it doesn't matter that the object is really a MyObject under the hood. The type of m2 is MyProtocol, not MyObject.

All your code sees is that m2 is *some* object conforming to MyProtocol, but it's not important what sort of object that is.

In other words, you don't really care that your employee may also have another job on the side, as long as it doesn't interfere with the duties you've hired him for.

Protocols are often used to define **delegates** but they come in handy for other uses as well, as you'll find out later on.

This concludes the quick recap of what you've seen so far of the Swift language. After all that theory, it's time to write some code!

Getting GPS coordinates

In this section you'll create the *MyLocations* project in Xcode and then use the Core Location framework to find the latitude and longitude of the user's location.

When you're done with this section, the app will look like this:

The first screen of the app

I know it's not very good looking yet, but you'll fix that later. For now, it's only important that you can obtain the GPS coordinates and show them on the screen.

As always, you first make things work and then make them look good.

➤ Fire up Xcode and make a new project. Choose the **Tabbed Application** template.

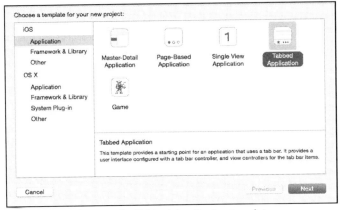

Choosing the Tabbed Application template

➤ Fill in the options as follows:

• Product Name: **MyLocations**

• Organization Name: Your own name or the name of your company

• Organization Identifier: Your own identifier in reverse domain notation

• Language: **Swift**

• Devices: **iPhone**

➤ Save the project.

If you run the app, it looks like this:

The app from the Tabbed Application template

The app has a tab bar along the bottom with two tabs: First and Second.

Even though it doesn't do much yet, the app already employs three view controllers:

1. its *root controller* is the `UITabBarController` that contains the tab bar and performs the switching between the different screens;

2. the view controller for the First tab;

3. the view controller for the Second tab.

The two tabs each have their own view controller. By default the Xcode template names them `FirstViewController` and `SecondViewController`.

The storyboard looks like this:

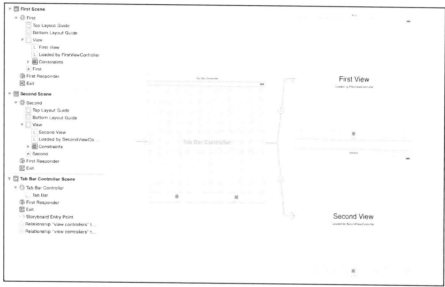

The storyboard from the Tabbed Application template

I already had to zoom it out to fit the whole thing on my screen. Storyboards are great but they sure take up a lot of space!

There are two changes you should make at this point: disabling Size Classes and disabling Auto Layout.

You've seen a glimpse of Auto Layout in the previous two tutorials where you used it to make the app fit on the different iPhone models. Auto Layout is a great technology for making complex user interfaces but it can also be quite confusing to get right – sometimes it's more trouble than it's worth. For this tutorial you disable Auto Layout altogether.

Size Classes are a new feature of iOS 8 that make it possible to have the same storyboard on the iPhone and iPad versions of the app. Because this app is only for iPhone, you don't need to use this feature. In the next tutorial you'll learn more about Size Classes and adaptive user interfaces.

➤ Go to the storyboard's **File inspector** and uncheck the **Use Auto Layout** option. This will also disable Size Classes.

Disabling Auto Layout in the File inspector for the storyboard

When Xcode asks you to confirm, click **Disable Size Classes** to continue.

The scenes in the storyboard now change from a square layout into a rectangular shape that is representative of the screen of the iPhone 5, 5c and 5s (320 points wide by 568 points tall). That is the device you'll be designing for. Later on you'll also make the app suitable for the smaller iPhone 4S and the larger iPhone 6 and 6 Plus models.

In this section you'll be working with the first tab only. In the second half of the tutorial you'll create the screen for the second tab and add a third tab as well.

Let's give FirstViewController a better name.

➤ In the project navigator, click **FirstViewController.swift** twice (but not too quickly) and rename it to **CurrentLocationViewController.swift**.

➤ Open **CurrentLocationViewController.swift** and change the class line to:

```
class CurrentLocationViewController: UIViewController {
```

➤ Switch to **Main.storyboard** and select the view controller connected to the first tab. In the **Identity inspector**, change the Class field from "FirstViewController" to **CurrentLocationViewController**:

Changing the class in Interface Builder

➤ Go into the **Project Settings** screen and de-select the Landscape Left and Landscape Right settings under **Deployment Info, Device Orientation**. Now the app is portrait-only.

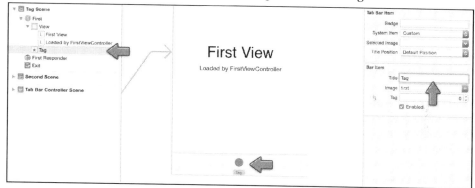

The app only works in portrait

➤ Run the app again just to make sure everything still works.

Whenever I change how things are hooked up in the storyboard, I find it useful to run the app and verify that the change was successful – it's way too easy to forget a step and you want to catch such mistakes right away.

As you've seen, a view controller that sits inside a navigation controller has a Navigation Item object that allows it to configure the navigation bar. Tab bars work the same way. Each view controller that represents a tab has a Tab Bar Item object.

➤ Select the Tab Bar Item object from the "First Scene" (this is the Current Location View Controller) and go to the **Attributes inspector**. Change the **Title** to **Tag**.

Changing the title of the Tab Bar Item

Later on you'll also set an image on the Tab Bar Item; it currently uses the default image of a circle from the template.

You will now design the screen for this first tab. It gets two buttons and a few labels that show the GPS coordinates and the street address. To save you some time, you'll add all the outlet properties in one go.

➤ Add the following to the class inside **CurrentLocationViewController.swift**:

```swift
@IBOutlet weak var messageLabel: UILabel!
@IBOutlet weak var latitudeLabel: UILabel!
@IBOutlet weak var longitudeLabel: UILabel!
@IBOutlet weak var addressLabel: UILabel!
@IBOutlet weak var tagButton: UIButton!
```

```
@IBOutlet weak var getButton: UIButton!

@IBAction func getLocation() {
  // do nothing yet
}
```

Design the UI to look as follows:

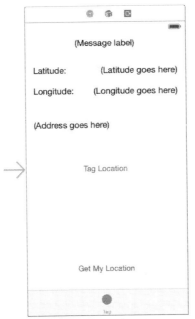

The design of the Current Location screen

➤ The **(Message label)** at the top should span the whole width of the screen. You'll use this label for status messages while the app is obtaining the GPS coordinates. Set the **Alignment** attribute to centered and connect the label to the messageLabel outlet.

➤ Make the **(Latitude goes here)** and **(Longitude goes here)** labels right-aligned and connect them to the latitudeLabel and longitudeLabel outlets respectively.

➤ The **(Address goes here)** label also spans the whole width of the screen and is 50 points high so it can fit two lines of text. Set its **Lines** attribute to 0 (that means it can fit a variable number of lines). Connect this label to the addressLabel outlet.

➤ The **Tag Location** button doesn't do anything yet but should be connected to the tagButton outlet.

➤ Connect the **Get My Location** button to the getButton outlet, and its Touch Up Inside event to the getLocation action.

➤ Run the app to see the new design in action.

So far, nothing special. With the exception of the tab bar this is stuff you've seen and done before. Time to add something new: let's play with Core Location!

Note: Because you're initially designing for the iPhone 5 screen size, it's best to use the iPhone 5s Simulator to run the app. The smaller iPhone 4S won't be able to show the entire user interface yet, and the app will look plain silly on the larger iPhone 6 and 6 Plus simulators. You'll fix this later in the tutorial.

Core Location

Most iOS-enabled devices have a way to let you know exactly where you are on the globe, either through communication with GPS satellites or Wi-Fi and cell tower triangulation. The Core Location framework puts that power into your own hands.

An app can ask Core Location for the user's current latitude and longitude. For devices with a compass it can also give the heading (you won't be using that in this tutorial). Core Location can also provide continuous location updates while you're on the move.

Getting a location from Core Location is pretty easy but there are some pitfalls that you need to avoid. Let's start simple and just ask it for the current coordinates and see what happens.

➤ At the very top of **CurrentLocationViewController.swift**, add an `import` statement:

```
import CoreLocation
```

That is all you have to do to add the Core Location framework to your project.

Core Location, as so many other parts of the iOS SDK, works with a delegate, so you should make the view controller conform to the `CLLocationManagerDelegate` protocol.

➤ Add `CLLocationManagerDelegate` to the view controller's `class` line:

```
class CurrentLocationViewController: UIViewController, CLLocationManagerDelegate {
```

➤ Also add a new constant property:

```
let locationManager = CLLocationManager()
```

The `CLLocationManager` is the object that will give you the GPS coordinates. You're putting the reference to this object in a constant (using `let`), not a variable (`var`). Once you have created the location manager object, the value of `locationManager` will never have to change.

The new `CLLocationManager` object doesn't give out GPS coordinates right away. To begin receiving coordinates, you have to call its `startUpdatingLocation()` method first.

Unless you're doing turn-by-turn navigation, you don't want your app to continuously receive GPS coordinates. That requires a lot of power and will quickly drain the battery. For this app, you only turn on the location manager when you want a location fix and turn it off again when you've received a usable location.

You'll implement that logic in a minute (it's more complex than you think it would be). For now, you're only interested in receiving something from Core Location, just so you know that it works.

➤ Change the `getLocation()` action method to the following:

```
@IBAction func getLocation() {
  locationManager.delegate = self
  locationManager.desiredAccuracy = kCLLocationAccuracyNearestTenMeters
  locationManager.startUpdatingLocation()
}
```

This method is hooked up to the Get My Location button. It tells the location manager that the view controller is its delegate and that you want to receive locations with an accuracy of up to ten meters. Then you start the location manager. From that moment on the CLLocationManager object will send location updates to its delegate, i.e. the view controller.

> Speaking of the delegate, add the following code to the bottom of the file:

```
// MARK: - CLLocationManagerDelegate

func locationManager(manager: CLLocationManager!, didFailWithError error: NSError!) {
  println("didFailWithError \(error)")
}

func locationManager(manager: CLLocationManager!,
                     didUpdateLocations locations: [AnyObject]!) {
  let newLocation = locations.last as! CLLocation
  println("didUpdateLocations \(newLocation)")
}
```

These are the delegate methods for the location manager. For the time being, you'll simply write a println() message to the debug area.

// MARK:

In the code above there is a comment line that starts with // MARK:. Such a comment gives a hint to Xcode that you have organized your source file into neat sections. You can see this from the Jump Bar:

The dash – makes Xcode draw a handy divider line. You can also use // TODO: and // FIXME: and Xcode will put those into the Jump Bar popup too.

> Run the app in the Simulator and press the Get My Location button.

Whoops, nothing seems to happen. That's because you need to ask for permission to use the user's location first. This is new as of iOS 8.

> Add the following lines to the top of getLocation():

```
let authStatus = CLLocationManager.authorizationStatus()
```

```
if authStatus == .NotDetermined {
  locationManager.requestWhenInUseAuthorization()
  return
}
```

This checks the current authorization status. If it is `.NotDetermined`, meaning that this app has not asked for permission yet, then the app will request "When In Use" authorization. That allows the app to get location updates while it is open and the user is interacting with it.

There is also "Always" authorization, which permits the app to check the user's location even when it is not active. For most apps, including MyLocations, when-in-use is what you want to ask for.

Just adding these lines of code is not enough. You also have to add a special key to the app's Info.plist.

➤ Open **Info.plist** (under Supporting Files). Right-click somewhere inside Info.plist and choose **Add Row** from the menu.

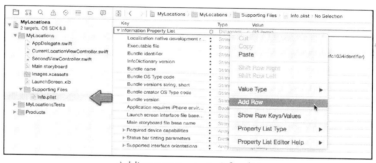

Adding a new row to Info.plist

➤ For the key, type **NSLocationWhenInUseUsageDescription**. Type the following text in the Value column:

This app lets you keep track of interesting places. It needs access to the GPS coordinates for your location.

This description tells the user what the app wants to use the location data for.

Adding the new item to Info.plist

➤ Run the app again and press the Get My Location button.

Core Location will pop up the following alert, asking the user for permission:

Users have to allow your app to use their location

If a user denies the request with the Don't Allow button, then Core Location will never give your app location coordinates.

➤ Press the **Don't Allow** button. Now press Get My Location again.

Xcode's debug area should now show the following message:

```
didFailWithError Error Domain=kCLErrorDomain Code=1 "The operation couldn't be completed.
(kCLErrorDomain error 1.)"
```

This comes from the locationManager(didFailWithError) delegate method. It's telling you that the location manager wasn't able to obtain a location.

The reason why is described by an NSError object, which is the standard object that the iOS SDK uses to convey error information. You'll see it in many other places in the SDK (there are plenty of places where things can go wrong!).

An NSError has a "domain" and a "code". The domain in this case is kCLErrorDomain meaning the error came from Core Location (CL). The code is 1, also known by the symbolic name CLError.Denied, which means the user did not allow the app to obtain location information.

> **Note:** The k prefix is often used by the iOS frameworks to signify that a name represents a constant value (I guess whoever came up with this prefix thought it was spelled "konstant"). This is an old convention and you won't see it used much in new frameworks or in Swift code, but it still pops up here and there.

➤ Stop the app from within Xcode and run it again.

When you now press the Get My Location button, the app does not ask for permission anymore but immediately gives you the same error message.

Let's make this a bit more user-friendly, because a normal user would never see that println().

➤ Add the following method to **CurrentLocationViewController.swift**:

```
func showLocationServicesDeniedAlert() {
  let alert = UIAlertController(title: "Location Services Disabled",
    message: "Please enable location services for this app in Settings.",
    preferredStyle: .Alert)

  let okAction = UIAlertAction(title: "OK", style: .Default, handler: nil)
  alert.addAction(okAction)

  presentViewController(alert, animated: true, completion: nil)
}
```

This pops up an alert with a helpful hint. This app is pretty useless without access to the user's location, so it should encourage the user to enable location services. It's not necessarily the user of the app who has denied access to the location data; a systems administrator or parent may have restricted location access.

➤ To show this alert, add the following lines to getLocation(), just before you set the locationManager's delegate:

```
if authStatus == .Denied || authStatus == .Restricted {
  showLocationServicesDeniedAlert()
  return
}
```

This shows the alert if the authorization status is denied or restricted. Notice the use of || here, the "logical or" operator. showLocationServicesDeniedAlert() will be called if either of those two conditions is true.

➤ Try it out. Run the app and tap Get My Location. You should now get the Location Services Disabled alert:

The alert that pops up when location services are not available

Fortunately, users can change their minds and enable location services for your app again. This is done from the iPhone's Settings app.

➤ Open the **Settings** app in the Simulator and go to **Privacy** → **Location**.

Location Services in the Settings app

> Click **MyLocations** and then **While Using the App** to enable location services again. Switch back to the app (or run it again from within Xcode) and press the Get My Location button.

When I tried this, the following message appeared in Xcode's debug area:

```
didFailWithError Error Domain=kCLErrorDomain Code=0 "The operation couldn't be completed.
(kCLErrorDomain error 0.)"
```

Again there is an error message but with a different code, 0. This is "location unknown" which means Core Location was unable to obtain a location for some reason.

That is not so strange, as you're running this from the Simulator, which obviously does not have a real GPS. Your Mac may have a way to obtain location information through Wi-Fi but this is not built into the Simulator. Fortunately, there is a way to fake it!

> With the app running, from the Simulator's menu bar at the top of the screen, choose **Debug → Location → Apple**.

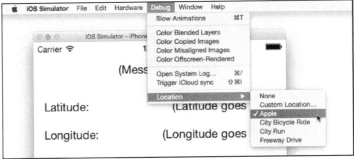

The Simulator's Location menu

You now should see messages like these in the debug area:

```
didUpdateLocations <+37.33259552,-122.03031802> +/- 500.00m (speed -1.00 mps / course -1.00)
@ 8/10/14 4:03:52 PM Central European Summer Time

didUpdateLocations <+37.33241023,-122.03051088> +/- 65.00m (speed -1.00 mps / course -1.00) @
8/10/14 4:03:54 PM Central European Summer Time

didUpdateLocations <+37.33233141,-122.03121860> +/- 50.00m (speed -1.00 mps / course -1.00) @
8/10/14 4:04:01 PM Central European Summer Time

didUpdateLocations <+37.33233141,-122.03121860> +/- 30.00m (speed 0.00 mps / course -1.00) @
8/10/14 4:04:03 PM Central European Summer Time

didUpdateLocations <+37.33233141,-122.03121860> +/- 10.00m (speed 0.00 mps / course -1.00) @
8/10/14 4:04:05 PM Central European Summer Time
```

It keeps going on and on, giving the app a new location every second or so, although after a short while the latitude and longitude readings do not change anymore. These particular coordinates point at the Apple headquarters in Cupertino, California.

Look carefully at the coordinates the app is receiving. The first one says "+/- 500.00m", the second one "+/- 65.00m", the third "+/- 50.00m". This number keeps getting smaller and smaller until it stops at about "+/- 5.00m".

This is the accuracy of the measurement, expressed in meters. What you see is the Simulator imitating what happens when you ask for a location on a real device.

If you go out with an iPhone and try to obtain location information, the iPhone uses three different ways to find your coordinates. It has onboard cell, Wi-Fi, and GPS radios that each give it location information in more detail:

- Cell tower triangulation will always work if there is a signal but it's not very precise.

- Wi-Fi positioning works better but that is only available if there are known Wi-Fi routers nearby. This system uses a big database that contains the locations of wireless networking equipment.

- The very best results come from the GPS (Global Positioning System) but that attempts a satellite communication and is therefore the slowest of the three. It also won't work very well indoors.

So your device has several ways of obtaining location data, ranging from fast but inaccurate (cell towers, Wi-Fi) to accurate but slow (GPS). And none of these are guaranteed to work. Some devices don't even have a GPS or cell radio at all and have to rely on just the Wi-Fi. Suddenly obtaining a location seems a lot trickier.

Fortunately for us, Core Location does all of the hard work of turning the location readings from its various sources into a useful number. Instead of making you wait for the definitive results from the GPS (which may never come), Core Location sends location data to the app as soon as it gets it, and then follows up with more and more accurate readings.

Exercise. If you have an iPhone, iPod touch or iPad nearby, try the app on your device and see what kind of readings it gives you. If you have more than one device, try the app on all of them and note the differences. ∎

Asynchronous operations

Obtaining a location is an example of an **asynchronous** process.

Sometimes apps need to do things that may take a while. You start an operation and then you have to wait until it gives you the results. If you're unlucky, those results may never come at all!

In the case of Core Location, it can take a second or two before you get the first location reading and then quite a few seconds more to get coordinates that are accurate enough for your app to use.

Asynchronous means that after you start such an operation, your app will continue on its merry way. The user interface is still responsive, new events are being sent and handled, and the user can still tap on things.

The asynchronous process is said to be operating "in the background". As soon as the operation is done, the app is notified through a delegate so that it can process the results.

The opposite is **synchronous** (without the a). If you start an operation that is synchronous, the app won't continue until that operation is done. In effect, it freezes up.

In the case of CLLocationManager that would cause a big problem: your app would be totally unresponsive for the couple of seconds that it takes to get a location fix. Those kinds of "blocking" operations are often a bad experience for the user.

For example, MyLocations has a tab bar at the bottom. If the app would block while getting the location, tapping on a tab during that time would have no effect. The user expects to always be able to switch between tabs but now it appears that the app is frozen, or worse, has crashed.

The designers of iOS decided that such behavior is unacceptable and therefore operations that take longer than a fraction of a second should be performed in an asynchronous manner.

In the next tutorial you'll see more asynchronous processing in action when we talk about network connections and downloading stuff from the internet.

By the way, iOS has something called the "watchdog timer". If your app is unresponsive for too long, then under certain circumstances the watchdog timer will kill your app without mercy – so don't do that!

The take-away is this: Any operation that takes long enough to be noticeable by the user should be done asynchronously, in the background.

Putting the coordinates on the screen

The locationManager(didUpdateLocations) delegate method gives you an array of CLLocation objects that contain the current latitude and longitude coordinates of the user. (These objects also have some additional information, such as the altitude and speed, but you don't use those in this app.)

You'll take the last CLLocation object from the array – because that is the most recent update – and display its coordinates in the labels that you added to the screen earlier.

➤ Add a new instance variable to **CurrentLocationViewController.swift**:

```
var location: CLLocation?
```

You will store the user's current location in this variable.

This needs to be an optional, because it is possible to *not* have a location, for example when you're stranded out in the Sahara desert somewhere and there is not a cell tower or GPS satellite in sight (it happens).

But even when everything works as it should, the value of location will still be nil until Core Location reports back with a valid CLLocation object, which as you've seen may take a few seconds. So an optional it is.

➤ Change the locationManager(didUpdateLocations) method to:

```
func locationManager(manager: CLLocationManager!,
                     didUpdateLocations locations: [AnyObject]!) {
  let newLocation = locations.last as! CLLocation
  println("didUpdateLocations \(newLocation)")

  location = newLocation
  updateLabels()
}
```

You store the CLLocation object that you get from the location manager into the instance variable and call a new updateLabels() method.

Keep the println() in there because it's handy for debugging.

➤ Add the updateLabels() method below:

```
func updateLabels() {
  if let location = location {
    latitudeLabel.text = String(format: "%.8f", location.coordinate.latitude)
    longitudeLabel.text = String(format: "%.8f", location.coordinate.longitude)
    tagButton.hidden = false
    messageLabel.text = ""
  } else {
    latitudeLabel.text = ""
    longitudeLabel.text = ""
    addressLabel.text = ""
    tagButton.hidden = true
    messageLabel.text = "Tap 'Get My Location' to Start"
  }
}
```

Because the location instance variable is an optional, you use the if let syntax to unwrap it.

Note that it's OK for the unwrapped variable to have the same name as the optional – here they are both called location. Inside the if-statement, location now refers to an actual CLLocation object; it can never be nil.

If there is a valid location object, you convert the latitude and longitude, which are values with type Double, into strings and put them into the labels.

You've seen *string interpolation* before to put values into strings, so why doesn't this code simply do:

```
latitudeLabel.text = "\(location.coordinate.latitude)"
```

That would certainly work, but it doesn't give you any control over how the latitude value appears. For this app, you want both latitude and longitude to be shown with 8 digits behind the decimal point.

For that sort of control, you need to use a so-called *format string*.

Like string interpolation, a format string uses placeholders that will be replaced by the actual value during runtime. These placeholders, or *format specifiers*, can be quite intricate.

To create the text for the latitude label you do this:

```
String(format: "%.8f", location.coordinate.latitude)
```

This creates a new `String` object using the format string `"%.8f"`, and the value to replace in that string, `location.coordinate.latitude`.

Placeholders always start with a `%` percent sign. Examples of common placeholders are: `%d` for integer values, `%f` for decimals, and `%@` for arbitrary objects.

Format strings are very common in Objective-C code but less so in Swift because string interpolation is much simpler, but also less powerful.

The `%.8f` format specifier does the same thing as `%f`: it takes a decimal number and puts it in the string. The `.8` means that there should always be 8 digits behind the decimal point.

➤ Run the app, select a location to simulate from the Simulator's **Debug** menu and tap the Get My Location button. You'll now see the latitude and longitude appear on the screen.

The app shows the GPS coordinates

When the app starts up it has no location object (`location` is still `nil`) and therefore should show the `"Tap 'Get My Location' to Start"` message at the top – see the `else` block in `updateLabels()` – but it doesn't do that yet.

That's because you don't call `updateLabels()` until the app receives its first coordinates. You should also call this method from `viewDidLoad()`.

➤ The view controller already has a `viewDidLoad()` method. Change it to:

```
override func viewDidLoad() {
  super.viewDidLoad()
  updateLabels()
}
```

➤ Run the app. Initially, the screen should now say, Tap 'Get My Location' to Start, and the latitude and longitude labels are empty.

Attributes and properties

Most of the attributes in Interface Builder's inspectors correspond directly to properties on the selected object. For example, a UILabel has the following attributes:

These are directly related to the following properties:

Text	label.text
Color	label.textColor
Font	label.font
Alignment	label.textAlignment
Lines	label.numberOfLines
Enabled	label.enabled
Baseline	label.baselineAdjustment
Line Breaks	label.lineBreakMode

And so on... As you can see, the names may not always be exactly the same ("Lines" and numberOfLines) but you can easily figure out which property goes with which attribute.

You can find the properties in the documentation for UILabel. From the Xcode **Help** menu, select **Documentation and API Reference**. Type "uilabel" into the search field to bring up the class reference for UILabel:

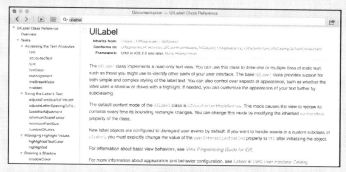

The documentation for UILabel may not list properties for all of the attributes from the inspectors. For example, in the Attributes inspector there is a section named "View". The attributes in this section come from UIView, which is the base class of UILabel. So if you can't find a property in the UILabel class, you may need to check the documentation under "Inherits from".

Handling errors

Getting GPS coordinates is error-prone. You may be somewhere where there is no clear line-of-sight to the sky (such as inside or in an area with lots of tall buildings), blocking your GPS signal.

There may not be many Wi-Fi routers around you, or they haven't been catalogued yet, so the Wi-Fi radio isn't much help getting a location fix either.

And of course your cell signal is so weak that triangulating your position doesn't offer particularly good results either.

All of that is assuming your device actually has a GPS or cell radio. I just went out with my iPod touch to capture coordinates and make some pictures for this tutorial. In the city center it was unable to obtain a location fix. My iPhone did better but it still wasn't ideal.

The moral of this story is that your location-aware apps had better know how to deal with errors and bad readings. There are no guarantees that you'll be able to get a location fix, and if you do then it might still take a few seconds.

This is where software meets the real world. You should add some error handling code to the app to let users know about problems getting those coordinates.

➤ Add these two instance variables to **CurrentLocationViewController.swift**:

```
var updatingLocation = false
var lastLocationError: NSError?
```

➤ Change the `locationManager(didFailWithError)` delegate method to the following:

```
func locationManager(manager: CLLocationManager!, didFailWithError error: NSError!) {
  println("didFailWithError \(error)")

  if error.code == CLError.LocationUnknown.rawValue {
    return
  }

  lastLocationError = error

  stopLocationManager()
  updateLabels()
}
```

The location manager may report errors for a variety of scenarios. You can look at the `code` property of the `NSError` object to find out what type of error you're dealing with.

Some of the Core Location errors:

- `CLError.LocationUnknown` – The location is currently unknown, but Core Location will keep trying.

- `CLError.Denied` – The user declined the app to use location services.

- `CLError.Network` – There was a network-related error.

There are more (having to do with the compass and geocoding), but you get the point. Lots of reasons for things to go wrong!

> **Note:** These error codes are defined in the CLError enumeration. Recall that an enumeration, or enum, is a list of values and names for these values.
>
> The error codes used by Core Location have simple integer values. Rather than using the values 0, 1, 2 and so on in your program, Core Location has given them symbolic names using the CLError enum. That makes these codes easier to understand and you're less likely to pick the wrong one.
>
> To convert these names back to an integer value you ask for the rawValue.

In your updated didFailWithError, you do:

```
if error.code == CLError.LocationUnknown.rawValue {
  return
}
```

The CLError.LocationUnknown error means the location manager was unable to obtain a location right now, but that doesn't mean all is lost. It might just need another second or so to get an uplink to the GPS satellite. In the mean time it's letting you know that for now it could not get any location information.

When you get this error, you will simply keep trying until you do find a location or receive a more serious error.

In the case of such a more serious error, didFailWithError stores the error object into a new instance variable, lastLocationError:

```
lastLocationError = error
```

That way you can look up later what kind of error you were dealing with. This comes in useful in updateLabels(). You'll be extending that method in a second to show the error to the user because you don't want to leave them in the dark about such things.

Exercise. Can you explain why lastLocationError is an optional? ∎

Answer: When there is no error, lastLocationError will not have a value. In other words it can be nil, and variables that can be nil must be optionals in Swift.

Finally, didFailWithError does:

```
stopLocationManager()
updateLabels()
```

The stopLocationManager() method is new. If obtaining a location appears to be impossible for wherever the user currently is on the globe, then you'll tell the location manager to stop. To conserve battery power the app should power down the iPhone's radios as soon as it doesn't need them anymore.

If this was a turn-by-turn navigation app, you'd keep the location manager running even in the case of a network error, because who knows, a couple of meters ahead you might get a valid location.

For this app the user will simply have to press the Get My Location button again if they want to try in another spot.

➤ Add the `stopLocationManager()` method:

```
func stopLocationManager() {
  if updatingLocation {
    locationManager.stopUpdatingLocation()
    locationManager.delegate = nil
    updatingLocation = false
  }
}
```

There's an if-statement in here that checks whether the boolean instance variable `updatingLocation` is `true` or `false`. If it is `false`, then the location manager wasn't currently active and there's no need to stop it.

The reason for having this `updatingLocation` variable is that you are going to change the appearance of the Get My Location button and the status message label when the app is trying to obtain a location fix, to let the user know the app is working on it.

➤ Put some extra code in `updateLabels()` to show the error message:

```
func updateLabels() {
  if let location = location {
    . . .
  } else {
    latitudeLabel.text = ""
    longitudeLabel.text = ""
    addressLabel.text = ""
    tagButton.hidden = true

    // The new code starts here:
    var statusMessage: String
    if let error = lastLocationError {
      if error.domain == kCLErrorDomain && error.code == CLError.Denied.rawValue {
        statusMessage = "Location Services Disabled"
      } else {
        statusMessage = "Error Getting Location"
      }
    } else if !CLLocationManager.locationServicesEnabled() {
      statusMessage = "Location Services Disabled"
    } else if updatingLocation {
      statusMessage = "Searching..."
    } else {
      statusMessage = "Tap 'Get My Location' to Start"
    }

    messageLabel.text = statusMessage
  }
}
```

The new code determines what to put in the `messageLabel` at the top of the screen. It uses a bunch of if-statements to figure out what the current status of the app is.

If the location manager gave an error, the label will show an error message.

The first error it checks for is `CLError.Denied` (in the error domain `kCLErrorDomain`, which means Core Location errors). In that case the user has not given this app permission to use the location services. That sort of defeats the purpose of this app but it can happen and you have to check for it anyway.

If the error code is something else then you simply say "Error Getting Location" as this usually means there was no way of obtaining a location fix.

Even if there was no error it might still be impossible to get location coordinates if the user disabled Location Services completely on her device (instead of just for this app). You check for that situation with the `locationServicesEnabled()` method of `CLLocationManager`.

Suppose there were no errors and everything works fine, then the status label will say "Searching..." before the first location object has been received.

If your device can obtain the location fix quickly then this text will be visible only for a fraction of a second, but often it might take a short while to get that first location fix. No one likes waiting, so it's nice to let the user know that the app is actively looking up her location. That is what you're using the `updatingLocation` boolean for.

> **Note:** You put all this logic into a single method because that makes it easy to change the screen when something has changed. Received a location? Simply call `updateLabels()` to refresh the contents of the screen. Received an error? Let `updateLabels()` sort it out...

➤ Also add the `startLocationManager()` method. I suggest you put it right above `stopLocationManager()`, to keep related functionality together:

```
func startLocationManager() {
  if CLLocationManager.locationServicesEnabled() {
    locationManager.delegate = self
    locationManager.desiredAccuracy = kCLLocationAccuracyNearestTenMeters
    locationManager.startUpdatingLocation()
    updatingLocation = true
  }
}
```

Starting the location manager used to happen in the `getLocation()` action method. Because you now have a `stopLocationManager()` method, it makes sense to move that code into a method of its own, `startLocationManager()`, just to keep things symmetrical.

The only difference with before is that this checks whether the location services are enabled. You also set the variable `updatingLocation` to `true`.

➤ Change `getLocation()` to:

```
@IBAction func getLocation() {
  let authStatus = CLLocationManager.authorizationStatus()

  if authStatus == .NotDetermined {
    . . .
  }

  if authStatus == .Denied || authStatus == .Restricted {
    . . .
  }

  startLocationManager()
  updateLabels()
}
```

There is one more small change to make. Suppose there was an error and no location could be obtained, but then you walk around for a bit and a valid location comes in. In that case it's a good idea to wipe the old error code.

➤ Change `locationManager(didUpdateLocations)` to:

```
func locationManager(manager: CLLocationManager!,
                      didUpdateLocations locations: [AnyObject]!) {
  let newLocation = locations.last as! CLLocation
  println("didUpdateLocations \(newLocation)")

  lastLocationError = nil
  location = newLocation
  updateLabels()
}
```

The only new line here is `lastLocationError = nil` to clear out the old error state. After receiving a valid coordinate, any previous error you may have encountered is no longer applicable.

➤ Run the app. While the app is waiting for incoming coordinates, the label at the top should say "Searching..." until it finds a valid coordinate or encounters a fatal error.

The app is waiting to receive GPS coordinates

Play around with the Simulator's location settings for a while.

Note that changing the Simulator's location to None isn't an error anymore. This still returns the `.LocationUnknown` error code but you ignore that because it's not a fatal error.

Tip: You can also simulate locations from within Xcode. If your app uses Core Location, the bar at the top of the debug area gets an arrow icon. Click on that icon to change the simulated location:

Simulating locations from within the Xcode debugger

Ideally you should not just test in the Simulator but also on your device, as you're more likely to encounter real errors that way.

Improving the results

Cool, you know how to obtain a `CLLocation` object from Core Location and you're able to handle errors. Now what?

Well, here's the thing: you saw in the Simulator that Core Location keeps giving you new location objects over and over, even though the coordinates may not have changed. That's because the user could be moving and then their coordinates do change.

However, you're not building a navigation app so for the purposes of this tutorial you just want to get a location that is accurate enough and then you can tell the location manager to stop sending updates.

This is important because getting location updates costs a lot of battery power as the device needs to keep its GPS/Wi-Fi/cell radios powered up for this. This app doesn't need to ask for GPS coordinates all the time, so it should stop when the location is accurate enough.

The problem is that you can't always get the accuracy you want, so you have to detect this. When the last couple of coordinates you received aren't increasing in accuracy then this is probably as good as it's going to get and you should let the radio power down.

➤ Change `locationManager(didUpdateLocations)` to the following:

```
func locationManager(manager: CLLocationManager!,
                     didUpdateLocations locations: [AnyObject]!) {
  let newLocation = locations.last as! CLLocation
  println("didUpdateLocations \(newLocation)")
  // 1
  if newLocation.timestamp.timeIntervalSinceNow < -5 {
    return
  }
  // 2
  if newLocation.horizontalAccuracy < 0 {
    return
  }
  // 3
  if location == nil || location!.horizontalAccuracy > newLocation.horizontalAccuracy {
    // 4
    lastLocationError = nil
    location = newLocation
    updateLabels()
    // 5
    if newLocation.horizontalAccuracy <= locationManager.desiredAccuracy {
      println("*** We're done!")
      stopLocationManager()
    }
  }
}
```

Let's take these changes one-by-one:

1. If the time at which the location object was determined is too long ago (5 seconds in this case), then this is a so-called *cached* result.

   Instead of returning a new location fix, the location manager may initially give you the most recently found location under the assumption that you might not have moved much since last time (obviously this does not take into consideration people with jet packs).

   You'll simply ignore these cached locations if they are too old.

2. To determine whether new readings are more accurate than previous ones you're going to be using the `horizontalAccuracy` property of the location object. However, sometimes locations may have a `horizontalAccuracy` that is less than 0, in which case these measurements are invalid and you should ignore them.

3. This is where you determine if the new reading is more useful than the previous one. Generally speaking, Core Location starts out with a fairly inaccurate reading and then gives you more and more accurate ones as time passes. However, there are no guarantees so you cannot assume that the next reading truly is always more accurate.

Note that a larger accuracy value means *less* accurate – after all, accurate up to 100 meters is worse than accurate up to 10 meters. That's why you check whether the previous reading, `location!.horizontalAccuracy`, is greater than the new reading, `newLocation.horizontalAccuracy`.

You also check for `location == nil`. Recall that `location` is the optional instance variable that stores the `CLLocation` object that you obtained in a previous call to `didUpdateLocations`. If `location` is `nil` then this is the very first location update you're receiving and in that case you should also continue.

So if this is the very first location reading (`location` is `nil`) or the new location is more accurate than the previous reading, you go on.

4. You've seen this before. It clears out any previous error if there was one and stores the new location object into the `location` variable.

5. If the new location's accuracy is equal to or better than the desired accuracy, you can call it a day and stop asking the location manager for updates. When you started the location manager in `startLocationManager()`, you set the desired accuracy to 10 meters (`kCLLocationAccuracyNearestTenMeters`), which is good enough for this app.

> **Note:** Because `location` is an optional you cannot access its properties directly – you first need to unwrap it. You could do that with `if let`, but if you're sure that the optional is not `nil` you can also *force unwrap* it with `!`.
>
> That's what you are doing in this line:
>
> ```
>     if location == nil || location!.horizontalAccuracy > newLocation.horizontalAccuracy {
> ```
>
> You wrote `location!.horizontalAccuracy` with an exclamation point instead of just `location.horizontalAccuracy`.
>
> But what if `location == nil`, won't the force unwrapping fail then? Not in this case, because it is never performed.
>
> The `||` operator (logical or) tests whether either of the two conditions is true. If the first one is true (`location` is `nil`), it will ignore the second condition. That's called *short circuiting*. There is no need for the app to check the second condition if the first one is already true.
>
> So the app will only look at `location!.horizontalAccuracy` when location is guaranteed to be non-`nil`. Blows your mind, eh?

> ➤ Run the app. First set the Simulator's location to None, then press Get My Location. The screen now says "Searching..."

> ➤ Switch to location Apple. After a brief moment, the screen is updated with GPS coordinates as they come in.

If you follow along in the debug area, you'll get about 10 location updates before it says "*** We're done!" and the location updates stop.

You as the developer can tell from the debug area when the location updates stop, but obviously the user won't see this.

The Tag Location button becomes visible as soon as the first location is received so the user can start tagging right away, but this location may not be accurate enough. So it's nice to show the user when the app has found the most accurate location.

To make this clearer, you are going to toggle the Get My Location button to say "Stop" when the location grabbing is active and switch it back to "Get My Location" when it's done. That gives a nice visual clue to the user. Later in this lesson you'll also show an animated activity spinner that makes this even more obvious.

To change the state of this button, you'll add a configureGetButton() method.

➤ Add the following method to **CurrentLocationViewController.swift**:

```
func configureGetButton() {
  if updatingLocation {
    getButton.setTitle("Stop", forState: .Normal)
  } else {
    getButton.setTitle("Get My Location", forState: .Normal)
  }
}
```

It's quite simple: if the app is currently updating the location then the button's title becomes Stop, otherwise it is Get My Location.

> **Note:** A button can be in different states. If nothing happens the button is in the "Normal" state (or as Interface Builder calls it, the "Default" state). But when the user touches the button, the state changes to "Highlighted".
>
> You've seen this in Bull's Eye when you gave the button different background images so it showed up different when tapped.
>
> The text on the button also depends on its state, so when you change the title you need to say which state it is for. Here you're using the state .Normal. The highlighted state will also use this new title, unless you explicitly set another title for .Highlighted.
>
> You should recognize .Normal and .Highlighted as being enum values (it's the dot that gives it away); a third possible state is .Disabled.

➤ Call configureGetButton() from the following places:

```
override func viewDidLoad() {
  super.viewDidLoad()
  updateLabels()
  configureGetButton()
}
```

```
@IBAction func getLocation() {
  . . .
  startLocationManager()
  updateLabels()
  configureGetButton()
}
```

```
func locationManager(manager: CLLocationManager!, didFailWithError error: NSError!) {
  . . .
  updateLabels()
  configureGetButton()
}
```

```
func locationManager(manager: CLLocationManager!,
                 didUpdateLocations locations: [AnyObject]!) {
    . . .
    if newLocation.horizontalAccuracy <= locationManager.desiredAccuracy {
      println("*** We're done!")
      stopLocationManager()
      configureGetButton()
    }
  }
}
```

Anywhere you did `updateLabels()`, you're now also calling `configureGetButton()`. In `locationManager(didUpdateLocations)` you only call it when you're done.

➤ Run the app again and perform the same test as before. The button changes to Stop when you press it. When there are no more location updates, it switches back.

The stop button

When a button says Stop you expect to be able to press it so you can interrupt the location updates. This is especially so when you're not getting any coordinates. Eventually Core Location may give an error but as a user you may not want to wait for that.

Currently, however, pressing Stop doesn't stop anything. You have to change `getLocation()` for this as taps on the button call this method.

➤ In `getLocation()`, replace the call to `startLocationManager()` with the following:

```
if updatingLocation {
  stopLocationManager()
} else {
  location = nil
  lastLocationError = nil
  startLocationManager()
}
```

Again you're using the `updatingLocation` flag to determine what state the app is in.

If the button is pressed while the app is already doing the location fetching, you stop the location manager.

Note that you also clear out the old location and error objects before you start looking for a new location.

➤ Run the app. Now pressing the Stop button will put an end to the location updates. You should see no more updates in the debug area after you press Stop.

Reverse geocoding

The GPS coordinates you've dealt with so far are just numbers. The coordinates 37.33240904, -122.03051218 don't really mean that much, but the address 1 Infinite Loop in Cupertino, California does.

Using a process known as **reverse geocoding**, you can turn that set of coordinates into a human-readable address. (Of course, regular or "forward" geocoding does the opposite: it turns an address into GPS coordinates. You can do both with the iOS SDK, but in this tutorial you only do the reverse one.)

You'll use the CLGeocoder object to turn the location data into a human-readable address and then display that address on the screen in the addressLabel outlet.

It's quite easy to do this but there are some rules. You're not supposed to send out a ton of these reverse geocoding requests at the same time. The process of reverse geocoding takes place on a server hosted by Apple and it costs them bandwidth and processor time to handle these requests. If you flood these servers with requests, Apple won't be happy.

The MyLocations app is only supposed to be used occasionally, so its users won't be spamming the Apple servers but you should still limit the geocoding requests to one at a time, and once for every unique location.

It makes no sense to reverse geocode the same set of coordinates over and over. Reverse geocoding needs an internet connection and anything you can do to prevent unnecessary use of the iPhone's radios is a good thing for your users.

➤ Add the following properties to **CurrentLocationViewController.swift**:

```
let geocoder = CLGeocoder()
var placemark: CLPlacemark?
var performingReverseGeocoding = false
var lastGeocodingError: NSError?
```

These mirror what you did for the location manager. CLGeocoder is the object that will perform the geocoding and CLPlacemark is the object that contains the address results.

The placemark variable needs to be a optional because it will have no value when there is no location yet, or when the location doesn't correspond to a street address (I don't think it will respond with "Sahara desert, Africa" but to be honest, I haven't been there to try).

You set performingReverseGeocoding to true when a geocoding operation is taking place, and lastGeocodingError will contain an NSError object if something went wrong (or nil if there is no error).

➤ You'll put the geocoder to work in locationManager(didUpdateLocations):

```
func locationManager(manager: CLLocationManager!,
                didUpdateLocations locations: [AnyObject]!) {
  . . .
  if location == nil || location!.horizontalAccuracy > newLocation.horizontalAccuracy {
    . . .
    if newLocation.horizontalAccuracy <= locationManager.desiredAccuracy {
```

```
    println("*** We're done!")
    stopLocationManager()
    configureGetButton()
  }

  // The new code begins here:
  if !performingReverseGeocoding {
    println("*** Going to geocode")

    performingReverseGeocoding = true

    geocoder.reverseGeocodeLocation(location, completionHandler: { placemarks, error in

      println("*** Found placemarks: \(placemarks), error: \(error)")
    })
  }
  // End of the new code
  }
}
```

The app should only perform a single reverse geocoding request at a time, so first you check whether it is not busy yet by looking at the `performingReverseGeocoding` variable. Then you start the geocoder.

The code looks straightforward enough, except... what is that `completionHandler` thing!?

Unlike the location manager, `CLGeocoder` does not use a delegate to tell you about the result, but something called a **closure**.

A closure is a block of code, much like a method or a function, that is written inline instead of in a separate method. The code inside a closure is usually not executed immediately but it is stored and performed at some later point.

Closures are an important Swift feature and you can expect to see them all over the place. (For Objective-C programmers, a closure is similar to a "block".)

Currently the closure contains just a `println()` – so you can see what's going on – but soon you'll add more code to it.

Unlike the rest of the code in the `locationManager(didUpdateLocations)` method, the code in this closure is not performed right away. After all, you can only print the geocoding results once the geocoding completes.

The closure is kept for later by the `CLGeocoder` object and is only performed after `CLGeocoder` finds an address or encounters an error.

So why does `CLGeocoder` use a closure instead of a delegate?

The problem with using a delegate to provide feedback is that you need to write one or more separate methods. For example, for `CLLocationManager` those are the `locationManager(didUpdateLocations)` and `locationManager(didFailWithError)` methods.

By making different methods you move the code that deals with the response away from the code that makes the request. With closures, on the other hand, you can put that handling code in the same place. That makes the code more compact and easier to read. (Some APIs do both and you have a choice between using a closure or becoming a delegate.)

So when you write,

```
geocoder.reverseGeocodeLocation(location, completionHandler: { placemarks, error in
    // put your statements here
}
```

you're telling the CLGeocoder object that you want to reverse geocode the location, and that the code in the block following completionHandler: should be executed as soon as the geocoding is completed.

The closure itself is:

```
{ placemarks, error in
    // put your statements here
}
```

The things before the in keyword – placemarks and error – are the parameters for this closure and they work just like parameters for a method or a function.

When the geocoder finds a result for the location object that you gave it, it invokes the closure and executes the statements within. The placemarks parameter will contain an array of CLPlacemark objects that describe the address information, and the error variable contains an error message in case something went wrong.

Just to rub it in: the statements in the closure are *not* executed right away when locationManager(didUpdateLocations) is called. Instead, the closure and everything inside it is given to CLGeocoder, which keeps it until later when it has performed the reverse geocoding operation. Only then will it execute the code from the closure.

It's the exact same principle as using delegate methods, except you're not putting the code into a separate method but in a closure.

It's OK if closures don't make any sense to you right now. You'll see them used many more times in this tutorial and the next.

➤ Run the app and pick a location. As soon as the first location is found, you can see in the debug area that the reverse geocoder kicks in (give it a second or two):

```
didUpdateLocations <+37.33240754,-122.03047460> +/- 65.00m (speed -1.00 mps / course -1.00) @
8/4/14, 1:43:25 PM Central European Summer Time

didUpdateLocations <+37.33233141,-122.03121860> +/- 50.00m (speed -1.00 mps / course -1.00) @
8/4/14, 1:43:30 PM Central European Summer Time

*** Going to geocode
*** Found placemarks: [Apple Inc.<GEOMapItemStorage: 0x7f8014919300> {
    placeData =    {
        component =    (
                    {
                "cache_control" = CACHEABLE;
                "start_index" = 0;
                . . .
```

If you choose the Apple location you'll see that some location readings are duplicates; the geocoder only does the first of those. Only when the accuracy of the reading improves does the app reverse geocode again. Nice!

➤ Add the following code to the closure, directly below the println() statement:

```
self.lastGeocodingError = error
```

```
if error == nil && !placemarks.isEmpty {
  self.placemark = placemarks.last as? CLPlacemark
} else {
  self.placemark = nil
}

self.performingReverseGeocoding = false
self.updateLabels()
```

Just as with the location manager, you store the error object so you can refer to it later, although you use a different instance variable this time, lastGeocodingError.

If there is no error and there are objects inside the placemarks array, then you take the last one. Usually there will be only one CLPlacemark object in the array but there is the odd situation where one location coordinate may refer to more than one address. This app can only handle one address, so you'll just pick the last one (which usually is the only one).

You're doing a bit of **defensive programming** here: you specifically check first whether the array has any objects in it. If there is no error then it should have at least one object, but you're not going to trust that it always will. Good developers are suspicious!

> **Note:** The placemarks array contains objects of type AnyObject. This happens because CLGeocoder was written in Objective-C, which isn't as expressive as Swift.
>
> Objects from Objective-C frameworks often appear as type AnyObject in Swift, which is not very helpful, and you'll have to tell Swift what sort of object it *really* is.
>
> Because the placemark instance variable is of type CLPlacemark, you have to **type cast** the object that you retrieve from the array to CLPlacemark, using the "as" operator:
>
> ```
>     self.placemark = placemarks.last as? CLPlacemark
> ```
>
> You're giving Swift your word (Scout's honor!) that objects from this array are always going to be CLPlacemark objects.
>
> In this case you need to use the optional cast, as?, because placemark is an optional instance variable. You'll learn more about casting soon.
>
> By the way, the last property refers to the last item from an array. You can also write placemarks[placemarks.count - 1] but that's not as tidy.

If there was an error during geocoding, you set placemark to nil. Note that you did not do that for the locations. If there was an error there, you kept the previous location object because it may actually be correct (or good enough) and it's better than nothing. But for the address that makes less sense.

You don't want to show an old address, only the address that corresponds to the current location or no address at all.

In mobile development, nothing is guaranteed. You may get coordinates back or you may not, and if you do, they may not be very accurate. The reverse geocoding will probably succeed if there is some type of network connection available, but you also need to be prepared to handle the case where there is none.

And not all GPS coordinates correspond to actual street addresses (there is no corner of 52nd and Broadway in the Sahara desert).

Note: Did you notice that inside the closure you used `self` to refer to the view controller's instance variables and methods? This is a Swift requirement.

Closures are said to *capture* all the variables they use and `self` is one of them. You may immediately forget about that; just know that Swift requires that all captured variables are explicitly mentioned.

Outside a closure you can also use `self` to refer to variables and methods (try it out), but it's not a requirement. However, it is a compiler error to leave out `self` inside a closure, so you don't have much choice there.

Let's make the address visible to the user as well.

➤ Change `updateLabels()` to:

```
func updateLabels() {
  if let location = location {
    . . .

    if let placemark = placemark {
      addressLabel.text = stringFromPlacemark(placemark)
    } else if performingReverseGeocoding {
      addressLabel.text = "Searching for Address..."
    } else if lastGeocodingError != nil {
      addressLabel.text = "Error Finding Address"
    } else {
      addressLabel.text = "No Address Found"
    }
  } else {
    . . .
  }
}
```

Because you only do the address lookup once the app has a location, you just have to change the code inside the first `if`.

If you've found an address, you show that to the user, otherwise you show a status message.

The code to format the `CLPlacemark` object into a string is placed in its own method, just to keep the code readable.

➤ Add the `stringFromPlacemark()` method:

```
func stringFromPlacemark(placemark: CLPlacemark) -> String {
  return "\(placemark.subThoroughfare) \(placemark.thoroughfare)\n" +
      "\(placemark.locality) \(placemark.administrativeArea) \(placemark.postalCode)"
}
```

Just so you know, `subThoroughfare` is the house number, `thoroughfare` is the street name, `locality` is the city, `administrativeArea` is the state or province, and `postalCode` is the zip code or postal code. The `\n` adds a line break into the string.

Tip: If you're ever wondering what some property or method name means, hold down the Option key and click the name to get a pop-up with a short description:

Viewing documentation by Option-clicking

(If you get an empty pop-up, then open the Xcode Preferences window and under Downloads first install the iOS 8 documentation.)

This also works for your own variables. Swift's type inference is great but it also makes it harder to see the data types of your variables. Option-click keeps you from having to dig through the code or API documentation to find that out:

Option-click your own variables to see their type

➤ In `getLocation()`, clear out the `placemark` and `lastGeocodingError` variables to start with a clean slate:

```
@IBAction func getLocation() {
  . . .

  if updatingLocation {
    stopLocationManager()
  } else {
    location = nil
    lastLocationError = nil
    placemark = nil
    lastGeocodingError = nil
    startLocationManager()
  }
  . . .
}
```

➤ Run the app again. Now you'll see that seconds after a location is found, the address label is filled in as well.

Reverse geocoding finds the address for the GPS coordinates

> **Note:** For some locations the address label can say "nil". This is because the CLPlacemark object may contain incomplete information, for example a missing street number. Later in this tutorial you'll improve how addresses are displayed.

Exercise. If you pick the City Bicycle Ride or City Run locations from the Simulator's Debug menu, you should see in the debug area that the app jumps through a whole bunch of different coordinates (it simulates someone moving from one place to another). However, the coordinates on the screen and the address label don't change nearly as often. Why is that? ∎

Answer: The logic in the MyLocations app was designed to find the most accurate set of coordinates for a stationary position. You only update the location variable when a new set of coordinates comes in that is more accurate than previous readings. Any new readings with a higher – or the same – horizontalAccuracy value are simply ignored, regardless of what the actual coordinates are.

With the City Bicycle Ride and City Run options the app doesn't receive the same coordinates with increasing accuracy but a series of completely different coordinates. That means this app doesn't work very well when you're on the move (unless you press Stop and try again), but that's also not what it was intended for.

Testing in practice

When I first wrote this source code I had only tested it out on the Simulator and there it worked fine. Then I put it on my iPod touch and guess what, not so good.

The problem with the iPod touch is that it doesn't have a GPS so it relies on Wi-Fi only to determine the location. But Wi-Fi might not be able to give you accuracy up to ten meters; I got +/- 100 meters at best.

Right now, you only stop the location updates when the accuracy of the reading falls within the desiredAccuracy setting – something that will never happen on my iPod.

That goes to show that you can't always rely on the Simulator to test your apps. You need to put them on your device and test them in the wild, especially when using location-based APIs. If you have more than one device, then test on all of them.

In order to deal with this situation, you will improve the didUpdateLocations delegate method some more.

➤ Change locationManager(didUpdateLocations) to:

```
func locationManager(manager: CLLocationManager!,
                     didUpdateLocations locations: [AnyObject]!) {
  let newLocation = locations.last as! CLLocation
  println("didUpdateLocations \(newLocation)")

  if newLocation.timestamp.timeIntervalSinceNow < -5 {
    return
  }

  if newLocation.horizontalAccuracy < 0 {
    return
  }

  var distance = CLLocationDistance(DBL_MAX)
```

```
if let location = location {
  distance = newLocation.distanceFromLocation(location)
}

if location == nil || location!.horizontalAccuracy > newLocation.horizontalAccuracy {

  lastLocationError = nil
  location = newLocation
  updateLabels()

  if newLocation.horizontalAccuracy <= locationManager.desiredAccuracy {
    println("*** We're done!")
    stopLocationManager()
    configureGetButton()

    if distance > 0 {
      performingReverseGeocoding = false
    }
  }

  if !performingReverseGeocoding {
    println("*** Going to geocode")

    performingReverseGeocoding = true

    geocoder.reverseGeocodeLocation(location, completionHandler: { placemarks, error in
      println("*** Found placemarks: \(placemarks), error: \(error)")

      self.lastGeocodingError = error
      if error == nil && !placemarks.isEmpty {
        self.placemark = placemarks.last as? CLPlacemark
      } else {
        self.placemark = nil
      }

      self.performingReverseGeocoding = false
      self.updateLabels()
    })
  }
} else if distance < 1.0 {
  let timeInterval = newLocation.timestamp.timeIntervalSinceDate(location!.timestamp)
  if timeInterval > 10 {
    println("*** Force done!")
    stopLocationManager()
    updateLabels()
    configureGetButton()
  }
}
}
```

It's a pretty long method now, but only the three highlighted sections were added. This is the first one:

```
var distance = CLLocationDistance(DBL_MAX)
if let location = location {
  distance = newLocation.distanceFromLocation(location)
}
```

This calculates the distance between the new reading and the previous reading, if there was one.

If there was no previous reading, then the distance is DBL_MAX. That is a built-in constant that represents the maximum value that a floating-point number can have. This little trick gives it a gigantic distance if this is the very first reading.

You're doing that so any of the following calculations still work even if you weren't able to calculate a true distance yet.

You also added an if-statement after where you stop the location manager:

```
if distance > 0 {
    performingReverseGeocoding = false
}
```

This forces a reverse geocoding for the final location, even if the app is already currently performing another geocoding request.

You absolutely want the address for that final location, as that is the most accurate location you've found. But if some previous location was still being reverse geocoded, this step would normally be skipped.

Simply by setting `performingReverseGeocoding` to `false`, you always force the geocoding to be done for this final coordinate.

(Of course, if `distance` is 0, then this location is the same as the location from a previous reading and you don't need to reverse geocode it anymore.)

The real improvement is found at the bottom of the method:

```
} else if distance < 1.0 {
    let timeInterval = newLocation.timestamp.timeIntervalSinceDate(location!.timestamp)
    if timeInterval > 10 {
        println("*** Force done!")
        stopLocationManager()
        updateLabels()
        configureGetButton()
    }
}
```

If the coordinate from this reading is not significantly different from the previous reading and it has been more than 10 seconds since you've received that original reading, then it's a good point to hang up your hat and stop.

It's safe to assume you're not going to get a better coordinate than this and you stop fetching the location.

This is the improvement that was necessary to make my iPod touch stop scanning eventually. It wouldn't give me a location with better accuracy than +/- 100 meters but it kept repeating the same one over and over.

I picked a time limit of 10 seconds because that seemed to give good results.

Note that you don't just say:

```
} else if distance == 0 {
```

The distance between subsequent readings is never exactly 0. It may be something like 0.0017632. Rather than checking for equals to 0, it's better to check for less than a certain distance, in this case one meter.

(By the way, did you notice you did `location!` to unwrap it before accessing the `timestamp` property? When the app gets inside this else-if, the value of `location` is guaranteed to be non-`nil`, so its safe to force unwrap the optional using the exclamation point.)

➤ Run the app and test that everything still works. It may be hard to recreate this situation on the Simulator but try it on your iPod touch or iPhone inside the house and see what the println()'s output to the debug area.

There is another improvement you can make to increase the robustness of this logic and that is to set a time-out on the whole thing. You can tell iOS to perform a method one minute from now. If by that time the app hasn't found a location yet, you stop the location manager and show an error message.

➤ First add a new instance variable:

```
var timer: NSTimer?
```

➤ Then change startLocationManager() to:

```
func startLocationManager() {
  if CLLocationManager.locationServicesEnabled() {
    . . .

    timer = NSTimer.scheduledTimerWithTimeInterval(60, target: self,
                      selector: Selector("didTimeOut"), userInfo: nil, repeats: false)
  }
}
```

The new lines set up a timer object that sends the "didTimeOut" message to self after 60 seconds; didTimeOut is of course the name of a method that you have to provide.

A *selector* is the term that Objective-C uses to describe the name of a method, and the Selector() syntax is how you make those selectors from Swift.

➤ Change stopLocationManager() to:

```
func stopLocationManager() {
  if updatingLocation {
    if let timer = timer {
      timer.invalidate()
    }
    . . .
  }
}
```

You have to cancel the timer in case the location manager is stopped before the time-out fires. This happens when an accurate enough location is found within one minute after starting, or when the user tapped the Stop button.

➤ Finally, add the didTimeOut() method:

```
func didTimeOut() {
  println("*** Time out")

  if location == nil {
    stopLocationManager()

    lastLocationError = NSError(domain: "MyLocationsErrorDomain", code: 1, userInfo: nil)

    updateLabels()
    configureGetButton()
  }
}
```

didTimeOut() is always called after one minute, whether you've obtained a valid location or not (unless stopLocationManager() cancels the timer first).

If after that one minute there still is no valid location, you stop the location manager, create your own error code, and update the screen.

By creating your own NSError object and putting it into the lastLocationError instance variable, you don't have to change any of the logic in updateLabels().

However, you do have to make sure that the error's domain is not kCLErrorDomain because this error object does not come from Core Location but from within your own app.

An error domain is simply a string, so "MyLocationsErrorDomain" will do. For the code I picked 1. The value of code doesn't really matter at this point because you only have one custom error, but you can imagine that when the app becomes bigger you'd have the need for multiple error codes.

Note that you don't always have to use an NSError object; there are other ways to let the rest of your code know that an error occurred. But in this case updateLabels() was already using an NSError anyway, so having your own error object just makes sense.

➤ Run the app. Set the Simulator location to None and press Get My Location.

After a minute, the debug area should say "*** Time out" and the Stop button reverts to Get My Location.

There should be an error message in the screen:

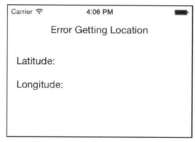

The error after a time out

Just getting a simple location from Core Location and finding the corresponding street address turned out to be a lot more hassle than it initially appeared. There are many different situations to handle. Nothing is guaranteed and everything can go wrong. (iOS development requires nerves of steel!)

To recap, the app either:

• finds a location with the desired accuracy,

• finds a location that is not as accurate as you'd like and you don't get any more accurate readings,

• doesn't find a location at all, or

• takes too long finding a location.

The code now handles all these situations, but I'm sure it's not perfect yet. No doubt the logic could be tweaked more but it will do for the purposes of this tutorial.

I hope it's clear that if you're releasing a location-based app, you need to do a lot of field testing!

Required Device Capabilities

The Info.plist file has a field, **Required device capabilities**, that lists the hardware that your app needs in order to run. This is the key that the App Store uses to determine whether a user can install your app on their device.

The default value is **armv7**, which is the CPU architecture of the iPhone 3GS and later models. If your app requires additional features, such as Core Location to retrieve the user's location, you should list them here.

➤ Add an item with the value `location-services` to **Info.plist**:

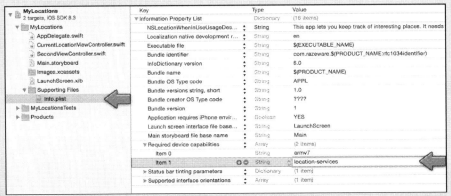

You could also add the item gps, in which case the app requires a GPS receiver. But when that item is present, users cannot install the app on iPod touch hardware and certain iPads.

For the full list of possible device capabilities, see the *iOS App Programming Guide* on the Apple Developer website.

P.S. You can now take the `println()` statements out of the app (or simply comment them out). Personally, I like to keep them in there as they're handy for debugging. In an app that you plan to upload to the App Store you'll definitely want to remove the `println()` statements.

Supporting other iPhone models

So far you've been designing and testing the app for the iPhone 5's 4-inch screen. But users of older models have screens with fewer pixels vertically and – like it or not – it's necessary for your apps to support those smaller screens.

➤ Run the app on the **iPhone 4s** Simulator or a 3.5-inch device.

It's a good thing you tried this because the Get My Location button is no longer visible. This button was very close to the bottom of the 4-inch screen already, and it simply drops off the screen of smaller devices. You will have to move the button up a bit or end up with 1-star reviews in the App Store.

The 'Get My Location' button is missing

Fortunately, this is really easy with **autosizing**.

Auto Layout is all the rage today (you used it in the previous two tutorials) but before Auto Layout was available, autosizing – also known as "springs & struts" – was the main tool for building resizable user interface layouts.

Each view has an autosizing setting that determines what happens to the size and position of that view when the size of its superview – i.e. the view that contains it – changes.

Because you disabled Auto Layout for this tutorial, you will use autosizing to keep the Get My Location button at a fixed distance from the bottom of the screen, no matter how large or small that screen is.

➤ Open the storyboard. Select the Get My Location button and go to the **Size inspector**. Change the autoresizing options to the following:

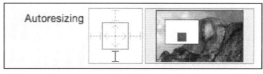

The autosizing options connect the button to the bottom of its superview

As you can see in the example animation on the right, the button (the red box) will now always be positioned relative to the bottom of its superview (the white box).

➤ Run the app. Now it works fine on 3.5-inch devices as well!

If you find your Tag Location button is now too close to Get My Location, then move it up a bit in the storyboard. Around Y = 250 should be fine.

➤ Now run the app on the **iPhone 6 Plus** Simulator:

The app on the iPhone 6 Plus

The labels are no longer aligned with the right edge of the screen and the Tag Location button isn't centered. That looks quite messy. Autosizing to the rescue!

➤ For the (**Message label**) and the **Tag Location** button, change the autoresizing settings to:

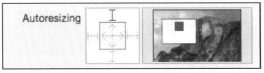

The autosizing settings for the message label and the button

Now the label and the button will always be centered horizontally in the main view.

➤ For the (**Latitude goes here**) and (**Longitude goes here**) labels, change the autoresizing settings to:

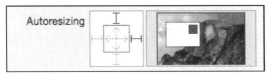

The autosizing settings for the coordinate labels

This keeps these two labels aligned with the right edge of the screen.

➤ Finally, for the (**Address goes here**) label, change the autoresizing settings to:

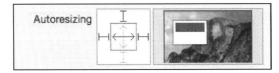

The autosizing settings for the address label

This stretches the address label to be as wide as the screen allows.

Now the app should look decent on the iPhone 6 and 6 Plus too. Try it out!

You can find the project files for this first part of the app under **01 - GPS Coordinates** in the tutorial's Source Code folder.

Objects vs. classes

Time for something new. Up until now I've been calling almost everything an object. However, to use proper object-oriented programming vernacular, we have to make a distinction between an object and its **class**.

When you do this,

```
class ChecklistItem: NSObject {
  . . .
}
```

You're really defining a class named ChecklistItem, not an object. An object is what you get when you **instantiate** a class:

```
let item = ChecklistItem()
```

The item variable now contains an object of the class ChecklistItem. You can also say: the item variable contains an **instance** of the class ChecklistItem. The terms object and instance mean the same thing.

In other words, "instance of class ChecklistItem" is the **type** of this item variable. The Swift language and the iOS frameworks already come with a lot of types built-in but you can also add types of your own by making new classes.

Let's use an example to illustrate the difference between a class and an instance / object.

You and me are both hungry, so we decide to eat some ice cream (my favorite subject next to programming!). Ice cream is the class of food that we're going to eat.

The ice cream class looks like this:

```
class IceCream: NSObject {

  var flavor: String
  var scoops: Int

  func eatIt() {
    // code goes in here
  }
}
```

You and I go on over to the ice cream stand and ask for two cones:

```
// one for you
let iceCreamForYou = IceCream()
iceCreamForYou.flavor = "Strawberry"
iceCreamForYou.scoops = 2

// and one for me
let iceCreamForMe = IceCream()
iceCreamForMe.flavor = "Pistachio"
iceCreamForMe.scoops = 3
```

Yep, I get more scoops but that's because I'm hungry from all this explaining. ;-)

Now the app has two instances of IceCream, one for you and one for me. There is just one class that describes what sort of food we're eating – ice cream – but there are two distinct objects. Your object has strawberry flavor, mine pistachio.

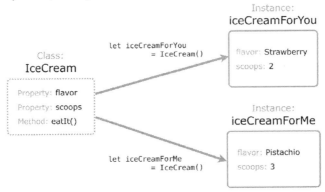

The class is a template for making new instances

The IceCream class is like a template that declares: objects of this type have two properties, flavor and scoops, and a method named eatIt().

Any new instance that is made from this template will have those instance variables and methods, but it lives in its own section of computer memory and therefore has its own values.

If you're more into architecture than food, then you can also think of a class as a blueprint for a building. It is the design of the building, but not the building itself. One blueprint can make many buildings, and you could paint each one – each instance – a different color if you wanted to.

Inheritance

Sorry, this is not where I tell you that you've inherited a fortune. We're talking about **class inheritance** here, one of the main principles of object-oriented programming.

Inheritance is a powerful feature that allows a class to be built on top of another class. The new class takes over all the data and functionality from that other class and adds its own specializations to it.

Take the IceCream class from the previous example. It is built on NSObject, the fundamental class in the iOS frameworks. You can see that in the class line that defines IceCream:

```
class IceCream: NSObject {
```

This means the IceCream class is actually the NSObject class with a few additions of its own, namely the flavor and scoops properties and the eatIt() method.

NSObject is the **base class** for almost all other classes in the iOS frameworks. Most objects that you'll encounter are made from a class that either directly inherits from NSObject or from another class that is ultimately based on NSObject. You can't escape it!

You've also seen class declarations that look like this:

```
class ChecklistViewController: UITableViewController
```

The `ChecklistViewController` class is really a `UITableViewController` class with your own additions. It does everything a `UITableViewController` can, plus whatever new data and functionality you've given it.

This inheritance thing is very handy because `UITableViewController` already does a lot of work for you behind the scenes. It has a table view, it knows how to deal with prototype cells and static cells, and it handles things like scrolling and a ton of other stuff. All you have to do is add your own customizations and you're ready to go.

`UITableViewController` itself is built on top of `UIViewController`, which is built on top of something called `UIResponder`, and ultimately that class is built on `NSObject`. This is called the inheritance tree.

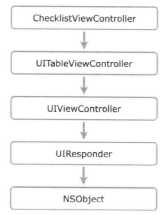

All framework classes stand on the shoulders of NSObject

The big idea here is that each object that is higher up performs a more specialized task than the one below it.

`NSObject`, the base class, only provides a few basic functions that are needed for all objects. For example, it contains an `alloc` method that is used to reserve memory space for the object's instance variables, and the basic `init` method.

`UIViewController` is the base class for all view controllers. If you want to make your own view controller, you extend `UIViewController`. To **extend** means that you make a class that inherits from this one. Other commonly used terms are **to derive from** or **to base on**. These phrases all mean the same thing.

You don't want to write all your own screen and view handling code. If you'd have to program each screen totally from scratch, you'd still be working on lesson 1!

Thank goodness that stuff has been taken care of by very smart people working at Apple and they've bundled it into `UIViewController`. You simply make a class that inherits from `UIViewController` and you get all that functionality for free. You just add your own data and logic to that class and off you go!

If your screen primarily deals with a table view then you'd make your class inherit from UITableViewController instead. This class does everything UIViewController does – because it inherits from it – but is more specialized for dealing with table views.

You could write all that code by yourself, but why would you when it's already available in a convenient package? Class inheritance lets you re-use existing code with minimal effort. It can save you a lot of time!

When programmers talk about inheritance, they'll often throw around the terms **superclass** and **subclass**.

In the example above, UITableViewController is the immediate superclass of ChecklistViewController, and conversely ChecklistViewController is a subclass of UITableViewController. The superclass is the class you derived from, while a subclass derives from your class.

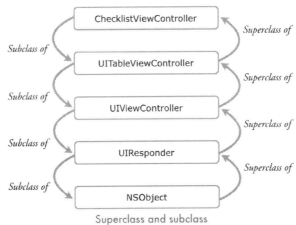

Superclass and subclass

A class in Swift can have many subclasses but only one immediate superclass. Of course, that superclass can have a superclass of its own. There are many different classes that inherit from UIViewController, for example:

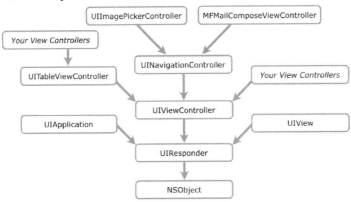

A small portion of the UIKit inheritance tree

Because nearly all classes extend from NSObject, they form a big hierarchy. It is important that you understand this class hierarchy so can you make your own objects inherit from the proper superclasses.

As you'll see later in this tutorial, there are many other types of hierarchies in programming. For some reason programmers seem to like them.

Note: In Objective-C code, all your classes should at least inherit from the NSObject class. This is not the case with Swift. You could also have written the IceCream class as follows:

```
class IceCream {
  . . .
}
```

Now IceCream does not have a base class at all. This is fine in pure Swift code, but it won't always work if you try to use IceCream instances in combination with the iOS frameworks (which are written in Objective-C).

For example, you cannot use IceCream with NSCoder and NSCoding unless you also make it an NSObject first. So sometimes you'll have to use the NSObject base class, even if you're writing the app in Swift only.

Overriding methods

Inheriting from a class means your new class gets to use the properties and methods from its superclass.

If you create a new base class Snack,

```
class Snack {
  var flavor: String
  func eatIt() {
    // code goes in here
  }
}
```

and make IceCream inherit from that class,

```
class IceCream: Snack {
  var scoops: Int
}
```

then elsewhere in your code you can do:

```
let iceCreamForMe = IceCream()
iceCreamForMe.flavor = "Chocolate"
iceCreamForMe.scoops = 1
iceCreamForMe.eatIt()
```

This works even though IceCream did not explicitly declare an eatIt() method or flavor instance variable. But Snack does! Because IceCream inherits from Snack, it automatically gets this method and instance variable for free.

IceCream can also provide its own eatIt() method if it's important for your app that eating ice cream is different from eating any other kind of snack (you may want to eat it faster, before it melts):

```
class IceCream: Snack {
  var scoops: Int

  override func eatIt() {
    // code goes in here
  }
}
```

Now when someone calls iceCreamForMe.eatIt(), this new version of the method is invoked. Note that Swift requires you to write the override keyword in front of any methods that you provide that already exist in the superclass.

A possible implementation of this overridden version of eatIt() could look like this:

```
class IceCream: Snack {
  var scoops: Int
  var isMelted: Bool

  override func eatIt() {
    if isMelted {
      throwAway()
    } else {
      super.eatIt()
    }
  }
}
```

If the ice cream has melted, you want to throw it in the trashcan. But if it's still edible, you'll call Snack's version of eatIt() using super.

Just like self refers to the current object, the super keyword refers to the object's superclass. That is the reason you've been calling super in various places in your code, to let any superclasses do their thing.

Methods can also be used for communicating between a class and its subclasses, so that the subclass can perform specific behavior in certain circumstances. That is what methods such as viewDidLoad() and viewWillAppear() are for.

These methods are defined and implemented by UIViewController but your own view controller subclass can override them.

For example, when its screen is about to become visible, the UIViewController class will call viewWillAppear(true). Normally this will invoke the viewWillAppear() method from UIViewController itself, but if you've provided your own version of this method in your subclass, then yours will be invoked instead.

By overriding viewWillAppear(), you get a chance to handle this event before the superclass does:

```
class MyViewController: UIViewController {
  override func viewWillAppear(animated: Bool) {
    // don't forget to call this!
    super.viewWillAppear(animated)

    // do your own stuff here
  }
}
```

That's how you can tap into the power of your superclass. A well-designed superclass provides such "hooks" that allow you to react to certain events.

Don't forget to call super's version of the method, though. If you neglect this, the superclass will not get its own notification and weird things may happen.

You've also seen override already in the table view data source methods:

```
override func tableView(tableView: UITableView,
                        didSelectRowAtIndexPath indexPath: NSIndexPath) {
    . . .
}
```

UITableViewController, the superclass, already implements these methods, so if you want to provide your own implementation you need to override the existing ones.

> **Note:** Inside those table view delegate and data source methods it's usually not necessary to call super. The iOS API documentation can tell you whether you need to call super or not.

When making a subclass, the init methods require special care.

If you don't want to change any of the init methods from your superclass or add any new init methods, then it's easy: you don't have to do anything. The subclass will automatically take over the init methods from the superclass.

Most of the time, however, you will want to override an init method or add your own, for example to put values into the subclass's new instance variables. In that case, you may have to override not just that one init method but all of them.

For example, in the next tutorial you'll create a class GradientView that extends UIView. The app from that tutorial uses init(frame) to initialize the GradientView object. GradientView overrides this method to set the background color:

```
class GradientView: UIView {
  override init(frame: CGRect) {
    super.init(frame: frame)
    backgroundColor = UIColor.blackColor()
  }

  required init(coder aDecoder: NSCoder) {
    super.init(coder: aDecoder)
  }
  . . .
}
```

But because UIView also has another init method, init(coder), GradientView needs to implement that method too even if it doesn't do anything but call super.

Also note that init(frame) is marked as override, but init(coder) is required. The required keyword is used to enforce that every subclass always implements this particular init method.

Swift wants to make sure that subclasses don't forget to add their own stuff to such required init methods (even if the app doesn't actually use that init method, as in the case of GradientView – it can be a bit of an over-concerned parent, that Swift).

The rules for inheritance of init methods are somewhat complicated – the official Swift Programming Guide devotes many pages to it – but at least if you make a mistake, Xcode will tell you what's wrong and what you should do to fix it.

Private parts

So... does a subclass get to use *all* the methods from its superclass? Not quite.

UIViewController and other UIKit classes have a lot more methods hidden away than you have access to. Often these secret methods do cool things, so it is tempting to use them. But they are not part of the official API, making them off-limits for mere mortals such as you and I.

If you ever hear other developers speak of "private APIs" in hushed tones and down dark alleys, then this is what they are talking about.

It is in theory possible to call such hidden methods if you know their names but this is not recommended. It may even get your app rejected from the App Store, as Apple is known to scan apps for these private APIs.

You're not supposed to use private APIs for two reasons: 1) these APIs may have unexpected side effects and not be as robust as their publicly available relatives; 2) there is no guarantee these methods will exist from one version of iOS to the next. Using them is very risky, as your apps may suddenly stop working.

Sometimes, however, using a private API is the only way to access certain functionality on the device. If so, you're out of luck. Fortunately, for most apps the official public APIs are more than enough and you won't need to resort to the private stuff.

Casts

Often your code will refer to an instance not by its own class but by one of its superclasses. That probably sounds very weird, so let's look at an example.

The app you're writing in this tutorial has a UITabBarController with three tabs, each of which is represented by a view controller.

The view controller for the first tab is CurrentLocationViewController. Later in this tutorial you'll add two others, LocationsViewController for the second tab and MapViewController for the third.

The designers of iOS obviously didn't know anything about those three particular view controllers when they created UITabBarController. The only thing the tab bar controller can reliably depend on is that each tab has a view controller that inherits from UIViewController.

So instead of talking to the CurrentLocationViewController class, the tab bar controller only sees its superclass part, UIViewController. As far as the tab bar controller is concerned it has three UIViewController instances and it doesn't know or care about the additions that you've made to them.

The structure of the app:

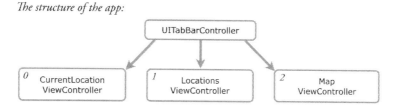

What the tab bar controller sees:

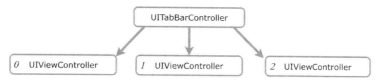

The UITabBarController does not see your subclasses

The same thing goes for `UINavigationController`. To the navigation controller, any new view controllers that get pushed on the navigation stack are all instances of `UIViewController`, nothing more, nothing less.

Sometimes that can be a little annoying. When you ask the navigation controller for one of the view controllers on its stack, it necessarily returns a reference to a `UIViewController` object, even though that is not the full type of that object.

If you want to treat that object as your own view controller subclass instead, you need to **cast** it to the proper type.

In the previous tutorial you did the following in `prepareForSegue(sender)`:

```
let navigationController = segue.destinationViewController as! UINavigationController
let controller = navigationController.topViewController as! ItemDetailViewController
controller.delegate = self
```

Here you wanted to get the top view controller from the navigation stack, which is an instance of `ItemDetailViewController`, and set its `delegate` property.

However, `UINavigationController`'s `topViewController` property won't give you an object of type `ItemDetailViewController`. The value it returns is of the plain `UIViewController` type, which naturally doesn't have your `delegate` property.

If you were to do it without the "`as! ItemDetailViewController`" bit, like so:

```
let controller = navigationController.topViewController
```

then Xcode gives an error on the line below it. Swift now infers that the type of `controller` should also be `UIViewController`, but `UIViewController` does not have the `delegate` property. That property is something you only added to the subclass, `ItemDetailViewController`.

You know that `topViewController` refers to an `ItemDetailViewController`, but Swift doesn't. Even though all `ItemDetailViewControllers` are `UIViewControllers`, not all `UIViewControllers` are `ItemDetailViewControllers`!

Just because your friend Chuck has no hair, that doesn't mean all bald guys are named Chuck.

To solve this problem, you have to cast the object to the proper type. You as the developer know this particular object is an `ItemDetailViewController`, so you use the as cast operator to tell the compiler, "I want to treat this object as an `ItemDetailViewController`."

With the cast, the code looks like this:

```
let controller = navigationController.topViewController as! ItemDetailViewController
```

Now you can treat the value from `controller` as an `ItemDetailViewController` object. The compiler doesn't check whether the thing you're casting really is that kind of object, so if you're wrong and it's not, your app will most likely crash.

Casts can fail for other reasons. For example, the value that you're trying to cast may actually be `nil`. If that's a possibility, it's a good idea to use the as? operator to make it an optional cast. You must also store the result of the cast into an optional value or use `if let` to safely unwrap it.

Note that a cast doesn't magically convert one type into another. You can't cast an `Int` into a `String`, for example. You only use a cast to make a type more specific, and the two types have to be compatible for this to work.

Casting is very common in Swift programs because of the Objective-C heritage of the iOS frameworks. You'll be doing a lot of it!

> **Note:** To summarize, there are three kinds of casts you can perform:
>
> **as?** for casts that are allowed to fail. This would happen if the object is `nil` or doesn't have a type that is compatible with the one you're trying to cast to. It will try to cast to the new type and if it fails, then no biggie. This cast returns an optional that you can unwrap with `if let`.
>
> **as!** for casts between a class and one of its subclasses. This is also known as a *downcast*. As with implicitly unwrapped optionals this cast is potentially unsafe and you should only use as! when you are certain it cannot possibly go wrong. You often need to use this cast when dealing with objects coming from UIKit and the other iOS frameworks. Better get used to all those exclamation marks!
>
> **as** for casts that can never possibly fail. Swift can sometimes guarantee that a type cast will always work, for example between `NSString` and `String`. In that case you can leave off the ? or the ! and just write as.
>
> It can sometimes be confusing to decide which of these three cast operators you need. If so, just type "as" and Xcode will suggest the correct variant. But nine times out of ten it will be as!.

The AnyObject type

Objective-C has a special type, `id`, that means "any object". It's similar to `NSObject` except that it doesn't make any assumptions at all about what kind of object it is. `id` doesn't have any methods, properties or instance variables, it's a completely naked object reference.

All objects in an Objective-C program can be treated as having type `id`. As a result, a lot of the APIs from the iOS frameworks depend on this special `id` type.

This is a powerful feature of Objective-C but unfortunately a dynamic type like `id` doesn't really fit in a *strongly typed* language such as Swift. Still, we can't avoid `id` because it's so prevalent in the iOS frameworks.

The Swift equivalent of `id` is the type `AnyObject`. You've already seen this in `prepareForSegue(sender)`:

```
override func prepareForSegue(segue: UIStoryboardSegue, sender: AnyObject?)
```

The `sender` parameter can be any kind of object and therefore has type `AnyObject` (thanks to the question mark it can also be `nil`).

If the segue is triggered from a table view, `sender` has type `UITableViewCell`. If triggered from a button, `sender` has type `UIBarButtonItem`, and so on.

`AnyObject` often appears in arrays. For example, in the `CLLocationManager` delegate method:

```
func locationManager(manager: CLLocationManager!, didUpdateLocations locations: [AnyObject]!)
```

The array of found locations is an array of `AnyObject` instances. That's why you need to write the following to obtain an actual `CLLocation` object from the array:

```
let newLocation = locations.last as! CLLocation
```

Without the cast to `CLLocation`, Swift doesn't know what sort of type it should give `newLocation`. It could be anything!

One final example: the `dequeueReusableCellWithIdentifier()` method returns an `AnyObject` value.

```
let cell = tableView.dequeueReusableCellWithIdentifier("ChecklistItem") as! UITableViewCell
```

This is a bit silly as it can't really be anything other than a `UITableViewCell`. But because the Objective-C code returns an `id` here, Swift sees it as an `AnyObject`. It can't be helped.

You want `cell` to have the type `UITableViewCell`, so you need to cast it. In fact, if you leave out the "`as! UITableViewCell`" bit, Xcode warns you that you should really add a cast.

In the above example, the "ChecklistItem" cell was a prototype cell from the storyboard. In those cases, calling `dequeueReusableCellWithIdentifier()` never returns `nil`. But elsewhere in the Checklists app, you do:

```
var cell: UITableViewCell! = tableView.dequeueReusableCellWithIdentifier(cellIdentifier)
                                       as? UITableViewCell
```

This is an *optional cast* because for this particular table view the dequeue method returns `nil` when there is no old cell available that can be recycled. Because the return value can be `nil`, `cell` must have the type `UITableViewCell!` and the cast must use the `as?` operator, which lets Swift know `nil` is also an acceptable value.

As you can see, it is very common to write "`as! SomeOtherType`" – or `as?` – in Swift code that talks to the iOS frameworks. In the future this may become less of an issue as the old Objective-C frameworks will start to integrate with Swift better. For now we're stuck with casting `AnyObject` values.

OK, that's enough theory for now. I hope this gives you a little more insight into objects and classes. It's no big deal if you're still confused. The only way to really get the hang of this object-oriented programming thing is do it, so let's continue with some coding.

The Tag Location screen

There is a big button on the main screen of the app that says Tag Location. It only becomes active when GPS coordinates have been captured, and you use it to add a description and a photo to that location.

In this section you'll build the Tag Location screen but you won't save the location object anywhere yet, that's the topic of the next section.

The Tag Location screen is a regular table view controller with static cells, so this is going to be very similar to what you did a few times already in the previous tutorial.

The finished Tag Location screen will look like this:

The Tag Location screen

The description cell at the top contains a UITextView for text. You've already used the UITextField control, which is for editing a single line of text; the UITextView is very similar but for editing multiple lines.

Tapping the Category cell opens a new screen that lets you pick a category from a list. This is very similar to the icon picker from the last tutorial, so no big surprises there either.

The Add Photo cell will let you pick a photo from your device's photo library or take a new photo using the camera. You'll skip this feature for now and build that later in this tutorial. Let's not get ahead of ourselves and try too much at once!

The other cells are read-only and contain the latitude, longitude and address information that you just captured, and the current date so you'll know when it was that you tagged this location.

Exercise. Try to implement this screen by yourself using the description I just gave you. You don't have to make the Category and Add Photo buttons work yet. Yikes, that seems like a big job! It sure is, but you should be able to pull this off. This screen doesn't do anything you haven't done in the previous tutorial. So if you feel brave, go ahead! ■

Adding the new view controller

➤ Add a new file to project using the **Swift File** template. Name the file **LocationDetailsViewController**.

You know what's next: create outlets and connect them to the controls on the storyboard. In the interest of saving time, I'll just give you the code that you're going to end up with.

➤ Replace the contents of **LocationDetailsViewController.swift** with the following:

```swift
import UIKit

class LocationDetailsViewController: UITableViewController {
  @IBOutlet weak var descriptionTextView: UITextView!
  @IBOutlet weak var categoryLabel: UILabel!
  @IBOutlet weak var latitudeLabel: UILabel!
  @IBOutlet weak var longitudeLabel: UILabel!
  @IBOutlet weak var addressLabel: UILabel!
  @IBOutlet weak var dateLabel: UILabel!

  @IBAction func done() {
    dismissViewControllerAnimated(true, completion: nil)
  }

  @IBAction func cancel() {
    dismissViewControllerAnimated(true, completion: nil)
  }
}
```

Nothing special here, just a bunch of outlet properties and two action methods that both dismiss the screen.

➤ In the storyboard, drag a new Table View Controller into the canvas and put it next to the Current Location View Controller.

➤ With the new Table View Controller selected, choose **Editor → Embed In → Navigation Controller** from Xcode's menu bar to put it inside a new navigation controller.

➤ **Ctrl-drag** from the Tag Location button to this new navigation controller and create a **modal** segue. Give it the identifier **TagLocation**.

➤ In the **Identity inspector**, change the **Class** attribute of the table view controller to **LocationDetailsViewController** to link it with the UITableViewController subclass you just created.

➤ Double-click the Location Details View Controller's navigation bar roughly in the center, and change the title to **Tag Location**.

➤ Switch the table content to **Static Cells** and its style to **Grouped**.

The storyboard now looks like this:

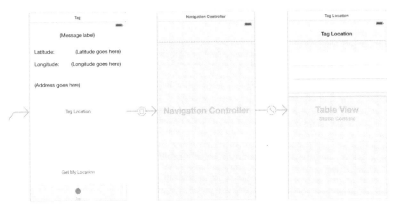

The Tag Location screen in the storyboard

➤ Run the app and make sure the Tag Location button works.

Of course, the screen won't do anything useful yet. Let's add some buttons.

➤ Drag a **Bar Button Item** into the left slot of the navigation bar. Make it a **Cancel** button and connect it to the **cancel** action. (Note: the thing that you're supposed to connect is the Bar Button Item's "selector", under Sent Actions.)

➤ Also drag a **Bar Button Item** into the right slot. Set both the style and identifier attributes to **Done**, and connect it to the **done** action.

➤ Run the app again and make sure you can close the Tag Location screen after you've opened it.

Making the cells

There will be three sections in this table view:

1. The description text view and the category cell. These can be changed by the user.

2. The photo. Initially this cell says Add Photo but once the user has picked a photo you'll display the actual photo inside the cell. So it's good to have that in a section of its own.

3. The latitude, longitude, address and date rows. These are read-only information.

➤ Open the storyboard. Select the table view and go to the **Attributes inspector**. Change the **Sections** field from 1 to 3.

When you do this, the contents of the first section are automatically copied to the next sections. That isn't quite what you want, so you'll have to remove some rows here and there. The first section will have 2 rows, the middle section will have just 1 row, and the last section will have 4 rows.

➤ Select one cell in the first section and delete it. (If it won't delete, make sure you selected the whole Table View Cell and not its Content View.)

➤ Delete two cells from the middle section.

➤ Select the last section object (that is easiest in the outline pane on the left of the storyboard editor) and in the **Attributes inspector** set its **Rows** to 4.

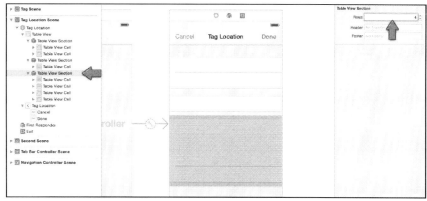

Adding a row to a table view section

(Alternatively you can drag a new Table View Cell from the Object Library into the table.)

The second row from the first section, and the first, second and fourth rows in the last section will all use a standard cell style.

➤ Select these cells and set their **Style** attribute to **Right Detail**.

The cells with the Right Detail style

The labels in these standard cell styles are still regular UILabels, so you can select them and change their properties.

➤ Name these labels from top to bottom: **Category, Latitude, Longitude,** and **Date**.

➤ Drag a new **Label** into the cell from the middle section (the one that's still empty). You cannot use a standard cell style for this one so you'll design it yourself. Name this label **Add Photo**. (Later on you'll also add an image view to this cell.)

➤ Change the font of the label to **System**, size **16**, so it's the same size as the labels from the Right Detail cell style. This font is slightly smaller than the default, so use **Editor → Size to Fit Content** to shrink the label to its optimal size.

➤ Put the Add Photo label at X: 15 (in the **Size inspector**) and vertically centered in its cell. You can use the **Editor → Align → Vertical Center in Container** menu option for this.

The table should now look like this:

The labels in the Tag Location screen

Note: You're going to make a bunch of changes that are the same for each cell. For some of these, it is easier if you select all the cells at once and then change the setting. That will save you some time.

My version of Xcode doesn't let you select more than one cell at a time when they are in different sections, but you can do it in the sidebar on the left by holding down ⌘ and clicking on multiple cells:

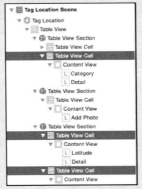

Unfortunately, some menu items are grayed out when you have a multiple selection, so you'll still have to change some of the settings for each cell individually.

Only the Category and Add Photo cells are tap-able, so you have to set the cell selection color to None on the other rows.

➤ Select all the cells except Category and Add Photo (this is easiest from the sidebar where you can select them all at once). In the **Attributes inspector**, set **Selection** to **None**.

➤ Select the Category and Add Photo cells and set **Accessory** to **Disclosure Indicator**.

Category and Add Photo now have a disclosure indicator

The empty cell in the last section is for the Address label. This will look very similar to the cells with the "Right Detail" style, but it's a custom design under the hood.

➤ Drag a new **Label** into that cell and name it **Address**. Put it on the left. Set the X position to 15.

➤ Drag another **Label** into the same cell and name it **Detail**. Put it on the right, X position 263.

➤ Change the font of both labels to **System**, size **16**.

➤ Change the **Alignment** of the address detail label to right-aligned and the **Color** to a medium gray (Red: 142, Green: 142, Blue: 147).

The detail label is special. Most likely the street address will be too long to fit in that small space, so you'll configure this label to have a variable number of lines. This requires a bit of programming in the view controller to make it work, but you also have to set up this label's attributes properly.

➤ In the **Attributes inspector** for the address detail label, set **Lines** to **0** and **Line Breaks** to **Word Wrap**. When the number of lines is 0, the label will resize vertically to fit all the text that you put into it, which is exactly what you need.

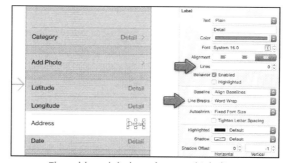

The address label can have multiple lines

So far you've left the cell at the top empty. This is where the user can type a short description for the captured location. Currently there is not much room to type anything, so first you'll make the cell larger.

➤ Click on the top cell to select it, then go into the **Size inspector** and type **88** into the **Row Height** field.

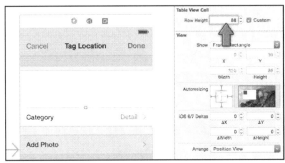

Changing the height of a row

You can also drag the cell to this new height by the handle at its bottom, but I prefer to simply type in the new value.

The reason I chose 88 is that mostly everything in the iOS interface has a size of 44 points. The navigation bar is 44 points high, regular table view cells are 44 points high, and so on. Choosing 44 or a multiple of it keeps the UI looking balanced.

➤ Drag a **Text View** into the cell. Give it the following position and size, X: 15, Y: 10, Width: 290, Height: 68.

➤ By default, Interface Builder puts a whole bunch of fake Latin text (Lorem ipsum dolor, etc) into the text view. Replace that text with "(Description goes here)". The user will never see that text, but it's handy to remind yourself what this view is for.

➤ Set the font to **System**, size **16**.

The attributes for the text view

➤ With the text view selected, go to the **Size inspector**. Change the **Autoresizing** settings to the following:

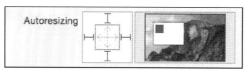

The autosizing settings for the text view

You're deactivating the two arrows in the center of the box – the "springs" – to stop the text view from autosizing.

> **Note:** With the springs enabled, the text view will automatically grow larger to fill up the extra space on the iPhone 6 and 6 Plus devices. That sounds like a good thing – and it is – except there appears to be a bug in either Xcode 6 or iOS 8 that makes the text view way too big when the springs are enabled. To work around this bug, you're disabling the autosizing behavior for the text view. Later you'll write some code to make the text view fit the larger screens of the iPhone 6 and 6 Plus. (Note: This bug appears to be fixed in the latest version of Xcode – yay! – so feel free to select those two arrows as well.)

One more thing to do and then the layout is complete. Because the top cell doesn't have a label to describe what it does – and it will initially be empty as well – the user may not know what it is for.

There really isn't any room to add a label in front of the text view, as you've done for the other rows, so let's add a header to the section. Table view sections can have a header and footer, and these can either be text or a complete view with controls of its own.

➤ Select the top-most Table View Section and in its **Attributes inspector** type **Description** into the **Header** field:

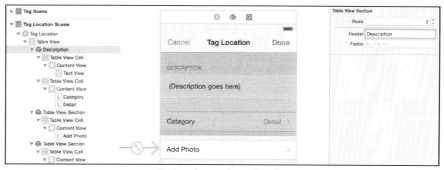

Giving the section a header

That's the layout done. The Tag Location screen should look like this in the storyboard:

The finished design of the Tag Location screen

Now you can actually make the screen do stuff.

➤ Connect the Detail labels and the text view to their respective outlets. It should be obvious which one goes where. (Tip: Ctrl-drag from the round yellow icon that represents the view controller to each of the labels. That's the quickest way.)

If you look at the **Connections inspector** for this view controller, you should see the following:

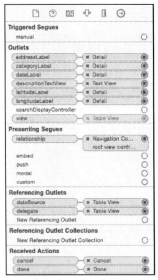

The connections of the Location Details View Controller

➤ Run the app to test whether everything works.

Of course, the screen still says "Detail" in the labels instead of the location's actual coordinates and address because you haven't given it this data yet.

Putting the location info into the screen

➤ Add two new properties to **LocationDetailsViewController.swift**:

```
var coordinate = CLLocationCoordinate2D(latitude: 0, longitude: 0)
var placemark: CLPlacemark?
```

You've seen the CLPlacemark object before. It contains the address information – street name, city name, and so on – that you've obtained through reverse geocoding. This is an optional because there is no guarantee that the geocoder finds an address.

The CLLocationCoordinate2D object is new. This contains the latitude and longitude from the CLLocation object that you received from the location manager. You only need those two fields, so there's no point in sending along the entire CLLocation object. The coordinate is not an optional, so you must give it some initial value.

Exercise. Why is coordinate not an optional? ■

Answer: You cannot tap the Tag Location button unless GPS coordinates have been found, so you'll never open the LocationDetailsViewController without a valid set of coordinates.

On the segue from the Current Location screen to the Tag Location screen you will fill in these two properties, and then the Tag Location screen can put their values into its labels.

Xcode isn't happy with the two lines you just added. It complains about "Use of unresolved identifier CLLocationCoordinate2D" and "CLPlacemark". That means Xcode does not know anything about these types yet.

That's because they are part of the Core Location framework – and before you can use anything from a framework you first need to import it.

➤ Add to the top of the file, below the import for UIKit:

```
import CoreLocation
```

Now Xcode's error messages should disappear after a second or two. If they don't, type ⌘+B to build the app again.

Structs

I said CLLocationCoordinate2D was an object, but unlike the objects you've seen before, it is not described by a class. CLLocationCoordinate2D is a so-called **struct**.

Structs are like classes but a little less powerful. They can have properties and methods, but unlike classes they cannot inherit from one another.

The definition for CLLocationCoordinate2D is as follows:

```
struct CLLocationCoordinate2D {
    var latitude: CLLocationDegrees
    var longitude: CLLocationDegrees
}
```

This struct has two fields, latitude and longitude. Both these fields have the data type CLLocationDegrees, which is a synonym for Double:

```
typealias CLLocationDegrees = Double
```

> The Double type is one of the primitive types built into the language. It's like a Float but with higher precision.
>
> Don't let these synonyms confuse you; CLLocationCoordinate2D is basically this:
>
> ```
> struct CLLocationCoordinate2D {
>     var latitude: Double
>     var longitude: Double
> }
> ```
>
> The reason the designers of Core Location used CLLocationDegrees instead of Double is that "CL Location Degrees" tells you what this type is intended for: it stores the degrees of a location.
>
> Underneath the hood it's a Double, but as a user of Core Location all you need to care about when you want to store latitude or longitude is that you can use the CLLocationDegrees type. The name of the type adds meaning.
>
> UIKit and the other iOS frameworks also use structs regularly. Common examples are CGPoint and CGRect.
>
> Structs are more lightweight than classes. If you just need to pass around a set of values it's often easier to bundle them into a struct and pass that struct around, and that is exactly what Core Location does with coordinates.

Back to the new properties that you just added to LocationDetailsViewController. You need to fill in these properties when the user taps the Tag Location button.

➤ Switch to **CurrentLocationViewController.swift** and add the prepareForSegue() method:

```
override func prepareForSegue(segue: UIStoryboardSegue, sender: AnyObject?) {
  if segue.identifier == "TagLocation" {
    let navigationController = segue.destinationViewController as! UINavigationController
    let controller = navigationController.topViewController as! LocationDetailsViewController
    controller.coordinate = location!.coordinate
    controller.placemark = placemark
  }
}
```

You've seen how this works before. You use some casting magic to obtain the proper destination view controller and then set its properties. Now when the segue is performed, the coordinate and address are given to the Tag Location screen.

Because location is an optional you need to unwrap it before you can access its coordinate property. It's perfectly safe to force unwrap at this point because the Tag Location button that triggers the segue won't be visible unless a location is found.

The placemark variable is also an optional, but so is the placemark property on LocationDetailsViewController, so you don't need to do anything special here.

viewDidLoad() is a good place to display these things on the screen.

➤ Add the viewDidLoad() method to **LocationDetailsViewController.swift**:

```
override func viewDidLoad() {
  super.viewDidLoad()

  descriptionTextView.text = ""
  categoryLabel.text = ""
```

```
   latitudeLabel.text = String(format: "%.8f", coordinate.latitude)
   longitudeLabel.text = String(format: "%.8f", coordinate.longitude)

   if let placemark = placemark {
     addressLabel.text = stringFromPlacemark(placemark)
   } else {
     addressLabel.text = "No Address Found"
   }

   dateLabel.text = formatDate(NSDate())
 }
```

This simply puts something in every label. It uses two helper methods that you haven't defined yet: `stringFromPlacemark()` to format the `CLPlacemark` object into a string, and `formatDate()` to do the same for an `NSDate` object.

➤ Add the `stringFromPlacemark()` method below `viewDidLoad()`:

```
func stringFromPlacemark(placemark: CLPlacemark) -> String {
  return "\(placemark.subThoroughfare) \(placemark.thoroughfare), \(placemark.locality), " +
       "\(placemark.administrativeArea) \(placemark.postalCode), \(placemark.country)"
}
```

This is fairly straightforward. It is similar to how you formatted the placemark on the main screen, except that you also include the country.

To format the date you'll use an `NSDateFormatter` object. You've seen this class in the previous tutorial. It converts the date and time that are encapsulated by the `NSDate` object into a human-readable string, taking into account the user's language and locale settings.

In the previous tutorial you created a new instance of `NSDateFormatter` every time you wanted to convert an `NSDate` to a string. Unfortunately, `NSDateFormatter` is a relatively expensive object to create. In other words, it takes quite long to initialize this object. If you do that many times over then it may slow down your app (and drain the phone's battery faster).

It is better to create `NSDateFormatter` just once and then re-use that same object over and over. The trick is that you won't create the `NSDateFormatter` object until the app actually needs it. This principle is called **lazy loading** and it's a very important pattern for iOS apps. The work that you don't do won't cost any battery power.

In addition, you'll only ever create one instance of `NSDateFormatter`. The next time you need to use `NSDateFormatter` you won't make a new instance but re-use the existing one.

To pull this off you'll use a *private global* constant. That's a constant that lives outside of the `LocationDetailsViewController` class (global) but it is only visible inside the **LocationDetailsViewController.swift** file (private).

➤ Add the following to the top of **LocationDetailsViewController.swift**, in between the `import` and `class` lines:

```
private let dateFormatter: NSDateFormatter = {
  let formatter = NSDateFormatter()
  formatter.dateStyle = .MediumStyle
  formatter.timeStyle = .ShortStyle
  return formatter
}()
```

What is going on here? You're creating a new constant named `dateFormatter` of type `NSDateFormatter`, that much should be obvious. This constant is `private` so it cannot be used outside of this Swift file.

You're also giving `dateFormatter` an initial value, but it's not an ordinary value – it looks like a bunch of source code in between { } brackets. That's because it is a closure.

Normally you'd create a new object like this:

```
private let dateFormatter = NSDateFormatter()
```

But to initialize the date formatter it's not enough to just make an instance of `NSDateFormatter`; you also want to set the `dateStyle` and `timeStyle` properties of this instance.

To create the object and set its properties in one go, you can use a closure:

```
private let dateFormatter: NSDateFormatter = {
  // the code that sets up the NSDateFormatter object
  return formatter
}()
```

Inside the closure is the code that creates and initializes the new `NSDateFormatter` object, and then returns it. This returned value is what gets put into `dateFormatter`.

The knack to making this work is the () at the end. Closures are like functions, and to perform the code inside the closure you call it just like you'd call a function.

> **Note:** If you leave out the (), Swift thinks you're assigning the closure itself to `dateFormatter` – in other words, `dateFormatter` will contain a block of code, not an actual `NSDateFormatter` object. That's not what you want.
>
> Instead you want to assign the *result* of that closure to `dateFormatter`. To make that happen, you use the () to perform or **evaluate** the closure – this runs the code inside the closure and returns the `NSDateFormatter` object.

Using a closure to create and configure an object all at once is a nifty trick; you can expect to see this often in Swift programs.

In Swift, globals are always created in a lazy fashion, which means the code that creates and sets up this `NSDateFormatter` object isn't performed until the very first time the `dateFormatter` global is used in the app.

That happens inside the new `formatDate()` method.

➤ Add this `formatDate()` method. It goes inside the class again:

```
func formatDate(date: NSDate) -> String {
  return dateFormatter.stringFromDate(date)
}
```

How simple is that? It just asks the `NSDateFormatter` to turn the `NSDate` into a `String` and returns that.

Exercise. How can you verify that the date formatter is really only created once? ■

Answer: Add a println() just before the return formatter line in the closure. This println() text should appear only once in the Xcode debug pane.

➤ Run the app. Choose the Apple location from the Simulator's Debug menu. Wait until the street address is visible and then press the Tag Location button.

The coordinates, address and date are all filled in:

Latitude	37.33240905
Longitude	-122.03051211
Address	2
Date	Sep 26, 2014, 10:25 AM

The Address label is too small to fit the entire address

The address seems to be missing something… only the first part of the address is visible (just the subthoroughfare or street number):

You have earlier configured the label to fit multiple lines of text, but the problem is that the table view doesn't know about that.

➤ Add the following method to **LocationDetailsViewController.swift**:

```
// MARK: - UITableViewDelegate

override func tableView(tableView: UITableView,
                        heightForRowAtIndexPath indexPath: NSIndexPath) -> CGFloat {
  if indexPath.section == 0 && indexPath.row == 0 {
    return 88
  } else if indexPath.section == 2 && indexPath.row == 2 {
    addressLabel.frame.size = CGSize(width: view.bounds.size.width - 115, height: 10000)
    addressLabel.sizeToFit()
    addressLabel.frame.origin.x = view.bounds.size.width - addressLabel.frame.size.width - 15
    return addressLabel.frame.size.height + 20
  } else {
    return 44
  }
}
```

This delegate method is called by the table view when it loads its cells. You use it to tell the table view how tall each cell is.

Usually, all the cells have the same height and you can simply set a property on the table view if you wanted to change the height of all the cells at once (using tableView.rowHeight or the Row Height attribute in the storyboard).

This table view, however, has three different cell heights:

• The Description cell at the top. You already set its height to 88 points in the storyboard.

• The Address cell. The height of this cell is variable. It may be anywhere from one line of text to several, depending on how big the address string is.

• The other cells. They all have the standard cell height of 44 points.

The three if-statements in `tableView(heightForRowAtIndexPath)` correspond to those three situations. Let's take a look at the code for sizing the Address label:

```
// 1
addressLabel.frame.size = CGSize(width: view.bounds.size.width – 115, height: 10000)
// 2
addressLabel.sizeToFit()
// 3
addressLabel.frame.origin.x = view.bounds.size.width – addressLabel.frame.size.width – 15
// 4
return addressLabel.frame.size.height + 20
```

This uses a bit of trickery to resize the `UILabel` to make all its text fit to the width of the cell (using word-wrapping), and then you use the newly calculated height of that label to determine how tall the cell must be.

The `frame` property is a `CGRect` that describes the position and size of a view.

`CGRect` is a struct that describes a rectangle. This rectangle has an origin made up of a `CGPoint` value with an (X, Y) coordinate, and a `CGSize` value for the width and height.

All `UIView` objects (and subclasses such as `UILabel`) have a frame rectangle. Changing the frame is how you can position views on the screen programmatically.

Step-by-step this is what the code does:

1. Change the width of the label to be 115 points less than the width of the screen, which makes it about 200 points wide on the iPhone 5. Those 115 points account for the "Address" label on the left, the margins at the edges of the cell (15 points each), and some extra space between the two labels.

   This code also makes the frame a whopping 10,000 points high. That is done to make the rectangle tall enough to fit a lot of text.

   Because you're changing the `frame` property, the multi-line `UILabel` will now word-wrap the text to fit the requested width. This works because you already set the text on the label in `viewDidLoad()`.

2. Now that the label has word-wrapped its contents, you'll have to size the label back to the proper height because you don't want a cell that is 10,000 points tall. Remember the Size to Fit Content menu option from Interface Builder that you can use to resize a label to fit its contents? You can also do that from code with `sizeToFit()`.

3. The call to `sizeToFit()` removed any spare space to the right and bottom of the label. It may also have changed the width so that the text fits inside the label as snugly as possible, but because of that the X-position of the label may no longer be correct.

   A "detail" label like this should be placed against the right edge of the screen with a 15-point margin between them. That's done by changing the `frame`'s `origin.x` position.

4. Now that you know how high the label is, you can add a margin (10 points at the top, 10 points at the bottom) to calculate the full height for the cell.

If you think this is a horrible way to figure out how large the contents are of a multiline label that does word wrapping, then I totally agree. But that's `UILabel` for you...

(This is one of those things that Auto Layout can help with, but Auto Layout brings its own set of problems related to labels. More about that in the next tutorial.)

➤ Run the app. Now the reverse geocoded address should completely fit in the Address cell (even on models with larger screens such as the iPhone 6). Try it out with a few different locations.

The label resizes to fit the address

Frame vs. bounds

In the code above, you do the following:

```
addressLabel.frame.size = CGSize(width: view.bounds.size.width - 115, height: 10000)
```

You use the view's bounds to calculate the address label's frame. Both frame and bounds are of type CGRect, which describes a rectangle. So what is the difference between the bounds and the frame?

The frame describes the position and size of a view in its parent view. If you want to put a 150×50 label at position X: 100, Y: 30, then its frame is (100, 30, 150, 50). To move a view from one position to another, you change its frame property (or its center property, which in turn will modify the frame).

Where the frame describes the outside of the view, the bounds describe the inside. The X and Y coordinates of the bounds are (0, 0) and the width and height will be the same as the frame. So for the label example, its bounds are (0, 0, 150, 50). It's a matter of perspective.

Sometimes it makes sense to use the bounds; sometimes you need to use the frame. The frame is actually derived from a combination of properties: the center position of the view, the bounds, and any transform that is set on the view. (Transforms are used for rotating or scaling the view.)

The description text view

Handling the description text view is very similar to what you did with the text fields in the previous tutorial.

➤ Add a new instance variable to **LocationDetailsViewController.swift**. This will store the description text.

```
var descriptionText = ""
```

➤ In viewDidLoad(), put the contents of this variable in the text view (previously you put an empty string literal in there):

```
override func viewDidLoad() {
  super.viewDidLoad()

  descriptionTextView.text = descriptionText
  . . .
```

You also need to add the text view delegate methods.

Previously when you made an object conform to a protocol, you added the name of that protocol to the class line. Here that would look something like this (don't actually make this change yet):

```
class LocationDetailsViewController: UITableViewController, UITextViewDelegate {
```

And then you'd place the implementations for the delegate methods directly into the class.

That would be a perfectly fine solution here too. However, I want to show you another feature of Swift called **extensions**.

With an extension you can add additional functionality to an existing object without having to change the source code for that object. This even works for objects from the iOS frameworks and you'll see an example of this later on in the tutorial.

You can also use extensions to organize your source code. Here you'll use an extension just for the UITextViewDelegate methods.

➤ Add the following to the very bottom of the file, *below* the final closing bracket:

```
extension LocationDetailsViewController: UITextViewDelegate {
  func textView(textView: UITextView,
         shouldChangeTextInRange range: NSRange, replacementText text: String) -> Bool {
    descriptionText = (textView.text as NSString).stringByReplacingCharactersInRange(
                                                        range, withString: text)
    return true
  }

  func textViewDidEndEditing(textView: UITextView) {
    descriptionText = textView.text
  }
}
```

This extension contains just the delegate callbacks from the text view, so they are not all tangled up with LocationDetailsViewController's other code. By putting it in its own thing, it keeps the responsibilities separate.

This makes it easy to spot which part of LocationDetailsViewController plays the role of text view delegate. All the text view stuff happens just in this extension, not in the main body of the class. (You could even place this extension in a separate Swift file if you wanted.)

The delegate methods simply update the contents of the descriptionText instance variable whenever the user types into the text view. Except for the extension bit, this is basically the same code you used in the Checklists tutorial.

Recall that to use the stringByReplacingCharactersInRange() method you first have to convert the text to an NSString object. You can do that in a single line – the type cast (textView.text as NSString) is done first because it's in parentheses, and after that stringByReplacingCharactersInRange() is called.

Of course, those delegate methods won't do any good if you don't also tell the text view that it has a delegate.

➤ Go into the storyboard and **Ctrl-drag** from the text view to the view controller and connect the **delegate** outlet.

➤ Just to test whether the descriptionText variable correctly captures whatever the user is typing into the text view, add a println() to the done() action:

```
@IBAction func done() {
  println("Description '\(descriptionText)'")
  dismissViewControllerAnimated(true, completion: nil)
}
```

➤ Run the app, tag a location and type something into the description text field. Press the Done button and verify that println() writes the text you just typed to the debug area. Cool.

> **Note:** You've just seen an example of a type cast that will never fail, between Swift's built-in String type and Objective-C's NSString. Those two types are *bridged*, meaning that you can always use NSString where String is used and vice versa. For those kinds of casts you use as, not as! or as?, because Swift guarantees 100% that it will always succeed. If not, you get your money back.

The category picker

When the user taps the Category cell, the app shows a list of category names:

The category picker

This is a new screen, so you also need a new view controller. The way it works is very similar to the icon picker from the previous tutorial. I'm just going to give you the source code and tell you how to hook it up.

➤ Add a new file to the project named **CategoryPickerViewController.swift**.

> Replace the contents of **CategoryPickerViewController.swift** with:

```swift
import UIKit

class CategoryPickerViewController: UITableViewController {
  var selectedCategoryName = ""

  let categories = [
    "No Category",
    "Apple Store",
    "Bar",
    "Bookstore",
    "Club",
    "Grocery Store",
    "Historic Building",
    "House",
    "Icecream Vendor",
    "Landmark",
    "Park"]

  var selectedIndexPath = NSIndexPath()

  // MARK: - UITableViewDataSource

  override func tableView(tableView: UITableView,
                          numberOfRowsInSection section: Int) -> Int {
    return categories.count
  }

  override func tableView(tableView: UITableView,
                          cellForRowAtIndexPath indexPath: NSIndexPath) -> UITableViewCell {
    let cell = tableView.dequeueReusableCellWithIdentifier("Cell") as! UITableViewCell

    let categoryName = categories[indexPath.row]
    cell.textLabel!.text = categoryName

    if categoryName == selectedCategoryName {
      cell.accessoryType = .Checkmark
      selectedIndexPath = indexPath
    } else {
      cell.accessoryType = .None
    }

    return cell
  }

  // MARK: - UITableViewDelegate

  override func tableView(tableView: UITableView,
                          didSelectRowAtIndexPath indexPath: NSIndexPath) {
    if indexPath.row != selectedIndexPath.row {
      if let newCell = tableView.cellForRowAtIndexPath(indexPath) {
        newCell.accessoryType = .Checkmark
      }
      if let oldCell = tableView.cellForRowAtIndexPath(selectedIndexPath) {
        oldCell.accessoryType = .None
      }
      selectedIndexPath = indexPath
    }
  }
}
```

There's nothing special going on here. This is a table view controller that shows a list of category names. It has table view data source and delegate methods.

The data source gets its rows from the `categories` array.

The only special thing is the `selectedIndexPath` instance variable. When the screen opens it shows a checkmark next to the currently selected category. This comes from the `selectedCategoryName` property, which is filled in when you segue to this screen.

When the user taps a row, you want to remove the checkmark from the previously selected cell and put it in the new cell.

In order to be able to do that, you need to know which row is the currently selected one. You can't use `selectedCategoryName` for this because that is a string, not a row number. Therefore, you first need to find the row number – or index-path – for the selected category name.

In `tableView(cellForRowAtIndexPath)`, which happens during the segue to this view controller, you compare the name of the row's category to `selectedCategoryName`. If they match, you store the row's index-path in the `selectedIndexPath` variable.

Now that you know the row number, you can remove the checkmark for this row later in `tableView(didSelectRowAtIndexPath)` when another row gets tapped.

It's a bit of work for such a small feature, but in a good app it's the details that matter.

➤ Open the storyboard and drag a new **Table View Controller** into the canvas. Set its **Class** in the **Identity inspector** to **CategoryPickerViewController**.

➤ Change the **Style** of the prototype cell to **Basic**, and give it the re-use identifier **Cell**.

➤ **Ctrl-drag** from the Category cell on the Location Details View Controller to this new view controller and choose **Selection Segue - push**.

➤ Give the segue the identifier **PickCategory**.

The Category Picker View Controller now has a navigation bar at the top. You could change its title to "Choose Category", but as of iOS 7 Apple recommends that you do not to give view controllers a title if their purpose is obvious. This helps to keep the navigation bar uncluttered.

The category picker in the storyboard

That's enough for the storyboard. Now all that remains is to handle the segue.

➤ Switch back to **LocationDetailsViewController.swift** and add a new instance variable categoryName. You'll use this to temporarily store the chosen category.

```
var categoryName = "No Category"
```

Initially you set the category name to "No Category". That is also the category at the top of the list in the category picker.

➤ Change viewDidLoad() to put categoryName into the label:

```
override func viewDidLoad() {
  super.viewDidLoad()

  descriptionTextView.text = descriptionText
  categoryLabel.text = categoryName

  . . .
```

➤ Finally, add the prepareForSegue(sender) method. Make sure you add this in the main class, not in the extension at the bottom of the file:

```
override func prepareForSegue(segue: UIStoryboardSegue, sender: AnyObject?) {
  if segue.identifier == "PickCategory" {
    let controller = segue.destinationViewController as! CategoryPickerViewController
    controller.selectedCategoryName = categoryName
  }
}
```

This simply sets the selectedCategoryName property of the category picker. And with that, the app has categories.

➤ Run the app and play with the category picker.

Selecting a new category

Hmm, it doesn't seem to work very well. You can choose a category but the screen doesn't close when you tap a row. When you press the Back button, the category you picked isn't shown on the screen.

Exercise. Which piece of the puzzle is missing? ∎

Answer: The CategoryPickerViewController currently does not have a way to communicate back to the LocationDetailsViewController that the user picked a new category.

I hope that at this point you're thinking, "Of course, dummy! You forgot to give the category picker a delegate protocol. That's why it cannot send any messages to the other view controller." (If so, awesome! You're getting the hang of this.)

A delegate protocol is a fine solution indeed, but I want to show you a new storyboarding feature that can accomplish the same thing with less work: **unwind segues**.

In case you were wondering what the orange "Exit" icons in the storyboard are for, you now have your answer: unwind segues.

Where a regular segue is used to open a new screen, an unwind segue closes the active screen. Sounds simple enough. However, making unwind segues is not very intuitive.

The orange Exit icons don't appear to do anything. Try Ctrl-dragging from the prototype cell to the Exit icon, for example. It won't let you make a connection.

First you have to add a special type of action method to the code.

➤ In **LocationDetailsViewController.swift**, add the following method:

```
@IBAction func categoryPickerDidPickCategory(segue: UIStoryboardSegue) {
  let controller = segue.sourceViewController as! CategoryPickerViewController
  categoryName = controller.selectedCategoryName
  categoryLabel.text = categoryName
}
```

This is an action method because it has the @IBAction annotation. What's different from a regular action method is the parameter, a UIStoryboardSegue object.

Normally if an action method has a parameter, it points to the control that triggered the action, such as a button or slider. But in order to make an unwind segue you need to define an action method that takes a UIStoryboardSegue parameter.

What happens inside the method is pretty straightforward. You look at the view controller that sent the segue (the sourceViewController), which of course is the CategoryPickerViewController, and then read the value of its selectedCategoryName property. Presumably that property contains the category that the user picked.

➤ Open the storyboard. **Ctrl-drag** from the prototype cell to the Exit button. This time it does allow you to make a connection:

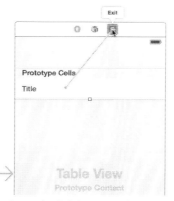

Ctrl-dragging to the Exit icon to make an unwind segue

From the popup choose **Selection Segue - categoryPickerDidPickCategory:**, the name of the unwind action method you just added.

(If Interface Builder doesn't let you make a connection, then make sure you're really Ctrl-dragging from the Cell, not from its Content View or the label.)

Now when you tap a cell in the category picker, the screen will close and this new method is called.

➤ Run the app to try it out. That was easy! Well, not quite. Unfortunately, the chosen category is ignored...

That's because `categoryPickerDidPickCategory()` looks at the `selectedCategoryName` property, but that property isn't filled in anywhere yet.

You need some kind of mechanism that is invoked when the unwind segue is triggered, at which point you can fill in the `selectedCategoryName` based on the row that was tapped.

What might such a mechanism be called? `prepareForSegue`, of course! This works for segues in both directions.

➤ Add the following method to **CategoryPickerViewController.swift**:

```
override func prepareForSegue(segue: UIStoryboardSegue, sender: AnyObject?) {
  if segue.identifier == "PickedCategory" {
    let cell = sender as! UITableViewCell
    if let indexPath = tableView.indexPathForCell(cell) {
      selectedCategoryName = categories[indexPath.row]
    }
  }
}
```

This looks at the selected index-path and puts the corresponding category name into the `selectedCategoryName` property.

This logic assumes the segue is named "PickedCategory", so you still have to set an identifier on the unwind segue.

Unfortunately, there is no visual representation of the unwind segue in the storyboard. There is no nice, big arrow that you can click on. To select the unwind segue you have to locate it in the document outline pane:

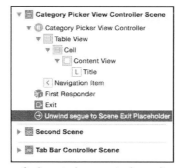

You can find unwind segues in the outline pane

➤ Select the unwind segue and go to the **Attributes inspector**. Give it the identifier **PickedCategory**.

➤ Run the app. Now the category picker should work properly. As soon as you tap the name of a category, the screen closes and the new category name is displayed.

Unwind segues are pretty cool and are often easier than using a delegate protocol, especially for simple picker screens such as this one.

Improving the user experience

The Tag Location screen is functional but it could do with some polish. These are the small details that will make your apps a delight to use and stand out from the competition.

Take a look at the design of the cell with the Description text view:

There is a margin between the text view and the cell border

There is 10-point margin between the text view and the cell border, but because the background of both the cell and the text view are white the user cannot see where the text view begins.

It is possible to tap inside the cell but just outside the text view. That is annoying when you want to start typing: you think that you're tapping in the text view but the keyboard doesn't appear.

There is no feedback to the user that she's actually tapping outside the text view, and she will think your app is broken. In my opinion, rightly so.

You'll have to make the app a little more forgiving. When the user taps anywhere inside that first cell, the text view should activate, even if the tap wasn't on the text view itself.

➤ Add the following two methods in the `// MARK: - UITableViewDelegate` section in **LocationDetailsViewController.swift**:

```
override func tableView(tableView: UITableView,
                        willSelectRowAtIndexPath indexPath: NSIndexPath) -> NSIndexPath? {
  if indexPath.section == 0 || indexPath.section == 1 {
    return indexPath
  } else {
    return nil
  }
}

override func tableView(tableView: UITableView,
                        didSelectRowAtIndexPath indexPath: NSIndexPath) {
  if indexPath.section == 0 && indexPath.row == 0 {
    descriptionTextView.becomeFirstResponder()
  }
}
```

The `tableView(willSelectRowAtIndexPath)` method limits taps to just the cells from the first two sections. The third section only has read-only labels anyway, so it doesn't need to allow taps.

The `tableView(didSelectRowAtIndexPath)` method handles the actual taps on the rows. You don't need to respond to taps on the Category or Add Photo rows as these cells are connected to segues. But if the user tapped in the first row of the first section – the row with the description text view – then you will give the input focus to that text view.

➤ Try it out. Run the app and click or tap somewhere along the edges of the first cell. Anywhere you tap inside that first cell should now bring up the keyboard.

Anything you can do to make screens less frustrating to use is worth putting in the effort.

Speaking of the text view, once you've activated it there's no way to get rid of the keyboard again. Because the keyboard takes up half of the screen that can be a bit annoying.

It would be nice if the keyboard disappeared after you tapped anywhere else on the screen. As it happens, that is not so hard to add.

➤ Add the following to the end of `viewDidLoad()`:

```
let gestureRecognizer = UITapGestureRecognizer(target: self,
                                               action: Selector("hideKeyboard:"))
gestureRecognizer.cancelsTouchesInView = false
tableView.addGestureRecognizer(gestureRecognizer)
```

A **gesture recognizer** is a very handy object that can recognize touches and other finger movements. You simply create the gesture recognizer object, give it a method to call when that particular gesture has been observed to take place, and add the recognizer object to the view.

You're using a `UITapGestureRecognizer`, which recognizes simple taps, but there are several others for swipes, pans, pinches and much more.

Notice the `Selector()` keyword again:

```
. . . target: self, action: Selector("hideKeyboard:")) . . .
```

You use this syntax to tell the `UITapGestureRecognizer` that it should call the method named by the `Selector()` whenever the gesture happens.

This pattern is known as **target-action** and you've already been using it all the time whenever you've connected `UIButtons`, `UIBarButtonItems`, and other controls to action methods.

The "target" is the object that the message should be sent to, which is often `self`, and "action" is the message to send.

Here you've chosen the message **hideKeyboard:** to be sent when a tap is recognized anywhere in the table view, so you also have to implement a method for that. The colon following the action name indicates that this method takes a single parameter, which in this case is a reference to the gesture recognizer. That will come in handy!

➤ Add the `hideKeyboard()` method to **LocationDetailsViewController.swift**. It doesn't really matter where you put it, but below `viewDidLoad()` is a good place:

```swift
func hideKeyboard(gestureRecognizer: UIGestureRecognizer) {
  let point = gestureRecognizer.locationInView(tableView)
  let indexPath = tableView.indexPathForRowAtPoint(point)
  if indexPath != nil && indexPath!.section == 0 && indexPath!.row == 0 {
    return
  }

  descriptionTextView.resignFirstResponder()
}
```

Whenever the user taps somewhere in the table view, the gesture recognizer calls this method. Conveniently, it also passes a reference to itself as the parameter, which lets you ask `gestureRecognizer` where the tap happened.

The `locationInView()` method returns a `CGPoint` value. This is common struct that you see all the time in UIKit. It contains two fields, x and y, that describe a position on the screen.

Using this `CGPoint`, you ask the table view which index-path is currently displayed at that position. This is important because you obviously don't want to hide the keyboard if the user tapped in the row with the description text view! If the user tapped anywhere else, you do hide the keyboard.

Exercise. Does the logic in the if-statement make sense to you? Explain how this works. ∎

Answer: It is possible that the user taps inside the table view but not on a cell, for example somewhere in between two sections or on the section header. In that case `indexPath` will be `nil`, making this an optional (of type `NSIndexPath?`). And to use an optional you need to unwrap it somehow, either with `if let` or with `!`.

> **Note:** You don't want to force unwrap an optional if there's a chance it might be `nil` or you risk crashing the app. Force unwrapping `indexPath!.section` and `indexPath!.row` may look dangerous here, but it is guaranteed to work thanks to the **short-circuiting** behavior of the `&&` operator.
>
> If `indexPath` equals `nil`, then everything behind the first `&&` is simply ignored. The condition can never become true anymore if one of the terms is false. So when the app gets to look at `indexPath!.section`, you know that the value of `indexPath` will never be `nil` at that point.

You only want to hide the keyboard if the index-path for the tap is *not* section 0, row 0, which is the cell with the text view. If the user did tap that particular cell, you bail out of `hideKeyboard()` with the return statement before the code reaches the call to `resignFirstResponder()`.

An alternative way to write this logic is:

```
if indexPath == nil || !(indexPath!.section == 0 && indexPath!.row == 0) {
  descriptionTextView.resignFirstResponder()
}
```

Can you wrap your head around that?

➤ Run the app. Tap in the text view to bring up the keyboard. (If the keyboard doesn't come up, press ⌘+K.) Tap anywhere else in the table view to hide the keyboard again.

The table view can also automatically dismiss the keyboard when the user starts scrolling. You can enable this in the storyboard.

➤ Open the storyboard and select the table view inside the Tag Location screen. In the **Attributes inspector** change the **Keyboard** option to **Dismiss on drag**. Now scrolling should also hide the keyboard.

The "Dismiss on drag" option for the keyboard

(If this doesn't work for you, try it on a real device. The keyboard in the Simulator can be a bit wonky.)

➤ Also try the **Dismiss interactively** option. Which one do you like best?

There's still something to fix with the text view. To see exactly what's wrong, first give the text view a different background color.

➤ In the **Attributes inspector** for the text view, change **Background** to something bright and shiny (you can find the Background setting near the bottom).

➤ Now run the app on the **iPhone 6 Plus** Simulator. It's obvious what's wrong: the text view is way too small.

There's a big space to the right of the text view

There are three ways to fix this:

1. Auto Layout. Not an option because we're not using Auto Layout in this tutorial.

2. Autosizing. This ought to work but due to a bug it doesn't. Try it out for yourself. In the size inspector for the text view, activate the red autosizing arrow to enable automatic horizontal resizing. Now the text view is much too wide! We just can't win… (Note: This bug appears to be fixed in the latest Xcode, so give it a try and see if using autosizing here works for you.)

3. Do it programmatically. When all else fails, you can always write some code.

➤ In **LocationDetailsViewController.swift**, add the following method:

```
override func viewWillLayoutSubviews() {
  super.viewWillLayoutSubviews()
  descriptionTextView.frame.size.width = view.frame.size.width - 30
}
```

The `viewWillLayoutSubviews()` method is called by UIKit as part of the layout phase of your view controller when it first appears on the screen. It's the ideal place for changing the `frames` of your views by hand.

Here, you set the width of the text view to the width of the screen minus 15 points margin on each side. That's all you need to do.

➤ Run the app again and now the text view looks all right:

That's better!

Be sure to put the background color back to white (or "Default") before you go on.

The HUD

There is one more improvement I wish to make to this screen, just to add a little spice. When you tap the Done button to close the screen, the app will show a quick animation to let the user know it successfully saved the location:

Before you close the screen it shows an animated checkmark

This type of overlay graphic is often called a HUD, for Heads-Up Display. Apps aren't quite fighter jets, but often HUDs are used to display a progress bar or spinner while files are downloading or another long-lasting task is taking place.

You'll show your own HUD view for a brief second before the screen closes. It adds a little extra liveliness to the app.

If you're wondering how you can display anything on top of a table, this HUD is simply a UIView subclass. You can add views on top of other views.

That's what you've been doing all along: the labels are views that are added on top of the cells, which are also views. The cells themselves are added on top of the table view, and the table view in turn is added on top of the navigation controller's content view.

So far, when you've made your own objects, they have always been view controllers or data model objects, but it's also possible to make your own views.

Often using the standard buttons and labels is sufficient, but when you want to do something that is not available as a standard view you can always make your own. You either subclass UIView or UIControl and do your own drawing. That's what you're going to do for the HUD view as well.

➤ Add a new file to the project using the **Cocoa Touch Class** template. Name it **HudView** and make it a subclass of **UIView**.

Let's build a minimal version of this class just so that you can get something on the screen. When that works, you'll make it look fancy.

➤ Replace the contents of **HudView.swift** with the following:

```
import UIKit

class HudView: UIView {
  var text = ""

  class func hudInView(view: UIView, animated: Bool) -> HudView {
    let hudView = HudView(frame: view.bounds)
    hudView.opaque = false
```

```
    view.addSubview(hudView)
    view.userInteractionEnabled = false

    hudView.backgroundColor = UIColor(red: 1, green: 0, blue: 0, alpha: 0.5)
    return hudView
  }
}
```

The `hudInView(animated)` method is known as a **convenience constructor**. It creates and returns a new `HudView` instance.

Normally you would create a new `HudView` object by writing:

```
let hudView = HudView()
```

But using the convenience constructor you'd write:

```
let hudView = HudView.hudInView(parentView, animated: true)
```

A convenience constructor is always a **class method,** i.e. a method that works on the class as a whole and not on any particular instance. You can tell because its declaration begins with `class func` instead of just `func`.

When you call `HudView.hudInView(parentView, animated: true)` you don't have an instance of `HudView` yet. The whole purpose of this method is to create an instance of the HUD view for you, so you don't have to do that yourself, and to place it on top of another view.

You can see that making an instance is actually the first thing this method does:

```
class func hudInView(view: UIView, animated: Bool) -> HudView {
  let hudView = HudView(frame: view.bounds)
  . . .
  return hudView
}
```

It calls `HudView()`, or actually `HudView(frame)` which is an `init` method inherited from `UIView`. At the end of the method that new instance is returned to the caller.

So why use this convenience constructor? As the name says, for convenience.

There are more steps needed than just initializing the view, and by putting these in the convenience constructor, the caller doesn't have to worry about any of this.

One of these additional steps is that this method adds the new `HudView` object as a subview on top of the `view` object. This is actually the navigation controller's view so the HUD will cover the entire screen.

It also sets the `view`'s `userInteractionEnabled` property to `false`. While the HUD is showing you don't want the user to interact with the screen anymore. The user has already pressed the Done button and the screen is in the process of closing.

Most users will leave the screen alone at this point but there's always some joker who wants to try and break things. By setting `userInteractionEnabled` to `false`, the view eats up any touches and all the underlying views become unresponsive.

Just for testing, the background color of the HUD view is 50% transparent red. That way you can see it covers the entire screen.

Let's add code to call the HUD, so that is out of the way.

➤ Change the done() method from **LocationDetailsViewController.swift** to:

```
@IBAction func done() {
  let hudView = HudView.hudInView(navigationController!.view, animated: true)
  hudView.text = "Tagged"
}
```

This creates a HudView object and adds it to the navigation controller's view with an animation. You also set a text property on the new object.

Previously, done() dismissed the view controller. For testing purposes you're not going to do that anymore. You want to have time to see what the HudView looks like as you're building it up step-by-step; if you immediately close the screen after showing the HUD, it will be hard to see what's going on (unless you have the ability to slow down time somehow). You'll put the code that closes the screen back later.

➤ Run the app. When you press the Done button, the screen will look like this:

The HUD view covers the whole screen

The app is now totally unresponsive because user interaction is disabled.

Often when you're working with views it's a good idea to set the background color to a bright color such as red or blue, so you can see exactly how big the view is.

➤ Remove the backgroundColor line from the hudInView(animated) method.

➤ Add the following method to **HudView.swift**:

```
override func drawRect(rect: CGRect) {
  let boxWidth: CGFloat = 96
  let boxHeight: CGFloat = 96

  let boxRect = CGRect(
    x: round((bounds.size.width - boxWidth) / 2),
    y: round((bounds.size.height - boxHeight) / 2),
    width: boxWidth,
    height: boxHeight)

  let roundedRect = UIBezierPath(roundedRect: boxRect, cornerRadius: 10)
```

```
  UIColor(white: 0.3, alpha: 0.8).setFill()
  roundedRect.fill()
}
```

The `drawRect()` method is invoked whenever UIKit wants your view to redraw itself. Recall that everything in iOS is event-driven. You don't draw anything on the screen unless UIKit sends you the `drawRect()` event. That means you should never call `drawRect()` yourself.

Instead, if you want to force your view to redraw then you should send it the `setNeedsDisplay()` message. UIKit will then trigger a `drawRect()` event when it is ready to perform the drawing. This may seem strange if you're coming from another platform. You may be used to redrawing the screen whenever you feel like it, but in iOS UIKit is in charge of who gets to draw when.

The above code draws a filled rectangle with rounded corners in the center of the screen. The rectangle is 96 by 96 points big (so I suppose it's really a square):

```
let boxWidth: CGFloat = 96
let boxHeight: CGFloat = 96
```

This declares two constants you'll be using in the calculations that follow. You're using constants because it's clearer to refer to the symbolic name `boxWidth` than the number 96. That number doesn't mean much by itself, but "box width" is a pretty clear description of its purpose.

Note that you force the type of these constants to be `CGFloat`, which is the type used by UIKit to represent decimal numbers. When working with UIKit or Core Graphics (CG, get it?) you use `CGFloat` instead of the regular `Float` or `Double`.

```
let boxRect = CGRect(
  x: round((bounds.size.width - boxWidth) / 2),
  y: round((bounds.size.height - boxHeight) / 2),
  width: boxWidth,
  height: boxHeight)
```

There is `CGRect` again, the struct that represents a rectangle. You use it to calculate the position for the HUD. The HUD rectangle should be centered horizontally and vertically on the screen. The size of the screen is given by `bounds.size` (this really is the size of `HudView` itself, which spans the entire screen).

The above calculation uses the `round()` function to make sure the rectangle doesn't end up on fractional pixel boundaries because that makes the image look fuzzy.

```
let roundedRect = UIBezierPath(roundedRect: boxRect, cornerRadius: 10)
UIColor(white: 0.3, alpha: 0.8).setFill()
roundedRect.fill()
```

`UIBezierPath` is a very handy object for drawing rectangles with rounded corners. You just tell it how large the rectangle is and how round the corners should be. Then you fill it with an 80% opaque dark gray color.

➤ Run the app. The result looks like this:

The HUD view has a partially transparent background

There are two more things to add to the HUD, a checkmark and a text label. The checkmark is an image.

➤ The Resources folder for this tutorial has two files in the **Hud Images** folder, **Checkmark@2x.png** and **Checkmark@3x.png**. Add these files to the asset catalog, **Images.xcassets**.

You can do this with the + button or simply drag them from Finder into the Xcode window with the asset catalog open. (The images are white so they are a bit hard to see inside the asset list.)

➤ Add the following code to `drawRect()`:

```
if let image = UIImage(named: "Checkmark") {
  let imagePoint = CGPoint(
    x: center.x - round(image.size.width / 2),
    y: center.y - round(image.size.height / 2) - boxHeight / 8)

  image.drawAtPoint(imagePoint)
}
```

This loads the checkmark image into a `UIImage` object. Then it calculates the position for that image based on the center coordinate of the HUD view (`center`) and the dimensions of the image (`image.size`).

Finally, it draws the image at that position.

➤ Run the app to see the HUD view with the image:

The HUD view with the checkmark image

> **Failable initializers**
>
> To create the UIImage you used if let to unwrap the resulting object. That's because UIImage(named) is a so-called *failable* initializer.
>
> It is possible that loading the image fails, because there is no image with the specified name or the file doesn't really contain a valid image. You can't fool UIImage into loading something that isn't an image!
>
> That's why UIImage's init(named) method is really defined as init?(named). The question mark indicates that this method returns an optional. If there was a problem loading the image, it returns nil instead of a brand spanking new UIImage object.
>
> You'll see these failable initializers through the iOS frameworks. Whenever it is possible that creating a new object will fail, the responsible init method will return an optional that you need to unwrap before you can use it.

Usually to draw text in your own view you'd add a UILabel object as a subview and let UILabel do all the hard work. However, for a view as simple as this you can also do your own text drawing.

➤ Complete drawRect() by adding the following code:

```
let attribs = [ NSFontAttributeName: UIFont.systemFontOfSize(16.0),
                NSForegroundColorAttributeName: UIColor.whiteColor() ]

let textSize = text.sizeWithAttributes(attribs)

let textPoint = CGPoint(
  x: center.x - round(textSize.width / 2),
  y: center.y - round(textSize.height / 2) + boxHeight / 4)

text.drawAtPoint(textPoint, withAttributes: attribs)
```

When drawing text you first need to know how big the text is, so you can figure out where to position it. String has a bunch of handy methods for doing both.

First, you create the UIFont object that you'll use for the text. This is a "System" font of size 16. The system font on iOS 8 is Helvetica Neue.

You also choose a color for the text, plain white. The font and foreground color are placed into a dictionary named attribs (short for "attributes").

Recall that a dictionary stores key-value pairs. To make a dictionary you write:

```
let myDictionary = [ key1: value1,
                     key2: value2,
                     key3: value3 ]
```

So in the dictionary from drawRect(), the NSFontAttributeName key is associated with the UIFont object, and the NSForegroundColorAttributeName key is associated with the UIColor object. In other words, this dictionary describes what the text will look like.

You use these attributes and the string from the text property to calculate how wide and tall the text will be. The result ends up in the textSize variable, which is of type CGSize. (CGPoint, CGSize and CGRect are types you use a lot when making your own views.)

Finally, you calculate where to draw the text and then draw it. Quite simple, really.

➤ Run the app to try it out. Lookin' good!

The HUD view with the checkmark and the text

➤ Make sure to test the HUD on the different Simulators. No matter the device dimensions, the HUD should still appear centered in the screen.

OK, this shows a rounded box with a checkmark, but it's still far from spectacular. Time to liven it up a little with an animation. You've already seen a bit about animations before – they're really easy to add.

➤ Add the showAnimated() method to **HudView.swift**:

```
func showAnimated(animated: Bool) {
  if animated {
    // 1
    alpha = 0
    transform = CGAffineTransformMakeScale(1.3, 1.3)
    // 2
    UIView.animateWithDuration(0.3, animations: {
      // 3
      self.alpha = 1
      self.transform = CGAffineTransformIdentity
    })
  }
}
```

In the Bull's Eye tutorial you made a crossfade animation using the Core Animation framework. UIView, however, has its own animation mechanism. That still uses Core Animation behind the scenes but it's a little more convenient to use.

The standard steps for doing UIView-based animations are as follows:

1. Set up the initial state of the view before the animation starts. Here you set alpha to 0, making the view fully transparent. You also set the transform to a scale factor of 1.3. We're not going to go into depth on transforms here, but basically this means the view is initially stretched out.

2. Call UIView.animateWithDuration(. . .) to set up an animation. You give this a closure that describes the animation. Recall that a closure is a piece of inline code that is not executed right away. UIKit will animate the properties that you change inside the closure from their initial state to the final state.

3. Inside the closure, set up the new state of the view that it should have after the animation completes. You set alpha to 1, which means the HudView is now fully opaque. You also set the transform to the "identity" transform, restoring the scale back to normal. Because this code is part of a closure, you need to use self to refer to the HudView instance and its properties. That's the rule for closures.

The HUD view will quickly fade in as its opacity goes from fully transparent to fully opaque, and it will scale down from 1.3 times its original size to its regular width and height.

This is only a simple animation but it looks quite smart.

➤ Change the `hudInView(animated)` method to call `showAnimated()` just before it returns:

```
class func hudInView(view: UIView, animated: Bool) -> HudView {
  . . .
  hudView.showAnimated(animated)
  return hudView
}
```

➤ Run the app and marvel at the magic of `UIView` animation.

You can actually do one better. iOS has something called "spring" animations, which bounce up and down and are much more visually interesting than the plain old animations. Using them is very simple.

➤ Replace the `UIView.animateWithDuration()` code with the following:

```
UIView.animateWithDuration(0.3, delay: 0, usingSpringWithDamping: 0.7,
  initialSpringVelocity: 0.5, options: UIViewAnimationOptions(0), animations: {
    self.alpha = 1
    self.transform = CGAffineTransformIdentity
  },
  completion: nil)
```

The code in the closure is still the same – it sets `alpha` to 1 and restores the identity transform – but the `animateWithDuration()` method has a lot more options. Feel free to play with these options to see what they do.

➤ Run the app and watch it bounce. Actually, the effect is very subtle, but subtle is good when it comes to user interfaces. You don't want your users to get seasick from using the app!

Back to **LocationDetailsViewController**... You still need to close the screen when the user taps Done.

There's a challenge here: you don't want to dismiss the screen right away. It won't look very good if the screen already closes before the HUD is finished animating. You didn't spend all that time writing `HudView` for nothing – you want to give your users a chance to see it.

➤ Add a new import at the top of **LocationDetailsViewController.swift**:

```
import Dispatch
```

This imports the Grand Central Dispatch framework, or GCD for short. GCD is a very handy but somewhat low-level library for handling asynchronous tasks. Telling the app to wait for a few seconds is a perfect example of such an "async" task.

➤ Add these lines to the bottom of the `done()` action method:

```
let delayInSeconds = 0.6
let when = dispatch_time(DISPATCH_TIME_NOW, Int64(delayInSeconds * Double(NSEC_PER_SEC)))
dispatch_after(when, dispatch_get_main_queue(), {
  self.dismissViewControllerAnimated(true, completion: nil)
})
```

Believe it or not, this gibberish tells the app to close the Tag Location screen after 0.6 seconds.

The magic happens in `dispatch_after()`. This function takes a closure as its final parameter. Inside that closure you tell the view controller to dismiss itself. This doesn't happen right away, though. That's the exciting thing about closures: even though the code is inline with all the other code in the method, everything that's inside the closure is ignored for now and kept for a later time.

The call to `dispatch_time()` converts the 0.6 second delay into some kind of internal time format – measured in nanoseconds because a second is an eternity for a computer – and then `dispatch_after()` uses that delay to schedule the closure for some point in the future. Until then, the app just sits there twiddling its thumbs.

After 0.6 seconds, the code from the closure finally runs and the screen closes.

> **Note:** I spent some time tweaking that number. The HUD view takes 0.3 seconds to fully fade in and then you wait another 0.3 seconds before the screen disappears. That felt right to me. You don't want to close the screen too quickly or the effect from showing the HUD is lost, but it shouldn't take too long either or it will annoy the user. Animations are cool but they shouldn't make the app more frustrating to use!

➤ Run the app. Press the Done button and watch how the screen disappears. This looks pretty smooth, if I do say so myself.

Now, I don't know about you but I find this Grand Central Dispatch stuff to be a bit messy. It's hard to see exactly what is going on with all this `DISPATCH_TIME_NOW` and `NSEC_PER_SEC` stuff. So let's clean up the code and make it easier to understand.

➤ Add a new file to the project. This time use the **Swift File** template. Name the file **Functions.swift**.

➤ Replace the contents of the new file with:

```
import Foundation
import Dispatch

func afterDelay(seconds: Double, closure: () -> ()) {
  let when = dispatch_time(DISPATCH_TIME_NOW, Int64(seconds * Double(NSEC_PER_SEC)))
  dispatch_after(when, dispatch_get_main_queue(), closure)
}
```

That looks very much like the code you just added to `done()`, except it now lives in its own function, `afterDelay()`.

This is a **free function**, not a method inside an object, and as a result can be used from anywhere in your code.

Take a good look at `afterDelay()`'s second parameter, `closure`. Its type is `() -> ()`.

That's not some weird emoticon; it is Swift notation for a parameter that takes a closure with no arguments and no return value.

The -> symbol means that the type represents a closure. The type for a closure generally looks like this:

```
(parameter list) -> return type
```

In this case, both the parameter list and the return value are empty, (). This can also be written as Void -> Void but I like the empty parentheses better.

So whenever you see a -> in the type annotation for a parameter, you know that this function takes a closure as one of its parameters.

afterDelay() simply passes this closure object along to dispatch_after().

You may be wondering why you're going through all this trouble. No fear! The reason why will become apparent after you've made the following change...

➤ Go back to **LocationDetailsViewController.swift** and change done() to:

```
@IBAction func done() {
  let hudView = HudView.hudInView(navigationController!.view, animated: true)
  hudView.text = "Tagged"

  afterDelay(0.6, {
    self.dismissViewControllerAnimated(true, completion: nil)
  })
}
```

Now that's the power of Swift! It only takes one look at this code to immediately understand what it does. After a delay, something happens.

By moving the nasty GCD stuff into a new function, afterDelay(), you have added a new **abstraction** into your code that makes it much easier to follow. Writing good programs is all about finding the right abstractions.

Note: Because the code to dismiss the view controller lives in a closure it needs to use self to call the method. Inside closures you always need to use self explicitly.

Also, because afterDelay() is a free function, not a method, you do not need to specify the closure: label for the second parameter.

You can make this read even more naturally. Change the code to:

```
afterDelay(0.6) {
  self.dismissViewControllerAnimated(true, completion: nil)
}
```

Now the closure sits *outside* of the call to afterDelay().

Swift has a handy rule that says you can put a closure behind a function call if it's the last parameter. This is known as **trailing closure syntax**.

By the way, you can remove the import Dispatch line again from **LocationDetailsViewController.swift**. This file no longer uses GCD directly and therefore doesn't need to import the framework.

➤ Run the app again to make sure the timing still works. Boo-yah!

You can find the project files for this section under **02 – Tagging Locations** in the tutorial's Source Code folder.

Value types and reference types

A type walks into a bar. "Do you have any variables?" he asks.

"Well, I don't know if it will be of much value," says the bartender, "but I can give you a reference!"

Anyway… Swift makes a distinction between **value types** and **reference types** and it uses different rules for each.

Objects that are made from classes are reference types. Anything else – all the basic types such as Int, Bool, Float and Double, String, Array and Dictionary, as well as enums – are all value types.

So what exactly is the difference between a value type and a reference type?

When you declare a variable as an Int or a CLLocationCoordinate2D – both value types – the compiler reserves a small portion of memory to hold the value that you wish to store. For an Int that is 8 bytes, for a CLLocationCoordinate2D that is 16 bytes (on a 64-bit CPU such as in the iPhone 5s and later models).

Variables for reference types are no different. When you create a UILabel outlet, for example, the compiler also reserves 8 bytes of memory, exactly the same as for an Int. But a label can hold several lines of text – surely that won't all fit into those measly 8 bytes?

When you put some values into these variables, the picture looks like this:

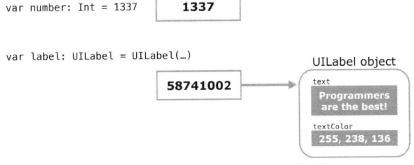

The label variable contains a reference to a UILabel object

The value 1337 is put directly into number's memory but the value of label is some weird number. It sure doesn't look like a text label. That number is not the actual UILabel object but the memory address where that UILabel object lives. It is a *reference* to the label object.

Every byte in memory has its own unique address, and in this case address 58741002 refers to the location in memory of the first byte of the UILabel object.

Obviously the 8 bytes that are reserved for the label variable are not enough to hold a UILabel object with the text "Programmers are the best!" and all the other label properties such as the text color.

So when the UILabel object is allocated, the computer puts it somewhere else in memory and returns the address of that memory location. That address – PO Box 58741002, Mike's iPhone, USA – is what gets put in the variable.

It's quite useful to think of a reference as a postal address. Your house is the actual object, but not every one of your acquaintances has a copy of your house. That would be silly. Instead, these people have a reference to your house: your address. To access your house (for example, to come over and eat ice cream), they look up the address so they can find where you live.

Don't worry if the distinction between value type and reference type doesn't quite make sense to you yet. It's a very powerful idea in computing and powerful ideas can take a while to sink in.

What you do need to know about the difference between value types and references types is this:

Rule 1. When you make a constant with let, you cannot change a value type once you have given it a value:

```
let coord1 = CLLocationCoordinate2D(latitude: 0, longitude: 0)
coord1.latitude = 37.33233141   // error

var coord2 = CLLocationCoordinate2D(latitude: 0, longitude: 0)
coord2.latitude = 37.33233141   // OK
```

But the object from a reference type can always be changed, even if you used let. For example:

```
let label = UILabel()
label.text = "Hello, world!"   // OK
label.text = "I like change"   // OK
```

What is constant is the reference itself; in other words you cannot put a new object into it:

```
let newLabel = UILabel()
label = newLabel              // error
```

Rule 2. When you put an object with a value type into a new variable or constant, it is copied. Arrays are value types in Swift. That means when you put an array into a new variable it will actually make a copy:

```
var a = [1, 2, 3]
let b = a
a.append(4)
println(a)    // prints [1, 2, 3, 4]
println(b)    // prints [1, 2, 3]
```

This doesn't happen with a reference type. The object itself isn't copied, only the reference:

```
var firstLabel = UILabel()
firstLabel.text = "Programmers are the best!"

var secondLabel = firstLabel
secondLabel.text = "I like ice cream"

println(firstLabel.text)   // prints "I like ice cream"
```

What happens is that secondLabel points to the same address as firstLabel, and therefore putting a new string in secondLabel's text property changes it for both.

Both label variables refer to the same object

Remember, only objects made from classes are reference types. Everything else is a value type.

Object ownership

Objects are rarely hermits, off by themselves on a mountain somewhere. Your apps will have many objects that all need to work together. They are a very cooperative bunch!

The relationships between the objects in your app are described by the **object graph**. For example, the CurrentLocationViewController has relationships with several objects:

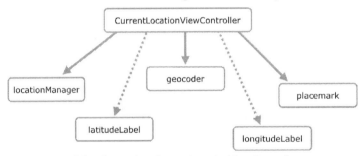

Some of the objects that CurrentLocationViewController owns

These are its instance variables and constants, in other words the objects it "owns". That's not the whole story. The CurrentLocationViewController itself is also owned by some object, as it belongs to a UITabBarController, which in turn belongs to the UIWindow.

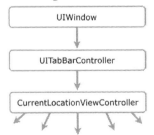

The UITabBarController owns CurrentLocationViewController

This is only a small part of the object graph for the app. It shows the ownership relations between the various objects. (Don't confuse this diagram with the class hierarchy, which shows how the types of the objects are related, but not the objects themselves.)

Object ownership is an important topic in iOS programming. You need to have a clear picture of which objects own what other objects, as the existence of those objects depends on it – and so does the proper functioning of your app!

An object that no longer has any owners is immediately deallocated – destroyed! – and that's a problem if your app does not expect that to happen. On the other hand, if an object has too many owners it will stay in memory forever, which may cause your app to run out of free memory and crash also.

So what does it mean to "own" an object? This is where the concept of **strong** and **weak** references comes in.

Most of the time when you declare a variable that holds a reference object, you are creating a strong relationship. This variable assumes ownership of the object, a responsibility that it shares with any other variables referencing the same object.

```
var image: UIImage          // a strong variable
```

In a weak relationship, there is no such ownership. A variable with a weak relationship to an object is not helping to keep this object alive. You need to explicitly declare this with the weak keyword (and make it an optional):

```
weak var weakImage: UIImage? // a weak variable
```

The lifetime of an object is determined by how many owners it has at any given point. As soon as there are no more strong references to an object, no matter how many weak references there are, the object is ruthlessly disposed of.

That's also when the object's deinit method is called, giving the object one last chance to get its affairs in order before it meets its maker.

So what's the point of weak?

It primarily exists to avoid the problem of **ownership cycles** where two objects end up owning each other. Because these objects keep each other alive, the app will never reclaim their memory after they've served their purpose. This slowly eats up the available memory for the app – memory leak! – until there is none left and the app crashes.

In the previous tutorial you learned to make delegates weak to avoid this kind of situation. Later on you'll see another example of an ownership cycle and how to fix it (hint: you'll use a weak reference).

Another common use of weak is with @IBOutlet properties. The reason outlets are weak is that the view controller isn't really their owner; instead, the outlets belong to the view controller's top-level view. Nothing untoward will happen if you have strong outlets, but by declaring them weak the view controller says, "I'm only renting these outlets, I don't need to own them."

Weak relationships have a cool side effect. If you have a weak reference to an object and that object is deallocated because its previous owners have all given up ownership, your reference automatically becomes nil.

That's a good thing too because if it didn't, you'd be pointing to a dead object and all sorts of mayhem would break loose if you tried to use it. (Using zombie objects is a common cause of crashes in languages that don't have weak references.)

This is also why weak variables must always be optionals (either ? or !) because they may become nil at some point.

> **Note:** Swift has a third type of relationship: unowned. Like weak this is used to break cycles. The difference is that unowned variables shouldn't be nil and therefore don't have to be optionals. It's less common than weak, but you'll probably run into unowned variables here or there. Just think of them as weak — it's what I do.

To recap: if you want to keep an object around for a while, you should store it with a strong relationship. But if you don't need to own the object and you don't mind it going away at some point, use a weak or unowned reference.

Let's look at a situation where there is more than one owner of an object.

For example, when the user taps the Tag Location button, the Current Location view controller passes a CLPlacemark object to the Location Details view controller. Both references are strong so from that moment on, the Location Details view controller assumes shared ownership of it. Now the CLPlacemark has two owners.

It's important to realize that the concept of shared ownership and object relationships only applies to reference types. Value types are always copied from one place to the other, so they never have more than one owner.

LocationDetailsViewController also has a coordinate property that is filled in upon the segue from the Tap Location button. This is a CLLocationCoordinate2D, a struct and therefore a value type.

In prepareForSegue(sender) the following happens:

```
override func prepareForSegue(segue: UIStoryboardSegue, sender: AnyObject?) {
  . . .
  controller.coordinate = location!.coordinate
  controller.placemark = placemark
}
```

The line that puts location!.coordinate into controller.coordinate makes a copy of that CLLocationCoordinate2D struct. Each view controller now has its own unique copy of those GPS coordinates.

For placemark the only thing that is copied is the reference. Both view controllers point to the same CLPlacemark object (or nil if placemark has no value).

The coordinate is copied but the placemark is a reference

Make sense? Great! If not, read it again. ☺

Seriously though, if you understand these concepts you're well on your way to programming greatness. And if not, don't give up. These can be tough ideas to grok. Just keep going until it does make sense (and I promise it will!).

> **Note:** If you want an object with a reference type to be copied when it is assigned to another variable, you can declare it as @NSCopying. This first creates a duplicate of the object and puts that in the new variable. Now the two variables each refer to their own object. @NSCopying is more of an Objective-C thing, but now you know what it's for should you come across it.

Storing the locations with Core Data

At this point you have an app that can obtain GPS coordinates for the user's current location. It also has a screen where the user can "tag" that location, which currently consists of entering a description and choosing a category. Later on, you'll also allow the user to pick a photo.

The next feature is to make the app remember the locations that the user has tagged and show them in a list.

The Locations screen will look like this:

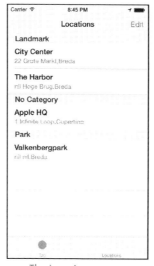

The Locations screen

You have to persist the data for these captured locations somehow, because they should be remembered even when the app terminates.

The last time you did this, you made data model objects that conformed to the NSCoding protocol and saved them to a .plist file using NSKeyedArchiver. That works fine but in this lesson I want to introduce you to a framework that can take a lot of work out of your hands: Core Data.

Core Data is an object persistence framework for iOS apps. If you've looked at Core Data before, you may have found the official documentation a little daunting but the principle is quite simple.

You've learned that objects get destroyed when there are no more references to it. In addition, all objects get destroyed when the app terminates.

With Core Data, you can designate some objects as being persistent so they will always be saved to a **data store**. Even when all references to such a **managed object** are gone and the instance gets destroyed, its data is still safely stored in Core Data and you can get it back at any time.

If you've worked with databases before, then you might be tempted to think of Core Data as a database but that's a little misleading. In some respects the two are similar but Core Data is about storing objects, not relational tables. It is just another way to make sure the data from certain objects doesn't get deleted when these objects are deallocated or the app terminates.

Adding Core Data to the app

Core Data requires the use of a data model. This is a special file that you add to your project to describe the objects that you want to persist. These *managed* objects, unlike regular objects, will keep their data in the data store unless you explicitly delete them.

➤ Add a new file to the project. Choose the **Data Model** template under the **Core Data** section:

Adding a Data Model file to the project

➤ Save it as **DataModel**.

This will add a new file to the project, DataModel.xcdatamodeld.

➤ Click **DataModel.xcdatamodeld** in the Project navigator to open the Data Model editor:

The empty data model

For each object that you want Core Data to manage, you have to add an **entity**.

An entity describes which data fields your objects will have. In a sense it serves the same purpose as a class but specifically for Core Data's data store. (If you've worked with SQL databases before, you can think of an entity as a table.)

This app will only have one entity, Location, which stores all the properties for a location that the user tagged. Each Location will keep track of the following data:

- latitude and longitude
- placemark (the street address)
- the date when the location was tagged
- the user's description
- category

These are the items from the Tag Location screen, except for the photo. Photos are potentially very big and can take up several megabytes of storage space. Even though the Core Data store can handle big "blobs" of data, it is usually better to store photos as separate files in the app's Documents directory. More about that later.

➤ Click the **Add Entity** button at the bottom of the data model editor. This adds a new entity under the ENTITIES heading. Name it **Location**. (You can rename the entity by clicking its name or from the Data Model inspector pane on the right.)

The new Location entity

To the right there are three sections: Attributes, Relationships and Fetched Properties. The Attributes are the entity's data fields. This app only has one entity, but often apps will have many entities that are all related to each other somehow.

With Relationships and Fetched Properties you can tell Core Data how your objects depend on each other. For this app you will only use the Attributes section.

➤ Click the **Add Attribute** button at the bottom of the editor (or the small + button below the Attributes section). Name the new attribute **latitude** and set its **Type** to **Double**:

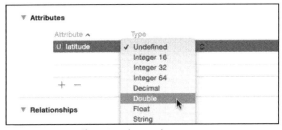

Choosing the attribute type

Attributes are basically the same as instance variables and therefore they have a type. You've seen earlier that the latitude and longitude coordinates really have the data type `Double`, so that's what you're choosing for the attribute as well.

Note: Don't let the change in terminology scare you. Just think:

entity = object (or class)

attribute = variable

If you're wondering where you'll define methods in Core Data, then the answer is: you don't. Core Data is only for storing the data portion of objects. That is what an entity describes, the data of an object, and optionally how that object relates to other objects if you use Relationships and Fetched Properties.

You are still going to define your own `Location` class in code by creating a Swift file, just as you've been doing all along. Because it describes a managed object, this class will be associated with the Location entity in the data model. But it's still a regular class, so you can add your own methods to it.

➤ Add the other attributes to the Location entity:

- **longitude**, type Double

- **date**, type Date

- **locationDescription**, type String

- **category**, type String

- **placemark**, type Transformable

The data model should look like this when you're done:

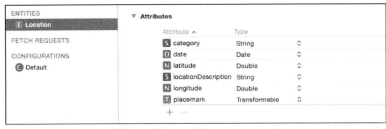

All the attributes of the Location entity

Why didn't you just call it "description" instead of "locationDescription"? As it turns out, description is the name of a method from NSObject. If you try to name an attribute "description", then this will cause a naming conflict with that method. Xcode will give you an error message if you try to do this.

The type of the placemark attribute is Transformable. Core Data only supports a limited number of data types right out the box, such as String, Double, and Date. The placemark is a CLPlacemark object and that is not in the list of supported data types.

Fortunately, Core Data has a provision for handling arbitrary data types. Any class that conforms to the NSCoding protocol can be stored in a Transformable attribute without additional work. Fortunately for us, CLPlacemark does conform to NSCoding, so you can store it in Core Data with no trouble.

By default, entity attributes are optional, meaning they can be nil. In our app, the only thing that can be nil is the placemark, in case reverse geocoding failed. It's a good idea to embed this constraint in the data model.

➤ Select the category attribute. In the inspectors panel, switch to the **Data Model inspector**. Uncheck the **Optional** setting:

Making the category attribute non-optional

➤ Repeat this for the other attributes, except for placemark. (Tip: you can select multiple attributes at the same time.)

There is one more change to make in the data model and then you're done here.

➤ Click on the Location entity to select it and go to the Data Model inspector.

The Data Model inspector

The Class field currently says "NSManagedObject". When you retrieve a Location entity from Core Data, it gives you an object of the class NSManagedObject.

That is the base class for all objects that are managed by Core Data. Regular objects inherit from NSObject, but objects from Core Data extend NSManagedObject.

Because using `NSManagedObject` directly is a bit limiting, you are going to use your own class instead.

➤ Change the **Class** field to **MyLocations.Location**. That is the name of the new class you are going to make.

You're not required to make your own classes for your entities, but it makes Core Data easier to use. When you now retrieve a Location entity from the data store, Core Data doesn't give you an `NSManagedObject` but an instance of your own `Location` class.

> **Note:** Swift apps consist of one or more **modules**. Each target in your project is compiled into its own module with its own namespace. Because of this, you need to tell Core Data in which module your `NSManagedObject` subclass lives, which is why you specified it as `MyLocations.Location`.
>
> The subclass itself is named `Location`, from the module `MyLocations`. That also happens to be the name of the app, because a simple app like this only has one module. (Actually, it has two. The other one is `MyLocationsTests`, for writing unit tests, but we're not using that in this tutorial.)

There's an Xcode trick that makes it easy to generate classes automatically from the data model.

➤ From the menu bar, choose **Editor → Create NSManagedObject Subclass**.

The assistant will now ask you for which data model and which entity you wish to create the class.

➤ Select **DataModel** and click **Next**.

Select the Location entity

➤ Make sure **Location** is selected and click **Next** again.

When asked where to save the source files, make sure Language is **Swift**. Put a checkmark in front of **Use scalar properties for primitive data types**:

The "Use scalar properties" option should be checked

➤ Press **Create** to finish.

> **Note:** It's possible that Xcode now asks you to install a so-called "bridging header". This is a piece of code that is necessary to combine Swift and Objective-C in a single project. If you get this, you forgot to choose Swift for the language.

This adds a new file to the project. It should be named **Location.swift** and look something like this:

```swift
import Foundation
import CoreData

class Location: NSManagedObject {

    @NSManaged var category: String
    @NSManaged var date: NSTimeInterval
    @NSManaged var latitude: Double
    @NSManaged var locationDescription: String
    @NSManaged var longitude: Double
    @NSManaged var placemark: AnyObject
}
```

It is possible that Xcode oddly named the new file **MyLocations.swift**. That's a bug in Xcode. If you get the same thing, rename the file to **Location.swift** and change the class line to say Location instead of MyLocations.

As you can see in the class line, the Location class extends NSManagedObject instead of the regular NSObject.

Xcode has also created properties for the attributes that you specified in the Data Model editor.

Because you made placemark a Transformable property, Xcode doesn't really know what kind of object this will be, so it chose the generic type AnyObject. You know it's going to be a CLPlacemark object, so you can make things easier for yourself by changing it.

➤ First import Core Location into **Location.swift**:

```swift
import CoreLocation
```

➤ Then change the placemark property to:

```swift
@NSManaged var placemark: CLPlacemark?
```

You're adding a question mark too, because placemark is optional.

➤ Also change the date property from NSTimeInterval to NSDate:

```swift
@NSManaged var date: NSDate
```

Both NSTimeInterval and NSDate can represent dates, but working with an NSDate object is a bit easier.

Because this is a *managed* object, and the data lives inside a data store, Swift will handle Location's variables in a special way. The @NSManaged keyword tells the compiler that these properties will be resolved at runtime by Core Data.

When you put a new value into one of these properties, Core Data will place that value into the data store for safekeeping, instead of in a regular instance variable.

This concludes the definition of the data model for this app. Now you have to hook it up to a data store.

The data store

On iOS, Core Data stores all of its data into a SQLite database. It's OK if you have no idea what that is. You'll take a peek into that database later, but you don't really need to know what goes on inside the data store in order to use Core Data.

However, you do need to initialize this data store when the app starts. The code for that is the same for just about any app that uses Core Data and it goes in the app delegate class.

The **app delegate** is the object that gets notifications that concern the application as a whole. This is where iOS notifies the app that it has started up, for example.

You're going to make a few changes to the project's AppDelegate class.

➤ Open **AppDelegate.swift** and import the Core Data framework at the very top:

```
import CoreData
```

➤ Add the following chunk of code inside the AppDelegate class:

```
lazy var managedObjectContext: NSManagedObjectContext = {
  if let modelURL = NSBundle.mainBundle().URLForResource("DataModel",
                                              withExtension: "momd") {
    if let model = NSManagedObjectModel(contentsOfURL: modelURL) {
      let coordinator = NSPersistentStoreCoordinator(managedObjectModel: model)

      let urls = NSFileManager.defaultManager().URLsForDirectory(.DocumentDirectory,
                                              inDomains: .UserDomainMask)
      let documentsDirectory = urls[0] as! NSURL
      let storeURL = documentsDirectory.URLByAppendingPathComponent("DataStore.sqlite")

      var error: NSError?
      if let store = coordinator.addPersistentStoreWithType(NSSQLiteStoreType,
                        configuration: nil, URL: storeURL, options: nil, error: &error) {
        let context = NSManagedObjectContext()
        context.persistentStoreCoordinator = coordinator
        return context
      } else {
        println("Error adding persistent store at \(storeURL): \(error!)")
      }
    } else {
      println("Error initializing model from: \(modelURL)")
    }
  } else {
    println("Could not find data model in app bundle")
  }

  abort()
}()
```

This is the code you need to load the data model that you've defined earlier, and to connect it to an SQLite data store.

This is very standard stuff that will be the same for almost any Core Data app you'll write. I won't bother you with the details of how it works just yet. Just know that this code creates a lazily loaded instance variable named managedObjectContext that is an object of type NSManagedObjectContext.

➤ Build the app to make sure it compiles without errors. If you run it you won't notice any difference because you're not actually using Core Data anywhere yet.

Passing around the context

When the user presses the Done button in the Tag Location screen, the app currently just closes the screen. Let's improve on that and make a tap on Done save a new `Location` object into the Core Data store.

I mentioned the `NSManagedObjectContext` object. This is the object that you use to talk to Core Data. It is often described as the "scratchpad". You first make your changes to the context and then you call its `save()` method to store those changes permanently in the data store.

That means every object that needs to do something with Core Data needs to have a reference to the `NSManagedObjectContext` object.

➤ Switch to **LocationDetailsViewController.swift**. Import Core Data into this file and then add a new instance variable:

```
var managedObjectContext: NSManagedObjectContext!
```

The problem is: how do you put the `NSManagedObjectContext` object from the app delegate into that property?

The context object is created by `AppDelegate` (in that big block of code you just added) but `AppDelegate` has no reference to the `LocationDetailsViewController`.

That's not so strange as the Location Details view controller doesn't exist until the user taps the Tag Location button. Prior to initiating that segue, there simply is no living `LocationDetailsViewController` object.

The answer is to put a reference to the `NSManagedObjectContext` object into this new `managedObjectContext` property when the Tag Location screen is opened. The logical place for this is `prepareForSegue()` in `CurrentLocationViewController`.

Now you need to find a way to get the `NSManagedObjectContext` object into the `CurrentLocationViewController` in the first place.

I come across a lot of code that does the following:

```
let appDelegate = UIApplication.sharedApplication().delegate as! AppDelegate
let context = appDelegate.managedObjectContext
// do something with the context
```

This depends on the `managedObjectContext` being a property on the app delegate. From anywhere in your source code you can get a reference to the context simply by asking the `AppDelegate`. Sounds like a good solution, right?

Not quite… Suddenly all your objects are dependent on the app delegate. This introduces a dependency that can make your code messy really quickly.

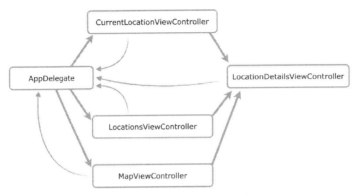

Bad: All classes depend on AppDelegate

As a general design principle, it is best to make your classes depend on each other as little as possible. The fewer interactions there are between the different parts of your program, the simpler it is to understand.

If many of your classes need to reach out to some shared object such as the app delegate, then you may want to rethink your design.

A better solution is to pass along the NSManagedObjectContext to each object that needs it.

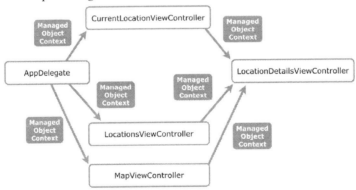

Good: The context object is passed from one object to the next

Using this architecture, AppDelegate gives the managed object context to CurrentLocationViewController, which in turn will pass it to the LocationDetailsViewController when it performs the segue. This technique is known as *dependency injection*.

This means CurrentLocationViewController needs its own property for the NSManagedObject context.

➤ Add the following property to **CurrentLocationViewController.swift**:

```
var managedObjectContext: NSManagedObjectContext!
```

Don't forget to also import Core Data or Xcode won't know what you mean by NSManagedObjectContext.

➤ Add the following line to prepareForSegue(sender), so that it passes on the context on to the Tag Location screen:

```
override func prepareForSegue(segue: UIStoryboardSegue, sender: AnyObject?) {
  if segue.identifier == "TagLocation" {
    . . .
    controller.coordinate = location!.coordinate
    controller.placemark = placemark
    controller.managedObjectContext = managedObjectContext
  }
}
```

This should also explain why the managedObjectContext variable is declared as an implicitly unwrapped optional using NSManagedObjectContext!.

You should know by now that variables in Swift must always have a value. If they can be nil – which means "not a value" – then the variable must be made optional.

If you were to declare managedObjectContext without the exclamation point,

```
var managedObjectContext: NSManagedObjectContext
```

then Swift demands you give it a value inside an init method. For objects loaded from a storyboard, such as view controllers, that is init(coder).

However, prepareForSegue() happens *after* the new view controller is instantiated, so also after the call to init(coder). As a result, inside init(coder) you can't know yet what the value for managedObjectContext is.

You have no choice but to leave the managedObjectContext variable nil for a short while until the segue happens, and therefore it must be an optional.

You could also have declared it like this:

```
var managedObjectContext: NSManagedObjectContext?
```

The difference between ? and ! is that the former requires you to manually unwrap the value with if let every time you want to use it.

That gets annoying fast, especially when you know that managedObjectContext will get a proper value during the segue and that it will never become nil afterwards again. In that case, the exclamation mark is the best type of optional to use.

These rules for optionals may seem very strict – and confusing – when you're coming from another language such as Objective-C, but they are there for a good reason. By only allowing certain variables to have no value, Swift can make your programs safer and reduce the number of programming mistakes.

The fewer optionals you use, the better, but sometimes you can't avoid them – as in this case with managedObjectContext.

Back in **AppDelegate.swift**, we need to find some way to pass the NSManagedObjectContext object to CurrentLocationViewController.

Unfortunately, Interface Builder does not allow you to make outlets for your view controllers on the App Delegate. Instead, you have to look up these view controllers by digging through the storyboard.

➤ Change the `application(didFinishLaunchingWithOptions)` method to:

```
func application(application: UIApplication,
            didFinishLaunchingWithOptions launchOptions: [NSObject : AnyObject]?) -> Bool {

  let tabBarController = window!.rootViewController as! UITabBarController

  if let tabBarViewControllers = tabBarController.viewControllers {
    let currentLocationViewController =
                            tabBarViewControllers[0] as! CurrentLocationViewController

    currentLocationViewController.managedObjectContext = managedObjectContext
  }
  return true
}
```

In order to get a reference to the `CurrentLocationViewController` you first have to find the `UITabBarController` and then look at its `viewControllers` array.

Once you have a reference to the `CurrentLocationViewController` object, you give it the `managedObjectContext`. It may not be immediately obvious from looking at the code, but something special happens at this point…

Remember you added that big chunk of code to `AppDelegate` earlier? This is what it looked like (I left out most of the actual code):

```
lazy var managedObjectContext: NSManagedObjectContext = {
  . . .
  return context
  . . .
}()
```

These lines declare an instance variable of type `NSManagedObjectContext`. It has an initial value because it says:

```
lazy var managedObjectContext: NSManagedObjectContext = something
```

And that something is a block of code in between { } braces:

```
{
  . . .
  return context
  . . .
}()
```

You may recognize this as a closure. You've already seen those a few times now. Normally a closure contains source code that is not performed right away, so you can store it for later use. Here, however, the parentheses at the end of the closure invoke it immediately.

To make this a bit clearer, here is another example:

```
var four: Int = { return 2 + 2 }()
```

The initial value of this variable is the result of the closure { `return 2 + 2` }. It's a bit silly to do this when you could have just written `var four = 4`, but in the case of `managedObjectContext` it is really handy.

Let's look at the code in its entirety and I'll explain the various parts:

```
lazy var managedObjectContext: NSManagedObjectContext = {
  // 1
  if let modelURL = NSBundle.mainBundle().URLForResource("DataModel",
                                              withExtension: "momd") {
    // 2
    if let model = NSManagedObjectModel(contentsOfURL: modelURL) {
      // 3
      let coordinator = NSPersistentStoreCoordinator(managedObjectModel: model)
      // 4
      let urls = NSFileManager.defaultManager().URLsForDirectory(.DocumentDirectory,
                                          inDomains: .UserDomainMask)
      let documentsDirectory = urls[0] as! NSURL
      let storeURL = documentsDirectory.URLByAppendingPathComponent("DataStore.sqlite")
      // 5
      var error: NSError?
      if let store = coordinator.addPersistentStoreWithType(NSSQLiteStoreType,
                      configuration: nil, URL: storeURL, options: nil, error: &error) {
        // 6
        let context = NSManagedObjectContext()
        context.persistentStoreCoordinator = coordinator
        return context
      // 7
      } else {
        println("Error adding persistent store at \(storeURL): \(error!)")
      }
    } else {
      println("Error initializing model from: \(modelURL)")
    }
  } else {
    println("Could not find data model in app bundle")
  }

  abort()
}()
```

To create an `NSManagedObjectContext` object, you need to do several things:

1. The Core Data model you created earlier is stored in your application bundle in a folder named "DataModel.momd". Here you create an `NSURL` object pointing at this folder. Paths to files and folders are often represented by URLs in the iOS frameworks.

2. Create an `NSManagedObjectModel` from that URL. This object represents the data model during runtime. You can ask it what sort of entities it has, what attributes these entities have, and so on. In most apps you don't need to use the `NSManagedObjectModel` object directly. (Note: this is another example of a *failable* initializer.)

3. Create an `NSPersistentStoreCoordinator` object. This object is in charge of the SQLite database.

4. The app's data is stored in an SQLite database inside the app's Documents folder. Here you create an `NSURL` object pointing at the DataStore.sqlite file.

5. Add the SQLite database to the store coordinator.

6. Finally, create the `NSManagedObjectContext` object and return it.

7. If something went wrong, then print an error message and abort the app. In theory, errors should never happen here but you definitely want to have some `println()`'s in place to help with debugging.

Most of this is boilerplate code that you'll see in any Core Data app. (If you create a new Xcode project and enable Core Data, the generated template contains a slightly different way to set up the Core Data stack. But if you look closely you'll see that it actually performs all the same steps.)

Now that you know what it does, you may be wondering why you didn't just put all of this code into a regular method and did something like this:

```
var managedObjectContext: NSManagedObjectContext

init() {
  managedObjectContext = createManagedObjectContext()
}

func createManagedObjectContext() -> NSManagedObjectContext {
  // all the initialization code here
  return context
}
```

That would certainly be possible, but now the initialization of managedObjectContext is spread over three different parts of the code: the declaration of the variable, the method that performs all the initialization logic, and the init method to tie it all together.

Isn't it nicer to keep all this stuff in one place, rather than chopped up into three different pieces? Swift lets you perform complex initialization right where you declare the variable. I think that's pretty nifty.

There's another thing going on here:

```
lazy var managedObjectContext: NSManagedObjectContext = { . . . }()
```

Notice the lazy keyword? That means the entire block of code in the { . . . }() closure isn't actually performed right away. The context object won't be created until you ask for it. This is another example of **lazy loading**.

> Run the app. Everything should still be the way it was, but behind the scenes a new database has been created for Core Data.

A peek inside the data store

When you initialized the persistent store coordinator, you gave it a path to a database file. That file is named **DataStore.sqlite** and it lives in the app's Documents folder.

You can see it in Finder if you go to **~/Library/CoreSimulator** and then to the folder that contains the data for the MyLocations app.

The easiest way to find this folder is to add a println() to the closure that sets up managedObjectContext.

Exercise. What value do you need to print out to find the data store file? ∎

Answer: Either println(storeURL) or print(documentsDirectory). On my computer this prints out:

```
file:///Users/matthijs/Library/Developer/CoreSimulator/Devices/078E984C-869F-4B9D-BA79-
521A9ACE6B04/data/Containers/Data/Application/22E1BE45-FDD1-48B7-AD17-CE342CDCC2BA/Documents/
```

> Open a new Finder window and press **Shift+⌘+G**. Then copy-paste the path without the file:// bit to go to the Documents folder:

The new database in the app's Documents directory

The **DataStore.sqlite-shm** and **-wal** files are also part of the data store.

This database is still empty because you haven't stored any objects inside it yet, but just for the fun of it you'll take a peek inside.

There are several handy (free!) tools that give you a graphical interface for interacting with your SQLite databases.

In this section you will use **Liya** to examine the data store file. Download it from the Mac App Store or http://www.cutedgesystems.com/software/liya/.

➤ Start Liya. It asks you for a database connection. Under **Database Type** choose **SQLite**.

Liya opens with this dialog box

➤ On the right of the Database Type field is a small icon. Click this to open a file picker.

You can navigate to the **CoreSimulator/.../Documents** folder, but that's a lot of work (it's a very deeply nested folder).

If you have the Finder window still open, it's easier to drag the DataStore.sqlite file from Finder directly into the open file picker. Click **Choose** when you're done.

The **Database URL** field should now contain the app's Document folder and **Database Name** should say DataStore.sqlite:

Choose from Saved Connections:

Connections

Database Type   SQLite

Database URL   /Users/matthijs/Library/Developer/CoreSimulator/Devices/1

Database Name   DataStore.sqlite

Trim Saved Connections...   Cancel   Login

Connecting to the SQLite database

> Click **Login** to proceed.

Tip: You can also simply right-click the DataStore.sqlite file in Finder and choose **Open With →** **Liya** from the popup menu.

The screen should look something like this:

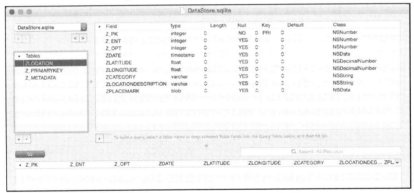

The empty DataStore.sqlite database in Liya

The ZLOCATION table is where your Location objects will be stored. It's currently empty but on the right you can already see the column names that correspond to your fields: ZDATE, ZLATITUDE, and so on. Core Data adds its own columns and tables (with the Z_ prefix).

You're not really supposed to change anything in this database by hand, but sometimes using a visual tool like this is handy to see what's going on. You'll come back to Liya once you've inserted new Location objects.

> **Note:** An alternative to Liya is SQLiteStudio, http://sqlitestudio.pl. You can find more tools, paid and free, on the Mac App Store by searching for "sqlite".

There is another handy tool for troubleshooting Core Data. By setting a special flag on the app, you can see the SQL statements that Core Data uses under the hood to talk to the data store.

Even if you have no idea of how to speak SQL, this is still valuable information. At least you can use it to tell whether Core Data is doing something or not. To enable this tool, you have to edit the project's scheme.

Schemes are how Xcode lets you configure your projects. A scheme is a bunch of settings for building and running your app. Standard projects have just one scheme but you can add additional schemes, which is handy when your project becomes bigger.

➤ Click on the left part of **MyLocations** > **iPhone** bar at the top of the screen and choose Edit Scheme... from the menu.

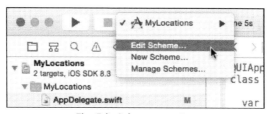

The Edit Scheme... option

The following screen should pop up:

The scheme editor

➤ Click the **Run** option on the left-hand side.

➤ Make sure the **Arguments** tab is selected.

➤ In the **Arguments Passed On Launch** section, add the following:

```
-com.apple.CoreData.SQLDebug 1
```

Adding the SQLDebug argument

➤ Press **Close** to close this dialog, and run the app.

When it starts, you should see something like this in the debug area:

```
CoreData: annotation: Connecting to sqlite database file at
"/Users/matthijs/Library/Developer/CoreSimulator/Devices/078E984C-869F-4B9D-BA79-
521A9ACE6B04/data/Containers/Data/Application/355C1E7A-CA9B-4E1F-8D44-
DF2ABD6856BE/Documents/DataStore.sqlite"

CoreData: sql: SELECT TBL_NAME FROM SQLITE_MASTER WHERE TBL_NAME = 'Z_METADATA'
```

```
CoreData: sql: pragma journal_mode=wal

CoreData: sql: pragma cache_size=200

CoreData: sql: SELECT Z_VERSION, Z_UUID, Z_PLIST FROM Z_METADATA
```

This is the debug output from Core Data. If you speak SQL, some of this will look familiar. The specifics don't matter, but it's clear that Core Data is connecting to the data store at this point. Excellent!

Saving the locations

You've successfully initialized Core Data and passed the NSManagedObjectContext to the Tag Location screen. Now it's time to make that screen put a new Location object into the data store when the Done button is pressed.

➤ Add the following instance variable to **LocationDetailsViewController.swift**:

```
var date = NSDate()
```

You're adding this variable because you need to store the current date in the new Location object.

➤ In viewDidLoad(), change the line that sets the dateLabel's text to:

```
dateLabel.text = formatDate(date)
```

➤ Change the done() method to the following:

```
@IBAction func done() {
  let hudView = HudView.hudInView(navigationController!.view, animated: true)
  hudView.text = "Tagged"

  // 1
  let location = NSEntityDescription.insertNewObjectForEntityForName("Location",
                             inManagedObjectContext: managedObjectContext) as! Location

  // 2
  location.locationDescription = descriptionText
  location.category = categoryName
  location.latitude = coordinate.latitude
  location.longitude = coordinate.longitude
  location.date = date
  location.placemark = placemark

  // 3
  var error: NSError?
  if !managedObjectContext.save(&error) {
    println("Error: \(error)")
    abort()
  }

  afterDelay(0.6) {
    self.dismissViewControllerAnimated(true, completion: nil)
  }
}
```

This is where you do all the work:

1. First, you create a new Location object. This is different from how you created objects before. If Location were a regular NSObject, you'd write Location() to create a new instance. However, this is a Core Data managed object, and they are created in a different manner.

You have to ask the NSEntityDescription class to insert a new object for your entity into the managed object context. It's a bit of a weird way to make new objects but that's how you do it in Core Data. The string "Location" is the name of the entity that you added in the data model earlier.

2. Once you have created the Location object, you can use it like any other object. Here you set its properties to whatever the user entered in the screen.

3. You now have a new Location object whose properties are all filled in, but if you were to look in the data store at this point you'd still see no objects there. That won't happen until you save the context.

Saving takes any objects that were added to the context, or any managed objects that had their contents changed, and permanently writes these changes into the data store. That's why they call the context the "scratchpad"; its changes aren't persisted until you save them.

NSError and &

The save() method takes a parameter, &error. The & ampersand character means that save() will put the results of the operation into an NSError object and then places that object into the error variable. This is sometimes called an *output parameter* or *pass-by-reference*.

Most of the time, parameters are used to send data into a method but an output parameter works the other way around.

This is really another holdover from Objective-C where methods can only return one value. Usually that is enough, but sometimes you want to return more than one value to the caller. In that case, you can use an output parameter.

Swift methods can return more than one value in the form of a so-called *tuple*. But Core Data, like the other iOS frameworks, is written in Objective-C and therefore can't use any of these fancy new Swift features.

The save() method returns a Bool to indicate whether the operation was successful or not. If not, then it also fills up the NSError object with additional error information. This is a pattern that you see a lot in the iOS SDK.

Because error can be nil – meaning no error occurred – it needs to be declared as an optional.

The important thing is to not forget the & or Xcode will give cryptic error messages such as: "Cannot convert the expression's type to NSErrorPointer". What Xcode really means to say is: You forgot the &, dummy!

➤ Run the app and tag a location. Enter a description and press the Done button.

If everything went well, Core Data will dump a whole bunch of debug information into the debug area:

```
CoreData: sql: BEGIN EXCLUSIVE
. . .
CoreData: sql: INSERT INTO ZLOCATION(Z_PK, Z_ENT, Z_OPT, ZCATEGORY, ZDATE, ZLATITUDE,
ZLOCATIONDESCRIPTION, ZLONGITUDE, ZPLACEMARK) VALUES(?, ?, ?, ?, ?, ?, ?, ?, ?)
CoreData: sql: COMMIT
. . .
CoreData: annotation: sql execution time: 0.0001s
```

These are the SQL statements that Core Data performs to store the new Location object in the database.

➤ If you have Liya open, then refresh the contents of the ZLOCATION table (press the Go button). There should now be one row in that table:

A new row was added to the table

(If you don't see any rows in the table, press the Stop button in Xcode first to exit the app. You can also try closing the Liya window and opening a new connection to the database.)

As you can see, the columns in this table contain the property values from the Location object. The only column that is not readable is ZPLACEMARK. Its contents have been encoded as a binary "blob" of data. That is because it's a Transformable attribute and the NSCoding protocol has converted its fields into a binary chunk of data.

If you don't have Liya or are a command line junkie, then there is another way to examine the contents of the database. You can use the Terminal app and the sqlite3 tool, but you'd better know your SQL's from your ABC's:

```
● ● ●                    Documents — bash — 104×21
$ cd /Users/matthijs/Library/Developer/CoreSimulator/Devices/078E984C-869F-4B9D-BA79-521A9ACE6804/data/C
ontainers/Data/Application/7F8E6078-EF95-41C1-8BD8-5280314ED9FD/Documents
$ sqlite3 DataStore.sqlite
SQLite version 3.8.5 2014-08-15 22:37:57
Enter ".help" for usage hints.
sqlite> select * from ZLOCATION;
1|1|1|433436327.353462|37.33165083|-122.03029752|Apple Store|Apple HQ|bplist00???X$versionX$objectsY$arc
hiverT$top
sqlite> .q
$ ▮
```

Examining the database from the Terminal

Handling Core Data errors

To save the contents of the context to the data store, you did:

```
var error: NSError?
if !managedObjectContext.save(&error) {
  println("Error: \(error)")
  abort()
}
```

What if something goes wrong with the save? In that case, the save() method returns false and you call abort(). True to its name, the abort() function will immediately kill the app and return the user to the iPhone's Springboard. That's a nasty surprise for the user, and therefore not recommended.

The good news is that Core Data only gives an error if you're trying to save something that is not valid. In other words, when there is some bug in your app.

Of course, you'll get all the bugs out during development so users will never experience any, right? The sad truth is that you'll never catch all your bugs. Some always manage to slip through.

The bad news is that there isn't much else to do but crash when Core Data does give an error. Something went horribly wrong somewhere and now you're stuck with invalid data. If the app were allowed to continue, things would likely only get worse, as there is no telling what state the app is in. The last thing you want to do is to corrupt the user's data.

Instead of making the app crash hard with abort(), it will be nice to tell the user about it first so at least they know what is happening. The crash is still inevitable, but now your users will know why the app suddenly stopped working.

In this section, you'll add a popup alert for handling such situations. Again, these errors should happen only during development, but just in case they do occur to an actual user, you'll try to handle it with at least a little bit of grace.

Here's a way to fake such a fatal error, just to illustrate what happens.

➤ Open the data model (**DataModel.xcdatamodeld** in the file list), and select the **placemark** attribute. In the inspector, uncheck the **Optional** flag.

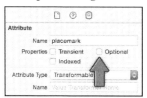

Making the placemark attribute non-optional

That means location.placemark may never be nil. This is a constraint that Core Data will enforce. When you try to save a Location object to the data store whose placemark property is nil, then Core Data will throw a tantrum. So that's exactly what you're going to do here.

➤ Run the app. Whoops, it crashes right away.

The app crashed in the initializer block for managedObjectContext from AppDelegate. The debug area says why:

```
. . . reason = "The model used to open the store is incompatible with the one used to create
the store";
```

You have just changed the data model by making changes to the placemark attribute. But these changes were only made to the data model inside the application bundle, not to the data store that is in the Documents folder.

The DataStore.sqlite file is now out of date with respect to the changed data model.

There are two ways to fix this: 1) simply throw away the DataStore.sqlite file from the Documents directory; 2) remove the entire app from the Simulator.

➤ Remove the DataStore.sqlite file, as well as the –shm and –wal files, and run the app again.

This wasn't actually the crash I wanted to show you, but it's important to know that changing the data model requires you to throw away the database file or Core Data cannot be initialized properly.

> **Note:** There is a migration mechanism in Core Data that is useful for when you release an update to your app with a new data model.
>
> Instead of crashing, this mechanism allows you to convert the contents of the user's existing data store to the new format. However, when developing it's just as easy to toss out the old database.
>
> If you're interested in learning more about Core Data migrations, then check out the following online tutorial: http://www.raywenderlich.com/27657/how-to-perform-a-lightweight-core-data-migration

➤ Now here's the trick. Tap the Get My Location button and then tap immediately on Tag Location. If you do that quickly enough, you can beat the reverse geocoder to it and the Tag Location screen will say: "No Address Found". It only says that when placemark is nil.

(If geocoding happens too fast for you, then you can also temporarily comment out the line self.placemark = placemarks.last in locationManager(didUpdateLocations) inside **CurrentLocationViewController.swift**. This will make it seem no address was found.)

➤ Tap the Done button to save the new Location object.

The app will crash on the call to abort():

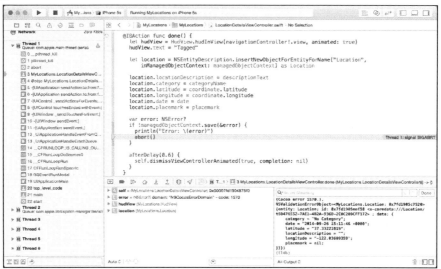

The app crashes after a Core Data error

In the debug area, you can see that it says:

```
The operation couldn't be completed . . . NSValidationErrorKey=placemark
```

This means the placemark attribute did not validate properly. Because you set it to non-optional, Core Data does not accept a placemark value that is nil.

This is what happens when you run the app from within Xcode. When it crashes, the debugger takes over and points at the line with the error. But that's not what the user sees.

➤ Stop the app. Now tap the app's icon in the Simulator to launch the app outside of Xcode. Repeat the same procedure to make the app crash. The app will simply cease functioning and disappear from the screen.

Imagine this happening to a user who just paid 99 cents (or more) for your app. They'll be horribly confused, "What just happened?!" They may even ask for their money back.

It's better to show an alert when this happens. After the user dismisses that alert, you'll still make the app crash, but at least the user knows the reason why. (The alert message should probably ask them to contact you and explain what they did, so you can fix that bug in the next version of your app.)

➤ At the top of **AppDelegate.swift**, directly below the import for Core Data, add the following code:

```
let MyManagedObjectContextSaveDidFailNotification =
                      "MyManagedObjectContextSaveDidFailNotification"

func fatalCoreDataError(error: NSError?) {
  if let error = error {
    println("*** Fatal error: \(error), \(error.userInfo)")
  }
  NSNotificationCenter.defaultCenter().postNotificationName(
                      MyManagedObjectContextSaveDidFailNotification, object: error)
}
```

This defines a new global function for handling fatal Core Data errors. More about how this works in sec.

➤ Replace the error handling code in the done() action with:

```
var error: NSError?
if !managedObjectContext.save(&error) {
  fatalCoreDataError(error)
  return
}
```

The call to fatalCoreDataError() has taken the place of println() and abort(). So what does that function do, actually?

It first outputs the error message to the Debug Area using println():

```
  if let error = error {
    println("*** Fatal error: \(error), \(error.userInfo)")
  }
```

This is not very different from what you did before, except that it makes sure error is not nil.

It is unlikely, but possible, that this function is called without a proper NSError object, which is why the error parameter has type NSError?.

After dumping the debug info, the function does the following:

```
NSNotificationCenter.defaultCenter().postNotificationName(
                    MyManagedObjectContextSaveDidFailNotification, object: error)
```

I've been using the term "notification" to mean any generic event or message being delivered, but iOS also has an object called the NSNotificationCenter (not to be confused with Notification Center on your phone).

The code above uses NSNotificationCenter to post a notification. Any object in your app can subscribe to such notifications and when these occur, NSNotificationCenter will call a certain method on those listener objects.

Using this official notification system is yet another way that your objects can communicate with each other. The handy thing is that the object that sends the notification and the object that receives the notification don't need to know anything about each other.

UIKit defines a lot of standard notifications that you can subscribe to. For example, there is a notification that lets you know that the app is about to be suspended when the user taps the Home button.

You can also define your own notifications, and that is what you've done here. The new notification is called MyManagedObjectContextSaveDidFailNotification.

The idea is that there is one place in the app that listens for this notification, pops up an alert view, and aborts. The great thing about using NSNotificationCenter is that your Core Data code does not need to care about any of this.

Whenever a saving error occurs, no matter at which point in the app, the fatalCoreDataError() function sends out this notification, safe in the belief that some other object is listening for the notification and will handle the error.

So who will handle the error? The app delegate is a good place for that. It's the top-level object in the app and you're always guaranteed this object exists.

➤ Add the following methods to **AppDelegate.swift**. Unlike fatalCoreDataError(), which is a global function, these go inside the class AppDelegate brackets:

```
func listenForFatalCoreDataNotifications() {
  // 1
  NSNotificationCenter.defaultCenter().addObserverForName(
    MyManagedObjectContextSaveDidFailNotification, object: nil,
    queue: NSOperationQueue.mainQueue(), usingBlock: { notification in
    // 2
    let alert = UIAlertController(title: "Internal Error", message:
        "There was a fatal error in the app and it cannot continue.\n\n"
      + "Press OK to terminate the app. Sorry for the inconvenience.",
        preferredStyle: .Alert)
    // 3
    let action = UIAlertAction(title: "OK", style: .Default) { _ in
      let exception = NSException(name: NSInternalInconsistencyException,
                          reason: "Fatal Core Data error", userInfo: nil)
      exception.raise()
    }
    alert.addAction(action)
```

```
  // 4
  self.viewControllerForShowingAlert().presentViewController(
                                       alert, animated: true, completion: nil)
  })
}
// 5
func viewControllerForShowingAlert() -> UIViewController {
  let rootViewController = self.window!.rootViewController!
  if let presentedViewController = rootViewController.presentedViewController {
    return presentedViewController
  } else {
    return rootViewController
  }
}
```

Here's how this works step-by-step:

1. Tell NSNotificationCenter that you want to be notified whenever a
   MyManagedObjectContextSaveDidFailNotification is posted. The actual code that is performed
   when that happens sits in a closure following usingBlock:.

   This closure has one parameter, notification, containing an NSNotification object. This object
   is not used anywhere inside the closure, so you could also have written: "_ in" to tell Swift you
   want to ignore the parameter. The _ is called the **wildcard** and you can use it whenever a name
   is expected but you don't really care about it.

2. Create a UIAlertController to show the error message.

3. Add an action for the alert's OK button. The code for handling the button press is again a
   closure (these things are everywhere!). Instead of calling abort(), the closure creates an
   NSException object. That's a bit nicer and it provides more information to the crash log. Note
   that this closure also uses the _ wildcard to ignore its parameter.

4. Finally, you present the alert.

5. To show the alert with presentViewController(animated, completion) you need a view
   controller that is currently visible, so this helper method finds one that is. Unfortunately you
   can't simply use the window's rootViewController – in this app that is the tab bar controller –
   because it will be hidden when the Location Details screen is open.

All that remains is calling this new listenForFatalCoreDataNotifications() method so that the
notification handler is registered with NSNotificationCenter.

➤ Add the following to application(didFinishLaunchingWithOptions), just before the return true
statement:

```
listenForFatalCoreDataNotifications()
```

➤ Run the app again and try to tag a location before the street address has been obtained. Now before the app crashes, at least it tells the user what's going on:

The app crashes with a message

Again, I should stress that you test your app very well to make sure you're not giving Core Data any objects that do not validate. You want to avoid these save errors at all costs!

Ideally, users should never have to see that alert view, but it's good to have it in place because there are no guarantees your app won't have bugs.

> **Note:** You can legitimately use `managedObjectContext.save()` to let Core Data validate user input. There is no requirement that you make your app crash after an unsuccessful save, only if the error was unexpected and definitely shouldn't have happened!
>
> Besides the "optional" flag, there are many more validation settings you can put on the attributes of your entities. If you let the user of your app enter data that needs to go into these attributes, then it's perfectly acceptable to use `save()` to perform the validation. If it returns `false`, then there was an error in whatever value the user entered and you should handle it.

➤ In the data model, set the **placemark** attribute back to optional. Remember to throw away the DataStore.sqlite files again!

Run the app just to make sure everything works as it should.

(If you commented out the line in `locationManager(didUpdateLocations)` to fake the error, then put that line back in.)

You can find the project files for the app up to this point under **03 - Core Data** in the tutorial's Source Code folder.

The Locations tab

You've set up the data model and gave the app the ability to save new locations to the data store. Now you'll show those locations in a table view in the second tab.

➤ Open the storyboard editor and delete the **Second Scene**. This is a leftover from the project template and you don't need it.

➤ Drag a new **Navigation Controller** into the canvas. (This has a table view controller attached to it, which is fine. You'll use that in a second.)

➤ **Ctrl-drag** from the Tab Bar Controller to this new Navigation Controller and select **Relationship Segue - view controllers**. This adds the navigation controller to the tab bar.

➤ The Navigation Controller now has a **Tab Bar Item** that is named "Item". Rename it to **Locations**.

➤ Double-click the navigation bar of the Root View Controller (the one attached to the new Navigation Controller) and change the title to **Locations**.

➤ In the **Identity inspector**, change the **Class** of this table view controller to **LocationsViewController**. This class doesn't exist yet but you'll make it in a minute.

The storyboard now looks like this:

The storyboard after adding the Locations screen

➤ Run the app and tap the Locations tab. It doesn't look very interesting yet:

The Locations screen in the second tab

Before you can show any data in the table, you first have to design the prototype cell.

> Set the prototype cell's Reuse Identifier to **LocationCell**.

> In the **Size inspector**, change **Row Height** to 57.

> Drag two **Labels** into the cell. Give the top one the text **Description** and the bottom one the text **Address**. This is just so you know what they are for.

> Set the font of the Description label to **System Bold**, size **17**. Give this label a tag of 100.

> Set the font of the Address label to **System**, size **14**. Set the Text color to black with 50% opacity (so its looks like a medium gray). Give it a tag of 101.

The cell will look something like this:

The prototype cell

Make sure that the labels are wide enough to span the entire cell.

Just changing the Row Height of the prototype cell isn't enough; you also have to tell the table view about the height of its rows.

> Select the table view and go to the **Size inspector**. Set the **Row Height** field to 57:

Setting the row height on the table view

Let's write the code for the view controller. You've seen table view controllers several times now, so this should be easy.

You're going to fake the content first, because it's a good idea to make sure that the prototype cell works before you have to deal with Core Data.

➤ Add a new file to the project and name it **LocationsViewController.swift**.

Tip: If you want to keep your list of source files neatly sorted by name in the project navigator, then right-click the MyLocations group (the yellow folder icon) and choose **Sort by Name** from the menu.

➤ Change the contents of **LocationsViewController.swift** to:

```swift
import UIKit
import CoreData
import CoreLocation

class LocationsViewController: UITableViewController {

  var managedObjectContext: NSManagedObjectContext!

  // MARK: - UITableViewDataSource

  override func tableView(tableView: UITableView,
                          numberOfRowsInSection section: Int) -> Int {
    return 1
  }

  override func tableView(tableView: UITableView,
                          cellForRowAtIndexPath indexPath: NSIndexPath) -> UITableViewCell {
    let cell = tableView.dequeueReusableCellWithIdentifier("LocationCell")
                        as! UITableViewCell

    let descriptionLabel = cell.viewWithTag(100) as! UILabel
    descriptionLabel.text = "If you can see this"

    let addressLabel = cell.viewWithTag(101) as! UILabel
    addressLabel.text = "Then it works!"

    return cell
  }
}
```

You're faking a single row with some placeholder text in the labels. You're also already giving this class an NSManagedObjectContext property even though you won't be using it yet.

➤ Run the app to make sure the table view works.

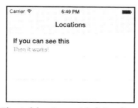

The table view with fake data

(If the table view remains empty, then go back to the storyboard. In the **Identity inspector**, remove the text from the **Class** field for the table view controller. Press ⌘+S to save the changes.

Then put Class back to **LocationsViewController** and run the app again. Chalk it up to another bug in Xcode.)

Excellent. Now it's time to fill up the table with the `Location` objects from the data store.

➤ Run the app and tag a handful of locations. If there is no data in the data store, then the app doesn't have much to show...

This part of the app doesn't know anything yet about the `Location` objects that you have added to the data store. In order to display them in the table view, you need to obtain references to these objects somehow. You can do that by asking the data store. This is called **fetching**.

➤ First, add a new instance variable to **LocationsViewController.swift**:

```
var locations = [Location]()
```

This array contains the list of `Location` objects.

➤ Add the `viewDidLoad()` method:

```
override func viewDidLoad() {
  super.viewDidLoad()
  // 1
  let fetchRequest = NSFetchRequest()
  // 2
  let entity = NSEntityDescription.entityForName("Location",
                          inManagedObjectContext: managedObjectContext)
  fetchRequest.entity = entity
  // 3
  let sortDescriptor = NSSortDescriptor(key: "date", ascending: true)
  fetchRequest.sortDescriptors = [sortDescriptor]
  // 4
  var error: NSError?
  let foundObjects = managedObjectContext.executeFetchRequest(fetchRequest, error: &error)
  if foundObjects == nil {
    fatalCoreDataError(error)
    return
  }
  // 5
  locations = foundObjects as! [Location]
}
```

This may look daunting but it's actually quite simple. You're going to ask the managed object context for a list of all `Location` objects in the data store, sorted by date.

1. The `NSFetchRequest` is the object that describes which objects you're going to fetch from the data store. To retrieve an object that you previously saved to the data store, you create a fetch request that describes the search parameters of the object – or multiple objects – that you're looking for.

2. The `NSEntityDescription` tells the fetch request you're looking for `Location` entities.

3. The `NSSortDescriptor` tells the fetch request to sort on the date attribute, in ascending order. In order words, the `Location` objects that the user added first will be at the top of the list. You can sort on any attribute here (later in this tutorial you'll sort on the `Location`'s category as well).

That completes the fetch request. It took a few lines of code, but basically you said: "Get all `Location` objects from the data store and sort them by date."

4. Now that you have the fetch request, you can tell the context to execute it. The `executeFetchRequest()` method returns an array with the sorted objects, or `nil` in case of an error.

5. If everything went well, you assign the contents of the `foundObjects` array to the `locations` instance variable, casting it from an array of `AnyObjects` to `Locations`.

Now that you've loaded the list of `Location` objects into an instance variable, you can change the table view's data source methods.

➤ Change the data source methods to:

```
override func tableView(tableView: UITableView, numberOfRowsInSection section: Int) -> Int {
  return locations.count
}
```

```
override func tableView(tableView: UITableView,
                    cellForRowAtIndexPath indexPath: NSIndexPath) -> UITableViewCell {
  let cell = tableView.dequeueReusableCellWithIdentifier("LocationCell") as! UITableViewCell

  let location = locations[indexPath.row]

  let descriptionLabel = cell.viewWithTag(100) as! UILabel
  descriptionLabel.text = location.locationDescription

  let addressLabel = cell.viewWithTag(101) as! UILabel
  if let placemark = location.placemark {
    addressLabel.text =
          "\(placemark.subThoroughfare) \(placemark.thoroughfare), \(placemark.locality)"
  } else {
    addressLabel.text = ""
  }

  return cell
}
```

This should have no surprises for you. You get the `Location` object for the row from the array and then use its properties to fill up the labels. Because `placemark` is an optional, you use `if let` to unwrap it.

➤ Run the app. Now switch to the Locations tab and... crap! It crashes.

The text in the debug area says something like:

```
fatal error: unexpectedly found nil while unwrapping an Optional value
```

Exercise. What did you forget? ∎

Answer: You added a `managedObjectContext` property to `LocationsViewController`, but never gave this property a value. Therefore, there is nothing to fetch Location objects from.

➤ Switch to **AppDelegate.swift**. In `application(didFinishLaunchingWithOptions)`, inside the `if let` block, add the following:

```
let navigationController = tabBarViewControllers[1] as! UINavigationController
let locationsViewController = navigationController.viewControllers[0]
                                    as! LocationsViewController
locationsViewController.managedObjectContext = managedObjectContext
```

This looks up the `LocationsViewController` in the storyboard and gives it a reference to the managed object context.

➤ Run the app again and switch to the Locations tab. Core Data properly fetches the objects and shows them on the screen:

The list of Locations

Note that the list doesn't update yet if you tag a new location. You have to restart the app to see the new `Location` object appear. You'll solve this later in the tutorial.

Creating a custom Table View Cell subclass

Using `cell.viewWithTag(xxx)` to find the labels from the table view cell works, but it doesn't look very object-oriented to me.

It would be much nicer if you could make your own `UITableViewCell` subclass and give it outlets for the labels. Fortunately, you can and it's pretty easy!

➤ Add a new file to the project using the **Cocoa Touch Class** template. Name it **LocationCell** and make it a subclass of **UITableViewCell.**

➤ Replace the contents of **LocationCell.swift** with the following:

```swift
import UIKit

class LocationCell: UITableViewCell {
  @IBOutlet weak var descriptionLabel: UILabel!
  @IBOutlet weak var addressLabel: UILabel!
}
```

➤ Open the storyboard and select the prototype cell that you made earlier. In the **Identity inspector**, set **Class** to **LocationCell.**

➤ Now you can connect the two labels to the two outlets. This time the outlets are not on the view controller but on the cell, so **Ctrl-drag** from the cell to the labels:

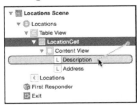

Connect the outlets to the cell

That is all you need to do to make the table view use your own table view cell class. You do need to update locationsViewController to make use of it.

➤ In **LocationsViewController.swift**, replace tableView(cellForRowAtIndexPath) with the following:

```
override func tableView(tableView: UITableView,
                      cellForRowAtIndexPath indexPath: NSIndexPath) -> UITableViewCell {
  let cell = tableView.dequeueReusableCellWithIdentifier("LocationCell") as! LocationCell

  let location = locations[indexPath.row]
  cell.configureForLocation(location)
  return cell
}
```

As before, this asks for a cell using dequeueReusableCellWithIdentifier, but now this will always be a LocationCell object instead of a regular UITableViewCell.

Note that "LocationCell" is the re-use identifier from the placeholder cell, but LocationCell is the class of the actual cell object that you're getting. They have the same name but one is a String and the other is a UITableViewCell subclass with extra properties. I hope that's not too confusing.

Once you have the cell reference, you call a new method, configureForLocation() to put the Location object into the table view cell.

➤ Add this new method to **LocationCell.swift**:

```
func configureForLocation(location: Location) {
  if location.locationDescription.isEmpty {
    descriptionLabel.text = "(No Description)"
  } else {
    descriptionLabel.text = location.locationDescription
  }

  if let placemark = location.placemark {
    addressLabel.text =
      "\(placemark.subThoroughfare) \(placemark.thoroughfare), \(placemark.locality)"
  } else {
    addressLabel.text = String(format: "Lat: %.8f, Long: %.8f", location.latitude,
                               location.longitude)
  }
}
```

Instead of using viewWithTag() to find the description and address labels, you now simply use the descriptionLabel and addressLabel properties of the cell.

➤ Run the app to make sure everything still works. If you have a location without a description the table cell will now say "(No Description)". If there is no placemark, the address label contains the GPS coordinates.

Using a custom subclass for your table view cells, there is no limit to how complex you can make them.

Editing the locations

You will now connect the LocationsViewController to the Location Details screen, so that when you tap a row in the table, it opens a screen that lets you edit that location.

You'll be re-using the `LocationDetailsViewController` for that, but have it edit an existing `Location` object rather than add a new one.

➤ Go to the storyboard. Select the prototype cell (the one with the "Description" and "Address" labels) and **Ctrl-drag** to the Navigation Controller that is connected to the Location Details screen. Add a **modal** segue and name it **EditLocation**.

After a bit of tidying up, the storyboard looks like this:

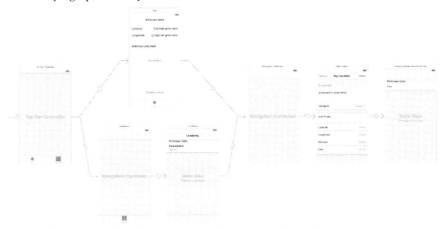

The Location Details screen is now also connected to the Locations screen

There are now two segues from two different screens going to the same view controller.

This is the reason why you should build your view controllers to be as independent of their "calling" controllers as possible, so that you can easily re-use them somewhere else in your app.

Soon you will be calling this same screen from yet another place. In total there will be three segues to it.

➤ Go to **LocationsViewController.swift** and add the `prepareForSegue()` method:

```
override func prepareForSegue(segue: UIStoryboardSegue, sender: AnyObject?) {
  if segue.identifier == "EditLocation" {
    let navigationController = segue.destinationViewController as! UINavigationController
    let controller = navigationController.topViewController
                                  as! LocationDetailsViewController
    controller.managedObjectContext = managedObjectContext

    if let indexPath = tableView.indexPathForCell(sender as! UITableViewCell) {
      let location = locations[indexPath.row]
      controller.locationToEdit = location
    }
  }
}
```

This method is invoked when the user taps a row in the Locations screen. It figures out which `Location` object belongs to this row and then puts it in the new `locationToEdit` property of `LocationDetailsViewController`. This property doesn't exist yet but you'll add it in a moment.

Note that you have to cast sender to UITableViewCell. The sender parameter from prepareForSegue(sender) is of type AnyObject, but indexPathForCell() expects a UITableViewCell object instead.

You and I both know that sender in this case really is a UITableViewCell because the only way to trigger this segue is to tap a table view cell. The cast tells Swift that it can safely interpret sender as a UITableViewCell.

(Of course, if you were to hook up this segue to something else, such as a button, then this assumption is no longer valid and the app will crash.)

When editing an existing Location object, you have to do a few things differently in the LocationDetailsViewController. The title of the screen shouldn't be "Tag Location" but "Edit Location". You also must put the values from the existing Location object into the various cells.

The value of the new locationToEdit property determines whether the screen operates in "adding" mode or in "editing" mode.

➤ Add this property to **LocationDetailsViewController.swift**:

```
var locationToEdit: Location?
```

This needs to be an optional because in "adding" mode it will be nil. That's how the LocationDetailsViewController tells the difference.

➤ Expand viewDidLoad() to check whether locationToEdit is set:

```
override func viewDidLoad() {
  super.viewDidLoad()

  if let location = locationToEdit {
    title = "Edit Location"
  }
  . . .
}
```

If locationToEdit is not nil, you're editing an existing Location object. In that case, the title of the screen becomes "Edit Location".

Now how do you get the values from that Location object into the text view and labels of this view controller? Swift has a really cool **property observer** feature that is perfect for this.

➤ Change the declaration of the locationToEdit property to the following:

```
var locationToEdit: Location? {
  didSet {
    if let location = locationToEdit {
      descriptionText = location.locationDescription
      categoryName = location.category
      date = location.date
      coordinate = CLLocationCoordinate2DMake(location.latitude, location.longitude)
      placemark = location.placemark
    }
  }
}
```

If a variable has a didSet block, then the code in this block is performed whenever you put a new value into the variable. Very handy!

Here, you take the opportunity to fill in the view controller's instance variables with the `Location` object's values.

Because `prepareForSegue()` – and therefore `locationToEdit`'s `didSet` – is called before `viewDidLoad()`, this puts the right values on the screen when it becomes visible.

➤ Run the app, go to the Locations tab and tap on a row. The Edit Location screen should now appear with the data from the selected location:

Editing an existing location

➤ Change the description of the location and press Done.

Nothing happened?! Well, that's not quite true. Stop the app and run it again. You will see that a new location has been added with the changed description, but the old one is still there as well.

There are two problems to solve:

1. when editing an existing location you must not insert a new one, and

2. the screen doesn't update to reflect any changes in the data model.

The first fix is easy.

➤ Still in **LocationDetailsViewController.swift**, change the top part of `done()`:

```
@IBAction func done() {
  let hudView = HudView.hudInView(navigationController!.view, animated: true)
  var location: Location
  if let temp = locationToEdit {
    hudView.text = "Updated"
    location = temp
  } else {
    hudView.text = "Tagged"
    location = NSEntityDescription.insertNewObjectForEntityForName("Location",
                            inManagedObjectContext: managedObjectContext) as! Location
  }

  location.locationDescription = descriptionText
  . . .
```

The change is very straightforward: you only ask Core Data for a new `Location` object if you don't already have one. You also make the text in the HUD say "Updated" when the user is editing an existing `Location`.

> **Note:** I've been harping on about the fact that Swift requires all non-optional variables to always have a value. But here you declare the local variable `location` without giving it an initial value. What gives?
>
> Well, the if-statement that follows this declaration always puts a value into `location`, either the unwrapped value of `locationToEdit`, or a new `Location` object obtained from Core Data. After the if-statement, `location` is guaranteed to have a value. Swift is cool with that.

➤ Run the app again and edit a location. Now the HUD should say "Updated".

➤ Stop the app and run it again to verify that the object was indeed properly changed. (You can also look at it directly in the SQLite database, of course.)

Exercise. Why do you think the table view isn't being updated after you change a `Location` object? Tip: Recall that the table view also doesn't update when you tag new locations. ■

Answer: You fetch the `Location` objects in `viewDidLoad()`. But `viewDidLoad()` is only performed once, when the app starts. After the initial load of the Locations screen, its contents are never refreshed.

In the Checklists app, you solved this by using a delegate, and that would be a valid solution here too. The `LocationDetailsViewController` could tell you through delegate methods that a location has been added or changed. But since you're using Core Data, there is a much cooler way to do this, and that's the topic of the next section.

Using NSFetchedResultsController

As you are no doubt aware by now, table views are everywhere in iOS apps. A lot of the time when you're working with Core Data, you want to fetch objects from the data store and show them in a table view.

And when those objects change, you want to live update the table view in response to show the changes to the user.

So far you've filled up the table view by manually fetching the results, but then you also need to manually check for changes and perform the fetch again to update the table. Thanks to `NSFetchedResultsController`, that suddenly becomes a lot easier.

It works like this: you give `NSFetchedResultsController` a fetch request, just like the `NSFetchRequest` you've made earlier, and tell it to go fetch the objects. So far nothing new.

But you don't put the results from that fetch into your own array. Instead, you read them straight from the fetched results controller. In addition, you make the view controller the delegate for the `NSFetchedResultsController`.

Through this delegate the view controller is informed that objects have been changed, added or deleted. In response it should update the table.

➤ In **LocationsViewController.swift**, replace the `locations` instance variable with the new `fetchedResultsController` variable:

```
lazy var fetchedResultsController: NSFetchedResultsController = {
  let fetchRequest = NSFetchRequest()
```

```
    let entity = NSEntityDescription.entityForName("Location",
                                  inManagedObjectContext: self.managedObjectContext)
    fetchRequest.entity = entity

    let sortDescriptor = NSSortDescriptor(key: "date", ascending: true)
    fetchRequest.sortDescriptors = [sortDescriptor]

    fetchRequest.fetchBatchSize = 20

    let fetchedResultsController = NSFetchedResultsController(
      fetchRequest: fetchRequest, managedObjectContext: self.managedObjectContext,
      sectionNameKeyPath: nil, cacheName: "Locations")

    fetchedResultsController.delegate = self
    return fetchedResultsController
}()
```

This again uses the lazy initialization pattern with a closure that sets everything up. It's good to get into the habit of lazily loading objects. You don't allocate them until you first use them. This makes your apps quicker to start and it saves memory.

The code in the closure does the same thing that you used to do in viewDidLoad(): it makes an NSFetchRequest and gives it an entity description and a sort descriptor.

> **Note:** One small difference is that you need to use self here to access the managedObjectContext variable. You're inside a closure, after all.

This is new:

```
fetchRequest.fetchBatchSize = 20
```

If you have a huge table with hundreds of objects then it requires a lot of memory to keep all of these objects around, even though you can only see a handful of them at a time.

The NSFetchedResultsController is pretty smart about this and will only fetch the objects that you can actually see, which cuts down on memory usage. This is all done in the background without you having to worry about it.

The fetch batch size setting allows you to tweak how many objects will be fetched at a time.

Once the fetch request is set up, you can create the star of the show:

```
let fetchedResultsController = NSFetchedResultsController(
  fetchRequest: fetchRequest, managedObjectContext: self.managedObjectContext,
  sectionNameKeyPath: nil, cacheName: "Locations")
```

The cacheName needs to be a unique name that NSFetchedResultsController uses to cache the search results. It keeps this cache around even after your app quits, so the next time the fetch request is lightning fast, as the NSFetchedResultsController doesn't have to make a round-trip to the database but can simply read from the cache.

We'll talk about the sectionNameKeyPath parameter shortly.

The line that sets fetchedResultsController.delegate to self gives an error message because LocationsViewController does not conform to the right delegate protocol yet. You'll fix that in minute.

Now that you have a fetched results controller, you can simplify viewDidLoad().

➤ Change `viewDidLoad()` to:

```
override func viewDidLoad() {
  super.viewDidLoad()
  performFetch()
}

func performFetch() {
  var error: NSError?
  if !fetchedResultsController.performFetch(&error) {
    fatalCoreDataError(error)
  }
}
```

You still perform the initial fetch in `viewDidLoad()`, using the new `performFetch()` helper method. However, if any `Location` objects change after that initial fetch, the `NSFetchedResultsController`'s delegate methods are called to let you know about the changes. I'll show you in a second how that works.

It's always a good idea to explicitly set the delegate to `nil` when you no longer need the `NSFetchedResultsController`, just so you don't get any more notifications that were still pending.

➤ For that reason, add a `deinit` method:

```
deinit {
  fetchedResultsController.delegate = nil
}
```

The `deinit` method is invoked when this view controller is destroyed. It may not strictly be necessary to `nil` out the delegate here, but it's a bit of defensive programming that won't hurt. (Note that in this app the `LocationsViewController` will never actually be deallocated because it's one of the top-level view controllers in the tab bar. Still, it's good to get into the habit of writing `deinit` methods.)

Because you removed the `locations` array, you should also change the table's data source methods.

➤ Change `tableView(numberOfRowsInSection)` to:

```
override func tableView(tableView: UITableView, numberOfRowsInSection section: Int) -> Int {
  let sectionInfo = fetchedResultsController.sections![section]
                                 as! NSFetchedResultsSectionInfo
  return sectionInfo.numberOfObjects
}
```

You simply ask the fetched results controller for the number of rows and return it. You'll learn more about this `NSFetchedResultsSectionInfo` object later on.

➤ Change `tableView(cellForRowAtIndexPath)` to:

```
override func tableView(tableView: UITableView,
                    cellForRowAtIndexPath indexPath: NSIndexPath) -> UITableViewCell {
  let cell = tableView.dequeueReusableCellWithIdentifier("LocationCell") as! LocationCell

  let location = fetchedResultsController.objectAtIndexPath(indexPath) as! Location
  cell.configureForLocation(location)

  return cell
}
```

Instead of looking into the locations array, you now ask the fetchedResultsController for the object at the requested index-path. Because it is designed to work closely together with table views, NSFetchedResultsController knows how to deal with index-paths, so that's very convenient.

➤ Make the same change in prepareForSegue(sender).

There is still one piece of the puzzle missing. You need to implement the delegate methods for NSFetchedResultsController in LocationsViewController. Let's use an extension for that, to keep these methods are organized.

➤ Add the following code to the bottom of the source file, outside of the class:

```swift
extension LocationsViewController: NSFetchedResultsControllerDelegate {

  func controllerWillChangeContent(controller: NSFetchedResultsController) {
    println("*** controllerWillChangeContent")
    tableView.beginUpdates()
  }

  func controller(controller: NSFetchedResultsController,
            didChangeObject anObject: AnyObject, atIndexPath indexPath: NSIndexPath?,
            forChangeType type: NSFetchedResultsChangeType, newIndexPath: NSIndexPath?) {
    switch type {
    case .Insert:
      println("*** NSFetchedResultsChangeInsert (object)")
      tableView.insertRowsAtIndexPaths([newIndexPath!], withRowAnimation: .Fade)

    case .Delete:
      println("*** NSFetchedResultsChangeDelete (object)")
      tableView.deleteRowsAtIndexPaths([indexPath!], withRowAnimation: .Fade)

    case .Update:
      println("*** NSFetchedResultsChangeUpdate (object)")
      if let cell = tableView.cellForRowAtIndexPath(indexPath!) as? LocationCell {
        let location = controller.objectAtIndexPath(indexPath!) as! Location
        cell.configureForLocation(location)
      }

    case .Move:
      println("*** NSFetchedResultsChangeMove (object)")
      tableView.deleteRowsAtIndexPaths([indexPath!], withRowAnimation: .Fade)
      tableView.insertRowsAtIndexPaths([newIndexPath!], withRowAnimation: .Fade)
    }
  }

  func controller(controller: NSFetchedResultsController,
            didChangeSection sectionInfo: NSFetchedResultsSectionInfo,
            atIndex sectionIndex: Int, forChangeType type: NSFetchedResultsChangeType) {
    switch type {
    case .Insert:
      println("*** NSFetchedResultsChangeInsert (section)")
      tableView.insertSections(NSIndexSet(index: sectionIndex), withRowAnimation: .Fade)

    case .Delete:
      println("*** NSFetchedResultsChangeDelete (section)")
      tableView.deleteSections(NSIndexSet(index: sectionIndex), withRowAnimation: .Fade)

    case .Update:
      println("*** NSFetchedResultsChangeUpdate (section)")

    case .Move:
      println("*** NSFetchedResultsChangeMove (section)")
    }
  }
}
```

```
  func controllerDidChangeContent(controller: NSFetchedResultsController) {
    println("*** controllerDidChangeContent")
    tableView.endUpdates()
  }
}
```

Yowza, that's a lot of code. Don't let this freak you out! This is the standard way of implementing these delegate methods. For many apps, this exact code will suffice and you can simply copy it over. Look it over for a few minutes to see if this code makes sense to you. You've made it this far, so I'm sure it won't be too hard.

NSFetchedResultsController will invoke these methods to let you know that certain objects were inserted, removed, or just updated. In response, you call the corresponding methods on the UITableView to insert, remove or update rows. That's all there is to it.

I put println() statements in these methods so you can follow along in the debug area with what is happening. Also note that you're using the switch statement here. A series of if's would have worked just as well but switch reads better.

➤ Run the app. Edit an existing location and press the Done button.

The debug area now shows:

```
*** controllerWillChangeContent
*** NSFetchedResultsChangeUpdate (object)
*** controllerDidChangeContent
```

NSFetchedResultsController noticed that an existing object was updated and, through updating the table, called your cell.configureForLocation() method to redraw the contents of the cell. By the time the Edit Location screen has disappeared from sight, the table view is updated and your change will be visible.

This also works for adding new locations.

➤ Tag a new location and press the Done button.

The debug area says:

```
*** controllerWillChangeContent
*** NSFetchedResultsChangeInsert (object)
*** controllerDidChangeContent
```

This time it's an "insert" notification. The delegate methods told the table view to do insertRowsAtIndexPaths(withRowAnimation) in response and the new Location object is inserted in the table.

That's how easy it is. You make a new NSFetchedResultsController object with a fetch request and implement the delegate methods.

The fetched results controller keeps an eye on any changes that you make to the data store and notifies its delegate in response.

It doesn't matter where in the app you make these changes, they can happen on any screen. When that screen saves the changes to the managed object context, the fetched results controller picks up on them right away.

Note: There is a nasty bug with Core Data in iOS 7 that also appears to be present in iOS 8. Here is how you can reproduce it:

1. Quit the app.
2. Run the app again and tag a new location.
3. Switch to the Locations tab.

You'd expect the new location to appear in the Locations tab, but it doesn't. Instead, the app crashes as soon as you switch tabs. The error message is:

```
CoreData: FATAL ERROR: The persistent cache of section information does not match the
current configuration.  You have illegally mutated the NSFetchedResultsController's fetch
request, its predicate, or its sort descriptor without either disabling caching or using
+deleteCacheWithName:
```

This does not happen when you switch to the Locations tab *before* you tag the new location. It also does not happen on iOS 6.

There are two possible fixes:

1. You can clear out the cache of the NSFetchedResultsController. To do this, add the following line to viewDidLoad(), before the call to performFetch():

```
    NSFetchedResultsController.deleteCacheWithName("Locations")
```

2. You can force the LocationsViewController to load its view immediately when the app starts up. Without this, it delays loading the view until you switch tabs, causing Core Data to get confused. To apply this fix, add the following to application(didFinishLaunchingWithOptions), immediately below the line that sets locationsViewController.managedObjectContext:

```
    let forceTheViewToLoad = locationsViewController.view
```

If this problem also affects you, then implement one of the above solutions (my suggestion is #2). Then throw away DataStore.sqlite and run the app again. Verify that the bug no longer occurs.

iOS is pretty great but unfortunately it's not free of bugs (what software is?). If you encounter what you perceive to be a bug, then report it at https://bugreport.apple.com. Feel free to report this Core Data bug as practice. ☺

Deleting Locations

Everyone makes mistakes so it's likely that users will want to delete locations from their list at some point. This is a very easy feature to add: you just have to remove the Location object from the data store and the NSFetchedResultsController will make sure it gets dropped from the table (again, through its delegate methods).

➤ Add the following method to **LocationsViewController.swift**:

```
override func tableView(tableView: UITableView,
                  commitEditingStyle editingStyle: UITableViewCellEditingStyle,
                  forRowAtIndexPath indexPath: NSIndexPath) {
  if editingStyle == .Delete {
    let location = fetchedResultsController.objectAtIndexPath(indexPath) as! Location
    managedObjectContext.deleteObject(location)

    var error: NSError?
    if !managedObjectContext.save(&error) {
```

```
    fatalCoreDataError(error)
  }
 }
}
```

You've seen `tableView(commitEditingStyle, forRowAtIndexPath)` before. It's part of the table view's data source protocol. As soon as you implement this method in your view controller, you enable swipe-to-delete.

This method gets the `Location` object from the selected row and then tells the context to delete that object. This will trigger the `NSFetchedResultsController` to send a notification to the delegate (`NSFetchedResultsChangeDelete`), which then removes the corresponding row from the table. That's all you need to do!

➤ Run the app and remove a location using swipe-to-delete. The `Location` object is dropped from the database and its row disappears from the screen with a brief animation.

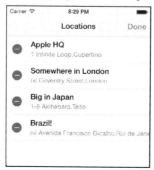

Swipe to delete rows from the table

Many apps have an Edit button in the navigation bar that triggers a mode that also lets you delete (and sometimes move) rows. This is extremely easy to add.

➤ Add the following line to `viewDidLoad()`:

```
navigationItem.rightBarButtonItem = editButtonItem()
```

That's all there is to it. Every view controller has a built-in Edit button that can be accessed through the `editButtonItem()` method. Tapping that button puts the table in editing mode:

Putting the screen into Edit mode

➤ Run the app and verify that you can now also delete rows by pressing the Edit button.

Pretty cool, huh. There's more cool stuff that NSFetchedResultsController makes really easy, such as splitting up the rows into sections.

Table view sections

The Location objects have a category field. It would be nice to group the locations by category in the table. The table view supports organizing rows into sections and each of those sections can have its own header.

Putting your rows into sections is a lot of work if you're doing it by hand, but NSFetchedResultsController practically gives you section support for free.

➤ Change the creation of the sort descriptors in the fetchedResultsController initialization block:

```
lazy var fetchedResultsController: NSFetchedResultsController = {
  . . .
  let sortDescriptor1 = NSSortDescriptor(key: "category", ascending: true)
  let sortDescriptor2 = NSSortDescriptor(key: "date", ascending: true)
  fetchRequest.sortDescriptors = [sortDescriptor1, sortDescriptor2]
  . . .
```

Instead of one sort descriptor object, you now have two. First this sorts the Location objects by category and inside each of these groups it sorts by date.

➤ Also change the initialization of the NSFetchedResultsController object:

```
let fetchedResultsController = NSFetchedResultsController(
      fetchRequest: fetchRequest, managedObjectContext: self.managedObjectContext,
      sectionNameKeyPath: "category", cacheName: "Locations")
```

The only difference here is that the sectionNameKeyPath parameter changed to "category", which means the fetched results controller will group the search results based on the value of the category attribute.

You're not done yet. The table view's data source also has methods for sections. So far you've only used the methods for rows, but now that you're adding sections to the table you need to implement a few additional methods.

➤ Add the following methods to the data source:

```
override func numberOfSectionsInTableView(tableView: UITableView) -> Int {
  return fetchedResultsController.sections!.count
}

override func tableView(tableView: UITableView,
                        titleForHeaderInSection section: Int) -> String? {
  let sectionInfo = fetchedResultsController.sections![section]
                                       as! NSFetchedResultsSectionInfo
  return sectionInfo.name
}
```

Because you let NSFetchedResultsController do all the work already, the implementation of these methods is very simple.

You ask the fetcher object for a list of the sections, which is an array of NSFetchedResultsSectionInfo objects, and then look inside that array to find out how many sections there are and what their names are.

Exercise. Why do you need to write sections! with an exclamation point? ∎

Answer: the sections property is an optional, so it needs to be unwrapped before you can use it.

Here you know for sure that sections will never be nil – after all, you just told NSFetchedResultsController to group the search results based on the value of their "category" field – so you can safely force unwrap it using the exclamation mark. Are you starting to get the hang of these optionals already?

➤ Run the app. Play with the categories on the locations and notice how the table view automatically updates. All thanks to NSFetchedResultsController!

The locations are now grouped in sections

You can find the project files for this section under **04 – Locations Tab** in the tutorial's Source Code folder.

Hierarchies

Programmers love to organize stuff into hierarchies – or **tree structures** as they like to call them.

You have to admit that the following pictures do look at bit like trees. The thing at the bottom is often called the root, all the other items are branches. Keeping with the tree analogy, the items at the very ends are known as the leaves.

There is the inheritance hierarchy of view controller classes:

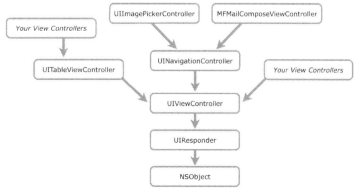

UIViewController inheritance tree (partial)

There is also an inheritance hierarchy of view classes:

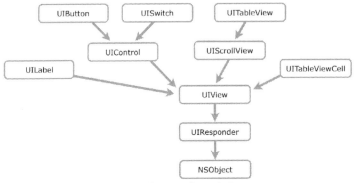

UIView and some of its subclasses

Often your data model classes will also have superclasses and subclasses:

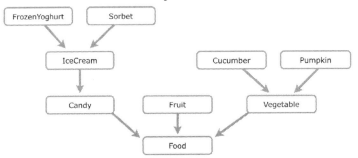

Data model class hierarchy for a grocery store

The arrows in these diagrams all represent **is-a** relationships between the classes.

A `UITableViewController` *is* a `UIViewController`, but with extra stuff. Likewise, a `UIButton` is a `UIView` that also knows how to respond to touches and can initiate actions when tapped.

Often people use the terms **parent** and **child** when they talk about such hierarchies. `UIViewController` is the parent of `UITableViewController`, while `UIButton` is a child of `UIView` and `UIControl`.

The above hierarchies are between data types. The object graph, on the other hand, is a hierarchy between actual object instances.

The type hierarchy is used only during the construction of your programs and is fixed, but the object graph can change dynamically while your app is running as new relationships are forged and old ones are broken.

The flow of screens in the MyLocations app can be expressed as a hierarchy between view controllers, with the `UITabBarController` as the root at the bottom:

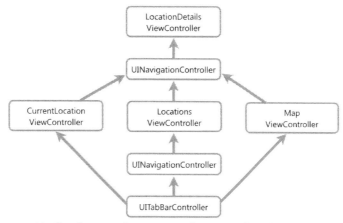

The flow between the screens in the app is also a hierarchy

This is essentially what your storyboard represents. Here the terms parent and child are used also: the UITabBarController is the parent of the view controllers for the Tag, Locations and Map screens (which you'll be adding next).

Views on the screen also have a hierarchy of subviews. The view controller's main view provides the backdrop for the screen, and it has many view objects layered on top of it:

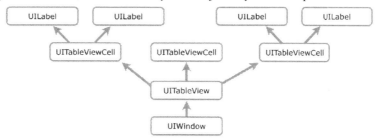

The view and subview objects in a screen with a table view

The graph of data model objects can also form a hierarchy:

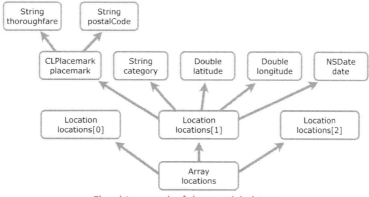

The object graph of data model objects

These are all known as **has-a** relationships. The Array instance *has* one or more Location objects (its children). Each Location object has latitude, longitude, category and placemark objects. And the CLPlacemark instance has a bunch of string objects of its own.

The world of computing is rife with examples of hierarchies and tree structures. For example, the contents of a plist or XML file, the organization of your source files into groups in the Xcode project, the file system itself with its infinitely nested directories, get-rich-quick Ponzi schemes, you name it.

Pins on a map

Showing the locations in a table view is useful but not very visually appealing. The iOS SDK comes with an awesome map view control and it would be a shame not to use it.

In this section you will add third tab to the app that looks like this:

The Map screen with some locations in my hometown

> First visit: the storyboard. From the Objects Library, drag a regular **View Controller** into the canvas (put it below the others).

> **Ctrl-drag** from the Tab Bar Controller to this new View Controller to add it to the tabs (choose **Relationship segue – view controllers**).

> The new view controller now has a **Tab Bar Item**. Rename it to say **Map**.

> Drag a **MapKit View** into the view controller. Make it cover the entire area of the screen, so that it sits partially below the tab bar. (The size of the Map View should be 320 × 568 points.)

> In the **Attributes inspector** for the Map View, enable **Shows User Location**. That will put a blue dot on the map at the user's current coordinates.

➤ Drag a **Navigation Bar** into the Map View Controller. Place it at Y = 20, against the bottom of the status bar. Change its title to **Map**. The navigation bar should also partially overlap the Map View.

➤ Drag a **Bar Button Item** into the left-hand slot of the navigation bar and give it the title **Locations**. Drag another into the right-hand slot but name it **User**. Later on you'll use nice icons for these buttons but for now these labels will do.

This part of the storyboard should look like this:

The design of the Map screen

The app won't run as-is. The app will compile without problems but crashes when you switch to the Map screen. MKMapView is not part of UIKit but of MapKit, so you need to add the MapKit framework first.

You'd think that adding import MapKit to the source of the app would be sufficient to solve this problem, but that doesn't seem to work (try it out). So let's add the framework by hand.

➤ Go to the **Project Settings** screen. On the **General** tab, scroll down to the section **Linked Frameworks and Libraries**.

The Linked Frameworks and Libraries section

➤ Click the + button and choose **MapKit.framework** from the list.

Adding the MapKit framework to the project

➤ Run the app. Choose a location in the Simulator's Debug menu and switch to the Map. The screen should look something like this:

The map shows the user's location

> **Note:** There is a gap between the top of the screen and the navigation bar. That happens because as of iOS 7 the status bar is no longer a separate area but is directly drawn on top of the view controller. You will fix this later in the tutorial.

Next, you're going to show the user's location in a little more detail because that blue dot could be almost anywhere in California!

➤ Add a new UIViewController subclass file to the project. Name it **MapViewController**. This is a regular view controller, not a table view controller!

➤ Replace the contents of **MapViewController.swift** with the following:

```
import UIKit
import MapKit
import CoreData

class MapViewController: UIViewController {
  @IBOutlet weak var mapView: MKMapView!

  var managedObjectContext: NSManagedObjectContext!

  @IBAction func showUser() {
    let region = MKCoordinateRegionMakeWithDistance(mapView.userLocation.coordinate,
                                              1000, 1000)
    mapView.setRegion(mapView.regionThatFits(region), animated: true)
  }

  @IBAction func showLocations() {
  }
}

extension MapViewController: MKMapViewDelegate {
}
```

This has an outlet property for the map view and two action methods that will be connected to the buttons in the navigation bar. The view controller is also the delegate of the map view, courtesy of the extension.

➤ In the storyboard, select the view controller and in the **Identity inspector** set its **Class** to **MapViewController**.

➤ Connect the Locations bar button item to the showLocations action and the User button to the showUser action. (In case you forgot, Ctrl-drag from the bar button items to the view controller.)

➤ Connect the Map View with the mapView outlet (Ctrl-drag from the view controller to the Map View), and its delegate with the view controller (Ctrl-drag the other way around).

Currently the view controller only implements the showUser() action method. When you press the **User** button, it zooms in the map to a region that is 1000 by 1000 meters (a little more than half a mile in both directions) around the user's position.

Try it out:

Pressing the User button zooms in to the user's location

> **Note:** If you're using the iPhone 5 Simulator (not the 5s), the app may crash at this point with an "Invalid Region" message. Unfortunately, Map Kit is quite buggy on the iPhone 5 Simulator. It should work OK on the other simulators.

The other button, Locations, will show the region that contains all the user's saved locations. Before you can do that, you first have to fetch those locations from the data store.

Even though this screen doesn't have a table view, you could still use an NSFetchedResultsController object to handle all the fetching and automatic change detection. But this time I want to make it hard on you, so you're going to do the fetching by hand.

➤ Add a new array to **MapViewController.swift**:

```
var locations = [Location]()
```

➤ Also add the updateLocations() method:

```
func updateLocations() {
  let entity = NSEntityDescription.entityForName("Location",
                                      inManagedObjectContext: managedObjectContext)

  let fetchRequest = NSFetchRequest()
  fetchRequest.entity = entity

  var error: NSError?
  let foundObjects = managedObjectContext.executeFetchRequest(fetchRequest, error: &error)
  if foundObjects == nil {
    fatalCoreDataError(error)
    return
  }

  mapView.removeAnnotations(locations)

  locations = foundObjects as! [Location]
  mapView.addAnnotations(locations)
}
```

The fetch request is nothing new, except this time you're not sorting the Location objects. The order of the Location objects in the array doesn't really matter to the map view, only their latitude and longitude coordinates.

Once you've obtained the Location objects, you call mapView.addAnnotations() to add a pin for each location on the map.

The idea is that updateLocations() will be executed every time there is a change in the data store. How you'll do that is of later concern, but the point is that the locations array may already exist and may contain Location objects. If so, you first tell the map view to remove the pins for these old objects.

➤ Add the viewDidLoad() method:

```
override func viewDidLoad() {
  super.viewDidLoad()
  updateLocations()
}
```

This fetches the Location objects and shows them on the map when the view loads. Nothing special here.

Before this class can use the managedObjectContext, you have to give it a reference to that object first. As before, that happens in AppDelegate.

➤ In **AppDelegate.swift,** extend application(didFinishLaunchingWithOptions) to pass the context object to the MapViewController as well. This goes inside the if-let statement:

```
let mapViewController = tabBarViewControllers[2] as! MapViewController
mapViewController.managedObjectContext = managedObjectContext
```

You're not quite done yet. The app builds without problems but crashes when you switch to the Map tab (try it out).

In updateLocations() you told the map view to add the Location objects as annotations (an annotation is a pin on the map). But MKMapView expects an array of MKAnnotation objects, not your own Location class. That's why it crashes.

Luckily, MKAnnotation is a protocol, so you can turn the Location objects into map annotations by making the class conform to that protocol.

➤ Change the class line from **Location.swift** to:

```
class Location: NSManagedObject, MKAnnotation {
```

Just because Location is an object that is managed by Core Data doesn't mean you can't add your own stuff to it. It's still an object!

Exercise. Xcode now says "Use of undeclared type MKAnnotation". Why is that? ■

Answer: You still need to import MapKit. Add that line to the top of the file.

Exercise. Xcode still gives a compiler error when you try to build the file. What is wrong now? ■

Answer: Because you said Location now conforms to the protocol MKAnnotation, you have to provide all the required features from that protocol inside **Location.swift.**

The MKAnnotation protocol requires the class to implement three properties: coordinate, title and subtitle.

It obviously needs to know the coordinate in order to place the pin in the correct place on the map. The title and subtitle are used for the "call-out" that appears when you tap on the pin.

➤ Add the following code to **Location.swift**:

```
var coordinate: CLLocationCoordinate2D {
  return CLLocationCoordinate2DMake(latitude, longitude)
}

var title: String! {
  if locationDescription.isEmpty {
    return "(No Description)"
  } else {
    return locationDescription
  }
}

var subtitle: String! {
  return category
}
```

Do you notice anything special here? All three items are instance variables (because of var), but they also have a block of source code associated with them.

These variables are **read-only computed properties**. That means they don't actually store a value into a memory location.

Whenever you access the coordinate, title, or subtitle variables, they perform the logic from their code blocks. That's why they are *computed* properties: they compute something. They are read-only because they only return a value; you can't give them a new value using the assignment operator.

The following is OK because it reads the value of the property:

```
let s = location.title
```

But you cannot do this:

```
location.title = "Time for a change"
```

The only way the title property can change is if the locationDescription value changes. You could also have written this as a method:

```
func title() -> String! {
  if locationDescription.isEmpty {
    return "(No Description)"
  } else {
    return locationDescription
  }
}
```

This is equivalent to using the computed property. Whether to use a method or a computed property is often a matter of taste and you'll see both ways used throughout the iOS frameworks.

(By the way, it is also possible to make read-write computed properties, but the MKAnnotation protocol doesn't use those.)

➤ Run the app and switch to the Map screen. It should now show pins for all the saved locations. If you tap on a pin, the callout shows the chosen description and category.

The map shows pins for the saved locations

Note: So far all the protocols you've seen were used for making delegates, but that's not the case here. `Location` is not a delegate of anything.

The `MKAnnotation` protocol simply lets you pretend that `Location` is an annotation that can be placed on a map view.

You can use this trick with any object you want; as long as the object implements the `MKAnnotation` protocol it can be shown on a map.

Protocols let objects wear different hats.

Pressing the User button makes the app zoom to the user's current coordinates but the same thing doesn't happen yet for the Locations button and the location pins.

By looking at the highest and lowest values for the latitude and longitude of all the `Location` objects, you can calculate a region and then tell the map view to zoom to that region.

➤ In **MapViewController.swift**, add a new method, `regionForAnnotations()`:

```
func regionForAnnotations(annotations: [MKAnnotation]) -> MKCoordinateRegion {
  var region: MKCoordinateRegion

  switch annotations.count {
    case 0:
      region = MKCoordinateRegionMakeWithDistance(mapView.userLocation.coordinate,
                                                  1000, 1000)
    case 1:
      let annotation = annotations[annotations.count - 1]
      region = MKCoordinateRegionMakeWithDistance(annotation.coordinate, 1000, 1000)

    default:
      var topLeftCoord = CLLocationCoordinate2D(latitude: -90, longitude: 180)
      var bottomRightCoord = CLLocationCoordinate2D(latitude: 90, longitude: -180)

      for annotation in annotations {
```

```
      topLeftCoord.latitude = max(topLeftCoord.latitude, annotation.coordinate.latitude)
      topLeftCoord.longitude = min(topLeftCoord.longitude, annotation.coordinate.longitude)
      bottomRightCoord.latitude = min(bottomRightCoord.latitude,
                                  annotation.coordinate.latitude)
      bottomRightCoord.longitude = max(bottomRightCoord.longitude,
                                  annotation.coordinate.longitude)
    }

    let center = CLLocationCoordinate2D(
      latitude: topLeftCoord.latitude -
            (topLeftCoord.latitude - bottomRightCoord.latitude) / 2,
      longitude: topLeftCoord.longitude -
            (topLeftCoord.longitude - bottomRightCoord.longitude) / 2)

    let extraSpace = 1.1
    let span = MKCoordinateSpan(
      latitudeDelta: abs(topLeftCoord.latitude - bottomRightCoord.latitude) * extraSpace,
      longitudeDelta:
            abs(topLeftCoord.longitude - bottomRightCoord.longitude) * extraSpace)

    region = MKCoordinateRegion(center: center, span: span)
  }

  return mapView.regionThatFits(region)
}
```

regionForAnnotations() has three situations to handle. It uses a switch statement to look at the number of annotations and then chooses the corresponding case:

- There are no annotations. You'll center the map on the user's current position.

- There is only one annotation. You'll center the map on that one annotation.

- There are two or more annotations. You'll calculate the extent of their reach and add a little padding. See if you can make sense of those calculations. The max() function looks at two values and returns the larger of the two; min() returns the smaller; abs() always makes a number positive (absolute value).

Note that this method does not use Location objects for anything. It assumes that all the objects in the array conform to the MKAnnotation protocol and it only looks at that part of the objects. As far as regionForAnnotations() is concerned, what it deals with are annotations.

That is the power of using protocols. It also allows you to use this method in any app that uses Map Kit, without modifications. Pretty neat.

➤ Change the showLocations() method to:

```
@IBAction func showLocations() {
  let region = regionForAnnotations(locations)
  mapView.setRegion(region, animated: true)
}
```

This calls regionForAnnotations() to calculate a reasonable region that fits all the Location objects and then sets that region on the map view.

➤ Finally, change viewDidLoad():

```
override func viewDidLoad() {
  super.viewDidLoad()
  updateLocations()
```

```
  if !locations.isEmpty {
    showLocations()
  }
}
```

It's a good idea to show the user's locations by default the first time you switch to the Map tab, so viewDidLoad() calls showLocations() too.

➤ Run the app and press the Locations button. The map view should now zoom in on your saved locations. (This only works well if the locations aren't too far apart, of course.)

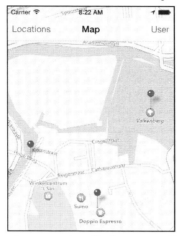

The map view zooms in to fit all your saved locations

Making your own pins

You made the MapViewController conform to the MKMapViewDelegate protocol but so far you haven't done anything with that.

This delegate is useful for creating your own annotation views. Currently a default pin and callout are being used, but you can change this to anything you like.

➤ Add the following code to **MapViewController.swift**, inside the extension at the bottom:

```
func mapView(mapView: MKMapView!, viewForAnnotation annotation: MKAnnotation!)
          -> MKAnnotationView! {
  // 1
  if annotation is Location {
    // 2
    let identifier = "Location"
    var annotationView = mapView.dequeueReusableAnnotationViewWithIdentifier(identifier)
                              as! MKPinAnnotationView!
    if annotationView == nil {
      annotationView = MKPinAnnotationView(annotation: annotation,
                                        reuseIdentifier: identifier)
      // 3
      annotationView.enabled = true
      annotationView.canShowCallout = true
      annotationView.animatesDrop = false
      annotationView.pinColor = .Green
      // 4
      let rightButton = UIButton.buttonWithType(.DetailDisclosure) as! UIButton
      rightButton.addTarget(self, action: Selector("showLocationDetails:"),
```

```
                          forControlEvents: .TouchUpInside)
    annotationView.rightCalloutAccessoryView = rightButton

  } else {
    annotationView.annotation = annotation
  }

  // 5
  let button = annotationView.rightCalloutAccessoryView as! UIButton
  if let index = find(locations, annotation as! Location) {
    button.tag = index
  }

  return annotationView
}

return nil
}
```

This is very similar to what a table view data source does in `cellForRowAtIndexPath`, except that you're not dealing with table view cells here but with `MKAnnotationView` objects. Step-by-step this is what happens:

1. Because `MKAnnotation` is a protocol, there may be other objects apart from the `Location` object that want to be annotations on the map. An example is the blue dot that represents the user's current location. You should leave such annotations alone, so you use the special "is" type check operator to determine whether the annotation is really a `Location` object. If so, you continue.

2. This looks very familiar to creating a table view cell. You ask the map view to re-use an annotation view object. If it cannot find a recyclable annotation view, then you create a new one.

   Note that you're not limited to using `MKPinAnnotationView` for your annotations. This is the standard annotation view class, but you can also create your own `MKAnnotationView` subclass and make it look like anything you want. Pins are only one option.

3. This just sets some properties to configure the look and feel of the annotation view. Previously the pins were red, but you make them green here.

4. This is where it gets interesting. You create a new `UIButton` object that looks like a detail disclosure button (a blue circled **i**). You use the target-action pattern to hook up the button's "Touch Up Inside" event with a new `showLocationDetails()` method, and add the button to the annotation view's accessory view.

5. Once the annotation view is constructed and configured, you obtain a reference to that detail disclosure button again and set its `tag` to the index of the `Location` object in the `locations` array. That way you can find the `Location` object later in `showLocationDetails()` when the button is pressed.

➤ Add the `showLocationDetails()` method but leave it empty for now. Put it inside the main class, not the extension.

```
func showLocationDetails(sender: UIButton) {
}
```

If you hadn't added this method at this point, then pressing the button on the annotation's callout would crash the app with an "unrecognized selector sent to instance" error.

> **Note:** When you specified `Selector("showLocationDetails:")` you placed a colon behind the name of the method. That colon means the method takes one parameter, usually called `sender`, that refers to the control that sent the action message.
>
> In this case the sender will be the (i) button. That's why the parameter of the `showLocationDetails()` method is written as (`sender: UIButton`).
>
> The reason a colon is used to indicate the existence of a parameter has everything to do with Objective-C, which is obsessed with colons and square brackets. If you've used it before, you know what I mean…

➤ Run the app. The pins are now green and the callout has a custom button. (If the pins stay red, then make sure you connected the view controller as the delegate of the map view in the storyboard.)

The annotations use your own view

What should this button do? Show the Edit Location screen, of course!

➤ Open the storyboard. Select the Map View Controller (the actual view controller, not some view inside it) and **Ctrl-drag** to the Navigation Controller that contains the Location Details View Controller.

Make this a new **modal** segue named **EditLocation**.

Tip: If making this connection gives you problems because the storyboard won't fit on your screen, then try Ctrl-dragging from the outline pane.

The storyboard now looks like this:

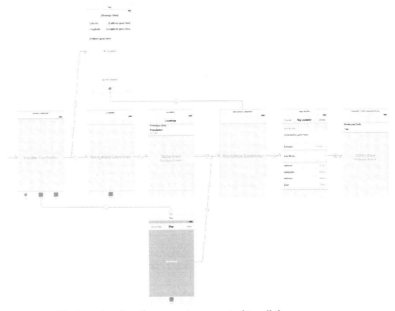

The Location Details screen is connected to all three screens

I had to zoom out the Storyboard in order to make the screen capture. It's not very readable at this level but you can see that there are now three segues going to the Location Details screen (or at least to its navigation controller).

> Back in **MapViewController.swift**, change the showLocationDetails() method to trigger the segue:

```
func showLocationDetails(sender: UIButton) {
  performSegueWithIdentifier("EditLocation", sender: sender)
}
```

Because the segue isn't connected to any particular control in the view controller, you have to perform it manually. You send along the button object as the sender, so you can read its tag property in prepareForSegue().

> Add the prepareForSegue(sender) method:

```
override func prepareForSegue(segue: UIStoryboardSegue, sender: AnyObject?) {
  if segue.identifier == "EditLocation" {
    let navigationController = segue.destinationViewController as! UINavigationController

    let controller = navigationController.topViewController
                                    as! LocationDetailsViewController
    controller.managedObjectContext = managedObjectContext

    let button = sender as! UIButton
    let location = locations[button.tag]
    controller.locationToEdit = location
  }
}
```

This is very similar to what you did in the Locations screen, except that now you get the Location object to edit from the locations array, using the tag property of the sender button as the index in that array.

➤ Run the app, tap on a pin and edit the location.

It works, except that the annotation on the map doesn't change until you tap the pin again. Likewise, changes on the other screens, such as adding or deleting a location, have no effect on the map. (The cells in the Locations screen changed immediately because you're using the NSFetchedResultsController there.)

This is the same problem you had earlier with the Locations screen. Because the list of Location objects is only fetched once in viewDidLoad(), any changes that happen afterwards are overlooked.

The way you're going to fix this for the Map screen is by using notifications. Recall that you have already put NSNotificationCenter to use for dealing with Core Data save errors.

As it happens, Core Data also sends out a bunch of notifications when certain changes happen to the data store. You can subscribe to these notifications and update the map view when you receive them.

➤ In **MapViewController.swift,** change the managedObjectContext property declaration to:

```
var managedObjectContext: NSManagedObjectContext! {
  didSet {
    NSNotificationCenter.defaultCenter().addObserverForName(
        NSManagedObjectContextObjectsDidChangeNotification, object: managedObjectContext,
        queue: NSOperationQueue.mainQueue()) { notification in
      if self.isViewLoaded() {
        self.updateLocations()
      }
    }
  }
}
```

This is another example of a property observer put to good use.

As soon as managedObjectContext is given a value – which happens in AppDelegate during app startup – the didSet block tells the NSNotificationCenter to add an observer for the NSManagedObjectContextObjectsDidChangeNotification.

This notification with the very long name is sent out by the managedObjectContext whenever the data store changes. In response you would like the following closure to be called. For clarity, here's what happens in the closure:

```
{ notification in
  if self.isViewLoaded() {
    self.updateLocations()
  }
}
```

This couldn't be simpler: you just call updateLocations() to fetch all the Location objects again. This throws away all the old pins and it makes new pins for all the newly fetched Location objects. Granted, it's not a very efficient method if there are hundreds of annotation objects, but for now it gets the job done.

> **Note:** You only call updateLocations() when the Maps screen's view is loaded.
>
> Because this screen sits in a tab, the view from MapViewController does not actually get loaded from the storyboard until the user switches to the Map tab.
>
> So the view may not have been loaded yet when the user tags a new location. In that case it makes no sense to call updateLocations() – it could even crash the app because the MKMapView object doesn't exist yet at that point!

➤ Run the app. First go to the Map screen to make sure it is loaded. Then tag a new location. The map should have added a new pin for it, although you may have to press the Locations bar button to make the new pin appear if it's outside the visible range

Have another look at that closure. The "notification in" bit is the parameter for the closure. Like functions and methods, closures can take parameters.

Because this particular closure gets called by NSNotificationCenter, you're given an NSNotification object in the notification parameter. Since you're not using this notification object anywhere in the closure, you could also write it like this:

```
{ _ in
  if self.isViewLoaded() {
    self.updateLocations()
  }
}
```

The _ wildcard symbol tells Swift you're not interested in that parameter. It also helps to reduce visual clutter in the source code; it's obvious at a glance that this parameter – whatever it may be – isn't being used in the closure.

Exercise. The NSNotification object has a userInfo dictionary. From that dictionary it is possible to figure out which objects were inserted/deleted/updated. For example, use the following println()s to examine this dictionary:

```
if let dictionary = notification.userInfo {
  println(dictionary["inserted"])
  println(dictionary["deleted"])
  println(dictionary["updated"])
}
```

This will print out an (optional) array of Location objects or nil if there were no changes. Your mission, should you choose to accept it: try to make the reloading of the locations more efficient by not re-fetching the entire list of Location objects, but by only inserting or deleting those that have changed. Good luck! (You can find the solutions from other readers on the raywenderlich.com forums.) ∎

That's it for the Map screen. Oh, one more thing. To fix the issue with the status bar you need to make the view controller the delegate for the navigation bar.

➤ Add a new extension at the bottom of **MapViewController.swift**:

```
extension MapViewController: UINavigationBarDelegate {
  func positionForBar(bar: UIBarPositioning) -> UIBarPosition {
    return .TopAttached
  }
}
```

This tells the navigation bar to extend under the status bar area.

➤ Finally, **Ctrl-drag** from the navigation bar to the view controller inside the storyboard to make the delegate connection.

Now the gap between the navigation bar and the top of the screen is gone:

The navigation bar extends to the top of the screen

You can find the project files for the app up to this point under **05 - Map View** in the tutorial's Source Code folder.

The photo picker

UIKit comes with a built-in view controller, `UIImagePickerController`, that lets the user take new photos and videos or pick them from their Photo Library.

You're going to make the Add Photo button from the Tag/Edit Location screen save the photo along with the location so the user has a nice picture to look at.

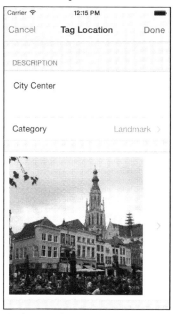

A photo in the Tag Location screen

> In **LocationDetailsViewController.swift**, add the following extension to the bottom of the source file:

```
extension LocationDetailsViewController: UIImagePickerControllerDelegate,
                                         UINavigationControllerDelegate {
  func takePhotoWithCamera() {
    let imagePicker = UIImagePickerController()
    imagePicker.sourceType = .Camera
    imagePicker.delegate = self
    imagePicker.allowsEditing = true
    presentViewController(imagePicker, animated: true, completion: nil)
  }
}
```

The UIImagePickerController is a view controller like any other, but it comes with UIKit and it takes care of the entire process of taking new photos and picking them from the user's photo library.

All you need to do is create a UIImagePickerController instance, set its properties to configure the picker, set its delegate, and then present it. When the user closes the image picker screen, the delegate methods will let you know what happened.

That's exactly how you've been designing your own view controllers. (You don't add the UIImagePickerController to the storyboard, though.)

> **Note:** You're doing this in an extension because it allows you to group all the photo-picking related functionality together.
>
> If you wanted to, you could put these methods into the main class body. That would work fine too, but view controllers tend to become very big with many methods that all do different things.
>
> As a way to preserve your sanity, it's nice to extract conceptually related methods – such as everything that has to do with picking photos – and place them together in their own extension.
>
> You could even move each of these extensions to their own source file, for example "LocationDetailsViewController+PhotoPicking.swift".

> Add the following methods to the extension:

```
func imagePickerController(picker: UIImagePickerController,
                           didFinishPickingMediaWithInfo info: [NSObject : AnyObject]) {
  dismissViewControllerAnimated(true, completion: nil)
}

func imagePickerControllerDidCancel(picker: UIImagePickerController) {
  dismissViewControllerAnimated(true, completion: nil)
}
```

Currently these delegate methods simply remove the image picker from the screen. Soon you'll be taking the image the user picked and add it to the Location object, but for now you just want to see that you can make the image picker show up.

Note that the view controller (in this case the extension) must conform to both UIImagePickerControllerDelegate and UINavigationControllerDelegate for this to work, but you don't have to implement any of the UINavigationControllerDelegate methods.

➤ Now change `tableView(didSelectRowAtIndexPath)` in the class:

```
override func tableView(tableView: UITableView,
                        didSelectRowAtIndexPath indexPath: NSIndexPath) {
  if indexPath.section == 0 && indexPath.row == 0 {
    descriptionTextView.becomeFirstResponder()
  }
  else if indexPath.section == 1 && indexPath.row == 0 {
    takePhotoWithCamera()
  }
}
```

Add Photo is the first row in the second section. When it's tapped, you call the `takePhotoWithCamera()` method that you just added.

➤ Run the app, tag a new location or edit an existing one, and press Add Photo.

If you're running the app in the Simulator, then bam! It crashes. The error message is this:

```
*** Terminating app due to uncaught exception 'NSInvalidArgumentException', reason: 'Source
type 1 not available'
```

The culprit for the crash is the line:

```
imagePicker.sourceType = .Camera
```

Not all devices have a camera, and neither does the Simulator. If you try to use the `UIImagePickerController` with a `sourceType` that is not supported by the device or the Simulator, the app crashes.

If you run the app on your device – and if it has a camera (which it probably does if it's a recent model) – then you should see this:

The camera interface

That is very similar to what you see when you take pictures using the iPhone's Camera app. (MyLocations doesn't let you record video, but you can certainly enable this feature in your own apps.)

You can still test the image picker on the Simulator, but instead of using the camera you have to use the photo library.

➤ Add the choosePhotoFromLibrary() method to the extension:

```
func choosePhotoFromLibrary() {
  let imagePicker = UIImagePickerController()
  imagePicker.sourceType = .PhotoLibrary
  imagePicker.delegate = self
  imagePicker.allowsEditing = true
  presentViewController(imagePicker, animated: true, completion: nil)
}
```

These two methods do essentially the same, except now you set the sourceType to .PhotoLibrary.

➤ Change didSelectRowAtIndexPath to call choosePhotoFromLibrary() instead of takePhotoWithCamera().

➤ Run the app in the Simulator and press Add Photo.

First, the user needs to give the app permission to access the photo library:

The user needs to allow the app to access the photo library

If they tap Don't Allow, the photo picker screen remains empty. (Users can undo this choice in the Settings app, under Privacy → Photos.)

➤ Choose **OK**. At this point you might see this:

There are no photos in the library

The simulator's photo library has no photos in it yet. It's also possible you already see a handful of stock images; this differs between Xcode versions.

➤ Stop the app and click on the built-in **Photos** app in the Simulator. This should display a handful of sample photos.

➤ Run the app again and try picking a photo. You may or may not see these sample photos now. If not, you'll have to add your own.

There are several ways you can add new photos to the Simulator. You can go into **Safari** (on the Simulator) and search the internet for an image. Then press down on the image until a menu appears and choose Save Image:

Adding images to the Simulator

Instead of surfing the internet for images, you can also simply drop an image file on top of the Simulator window. This adds the picture to your library in the Photos app.

Finally, you can use the Terminal and the simctl command. Type all on one line:

```
/Applications/Xcode.app/Contents/Developer/usr/bin/simctl addphoto booted
~/Desktop/MyPhoto.JPG
```

The simctl tool can be used to manage your Simulators (type simctl help for a list of options). The command "addphoto booted" adds the specified image to the active Simulator's photo library.

➤ Run the app again. Now you can choose a photo from the Photo Library:

The photos in the library

➤ Choose one of the photos. The screen now changes to:

The user can tweak the photo

This happens because you set the image picker's `allowsEditing` property to `true`. With this setting enabled, the user can do some quick editing on the photo before making his final choice.

So there are two types of image pickers you can use, the camera and the Photo Library, but the camera won't work everywhere. It's a bit limiting to restrict the app to just picking photos from the library, though.

You'll have to make the app a little smarter and allow the user to choose the camera when it is present. First you check whether the camera is available. When it is, you show an **action sheet** to let the user choose between the camera and the Photo Library.

➤ Add the following methods to **LocationDetailsViewController.swift**, in the photo picking extension:

```swift
func pickPhoto() {
  if UIImagePickerController.isSourceTypeAvailable(.Camera) {
    showPhotoMenu()
  } else {
    choosePhotoFromLibrary()
  }
}

func showPhotoMenu() {
  let alertController = UIAlertController(title: nil, message: nil,
                                          preferredStyle: .ActionSheet)

  let cancelAction = UIAlertAction(title: "Cancel", style: .Cancel, handler: nil)
  alertController.addAction(cancelAction)

  let takePhotoAction = UIAlertAction(title: "Take Photo", style: .Default, handler: nil)
  alertController.addAction(takePhotoAction)

  let chooseFromLibraryAction = UIAlertAction(title: "Choose From Library",
                                          style: .Default, handler: nil)
  alertController.addAction(chooseFromLibraryAction)

  presentViewController(alertController, animated: true, completion: nil)
}
```

You're using `UIImagePickerController`'s `isSourceTypeAvailable()` method to check whether there's a camera present. If not, you call `choosePhotoFromLibrary()` as that is the only option then. But when the device does have a camera you show a `UIAlertController` on the screen.

Unlike the alert controllers you've used before, this one has the `.ActionSheet` style. An action sheet works very much like an alert view, except that it slides in from the bottom of the screen.

➤ In `didSelectRowAtIndexPath`, change the call to `choosePhotoFromLibrary()` to `pickPhoto()` instead. This is the last time you're changing this line, honest.

➤ Run the app on your device to see the action sheet in action:

The action sheet that lets you choose between camera and photo library

Tapping any of the buttons in the action sheet simply dismisses the action sheet but doesn't do anything else yet.

By the way, if you want to test this action sheet on the Simulator, then you can fake the availability of the camera by writing the following in `pickPhoto()`:

```
if true || UIImagePickerController.isSourceTypeAvailable(.Camera) {
```

That will always show the action sheet because the condition is now always true.

The choices in the action sheet are provided by `UIAlertAction` objects. The `handler:` parameter determines what happens when you press the alert action's button in the action sheet.

Right now the handlers for all three choices – Take Photo, Choose From Library, Cancel – are `nil`, so nothing will happen.

➤ Change these lines to the following:

```
let takePhotoAction = UIAlertAction(title: "Take Photo", style: .Default,
                            handler: { _ in self.takePhotoWithCamera() })
```

```
let chooseFromLibraryAction = UIAlertAction(title: "Choose From Library", style: .Default,
                            handler: { _ in self.choosePhotoFromLibrary() })
```

This gives `handler:` a closure that calls the corresponding method from the extension. You use the `_` wildcard to ignore the parameter that is passed to this closure (which is a reference to the `UIAlertAction` itself).

➤ Run the app make sure the buttons from the action sheet work properly.

There may be a small delay between pressing any of these buttons before the image picker appears but that's because it's a big component and iOS needs a few seconds to load it up.

Notice that the Add Photo cell remains selected (dark gray background) when you cancel the action sheet. That doesn't look so good.

➤ In `tableView(didSelectRowAtIndexPath)`, add the following line before the call to `pickPhoto()`:

```
tableView.deselectRowAtIndexPath(indexPath, animated: true)
```

This first deselects the Add Photo row. Try it out, it looks better this way. The cell background quickly fades from gray back to white as the action sheet slides into the screen.

By the way, if you still have the Core Data debug output enabled, then you should see a whole bunch of output in the Xcode Debug Area when the image picker is active. Apparently the `UIImagePickerController` uses Core Data as well!

Showing the image

Now that the user can pick a photo, you should display it somewhere (otherwise, what's the point?). After picking a photo, you'll change the Add Photo cell to hold the photo. The cell will grow to fit the photo and the Add Photo label is gone.

➤ Add two new outlets to the class in **LocationDetailsViewController.swift**:

```
@IBOutlet weak var imageView: UIImageView!
@IBOutlet weak var addPhotoLabel: UILabel!
```

➤ In the storyboard, drag an **Image View** into the Add Photo cell. It doesn't really matter how big it is or where you put it. You'll programmatically move it to the proper place later. (This is the reason you made this a custom cell way back when, so you could add this image view into it.)

Adding an Image View to the Add Photo cell

➤ Connect the Image View to the view controller's `imageView` outlet. Also connect the Add Photo label to the `addPhotoLabel` outlet.

➤ Select the Image View. In the **Attributes inspector**, check its **Hidden** attribute (in the Drawing section). This makes the image view initially invisible, until you have a photo to give it.

Now that you have an image view, let's make it display something.

➤ Add a new instance variable to **LocationDetailsViewController.swift**:

```
var image: UIImage?
```

If no photo is picked yet, `image` is `nil`, so this must be an optional.

➤ Add the `showImage()` method to the class:

```
func showImage(image: UIImage) {
  imageView.image = image
  imageView.hidden = false
  imageView.frame = CGRect(x: 10, y: 10, width: 260, height: 260)
  addPhotoLabel.hidden = true
}
```

This puts the image into the image view, makes the image view visible and gives it the proper dimensions. It also hides the Add Photo label because you don't want it to overlap the image view.

➤ Change the imagePickerController(didFinishPickingMediaWithInfo) method from the photo picking extension to the following:

```
func imagePickerController(picker: UIImagePickerController,
                          didFinishPickingMediaWithInfo info: [NSObject : AnyObject]) {

  image = info[UIImagePickerControllerEditedImage] as? UIImage

  if let image = image {
    showImage(image)
  }

  dismissViewControllerAnimated(true, completion: nil)
}
```

This is the method that gets called when the user has selected a photo in the image picker.

You can tell by the notation [NSObject : AnyObject] that the info parameter is a dictionary. Whenever you see [A : B] you're dealing with a dictionary that has keys of type "A" and values of type "B".

The info dictionary contains a variety of data describing the image that the user picked. You use the UIImagePickerControllerEditedImage key to retrieve a UIImage object that contains the image from after the Move and Scale operation. (You can also get the original image if you wish.)

Once you have the photo, you store it in the image instance variable so you can use it later.

Dictionaries always return optionals, because there is a theoretical possibility that the key you asked for – UIImagePickerControllerEditedImage in this case – doesn't actually exist in the dictionary.

Under normal circumstances you'd unwrap this optional but here the image instance variable is an optional itself so no unwrapping is necessary.

If info[UIImagePickerControllerEditedImage] is nil, then image will be nil too. You do need to cast the value from the meaningless AnyObject to UIImage using the as? operator.

Once you have the image and it is not nil, the call to showImage() puts it in the Add Photo cell.

Exercise. See if you can rewrite the above logic to use a didSet property observer on the image instance variable. If you succeed, then placing the photo into image will automatically update the UIImageView, without needing to call showImage(). ∎

➤ Run the app and choose a photo. Whoops, it looks like you have a small problem here:

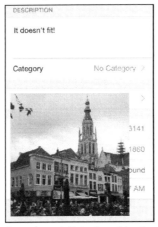

The photo doesn't fit in the table view cell

(It's also possible that the photo doesn't overlap the rows below it but simply gets cut off. In any case, it doesn't look good…)

The `showImage()` method made the image view 260-by-260 points tall but the table view cell doesn't automatically resize to fit that image view. As a result, the photo overlaps the cells below.

You'll have to add some logic to the `heightForRowAtIndexPath` table view method to make the table view cell resize.

➤ Change the `tableView(heightForRowAtIndexPath)` method:

```
override func tableView(tableView: UITableView,
                     heightForRowAtIndexPath indexPath: NSIndexPath) -> CGFloat {
  if indexPath.section == 0 && indexPath.row == 0 {
    return 88
  } else if indexPath.section == 1 {
    if imageView.hidden {
      return 44
    } else {
      return 280
    }
  } else if indexPath.section == 2 && indexPath.row == 2 {
    . . .
```

If there is no image, then the height for the Add Photo cell is 44 points just like a regular cell. But if there is an image, it's a lot higher: 280 points. That is 260 points for the image view plus 10 points margin on the top and bottom.

➤ Add the following line to `imagePickerController(didFinishPickingMediaWithInfo)`, just before you dismiss the view controller:

```
tableView.reloadData()
```

This refreshes the table view and sets the photo row to the proper height.

➤ Try it out. The row now resizes and is big enough for the whole photo. The image does appear to be stretched out a little, though.

The photo is stretched out a bit

The image view is square but most photos won't be. By default, an image view will stretch the image to fit the entire content area. That's probably not what you want for this app.

➤ Go to the storyboard and select the Image View (it may be hard to see on account of it being hidden, but you can still find it in the outline pane). In the **Attributes inspector**, set its **Mode** to **Aspect Fit**.

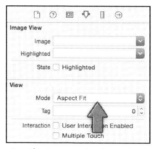

Changing the image view's content mode

This will keep the image's aspect ratio intact as it is resized to fit into the image view. Play a bit with the other content modes to see what they do. (Aspect Fill is similar to Aspect Fit, except that it tries to fill up the entire view.)

The aspect ratio of the photo is kept intact

That looks a bit better, although there are now larger margins at the top and bottom of the image.

Exercise. Make the height of the photo table view cell dynamic, depending on the aspect ratio of the image. This is a tough one! You can keep the width of the image view at 260 points. This should correspond to the width of the `UIImage` object. You get the aspect ratio by doing `image.size.width` / `image.size.height`. With this ratio you can calculate what the height of the image view and the cell should be. Good luck! You can find solutions from other readers at raywenderlich.com/forums ∎

Notice how the if-statements in `tableView(heightForRowAtIndexPath)` all look at the index-path's section and/or row?

```
if indexPath.section == 0 && indexPath.row == 0 {
  . . .
} else if indexPath.section == 1 {
  . . .
} else if indexPath.section == 2 && indexPath.row == 2 {
  . . .
} else {
  . . .
}
```

Whenever you see `if` – `else if` – `else if` – `else` where the conditions all check the same thing, it's a good opportunity to use a `switch` statement instead.

➤ Change the `tableView(heightForRowAtIndexPath)` method to:

```
override func tableView(tableView: UITableView,
                    heightForRowAtIndexPath indexPath: NSIndexPath) -> CGFloat {

  switch (indexPath.section, indexPath.row) {
    case (0, 0):
      return 88

    case (1, _):
      return imageView.hidden ? 44 : 280

    case (2, 2):
      addressLabel.frame.size = CGSize(width: view.bounds.size.width - 115, height: 10000)
      addressLabel.sizeToFit()
      addressLabel.frame.origin.x = view.bounds.size.width -
                            addressLabel.frame.size.width - 15
      return addressLabel.frame.size.height + 20

    default:
      return 44
  }
}
```

The logic inside each of the sections is the same as before, but now the different cases are easier to distinguish:

```
switch (indexPath.section, indexPath.row) {
  case (0, 0):
  case (1, _):
  case (2, 2):
  default:
}
```

This `switch` statement puts `indexPath.section` and `indexPath.row` into a **tuple**, and then uses *pattern matching* to look for the different cases:

- `case (0, 0)` corresponds to section 0, row 0.

- `case (1, _)` corresponds to section 1, any row. The _ is the wildcard again, which means any value for `indexPath.row` is accepted here.

- `case (2, 2)` corresponds to section 2, row 2.

- The `default` case is for any other rows in sections 0 and 2.

Using `switch` is very common in Swift because it makes large blocks of `if – else if` statements much easier to read.

> **Note:** A tuple is nothing more than a list of values inside ( ) parentheses. For example, `(10, 3.14, "Hello")` is a tuple with three elements.
>
> Tuples have various uses, such as allowing a method to return more than one value (simply put the different values into a tuple and return that). They are also very convenient in `switch` statements.

There's another change. The following lines have changed from this,

```
if imageView.hidden {
  return 44
} else {
  return 280
}
```

into this:

```
return imageView.hidden ? 44 : 280
```

The `? :` construct is the **ternary conditional** operator. It works like an `if – else` statement compressed into a single line.

If the thing before the `?` is true (`imageView.hidden`) it returns the first value, 44; if false, it returns the second value, 280.

Using `? :` is often simpler than writing it out as `if – else`.

Be careful: there must be a space between `imageView.hidden` and `?` or else Swift thinks `hidden` is an optional that you're trying to unwrap, which results in an error. This is a case where the same symbol, `?`, can mean more than one thing.

Going to the background

The user can take or pick a photo now but the app doesn't save it yet in the data store. Before you get to that, there are still a few improvements to make with the image picker.

Apple recommends that apps remove any alert or action sheet from the screen when the user presses the Home button to put the app in the background.

The user may return to the app hours or days later and they will have forgotten what they were going to do. The presence of the alert or action sheet is confusing and the user will be thinking, "What's that thing doing here?!"

To prevent this from happening, you'll make the Tag Location screen a little more attentive. When the app goes to the background, it will dismiss the action sheet if that is currently showing. You'll do the same for the image picker.

You've seen in the Checklists tutorial that the AppDelegate is notified by the operating system when the app is about to go into the background, through its applicationDidEnterBackground() method.

View controllers don't have such a method, but fortunately iOS sends out "going to the background" notifications through NSNotificationCenter that you can make the view controller listen to.

Earlier you used the notification center to observe the notifications from Core Data. This time you'll listen for the UIApplicationDidEnterBackgroundNotification.

➤ In **LocationDetailsViewController.swift**, add a new method:

```
func listenForBackgroundNotification() {
  NSNotificationCenter.defaultCenter().addObserverForName(
      UIApplicationDidEnterBackgroundNotification, object: nil,
      queue: NSOperationQueue.mainQueue()) { notification in

    if self.presentedViewController != nil {
      self.dismissViewControllerAnimated(false, completion: nil)
    }

    self.descriptionTextView.resignFirstResponder()
  }
}
```

This adds an observer for UIApplicationDidEnterBackgroundNotification. When this notification is received, NSNotificationCenter will call the closure.

(Notice that you're using the "trailing" closure syntax here; the closure is not a parameter to addObserverForName() but immediately follows the method call.)

If there is an active image picker or action sheet, you dismiss it. You also hide the keyboard if the text view was active.

The image picker and action sheet are both presented as modal view controllers that lie on top of everything else. If such a modal view controller is active, UIViewController's presentedViewController property has a reference to that modal view controller.

So if presentedViewController is not nil you call dismissViewControllerAnimated() to close the modal screen. This has no effect on the category picker; that does not use a modal but a push segue.

➤ Call the listenForBackgroundNotification() method from within viewDidLoad().

➤ Try it out. Open the image picker (or the action sheet if you're on a device that has a camera) and tap the Home button to put the app to sleep.

Then tap the app's icon to activate the app again. You should now be back on the Tag Location screen (or Edit Location screen if you opted to edit an existing tag). The image picker (or action sheet) has automatically closed.

Cool, that seems to work.

There's one more thing to do. You should tell the NSNotificationCenter to stop sending these background notifications when the Tag/Edit Location screen closes. You don't want NSNotificationCenter to send notifications to an object that no longer exists, that's just asking for trouble! The deinit method is a good place to tear this down.

➤ First, add a new instance variable:

```
var observer: AnyObject!
```

This will hold a reference to the observer, which is necessary to unregister it later.

The type of this variable is AnyObject!, meaning that you don't really care what sort of object this is (the exclamation point is used for its regular purpose, to make this an implicitly unwrapped optional).

➤ In listenForBackgroundNotification(), change the first line so that it stores the return value of addObserverForName() into this new instance variable:

```
func listenForBackgroundNotification() {
  observer = NSNotificationCenter.defaultCenter().addObserverForName(...
```

➤ Finally, add the deinit method:

```
deinit {
  println("*** deinit \(self)")
  NSNotificationCenter.defaultCenter().removeObserver(observer)
}
```

You're also adding a println() here so you can see some proof that the view controller really does get destroyed when you close the Tag/Edit Location screen.

➤ Run the app, edit an existing location, and tap Done to close the screen.

I don't know about you but I don't see the *** deinit message anywhere in the Xcode debug pane.

Guess what? The LocationDetailsViewController doesn't get destroyed for some reason. Of course, this was all a big setup on my part so I can tell you about closures and capturing.

Remember that in closures you always have to specify self when you want to access an instance variable or call a method? That is because closures **capture** any variables that are used inside the closure.

When it captures a variable, the closure simply stores a reference to that variable. This allows it to use the variable at some later point when the closure is actually performed.

Why is this important? If the code inside the closure uses a local variable, the method that created this variable may no longer be active by the time the closure is performed. Normally when a method ends, all locals are destroyed. But when such a local is captured by a closure, it stays alive until the closure is also done with it.

Because the closure needs to keep the objects from those captured variables alive in the time between capturing and actually performing the closure, it stores a *strong* reference to those objects. In other words, capturing means the closure becomes a shared owner of the captured objects.

What may not be immediately obvious is that self is also one of those variables and therefore gets captured by the closure. Sneaky! That's why Swift requires you to explicitly write out self inside closures, so you won't forget this value is being captured. It puts it right there in your face.

Because self is captured, the closure creates a strong reference to the active LocationDetailsViewController object and becomes a co-owner of this view controller. I bet you didn't expect that!

Remember, as long as an object has owners it is being kept alive. So this closure is keeping the view controller alive, even after you closed it!

This is known as an **ownership cycle**, because the view controller itself has a strong reference back to the closure through the observer variable.

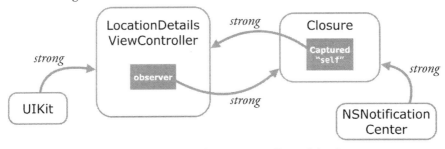

The relationship between the view controller and the closure

(In case you're wondering, the view controller's other owner is UIKit. The observer is also being kept alive by NSNotificationCenter.)

This sounds like a classic Catch-22 problem! Fortunately, there is a way to break the ownership cycle. You can give the closure a so-called **capture list**.

➤ Change listenForBackgroundNotification() to the following:

```
func listenForBackgroundNotification() {
  observer = NSNotificationCenter.defaultCenter().addObserverForName(
    UIApplicationDidEnterBackgroundNotification, object: nil,
    queue: NSOperationQueue.mainQueue()) { [weak self] notification in

    if let strongSelf = self {
      if strongSelf.presentedViewController != nil {
        strongSelf.dismissViewControllerAnimated(false, completion: nil)
      }

      strongSelf.descriptionTextView.resignFirstResponder()
    }
  }
}
```

There are a couple of new things here. Let's look at the first part of the closure:

```
{ [weak self] notification in
  . . .
}
```

The `[weak self]` bit is the capture list for the closure. It tells the closure that the variable `self` will still be captured, but as a weak reference, not strong. As a result, the closure no longer keeps the view controller alive.

Weak references are allowed to become `nil`, which means the captured `self` is now an optional inside the closure. You need to unwrap it with `if let` before you can send messages to the view controller.

Other than that, the closure still does the exact same things as before.

➤ Try it out. Open the Tag/Edit Location screen and close it again. You should now see the `println()` from `deinit` in the Xcode debug pane.

That means the view controller gets destroyed properly and the notification observer is removed from `NSNotificationCenter`.

Exercise. What happens if you remove the call to `removeObserver()` from `deinit`? Hint: add `println(self)` inside the closure. ∎

Answer: Because the observer is not removed, it says alive and active. The next time you put the app in the background, even if you're not on the Tag/Edit Location screen, this closure from this "old" observer is called again but `self` is now `nil` (the object that it captured no longer exists).

This may seem innocuous but it's a serious bug. Every time the user opens and closes the Tag/Edit Location screen you end up with a new observer that stays in memory forever. The `if let` prevents the app from crashing on a `nil` dereference of `self`, but over time all these leftover observers will eat up the app's available memory.

That's why it's always a good idea to clean up after yourself. Use `println()`'s to make sure your objects really get deallocated! (Xcode also comes with a handy tool, Instruments, that you can use to detect such issues.)

Saving photos

The ability to pick photos is rather useless if the app doesn't also save them, so that's what you'll do here.

It is possible to store images inside the Core Data store as "blobs" (Binary Large OBjects), but that is not recommended. Large blocks of data are better off stored as regular files in the app's Documents directory.

> **Note:** Core Data has an "Allows external storage" feature that is designed to make this process completely transparent for the developer. In theory, you can put data of any size into your entities and Core Data automatically decides whether to put the data into the SQLite database or store it as an external file.
>
> Unfortunately, this feature doesn't work very well in practice. It just has too many bugs to be useful. So until this part of Core Data becomes rock solid, we'll be doing it by hand.

When the image picker gives you a UIImage object with a photo, that photo only lives in the iPhone's working memory.

The photo may also be stored as a file somewhere if the user picked it from the photo library, but that's not the case if she just snapped a new picture. Besides, the user may have resized or cropped the photo.

So you have to save that UIImage to a file of your own if you want to keep it. The photos from this app will be saved in the JPEG format.

You need a way to associate that JPEG file with your Location object. The obvious solution is to store the filename in the Location object. You won't store the entire filename, just an ID, which is a positive number.

The image file itself will be named **Photo-XXX.jpg**, where XXX is the numeric ID.

➤ Open the Data Model editor. Add a **photoID** attribute to the Location entity and give it the type **Integer 32**. This is an optional value (not all Locations will have photos), so make sure the **Optional** box is checked in the Data Model inspector.

➤ Add a property for this new attribute to **Location.swift**:

```
@NSManaged var photoID: NSNumber?
```

Remember that in an object that is managed by Core Data, you have to declare the property as @NSManaged.

You may be wondering why you're declaring the type of photoID as NSNumber and not as Int (or more precisely Int32). Remember that Core Data is an Objective-C framework, so you're limited by the possibilities of that language.

For various reasons you can't represent an Int value as an optional in Objective-C, so instead you'll use the NSNumber class. Swift will automatically convert between Int values and this NSNumber, so it's no big deal.

You'll now add some other properties to the Location object to make working with the photo file a little easier.

➤ Add the hasPhoto computed property:

```
var hasPhoto: Bool {
  return photoID != nil
}
```

This determines whether the Location object has a photo associated with it or not. Swift's optionals make this easy.

➤ Add the photoPath property:

```
var photoPath: String {
  assert(photoID != nil, "No photo ID set")
  let filename = "Photo-\(photoID!.integerValue).jpg"
  return applicationDocumentsDirectory.stringByAppendingPathComponent(filename)
}
```

This property computes the full path to the JPEG file for the photo. You'll save these files inside the app's Documents directory.

Notice the use of `assert()` to make sure the `photoID` is not `nil`. An **assertion** is a special debugging tool that is used to check that your code always does something valid. If not, the app will crash with a helpful error message. You'll see more of this later when we talk about finding bugs – and squashing them.

Assertions are a form of defensive programming. Most of the crashes you've seen so far were actually caused by assertions in UIKit. They allow the app to crash in a controlled manner. Without these assertions, programming mistakes could crash the app at random moments, making it very hard to find out what went wrong.

If the app were to ask a `Location` object for its `photoPath` without having given it a valid `photoID` earlier, the app will crash with the message "No photo ID set". If so, there is a bug in the code somewhere because this is not supposed to happen. Internal consistency checks like this can be very useful.

Assertions are usually enabled only while you're developing and testing your app and disabled when you upload the final build of your app to the App Store. By then there should be no more bugs in your app (or so you would hope!). It's a good idea to use `assert()` in strategic places to catch yourself making programming errors.

Speaking of errors, Xcode complains that "applicationDocumentsDirectory" is an unresolved identifier. That's correct because you haven't added that yet. You could make a method for this as you did in the Checklists tutorial, but I've got a better idea: let's make it a global.

➤ Open **Functions.swift** and add the following code:

```
let applicationDocumentsDirectory: String = {
  let paths = NSSearchPathForDirectoriesInDomains(.DocumentDirectory, .UserDomainMask, true)
                      as! [String]
  return paths[0]
}()
```

This creates a new global constant, `applicationDocumentsDirectory`, containing the path to the app's Documents directory. It's a global because you're not putting this inside a class. This constant will exist for the duration of the app; it never goes out of scope.

As before you're using a closure to provide the code that initializes this string. Like all globals, this is evaluated lazily the very first time it is used.

> **Note:** Globals have a bad reputation. Many programmers avoid them at all costs. The problem with globals is that they create hidden dependencies between the various parts of your program. And dependencies make the program hard to change and hard to debug.
>
> But used well, globals can be very handy. It's feasible that your app will need to know the path to the Documents directory in several different places. Putting it in a global constant is a great way to solve that design problem.

➤ Switch back to **Location.swift** and add the `photoImage` property:

```
var photoImage: UIImage? {
  return UIImage(contentsOfFile: photoPath)
}
```

This method returns a `UIImage` object by loading the image file. You'll need this later to show the photos for existing `Location` objects.

Note that this property has the optional type `UIImage?` – that's because loading the image may fail if the file is damaged or removed. Of course, that *shouldn't* happen, but you've heard of Murphy's Law. It's good to get into the habit of defensive programming.

There is one more thing to add, the `nextPhotoID()` method. This is a class method, meaning that you don't need to have a `Location` object to call it. You can call this method anytime from anywhere.

➤ Add the `nextPhotoID()` method:

```
class func nextPhotoID() -> Int {
  let userDefaults = NSUserDefaults.standardUserDefaults()
  let currentID = userDefaults.integerForKey("PhotoID")
  userDefaults.setInteger(currentID + 1, forKey: "PhotoID")
  userDefaults.synchronize()
  return currentID
}
```

You need to have some way to generate a unique ID for each `Location` object. All `NSManagedObjects` have an `objectID` method, but that returns something unreadable such as:

```
<x-coredata://C26CC559-959C-49F6-BEF0-F221D6F3F04A/Location/p1>
```

You can't really use that in a filename. So instead, you're going to put a simple integer in `NSUserDefaults` and update it every time the app asks for a new ID. (This is similar to what you did in the last tutorial to make `ChecklistItem` IDs for use with local notifications.)

It may seem a little silly to use `NSUserDefaults` for this when you're already using Core Data as the data store, but with `NSUserDefaults` the `nextPhotoID()` method is only five lines. You've seen how verbose the code is for fetching something from Core Data and then saving it again. This is just as easy. (As an exercise, you could try to implement these IDs using Core Data.)

That does it for `Location`. Now you have to save the photo in the Tag/Edit Location screen and fill in the `Location` object's `photoID` field. This happens in the Location Details View Controller's `done()` action.

➤ In **LocationDetailsViewController.swift**, in the `done()` method, add the following in between where you set the properties of the `Location` object and where you save the managed object context:

```
if let image = image {
  // 1
  if !location.hasPhoto {
    location.photoID = Location.nextPhotoID()
  }
  // 2
  let data = UIImageJPEGRepresentation(image, 0.5)
  // 3
  var error: NSError?
  if !data.writeToFile(location.photoPath, options: .DataWritingAtomic, error: &error) {
    println("Error writing file: \(error)")
  }
}
```

This code is only performed if `image` is not `nil`, in other words, when the user has picked a photo.

1. You need to get a new ID and assign it to the Location's photoID property, but only if you're adding a photo to a Location that didn't already have one. If a photo existed, you simply keep the same ID and overwrite the existing JPEG file.

2. The UIImageJPEGRepresentation() function converts the UIImage into the JPEG format and returns an NSData object. NSData is an object that represents a blob of binary data, usually the contents of a file.

3. Here you save the NSData object to the path given by the photoPath property. (Also notice the use of the NSError pattern again.)

➤ Before you run the app, first remove the old **DataStore.sqlite** file (or simply reset the Simulator or remove the app from your test device). You have added a new attribute to the data model (photoID), so the data source is out of sync.

➤ Run the app, tag a location, choose a photo, and press Done to exit the screen. Now the photo you picked should be saved in the app's Documents directory as a regular JPEG file.

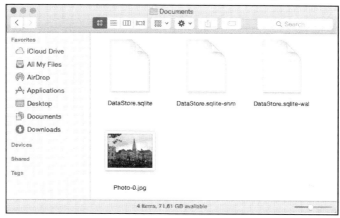

The photo is saved in the app's Documents folder

➤ Tag another location and add a photo to it. Hmm... if you look into the app's Documents directory, this seems to have overwritten the previous photo.

Exercise. Try to debug this one on your own. What is going wrong here? This is a tough one! ∎

Answer: When you create a new Location object, its photoID property gets a default value of 0. That means each Location initially has a photoID of 0. That should really be nil, which means "no photo".

➤ In **LocationDetailsViewController.swift**, add the following line near the top of done():

```
@IBAction func done() {
  . . .
  } else {
    hudView.text = "Tagged"
    location = NSEntityDescription.insertNewObjectForEntityForName("Location",
                       inManagedObjectContext: managedObjectContext) as! Location
    location.photoID = nil
  }
  . . .
}
```

You now give new `Location` objects a `photoID` of nil so that the `hasPhoto` property correctly recognizes that these `Locations` do not have a photo yet.

➤ Run the app again and tag multiple locations with photos. Verify that now each photo is saved individually.

If you have Liya or another SQLite inspection tool, you can verify that each `Location` object has been given a unique `photoID` value (in the ZPHOTOID column):

The Location objects with unique photoId values in Liya

Editing photos

So far all the changes you've made were for the Tag Location screen and adding new locations. Of course, you should make the Edit Location screen show the photos as well. The change to `LocationDetailsViewController` is quite simple.

➤ Change `viewDidLoad()` in **LocationDetailsViewController.swift** to:

```
override func viewDidLoad() {
  super.viewDidLoad()

  if let location = locationToEdit {
    title = "Edit Location"
    if location.hasPhoto {
      if let image = location.photoImage {
        showImage(image)
      }
    }
  }
  . . .
```

If the `Location` that you're editing has a photo, this calls `showImage()` to display it in the photo cell.

Recall that the `photoImage` property returns an optional, `UIImage?`, so you use `if let` to unwrap it. This is another bit of defensive programming.

Sure, if `hasPhoto` is `true` there should always be a valid image file present. But it's possible to imagine a scenario where there isn't – the JPEG file could have been erased or corrupted – even though that "should" never happen. (I'm sure you've had your own share of computer gremlins eating important files.)

Note also what you **don't** do here: the Location's image is *not* assigned to the image instance variable. If the user doesn't change the photo, then you don't need to write it out to a file again – it's already in that file and doing perfectly fine, thank you.

If you were to put the photo in the image variable, then done() would overwrite that existing file with the exact same data, which is a little silly. Therefore, the image instance variable will only be set when the user picks a new photo.

➤ Run the app and take a peek at the existing locations from the Locations or Map tabs. The Edit Location screen should now show the photos for the locations you're editing.

➤ Verify that you can also change the photo and that the JPEG file in the app's Documents directory gets overwritten when you press the Done button.

There's another editing operation the user can perform on a location: deletion. What happens to the image file when the location is deleted? At the moment, nothing. That photo stays forever in the app's Documents directory.

Let's do something about that and remove the file when the Location object is deleted.

➤ First add a new method to **Location.swift**:

```
func removePhotoFile() {
  if hasPhoto {
    let path = photoPath
    let fileManager = NSFileManager.defaultManager()
    if fileManager.fileExistsAtPath(path) {
      var error: NSError?
      if !fileManager.removeItemAtPath(path, error: &error) {
        println("Error removing file: \(error!)")
      }
    }
  }
}
```

This is a code snippet that you can use to remove any file or folder. The NSFileManager class has all kinds of useful methods for dealing with the file system.

➤ Deleting locations happens in **LocationsViewController.swift**. Add the following line to tableView(commitEditingStyle, forRowAtIndexPath):

```
override func tableView(tableView: UITableView,
                  commitEditingStyle editingStyle: UITableViewCellEditingStyle,
                  forRowAtIndexPath indexPath: NSIndexPath) {
  if editingStyle == .Delete {
    let location = fetchedResultsController.objectAtIndexPath(indexPath) as! Location
    location.removePhotoFile()
    managedObjectContext.deleteObject(location)
    . . .
```

The new line calls removePhotoFile() on the Location object.

➤ Try it out. Add a new location and give it a photo. You should see the JPEG file in the Documents directory.

Delete the new location from the Locations screen and look in the Documents directory to make sure the JPEG file truly is a goner.

Thumbnails of the photos

Now that locations can have photos, it's a good idea to show thumbnails for these photos in the Locations tab. That will liven up this screen a little... a plain table view with just a bunch of text isn't particularly exciting.

➤ Go to the storyboard editor. In the prototype cell on the **Locations View Controller,** move the two labels to X = 82. Make them 238 points wide.

➤ Drag a new **Image View** into the cell. Place it at the top-left corner of the cell. Give it the following position: X = 15, Y = 2. Make it 52 by 52 points big.

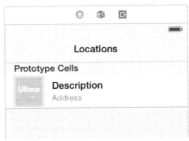

The table view cell has an image view

➤ Connect the image view to a new `UIImageView` outlet on `LocationCell`, named **photoImageView.**

Exercise. Make this connection with the Assistant editor. Tip: you should connect the image view to the cell, not to the view controller. ∎

Now you can put any image into the table view cell simply by placing it inside the image view from `LocationCell`'s `photoImageView` property.

➤ Go to **LocationCell.swift** and add the following method:

```
func imageForLocation(location: Location) -> UIImage {
  if location.hasPhoto {
    if let image = location.photoImage {
      return image
    }
  }
  return UIImage()
}
```

This returns either the image from the Location or an empty placeholder image.

➤ Call this new method from the bottom of `configureForLocation()`:

```
photoImageView.image = imageForLocation(location)
```

➤ Try it out. The Locations tab should now look something like this:

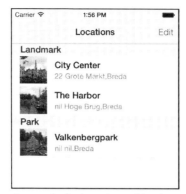

Images in the Locations table view

You've got thumbnails, all right!

But look closely and you'll see that the images are a little squashed again. That's because you didn't set the Aspect Fit content mode on the image view – but there's a bigger problem here. Literally.

These photos are potentially huge (2592 by 1936 pixels or more), even though the image view is only 52 pixels square. To make them fit, the image view needs to scale down the images by a lot (which is also why they look a little "gritty").

What if you have tens or even hundreds of locations? That is going to require a ton of memory and processing speed just to display these tiny thumbnails. A better solution is to scale down the images before you put them into the table view cell.

And what better way to do that than to use an extension?

Extensions

So far you've used extensions on your view controllers to group related functionality together, such as delegate methods. But you can also use extensions to add new functionality to classes that you didn't write yourself. That includes classes from the iOS frameworks, such as `UIImage`.

If you ever catch yourself thinking, "Gee, I wish object X had such-or-so method" then you can probably give it that method by making an extension.

Suppose you want `String` to have a method for adding random words to the string. You could add the `addRandomWord()` method to `String` as follows.

First you create a new source file, for example **String+RandomWord.swift**. It would look like this:

```
import Foundation

extension String {
  func addRandomWord() -> String {
    let value = arc4random_uniform(3)

    var word: String

    switch value {
    case 0:
      word = "rabbit"
    case 1:
      word = "banana"
```

```
        case 2:
            word = "boat"
        default:
            word = ""
        }
        return self + word
    }
}
```

Anywhere in your code you can now call `addRandomWord()` on any `String` value:

```
let someString = "Hello, "
let result = someString.addRandomWord()
println("The queen says: \(result)")
```

Extensions are pretty cool because they make it simple to add new functionality into an existing class. In other programming languages you would have to make a subclass and put your new methods in there, but extensions are often a cleaner solution.

You can also use extensions on types that don't even allow inheritance, such as `structs` and `enums`. Besides new methods you can also add new computed properties, but you can't add regular instance variables.

You are going to add an extension to `UIImage` that lets you resize the image. You'll use it as follows:

```
return image.resizedImageWithBounds(CGSize(width: 52, height: 52))
```

The `resizedImageWithBounds()` method is new. The "bounds" is the size of the rectangle (or square in this case) that encloses the image. If the image itself is not square, then the resized image may actually be smaller than the bounds.

Let's write the extension.

➤ Add a new file to the project and choose the **Swift File** template. Name the file **UIImage+Resize.swift**.

➤ Replace the contents of this new file with:

```
import UIKit

extension UIImage {
  func resizedImageWithBounds(bounds: CGSize) -> UIImage {
    let horizontalRatio = bounds.width / size.width
    let verticalRatio = bounds.height / size.height
    let ratio = min(horizontalRatio, verticalRatio)
    let newSize = CGSize(width: size.width * ratio, height: size.height * ratio)

    UIGraphicsBeginImageContextWithOptions(newSize, true, 0)
    drawInRect(CGRect(origin: CGPoint.zeroPoint, size: newSize))
    let newImage = UIGraphicsGetImageFromCurrentImageContext()
    UIGraphicsEndImageContext()

    return newImage
  }
}
```

This method first calculates how big the image can be in order to fit inside the bounds rectangle. It uses the "aspect fit" approach to keep the aspect ratio intact.

Then it creates a new image context and draws the image into that. We haven't really dealt with graphics contexts before, but they are an important concept in Core Graphics (it has nothing to do with the managed object context from Core Data, even though they're both called "context").

Lets put this extension in action.

➤ Switch to **LocationCell.swift**. Update the imageForLocation() method:

```
func imageForLocation(location: Location) -> UIImage {
  if location.hasPhoto {
    if let image = location.photoImage {
      return image.resizedImageWithBounds(CGSize(width: 52, height: 52))
    }
  }
  return UIImage()
}
```

➤ Run the app. The thumbnails look like this:

City Center
22 Grote Markt,Breda

The photos are shrunk to the size of the thumbnails

The images are a little blurry, and they still seem to be stretched out. This is because the content mode on the image view is still wrong.

Previously it shrunk the big photos to 52 by 52 points, but now the thumbnails may actually be smaller than 52 points (unless the photo was perfectly square) and they get scaled up to fill the entire image view rectangle.

➤ Go to the storyboard and set the **Mode** of the image view to **Center**.

➤ Run the app again and now the photos look A-OK:

City Center
22 Grote Markt,Breda

The thumbnails now have the correct aspect ratio

Exercise. Change the resize function in the UIImage extension to resize using the "Aspect Fill" rules instead of the "Aspect Fit" rules. Both keep the aspect ratio intact but Aspect Fit keeps the entire image visible while Aspect Fill fills up the entire rectangle and may cut off parts of the sides. In other words, Aspect Fit scales to the longest side but Aspect Fill scales to the shortest side. ■

Aspect Fit
Keeps the entire image
but adds empty border

Aspect Fill
Fills up the whole frame
but cuts off sides

Aspect Fit vs. Aspect Fill

Handling low-memory situations

The UIImagePickerController is very memory-hungry. Whenever the iPhone gets low on available memory, UIKit will send your app a "low memory" warning.

```
2014-09-27 14:06:29.556 MyLocations[17575:545318] Received memory warning.



All Output ⌄                                                              🗑 ▢▢
```

When that happens you should reclaim as much memory as possible, or iOS might be forced to terminate the app. And that's something to avoid – users generally don't like apps that suddenly quit on them!

Chances are that your app gets one or more low-memory warnings while the image picker is open, especially when you run it on a device that has other apps suspended in the background. Photos take up a lot of space – especially when your camera is 5 or more megapixels – so it's no wonder that memory fills up quickly.

You can respond to low-memory warnings by overriding the didReceiveMemoryWarning() method in your view controllers to free up any memory you no longer need. This is often done for things that can easily be recalculated or recreated later, such as thumbnails or other cached objects.

UIKit is already pretty smart about low memory situations and it will do everything it can to release memory, including the thumbnail images of rows that are not (or no longer) visible in your table view.

For MyLocations there's not much that you can or need to do to free up additional memory; you can rely on UIKit to automatically take care of it. But in your own apps you might want to take extra measures, depending on the sort of cached data that you have.

By the way, on the Simulator you can trigger a low memory warning using the **Hardware →
Simulate Memory Warning** menu item. It's smart to test your apps under low memory conditions, because that's what they are going to encounter out in the wild once they're running on real users' devices.

Great, that concludes all the functionality for this app. Now it's time to fine-tune its looks.

You can find the project files for the app up to this point under **06 – Photo Picker** in the tutorial's Source Code folder.

Making the app look good

Apps with appealing visuals sell better than ugly ones. Usually I don't wait with the special sauce until the end of a project, but for these tutorials it's clearer if you first get all the functionality in before you improve the looks. Now that the app works as it should, let's make it look good!

You're going to go from this,

to this:

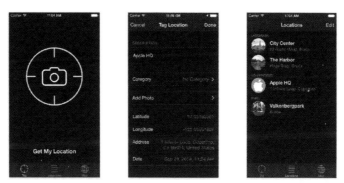

The main screen gets the biggest makeover, but you'll also tweak the others a little.

No more 'nil' in placemarks

You may have noticed that the reverse geocoded street address often contains the text "nil". That means one or more of its fields do not have a value. Whenever you convert a nil object into a string, it – surprise! – says "nil".

That's not very user-friendly, so you'll make the logic for displaying placemarks a little smarter.

If you haven't noticed any "nil" before, then launch the app in the Simulator and set the simulated location to London, England (in the Xcode Debugger pane). You'll see missing house numbers and/or street names, for example:

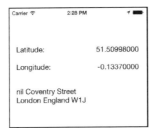

No street name was found for this location

> **Note:** For some reason, UK postal codes are missing the last few characters. The above address should really be London England W1J 9HP. This appears to be a bug in Core Location.

There are three places where you convert CLPlacemark objects into strings:

- CurrentLocationViewController, the main screen
- LocationDetailsViewController, the Tag/Edit Location screen
- LocationsViewController, the list of saved locations

Let's start with the main screen. CurrentLocationViewController has a method named stringFromPlacemark() where this conversion happens. It currently does this:

```
func stringFromPlacemark(placemark: CLPlacemark) -> String {
  return "\(placemark.subThoroughfare) \(placemark.thoroughfare)\n" +
       "\(placemark.locality) \(placemark.administrativeArea) \(placemark.postalCode)"
}
```

It may be a little hard to read with all those \( ) symbols, but this returns a string that looks like:

```
subThoroughfare thoroughfare
locality administrativeArea postalCode
```

This string goes into a UILabel that has room for two lines, so you use the \n character sequence to create a line-break between the thoroughfare and locality.

The problem is that any of these fields may be nil. You'll make the code smarter so that it skips these empty fields.

> In **CurrentLocationViewController.swift**, change stringFromPlacemark() to the following:

```
func stringFromPlacemark(placemark: CLPlacemark) -> String {
  // 1
  var line1 = ""
  // 2
  if placemark.subThoroughfare != nil {
    line1 += placemark.subThoroughfare
  }
  // 3
  if placemark.thoroughfare != nil {
    if !line1.isEmpty {
      line1 += " "
    }
    line1 += placemark.thoroughfare
  }
  // 4
  var line2 = ""
```

```
  if placemark.locality != nil {
    line2 += placemark.locality
  }
  if placemark.administrativeArea != nil {
    if !line2.isEmpty {
      line2 += " "
    }
    line2 += placemark.administrativeArea
  }
  if placemark.postalCode != nil {
    if !line2.isEmpty {
      line2 += " "
    }
    line2 += placemark.postalCode
  }
  // 5
  return line1 + "\n" + line2
}
```

Let's look at this in detail:

1. Create new string variable for the first line of text.

2. If the placemark has a subThoroughfare, add it to the string.

3. Adding the thoroughfare is done similarly, but you also put a space between it and subThoroughfare so they don't get glued together. If there was no subThoroughfare in the placemark, then you don't want to add that space.

4. The same logic goes for the second line. This adds the locality, administrative area, and postal code, with spaces between them where appropriate.

5. Finally, the two lines are concatenated (added together) with a newline character in between.

Try it out, there should no longer be any "nil" in the address label – but there's a lot of repetition going on in this method. You can refactor this.

Exercise. Try to make this method simpler by moving the common logic into a new method. ∎

Answer: Here is how I did it.

➤ Add the following method:

```
func addText(text: String?, toLine line: String, withSeparator separator: String) -> String {
  var result = line
  if let text = text {
    if !line.isEmpty {
      result += separator
    }
    result += text
  }
  return result
}
```

This adds text (an optional string because it may be nil) to a regular string, with a separator such as a space or comma. The separator is only used if line isn't empty.

➤ Now you can rewrite stringFromPlacemark() as follows:

```
func stringFromPlacemark(placemark: CLPlacemark) -> String {
  var line1 = ""
  line1 = addText(placemark.subThoroughfare, toLine: line1, withSeparator: "")
  line1 = addText(placemark.thoroughfare, toLine: line1, withSeparator: " ")
```

```
var line2 = ""
line2 = addText(placemark.locality, toLine: line2, withSeparator: "")
line2 = addText(placemark.administrativeArea, toLine: line2, withSeparator: " ")
line2 = addText(placemark.postalCode, toLine: line2, withSeparator: " ")

if line1.isEmpty {
  return line2 + "\n "
} else {
  return line1 + "\n" + line2
}
}
```

That is a lot cleaner.

But what's up with the if-statement at the bottom? UILabel always centers its text vertically. You made the label big enough to fit two lines of text, but if there's only one line's worth then that text will be positioned in the middle of the label, not at the top. For some apps that might be fine, but here I want to always align the text at the top.

If there is no text in the line1 string, then you add a newline and a space to the end of line2. This will force the UILabel to always draw two lines of text, even if the second one looks empty (it only has a space).

➤ Run the app to see if it works.

That settles CurrentLocationViewController. What about the other two controllers? Well, they probably need to do something very similar.

You could either copy the addText(toLine, withSeparator) method into the other two view controllers, which causes code duplication, or... you can put it into an extension on String. I bet you can guess which one we're going to pick.

➤ Add a new file to the project using the **Swift File** template. Name it **String+ AddText**.

➤ Replace the contents of **String+AddText.swift** with:

```
extension String {
  mutating func addText(text: String?, withSeparator separator: String) {
    if let text = text {
      if !isEmpty {
        self += separator
      }
      self += text
    }
  }
}
```

You've simply moved the method into this new extension.

The only difference is that the toLine: parameter is no longer necessary because this method now always modifies the string object that it belongs to. It adds the text and the separator to self.

Mutating

Notice the mutating keyword. You haven't seen this before. Sorry, it doesn't have anything to do with X-men – programming is certainly fun but it isn't *that* exciting.

When a method changes the value of a struct, it must be marked as mutating. Recall that String is a struct, which is a value type, and therefore cannot be modified when declared with let.

The mutating keyword tells Swift that the addText(withSeparator) method can only be used on strings that are made with var, but not on strings made with let.

If you try to modify self in a method on a struct that is not marked as mutating, Swift considers this an error.

You don't need to use the mutating keyword on methods inside a class because classes are reference types and can always be mutated, even if they are declared with let.

➤ Back in **CurrentLocationViewController.swift**, change stringFromPlacemark() to the following:

```swift
func stringFromPlacemark(placemark: CLPlacemark) -> String {
  var line1 = ""
  line1.addText(placemark.subThoroughfare, withSeparator: "")
  line1.addText(placemark.thoroughfare, withSeparator: " ")

  var line2 = ""
  line2.addText(placemark.locality, withSeparator: "")
  line2.addText(placemark.administrativeArea, withSeparator: " ")
  line2.addText(placemark.postalCode, withSeparator: " ")

  if line1.isEmpty {
    return line2 + "\n "
  } else {
    return line1 + "\n" + line2
  }
}
```

➤ Remove the addText(toLine, withSeparator) method; it's no longer used for anything.

There's still a small thing you can do to improve the new addText(withSeparator) method from the String extension.

➤ In **String+AddText.swift**, change the line that defines the method to:

```swift
mutating func addText(text: String?, withSeparator separator: String = "") {
```

You've added the = "" bit behind the separator parameter. This is known as a **default parameter value**. If a parameter has a default value, it allows callers of this method to leave out that parameter.

When you now write,

```swift
line1.addText(placemark.subThoroughfare)
```

it does the same thing as:

```swift
line1.addText(placemark.subThoroughfare, withSeparator: "")
```

In this case the default value for separator is the empty string. If the withSeparator parameter is left out, separator will be "".

➤ Make these changes in **CurrentLocationViewController.swift**:

```swift
func stringFromPlacemark(placemark: CLPlacemark) -> String {

  line1.addText(placemark.subThoroughfare)
  . . .

  line2.addText(placemark.locality)
  . . .
```

Where the separator was the empty string, you leave out the `withSeparator: ""` part of the method call.

Now you have a pretty clean solution that you can re-use in the other two view controllers.

➤ Go to **LocationDetailsViewController.swift**. Change its `stringFromPlacemark()` method to:

```swift
func stringFromPlacemark(placemark: CLPlacemark) -> String {
  var line = ""
  line.addText(placemark.subThoroughfare)
  line.addText(placemark.thoroughfare, withSeparator: " ")
  line.addText(placemark.locality, withSeparator: ", ")
  line.addText(placemark.administrativeArea, withSeparator: ", ")
  line.addText(placemark.postalCode, withSeparator: " ")
  line.addText(placemark.country, withSeparator: ", ")
  return line
}
```

It's slightly different from how the main screen does it.

Here you make a string that looks like: `"subThoroughfare thoroughfare, locality, administrativeArea postalCode, country"`.

There are no \n newline characters and some of the elements are separated by commas instead of just spaces. Newlines aren't necessary here because the label will word-wrap.

The final place where placemarks are shown is `LocationsViewController`. However, this class doesn't have a `stringFromPlacemark()` method. Instead, the logic for formatting the address lives in `LocationCell`.

➤ Go to **LocationCell.swift**. Change the relevant part of `configureForLocation()`:

```swift
func configureForLocation(location: Location) {
  . . .
  if let placemark = location.placemark {
    var text = ""
    text.addText(placemark.subThoroughfare)
    text.addText(placemark.thoroughfare, withSeparator: " ")
    text.addText(placemark.locality, withSeparator: ", ")
    addressLabel.text = text

  } else {
    . . .
```

You only show the street and the city so the conversion is simpler. The string will be `"subThoroughfare thoroughfare, locality"`.

If there is now a bit of missing data, such as the `subThoroughfare` that often is `nil`, the app simply won't display it. That's a lot nicer than showing the text "nil" to the user.

And that's it for placemarks.

The labels no longer say "nil"

Back to black

Right now the app looks like a typical standard iOS 8 app: lots of white, gray tab bar, blue tint color. Let's go for a radically different look and paint the whole thing black.

➤ Open the storyboard and go to the **Current Location View Controller**. Select the top-level view and change its **Background Color** to **Black Color**.

➤ Select all the labels (probably easiest from the outline pane since they are now invisible) and set their **Color** to **White Color**.

➤ Change the **Font** of the **(Latitude/Longitude goes here)** labels to **System Bold 17**.

➤ Select the two buttons and change their **Font** to **System Bold 20**, to make them slightly larger. You may need to resize their frames to make the text fit (remember, ⌘= is the magic keyboard shortcut).

➤ In the **File inspector**, change **Global Tint** to the color **Red: 255, Green: 238, Blue: 136**. That makes the buttons and other interactive elements yellow, which stands out nicely against the black background.

➤ Select the Get My Location button and change its **Text Color** to **White Color**. This provides some contrast between the two buttons.

The storyboard should look like this:

The new yellow-on-black design

When you run the app, there are two obvious problems:

1. the status bar text has become invisible (it is black text on a black background)

2. the grey tab bar sticks out like a sore thumb (also, the yellow tint color doesn't get applied to the tab bar icons)

To fix this, you can use the UIAppearance API. This is a set of methods that lets you customize the look of the standard UIKit controls.

You can customize on a per-control basis, or you can use the "appearance proxy" to change the look of all of the controls of a particular type at once. That's what you're going to do here.

➤ Add the following method to **AppDelegate.swift**:

```
func customizeAppearance() {
  UINavigationBar.appearance().barTintColor = UIColor.blackColor()

  UINavigationBar.appearance().titleTextAttributes = [
              NSForegroundColorAttributeName: UIColor.whiteColor() ]

  UITabBar.appearance().barTintColor = UIColor.blackColor()

  let tintColor = UIColor(red: 255/255.0, green: 238/255.0, blue: 136/255.0, alpha: 1.0)
  UITabBar.appearance().tintColor = tintColor
}
```

This changes the "bar tint" or background color of all navigation bars and tab bars in the app to black in one fell swoop. It also sets the color of the navigation bar's title label to white and applies the tint color to the tab bar.

➤ Call this method from the top of application(didFinishLaunchingWithOptions):

```
func application(application: UIApplication,
            didFinishLaunchingWithOptions launchOptions: [NSObject : AnyObject]?) -> Bool {
  customizeAppearance()
  . . .
}
```

This looks better already.

The tar bar is now nearly black and has yellow icons

On the Locations and Map screens you can clearly see that the bars now have a dark tint:

The navigation and tab bars appear in a dark color

Keep in mind that the bar tint is not the true background color. The bars are still translucent, which is why they appear as a medium gray rather than pure black.

Tab bar icons

The icons in the tab bar could also do with some improvement. The Xcode Tabbed Application template put a bunch of cruft in the app that you're no longer using, so let's get rid of it.

➤ Remove the **SecondViewController.swift** file from the project.

➤ Remove the **first** and **second** images from the asset catalog (Images.xcassets).

Tab bar images should be basic grayscale images of up to 30 × 30 points (that is 60 × 60 pixels for Retina and 90 × 90 pixels for Retina HD). You don't have to tint the images; iOS will automatically draw them in the proper color.

➤ The resources for this tutorial include an **Images** directory. Add the files from this folder to the asset catalog. (Most of these images are in white, which makes them hard to see on the white background of the asset catalog, but trust me they are there.)

➤ Go to the storyboard. Select the **Tab Bar Item** of the Current Location screen. In the **Attributes inspector,** under **Image** choose **Tag.**

Choosing an image for a Tab Bar Item

➤ For the Tab Bar Item from the navigation controller attached to the Locations screen, choose the **Locations** image.

➤ For the Tab Bar Item from the Map View Controller, choose the **Map** image.

Now the tab bar looks a lot more appealing:

The tab bar with proper icons

The status bar

The status bar is currently invisible on the Tag screen and appears as black text on dark gray on the other two screens. It will look better if the status bar text is white instead.

To do this, you need to override the preferredStatusBarStyle() method in your view controllers and make it return the value .LightContent.

For some reason that won't work for view controllers embedded in a Navigation Controller, such as the Locations tab and the Tag/Edit Location screens.

The simplest way to make the status bar white for all your view controllers in the entire app is to replace the UITabBarController with your own subclass.

➤ Add a new file to the project using the **Swift File** template. Name it **MyTabBarController**.

➤ Replace the contents of **MyTabBarController.swift** with:

```
import UIKit

class MyTabBarController: UITabBarController {
  override func preferredStatusBarStyle() -> UIStatusBarStyle {
    return .LightContent
  }
}
```

```
override func childViewControllerForStatusBarStyle() -> UIViewController? {
    return nil
  }
}
```

By returning `nil` from `childViewControllerForStatusBarStyle()`, the tab bar controller will look at its own `preferredStatusBarStyle()` method.

➤ In the storyboard, select the Tab Bar Controller and in the **Identity inspector** change its **Class** to **MyTabBarController**. This tells the storyboard that it should now create an instance of your subclass when the app starts up.

That's right, you can replace standard UIKit components with your own subclass!

Subclassing lets you change what the built-in UIKit objects do – that's the power of object-oriented programming – although you probably shouldn't get carried away and alter their behavior *too* much. Before you know it, your app ends up with an identity crisis!

`MyTabBarController` still does everything that the standard `UITabBarController` does. You only overrode `preferredStatusBarStyle()` to change the status bar color.

You can plug this `MyTabBarController` class into any app that uses a tab bar controller, and from then on all its view controllers have a white status bar.

You also need to make a subclass for the Navigation Controller that embeds the Tag/Edit Location screen, because that is presented modally on top of the other screens and is therefore not part of the Tab Bar Controller hierarchy.

➤ Add a new file to the project using the **Swift File** template. Name it **MyNavigationController**.

➤ Replace the contents of **MyNavigationController.swift** with:

```
import UIKit

class MyNavigationController: UINavigationController {
  override func preferredStatusBarStyle() -> UIStatusBarStyle {
    return .LightContent
  }
}
```

➤ In the storyboard, select the Navigation Controller that is connected to the Location Details View Controller. Change its **Class** to **MyNavigationController**.

(You don't have to change the other navigation controller, although it wouldn't cause any trouble if you did.)

Now the status bar is white everywhere:

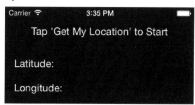

The status bar is visible again

Well, almost everywhere… When you open the photo picker, the status bar fades to black again. You can probably guess what the solution is…

➤ Add a new file to the project using the **Swift File** template. Name it **MyImagePickerController**. (Getting a sense of déjà vu?)

➤ Replace the contents of **MyImagePickerController.swift** with:

```
import UIKit

class MyImagePickerController: UIImagePickerController {
  override func preferredStatusBarStyle() -> UIStatusBarStyle {
    return .LightContent
  }
}
```

Now instead of instantiating the standard `UIImagePickerController` to pick a photo, you'll use this new subclass instead.

➤ Go to **LocationDetailsViewController.swift**. In `takePhotoWithCamera()` and `choosePhotoFromLibrary()`, change the line that creates the image picker to:

```
let imagePicker = MyImagePickerController()
```

This is allowed because `MyImagePickerController` is a subclass of the standard `UIImagePickerController`, so it has the same properties and methods. As far as UIKit is concerned, the two are interchangeable. So you can use your subclass anywhere you'd use `UIImagePickerController`.

While you're at it, the photo picker still uses the standard blue tint color. That makes its navigation bar buttons hard to read (blue text on a dark gray navigation bar). The fix is simple: set the tint color on the Image Picker Controller just before you present it.

➤ Also add the following line to the two methods:

```
imagePicker.view.tintColor = view.tintColor
```

Now the Cancel button appears in yellow instead of blue.

The photo picker with the new colors

There is one more thing to change. When the app starts up, iOS looks in the Info.plist file to determine whether it should show a status bar while the app launches, and if so, what color that status bar should be.

Right now, it's set to Default, which is the black status bar.

➤ Just to be thorough, go to the **Project Settings** screen. In the **General** tab, under **Deployment Info** is a **Status Bar Style** option. Change this to **Light**.

Changing the status bar style for app startup

And now the status bar really is white everywhere!

The map screen

The Map screen currently has a somewhat busy navigation bar with three pieces of text in it: the title and the two buttons.

The bar button items have text labels

The design advice that Apple gives for iOS 8 apps is to prefer text to icons because icons tend to be harder to understand. The disadvantage of using text is that it makes your navigation bar more crowded.

There are two possible solutions:

1. Remove the title. If the purpose of the screen is obvious, which it is in this case, then the title "Map" is superfluous. You might as well remove it.

2. Keep the title but replace the button labels with icons.

For this app you'll choose the second option.

➤ Go to the Map scene in the storyboard and select the **Locations** bar button item. In the **Attributes inspector**, under **Image** choose **Pin**. This will remove the text from the button.

➤ For the User bar button item, choose the **User** image.

The Map screen now looks like this:

The Map screen with the button icons

Notice that the dot for the user's current location is drawn in the yellow tint color (it was a blue dot before).

The **(i)** button on the map annotation also appears in yellow, making it hard to see on the white callout. Fortunately, you can override the tint color on a per-view basis.

➤ In **MapViewController.swift**, in the method mapView(viewForAnnotation), add this below the line that sets annotationView.pinColor:

```
annotationView.tintColor = UIColor(white: 0.0, alpha: 0.5)
```

This sets the annotation's tint color to half-opaque black:

The callout button is now easier to see

Fixing up the table views

The app is starting to shape up but there are still some details to take care of. The table views, for example, are still very white.

Unfortunately, what UIAppearance can do for table views is very limited, so you'll have to customize each of the table views individually.

➤ Add the following lines to viewDidLoad() in **LocationsViewController.swift**:

```
tableView.backgroundColor = UIColor.blackColor()
tableView.separatorColor = UIColor(white: 1.0, alpha: 0.2)
tableView.indicatorStyle = .White
```

This makes the table view itself black but does not alter the cells.

➤ In **LocationCell.swift**, add the `awakeFromNib()` method to change the appearance of the actual cells:

```
override func awakeFromNib() {
  super.awakeFromNib()

  backgroundColor = UIColor.blackColor()
  descriptionLabel.textColor = UIColor.whiteColor()
  descriptionLabel.highlightedTextColor = descriptionLabel.textColor
  addressLabel.textColor = UIColor(white: 1.0, alpha: 0.4)
  addressLabel.highlightedTextColor = addressLabel.textColor
}
```

Every object that comes from a storyboard has the `awakeFromNib()` method. This method is invoked when UIKit loads the object from the storyboard. It's the ideal place to customize its looks.

> **Note:** In case you're wondering why it's not called `awakeFromStoryboard()`, this is simply for historical reasons when nibs were all we had. A nib (or XIB) is like a storyboard but it can only hold the design of a single screen. Even though they are not as popular as they once were, you can still use nibs. In the next tutorial you'll see an example of that.

➤ Run the app. That's starting to look pretty good already:

The table view cells are now white-on-black

There is a small issue. When you tap a cell it still lights up in a bright color, which is a little extreme. It would look better if the selection color was more subdued.

There is no "selectionColor" property on `UITableViewCell`, but you can give it a different view to display when it is selected.

➤ Add the following to the bottom of `awakeFromNib()`:

```
let selectionView = UIView(frame: CGRect.zeroRect)
selectionView.backgroundColor = UIColor(white: 1.0, alpha: 0.2)
selectedBackgroundView = selectionView
```

This creates a new `UIView` filled with a dark gray color. This new view is placed on top of the cell's background when the user taps on the cell. It looks like the following image:

The selected cell (The Harbor) has a subtly different background color

The section headers are also on the heavy side. There is no easy way to customize the existing headers but you can replace them with a view of your own.

➤ Go to **LocationsViewController.swift** and add the following method:

```
// MARK: - UITableViewDelegate

override func tableView(tableView: UITableView,
                        viewForHeaderInSection section: Int) -> UIView? {

  let labelRect = CGRect(x: 15, y: tableView.sectionHeaderHeight - 14,
                         width: 300, height: 14)
  let label = UILabel(frame: labelRect)
  label.font = UIFont.boldSystemFontOfSize(11)

  label.text = tableView.dataSource!.tableView!(tableView, titleForHeaderInSection: section)

  label.textColor = UIColor(white: 1.0, alpha: 0.4)
  label.backgroundColor = UIColor.clearColor()

  let separatorRect = CGRect(x: 15, y: tableView.sectionHeaderHeight - 0.5,
                             width: tableView.bounds.size.width - 15, height: 0.5)
  let separator = UIView(frame: separatorRect)
  separator.backgroundColor = tableView.separatorColor

  let viewRect = CGRect(x: 0, y: 0, width: tableView.bounds.size.width,
                        height: tableView.sectionHeaderHeight)
  let view = UIView(frame: viewRect)
  view.backgroundColor = UIColor(white: 0, alpha: 0.85)
  view.addSubview(label)
  view.addSubview(separator)

  return view
}
```

This is a UITableView delegate method. It gets called once for each section in the table view.

Here you create a label for the section name, a 1-pixel high view that functions as a separator line, and a container view to hold these two subviews.

It looks like this:

The section headers now draw much less attention to themselves

> **Note:** Did you notice anything special about the following line?
>
> ```
> label.text = tableView.dataSource!.tableView!(tableView,
>                                 titleForHeaderInSection: section)
> ```
>
> The dataSource property is an optional so you're using ! to unwrap it. But that's not the only ! in this line…
>
> You're calling the tableView(titleForHeaderInSection) method on the table view's data source, which is of course the LocationsViewController itself.
>
> But this method is an optional method – not all data sources need to implement it. Because of that you have to *unwrap the method* with the exclamation mark in order to use it. Unwrapping methods… does it get any crazier than that?
>
> By the way, you can also write this as:
>
> ```
> label.text = self.tableView(tableView, titleForHeaderInSection: section)
> ```
>
> Here you use self to directly access that method on LocationsViewController. Both ways achieve exactly the same thing.

Another small improvement you can make is to always put the section headers in uppercase.

➤ Change the tableView(titleForHeaderInSection) data source method to:

```
override func tableView(tableView: UITableView,
                    titleForHeaderInSection section: Int) -> String? {
  let sectionInfo = fetchedResultsController.sections![section]
                                as! NSFetchedResultsSectionInfo
  return sectionInfo.name!.uppercaseString
}
```

Now the section headers look even better:

The section header text is in uppercase

Currently if a location does not have a photo, there is a black gap where the thumbnail is supposed to be. That doesn't look very professional.

It's better to show a placeholder image. You already added one to the asset catalog when you imported the Images folder.

> In **LocationCell.swift**'s `imageForLocation()`, replace the line that returns an empty `UIImage` with:

```
return UIImage(named: "No Photo")!
```

Recall that `UIImage(named)` is a failable initializer, so it returns an optional. Don't forget the exclamation point to unwrap the optional.

Now locations without photos appear like so:

A location using the placeholder image

That makes it a lot clearer to the user that the photo is missing. (As opposed to, say, being a photo of a black hole.)

The placeholder image is round. That's the fashion for thumbnail images on iOS these days, and it's pretty easy to make the other thumbnails rounded too.

> Still in **LocationCell.swift**, add the following lines to the bottom of `awakeFromNib()`:

```
photoImageView.layer.cornerRadius = photoImageView.bounds.size.width / 2
photoImageView.clipsToBounds = true
separatorInset = UIEdgeInsets(top: 0, left: 82, bottom: 0, right: 0)
```

This gives the image view rounded corners with a radius that is equal to half the width of the image, which makes it a perfect circle.

The `clipsToBounds` setting makes sure that the image view respects these rounded corners and does not draw outside them.

The `separatorInset` moves the separator lines between the cells a bit to the right so there are no lines between the thumbnail images.

The thumbnails live inside little circles

> **Note:** The rounded thumbnails don't look very good if the original photo isn't square. You may want to change the Mode of the image view back to Aspect Fill or Scale to Fill so that the thumbnail always fills up the entire image view.

The labels in this screen have one final problem: they are not big enough on the iPhone 6 or 6 Plus. Remember that the screens of these models are wider than the 320 points you've been designing for (375 and 414 points, respectively).

The obvious solution, setting autosizing on the labels so they automatically resize, was unfortunately broken in iOS 8.0. Autosizing worked fine outside of table view cells but inside a table view it made the labels way too large. Fortunately, this bug appears to be fixed in iOS 8.1 and up.

Give autosizing a try. If it doesn't work and the labels become too large when you run the app, then add the following lines of code to LocationCell to do the layout manually.

➤ Add this method to **LocationCell.swift**:

```
override func layoutSubviews() {
  super.layoutSubviews()
  if let sv = superview {
    descriptionLabel.frame.size.width = sv.frame.size.width -
                                 descriptionLabel.frame.origin.x - 10
    addressLabel.frame.size.width = sv.frame.size.width - addressLabel.frame.origin.x - 10
  }
}
```

UIKit calls layoutSubviews() just before it makes the cell visible. Here you resize the frames of the labels to take up all the remaining space in the cell, with 10 points margin on the right.

The superview property refers to the table view cell's Content View – you've seen this in Interface Builder (see the outline pane). Labels are never added directly to the cell but to its Content View.

Note that superview is an optional – a cell that is not yet part of a table view doesn't have a superview yet – hence the use of if let to unwrap it.

Tip: To verify that the labels now take advantage of all the available screen space on the larger iPhones, give them a non-transparent background color.

➤ Add these lines to awakeFromNib() and run the app:

```
descriptionLabel.backgroundColor = UIColor.blueColor()
addressLabel.backgroundColor = UIColor.redColor()
```

This is what it looks like on the iPhone 6 Plus:

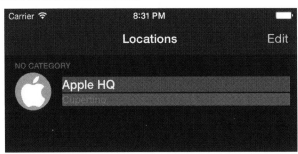

The labels resize to fit the iPhone 6

When you're done testing, don't forget to remove the lines that set the background color. It's useful as a debugging tool but not particularly pretty to look at.

There are two other table views in the app and they get a similar treatment.

➤ Add these lines to viewDidLoad() in **LocationDetailsViewController.swift**:

```
tableView.backgroundColor = UIColor.blackColor()
tableView.separatorColor = UIColor(white: 1.0, alpha: 0.2)
tableView.indicatorStyle = .White

descriptionTextView.textColor = UIColor.whiteColor()
descriptionTextView.backgroundColor = UIColor.blackColor()

addPhotoLabel.textColor = UIColor.whiteColor()
addPhotoLabel.highlightedTextColor = addPhotoLabel.textColor

addressLabel.textColor = UIColor(white: 1.0, alpha: 0.4)
addressLabel.highlightedTextColor = addressLabel.textColor
```

This is similar to what you did before. It changes the colors of the table view (but not the cells) and some of the other controls.

This table view controller has static cells so there is no cellForRowAtIndexPath data source method that you can use to change the colors of the cells and their labels.

However, the table view delegate has a handy method that comes in useful here.

➤ Add the following method:

```
override func tableView(tableView: UITableView,
        willDisplayCell cell: UITableViewCell, forRowAtIndexPath indexPath: NSIndexPath) {
  cell.backgroundColor = UIColor.blackColor()
```

```
    if let textLabel = cell.textLabel {
      textLabel.textColor = UIColor.whiteColor()
      textLabel.highlightedTextColor = textLabel.textColor
    }
    if let detailLabel = cell.detailTextLabel {
      detailLabel.textColor = UIColor(white: 1.0, alpha: 0.4)
      detailLabel.highlightedTextColor = detailLabel.textColor
    }

    let selectionView = UIView(frame: CGRect.zeroRect)
    selectionView.backgroundColor = UIColor(white: 1.0, alpha: 0.2)
    cell.selectedBackgroundView = selectionView
}
```

The "willDisplayCell" delegate method is called just before a cell becomes visible. Here you can do some last-minute customizations on the cell and its contents.

You're using if let to unwrap cell.textLabel and cell.detailTextLabel because they are optionals. Not all cell types come with these built-in labels, in which case these properties are nil.

If you run the app now and tag a new location, you'll see that the label that used to say "Address" is not visible (try it out). That's because this cell does not use one of the built-in cell types so it does not have anything connected to the textLabel and detailTextLabel properties.

You could make a new outlet for this label but you can also do it as follows:

➤ Set the **Tag** of the "Address" label to 100 in the storyboard.

➤ Add these lines to tableView(willDisplayCell, forRowAtIndexPath):

```
if indexPath.row == 2 {
  let addressLabel = cell.viewWithTag(100) as! UILabel
  addressLabel.textColor = UIColor.whiteColor()
  addressLabel.highlightedTextColor = addressLabel.textColor
}
```

The Tag Location screen now looks like this:

The Tag Location screen with styling applied

The final table view is the category picker.

➤ Add a `viewDidLoad()` method to **CategoryPickerViewController.swift**:

```
override func viewDidLoad() {
  super.viewDidLoad()
  tableView.backgroundColor = UIColor.blackColor()
  tableView.separatorColor = UIColor(white: 1.0, alpha: 0.2)
  tableView.indicatorStyle = .White
}
```

➤ And give this class a `willDisplayCell` method too:

```
override func tableView(tableView: UITableView,
        willDisplayCell cell: UITableViewCell, forRowAtIndexPath indexPath: NSIndexPath) {
  cell.backgroundColor = UIColor.blackColor()

  if let textLabel = cell.textLabel {
    textLabel.textColor = UIColor.whiteColor()
    textLabel.highlightedTextColor = textLabel.textColor
  }

  let selectionView = UIView(frame: CGRect.zeroRect)
  selectionView.backgroundColor = UIColor(white: 1.0, alpha: 0.2)
  cell.selectedBackgroundView = selectionView
}
```

Now the category picker is dressed in black as well. It's a bit of work to change the visuals of all these table views by hand, but it's worth it.

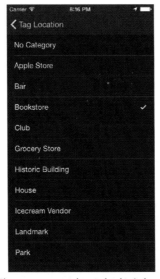

The category picker is lookin' sharp

Polishing the main screen

I'm pretty happy with all the other screens but the main screen needs a bit more work to be presentable.

Here's what you'll do:

- Show a logo when the app starts up. Normally such splash screens are bad for the user experience, but here you can get away with it.

- Make the logo disappear with an animation when the user taps Get My Location.

- While the app is fetching the coordinates, show an animated activity spinner to make it even clearer to the user that something is going on.

- Hide the Latitude: and Longitude: labels until the app has found coordinates.

You will first hide the text labels from the screen until the app actually has some coordinates to display. The only label that will be visible until then is the one on the top and it will say "Searching..." or give some kind of error message.

In order to do this, you must have outlets for these two labels.

➤ Add the following properties to **CurrentLocationViewController.swift**:

```
@IBOutlet weak var latitudeTextLabel: UILabel!
@IBOutlet weak var longitudeTextLabel: UILabel!
```

You'll put the logic for updating these labels into a single place, the updateLabels() method, so that hiding and showing them is pretty straightforward.

➤ Change the updateLabels() method in **CurrentLocationViewController.swift**:

```
func updateLabels() {
  if let location = location {
    . . .
    latitudeTextLabel.hidden = false
    longitudeTextLabel.hidden = false
  } else {
    . . .
    latitudeTextLabel.hidden = true
    longitudeTextLabel.hidden = true
  }
}
```

➤ Connect the **Latitude:** and **Longitude:** labels in the storyboard editor to the latitudeTextLabel and longitudeTextLabel outlets.

➤ Run the app and verify that the **Latitude:** and **Longitude:** labels only appear when you have obtained GPS coordinates.

The first impression

The main screen looks decent and is completely functional but it could do with more pizzazz. It lacks the "Wow!" factor. You want to impress users the first time they start your app, in order to keep them coming back. To pull this off, you'll add a logo and a cool animation.

When the user hasn't yet pressed the Get My Location button, there are no GPS coordinates and the Tag Location button is hidden. Instead of showing the upper panel with absolutely no information in it, you can show a large version of the app's icon:

The welcome screen of MyLocations

When the user taps the Get My Location button, the icon rolls out of the screen (it's round so that kinda makes sense) while the panel with the GPS status slides in:

The logo rolls out of the screen while the panel slides in

This is pretty easy to program thanks to the power of Core Animation and it makes the app a whole lot more impressive to first-time users.

First you need to move the labels into a new container subview.

➤ Open the storyboard and go to the **Current Location View Controller**. In the outline pane, select the six labels and the Tag Location button. With these seven views selected, choose **Editor** → **Embed In** → **View** from the Xcode menu bar.

This creates a blank, white UIView and puts these labels and the button inside that new view.

➤ Change the **Background Color** of this new container view to **Clear Color**, so that everything becomes visible again.

The layout of the screen hasn't changed; you have simply reorganized the view hierarchy so that you can easily manipulate and animate this group of labels as a whole. Grouping views in a container view is a common technique for building complex layouts.

➤ To avoid problems on 3.5-inch devices, make sure that the **Get My Location** button sits higher up in the view hierarchy than the container view. If the button sits under another view you cannot tap it anymore.

Unintuitively, in the outline pane the button must sit *below* the container view. If it doesn't, drag to rearrange:

Get My Location must sit below the container view in the outline pane

Note: When you drag the Get My Location button, make sure you're not dropping it into the container view. "View" and "Get My Location" should sit at the same level in the view hierarchy.

➤ Add the following outlet to **CurrentLocationViewController.swift**:

```
@IBOutlet weak var containerView: UIView!
```

➤ In the storyboard, connect the UIView that contains all these labels to the containerView outlet.

Now onto the good stuff!

➤ Add the following instance variables to **CurrentLocationViewController.swift**:

```
var logoVisible = false

lazy var logoButton: UIButton = {
  let button = UIButton.buttonWithType(.Custom) as! UIButton
  button.setBackgroundImage(UIImage(named: "Logo"), forState: .Normal)
  button.sizeToFit()
  button.addTarget(self, action: Selector("getLocation"), forControlEvents: .TouchUpInside)
  button.center.x = CGRectGetMidX(self.view.bounds)
  button.center.y = 220
  return button
}()
```

The logo image is actually a button, so that you can tap the logo to get started. The app will show this button when it starts up, and when it doesn't have anything better to display (for example, after you press Stop and there are no coordinates and no error). To orchestrate this, you'll use the boolean logoVisible.

The button is a "custom" type UIButton, meaning that it has no title text or other frills. It draws the **Logo.png** image and calls the getLocation() method when tapped. This is another one of those lazily loaded properties; I did that because it's nice to keep all the initialization logic inline with the declaration of the property.

➤ Add the following method:

```
// MARK: - Logo View

func showLogoView() {
  if !logoVisible {
    logoVisible = true
    containerView.hidden = true
    view.addSubview(logoButton)
  }
}
```

This hides the container view so the labels disappear, and puts the `logoButton` object on the screen. This is the first time `logoButton` is accessed, so at this point the lazy loading kicks in.

➤ In `updateLabels()`, change the line that says,

```
statusMessage = "Tap 'Get My Location' to Start"
```

into:

```
statusMessage = ""
showLogoView()
```

This new logic makes the logo appear when there are no coordinates or error messages to display. That's also the state at startup time, so when you run the app now, you should be greeted by the logo.

➤ Run the app to check it out.

What you see when you start the app

When you tap the logo (or Get My Location), the logo should disappear and the panel with the labels ought to show up. That doesn't happen yet, so let's write some more code.

➤ Add the following method:

```
func hideLogoView() {
  logoVisible = false
```

```
    containerView.hidden = false
    logoButton.removeFromSuperview()
}
```

This is the counterpart to showLogoView(). For now, it simply removes the button with the logo and un-hides the container view with the GPS coordinates.

➤ Add the following to getLocation(), right after the authorization status checks:

```
if logoVisible {
  hideLogoView()
}
```

Before it starts the location manager, this first removes the logo from the screen if it was visible.

Currently there is no animation code to be seen. When doing complicated layout stuff such as this, I always first want to make sure the basics work. If they do, you can make it look fancy with an animation.

➤ Run the app. You should see the screen with the logo. Press the Get My Location button and the logo is replaced by the coordinate labels.

Great, now that works you can add the animation. The only method you have to change is hideLogoView().

➤ First add an import for QuartzCore, the framework that provides Core Animation. This goes all the way at the top of the file, as usual:

```
import QuartzCore
```

➤ Then replace hideLogoView() with:

```
func hideLogoView() {
  if !logoVisible { return }

  logoVisible = false
  containerView.hidden = false

  containerView.center.x = view.bounds.size.width * 2
  containerView.center.y = 40 + containerView.bounds.size.height / 2

  let centerX = CGRectGetMidX(view.bounds)

  let panelMover = CABasicAnimation(keyPath: "position")
  panelMover.removedOnCompletion = false
  panelMover.fillMode = kCAFillModeForwards
  panelMover.duration = 0.6
  panelMover.fromValue = NSValue(CGPoint: containerView.center)
  panelMover.toValue = NSValue(CGPoint: CGPoint(x: centerX, y: containerView.center.y))
  panelMover.timingFunction = CAMediaTimingFunction(name: kCAMediaTimingFunctionEaseOut)
  panelMover.delegate = self
  containerView.layer.addAnimation(panelMover, forKey: "panelMover")

  let logoMover = CABasicAnimation(keyPath: "position")
  logoMover.removedOnCompletion = false
  logoMover.fillMode = kCAFillModeForwards
  logoMover.duration = 0.5
  logoMover.fromValue = NSValue(CGPoint: logoButton.center)
  logoMover.toValue = NSValue(CGPoint: CGPoint(x: -centerX, y: logoButton.center.y))
  logoMover.timingFunction = CAMediaTimingFunction(name: kCAMediaTimingFunctionEaseIn)
  logoButton.layer.addAnimation(logoMover, forKey: "logoMover")
```

```
    let logoRotator = CABasicAnimation(keyPath: "transform.rotation.z")
    logoRotator.removedOnCompletion = false
    logoRotator.fillMode = kCAFillModeForwards
    logoRotator.duration = 0.5
    logoRotator.fromValue = 0.0
    logoRotator.toValue = -2 * M_PI
    logoRotator.timingFunction = CAMediaTimingFunction(name: kCAMediaTimingFunctionEaseIn)
    logoButton.layer.addAnimation(logoRotator, forKey: "logoRotator")
}
```

This creates three animations that are played at the same time:

1. the containerView is placed outside the screen (somewhere on the right) and moved to the center, while

2. the logo image view slides out of the screen, and

3. at the same time rotates around its center, giving the impression that it's rolling away.

Because the "panelMover" animation takes longest, you set a delegate on it so that you will be notified when the entire animation is over.

The methods for this delegate are not declared in a protocol, so there is no need to add anything to your class line. (This is also known as an *informal* protocol. It's a holdover from the early days of Objective-C.)

➤ Add the following method below hideLogoView():

```
override func animationDidStop(anim: CAAnimation!, finished flag: Bool) {
  containerView.layer.removeAllAnimations()
  containerView.center.x = view.bounds.size.width / 2
  containerView.center.y = 40 + containerView.bounds.size.height / 2

  logoButton.layer.removeAllAnimations()
  logoButton.removeFromSuperview()
}
```

This cleans up after the animations and removes the logo button, as you no longer need it.

➤ Run the app. Tap on Get My Location to make the logo disappear. I think the animation looks pretty cool.

Tip: To get the logo back so you can try again, first choose **Location** → **None** from the Simulator's **Debug** menu. Then tap Get My Location followed by Stop to make the logo reappear.

Apple says that good apps should "surprise and delight" and modest animations such as these really make your apps more interesting to use – as long as you don't overdo it!

Adding an activity indicator

When the user taps the Get My Location button, you change the button's text to Stop to indicate the change of state. You can make it even clearer to the user that something is going on by adding an animated activity "spinner".

It will look like this:

The animated activity spinner shows that the app is busy

UIKit comes with a standard control for this, UIActivityIndicatorView. You're going to create this spinner control programmatically, because not everything has to be done in Interface Builder (even though you could).

The code to change the appearance of the Get My Location button sits in the configureGetButton() method, so that's also a good place to show and hide the spinner.

➤ Change configureGetButton() to the following:

```
func configureGetButton() {
  let spinnerTag = 1000

  if updatingLocation {
    getButton.setTitle("Stop", forState: .Normal)

    if view.viewWithTag(spinnerTag) == nil {
      let spinner = UIActivityIndicatorView(activityIndicatorStyle: .White)
      spinner.center = messageLabel.center
      spinner.center.y += spinner.bounds.size.height/2 + 15
      spinner.startAnimating()
      spinner.tag = spinnerTag
      containerView.addSubview(spinner)
    }
  } else {
    getButton.setTitle("Get My Location", forState: .Normal)

    if let spinner = view.viewWithTag(spinnerTag) {
      spinner.removeFromSuperview()
    }
  }
}
```

In addition to changing the button text to "Stop", you create a new UIActivityIndicatorView instance. Then you do some calculations to position the spinner view below the message label at the top of the screen.

The call to addSubview() makes the spinner visible on the screen.

To keep track of this spinner view, you give it a tag of 1000. You could use an instance variable but this is just as easy and it keeps everything local to the configureGetButton() method. It's nice to have everything in one place.

When it's time to revert the button to its old state, you call removeFromSuperview() to remove the activity indicator view from the screen.

And that's all you need to do.

➤ Run the app. There should now be a cool little animation while the app is busy talking to the GPS satellites.

Make some noise

Visual feedback is important but you can't expect users to keep their eyes glued to the screen all the time, especially if an operation might take a few seconds or more.

Emitting an unobtrusive sound is a good way to alert the user that a task is complete. When your iPhone has sent an email, for example, you hear a soft "Whoosh" sound.

You're going to add a sound effect to the app too, which is to be played when the first reverse geocoding successfully completes. That seems like a reasonable moment to alert the user that GPS and address information has been captured.

There are many ways to play sound on iOS but you're going to use one of the simplest: system sounds. The System Sound API is intended for short beeps and other notification sounds, which is exactly the type of sound that you want to play here.

➤ Add an import for AudioToolbox, the framework for playing system sounds, to the top of **CurrentLocationViewController.swift**:

```
import AudioToolbox
```

➤ Add the soundID instance variable:

```
var soundID: SystemSoundID = 0
```

Because writing just 0 would normally give you a variable of type Int, you explicitly mention the type that you want it to be: SystemSoundID. This is a numeric identifier – sometimes called a "handle" – that refers to a system sound object. 0 means no sound has been loaded yet.

➤ Add the following methods to the bottom of the class:

```
// MARK: - Sound Effect

func loadSoundEffect(name: String) {
  if let path = NSBundle.mainBundle().pathForResource(name, ofType: nil) {
    let fileURL = NSURL.fileURLWithPath(path, isDirectory: false)
    if fileURL == nil {
      println("NSURL is nil for path: \(path)")
      return
    }

    let error = AudioServicesCreateSystemSoundID(fileURL, &soundID)
    if Int(error) != kAudioServicesNoError {
      println("Error code \(error) loading sound at path: \(path)")
      return
    }
  }
}

func unloadSoundEffect() {
  AudioServicesDisposeSystemSoundID(soundID)
  soundID = 0
}

func playSoundEffect() {
  AudioServicesPlaySystemSound(soundID)
}
```

The `loadSoundEffect()` method loads the sound file and puts it into a new sound object. The specifics don't really matter, but you end up with a reference to that object in the `soundID` instance variable.

➤ Call `loadSoundEffect()` in `viewDidLoad()`:

```
loadSoundEffect("Sound.caf")
```

➤ In `locationManager(didUpdateLocations)`, in the geocoder's completion block, change the following code:

```
self.lastGeocodingError = error
if error == nil && !placemarks.isEmpty {
  if self.placemark == nil {
    println("FIRST TIME!")
    self.playSoundEffect()
  }
  self.placemark = placemarks.last as? CLPlacemark
} else {
  self.placemark = nil
}
```

The added if-statement simply checks whether the `self.placemark` instance variable is still `nil`, in which case this is the first time you've reverse geocoded an address. It then plays a sound using the `playSoundEffect()` method.

Of course, you shouldn't forget to include the actual sound effect into the project!

➤ Add the **Sound** folder from this tutorial's Resources to the project. Make sure **Copy items if needed** is selected.

➤ Run the app and see if you can let it make some noise. The sound should only be played for the first address it finds – when you see the FIRST TIME! `println` – even if more precise locations keep coming in afterwards.

Note: If you don't hear the sound on the Simulator, try the app on a device. There have been reports that system sounds are not playing in the iOS 8 simulators.

CAF audio files

The Sound folder contains a single file, **Sound.caf**. The **caf** extension stands for Core Audio Format, and it's the preferred file format for these kinds of short audio files on iOS.

If you want to use your own sound file but it is in a different format than CAF and your audio software can't save CAF files, then you can use the `afconvert` utility to convert the audio file. You need to run it from the Terminal:

```
$ /usr/bin/afconvert -f caff -d LEI16 Sound.wav Sound.caf
```

This converts the Sound.wav file into Sound.caf. You don't need to do this for the audio file from this tutorial's Sound folder because that file is already in the correct format.

But if you want to experiment with your own audio files, then knowing how to use `afconvert` might be useful. (By the way, iOS can play .wav files just fine, but .caf is more optimal.)

The icon and launch images

The Resources folder for this tutorial contains an **Icon** folder with the icons for this app.

➤ Import the icon images into the asset catalog. Simply drag them from Finder into the **AppIcon** group.

It's best to drag them one-by-one into their respective slots (if you drag the whole set of icons into the group at once, Xcode can get confused):

The icons in the asset catalog

The app also has a launch file, **LaunchScreen.xib**, that provides the "splash" image while the app loads.

Having a launch file is required to take advantage of the larger screens of the iPhone 6 and 6 Plus. Without this launch file, the app will think it's running on a 4-inch screen (like the iPhone 5s) but gets scaled up to fill the extra pixels on the iPhone 6 models. That doesn't look very good, except maybe for games. So you definitely want the app to use a launch file.

Instead of using a XIB for the launch screen (or the storyboard as you did in the previous tutorial) you can also supply a set of images. Let's do that for this app.

➤ In the **Project Settings** screen, in the **General** tab, find the **App Icons and Launch Images** section. Click the **Use Asset Catalog** button next to **Launch Images Source**:

Using the asset catalog for launch images

Xcode now asks if you want to migrate the launch images. Click **Migrate**.

➤ Make the field for **Launch Screen File** empty. Also remove **LaunchScreen.xib** from the project.

➤ Open **Images.xcassets**. There is now a **LaunchImage** item in the list. Select it and go to the Attributes inspector. Under both **iOS 8 and Later** and **iOS 7 and Later,** put checkmark by **iPhone Portrait:**

Enabling the launch images for iPhone portrait

You now have four slots for dropping the launch images into.

The Resources folder for this tutorial contains a **Launch Images** folder. Let's take a look at one of those images, **Launch Image Retina 4.png:**

The launch image for this app

The launch image only has the tab bar and the logo button, but no status bar or any buttons. The reason it has no "Get My Location" button is that you don't want users to try and tap it while the app is still loading (it's not really a button!).

To make this launch image, I ran the app in the Simulator and chose **File → Save Screen Shot.** This puts a new PNG file on the Desktop. I then opened this image in Photoshop and blanked out any text and the status bar portion of the image. The iPhone will draw its own status bar on top anyway.

➤ Drag the files from the **Launch Images** folder into the asset catalog, one at a time. It should be pretty obvious into which slot each image goes.

Done. That was easy. :-)

And with that, the MyLocations app is complete! Woohoo!

You can find the final project files for the app under **07 - Finished App** in the tutorial's Source Code folder.

The end

Congrats for making it this far! This has been another lengthy lesson with a lot of theory to boot. I hoped you learned a lot of useful stuff.

The final storyboard for the MyLocations app looks like this:

The final storyboard

In this lesson you took a more detailed look at Swift but there is still plenty to discover. To learn more about the Swift programming language, I recommend that you read the following books:

- **The Swift Programming Language** by Apple. This is a free download on the iBooks Store. If you don't want to read the whole thing, at least take the Swift tour. It's a great introduction to the language,

- **Swift by Tutorials: A Hands-On Approach** by Colin Eberhart and Matt Galloway. This book is for intermediate to advanced developers, who already know the basics of programming but want to learn how to use the Swift programming language.
  http://www.raywenderlich.com/store/swift-by-tutorials

There are several good Core Data beginner books on the market. Here are two recommendations:

- **Core Data by Tutorials** by Saul Mora and Pietro Rea. One of the few Core Data books that is completely up-to-date with iOS 8 and Swift. This book is for intermediate iOS developers who already know the basics of iOS and Swift development but want to learn how to use Core Data to save data in their apps. http://www.raywenderlich.com/store/core-data-tutorials-ios-8-swift-edition

- **Core Data Programming Guide** by Apple. If you want to get into the nitty gritty, then Apple's official guide is a must-read. The code samples are in Objective-C, not Swift, but you can still learn a ton from this guide.
  https://developer.apple.com/library/mac/documentation/Cocoa/Conceptual/CoreData/cdProgrammingGuide.html

Credits for this tutorial:

- Sound effect based on a flute sample by elmomo, downloaded from The Freesound Project (http://freesound.org)

- Image resizing category is based on code by Trevor Harmon (http://vocaro.com/trevor/blog/2009/10/12/resize-a-uiimage-the-right-way/)

- HudView code is based on MBProgressHud by Matej Bukovinski (https://github.com/matej/MBProgressHUD)

Are you ready for the final lesson? Then continue on to tutorial 4, where you'll make an app that communicates over the network to a web service!

Tutorial 4: StoreSearch

One of the most common things that mobile apps do is talking to a server on the internet. It's beyond question: if you're writing mobile apps, you need to know how to upload and download data.

In this lesson you'll learn how to do HTTP GET requests to a web service, how to parse JSON data, and how to download files such as images.

You are going to build an app that lets you search the iTunes store. Of course, your iPhone already has apps for that ("App Store" and "iTunes Store" to name two), but what's the harm in writing another one?

Apple has made a web service available for searching the entire iTunes store and you'll be using that to learn about networking.

The finished app will look like this:

The finished StoreSearch app

You will add search capability to your old friend, the table view.

There is an animated pop-up with extra information when you tap an item in the table.

And when you flip the iPhone over to landscape, the layout of the app completely changes to show the search results in a different way.

There is also an iPad version of the app:

The app on the iPad

The to-do list for building **StoreSearch** is roughly as follows:

• Create a table view (yes, again!) with a search bar.

• Perform a search on the iTunes store using their web service.

• Understand the response from the iTunes store and put the search results into the table view.

• Each search result has an artwork image associated with it. You'll need to download these images separately and place them in the table view as well.

• Add the pop-up screen with extra info that appears when you touch an item.

• When you flip to landscape, the whole user interface changes and you'll show all of the icons in a paging scroll view.

• Add support for other languages. Having your app available in languages besides English dramatically increases its audience.

• Make the app universal so it runs on the iPad.

This tutorial fills in the missing pieces and rounds off the knowledge you have obtained from the previous tutorials.

You will also learn how to distribute your app to beta testers with so-called Ad Hoc Distribution, and how to submit it to the App Store.

There's a lot of work ahead of you, so let's get started!

In the beginning...

Fire up Xcode and make a new project. Choose the **Single View Application** template and fill in the options as follows:

• Product Name: **StoreSearch**

• Organization Name: your name

• Company Identifier: com.yourname

• Language: **Swift**

- Devices: **iPhone**
- Use Core Data: leave this unchecked

When you save the project Xcode gives you the option to create a so-called **Git repository**. You've ignored this option thus far but now you should enable it:

Creating a Git repository for the project

> ### Git and version control
>
> Git is a so-called **revision control system**. In short, Git allows you to make snapshots of your work so you can always go back later and see a history of what you did. Its principle is similar to Xcode's Snapshots feature but it offers a lot of extra goodies that are important when you're working on the same code with multiple people.
>
> Imagine what happens if two programmers changed the same source file at the same time. Things will go horribly wrong! It's quite likely your changes will accidentally be overwritten by a colleague's. I once had a job where I had to shout down the hall to another programmer, "Are you using file X?" just so we wouldn't be destroying each other's work.
>
> With a revision control system such as Git, each programmer can work independently on the same files, without a fear of undoing the work of others. Git is smart enough to automatically merge all of the changes, and if there are any conflicting edits it will let you resolve them before breaking anything.
>
> Git is not the only revision control system out there but it's the most popular one for iOS. A lot of iOS developers share their source code on GitHub (https://github.com), a free collaboration site that uses Git as its engine. Another popular system is Subversion, often abbreviated as SVN. Xcode has built-in support for both Git and Subversion.
>
> In this tutorial I'll show you some of the basics of using Git. Even if you work alone and don't have to worry about other programmers messing up your code, it still makes sense to use it. After all, *you* might be the one messing up your own code and with Git you'll always have a way to go back to your old – working! – version of the code.

The first screen in StoreSearch will have a table view with a search bar, so let's make the view controller for that screen.

> In the project navigator, rename **ViewController** to **SearchViewController**.

> In **SearchViewController.swift**, change the class line to:

```
class SearchViewController: UIViewController {
```

Note that this is a plain `UIViewController`, not a table view controller.

➤ Open the storyboard. It should look like this:

The empty view controller in the storyboard

The scene is square thanks to iOS 8's "Size Classes" feature, which is enabled by default in all new projects. This 600×600 point canvas does not correspond to the size of any real iPhone or iPad device (maybe the future iSquare?). It is a canvas for device-independent designs.

Size Classes allow you to build *adaptive user interfaces* that can scale to any type of device, whether it's a small iPhone, a big iPhone, or an even bigger iPad.

Instead of having to supply a different storyboard for each device type, you only need to design the user interface once. The app can use the same storyboard regardless of what type of device it's running on. The things inside the storyboard automatically "adapt" to the true screen size.

That doesn't mean the iPad version of the app will look exactly the same as the iPhone version, only bigger. The storyboard allows you to supply different rules depending on the *size class* of the device, for example to show additional UI elements when there is room to display them.

In this tutorial you'll put Size Classes and adaptive user interfaces into action to make StoreSearch run on both the iPhone and the iPad. You'll also be upgrading your knowledge of Auto Layout because adaptive design and Auto Layout go hand in hand.

➤ In the storyboard, change the **Custom Class** for the view controller to **SearchViewController** (in the Identity inspector).

➤ For good measure, run the app to make sure everything works. You should see a white screen with the status bar on top.

Notice that the project navigator now shows **M** and **A+** icons next to some of the filenames in the list:

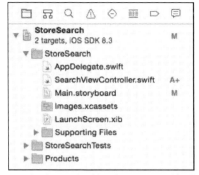

Xcode shows the files that are modified

If you don't see these icons, then choose the **Source Control → Refresh Status** option from the Xcode menu bar. (If that gives an error message or still doesn't work, simply restart Xcode. That's a good tip in general: if Xcode is acting weird, restart it.)

An M means the file has been modified since the last "commit" and an A means this is a file that has been added since then.

So what is a commit?

When you use a revision control system such as Git, you're supposed to make a snapshot every so often. Usually you'll do that after you've added a new feature to your app or when you've fixed a bug, or whenever you feel like you've made changes that you want to keep. That is called a **commit**.

When you created the project, Xcode made the initial commit. You can see that in the Project History window.

➤ Choose **Source Control → History…**

The history of commits for this project

You may get a popup at this point asking for permission to access your contacts. That allows Xcode to add contact information to the names in the commit history. This can be useful if you're collaborating with other developers. You can always change this later under Security & Privacy in System Preferences.

➤ Let's commit the change you just made. Close the history window. From the **Source Control** menu, choose **Commit**:

The Commit menu option

This opens a new window that shows in detail what changes you made. This a good time to quickly review the differences, just to make sure you're not committing anything you didn't intend to:

Xcode shows the changes you've made since the last commit

> Check the boxes for the files on the left-hand side that you want to include in the commit:

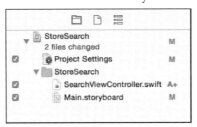

Selecting the files to commit

Note: You may see a User Data folder in this list too. The User Data folder is usually not included in the commit. This folder contains user-specific settings such as the size of your Xcode window, the name of the file you last opened, any breakpoints you have set, and other temporary data. Most developers do not add this into their repositories.

It's always a good idea to write a short but clear reason for the commit in the text box at the bottom. Having a good description here will help you later to find specific commits in your project's history.

> Write: **Renamed ViewController to SearchViewController.**

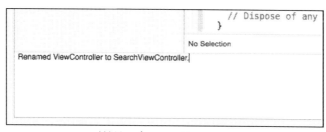

Writing the commit message

➤ Press the **Commit 4 Files** button. You'll see that in the project navigator the M and A icons are gone (at least until you make the next change).

If you're wondering why it said "Commit 4 Files" even though there were only three files in the list, renaming ViewController.swift counts as two – deleting the old file and adding it back with the new name – so in total four files were modified.

The **Source Control → History** window now shows two commits:

Your commit is listed in the project history

If you click **Show 4 modified files**, Xcode will show you what has changed with that commit. You'll be doing commits on a regular basis and by the end of the tutorial you'll be a pro at it.

Creating the UI

The app still doesn't do much yet. In this section, you'll build the UI to look like this, a search bar on top of a table view:

The app with a search bar and table view

Even though this screen uses the familiar table view, it is not a *table* view controller but a regular `UIViewController`.

You are not required to use a `UITableViewController` if you have a table view and for this app I will show you how to do without.

UITableViewController vs. UIViewController

So what exactly is the difference between a *table* view controller and a regular view controller?

First off, `UITableViewController` is a subclass of `UIViewController` so it can do everything that a regular view controller can. However, it is optimized for use with table views and has some cool extra features.

For example, when a table cell contains a text field, tapping that text field will bring up the on-screen keyboard. `UITableViewController` automatically scrolls the cells out of the way of the keyboard so you can always see what you're typing.

You don't get that behavior for free with a plain `UIViewController`, so if you want this feature you'll have to program it yourself.

`UITableViewController` does have a big restriction: its main view must be a `UITableView` that takes up the entire space (except for a possible navigation bar at the top, and a toolbar or tab bar at the bottom).

If your screen consists of just a `UITableView`, then it makes sense to make it a `UITableViewController`. But if you want to have other views as well, a basic `UIViewController` is your only option.

That's the reason you're not using a `UITableViewController` in this app. Besides the table view there is another view, a `UISearchBar`. It is possible to put the search bar *inside* the table view as a special header view, but for this app it will always be sitting on top.

➤ Open the storyboard and drag a new **Table View** into the view controller.

➤ Make the Table View as big as the main view (600 by 600 points) and then use the **Pin menu** at the bottom to attach the Table View to the edges of the screen:

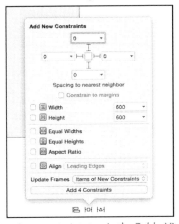

Creating constraints to pin the Table View

Remember how this works? This app uses Auto Layout, which you learned about in the Bull's Eye and Checklists tutorials. With Auto Layout you create **constraints** that determine how big the views are and where they go on the screen.

➤ First, uncheck **Constrain to margins**. Each screen has 16-point margins on the left and right (although you can change their size). When "Constrain to margins" is enabled you're pinning to these margins. That's no good here; you want to pin the Table View to the edge of the screen instead.

➤ In the **Spacing to nearest neighbor** section, select the four red T-bars to make four constraints, one on each side of the Table View. Keep the spacing values at 0.

This pins the Table View to the edges of its superview. Now the table will always fill up the entire screen, regardless of whether you're running the app on a 3.5-inch or a 5.5-inch device.

➤ Make sure **Update Frames** says **Items of New Constraints**.

➤ Click the **Add 4 Constraints** button to finish.

If you were successful, there are now four blue bars surrounding the table view, one for each constraint. In the outline pane there is also a new Constraints section:

The new constraints in the outline pane

➤ Drag a **Search Bar** component into the view. (Be careful to pick the Search Bar and not "Search Bar and Search Display Controller".) Place it at Y = 20 so it sits right under the status bar.

Make sure the Search Bar is not placed inside the table view. It should sit on the same level as the table view in the outline pane:

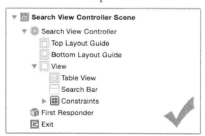 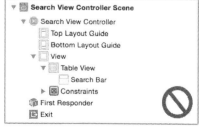

Search Bar must be below of Table View (left), not inside (right)

➤ Pin the Search Bar to the top and left and right edges, 3 constraints in total.

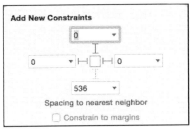

The constraints for the Search Bar

You don't need to pin the bottom of the Search Bar or give it a height constraint. Search Bars have an *intrinsic* height of 44 points.

> In the **Attributes inspector** for the Search Bar, change the **Placeholder** text to **App name, artist, song, album, e-book**.

The view controller's design should look like this:

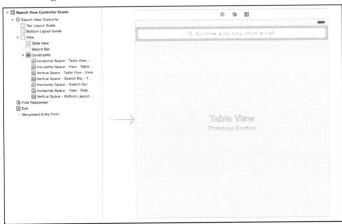

The search view controller with Search Bar and Table View

You know what's coming next: connecting the Search Bar and the Table View to outlets on the view controller.

> Add the following outlets to **SearchViewController.swift**:

```
@IBOutlet weak var searchBar: UISearchBar!
@IBOutlet weak var tableView: UITableView!
```

Recall that as soon as an object no longer has any strong references, it goes away – it is deallocated – and any weak references to it become `nil`.

Per Apple's recommendation you've been making your outlets weak. You may be wondering, if the references to these view objects are weak, then won't the objects get deallocated too soon?

Exercise. What is keeping these views from being deallocated? ■

Answer: Views are always part of a view hierarchy and they will always have an owner with a strong reference: their superview.

The SearchViewController's main view object holds a reference to both the search bar and the table view. This is done inside UIKit and you don't have to worry about it. As long as the view controller exists, so will these two outlets.

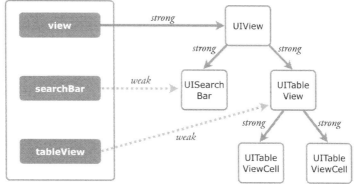

Outlets can be weak because the view hierarchy already has strong references

➤ Switch back to the storyboard and connect the Search Bar and the Table View to their respective outlets. (Ctrl-drag from the view controller to the object that you want to connect.)

If you run the app now, you'll notice a small problem: the first rows of the Table View are hidden beneath the Search Bar.

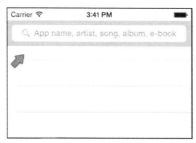

The first row is only partially visible

That's not so strange because you put the Search Bar on top of the table, obscuring part of the table view below.

To fix this you could nudge the Table View down a few pixels. However, according to the iOS design guidelines the content of a view controller should take up the entire screen space.

It's better to leave the size of the Table View alone and to make the Search Bar partially translucent to let the contents of the table cells shine through. But it would still be nice to see the first few rows in their entirety.

You can compensate for this with the **content inset** attributes of the Table View. Unfortunately, with Auto Layout enabled this attribute is unavailable in Interface Builder (at least in Xcode 6.3) so you'll have to do this from code.

➤ Add the following line to viewDidLoad() in **SearchViewController.swift**:

```
override func viewDidLoad() {
  super.viewDidLoad()
  tableView.contentInset = UIEdgeInsets(top: 64, left: 0, bottom: 0, right: 0)
}
```

This tells the table view to add a 64-point margin at the top, made up of 20 points for the status bar and 44 points for the Search Bar.

Now the first row will always be visible, and when you scroll the table view the cells still go under the search bar. Nice.

Doing fake searches

Before you search the iTunes store, it's good to understand how the UISearchBar component works.

In this section you'll get the text to search for from the search bar and use that to put some fake search results into the table view. Once you've got that working, you can build in the web service. Small steps!

➤ Run the app. If you tap in the search bar, the on-screen keyboard will appear, but it still doesn't do anything when you tap the Search button.

Keyboard with Search button

(If you're using the Simulator you may need to press ⌘K to bring up the keyboard.)

Listening to the search bar is done – how else? – with a delegate. Let's put this delegate code into an extension.

➤ Add the following to the bottom of **SearchViewController.swift**, below the final closing bracket:

```
extension SearchViewController: UISearchBarDelegate {
  func searchBarSearchButtonClicked(searchBar: UISearchBar) {
    println("The search text is: '\(searchBar.text)'")
  }
}
```

Recall that you can use extensions to organize your source code. By putting all the UISearchBarDelegate stuff into its own extension you keep it together in one place and out of the way of the rest of the code.

The UISearchBarDelegate protocol has a method searchBarSearchButtonClicked() that is invoked when the user taps the Search button on the keyboard. You will implement this method to put some fake data into the table.

In a little while you'll make this method send a network request to the iTunes store to find songs, movies and e-books that match the search text that the user typed, but let's not do too many new things at once!

> **Tip:** I always put strings in between single quotes when I use println() to print them. That way you can easily see whether there are any trailing or leading spaces in the string.

➤ In the storyboard, **Ctrl-drag** from the Search Bar to Search View Controller (or the yellow circle at the top). Connect to **delegate**.

➤ Run the app, type something in the search bar and press the Search button. The Xcode Debug pane should now print the text you typed.

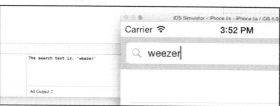

The search text in the debug pane

➤ Add the following two (empty) extensions to **SearchViewController.swift**:

```
extension SearchViewController: UITableViewDataSource {
}

extension SearchViewController: UITableViewDelegate {
}
```

Adding the UITableViewDataSource and UITableViewDelegate protocols wasn't necessary in the previous tutorials because you used a UITableViewController there, which by design already conforms to these protocols.

For this app you're using a regular view controller and therefore you'll have to hook up the data source and delegate protocols yourself.

➤ In the storyboard, **Ctrl-drag** from the Table View to Search View Controller. Connect to **dataSource**. Repeat and connect to **delegate**.

Note that you connected something to Search View Controller's "delegate" twice: the Search Bar and the Table View. The way Interface Builder presents this is a little misleading: the delegate outlet is not from SearchViewController, but belongs to the thing that you Ctrl-dragged from.

So you connected the SearchViewController to the delegate outlet on the Search Bar and also to the delegate (and dataSource) outlets on the Table View:

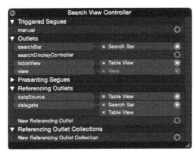

The connections from Search View Controller to the other objects

➤ Build the app. Whoops… Xcode says, "Not so fast, buddy!"

By making the extension you said the `SearchViewController` would play the role of table view data source but you didn't actually implement any of those data source methods yet.

➤ Change the extension to:

```
extension SearchViewController: UITableViewDataSource {
  func tableView(tableView: UITableView, numberOfRowsInSection section: Int) -> Int {
    return 0
  }

  func tableView(tableView: UITableView,
            cellForRowAtIndexPath indexPath: NSIndexPath) -> UITableViewCell {
    return UITableViewCell()
  }
}
```

This simply tells the table view that it has no rows yet. Soon you'll give it some fake data to display, but for now you just want to be able to run the app without errors.

Often you can declare to conform to a protocol without implementing any of its methods. This works fine for `UISearchBarDelegate` and `UITableViewDelegate`, but obviously not in the case of `UITableViewDataSource`!

A protocol can have optional and required methods and if you forget a required method, a compiler error is your reward. (Swift is more strict about this than Objective-C, which simply crashes if a required method is missing.)

➤ Build and run the app to make sure everything still works.

> **Note:** Did you notice a difference between these data source methods and the ones from the previous tutorials? If not, look closely…
>
> **Answer:** They don't have the `override` keyword in front of them.
>
> In the previous apps, `override` was necessary because you were dealing with a subclass of `UITableViewController`, which already provides its own version of the `tableView(numberOfRowsInSection)` and `cellForRowAtIndexPath` methods.
>
> In those apps you were "overriding" or replacing those methods with your own versions, hence the need for the `override` keyword.

> Here, however, your base class is not a table view controller but a regular UIViewController.
> Such a view controller doesn't have any table view methods yet, so you're not overriding
> anything here.

As you know by now, a table view needs some kind of data model. Let's start with a simple Array.

➤ Add an instance variable for the array:

```
var searchResults = [String]()
```

This creates an empty array object that can hold strings.

The search bar delegate method will put some fake data into this array and then use it to fill up
the table.

➤ Replace the searchBarSearchButtonClicked() method with:

```
func searchBarSearchButtonClicked(searchBar: UISearchBar) {
  searchResults = [String]()

  for i in 0...2 {
    searchResults.append(String(format: "Fake Result %d for '%@'", i, searchBar.text))
  }

  tableView.reloadData()
}
```

Here you instantiate a new [String] array and put it into the searchResults instance variable. This
is done each time the user performs a search. If there was already a previous array then it is
thrown away and deallocated.

You add a string with some text into the array. Just for fun, that is repeated 3 times so your data
model will have three rows in it.

When you write for i in 0...2, it creates a loop that repeats three times because the *closed range*
0...2 contains the numbers 0, 1, and 2. You could also have written this as 1...3 but
programmers like to start counting at 0.

You've seen format strings before. The format specifier %d is a placeholder for integer numbers.
Likewise, %f is for numbers with a decimal point (the floating-point numbers). The placeholder
%@ is for all other kinds of objects, such as strings.

The last statement in the method reloads the table view to make the new rows visible, which
means you have to adapt the data source methods to read from this array as well.

➤ Change the tableView(numberOfRowsInSection) method to:

```
func tableView(tableView: UITableView, numberOfRowsInSection section: Int) -> Int {
  return searchResults.count
}
```

This simply returns the number of elements in the searchResults array. When the app first starts
up, searchResults will have an empty array because no search is done yet and simply returns 0.

➤ Finally, change tableView(cellForRowAtIndexPath) to:

```
func tableView(tableView: UITableView,
               cellForRowAtIndexPath indexPath: NSIndexPath) -> UITableViewCell {
  let cellIdentifier = "SearchResultCell"

  var cell = tableView.dequeueReusableCellWithIdentifier(cellIdentifier) as! UITableViewCell!
  if cell == nil {
    cell = UITableViewCell(style: .Default, reuseIdentifier: cellIdentifier)
  }

  cell.textLabel!.text = searchResults[indexPath.row]
  return cell
}
```

You've seen this before. You create a UITableViewCell by hand and put the data for this row into its text label.

➤ Run the app. If you search for anything, a couple of fake results get added to the data model and are shown in the table.

Search for something else and the table view updates with new fake results.

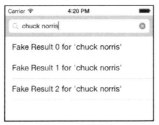

The app shows fake results when you search

There are some improvements you can make. To begin with, it's not very nice that the keyboard stays on the screen after you press the Search button. It obscures about half of the table view and there is no way to dismiss the keyboard by hand.

➤ Add the following line at the start of searchBarSearchButtonClicked():

```
func searchBarSearchButtonClicked(searchBar: UISearchBar) {
  searchBar.resignFirstResponder()
  . . .
```

This tells the UISearchBar that it should no longer listen to keyboard input. As a result, the keyboard will hide itself until you tap inside the search bar again.

You can also configure the table view to dismiss the keyboard with a gesture.

➤ In the storyboard, select the Table View. Go to the **Attributes inspector** and set **Keyboard** to **Dismiss interactively**.

The search bar still has an ugly white gap above it. It would look a lot better if the status bar area was unified with the search bar. Recall that the navigation bar in the Map screen from the MyLocations tutorial had a similar problem. You can use the same trick to fix it.

➤ Add the following method to the SearchBarDelegate extension:

```
func positionForBar(bar: UIBarPositioning) -> UIBarPosition {
  return .TopAttached
}
```

If you were to look in the API documentation for UISearchBarDelegate you wouldn't find this method. Instead, it is part of the UIBarPositioningDelegate protocol, which the UISearchBarDelegate protocol extends. (Like classes, protocols can inherit from other protocols.)

Now the app looks a lot smarter:

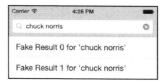

The search bar is "attached" to the top of the screen

The API documentation

Xcode comes with a big library of documentation for developing iOS apps. Basically everything you need to know is in here. Learn to use the Xcode Documentation browser – it will become your best friend!

There are a few ways to get documentation about a certain item in Xcode. There is **Quick Help**, which shows info about the thing under the text cursor:

Simply have the **Quick Help inspector** open (the second tab in the inspector pane) and it will show context-sensitive help. Put the text cursor on the thing you want to know more about and the inspector will give a summary on it. You can click any of the blue text to jump to the full documentation.

You can also get pop-up help. Hold down the **Option** (Alt) key and hover over the item that you want to learn more about. Then click the mouse:

And of course, there is the full-fledged Documentation window. You can access it from the **Help** menu, under **Documentation and API Reference**. Use the bar at the top to search for the item that you want to know more about:

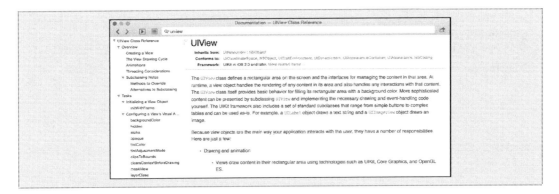

Improving the data model

So far you've added String objects to the searchResults array, but that's a bit limited. The search results that you'll get back from the iTunes store include the product name, the name of the artist, a link to an image, the purchase price, and much more.

You can't fit all of that in a single string, so let's create a new class to hold this data.

➤ Add a new file to the project using the **Swift File** template. Name the new class **SearchResult**.

➤ Replace the contents of **SearchResult.swift** with:

```
class SearchResult {
  var name = ""
  var artistName = ""
}
```

This adds two properties to the new SearchResult class. In a little while you'll add several others.

In the SearchViewController you will no longer add Strings to the searchResults array, but instances of SearchResult.

➤ In **SearchViewController.swift**, change the search bar delegate method to:

```
func searchBarSearchButtonClicked(searchBar: UISearchBar) {
  searchBar.resignFirstResponder()

  searchResults = [SearchResult]()

  for i in 0...2 {
    let searchResult = SearchResult()
    searchResult.name = String(format: "Fake Result %d for", i)
    searchResult.artistName = searchBar.text
    searchResults.append(searchResult)
  }

  tableView.reloadData()
}
```

This creates the new SearchResult object and simply puts some fake text into its name and artistName properties. Again, you do this in a loop because just having one search result by itself is a bit lonely.

Exercise. At this point Xcode gives a number of error messages. Can you explain why? ∎

Answer: The type of searchResults is array-of-String, but here you're trying to put SearchResult objects into the array. To make it accept SearchResult objects, you also need to change the declaration of searchResults to:

```
var searchResults = [SearchResult]()
```

➤ At this point, tableView(cellForRowAtIndexPath) still expects the array to contain strings so also update that method:

```
func tableView(tableView: UITableView,
               cellForRowAtIndexPath indexPath: NSIndexPath) -> UITableViewCell {
  let cellIdentifier = "SearchResultCell"

  var cell = tableView.dequeueReusableCellWithIdentifier(cellIdentifier) as! UITableViewCell!
  if cell == nil {
    cell = UITableViewCell(style: .Subtitle, reuseIdentifier: cellIdentifier)
  }

  let searchResult = searchResults[indexPath.row]
  cell.textLabel!.text = searchResult.name
  cell.detailTextLabel!.text = searchResult.artistName
  return cell
}
```

Instead of a regular table view cell this now uses a "subtitle" cell style. You put the contents of the artistName property into the detail (subtitle) text label.

➤ Run the app; it should look like this:

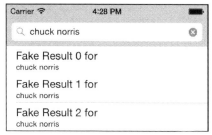

Fake results in a subtitle cell

Nothing found

When you add searching capability to your apps, you'll usually have to handle the following situations:

1. The user did not perform a search yet.

2. The user performed the search and received one or more results. That's what happens in the current version of the app: for every search you'll get back a handful of SearchResult objects.

3. The user performed the search and there were no results. It's usually a good idea to explicitly tell the user there were no results. If you display nothing at all the user may wonder whether the search was actually performed or not.

Even though the app doesn't do any actual searching yet – everything is fake – there is no reason why you cannot fake the latter situation as well.

For the sake of good taste, the app will return 0 results when the user searches for "justin bieber", just so you know the app can handle this kind of situation.

➤ In searchBarSearchButtonClicked(), put the following if-statement around the for loop:

```
if searchBar.text != "justin bieber" {
  for i in 0...2 {
    . . .
  }
}
```

The change here is pretty simple. You have added an if-statement that compares the search text to "justin bieber". Only if there is no match will this create the SearchResult objects and add them to the array.

➤ Run the app and do a search for "justin bieber" (all lowercase). The table should stay empty.

You can improve the user experience by showing the text "(Nothing found)" instead, so the user knows beyond a doubt that there were no search results.

➤ Change the bottom part of tableView(cellForRowAtIndexPath) to:

```
if searchResults.count == 0 {
  cell.textLabel!.text = "(Nothing found)"
  cell.detailTextLabel!.text = ""
} else {
  let searchResult = searchResults[indexPath.row]
  cell.textLabel!.text = searchResult.name
  cell.detailTextLabel!.text = searchResult.artistName
}
```

That alone is not enough. When there is nothing in the array, searchResults.count is 0, right? But that also means the data source's numberOfRowsInSection will return 0 and the table view stays empty – this "Nothing found" row will never show up.

➤ Change tableView(numberOfRowsInSection) to:

```
func tableView(tableView: UITableView, numberOfRowsInSection section: Int) -> Int {
  if searchResults.count == 0 {
    return 1
  } else {
    return searchResults.count
  }
}
```

If there are no results this returns 1, for the row with the text "(Nothing Found)". This works because both numberOfRowsInSection and cellForRowAtIndexPath check for this special situation.

➤ Try it out:

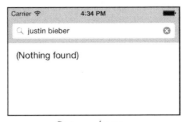

One can hope...

Unfortunately, the text "Nothing found" also appears when the user did not actually search for anything yet. That's a little silly.

The problem is that you have no way to distinguish between "not searched yet" and "nothing found". Right now, you can only tell whether the searchResults array is empty but not what caused this.

Exercise. How would you solve this little problem? ∎

There are two obvious solutions that come to mind:

• Make searchResults into an optional. If it is nil, i.e. it has no value, then the user hasn't searched yet. That's different from the case where the user did search and no matches were found.

• Use a separate boolean variable to keep track of this.

It may be tempting to choose the optional, but it's best to avoid optionals if you can. They make the logic more complex, can cause the app to crash if you don't unwrap them properly, and require if let statements everywhere. Optionals certainly have their uses, but here they are not really necessary.

So we'll opt for the boolean. (But feel free to come back and try the optional as well, and compare the differences. It'll be a great exercise!)

➤ Add the new instance variable:

```
var hasSearched = false
```

➤ In the search bar delegate method, set this variable to true. It doesn't really matter where you do this, as long as it happens before the table view is reloaded.

```
func searchBarSearchButtonClicked(searchBar: UISearchBar) {
  . . .
  hasSearched = true
  . . .
  tableView.reloadData()
}
```

➤ And finally, change tableView(numberOfRowsInSection) to look at the value of this new variable:

```
func tableView(tableView: UITableView, numberOfRowsInSection section: Int) -> Int {
  if !hasSearched {
    return 0
  } else if searchResults.count == 0 {
    return 1
  } else {
    return searchResults.count
  }
}
```

Now the table view remains empty until you first search for something. Try it out! (Later on in the tutorial you'll see a much better way to handle this using an enum – and it will blow your mind!)

One more thing, if you currently tap on a row it will become selected and stays selected.

➤ To fix that, add the following methods inside the UITableViewDelegate extension:

```
func tableView(tableView: UITableView, didSelectRowAtIndexPath indexPath: NSIndexPath) {
  tableView.deselectRowAtIndexPath(indexPath, animated: true)
}

func tableView(tableView: UITableView,
               willSelectRowAtIndexPath indexPath: NSIndexPath) -> NSIndexPath? {
  if searchResults.count == 0 {
    return nil
  } else {
    return indexPath
  }
}
```

The `tableView(didSelectRowAtIndexPath)` method will simply deselect the row with an animation, while `willSelectRowAtIndexPath` makes sure that you can only select rows with actual search results.

If you tap on the (Nothing Found) row now you will notice that it does not turn gray at all. (Actually, the row may still turn gray if you press down on it for a short while. That happens because you did not change the `selectionStyle` property of the cell. You'll fix that in the next section.)

➤ This is a good time to commit the app. Go to **Source Control** → **Commit** (or press the ⌘+**Option+C** keyboard shortcut).

Make sure all the files are selected, review your changes, and type a good commit message – something like "Added a search bar and table view. The search puts fake results in the table for now." Press the **Commit** button to finish.

If you ever want to look back through your commit history, you can either do that from the **Source Control** → **History** window or from the Version editor, pictured below:

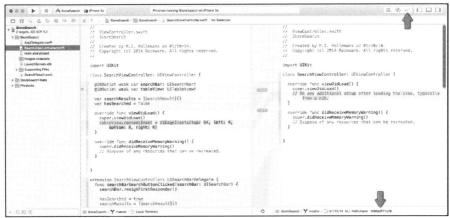

Viewing revisions in the Version editor

You switch to the Version editor with the button in the toolbar at the top of the Xcode window.

In the screenshot above, the current version is shown on the left and the previous version on the right. You can switch versions with the bar at the bottom. The Version editor is a very handy tool for viewing the history of changes in your source files.

The app isn't very impressive yet but you've laid the foundation for what is to come. You have a search bar and know how to take action when the user presses the Search button. The app also has a simple data model that consists of an array with SearchResult objects, and it can display these search results in a table view.

You can find the project files for the first part of this app under **01 - Search Bar** in the tutorial's Source Code folder.

Before you make the app do a real search on the iTunes store, first let's make the table view look a little better. Appearance does matter!

Custom table cells and nibs

In the previous tutorials you used prototype cells to create your own table view cell layouts. That works great but there's another way: in this tutorial you'll create a "nib" file with the design for the cell and load your table view cells from that. The principle is very similar to prototype cells.

A nib, also called a xib, is very much like a storyboard except that it only contains the design for a single thing. That thing can be a view controller but it can also be an individual view or table view cell. A nib is really nothing more than a container for a "freeze dried" object that you can edit in Interface Builder.

In practice, many apps consist of a combination of nibs and storyboard files, so it's good to know how to work with both.

This is what you're going to make in this section:

The app with better looks

The app still uses the same fake data, but you'll make it look a bit better.

➤ First, add the contents of the **Images** folder from this tutorials's resources into the project's asset catalog, **Images.xcassets**.

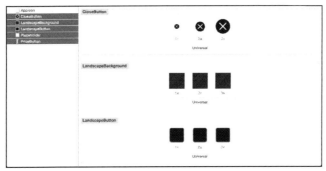

Imported images in the asset catalog

Each of the images comes in three versions: 1x, 2x, and 3x. Previously you only had 2x and 3x images but because this app will also run on iPads, you need 1x versions of the images too (the iPad 2 and first generation iPad mini are the only low-resolution devices that can run iOS 8).

➤ Add a new file to the project. Choose the **Empty** template from the **User Interface** category. This will create a new nib without anything in it.

Adding an empty nib to the project

➤ Click **Next** and save the new file as **SearchResultCell**.

This adds a nib with no contents to the project. Open **SearchResultCell.xib** and you will see an empty canvas.

Xib or nib

I've been calling it a nib but the file extension is **.xib**. So what is the difference? In practice these terms are used interchangeably. Technically speaking, a xib file is compiled into a nib file that is put into your application bundle. The term nib mostly stuck for historical reasons (it stands for *NeXT Interface Builder*).

You can consider the terms "xib file" and "nib file" to be equivalent. The preferred term seems to be nib, so that is what I will be using from now on. (This won't be the last time computer terminology is confusing, ambiguous or inconsistent. The world of programming is full of colorful slang.)

➤ From the Object Library, drag a new **Table View Cell** into the canvas:

The Table View Cell in the Object Library

➤ Select the new Table View Cell and go to the **Size inspector**. Type 80 in the **Height** field (not Row Height).

The cell now looks like this:

An empty table view cell

➤ Drag an **Image View** and two **Labels** into the cell, like this:

The design of the cell

➤ The Image View is positioned at X:15, Y:10, Width:60, Height:60.

➤ The **Name** label is at X:90, Y:15, Width:222, Height:22. Its font is **System 18.0**.

➤ The **Artist Name** label is at X:90, Y:44, Width:222, Height:18. Font is **System 15.0** and Color is black with 50% opacity.

As you can see, editing a nib is just like editing a storyboard. The difference is that the canvas isn't square, but that's because you're only editing a single table view cell, not an entire view controller (prototype cells also aren't square).

➤ The Table View Cell itself needs to have a reuse identifier. You can set this in the **Attributes inspector** to the value **SearchResultCell**.

The image view will hold the artwork for the found item, such as an album cover, book cover, or an app icon. It may take a few seconds for these images to be loaded, so until then it's a good idea to show a placeholder image. That placeholder is part of the image files you just added to the project.

➤ Select the Image View. In the **Attributes inspector**, set **Image** to **Placeholder**.

The cell design now looks like this:

The cell design with placeholder image

You're not done yet. The design for the cell is only 320 points wide but the iPhone 6 and 6 Plus are wider than that. The cell itself will resize to accommodate those larger screens but the labels won't, potentially causing their text to be cut off. You'll have to add some Auto Layout constraints to make the labels resize along with the cell.

➤ Select the **Name** label and open the **Pin menu**. Uncheck **Constrain to margins** and select the **top**, **left**, and **right** T-bars:

The constraints for the Name label

This time, leave **Update Frames** set to **None**. When enabled, the Update Frames option will move and resize the label according to the constraints you've set on it. That will not do the correct thing in this case (if you're curious, try it out and see what happens).

➤ Click **Add 3 Constraints** to finish. The nib now looks like this:

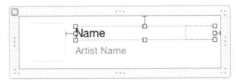

The Name label has insufficient constraints

The orange rectangle indicates that something's not right with the constraints from the Name label. Apparently the width of the label is incorrect; the dotted box over on the right is what Auto Layout thinks should be the size and position for the label according to the constraints.

> **Note:** If you had set Update Frames to "Items of New Constraints", then Interface Builder would have moved the label to where the dotted box is. That's why you left it set to None because you didn't want it to do that here.

Auto Layout is entitled to its opinion, of course, but over in the corner is not where *you* want the label to be. Its current position is just fine, so you'll have to add a couple more constraints to tell Auto Layout that this is really what you intended.

The solution is to pin the Image View. Remember that each view always needs to have enough constraints to uniquely determine its position and size. The Name label is connected to the Image View on the left, but the Image View doesn't have any constraints of its own.

➤ Select the **Image View** and pin it to the **top** and **left** sides of the cell. Also give it **Width** and **Height** constraints so that its size is always fixed to 60 by 60 points:

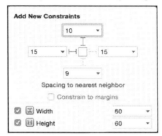

The constraints for the Image View

The orange box from the Name label should have disappeared. If you select this label, it should show three blue bars and nothing in orange.

➤ Finally, pin the **Artist Name** label to the **left**, **right**, and **bottom**.

That concludes the design for this cell. Now you have to tell the app to use this nib.

➤ In **SearchViewController.swift**, add these lines to the bottom of `viewDidLoad()`:

```
var cellNib = UINib(nibName: "SearchResultCell", bundle: nil)
tableView.registerNib(cellNib, forCellReuseIdentifier: "SearchResultCell")
```

The `UINib` class is used to load nibs. Here you tell it to load the nib you just created (note that you don't specify the .xib file extension). Then you ask the table view to register this nib for the reuse identifier "SearchResultCell".

From now on, when you call `dequeueReusableCellWithIdentifier()` for the identifier "SearchResultCell", `UITableView` will automatically make a new cell from the nib – or reuse an existing cell if one is available, of course. And that's all you need to do.

➤ Change `tableView(cellForRowAtIndexPath)` to:

```
func tableView(tableView: UITableView,
            cellForRowAtIndexPath indexPath: NSIndexPath) -> UITableViewCell {

  let cell = tableView.dequeueReusableCellWithIdentifier(
                  "SearchResultCell", forIndexPath: indexPath) as! UITableViewCell

  if searchResults.count == 0 {
    . . .
  } else {
    . . .
  }
  return cell
}
```

You were able to replace this chunk of code,

```
let cellIdentifier = "SearchResultCell"

var cell = tableView.dequeueReusableCellWithIdentifier(cellIdentifier) as! UITableViewCell!
if cell == nil {
  cell = UITableViewCell(style: .Subtitle, reuseIdentifier: cellIdentifier)
}
```

with just one statement. It's almost exactly like using prototype cells, except that you have to create your own nib object and you need to register it with the table view beforehand.

> Note: The call to dequeueReusableCellWithIdentifier() now takes a second parameter, forIndexPath. This variant of the dequeue method lets the table view be a bit smarter, but it only works when you have registered a nib with the table view.

➤ Run the app and do a (fake) search. Hmm, that doesn't look too good:

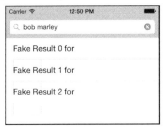

Uh oh...

There are two problems here. First of all, these rows aren't 80 points high. The table view isn't smart enough to figure out that these custom cells need to be higher. Fortunately this is easily fixed.

➤ Add the following line to viewDidLoad():

```
tableView.rowHeight = 80
```

The second problem is more serious: the text doesn't end up in the right place and overlaps the image view.

Exercise. Any ideas why? ∎

Answer: Because you made your own cell design, you should no longer use the textLabel and detailTextLabel properties of UITableViewCell.

Every table view cell – even custom ones that you load from a nib – has a few labels and an image view of its own, but you should only employ these when you're using one of the standard cell styles: .Default, .Subtitle, etc. If you use them on custom cells then these labels get in the way of your own labels.

So here you shouldn't use textLabel and detailTextLabel to put text into the cell, but make your own properties for your own labels.

Where do you put these properties? In a new class, of course. You're going to make a new class named SearchResultCell that extends UITableViewCell and that has properties (and logic) for displaying the search results in this app.

➤ Add a new file to the project using the **Cocoa Touch Class** template. Name it **SearchResultCell** and make it a subclass of **UITableViewCell**. ("Also create XIB file" should be unchecked as you already have one.)

This creates the Swift file to accompany the nib file you created earlier.

➤ Open **SearchResultCell.xib** and select the Table View Cell. (Make sure you select the actual Table View Cell object, not its Content View.)

➤ In the **Identity inspector,** change its class from "UITableViewCell" to **SearchResultCell.**

You do this to tell the nib that the top-level view object it contains is no longer a UITableViewCell but your own SearchResultCell subclass:

The nib's top-level view is now a SearchResultCell

(If you don't see the outline pane, click the tiny button at the bottom of the Interface Builder window to expand it.)

From now on, whenever you do dequeueReusableCellWithIdentifier(), the table view will return an object of type SearchResultCell.

➤ Add the following outlet properties to **SearchResultCell.swift**:

```
@IBOutlet weak var nameLabel: UILabel!
@IBOutlet weak var artistNameLabel: UILabel!
@IBOutlet weak var artworkImageView: UIImageView!
```

➤ Hook these outlets up to the respective labels and image view in the nib. It is easiest to do this from the Connections inspector for SearchResultCell:

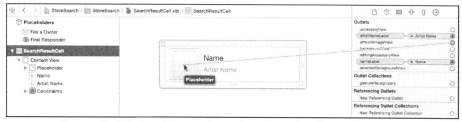

Connect the labels and image view to Search Result Cell, not File's Owner

You can also open the Assistant editor and Ctrl-drag from the labels and image view to their respective outlet definitions. (If you've used nib files before you might be tempted to connect the outlets to File's Owner but that won't work in this case.)

Now that this is all set up, you can tell the `SearchViewController` to use these new `SearchResultCell` objects.

> In **SearchViewController.swift**, change `cellForRowAtIndexPath` to:

```
func tableView(tableView: UITableView,
               cellForRowAtIndexPath indexPath: NSIndexPath) -> UITableViewCell {
  let cell = tableView.dequeueReusableCellWithIdentifier(
                     "SearchResultCell", forIndexPath: indexPath) as! SearchResultCell

  if searchResults.count == 0 {
    cell.nameLabel.text = "(Nothing found)"
    cell.artistNameLabel.text = ""
  } else {
    let searchResult = searchResults[indexPath.row]
    cell.nameLabel.text = searchResult.name
    cell.artistNameLabel.text = searchResult.artistName
  }
  return cell
}
```

Notice the change in the first line. Previously this returned a `UITableViewCell` object but now that you've changed the class in the nib, you're guaranteed to always receive a `SearchResultCell`.

Given that cell, you can put the name and artist name from the search result into the proper labels. You're now using the cell's `nameLabel` and `artistNameLabel` outlets instead of `textLabel` and `detailTextLabel`. (You also no longer need to write `!` to unwrap because the outlets are implicitly unwrapped optionals, not true optionals.)

> Run the app and it should look something like this:

Much better!

There are a few more things to improve. Notice that you've been using the string literal `"SearchResultCell"` in a few different places? It's generally better to create a *constant* for such occasions.

Suppose you – or one of your co-workers – renamed the reuse identifier in one place (for whatever reason). Then you'd also have to remember to change it in all the other places where `"SearchResultCell"` is used.

It's better to limit those changes to one single spot by using a symbolic name instead.

> Add the following to **SearchViewController.swift**, somewhere inside the class:

```
struct TableViewCellIdentifiers {
  static let searchResultCell = "SearchResultCell"
}
```

This defines a new struct, `TableViewCellIdentifiers`, containing a constant named `searchResultCell` with the value `"SearchResultCell"`.

Should you want to change this value, then you only have to do it here and any code that uses `TableViewCellIdentifiers.searchResultCell` will be automatically updated.

There is another reason for using a symbolic name rather than the actual value: it gives extra meaning. Just seeing the text `"SearchResultCell"` says less about its intended purpose than the symbol `TableViewCellIdentifiers.searchResultCell`.

> **Note:** Putting symbolic constants as `static let` members inside a `struct` is a common trick in Swift. A `static` value can be used without an instance so you don't need to instantiate `TableViewCellIdentifiers` before you can use it (like you would need to do with a class).
>
> It's allowed in Swift to place a struct *inside* a class, which permits different classes to all have their own `struct TableViewCellIdentifiers`. This wouldn't work if you placed the struct outside the class – then you'd have more than one struct with the same name in the global namespace, which is not allowed.

➤ Anywhere else in **SearchViewController.swift**, replace the string `"SearchResultCell"` with `TableViewCellIdentifiers.searchResultCell`.

For example, `viewDidLoad()` will now look like this:

```
override func viewDidLoad() {
  super.viewDidLoad()
  tableView.contentInset = UIEdgeInsets(top: 64, left: 0, bottom: 0, right: 0)
  tableView.rowHeight = 80

  var cellNib = UINib(nibName: TableViewCellIdentifiers.searchResultCell, bundle: nil)
  tableView.registerNib(cellNib,
                      forCellReuseIdentifier: TableViewCellIdentifiers.searchResultCell)
}
```

The other change is in `tableView(cellForRowAtIndexPath)`.

➤ Run the app to make sure everything still works.

A new "Nothing Found" cell

Remember our friend Justin Bieber? Searching for him now looks like this:

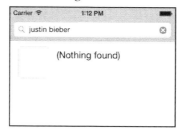

The Nothing Found label now draws like this

That's not very pretty. It will be nicer if you gave this its own cell. That's not too hard: you can simply make another nib for it.

> Add another nib file to the project. Again this will be an **Empty** nib. Name it **NothingFoundCell.xib**.

> Drag a new **Table View Cell** into the canvas. Set its **Height** to 80 and give it the reuse identifier **NothingFoundCell**.

> Drag a **Label** into the cell and give it the text **Nothing Found**. Make the text color 50% opaque black and the font **System 15**.

> Use **Editor** → **Size to Fit Content** to make the label fit the text exactly (you may have to deselect and select the label again to enable this menu option).

> Center the label in the cell, using the blue guides to snap it exactly to the center.

It should look like this:

Design of the Nothing Found cell

In order to keep the text centered on all devices, select the label and open the Align menu:

Creating the alignment constraints

> Choose **Horizontal Center in Container** and **Vertical Center in Container**. Set Update Frames to **Items of New Constraints**.

The constraints should look like this:

The constraints for the label

One more thing to fix. Remember that in `willSelectRowAtIndexPath` you return `nil` if there are no search results to prevent the row from being selected? Well, if you are persistent enough you can still make the row appear gray as if it were selected.

For some reason, UIKit draws the selected background if you press down on the cell for long enough, even though this doesn't count as a real selection. To prevent this, you have to tell the cell not to use a selection color.

➤ Select the cell itself. In the **Attributes inspector**, set **Selection** to **None**. Now tapping or holding down on the Nothing Found row will no longer show any sort of selection.

You don't have to make a `UITableViewCell` subclass for this cell because there is no text to change or properties to set. All you need to do is register this nib with the table view.

➤ Add to the struct in **SearchViewController.swift**:

```
struct TableViewCellIdentifiers {
  static let searchResultCell = "SearchResultCell"
  static let nothingFoundCell = "NothingFoundCell"
}
```

➤ Add these lines to `viewDidLoad()`, below the other code that registers the nib:

```
cellNib = UINib(nibName: TableViewCellIdentifiers.nothingFoundCell, bundle: nil)
tableView.registerNib(cellNib,
                   forCellReuseIdentifier: TableViewCellIdentifiers.nothingFoundCell)
```

➤ And finally, change `tableView(cellForRowAtIndexPath)` to:

```
func tableView(tableView: UITableView,
            cellForRowAtIndexPath indexPath: NSIndexPath) -> UITableViewCell {

  if searchResults.count == 0 {
    return tableView.dequeueReusableCellWithIdentifier(
      TableViewCellIdentifiers.nothingFoundCell, forIndexPath: indexPath) as! UITableViewCell

  } else {
    let cell = tableView.dequeueReusableCellWithIdentifier(
                      TableViewCellIdentifiers.searchResultCell, forIndexPath: indexPath)
                      as! SearchResultCell

    let searchResult = searchResults[indexPath.row]
    cell.nameLabel.text = searchResult.name
    cell.artistNameLabel.text = searchResult.artistName

    return cell
  }
}
```

The logic here has been restructured a little. You only make a `SearchResultCell` if there are actually any results. If the array is empty, you'll simply dequeue the cell for the `nothingFoundCell` identifier and return it. There is nothing to configure for that cell so this one-liner will do.

➤ Run the app. The search results for Justin Bieber now look like this:

The new Nothing Found cell in action

Also try it out on the larger iPhones. The label should always be centered in the cell.

Sweet. It has been a while since your last commit, so this seems like a good time to secure your work.

➤ Commit the changes to the repository. I used the message "Now uses custom cells for search results."

Changing the look of the app

As I write this, it's gray and rainy outside. The app itself also looks quite gray and dull. Let's cheer it up a little by giving it more vibrant colors.

➤ Add the following method to **AppDelegate.swift**:

```
func customizeAppearance() {
  let barTintColor = UIColor(red: 20/255, green: 160/255, blue: 160/255, alpha: 1)
  UISearchBar.appearance().barTintColor = barTintColor

  window!.tintColor = UIColor(red: 10/255, green: 80/255, blue: 80/255, alpha: 1)
}
```

This changes the appearance of the UISearchBar – in fact, it changes *all* search bars in the application. You only have one, but if you had several then this changes the whole lot in one swoop.

The UIColor(red, green, blue, alpha) method makes a new UIColor object based on the RGB and alpha color components that you specify.

Many painting programs let you pick RGB values going from 0 to 255 so that's the range of color values that many programmers are accustomed to thinking in. The UIColor initializer, however, accepts values between 0.0 and 1.0, so you have to divide these numbers by 255 to scale them down to that range.

➤ Call this new method from application(didFinishLaunchingWithOptions):

```
func application(application: UIApplication,
            didFinishLaunchingWithOptions launchOptions: [NSObject: AnyObject]?) -> Bool {
  customizeAppearance()
  return true
}
```

➤ Run the app and notice the difference:

The search bar in the new teal-colored theme

The search bar is bluish-green, but still slightly translucent. The overall tint color is now a dark shade of green instead of the default blue. (You can currently only see the tint color in the text field's cursor but it will become more obvious later on.)

Aside: The role of App Delegate

The poor AppDelegate is often abused. People give it too many responsibilities. Really, there isn't that much for the app delegate to do.

It gets a number of callbacks about the state of the app – whether the app is about to be closed, for example – and handling those events should be its primary responsibility. The app delegate also owns the main window and the top-level view controller. Other than that, it shouldn't do much.

Some developers use the app delegate as their data model. That is just bad design. You should really have a separate class for that (or several). Others make the app delegate their main control hub. Wrong again! Put that stuff in your top-level view controller.

If you ever see the following type of thing in someone's source code, it's a pretty good indication that the application delegate is being used the wrong way:

```
let appDelegate = UIApplication.sharedApplication().delegate as! AppDelegate
appDelegate.property = . . .
```

This happens when an object wants to get something from the app delegate. It works but it's not good architecture.

In my opinion, it's better to design your code the other way around: the app delegate may do a certain amount of initialization, but then it gives any data model objects to the root view controller, and hands over control. The root view controller passes these data model objects to any other controller that needs them, and so on.

This is also called *dependency injection*. I described this principle in the section "Passing around the context" in the MyLocations tutorial.

Currently, tapping a row gives it a gray selection. This doesn't go so well with the teal-colored theme so you'll give the row selection the same bluish-green tint.

That's very easy to do because all table view cells have a selectedBackgroundView property. The view from that property is placed on top of the cell's background, but below the other content, when the cell is selected.

➤ Add the following code to `awakeFromNib()` in **SearchResultCell.swift**:

```
override func awakeFromNib() {
  super.awakeFromNib()

  let selectedView = UIView(frame: CGRect.zeroRect)
  selectedView.backgroundColor = UIColor(red: 20/255, green: 160/255, blue: 160/255,
                                         alpha: 0.5)
  selectedBackgroundView = selectedView
}
```

The `awakeFromNib()` method is called after this cell object has been loaded from the nib but before the cell is added to the table view. You can use this method to do additional work to prepare the object for use. That's perfect for creating the view with the selection color.

Why don't you do that in an init method, such as `init(coder)`? To be fair, in this case you could. But it's worth noting that `awakeFromNib()` is called some time after `init(coder)` and also after the objects from the nib have been connected to their outlets.

For example, in `init(coder)` the `nameLabel` and `artistNameLabel` outlets will still be `nil` but in `awakeFromNib()` they will be properly hooked up to their `UILabel` objects. So if you wanted to do something with those outlets in code, you'd need to do that in `awakeFromNib()`, not in `init(coder)`.

That's why `awakeFromNib()` is the ideal place for this kind of thing. (It's similar to what you use `viewDidLoad()` for in a view controller.)

Don't forget to first call `super.awakeFromNib()`, which is required. If you forget, then the superclass `UITableViewCell` – or any of the other superclasses – may not get a chance to initialize themselves.

Tip: It's always a good idea to call `super.methodName(...)` in methods that you're overriding – such as `viewDidLoad()`, `viewWillAppear()`, `awakeFromNib()`, and so on – unless the documentation says otherwise.

When you run the app, it should look as follows:

The selection color is now green

While you're at it, you might as well give the app an icon.

➤ Open the asset catalog (**Images.xcassets**) and select the **AppIcon** group.

Later in this tutorial you will convert this app to run on the iPad, so you also need to add the icons for the iPad version.

➤ Open the **Attributes inspector** and put a checkmark in front of **iPad, iOS 7.0 and Later Sizes**:

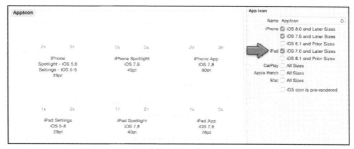

Enabling iPad icons

This adds six new slots for the iPad icons.

➤ Drag the images from the **Icon** folder from this tutorial's resources into the slots.

Keep in mind that for the 2x slots you need to use the image with twice the size in pixels. For example, you drag the **Icon-152.png** file into **iPad App 76pt, 2x**. For 3x you need to multiply the image size by 3.

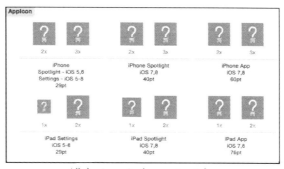

All the icons in the asset catalog

➤ Run the app and notice that it has a nice icon:

The app icon

One final user interface tweak I'd like to make is that the keyboard will be immediately visible when you start the app so the user can start typing right away.

➤ Add the following line to viewDidLoad() in **SearchViewController.swift**:

```
searchBar.becomeFirstResponder()
```

This is the inverse of `resignFirstResponder()` that you used earlier. Where "resign" got rid of the keyboard, `becomeFirstResponder()` will show the keyboard and anything you type will end up in the search bar.

➤ Try it out and commit your changes. You styled the search bar and added the icon.

Tagging the commits

If you look through the various commits you've made so far, you'll notice a bunch of strange numbers, such as "4e02ea387802":

The commits are listed in the history window but have weird numbers

Those are internal numbers that Git uses to uniquely identify commits (known as the "hash"). Such numbers aren't very nice for us humans so Git also allows you to "tag" a certain commit with a more friendly label.

Unfortunately, at the time of writing, Xcode does not support this tag command. You can do it from a Terminal window, though.

➤ Open the **Terminal** (from **Applications/Utilities**).

➤ Type "**cd** " (with a space behind it) and from Finder drag the folder that contains the StoreSearch project into the Terminal. Then press Enter. This will make the Terminal go to your project directory.

➤ Type the command "**git tag v0.1**".

Doing git tag from the Terminal

Later you can refer to this particular commit as "v0.1".

Note: If typing the **git** command in Terminal gives you a "command not found" error, then type the command **xcode-select --install** first.

It's a bit of a shame that Xcode doesn't show these Git tags, as they're really handy, but third-party tools such as Tower do.

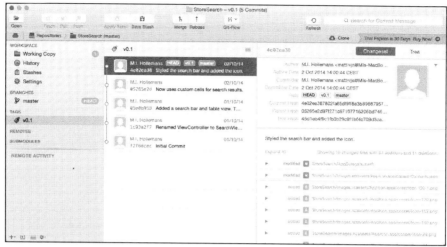

Viewing the Git repository with Tower

Xcode works quite well with Git but it only supports the basic features. To take full advantage of Git you'll probably need to learn how to use the Terminal or get a tool such as Tower (git-tower.com, free 30-day trial), SourceTree (free on the Mac App Store), GitX (gitx.frim.nl, free), or GitHub for Mac (mac.github.com, free).

You can find the project files for the app up to this point under **02 - Custom Table Cells** in the tutorial's Source Code folder.

The debugger

Xcode has a built-in **debugger**. Unfortunately, a debugger doesn't actually get the bugs out of your programs; it just lets them crash in slow motion so you can get a better idea of what is wrong.

Like a police detective, the debugger lets you dig through the evidence after the damage has been done, in order to find the scoundrel who did it.

Let's introduce a bug into the app so that it crashes. Knowing what to do when your app crashes is very important.

Thanks to the debugger, you don't have to stumble in the dark with no idea what just happened. Instead, you can use it to quickly pinpoint what went wrong and where. Once you know that, figuring out *why* it went wrong becomes a lot easier.

➤ Change **SearchViewController.swift**'s `numberOfRowsInSection` method to:

```
func tableView(tableView: UITableView, numberOfRowsInSection section: Int) -> Int {
  if !hasSearched {
    return 0
  } else if searchResults.count == 0 {
    return 1
  } else {
    return searchResults.count + 1
  }
}
```

➤ Now run the app and search for something. The app crashes and the Xcode window changes to something like this:

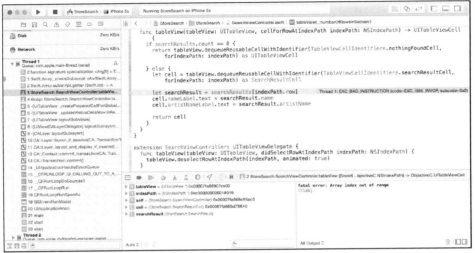

The Xcode debugger appears when the app crashes

The crash is: **Thread 1: signal EXC_BAD_INSTRUCTION**. Sounds nasty!

There are different types of crashes, with wonderful names such as SIGABRT, EXC_BAD_ACCESS, and the one you have here, EXC_BAD_INSTRUCTION.

This is actually a pretty good crash to have – as far as that's possible anyway. It means your app died in a controlled fashion. You did something you were not supposed to and Swift caught this and politely terminated the app with an error message.

That error message is an important clue and you can find it in Xcode's Debug area:

```
fatal error: Array index out of range
```

According to the error message, the index that was used on the array is larger than the number of items inside the array. In other words, the index is "out of range". That is a common error with arrays and you're likely to make this mistake more than once in your programming career.

Now that you know what went wrong, the big question is: *where* did it go wrong? You may have many calls to array[index] in your app, and you don't want to have to dig through the entire code to find the culprit.

Thankfully, you have the debugger to help you out. In the source code editor it already points at the offending line:

```
        } else {
            let cell = tableView.dequeueReusableCellWithIdentifier(TableViewCellIdentifiers.searchResultCell,
                forIndexPath: indexPath) as SearchResultCell

            let searchResult = searchResults[indexPath.row]        Thread 1: EXC_BAD_INSTRUCTION (code=EXC_I386_INVOP, subcode=0x0)
            cell.nameLabel.text = searchResult.name
            cell.artistNameLabel.text = searchResult.artistName

            return cell
        }
    }
}
```

The debugger points at the line that crashed

Important: This line isn't necessarily the *cause* of the crash – after all, you didn't change anything in this method – but it is where the crash happens. From here you can find your way backwards to the cause.

The array is searchResults and the index is given by indexPath.row. It would be great to get some insight into the row number but unfortunately there is no easy way to see the value of indexPath.row in the debugger.

You'll have to resort to using the debugger's command line interface, like a hacker whiz kid from the movies.

➤ Behind the **(lldb)** prompt, type **p indexPath.row** and press enter:

```
fatal error: Array index out of range
(lldb) p indexPath.row
(Int) $R1 = 3
(lldb)



All Output ○                                              🗑 □□
```

Printing the value of indexPath.row

The output should be something like:

```
(Int) $R1 = 3
```

This means the value of indexPath.row is 3 and the type is Int. (You can ignore the $R1 bit.)

Let's also find out how many items are in the array.

➤ Type **p searchResults**:

```
fatal error: Array index out of range
(lldb) p indexPath.row
(Int) $R1 = 3
(lldb) p searchResults
([(StoreSearch.SearchResult)]) $R2 = 3 values {
  [0] = 0x00007fa668cc1760 (name = "Fake Result 0 for", artistName = "sds")
  [1] = 0x00007fa668cc99f0 (name = "Fake Result 1 for", artistName = "sds")
  [2] = 0x00007fa66b01de30 (name = "Fake Result 2 for", artistName = "sds")
}
```

Printing the searchResults array

The output shows an array with three items.

You can now reason about the problem: the table view is asking for a cell for the fourth row (i.e. the one at index 3) but apparently there are only three rows in the data model (rows 0 through 2).

The table view knows how many rows there are from the value that is returned from numberOfRowsInSection, so maybe that method is returning the wrong number of rows. That is indeed the cause, of course, as you intentionally introduced the bug in that method.

I hope this illustrates how you should deal with crashes: first find out where the crash happens and what the actual error is, then reason your way backwards until you find the cause.

➤ Restore numberOfRowsInSection to what it was and then add a new outlet property to **SearchViewController.swift**:

```
@IBOutlet weak var searchBar2: UISearchBar!
```

➤ Open the storyboard and **Ctrl-drag** from Search View Controller to the Search Bar. Select **searchBar2** from the popup.

Now the search bar is also connected to this new `searchBar2` outlet. (It's perfectly fine for an object to be connected to more than one outlet at a time.)

> Remove the `searchBar2` outlet property from **SearchViewController.swift**.

This is a dirty trick on my part to make the app crash. The storyboard contains a connection to a property that no longer exists. (If you think this a convoluted example, then wait until you make this mistake in one of your own apps. It happens more often than you may think!)

> Run the app and it immediately crashes. The crash is "Thread 1: signal SIGABRT".

The Debug pane says:

```
*** Terminating app due to uncaught exception 'NSUnknownKeyException', reason:
'[<StoreSearch.SearchViewController 0x7ff47a6242c0> setValue:forUndefinedKey:]: this class is
not key value coding-compliant for the key searchBar2.'
*** First throw call stack:
(
   0   CoreFoundation      0x00000001099a63f5 __exceptionPreprocess + 165
   1   libobjc.A.dylib     0x000000010b4d4bb7 objc_exception_throw + 45
  . . .
```

The first part of this message is very important: it tells you that the app was terminated because of an "NSUnknownKeyException". On some platforms exceptions are a commonly used error handling mechanism, but on iOS an exception is only thrown when some fatal error happens.

The bit that should pique your interest is this:

```
this class is not key value coding-compliant for the key searchBar2
```

Hmm, that is a bit cryptic. It does mention "searchBar2" but what does "key value-coding compliant" mean? I've seen this error enough times to know what is wrong but if you're new to this game a message like that isn't very enlightening.

So let's see where Xcode thinks the crash happened:

Crash in AppDelegate?

That also isn't very useful. Xcode says the app crashed in **AppDelegate**, but that's not really true.

Xcode goes through the **call stack** until it finds a method that it has source code for and that's the one it shows. The call stack is the list of methods that have been called most recently. You can see it on the left of the Debugger window.

> Click the left-most icon at the bottom of the Debug navigator to see more info:

A more detailed call stack

The method at the top, __pthread_kill, was the last method that was called (it's actually a function, not a method). It got called from pthread_kill, which was called from abort, which was called from abort_message, and so on, all the way back to the main function, which is the entry point of the app and the very first function that was called when the app started.

All of the methods and functions that are listed in this call stack are from system libraries, which is why they are grayed out. If you click on one, you'll get a bunch of unintelligible assembly code:

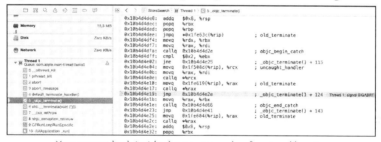

You cannot look inside the source code of system libraries

So clearly this approach is not getting you anywhere. However, there is another thing you can try and that is to set an **Exception Breakpoint**.

> A **breakpoint** is a special marker in your code that will pause the app and jump into the debugger.
>
> When your app hits a breakpoint, the app will pause at that exact spot. Then you can use the debugger to step line-by-line through your code in order to run it in slow motion. That can be a handy tool if you really cannot figure out why something crashes.
>
> You're not going to step through code in this tutorial, but you can read more about it in the Xcode Overview guide, in the section Debug Your App. You can find it in the iOS Developer Library. https://developer.apple.com/library/ios/

You are going to set a special breakpoint that is triggered whenever a fatal exception occurs. This will halt the program just as it is about to crash, which should give you more insight into what is going on.

➤ Switch to the **Breakpoint navigator** (the arrow-shaped button to the right of the Debug navigator) and click the + button at the bottom to add an Exception Breakpoint:

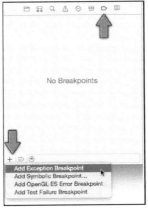

Adding an Exception Breakpoint

This will put a new breakpoint in the list:

After adding the Exception Breakpoint

➤ Now run the app again. It will still crash, but Xcode shows a lot more info:

Xcode now halts the app as the exception is being thrown

There are many more methods in the call stack now. Let's see if we can find some clues as to what is going on.

What catches my attention is the call to something called [UIViewController _loadViewFromNibNamed:bundle:]. That's a pretty good hint that this has error occurs when loading a nib file, or the storyboard in this case.

Using these hints and clues, and the somewhat cryptic error message that you got without the Exception Breakpoint, you can usually figure out what is making your app crash.

In this case we've established that the app crashes when it's loading the storyboard, and the error message mentioned "searchBar2". Put two and two together and you've got your answer.

A quick peek in the source code confirms that the searchBar2 outlet no longer exists on the view controller but the storyboard still refers to it.

➤ Open the storyboard and disconnect Search View Controller from **searchBar2** to fix the crash. That's another bug squashed!

> **Note:** Enabling the Exception Breakpoint means that you no longer get a useful error message in the Debug pane if you app crashes (because the exception was never actually thrown). If sometime later during development your app crashes on another bug, you may want to disable this breakpoint again to actually see the error message. You can do that from the Breakpoint navigator.

To summarize:

- If your app crashes with EXC_BAD_INSTRUCTION or SIGABRT, the Xcode debugger will often show you an error message and where in the code the crash happens.

- If Xcode thinks the crash happened on **AppDelegate** (not very useful!), enable the Exception Breakpoint to get more info.

- If the app crashes with a SIGABRT but there is no error message, then disable the Exception Breakpoint and make the app crash again. (Alternatively, click the **Continue program execution** button from the debugger toolbar a few times. That will also show the error message.)

- An EXC_BAD_ACCESS error usually means something went wrong with your memory management. An object may have been "released" one time too many or not "retained" enough. With Swift these problems are mostly a thing of the past because the compiler will usually make sure to do the right thing. However, it's still possible to mess up if you're talking to Objective-C code or low-level APIs.

- EXC_BREAKPOINT is not an error. The app has stopped on a breakpoint, the blue arrow pointing at the line where the app is paused. You set breakpoints to pause your app at specific places in the code, so you can examine the state of the app inside the debugger. The "Continue program execution" button resumes the app.

This should help you get to the bottom of most of your crashes!

The build log

If you're wondering what Xcode actually does when it builds your app, then take a peek at the **Log navigator**. It's the last icon in the navigator pane.

The Log navigator keeps track of your builds, debug sessions and commits so you can look back at what happened. It even remembers the debug output of previous runs of the app.

To get more information about a particular log item, hover over it and click the little icon that appears on the right. The line will expand and you'll see exactly which commands Xcode executed and what the result was.

Should you run into some weird compilation problem, then this is the place for troubleshooting. Besides, it's interesting to see what Xcode is up to from time to time.

It's all about the networking

Now that the preliminaries are out of the way, you can finally get to the good stuff: adding networking to the app.

The iTunes store sells a lot of products: songs, e-books, movies, software, TV episodes... you name it. You can sign up as an affiliate and earn a commission on each sale that happens because you recommended a product (even your own apps!).

To make it easier for affiliates to find products, Apple made available a web service that queries the iTunes store. You're not going to sign up as an affiliate for this tutorial but you will use that free web service to perform searches.

So what is a **web service**? Your app (also known as the "client") will send a message over the network to the iTunes store (the "server") using the HTTP protocol.

Because the iPhone can be connected to different types of networks – Wi-Fi or a cellular network such as LTE, 3G, or GPRS – the app has to "speak" a variety of networking protocols to communicate with other computers on the Internet.

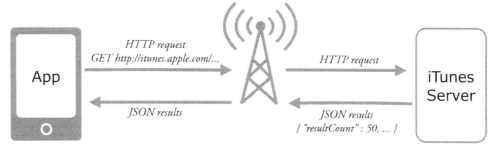

The HTTP requests fly over the network

Fortunately you don't have to worry about any of that as the iPhone firmware will take care of this complicated subject matter. All you need to know is that you're using HTTP.

HTTP is the exact same protocol that your web browser uses when you visit a web site. In fact, you can play with the iTunes web service using a web browser. That's a great way to figure out how this web service works.

This trick won't work with all web services (some require "POST" requests instead of "GET" requests) but often you can get quite far with just a web browser.

Open your favorite web browser (I'm using Safari) and go to the following URL:

```
http://itunes.apple.com/search?term=metallica
```

The browser should show something like this:

Using the iTunes web service from the Safari web browser

Those are the search results that the iTunes web service gives you. The data is in a format named JSON, which stands for JavaScript Object Notation.

JSON is commonly used to send structured data back-and-forth between servers and clients (i.e. apps). Another data format that you may have heard of is XML, but that's quickly going out of favor for JSON.

There are a variety of tools that you can use to make the JSON output more readable for mere humans. I have a Quick Look plug-in installed that renders JSON files in a colorful view (http://www.sagtau.com/quicklookjson.html).

You do need to save the output from the server to a file first:

A more readable version of the output from the web service

That makes a lot more sense.

> **Note:** You can find extensions for Safari (and most other browsers) that can prettify JSON directly inside the browser. github.com/rfletcher/safari-json-formatter is a good one.
>
> There are also dedicated tools on the Mac App Store, for example Visual JSON, that let you directly perform the request on the server and show the output in a structured and readable format.

Browse through the JSON text for a bit. You'll see that the server gave back a list of items, some of which are songs; others are audiobooks or music videos.

Each item has a bunch of data associated with it, such as an artist name ("Metallica", which is what you searched for), a track name, a genre, a price, a release date, and so on.

You'll store some of these fields in the SearchResult class so you can display them on the screen.

The results you get from the iTunes store might be different from mine. By default the search returns at most 50 items and since the store has quite a bit more than fifty entries that match "metallica", each time you do the search you may get back a different set of 50 results.

Also notice that some of these fields, such as artistViewUrl and artworkUrl60 and previewUrl are links (URLs). For example, from the search result for the song "One" from the album "...And Justice for All":

```
artistViewUrl:
https://itunes.apple.com/us/artist/metallica/id3996865?uo=4

artworkUrl60:
http://a3.mzstatic.com/us/r30/Features4/v4/3b/e2/5f/3be25fec-ba01-8c4c-d694-
cf7725f5c0fd/dj.rarclwth.60x60-50.jpg

previewUrl:
http://a899.phobos.apple.com/us/r30/Music/v4/b7/61/2d/b7612d40-bf5b-8fe7-57a6-
755f1aaea785/mzaf_7142718067413325399.aac.m4a
```

Go ahead and copy-paste these URLs in your browser (use the ones from your own search results).

The artistViewUrl will open an iTunes Preview page for the artist, the artworkUrl60 loads a thumbnail image, and the previewUrl opens a 30-second audio preview.

This is how the server tells you about additional resources. The images and so on are not embedded directly into the search results, but you're given a URL that allows you to download them separately. Try some of the other URLs from the JSON data and see what they do!

Back to the original HTTP request. You made the web browser go to the following URL:

```
http://itunes.apple.com/search?term=the search term
```

You can add other parameters as well to make the search more specific. For example:

```
http://itunes.apple.com/search?term=metallica&entity=song
```

Now the results won't contain any music videos or podcasts, only songs.

If the search term has a space in it you should replace it with a + sign, as in:

```
http://itunes.apple.com/search?term=angry+birds&entity=software
```

This searches for all apps that have something to do with angry birds (you may have heard of some of them).

The fields in the JSON results for this particular query are slightly different than before. There is no more previewUrl but there are several screenshot URLs per entry. Different kinds of products – songs, movies, software – return different types of data.

That's all there is to it. You construct a URL to itunes.apple.com with the search parameters and then use that URL to make an HTTP request. The server will send JSON gobbledygook back to the app and you'll have to somehow turn that into SearchResult objects and put them in the table view. Let's get on it!

Sending the HTTP request to the iTunes server

Synchronous networking = bad

Before you begin, I should point out that there is a bad way to do networking in your apps and a good way. The bad way is to perform the HTTP requests on your app's **main thread**.

This is simple to program but it will block the user interface and make your app unresponsive while the networking is taking place. Because it blocks the rest of the app, this is called synchronous networking.

Unfortunately, many programmers insist on doing networking the wrong way in their apps, which makes for apps that are slow and prone to crashing.

I will begin by demonstrating the easy-but-bad way, just to show you how *not* to do this. It's important that you realize the consequences of synchronous networking, so you will avoid it in your own apps.

After I have convinced you of the evilness of this approach, I will show you how to do it the right way. That only requires a small modification to the code but may require a big change in how you think about these problems.

Asynchronous networking (the right kind, with an "a") makes your apps much more responsive, but also brings with it additional complexity that you need to deal with.

The to-do list for this section:

- Create the URL with the search parameters.
- Do the request on the iTunes server and see if you get any data back.
- Turn the JSON data into something more useful, i.e. SearchResult objects.
- Show these SearchResult objects in the table view.
- Take care of errors. There may be no network connection (or a very bad one), or the iTunes server may send back data that the app does not know how to interpret. The app should be able to recover from such situations.

You will not worry about downloading the artwork images for now; just the list of products will be plenty for our poor brains to handle.

➤ Add a new method to **SearchViewController.swift**:

```
func urlWithSearchText(searchText: String) -> NSURL {
  let urlString = String(format: "http://itunes.apple.com/search?term=%@", searchText)
  let url = NSURL(string: urlString)
  return url!
}
```

This first builds the URL as a string by placing the text from the search bar behind the "term=" parameter, and then turns this string into an NSURL object.

Because NSURL(string) is one of those *failable* initializers, it returns an optional. You force unwrap that using url! to return an actual NSURL object.

➤ Change searchBarSearchButtonClicked() to:

```
func searchBarSearchButtonClicked(searchBar: UISearchBar) {
  if !searchBar.text.isEmpty {
    searchBar.resignFirstResponder()

    hasSearched = true
    searchResults = [SearchResult]()

    let url = urlWithSearchText(searchBar.text)
    println("URL: '\(url)'")

    tableView.reloadData()
  }
}
```

You've removed the code that creates the fake SearchResult items, and instead call the new urlWithSearchText() method. For testing purposes you log the NSURL object that this method returns.

This logic sits inside the if-statement so that none of this happens unless the user actually typed text into the search bar – it doesn't make much sense to search the iTunes store for "nothing".

➤ Run the app and type in some search text, for example "metallica" (or one of your other favorite metal bands), and press the Search button.

Xcode should now show this in its Debug pane:

```
URL: 'http://itunes.apple.com/search?term=metallica'
```

That looks good.

➤ Now type "angry birds" into the search box.

Whoops, the app crashes!

The crash after searching for "angry birds"

Look into the left-hand pane of the Xcode debugger and you'll see that the value of the url constant is nil (this may also show up as 0x0000… followed by a whole bunch of zeros).

The app apparently did not create a valid NSURL object. But why?

A space is not a valid character in a URL. Many other characters aren't valid either (such as the < or > signs) and therefore must be **escaped**. Another term for this is **URL encoding**.

A space, for example, can be encoded as the + sign (you did that earlier when you typed the URL into the web browser) or as the character sequence %20.

➤ Fortunately, String can do this encoding already, so you only have to add one extra statement to the app to make this work:

```
func urlWithSearchText(searchText: String) -> NSURL {
  let escapedSearchText = searchText.stringByAddingPercentEscapesUsingEncoding(
                                          NSUTF8StringEncoding)!
  let urlString = String(format: "http://itunes.apple.com/search?term=%@", escapedSearchText)
  let url = NSURL(string: urlString)
  return url!
}
```

This calls the stringByAddingPercentEscapesUsingEncoding() method to escape the special characters, which returns a new string that you then use for the search term.

In theory this method can return nil for certain encodings but because you chose the UTF-8 encoding here that won't ever happen, so you can safely force-unwrap the return value with the exclamation point at the end. (You could also have used if let.)

> **Note:** There are many different ways to encode text. You've probably heard of ASCII and Unicode, the two most common encodings.
>
> UTF-8 is a version of Unicode that is very efficient for storing regular text, but less so for special symbols or non-Western alphabets. Still, it's the most popular way to deal with Unicode text today.

Normally you don't have to worry about how your strings are encoded but when sending requests to a web service you need to transmit the text in the proper encoding. Tip: When in doubt, use UTF-8, it will almost always work.

➤ Run the app and search for "angry birds" again. This time a valid NSURL object can be created, and it looks like this:

```
URL: 'http://itunes.apple.com/search?term=angry%20birds'
```

The space has been turned into the character sequence %20. The % indicates an escaped character and 20 is the UTF-8 value for a space. Also try searching for terms with other special characters, such as # and * or even Emoji, and see what happens.

Now that you have an NSURL object, you can do some actual networking!

➤ Add a new method to **SearchViewController.swift**:

```
func performStoreRequestWithURL(url: NSURL) -> String? {
  var error: NSError?
  if let resultString = String(contentsOfURL: url, encoding: NSUTF8StringEncoding,
                               error: &error) {
    return resultString
  } else if let error = error {
    println("Download Error: \(error)")
  } else {
    println("Unknown Download Error")
  }
  return nil
}
```

The meat of this method is the call to String(contentsOfURL, encoding, error), a constructor of the String class that returns a new string object with the data that it receives from the server at the other end of the URL.

If something goes wrong, the string is nil and the NSError variable contains more details about the error. (That's also why this method returns an optional.)

➤ Add the following lines to searchBarSearchButtonClicked(), below the println() line:

```
if let jsonString = performStoreRequestWithURL(url) {
  println("Received JSON string '\(jsonString)'")
}
```

This invokes performStoreRequestWithURL(), which takes the NSURL object as a parameter and returns the JSON data that is received from the server.

If everything goes according to plan, this method returns a new string object that contains the JSON data that you're after. Let's try it out!

➤ Run the app and search for your favorite band. After a second or so, a whole bunch of data will be dumped to the Xcode Debug pane:

```
URL: 'http://itunes.apple.com/search?term=metallica'

Received JSON string '

{
  "resultCount":50,
```

```
 "results": [
{"wrapperType":"track", "kind":"song", "artistId":3996865, "collectionId":579372950,
"trackId":579373079, "artistName":"Metallica", "collectionName":"Metallica",
"trackName":"Enter Sandman", "collectionCensoredName":"Metallica", "trackCensoredName":"Enter
Sandman",
. . . and so on . . .
```

Congratulations! You've successfully made the app talk to a web service.

The `println()` prints the same stuff you saw in the web browser earlier. Right now it's all contained in a single `String` object, which isn't really convenient for our purposes, but you'll convert it to a more useful format in a minute.

Of course, it's possible that you received an error. In that case, the output will be something like this:

```
Download Error: Error Domain=NSCocoaErrorDomain Code=256 "The operation couldn't be
completed. (Cocoa error 256.)" UserInfo=0x7fc7e580bb10
{NSURL=http://itunes.apple.com/search?term=metallica}
```

You'll add better error handling to the app later, but if you get such an error at this point, then make sure your computer is connected to the Internet (or your iPhone in case you're running the app on the device and not in the Simulator). Also try the URL directly in your web browser and see if that works.

Parsing JSON

Now that you have managed to download a chunk of JSON data from the server, what do you do with it?

JSON is a so-called *structured* data format. It typically consists of arrays and dictionaries that contain other arrays and dictionaries, as well as regular data such as string and numbers.

The JSON from the iTunes store roughly looks like this:

```
{
  "resultCount": 50,
  "results": [ . . . a bunch of other stuff . . . ]
}
```

The { } brackets surround a dictionary. This particular dictionary has two keys: `resultCount` and `results`. The first one, `resultCount`, has a numeric value, the number of items that matched the search query. By default the limit is a maximum of 50 items but as you shall later see you can increase this upper limit.

The `results` key contains an array, which is delineated by the [ ] brackets. Inside that array are more dictionaries, each of which describes a single product from the store. You can tell these things are dictionaries because they have the { } brackets again.

Here are two of these items from the array:

```
{
  "wrapperType": "track",
  "kind": "song",
  "artistId": 3996865,
  "artistName": "Metallica",
  "trackName": "Enter Sandman",
```

```
. . . and so on . . .
},
{
  "wrapperType": "track",
  "kind": "song",
  "artistId": 3996865,
  "artistName": "Metallica",
  "trackName": "Nothing Else Matters",
  . . . and so on . . .
},
```

Each product is represented by a dictionary with several keys. The values of the `kind` and `wrapperType` keys determine what sort of product this is: a song, a music video, an audiobook, and so on. The other keys describe the artist and the song itself.

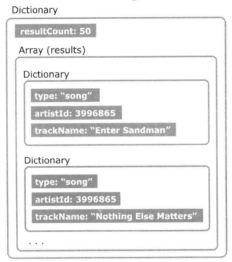

The structure of the JSON data

To summarize, the JSON data represents a dictionary, inside that dictionary is an array of more dictionaries. Each of the dictionaries from the array represents one search result.

Currently all of this sits in a `String`, which isn't very handy, but using a so-called **JSON parser** you can turn this data into actual `Dictionary` and `Array` objects.

JSON vs. XML

JSON is not the only structured data format out there. A slightly more formal standard is XML, which stands for Extensible Markup Language. Both formats serve the same purpose but they look a bit different. If the iTunes store would return its results as XML, the output would look more like this:

```
<?xml version="1.0" encoding="utf-8"?>
<iTunesSearch>
  <resultCount>5</resultCount>
  <results>
    <song>
      <artistName>Metallica</artistName>
      <trackName>Enter Sandman</trackName>
    </song>
    <song>
```

```
            <artistName>Metallica</artistName>
            <trackName>Nothing Else Matters</trackName>
        </song>

        . . . and so on . . .

    </results>
</iTunesSearch>
```

These days most developers prefer JSON because it's simpler than XML and easier to parse. But it's perfectly possible that if you want your app to talk to a particular web service that you'll be expected to speak XML.

In the past, if you wanted to parse JSON it used to be necessary to include a third-party framework into your apps but these days iOS comes with its own JSON parser, so that's easy.

➤ Add the following method somewhere in **SearchViewController.swift**:

```
func parseJSON(jsonString: String) -> [String: AnyObject]? {
  if let data = jsonString.dataUsingEncoding(NSUTF8StringEncoding) {
    var error: NSError?
    if let json = NSJSONSerialization.JSONObjectWithData(data,
              options: NSJSONReadingOptions(0), error: &error) as? [String: AnyObject] {
      return json
    } else if let error = error {
      println("JSON Error: \(error)")
    } else {
      println("Unknown JSON Error")
    }
  }
  return nil
}
```

You're using the NSJSONSerialization class here to convert the JSON search results to a Dictionary.

The dictionary is of type [String: AnyObject]. The dictionary keys will always be strings but the values from these keys can be anything from a string to a number to a boolean. That's why the type of the values is AnyObject.

Because the JSON data is currently in the form of a string, you have to put it into an NSData object first. Then you convert the NSData object into a Dictionary using NSJSONSerialization.JSONObjectWithData(options, error). Or at least, you *hope* you can convert it into a dictionary…

Note: When you write apps that talk to other computers on the Internet, one thing to keep in mind is that your conversational partners may not always say the things you expect them to say.

There could be an error on the server and instead of valid JSON data it may send back some error message. In that case, NSJSONSerialization will not be able to parse the data and the app will return nil from parseJSON().

Another thing that could happen is that the owner of the server changes the format of the data that they send back. Usually they will do this in a new version of the web service that runs on some other URL or that requires you to send along a "version" parameter.

But not everyone is careful like that and by changing what the server does, they may break apps that depend on the data coming back in a specific format.

Just because `NSJSONSerialization` was able to turn the string into valid Swift objects, doesn't mean that it returns a `Dictionary`! It could have returned an `Array` or even a `String` or a number...

In the case of the iTunes store web service, the top-level object *should* be a `Dictionary`, but you can't control what happens on the server. If for some reason the server programmers decide to put [ ] brackets around the JSON data, then the top-level object will no longer be a `Dictionary` but an `Array`.

Being paranoid about these kinds of things and showing an error message in the unlikely event this happens is a lot better than your application suddenly crashing when something changes on a server that is outside of your control.

Just to be sure, you're using the `as?` cast and `if let` to check that the object returned by `NSJSONSerialization` is truly a `Dictionary`. Should the conversion to a `Dictionary` fail, then the app doesn't burst into flames but simply returns `nil` to signal an error.

It's good to add checks like these to the app to make sure you get back what you expect. If you don't own the servers you're talking to, it's best to program defensively.

➤ Add the following lines to `searchBarSearchButtonClicked()`, inside the `if let jsonString` block:

```
if let dictionary = parseJSON(jsonString) {
  println("Dictionary \(dictionary)")
}
```

You simply call the new `parseJSON()` method and print its return value.

➤ Run the app and search for something. The Xcode Debug pane now prints the following:

```
Dictionary [results: (
        {
        artistId = 3996865;
        artistName = Metallica;
        kind = song;
        trackName = "Enter Sandman";
        . . . more fields . . .
    },
        {
        artistId = 3996865;
        artistName = Metallica;
        kind = song;
        trackName = "Nothing Else Matters";
        . . . more fields . . .
    },
    . . . and so on . . .
), resultCount: 50]
```

This should look very familiar to the JSON data – which is not so strange because it represents the exact same thing – except that now you're looking at the contents of a Swift `Dictionary` object.

You have converted a bunch of text that was all packed together in a single string into actual objects that you can use.

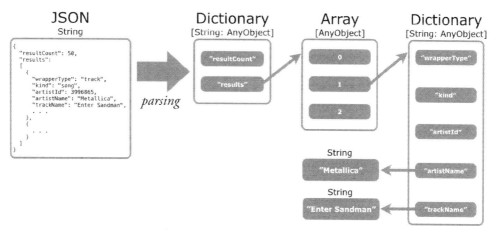

Parsing JSON turns text into objects

Let's add an alert to handle potential errors. It's inevitable that something goes wrong somewhere, so it's best to be prepared.

➤ Add the following method:

```
func showNetworkError() {
  let alert = UIAlertController(title: "Whoops...",
    message: "There was an error reading from the iTunes Store. Please try again.",
    preferredStyle: .Alert)

  let action = UIAlertAction(title: "OK", style: .Default, handler: nil)
  alert.addAction(action)

  presentViewController(alert, animated: true, completion: nil)
}
```

Nothing you haven't seen before; it simply presents an alert controller with an error message.

➤ Change searchBarSearchButtonClicked() to the following:

```
func searchBarSearchButtonClicked(searchBar: UISearchBar) {
  if !searchBar.text.isEmpty {
    searchBar.resignFirstResponder()

    hasSearched = true
    searchResults = [SearchResult]()

    let url = urlWithSearchText(searchBar.text)

    if let jsonString = performStoreRequestWithURL(url) {
      if let dictionary = parseJSON(jsonString) {
        println("Dictionary \(dictionary)")

        tableView.reloadData()
        return
      }
    }
    showNetworkError()
  }
}
```

You moved the call to `tableView.reloadData()` into the innermost `if let` statement and added a `return` statement. If the code made it there, then everything went OK. But if something goes wrong, one of these `if let` statements is false, and you call `showNetworkError()` to show an alert box.

If you did everything correctly up to this point then the web service should always have worked. Still it's a good idea to test a few error situations, just to make sure the error handling is working for those unlucky users with bad network connections.

➤ Try this: In the `urlWithSearchText()` method, temporarily change the itunes.apple.com part of the URL to "NOMOREitunes.apple.com".

You should now get an error alert when you try a search because no such server exists at that address. This simulates the iTunes server being down. Don't forget to change the URL back when you're done testing.

Tip: To simulate no network connection you can pull the network cable and/or disable Wi-Fi on your Mac, or run the app on your device in Airplane Mode.

The app shows an alert when there is a network error

Interestingly enough, a little while ago I was also able to make the app fail simply by searching for "photoshop". The Xcode Debug pane said:

```
JSON Error: Error Domain=NSCocoaErrorDomain Code=3840 "The operation couldn't be completed.
(Cocoa error 3840.)" (Missing low code point in surrogate pair around character 92893.)
UserInfo=0x6eb3110 {NSDebugDescription=Missing low code point in surrogate pair around
character 92893.}
```

This may sound like gibberish, but it means that `NSJSONSerialization` was unable to convert the data to Swift objects because it thinks there is some error in the data. However, when I typed the URL into my web browser it seemed to return valid JSON data, which I verified with JSONLint (http://jsonlint.com/).

So who was right? It could have been a bug in `NSJSONSerialization` or it could be that the iTunes web service did something naughty... As of the current revision of this tutorial, searching for "photoshop" works again.

In any case, it should be obvious that when you're doing networking things can – and will! – go wrong, often in unexpected ways.

Turning the JSON into SearchResult objects

So far you've managed to send a request to the iTunes web service and you parsed the JSON data into a bunch of Dictionary objects. That's a great start, but now you are going to turn this into an array of SearchResult objects because they're much easier to work with.

The iTunes store sells different kinds of products – songs, e-books, software, movies, and so on – and each of these has its own structure in the JSON data. A software product will have screenshots but a movie will have a video preview. The app will have to handle these different kinds of data.

You're not going to support everything the iTunes store has to offer, only these items:

• Songs, music videos, movies, TV shows and podcasts

• Audio books

• Software (apps)

• E-books

The reason I split them up like this is because that's how the iTunes store does it. Songs and music videos, for example, share the same set of fields, but audiobooks and software have different data structures. The JSON data makes this distinction using the kind and wrapperType fields.

➤ Add a new method, parseDictionary(), to **SearchViewController.swift**:

```
func parseDictionary(dictionary: [String: AnyObject]) {
  // 1
  if let array: AnyObject = dictionary["results"] {
    // 2
    for resultDict in array as! [AnyObject] {
      // 3
      if let resultDict = resultDict as? [String: AnyObject] {
        // 4
        if let wrapperType = resultDict["wrapperType"] as? String {
          if let kind = resultDict["kind"] as? String {
            println("wrapperType: \(wrapperType), kind: \(kind)")
          }
        }
      // 5
      } else {
        println("Expected a dictionary")
      }
    }
  } else {
    println("Expected 'results' array")
  }
}
```

This method goes through the top-level dictionary and looks at each search result in turn. Here's what happens step-by-step:

1. First there is a bit of defensive programming to make sure the dictionary has a key named results that contains an array. It probably will, but better safe than sorry.

2. Once it is satisfied that array exists, the method uses a for-loop to look at each of the array's elements in turn.

3. Each of the elements from the array is another dictionary. Because you're dealing with an Objective-C API here, you don't actually receive nice `Dictionary` and `Array` objects, but objects of type `AnyObject`. (Recall that `AnyObject` exists to make Swift compatible with Objective-C and the iOS frameworks.)

   To make sure these objects really do represent a dictionary, you have to cast them to the right type first. You're using the optional cast `as?` here as another defensive measure. In theory it's possible `resultDict` doesn't actually hold a `[String: AnyObject]` dictionary and then you don't want to continue.

4. For each of the dictionaries, you print out the value of its `wrapperType` and `kind` fields. Indexing a dictionary always gives you an optional, which is why you're using `if let`. And because the dictionary only contains values of type `AnyObject`, you also cast to the more useful `String`.

5. If something went wrong, print out an error message. That's always useful for debugging.

➤ Call this method from `searchBarSearchButtonClicked()`, just before the line that reloads the table view.

```
parseDictionary(dictionary)
```

➤ Run the app and do a search. Look at the Xcode output.

When I did this, Xcode showed three different types of products, with the majority of the results being songs. What you see may vary, depending on what you search for.

```
wrapperType: track, kind: song
wrapperType: track, kind: feature-movie
wrapperType: track, kind: music-video
```

To turn these things into `SearchResult` objects, you're going to look at value of the `wrapperType` field first. If that is "track" then you know that the product in question is a song, movie, music video, podcast or episode of a TV show.

Other values for `wrapperType` are "audiobook" for audio books and "software" for apps, and you will interpret these differently than "tracks".

But before you get to that, let's first add some new properties to the `SearchResult` object.

Documentation!

If you're wondering how I knew how to interpret the data from the iTunes web service, or even how to make the URLs to use the service in the first place, then you should know there is no way you can be expected to use a web service if there is no documentation.

Fortunately, for the iTunes store web service there is a pretty good document that explains how to use it:

http://www.apple.com/itunes/affiliates/resources/documentation/itunes-store-web-service-search-api.html

Just reading the docs is often not enough. You have to play with the web service for a bit to know what you can and cannot do.

There are some things that the StoreSearch app needs to do with the search results that were not clear from reading the documentation. For example, e-books do not include a wrapperType field for some reason.

So first read the docs and then play with it. That goes for any API, really, whether it's something from the iOS SDK or a web service.

A better SearchResult

The current SearchResult class only has two properties: name and artistName. As you've seen, the iTunes store returns a lot more information than that, so you'll need to add a few new properties.

➤ Add the following instance variables to **SearchResult.swift**:

```
var artworkURL60 = ""
var artworkURL100 = ""
var storeURL = ""
var kind = ""
var currency = ""
var price = 0.0
var genre = ""
```

You're not including *everything* that the iTunes store returns, only the fields that are interesting to this app.

SearchResult stores two artwork URLs, one for a 60×60 pixel image and the other for a 100×100 pixel image. It also stores the kind and genre of the item, its price and the currency (US dollar, Euro, British Pounds, etc.), as well as a link to the product's page on the iTunes store itself.

All right, now that you have some place to put this data, let's get it out of the dictionaries and into the SearchResult objects.

➤ Back in **SearchViewController.swift**, make the following changes to the parseDictionary() method:

```
func parseDictionary(dictionary: [String: AnyObject]) -> [SearchResult] {
  var searchResults = [SearchResult]()

  if let array: AnyObject = dictionary["results"] {
    . . .
  }
  return searchResults
}
```

You're making the method return an array of SearchResult objects. (If something went wrong during parsing, it simply returns an empty array.)

➤ Change the inside of the if let resultDict block in parseDictionary() to the following (replace the existing code inside that if-statement):

```
var searchResult: SearchResult?

if let wrapperType = resultDict["wrapperType"] as? String {
  switch wrapperType {
    case "track":
      searchResult = parseTrack(resultDict)
    default:
```

```
      break
  }
}

if let result = searchResult {
  searchResults.append(result)
}
```

If the found item is a "track" then you create a SearchResult object for it, using a new method parseTrack(), and add it to the searchResults array.

For any other types of products, the temporary variable searchResult remains nil and doesn't get added to the array (that's why it's an optional).

You'll be adding more wrapper types to the switch soon but for now you're limiting it to just the "track" type, which is used for songs, movies, and TV episodes.

> Also add the parseTrack() method:

```
func parseTrack(dictionary: [String: AnyObject]) -> SearchResult {
  let searchResult = SearchResult()

  searchResult.name = dictionary["trackName"] as! String
  searchResult.artistName = dictionary["artistName"] as! String
  searchResult.artworkURL60 = dictionary["artworkUrl60"] as! String
  searchResult.artworkURL100 = dictionary["artworkUrl100"] as! String
  searchResult.storeURL = dictionary["trackViewUrl"] as! String
  searchResult.kind = dictionary["kind"] as! String
  searchResult.currency = dictionary["currency"] as! String

  if let price = dictionary["trackPrice"] as? Double {
    searchResult.price = price
  }
  if let genre = dictionary["primaryGenreName"] as? String {
    searchResult.genre = genre
  }
  return searchResult
}
```

It's a big chunk of code but what happens here is quite simple. You first instantiate a new SearchResult object, then get the values out of the dictionary and put them into the SearchResult's properties.

All of these things are strings, except the track price, which is a number. Because the dictionary is defined as having AnyObject values, you first need to cast to String and Double here.

> **Note:** Something else interesting is going on here; did you spot it? You've learned that indexing a dictionary always gives you an optional. If that is true, then why don't you need to use if let with lines such as these:
>
> ```
> searchResult.name = dictionary["trackName"] as! String
> ```
>
> After all, dictionary["trackName"] is an optional but searchResult.name is definitely not... How come you can assign an optional value to a non-optional?
>
> The trick is in the cast. When you write "as! <something>", you're telling the compiler that you're sure this isn't an optional. (Of course if it turns out you're wrong, the app will crash.)

If you wanted to keep the optional status, you'd have to write "as! String?" or "as? String".
The former means you're casting to an optional String; the latter means you're trying to cast to
a regular String but it might fail and be nil because it's not really a string. It's a subtle
difference.

With these latest changes, parseDictionary() returns an array of SearchResult objects, but you're
not doing anything with that array yet.

➤ In searchBarSearchButtonClicked(), change the line that calls parseDictionary() to the
following:

```
searchResults = parseDictionary(dictionary)
```

Now the returned array is placed into the instance variable and the table view can show the actual
search result objects.

➤ Run the app and search for your favorite musician. After a second or so you should see a whole
bunch of results appear in the table. Cool!

You don't have to search for music, of course. You can also search for names of books, software,
or authors. For example, a search for Stephen King brings up results such as these:

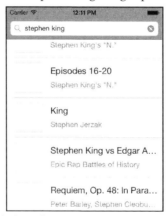

The results from the search now show up in the table

You might be wondering what "Requiem, Op. 48" and "Epic Rap Battles of History" have to do
with Stephen King (they're not new novels!).

The search results may include podcasts, songs, or other related products. It would be useful to
make the table view display what type of product it is showing, so let's improve
tableView(cellForRowAtIndexPath) a little.

➤ In cellForRowAtIndexPath, change the line that sets cell.artistNameLabel to the following:

```
if searchResult.artistName.isEmpty {
  cell.artistNameLabel.text = "Unknown"
} else {
  cell.artistNameLabel.text = String(format: "%@ (%@)", searchResult.artistName,
                                             searchResult.kind)
}
```

The first change is that you now check that the SearchResult's artistName is not empty. When testing the app I noticed that sometimes a search result did not include an artist name. In that case you make the cell say "Unknown".

You also add the value of the kind property to the artist name label, which should tell the user what kind of product they're looking at:

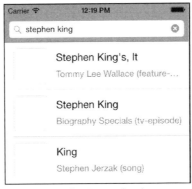

Yup, they're not books

There is one problem with this. The value of kind comes straight from the server and it is more of an internal name than something you'd want to show directly to the user.

What if you want it to say "TV Episode" or "TV Series" instead, or maybe you want to translate the app to another language (something you'll do later in this tutorial).

It's better to convert this internal identifier ("tv-episode") into the text that you want to show to the user ("TV Episode").

➤ Add this new method:

```
func kindForDisplay(kind: String) -> String {
  switch kind {
  case "album": return "Album"
  case "audiobook": return "Audio Book"
  case "book": return "Book"
  case "ebook": return "E-Book"
  case "feature-movie": return "Movie"
  case "music-video": return "Music Video"
  case "podcast": return "Podcast"
  case "software": return "App"
  case "song": return "Song"
  case "tv-episode": return "TV Episode"
  default: return kind
  }
}
```

These are the types of products that this app understands.

It's possible that I missed one or that the iTunes Store adds a new product type at some point. If that happens, the switch jumps to the default: case and you'll simply return the original kind value (and hopefully fix this in an update of the app).

➤ In tableView(cellForRowAtIndexPath), change the line that sets the artist name label to:

```
cell.artistNameLabel.text = String(format: "%@ (%@)", searchResult.artistName,
                                    kindForDisplay(searchResult.kind))
```

Now the text inside the parentheses is no longer the internal identifier from the iTunes web service, but the one you gave it:

The product type is a bit more human-friendly

All right, let's put in the other types of products. This is very similar to what you just did.

➤ Add the following methods below `parseTrack()`:

```
func parseAudioBook(dictionary: [String: AnyObject]) -> SearchResult {
  let searchResult = SearchResult()
  searchResult.name = dictionary["collectionName"] as! String
  searchResult.artistName = dictionary["artistName"] as! String
  searchResult.artworkURL60 = dictionary["artworkUrl60"] as! String
  searchResult.artworkURL100 = dictionary["artworkUrl100"] as! String
  searchResult.storeURL = dictionary["collectionViewUrl"] as! String
  searchResult.kind = "audiobook"
  searchResult.currency = dictionary["currency"] as! String

  if let price = dictionary["collectionPrice"] as? Double {
    searchResult.price = price
  }
  if let genre = dictionary["primaryGenreName"] as? String {
    searchResult.genre = genre
  }
  return searchResult
}
```

```
func parseSoftware(dictionary: [String: AnyObject]) -> SearchResult {
  let searchResult = SearchResult()
  searchResult.name = dictionary["trackName"] as! String
  searchResult.artistName = dictionary["artistName"] as! String
  searchResult.artworkURL60 = dictionary["artworkUrl60"] as! String
  searchResult.artworkURL100 = dictionary["artworkUrl100"] as! String
  searchResult.storeURL = dictionary["trackViewUrl"] as! String
  searchResult.kind = dictionary["kind"] as! String
  searchResult.currency = dictionary["currency"] as! String

  if let price = dictionary["price"] as? Double {
    searchResult.price = price
  }
  if let genre = dictionary["primaryGenreName"] as? String {
    searchResult.genre = genre
  }
  return searchResult
}
```

```
func parseEBook(dictionary: [String: AnyObject]) -> SearchResult {
  let searchResult = SearchResult()
  searchResult.name = dictionary["trackName"] as! String
  searchResult.artistName = dictionary["artistName"] as! String
  searchResult.artworkURL60 = dictionary["artworkUrl60"] as! String
  searchResult.artworkURL100 = dictionary["artworkUrl100"] as! String
  searchResult.storeURL = dictionary["trackViewUrl"] as! String
  searchResult.kind = dictionary["kind"] as! String
  searchResult.currency = dictionary["currency"] as! String

  if let price = dictionary["price"] as? Double {
    searchResult.price = price
  }
  if let genres: AnyObject = dictionary["genres"] {
    searchResult.genre = ", ".join(genres as! [String])
  }
  return searchResult
}
```

Two interesting points here:

- Audio books don't have a "kind" field, so you have to set the kind property to "audiobook" yourself.

- E-books don't have a "primaryGenreName" field, but an array of genres. You use the join() method to glue these genre names into a single string, separated by commas. (Yep, you're calling join() on a string literal, cool huh!)

You still need to call these new methods, based on the value of the wrapperType field.

➤ Change the if let wrapperType statement in parseDictionary() to:

```
if let wrapperType = resultDict["wrapperType"] as? String {
  switch wrapperType {
  case "track":
    searchResult = parseTrack(resultDict)
  case "audiobook":
    searchResult = parseAudioBook(resultDict)
  case "software":
    searchResult = parseSoftware(resultDict)
  default:
    break
  }
} else if let kind = resultDict["kind"] as? String {
  if kind == "ebook" {
    searchResult = parseEBook(resultDict)
  }
}
```

For some reason, e-books do not have a wrapperType field, so in order to determine whether something is an e-book you have to look at the kind field instead.

Depending on the value of wrapperType or kind, you call one of the parse methods to get a SearchResult object.

If there is a wrapperType or kind that the app does not support, no SearchResult object gets created, the value of searchResult is nil, and you simply skip that item.

Default and break

Switch statements often have a `default:` case at the end that just says `break`.

In Swift, a `switch` must be exhaustive, meaning that it must have a case for all possible values of the thing that you're looking at.

Here you're looking at `wrapperType`. Swift needs to know what to do when `wrapperType` is not "track", "audiobook", or "software". That's why you're required to include the `default:` case, as a catch-all for any other possible values of `wrapperType`.

Because a case cannot be empty in Swift, you add a `break` statement to keep the compiler happy. The `break` doesn't do anything – it just says "Nothing to see here, move along."

By the way: unlike in other languages, the `case` statements in Swift do not need to say `break` at the end (they do not automatically fall through from one case to the other as they do in Objective-C).

➤ Run the app and search for software, audio books or e-books to see that the parsing code works. It can take a few tries before you find some because of the enormous quantity of products on the store.

Later in this tutorial you'll add a control that lets you pick the type of products that you want to search for, which makes it a bit easier to find just e-books or audiobooks.

The app shows a varied range of products now

Sorting the search results

It would be nice to sort the search results alphabetically. That's quite easy, actually. `Array` already has a method to sort itself – all you have to do is tell it what to sort on.

➤ In `searchBarSearchButtonClicked()`, between the lines that call `parseDictionary()` and reload the table view, add the following:

```
searchResults.sort({ result1, result2 in
  return result1.name.localizedStandardCompare(result2.name) ==
                                      NSComparisonResult.OrderedAscending
})
```

Before reloading the table, you first call `sort()` on the `searchResults` array with a closure that determines the sorting rules (the code in between the { } brackets). This is identical to what you did in the Checklists tutorial to sort the to-do lists.

In order to sort the contents of the `searchResults` array, the closure will compare the `SearchResult` objects with each other and return `true` if `result1` comes before `result2`. The closure is called repeatedly on different pairs of `SearchResult` objects until the array is completely sorted.

The actual sorting rule calls `localizedStandardCompare()` to compare the names of the `SearchResult` objects. Because you used `.OrderedAscending`, the closure returns `true` only if `result1.name` comes before `result2.name` – in other words, the array gets sorted from A to Z.

➤ Run the app and verify that the search results are sorted alphabetically.

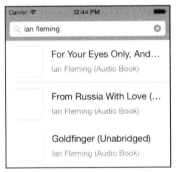

The search results are sorted by name

Sorting was pretty easy to add but there is an even easier way to write this. Change the sorting code to:

```
searchResults.sort { $0.name.localizedStandardCompare($1.name) ==
                                  NSComparisonResult.OrderedAscending }
```

This uses the *trailing* closure syntax to put the closure behind the method name, rather than inside the traditional ( ) parentheses as a parameter. It's a small improvement in readability.

More importantly, inside the closure you're no longer referring to the two `SearchResult` objects by name but with the special syntax `$0` and `$1`. Using these shorthand symbols instead of full parameter names is common in Swift closures. There is also no longer a `return` statement.

➤ Verify that this works.

Believe it or not, you can do even better. Swift has a very cool feature called **operator overloading**. It allows you to take the standard operators such as + and * and apply them to your own objects. You can even create completely new operator symbols.

It's not a good idea to go overboard with this feature and make operators do something completely unexpected – don't overload / to do multiplications, eh? – but it comes in very handy when doing sorting.

➤ Open **SearchResult.swift** and add the following code, outside of the class:

```
import Foundation

func < (lhs: SearchResult, rhs: SearchResult) -> Bool {
  return lhs.name.localizedStandardCompare(rhs.name) == NSComparisonResult.OrderedAscending
}
```

This should look familiar! You're creating a function named < that contains the same code as the closure from earlier.

This time the two SearchResult objects are called lhs and rhs, for left-hand side and right-hand side, respectively. (The import for Foundation is necessary or Swift won't know what an NSComparisonResult is.)

You have now overloaded the less-than operator so that it takes two SearchResult objects and returns true if the first one should come before the second, and false otherwise. Like so:

```
searchResultA.name = "Waltz for Debby"
searchResultB.name = "Autumn Leaves"

searchResultA < searchResultB  // false
searchResultB < searchResultA  // true
```

➤ Back in **SearchViewController.swift**, change the sorting code to:

```
searchResults.sort { $0 < $1 }
```

That's pretty sweet. Using the < operator makes it very clear that you're sorting the items from the array in ascending order. But wait, you can write it even shorter:

```
searchResults.sort(<)
```

Wow, it doesn't get much simpler than that! This line literally says, "Sort this array in ascending order".

Of course, this only works because you added your own func < to overload the less-than operator so it takes two SearchResult objects and compares them.

➤ Run the app again and make sure everything is still sorted.

Exercise. See if you can make the app sort by the artist name instead. ∎

Exercise. Try to sort in descending order, from Z to A. Tip: use the > operator. ∎

Excellent! You made the app talk to a web service and you were able to convert the data that was received into your own data model objects.

The app may not support every product that's shown on the iTunes store, but I hope I illustrated the principle of how you can take data that comes in slightly different forms and convert it to objects that are more convenient to use in your own apps.

Feel free to dig through the web service API documentation to add the remaining items that the iTunes store sells: http://www.apple.com/itunes/affiliates/resources/documentation/itunes-store-web-service-search-api.html

➤ Commit your changes.

You can find the project files for this section under **03 - Using Web Service** in the tutorial's Source Code folder.

> **SDKs for APIs**
>
> Often third-party services already have their own SDK (Software Development Kit) that lets you talk to their web service. In that case you don't have to write your own networking and JSON parsing code but you simply add a framework to your app and use the classes from that framework.
>
> For example:
>
> • Facebook https://developers.facebook.com/docs/ios/sample-apps
>
> • Wordnik http://developer.wordnik.com
>
> • Amazon Web Services http://aws.amazon.com/mobile/sdk/
>
> and many others.
>
> If you're really lucky, support for the web service is already built into iOS itself, such as the Social Framework that makes it very easy to put Twitter and Facebook into your apps.

Asynchronous networking

That wasn't so bad, was it? Yes it was, and I'll show you why! Did you notice that whenever you performed a search, the app became unresponsive?

While the network request was taking place, you could not scroll the table view up or down, or type anything new into the search bar. The app was completely frozen for a few seconds.

You may not have seen this if your network connection was very fast but if you're using your iPhone out in the wild the network will be a lot slower than your home or office Wi-Fi, and a search can easily take ten seconds or more.

So what if the app is unresponsive while the search is taking place? After all, there is nothing for the user to do at that point anyway...

However, to most users an app that does not respond is an app that has crashed. The screen looks empty, there is no indication of what is going on, and even an innocuous gesture such as sliding your finger up and down does not bounce the table view like you'd expect it to.

Conclusion: the app has crashed.

The user will press the Home button and try again – or more likely, delete your app, give it a bad rating on the App Store, and switch to a competing app.

Still not convinced? Let's slow down the network connection to pretend the app is running on an iPhone that someone may be using on a bus or in a train, not in the ideal conditions of a fast home or office network.

First off, you'll increase the amount of data that the app will get back. By adding a "limit" parameter to the URL you set the maximum number of results that the web service will return. The default value is 50, the maximum is 200.

➤ In urlWithSearchText(), change the following line:

```
let urlString = String(format: "http://itunes.apple.com/search?term=%@&limit=200",
                        escapedSearchText)
```

You added &limit=200 to the URL. Just so you know, parameters in URLs are separated by the & sign, also known as the "and" sign.

➤ If you run the app now, the search should be quite a bit slower.

Still too fast? Then download and install the **Network Link Conditioner**. This adds a new pane to your System Preferences window that lets you simulate different network conditions, including bad cell phone networks.

➤ From Xcode's menu choose **Open Developer Tool → More Developer Tools…** This opens the Apple developer website. From the Downloads for Apple Developers page, download the latest **Hardware IO Tools for Xcode** package.

Open the downloaded file and double-click **Network Link Conditioner.prefPane** to install it.

➤ Open the **System Preferences** on your Mac and locate **Network Link Conditioner** (it should be at the bottom).

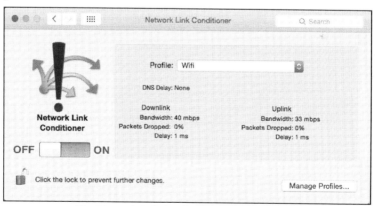

The Network Link Conditioner preference pane

➤ Click on **Manage Profiles** and create a new profile with the following settings:

• Name: Very slow connection

• Downlink Bandwidth: 48 Kbps

• Downlink Packets Dropped: 0 %

• Downlink Delay: 5000 ms (i.e. 5 seconds)

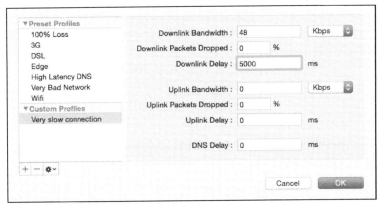

Adding the profile for a very slow connection

Press **OK** to add this profile and return to the main page. Make sure this new profile is selected and flick the switch to ON to start.

➤ Now run the app and search for something. The Network Link Conditioner tool will delay the HTTP request by 5 seconds in order to simulate a slow connection, and then downloads the data at a very slow speed.

> **Tip:** If the download still appears very fast, then try searching for some term you haven't used before; the system may be caching the results from a previous search.

Notice how the app totally doesn't respond during this time? It feels like something is wrong. Did the app crash or is it still doing something? It's impossible to tell and very confusing to your users when this happens.

Even worse, if your program is unresponsive for too long, iOS may actually kill it by force, in which case it really did crash. You don't want that to happen!

"Ah," you say, "let's show some type of animation to let the user know that the app is communicating with a server. Then at least they will know that the app is busy."

That sounds like a decent thing to do, so let's get to it.

> **Tip:** Even better than pretending to have a lousy connection on the Simulator is to use Network Link Conditioner on your device, so you can also test bad network connections on your actual iPhone.
>
> You can find it under **Settings → Developer → Network Link Conditioner:**

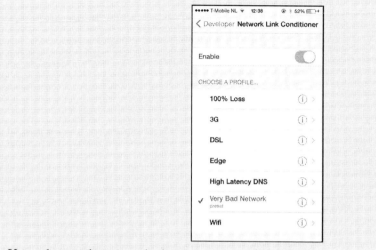

Using these tools to test whether your app can deal with real-world network conditions is a must! Not every user has the luxury of broadband...

The activity indicator

You've used the spinning activity indicator before in MyLocations to show the user that the app was busy. Let's create a new table view cell to show while the app is querying the iTunes store. It will look like this:

The app shows that it is busy

➤ Create a new, empty nib file. Call it **LoadingCell.xib**.

➤ Drag a new **Table View Cell** into the canvas. Set its height to 80 points.

➤ Set the reuse identifier of the cell to **LoadingCell** and set the **Selection** attribute to **None**.

➤ Drag a new **Label** into the cell. Rename it to **Loading...** and change the font to **System 15.0**. The label's text color should be 50% opaque black.

➤ Drag a new **Activity Indicator View** into the cell and put it next to the label. Change its **Style** to **Gray** and give it the **Tag** 100.

The design looks like this:

The design of the LoadingCell nib

To make this cell work properly on the larger iPhone 6 models you'll add constraints that keep the label and the activity spinner centered in the cell. The easiest way to do this is to place these two items inside a container view and center that.

➤ Select both the Label and the Activity Indicator View (hold down ⌘ to make a multiple selection). From the Xcode menu bar, choose **Editor** → **Embed In** → **View**. This puts a larger, white, view behind them.

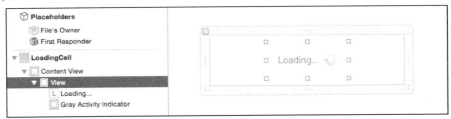

The label and the spinner now sit in a container view

➤ With this container view selected, choose **Editor** → **Align** → **Horizontal Center in Container**, followed by **Vertical Center in Container**. (This does the same thing as the Align popup that you're already familiar with.)

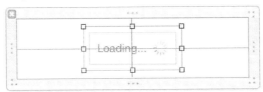

The container view has orange constraints

You end up with a number of orange constraints. That's no good; we want to see blue ones. The reason your new constraints are empty is that Auto Layout does not know yet how large this container view should be; you've only added constraints for the view's position, not its size.

To fix this, you're going to add constraints to the label and activity indicator as well, so that the width and height of the container view are determined by the size of the two things inside it.

That is especially important for later when you're going to translate the app to another language. If the Loading… text becomes larger or smaller, then so should the container view, in order to stay centered inside the cell.

➤ Select the label and open the **Pin** menu. Simply pin it to all four sides. Leave Update Frames set to **None** for now:

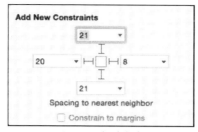

Pinning the label

(Don't worry about the numbers. If they are different for you, then just leave them as they are.)

➤ Repeat this for the Activity Indicator View. You don't need to pin it to the left because that constraint already exists (pinning the label added it).

Now the T-bars for the label and the activity indicator should be all blue.

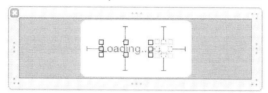

The label and spinner have blue constraints

However, the container view may still have orange lines. If so, select it and choose **Editor** → **Resolve Auto Layout Issues** → **Update Frames** (under Selected Views). This will move the container view into the position dictated by its constraints.

Cool, you now have a cell that automatically adjusts itself to any size device.

To make this special table view cell appear you'll follow the same steps as for the "Nothing Found" cell.

➤ Add the following line to the struct TableViewCellIdentifiers in **SearchViewController.swift**:

```
static let loadingCell = "LoadingCell"
```

➤ And register the nib in viewDidLoad():

```
cellNib = UINib(nibName: TableViewCellIdentifiers.loadingCell, bundle: nil)
tableView.registerNib(cellNib, forCellReuseIdentifier: TableViewCellIdentifiers.loadingCell)
```

Now you have to come up with some way to let the table view's data source know that the app is currently in a state of downloading data from the server.

The simplest way to do that is to keep a boolean flag. If this variable is true, then the app is downloading stuff and the new Loading... cell should be shown; if the variable is false, you show the regular contents of the table view.

➤ Add a new instance variable:

```
var isLoading = false
```

➤ Change tableView(numberOfRowsInSection) to:

```swift
func tableView(tableView: UITableView, numberOfRowsInSection section: Int) -> Int {
  if isLoading {
    return 1
  } else if !hasSearched {
    return 0
  } else if searchResults.count == 0 {
    return 1
  } else {
    return searchResults.count
  }
}
```

You've added the if isLoading statement to return 1, because you need a row in order to show a cell.

> Add the following to the top of tableView(cellForRowAtIndexPath):

```swift
func tableView(tableView: UITableView,
              cellForRowAtIndexPath indexPath: NSIndexPath) -> UITableViewCell {

  if isLoading {
    let cell = tableView.dequeueReusableCellWithIdentifier(
          TableViewCellIdentifiers.loadingCell, forIndexPath:indexPath) as! UITableViewCell

    let spinner = cell.viewWithTag(100) as! UIActivityIndicatorView
    spinner.startAnimating()

    return cell
  }
  else if searchResults.count == 0 {
    . . .
```

You added an if-statement to return an instance of the new Loading... cell. It also looks up the UIActivityIndicatorView by its tag and then tells the spinner to start animating. The rest of the method stays the same.

> Change tableView(willSelectRowAtIndexPath) to:

```swift
func tableView(tableView: UITableView,
              willSelectRowAtIndexPath indexPath: NSIndexPath) -> NSIndexPath? {
  if searchResults.count == 0 || isLoading {
    return nil
  } else {
    return indexPath
  }
}
```

Just like you don't want the users to select the "Nothing Found" cell, you also don't want them to select the "Loading..." cell, so you return nil in both cases.

That leaves only one thing to do: you should set isLoading to true before you make the HTTP request to the iTunes server, and also reload the table view to make the Loading... cell appear.

> Change searchBarSearchButtonClicked() to:

```swift
func searchBarSearchButtonClicked(searchBar: UISearchBar) {
  if !searchBar.text.isEmpty {
    searchBar.resignFirstResponder()

    isLoading = true
    tableView.reloadData()
```

```
. . . here is the networking code . . .

    isLoading = false
    tableView.reloadData()
    return
    . . .
}
```

Before you do the networking request, you set `isLoading` to `true` and reload the table to show the activity indicator.

After the request completes and you have the search results, you set `isLoading` back to `false` and reload the table again to show the `SearchResult` objects.

Makes sense, right? Let's fire up the app and see this in action.

➤ Run the app and perform a search. While search is taking place the Loading... cell with the spinning activity indicator should appear...

...or should it?!

The sad truth is that there is no spinner to be seen. And in the unlikely event that it does show up for you, it won't be spinning. (Try it with Network Link Conditioner enabled.)

➤ To show you why, first change `searchBarSearchButtonClicked()` to the following.

You don't have to remove anything from the code, simply comment out everything after the first call to `tableView.reloadData()`.

```
func searchBarSearchButtonClicked(searchBar: UISearchBar) {
  if !searchBar.text.isEmpty {
    searchBar.resignFirstResponder()

    isLoading = true
    tableView.reloadData()

    /*
       . . . the networking code (commented out) . . .
    */
  }
}
```

➤ Run the app and do a search. Now the activity spinner does show up!

So at least you know that part of the code is working fine. But with the networking code enabled the app isn't only totally unresponsive to any input from the user, it also doesn't want to redraw its screen. What's going on here?

The main thread

The CPU (Central Processing Unit) in older iPhone and iPad models has one core, which means it can only do one thing at the time. More recent models have a CPU with two cores, which allows for a whopping two computations to happen simultaneously. Your Mac may have 4 cores.

With so few cores available, how come modern computers can have many more applications and other processes running at the same time? (I count 287 active processes on my Mac right now.)

To get around the hardware limitation of having only one or two CPU cores, most computers including the iPhone and iPad use **preemptive multitasking** and **multithreading** to give the illusion that they can do many things at once.

Multitasking is something that happens between different apps. Each app is said to have its own **process** and each process is given a small portion of each second of CPU time to perform its jobs. Then it is *pre-empted* and control is given to the next process.

Apple only introduced multitasking between apps with iOS 4 but in truth all iPhones since version 1.0 have been running true multitasked processes – you simply weren't able to take advantage of that as a user until iOS 4.

Each process contains one or more **threads**. I just mentioned that each process in turn is given a bit of CPU time to do its work. The process splits up that time among its threads. Each thread typically performs its own work and is as independent as possible from the other threads within that process.

An app can have multiple threads and the CPU switches between them:

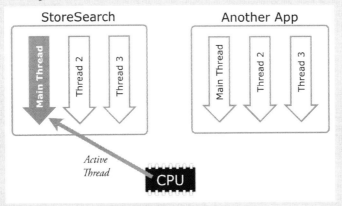

If you go into the Xcode debugger and pause the app, the debugger will show you which threads are currently active and what they were doing before you stopped them.

For the StoreSearch app, there were apparently four threads at that time:

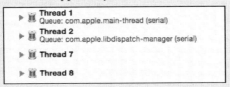

Most of these threads are managed by iOS itself and you don't have to worry about them (you may see more than four). However, there is one thread that requires special care: the **main thread**. In the image above, that is Thread 1.

The main thread is the app's initial thread and from there all the other threads are spawned. The main thread is responsible for handling user interface events and also for drawing the UI. Most of your app's activities take place on the main thread. Whenever the user taps a button in your app, it is the main thread that performs your action method.

Because it's so important, you should be careful not to "block" the main thread. If your action method takes more than a fraction of a second to run, then doing all these computations on the main thread is not a good idea for the reasons you saw earlier.

The app becomes unresponsive because the main thread cannot handle any UI events while you're keeping it busy doing something else – and if the operation takes too long the app may even be killed by the system.

In StoreSearch, you're doing a lengthy network operation on the main thread. It could potentially take many seconds, maybe even minutes, to complete.

After you set the isLoading flag to true, you tell the tableView to reload its data so that the user can see the spinning animation. But that never comes to pass. Telling the table view to reload schedules a "redraw" event, but the main thread gets no chance to handle that event as you immediately start the networking operation, keeping the thread busy all the time.

This is why I said the current synchronous approach to doing networking was bad: **Never block the main thread.** It's one of the seven deadly sins of iOS programming!

Making it asynchronous

To prevent locking up the main thread, any operation that might take a while to complete should be **asynchronous**. That means the operation happens off in the background somewhere and in the mean time the main thread is free to process new events.

That is not to say you should create your own thread. If you've programmed on other platforms before you may not think twice about creating new threads, but on iOS that is often not the best solution.

You see, threads are tricky. Not threads per se, but doing things in parallel. Our human minds are very bad at handling the complexity that comes from doing more than one thing at a time – at least when it comes to computations.

I won't go into too much detail here, but generally you want to avoid the situation where two threads are modifying the same piece of data at the same time. That can lead to very surprising (but not very pleasant!) results.

Rather than making your own threads, iOS has several more convenient ways to start background processes. For this app you'll be using **queues** and **Grand Central Dispatch** (or GCD). GCD greatly simplifies tasks that require parallel programming. You've already briefly played with GCD in the MyLocations tutorial, but now you'll put it to real use.

In short, GCD has a number of queues with different priorities. To perform a job in the background, you put it in a closure and then give that closure to a queue and forget about it. It's as simple as that.

GCD will pull the closures – or "blocks" as it calls them – from the queues one-by-one and perform their code in the background. Exactly how it does that is not important, you're only guaranteed it happens on a background thread somewhere. Queues are not exactly the same as threads, but they use threads to do their dirty work.

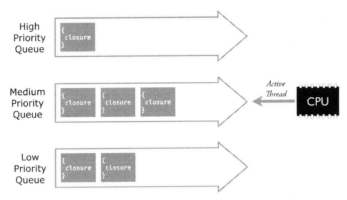

Queues have a list of closure to perform on a background thread

To make the web service requests asynchronous, you're going to put the networking part from `searchBarSearchButtonClicked()` into a closure and then place that closure on a medium priority queue.

➤ Change `searchBarSearchButtonClicked()` to the following:

```
func searchBarSearchButtonClicked(searchBar: UISearchBar) {
  if !searchBar.text.isEmpty {
    searchBar.resignFirstResponder()

    isLoading = true
    tableView.reloadData()

    hasSearched = true
    searchResults = [SearchResult]()

    // 1
    let queue = dispatch_get_global_queue(DISPATCH_QUEUE_PRIORITY_DEFAULT, 0)
    // 2
    dispatch_async(queue) {
      let url = self.urlWithSearchText(searchBar.text)

      if let jsonString = self.performStoreRequestWithURL(url) {
        if let dictionary = self.parseJSON(jsonString) {

          self.searchResults = self.parseDictionary(dictionary)
          self.searchResults.sort(<)

          // 3
          println("DONE!")
          return
        }
      }
      println("Error!")
    }
  }
}
```

Here is the new stuff:

1. This gets a reference to the queue. GCD uses regular functions, not classes and methods, because it is not limited to Swift and can also be used from Objective-C, C++, and even C programs. Most iOS frameworks are object-oriented but GCD isn't. (We won't hold that against it.)

2. Once you have the queue, you can dispatch a closure on it:

```
dispatch_async(queue) {
  // this is the closure
}
```

The closure, as usual, is everything between the { and } symbols. Whatever code is in the closure will be put on the queue and executed asynchronously in the background. After scheduling this closure, the main thread is free to continue. It is no longer blocked.

3. Inside the closure I have removed the code that reloads the table view after the search is done, as well as the error handling code. For now this has been replaced by println() statements. There is a good reason for this that we'll get to in a second. First let's try the app again.

➤ Run the app and do a search. The "Loading..." cell should be visible – complete with animating spinner! After a short while you should see the "DONE!" message appear in the debug pane.

Of course, the Loading... cell sticks around forever because you haven't told it yet to go away.

The reason I removed all the user interface code from the block is that UIKit has a rule that all UI code should always be performed on the main thread. This is important!

Accessing the same data from multiple threads can create all sorts of misery, so the designers of UIKit decided that changing the UI from other threads would not be allowed. That means you cannot reload the table view from within this closure because it runs on a queue that is backed by a thread other than the main thread.

As it happens, there is also a so-called "main queue" that is associated with the main thread. If you need to do anything on the main thread from a background queue, you can simply create a new closure and schedule that on the main queue.

➤ Replace the line that says println("DONE!") with:

```
dispatch_async(dispatch_get_main_queue()) {
  self.isLoading = false
  self.tableView.reloadData()
}
```

The dispatch_get_main_queue() function returns a reference to the main queue and dispatch_async() schedules a new closure on that queue.

This new closure sets isLoading back to false and reloads the table view. Note that self is required because this code sits inside a closure.

➤ Replace the line that says println("Error!") with:

```
dispatch_async(dispatch_get_main_queue()) {
  self.showNetworkError()
}
```

You also schedule the call to showNetworkError() on the main queue. That method shows a UIAlertController, which is UI code and therefore needs to happen on the main thread.

➤ Try it out. With those changes in place, your networking code no longer occupies the main thread and the app suddenly feels a lot more responsive!

➤ I think with this important improvement the app deserves a new version number, so commit the changes and create a tag for **v0.2**.

You can find the project files for this section under **04 - Async Networking** in the tutorial's Source Code folder.

> **Note:** When working with GCD you will often see this pattern:
>
> ```
> let queue = dispatch_get_global_queue(. . .)
> dispatch_async(queue) {
>   // code that needs to run in the background
>   dispatch_async(dispatch_get_main_queue()) {
>     // update the user interface
>   }
> }
> ```
>
> There is also dispatch_sync(), without the "a", which takes the next closure from the queue and performs it in the background, but makes you wait until that closure is done. That can be useful in some cases but most of the time you'll want to use dispatch_async(). No one likes to wait!

NSURLSession

So far you've used the String(contentsOfURL, encoding, error) method to perform the search on the iTunes web service. That is great for simple apps, but I want to show you another way to do networking that is more powerful.

iOS itself comes with a number of different classes for doing networking, from low-level sockets stuff that is only interesting to really hardcore network programmers, to convenient classes such as NSURLConnection and NSURLSession.

In this section you'll replace the existing networking code with the NSURLSession API. That is the API the pros use for building real apps, but don't worry, it's not more difficult than what you've done before – just more powerful.

Branch it

Whenever you make a big change to the code, such as replacing all the networking stuff with NSURLSession, there is a possibility that you'll mess things up. I certainly do often enough! That's why it's smart to create a so-called Git **branch** first.

The Git repository contains a history of all the app's code, but it can also contain this history along different paths.

You just finished the first version of the networking code and it works pretty well. Now you're going to completely replace that with a – hopefully! – better solution. In doing so, you may want to commit your progress at several points along the way.

What if it turns out that switching to NSURLSession wasn't such a good idea after all? Then you'd have to restore the source code to a previous commit from before you started making those changes. In order to avoid this potential mess, you can make a branch instead.

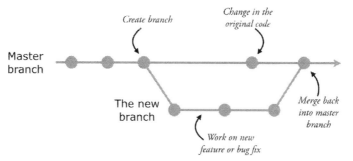

Branches in action

Every time you're about to add a new feature to your code or have a bug to fix, it's a good idea to make a new branch and work on that. When you're done and are satisfied that everything works as it should, merge your changes back into the master branch. Different people use different branching strategies but this is the general principle.

So far you have been committing your changes to the "master" branch. Now you're going to make a new branch, let's call it "NSURLSession", and commit your changes to that. When you're done with this new feature you will merge everything back into the master branch.

You can find the branches for your repository in the **Source Control** menu:

The Source Control branch menu

➤ Select **StoreSearch – master** (the name of the active branch), and choose **Configure StoreSearch...** to bring up the following panel:

There is currently only one branch in the repository

➤ Go to the **Branches** tab and click the + button at the bottom. In the screen that appears, type **NSURLSession** for the branch name and click **Create**.

Creating a new branch

When Xcode is done, you'll see that a new "NSURLSession" branch has been added and that it is made the current one.

This new branch contains the exact same source code and history as the master branch. But from here on out the two paths will diverge – any changes you make happen on the "NSURLSession" branch only.

Putting NSURLSession into action

Good, now that you're in a new branch it's safe to experiment with these new APIs.

➤ First, remove the `performStoreRequestWithURL()` method from **SearchViewController.swift**. Yup, that's right, you won't be needing it anymore.

Don't be afraid to remove old code. Some developers only comment out the old code but leave it in the project, just in case they may need it again some day.

You don't have to worry about that because you're using source control. Should you really need it, you can always find the old code in the Git history. Besides, if the experiment should fail, you can simply throw away this branch and switch back to the "official" one.

Anyway, on to `NSURLSession`. This is a closured-based API, meaning that instead of making a delegate for it, you give it a closure containing the code that should be performed once the response from the server has been received. `NSURLSession` calls this closure the "completion handler".

➤ Change `searchBarSearchButtonClicked()` to the following:

```swift
func searchBarSearchButtonClicked(searchBar: UISearchBar) {
  if !searchBar.text.isEmpty {
    searchBar.resignFirstResponder()

    isLoading = true
    tableView.reloadData()

    hasSearched = true
    searchResults = [SearchResult]()

    // 1
    let url = self.urlWithSearchText(searchBar.text)
    // 2
    let session = NSURLSession.sharedSession()
    // 3
    let dataTask = session.dataTaskWithURL(url, completionHandler: { data, response, error in
      // 4
      if let error = error {
        println("Failure! \(error)")
      } else {
        println("Success! \(response)")
      }
    })
```

```
    // 5
    dataTask.resume()
  }
}
```

This is what the changes do:

1. Create the NSURL object with the search text like before.

2. Obtain the NSURLSession object. This grabs the "shared" session, which always exists and uses a default configuration with respect to caching, cookies, and other web stuff.

   If you want to use a different configuration – for example, to restrict networking to when Wi-Fi is available but not when there is only cellular access – then you have to create your own NSURLSessionConfiguration and NSURLSession objects. But for this app the default one will be fine.

3. Create a data task. Data tasks are for sending HTTP GET requests to the server at url. The code from the completion handler will be invoked when the data task has received the reply from the server.

4. Inside the closure you're given three parameters: data, response, and error. These are all ! optionals so they can be nil, but you don't have to unwrap them.

   If there was a problem, error contains an NSError object describing what went wrong. This happens when the server cannot be reached or the network is down or some other hardware failure.

   If error is nil, the communication with the server succeeded; response holds the server's response code and headers, and data contains the actual thing that was sent back from the server, in this case a blob of JSON.

   For now you simply use an println() to show success or failure.

5. Finally, once you have created the data task, you need to call resume() to start it. This sends the request to the server. That all happens on a background thread, so the app is immediately free to continue (NSURLSession is as asynchronous as they come).

With those changes made, you can run the app and see what NSURLSession makes of it.

➤ Run the app and search for something. After a second or two you should see the debug output say "Success!" followed by a dump of the HTTP response headers.

Excellent!

A brief review of closures

You've seen closures a few times now. They are a really powerful feature of Swift and you can expect to be using them all the time when you're working with Swift code. So it's good to have at least a basic understanding of how they work.

A closure is simply a piece of source code that you can pass around just like any other type of object. The difference between a closure and regular source code is that the code from the closure does not get performed right away. It is stored in a "closure object" and can be performed at a later point, even more than once.

That's exactly what NSURLSession does: it keeps hold of the "completion handler" closure and only performs it when a response is received from the web server or when a network error occurs.

A closure typically looks like this:

```
let dataTask = session.dataTaskWithURL(url, completionHandler: {
    data, response, error in
    . . . source code . . .
})
```

The thing behind completionHandler inside the { } brackets is the closure. The form of a closure is always:

```
{ parameters in
  your source code
}
```

or without parameters:

```
{
  your source code
}
```

Just like a method or function, a closure can accept parameters. They are separated from the source code by the "in" keyword. In NSURLSession's completion handler the parameters are data, response, and error.

Thanks to Swift's type inference you don't need to specify the data types of the parameters. However, you could write them out in full if you wanted to:

```
let dataTask = session.dataTaskWithURL(url, completionHandler: {
    (data: NSData!, response: NSURLResponse!, error: NSError!) in
    . . .
})
```

Tip: For a parameter without a type annotation, you can Option-click to find out what its type is. This trick works for any symbol in your programs.

If you don't care about a particular parameter you can substitute it with _, the *wildcard* symbol:

```
let dataTask = session.dataTaskWithURL(url, completionHandler: {
    data, _, error in
    . . .
})
```

If a closure is really simple, you can leave out the parameter list and use $0, $1, and so on as the parameter names.

```
let dataTask = session.dataTaskWithURL(url, completionHandler: {
    println("My parameters are \($0), \($1), \($2)")
})
```

You wouldn't do that with NSURLSession's completion handler, though. It's much easier if you know the parameters are called data, response, and error than remembering what $0, $1, and $2 stand for.

If a closure is the last parameter of a method, you can use *trailing* syntax to simplify the code a little:

```
let dataTask = session.dataTaskWithURL(url) {
    data, response, error in
```

```
    . . .
  }
```

Now the closure sits behind the closing parenthesis, not inside. Many people, myself included, find this more natural to read.

Closures are useful for other things too, such as initializing objects and lazy loading:

```
lazy var dateFormatter: NSDateFormatter = {
  let formatter = NSDateFormatter()
  formatter.dateStyle = .MediumStyle
  formatter.timeStyle = .ShortStyle
  return formatter
}()
```

The code to create and initialize the NSDateFormatter object sits inside a closure. The () at the end causes the closure to be *evaluated* and the returned object is put inside the dataFormatter variable. This is a common trick for placing complex initialization code right next to the variable declaration.

It's no coincidence that closures look a lot like functions. In Swift closures, methods and functions are really all the same thing. For example, you can supply the name of a method or function when a closure is expected, as long as the parameters match:

```
let dataTask = session.dataTaskWithURL(url,
                          completionHandler: myCompletionHandlerMethod)
. . .

func myCompletionHandlerMethod(data: NSData!, response: NSURLResponse!,
                    error: NSError!) {
  . . .
}
```

That somewhat negates one of the prime benefits of closures – keeping all the code in the same place – but there are situations where this is quite useful (the method acts as a "mini" delegate.)

One final thing to be aware of with closures is that they *capture* any variables used inside the closure, including self. This can create ownership cycles, often leading to memory leaks. To avoid this, you can supply a *capture list*:

```
let dataTask = session.dataTaskWithURL(url) {
  [weak self] data, response, error in
  . . .
}
```

SearchViewController doesn't have to worry about NSURLSession capturing self because the data task is only short-lived, while the view controller sticks around for as long as the app itself. This ownership cycle is quite harmless. Later on in the tutorial you *will* have to use [weak self] with NSURLSession, though, or the app might crash and burn!

Note: Swift 1.2 introduces the concept of "no escape" closures. We won't go into that here, except to mention that no-escape closures don't capture self, so you don't have to write "self." everywhere. Nice!

After a successful request, the app prints the HTTP response from the server. The response object might look something like this:

```
Success! <NSHTTPURLResponse: 0x7f8b19e38d10> { URL:
http://itunes.apple.com/search?term=metallica&limit=200 } { status code: 200, headers {
    "Cache-Control" = "no-transform, max-age=41";
```

```
    Connection = "keep-alive";
    "Content-Encoding" = gzip;
    "Content-Length" = 34254;
    "Content-Type" = "text/javascript; charset=utf-8";
    Date = "Sat, 04 Oct 2014 07:53:20 GMT";
    . . .
} }
```

If you've done any web development before, this should look familiar. These "HTTP headers" are always the first part of the response from a web server that precedes the actual data you're receiving. The headers give additional information about the communication that just happened.

What you're especially interested in is the status code. The HTTP protocol has defined a number of status codes that tell clients whether the request was successful or not. No doubt you're familiar with 404, web page not found.

The status code you want to see is 200 OK, which indicates success. (Wikipedia has the complete list of codes, wikipedia.org/wiki/List_of_HTTP_status_codes.)

To make the error handling of the app a bit more robust, let's check to make sure the HTTP response code really was 200. If not, something has gone wrong and we can't assume that data contains the JSON we're after.

➤ Change the contents of the `completionHandler` to:

```
if let error = error {
  println("Failure! \(error)")
} else if let httpResponse = response as? NSHTTPURLResponse {
  if httpResponse.statusCode == 200 {
    println("Success! \(data)")
  } else {
    println("Failure! \(response)")
  }
}
```

The response parameter has the data type `NSURLResponse` but that doesn't have a property for the status code. Because you're using the HTTP protocol what you've really received is an `NSHTTPURLResponse` object, a subclass of `NSURLResponse`.

So first you cast it to the proper type and then look at its `statusCode` property. Only if it is 200 you'll consider the job a success.

➤ Run the app and search for something. You should now see something like:

```
Success! <0a0a0a7b 0a202272 6573756c 74436f75 6e74223a 3230302c 0a202272 6573756c 7473223a
205b0a7b 22777261 70706572 54797065 223a2274 7261636b 222c2022 6b696e64 223a2266 65617475
72652d6d 6f766965 222c2022 74726163 6b496422 3a353338 38303035 39382c20 22617274 6973744e
616d6522 3a224c69 . . .
```

This is the data object with the JSON search results. The JSON is really text but because data is in the form of an `NSData` object it prints out its contents as binary (hexadecimal to be precise). In a minute you'll turn this into real JSON objects.

It's always a good idea to actually test your error handling code, so let's first fake an error and get that out of the way.

➤ In `urlWithSearchText()`, change the string to:

```
"http://itunes.apple.com/searchLOL?term=%@&limit=200"
```

Here I've changed the endpoint from search to searchLOL. It doesn't really matter what you type there, as long as it's something that cannot possibly exist on the iTunes server.

➤ Run the app again. Now a search should respond with something like this:

```
Failure! <NSHTTPURLResponse: 0x7ff76b42d4b0> { URL:
http://itunes.apple.com/searchLOL?term=metallica&limit=200 } { status code: 404, headers {
    Connection = "keep-alive";
    "Content-Length" = 207;
    "Content-Type" = "text/html; charset=iso-8859-1";
    . . .
} }
```

As you can see, the status code is now 404 – there is no searchLOL page – and the app correctly considers this a failure. That's a good thing too, because data now contains the following:

```
<!DOCTYPE HTML PUBLIC "-//IETF//DTD HTML 2.0//EN">
<html><head>
<title>404 Not Found</title>
</head><body>
<h1>Not Found</h1>
<p>The requested URL /searchLOL was not found on this server.</p>
</body></html>
```

That is definitely not JSON. If you tried to convert that into JSON objects, you'd fail horribly.

Great, so the error handling works. Let's add JSON parsing to the code.

➤ First, put urlWithSearchText() back to the way it was (⌘+Z to undo).

➤ Then change parseJSON() to the following:

```
func parseJSON(data: NSData) -> [String: AnyObject]? {
  var error: NSError?
  if let json = NSJSONSerialization.JSONObjectWithData(data,
                  options: NSJSONReadingOptions(0), error: &error) as? [String: AnyObject] {
    return json
  } else if let error = error {
    println("JSON Error: \(error)")
  } else {
    println("Unknown JSON Error")
  }
  return nil
}
```

Previously this method took a String parameter and converted it into an NSData object that it passed to NSJSONSerialization.JSONObjectWithData(…). Now you already have the JSON text in an NSData object, so you no longer have to do that conversion and the method has become a bit simpler (you just removed the first if-statement).

The app is not doing anything yet with the search results, but you already wrote all the code you need for that, so let's put it in the closure.

➤ In the completionHandler, replace the println("Success! \(data)") line with:

```
if let dictionary = self.parseJSON(data) {
  self.searchResults = self.parseDictionary(dictionary)
  self.searchResults.sort(<)
```

```
dispatch_async(dispatch_get_main_queue()) {
  self.isLoading = false
  self.tableView.reloadData()
}
return
}
```

This gives the object from the `data` parameter to `parseJSON()` to convert it into a dictionary, and then calls `parseDictionary()` to turn the dictionary's contents into `SearchResult` objects, just like you did before. Finally, you sort the results and put everything into the table view. This should look very familiar.

It's important to realize that the completion handler closure won't be performed on the main thread. Because `NSURLSession` does all the networking asynchronously, it will also call the completion handler on a background thread.

Parsing the JSON and sorting the list of search results could potentially take a while (not seconds but possibly long enough to be noticeable). You don't want to block the main thread while that is happening, so it's preferable that this happens in the background too.

But when the time comes to update the UI, you need to switch back to the main thread. Them's the rules. That's why you wrap the reloading of the table view into `dispatch_async()` on the main queue.

(If you forget to do this, your app may still appear to work. That's the insidious thing about working with multiple threads. However, it may also crash in all kinds of mysterious ways. So remember, UI stuff should always happen on the main thread. Write it on a Post-It note and stick it to your screen!)

➤ Run the app. The search should work again. You have successfully replaced the old networking code with `NSURLSession`!

> **Tip:** To tell whether a particular piece of code is being run on the main thread, add the following code snippet:
>
>   `println("On the main thread? " + (NSThread.currentThread().isMainThread ? "Yes" : "No"))`
>
> Go ahead, paste this at the top of the `completionHandler` closure and see what it says.
>
> Of course, the official framework documentation should be your first stop. Usually when a method takes a closure the docs mention whether it is performed on the main thread or not. But if you're not sure, or just can't find it in the docs, add the above `println()` and be enlightened.

➤ At the very bottom of the completion handler closure, below the if-statements, add the following:

```
dispatch_async(dispatch_get_main_queue()) {
  self.hasSearched = false
  self.isLoading = false
  self.tableView.reloadData()
  self.showNetworkError()
}
```

The code gets here if something went wrong. You call `showNetworkError()` to let the user know about the problem.

Note that you do `tableView.reloadData()` here too, because the contents of the table view need to be refreshed to get rid of the Loading… indicator. And of course, all this happens on the main thread.

Exercise. Why doesn't the error alert show up on success? After all, the above piece of code sits at the bottom of the closure, so doesn't it always get executed? ∎

Answer: Upon success, the `return` statement exits the closure after the search results get displayed in the table view. So in that case execution never reaches the bottom of the closure.

➤ Fake an error situation to test that the error handling code really works.

Testing errors is not a luxury! The last thing you want is your app to crash when a networking error occurs because of faulty error handling code. I've worked on codebases where it was obvious the previous developer never bothered to verify that the app was able to recover from errors. (That's probably why they were the *previous* developers.)

Things *will* go wrong in the wild and your app better be prepared to deal with it. As the MythBusters say, "failure is always an option".

Does the error handling code work? Great! Time to add some new networking features to the app.

➤ This is a good time to commit your changes.

Canceling operations

What happens when a search takes very long and the user already starts a second search when the first one is still going? The app doesn't disable the search bar so it's possible for the user to pull this off. When dealing with networking – or any asynchronous process, really – you have to think these kinds of situations through.

There is no way to predict what happens, but it will most likely be a strange experience for the user. He might see the results from his first search, which he is no longer expecting (confusing!), only to be replaced by the results of the second search a few seconds later.

But there is no guarantee the first search completes before the second, so the results from search 2 may arrive first and then get overwritten by the results from search 1, which is definitely not what the user wanted to see either.

Because you're no longer blocking the main thread, the UI always accepts user input, and you cannot assume the user to sit still and wait until the request is done.

You can usually fix this dilemma in one of two ways:

1. Disable all controls. The user cannot tap anything while the operation is taking place. This does not mean you're blocking the main thread; you're just making sure the user cannot mess up the order of things.

2. Cancel the on-going request when the user starts a new one.

For this app you're going to pick the second solution because it makes for a nicer user experience. Every time the user performs a new search you cancel the previous request. NSURLSession makes this easy: data tasks have a cancel() method.

When you created the data task, you were given an NSURLSessionDataTask object, and you placed this into the local constant named dataTask. Cancelling the task, however, needs to happen the *next* time searchBarSearchButtonClicked() is called.

Storing the NSURLSessionDataTask object into a local variable isn't good enough anymore; you need to keep that reference beyond the scope of this method. In other words, you have to put it into an instance variable.

> Add the following instance variable to **SearchViewController.swift**:

```
var dataTask: NSURLSessionDataTask?
```

This is an optional because you won't have a data task yet until the user performs a search.

> Inside searchBarSearchButtonClicked(), change the line that creates the new data task object to:

```
dataTask = session.dataTaskWithURL(url, completionHandler: {
```

You've removed the let keyword because dataTask should no longer be a local; it now refers to the instance variable.

> At the bottom of the method, change the line that starts the task:

```
dataTask?.resume()
```

Because dataTask is an optional, you have to unwrap the optional somehow. Here you're using optional chaining.

> Finally, near the top of the method before you set isLoading to true, add:

```
dataTask?.cancel()
```

If there was an active data task this cancels it, making sure that no old searches can ever get in the way of the new search.

Thanks to the optional chaining, if no search was done yet and dataTask is still nil, this simply ignores the call to cancel(). You could also unwrap the optional with if let, but using the question mark is shorter and just as safe.

Exercise. Why can't you write dataTask!.cancel() to unwrap the optional? ∎

Answer: If an optional is nil, using ! will crash the app. You're only supposed to use ! to unwrap an optional when you're sure it won't be nil. But the very first time the user types something into the search bar, dataTask will still be nil, and using ! is not a good idea.

> Test the app with and without this call to dataTask.cancel() to experience the difference.

Use the Network Link Conditioner preferences pane to delay each query by a few seconds so it's easier to get two requests running at the same time.

Hmm... you may have noticed something odd. When the data task gets cancelled, you get the error popup and the Debug pane says:

```
Failure! Error Domain=NSURLErrorDomain Code=-999 "cancelled" UserInfo= . . .
{NSErrorFailingURLKey=http://itunes.apple.com/search?term=monkeys&limit=200,
NSLocalizedDescription=cancelled, NSErrorFailingURLStringKey= . . .}
```

As it turns out, when a data task gets cancelled its completion handler is still invoked but with an NSError object that has error code -999. That's what caused the error alert to pop up.

You'll have to make the error handler a little smarter to ignore code -999. After all, the user cancelling the previous search is no cause for panic.

➤ In the completionHandler, change the if let error section to:

```
if let error = error {
  println("Failure! \(error)")
  if error.code == -999 { return }

} else if let httpResponse = . . .
```

This new line simply ends the closure when there is an error with code -999. The rest of the closure gets skipped.

➤ If you're satisfied it works, commit the changes to the repository.

> **Note:** Maybe you don't think it's worth making a commit when you've only changed a few lines, but many small commits are often better than a few big ones. Each time you fix a bug or add a new feature is a good time to commit.

Searching different categories

The iTunes store has a vast collection of products and each search returns at most 200 items. It can be hard to find what you're looking for by name alone, so you'll add a control to the screen that lets you pick the category that you want to search in. It looks like this:

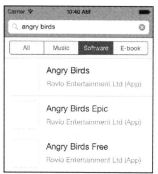

Searching in the Software category

This type of control is called a **segmented control** and is used to pick one option out of multiple choices.

➤ Open the storyboard. Drag a new **Navigation Bar** into the view and put it below the Search Bar. You're using the Navigation Bar purely for decorative purposes, as a container for the segmented control.

Make sure the Navigation Bar doesn't get added inside the Table View. It may be easiest to drag it from the Object Library directly into the outline pane and drop it below the Search Bar. Then change its Y-position to 64.

➤ With the Navigation Bar selected, open the **Pin menu** and pin its **top, left,** and **right** sides.

➤ Drag a new **Segmented Control** from the Object Library on top of the Navigation Bar's title (so it will replace the title).

The design now looks like this:

The Segmented Control sits in a Navigation Bar below the Search Bar

➤ Select the Segmented Control. Set its **Width** to 300 points (make sure you change the width of the entire control, not of the individual segments).

➤ In the **Attributes inspector**, set the number of segments to 4.

➤ Change the title of the first segment to **All**. Then select the second segment and set its title to **Music**. The title for the third segment should be **Software** and the fourth segment is **E-books**.

You can change the segment title by double-clicking inside the segment or inside the Attributes inspector.

The scene should look like this now:

The finished Segmented Control

Next you'll add a new outlet and action method for the Segmented Control. This is a good opportunity to practice using the Assistant editor.

➤ Press **Option+⌘+Enter** to open the Assistant editor and then Ctrl-drag from the Segmented Control into the view controller source code to add the new outlet:

```
@IBOutlet weak var segmentedControl: UISegmentedControl!
```

To add the action method you can also use the Assistant editor. Ctrl-drag from the Segmented Control into the source code again, but this time choose:

• Connection: **Action**

• Name: **segmentChanged**

- Type: **UISegmentedControl**
- Event: Value Changed
- Arguments: Sender

Adding an action method for the segmented control

➤ Press **Connect** to add the action method. Also add a `println()` statement to it:

```
@IBAction func segmentChanged(sender: UISegmentedControl) {
  println("Segment changed: \(sender.selectedSegmentIndex)")
}
```

Type ⌘+**Enter** (without Option) to close the Assistant editor again. These are very handy keyboard shortcuts to remember.

➤ Run the app to make sure everything still works. Tapping a segment should log a number (the index of that segment) to the debug pane.

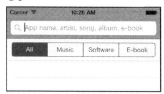

The segmented control in action

Notice that the first row of the table view is partially obscured again. Because you placed a navigation bar below the search bar, you need to add another 44 points to the table view's content inset.

➤ Change that line in `viewDidLoad()` to:

```
tableView.contentInset = UIEdgeInsets(top: 108, left: 0, bottom: 0, right: 0)
```

You will be using the segmented control in two ways. First of all, it determines what sort of products the app will search for. Second, if you have already performed a search and you tap on one of the other segment buttons, the app will search again for that new product category.

That means a search can now be triggered by two different events: tapping the Search button on the keyboard and tapping in the Segmented Control.

➤ Rename the `searchBarSearchButtonClicked()` method to `performSearch()` and also remove the `searchBar` parameter.

You're doing this to put the search logic into a separate method that can be invoked from more than one place. Removing `searchBar` as the parameter of this method is no problem because there is also an `@IBOutlet` instance variable with that name and `performSearch()` will simply use that.

➤ Now add a new version of `searchBarSearchButtonClicked()` back into the source code:

```
func searchBarSearchButtonClicked(searchBar: UISearchBar) {
  performSearch()
}
```

➤ Also replace the `segmentChanged()` action method with:

```
@IBAction func segmentChanged(sender: UISegmentedControl) {
  performSearch()
}
```

The app will now call `performSearch()` if the user presses the Search button on the keyboard or taps on the segmented control.

➤ Run the app and verify that searching still works. When you tap on the different segments the search should be performed again as well.

> **Note:** The second time you search for the same thing the app may return results very quickly. The networking layer is now returning a *cached* response so it doesn't have to download the whole thing again, which is usually a performance gain on mobile devices. (There is an API to turn off this caching behavior if that makes sense for your app.)

You still have to tell the app to use the category from the selected segment for the search. You've already seen that you can get the index of the selected segment with the `selectedSegmentIndex` property. This returns an `Int` value (0, 1, 2, or 3).

➤ Change the `urlWithSearchText()` method so that it accepts this `Int` as a parameter and then builds up the request URL accordingly:

```
func urlWithSearchText(searchText: String, category: Int) -> NSURL {
  var entityName: String
  switch category {
    case 1: entityName = "musicTrack"
    case 2: entityName = "software"
    case 3: entityName = "ebook"
    default: entityName = ""
  }

  let escapedSearchText = searchText.stringByAddingPercentEscapesUsingEncoding(
                                    NSUTF8StringEncoding)!

  let urlString = String(format:"http://itunes.apple.com/search?term=%@&limit=200&entity=%@",
                    escapedSearchText, entityName)
  let url = NSURL(string: urlString)
  return url!
}
```

This first turns the category index from a number into a string. (Note that the category index is passed to the method as a new parameter.)

Then it puts this string behind the `&entity=` parameter in the URL. For the "All" category, the entity value is empty but for the other categories it is "musicTrack", "software" and "ebook", respectively.

➤ In the `performSearch()` method, change the line that used to call `urlWithSearchText:` into the following:

```
let url = self.urlWithSearchText(searchBar.text,
                        category: segmentedControl.selectedSegmentIndex)
```

And that should do it.

> **Note:** You could have used `segmentedControl.selectedSegmentIndex` directly inside `urlWithSearchText()` instead of passing the category index as a parameter. Using the parameter is the better design, though. It makes it possible to reuse the same method with a different type of control, should you decide that a Segmented Control isn't really the right component for this app. It is always a good idea to make methods as independent from each other as possible.

➤ Run the app and search for "stephen king". In the All category that gives results for anything from movies to podcasts to audio books. In the Music category it matches mostly artists with the word "King" in their name. There doesn't seem to be a lot of Stephen King-related software, but in the E-Books category you finally find some of his novels.

You can now limit the search to just e-books

This finalizes the UI design of the main screen. This is as good a point as any to replace the silly launch file from the template.

➤ Remove the **LaunchScreen.xib** file from the project.

➤ In the **Project Settings** screen, under **App Icons and Launch Images**, change **Launch Screen File** to **Main.storyboard**.

Now when the app starts up it uses the initial view controller from the storyboard as the launch image. Also verify that the app works properly on the smaller iPhone 4S and the larger iPhone 6 and 6 Plus models.

➤ Commit the changes and get ready for some more networking!

Downloading the artwork images

The JSON search results contain a number of URLs to images and you put two of those – `artworkURL60` and `artworkURL100` – into the `SearchResult` object. Now you are going to download these images over the internet and put them into the table view cells.

Downloading images, just like using a web service, is simply a matter of doing an HTTP GET request to a server that is connected to the internet. An example of such a URL is:

http://a5.mzstatic.com/us/r30/Music/5c/16/8d/mzi.ezpjahaj.100x100-75.jpg

Click that link and it will open the picture in a new web browser window. The server where this picture is stored is apparently not itunes.apple.com but a5.mzstatic.com, but that doesn't matter anything to the app.

As long as it has a valid URL, it will just go fetch the file at that location, no matter where it is and no matter what kind of file that is.

There are various ways that you can download files from the internet. You're going to use NSURLSession and write a handy UIImageView extension to make this really convenient. Of course, you'll be downloading these images asynchronously!

First, you will move the logic for configuring the contents of the table view cells into the SearchResultCell class. That's a better place for it. Logic related to an object should live inside that object as much as possible, not somewhere else.

Many developers have a tendency to stuff everything into their view controllers, but if you can move some of the logic into other objects that makes for a much cleaner program.

➤ Add the following method to **SearchResultCell.swift**:

```
func configureForSearchResult(searchResult: SearchResult) {
  nameLabel.text = searchResult.name

  if searchResult.artistName.isEmpty {
    artistNameLabel.text = "Unknown"
  } else {
    artistNameLabel.text = String(format: "%@ (%@)", searchResult.artistName,
                                  kindForDisplay(searchResult.kind))
  }
}
```

This is the same as what you used to do in tableView(cellForRowAtIndexPath). The only problem is that this class doesn't have the kindForDisplay() method yet.

➤ Cut the kindForDisplay() method out of **SearchViewController.swift** and paste it into **SearchResultCell.swift**.

It's easy to move this method from one class to another because it doesn't depend on any instance variables. It is completely self-contained. You should strive to write your methods in that fashion as much as possible.

➤ Finally, change tableView(cellForRowAtIndexPath) to the following:

```
func tableView(tableView: UITableView,
               cellForRowAtIndexPath indexPath: NSIndexPath) -> UITableViewCell {
  if isLoading {
    . . .
  } else if searchResults.count == 0 {
    . . .
  } else {
    let cell = tableView.dequeueReusableCellWithIdentifier(
                    TableViewCellIdentifiers.searchResultCell, forIndexPath: indexPath)
                    as! SearchResultCell

    let searchResult = searchResults[indexPath.row]
    cell.configureForSearchResult(searchResult)

    return cell
  }
}
```

This small refactoring of moving some code from one class (SearchViewController) into another (SearchResultCell) was necessary to make the next bit work right.

In hindsight, it makes more sense to do this sort of thing in SearchResultCell anyway, but until now it did not really matter. Don't be afraid to refactor your code! (Remember, if you screw up you can always go back to the Git history.)

➤ Run the app to make sure everything still works as before.

OK, here comes the cool part. You will now make an extension for UIImageView that loads the image and automatically puts it into the image view on the table view cell with just one line of code.

As you know, an extension can be used to extend the functionality of an existing class without having to subclass it. This works even for classes from the system frameworks.

UIImageView doesn't have built-in support for downloading images, but this is a very common thing to do in apps. It's great that you can simply plug in your own extension – from then on every UIImageView in your app has this new ability.

➤ Add a new file to the project using the **Swift File** template, and name it **UIImageView+DownloadImage.swift**.

➤ Replace the contents of this new file with the following:

```swift
import UIKit

extension UIImageView {
  func loadImageWithURL(url: NSURL) -> NSURLSessionDownloadTask {
    let session = NSURLSession.sharedSession()
    //1
    let downloadTask = session.downloadTaskWithURL(url, completionHandler: {
      [weak self] url, response, error in
      // 2
      if error == nil && url != nil {
        // 3
        if let data = NSData(contentsOfURL: url) {
          if let image = UIImage(data: data) {
            // 4
            dispatch_async(dispatch_get_main_queue()) {
              if let strongSelf = self {
                strongSelf.image = image
              }
            }
          }
        }
      }
    })
    // 5
    downloadTask.resume()
    return downloadTask
  }
}
```

This should look very similar to what you did before with NSURLSession, but there are some differences:

1. After obtaining a reference to the shared NSURLSession, you create a download task. This is similar to a data task but it saves the downloaded file to a temporary location on disk instead of keeping it in memory.

2. Inside the completion handler for the download task you're given a URL where you can find the downloaded file (this URL points to a local file rather than an internet address). Of course, you must also check that `error` is `nil` before you continue.

3. With this local URL you can load the file into an `NSData` object and then make an image from that. It's possible that constructing the `UIImage` fails, when what you downloaded was not a valid image but a 404 page or something else unexpected. As you can tell, when dealing with networking code you need to check for errors every step of the way!

4. Once you have the image you can put it into the `UIImageView`'s `image` property. Because this is UI code you need to do this on the main thread.

Here's the tricky thing: it is theoretically possible that the `UIImageView` no longer exists by the time the image arrives from the server. After all, it may take a few seconds and the user can still navigate through the app in the mean time.

That won't happen in this part of the app because the image view is part of a table view cell and they get recycled but not thrown away. But later in the tutorial you'll use this same code to load an image on a detail pop-up that may be closed while the image is still downloading. In that case you don't want to set the image on the `UIImageView` anymore.

That's why the capture list for this closure includes [weak self], where `self` now refers to the `UIImageView`. Inside the `dispatch_async()` block you need to check whether "self" still exists; if not, then there is no more `UIImageView` to set the image on.

5. After creating the download task you call `resume()` to start it, and then return the `NSURLSessionDownloadTask` object to the caller. Why return it? That gives the app the opportunity to call `cancel()` on the download task. You'll see how that works in a minute.

And that's all you need to do. From now on you can call `loadImageWithURL()` on any `UIImageView` object in your project. Cool, huh!

> **Note:** Swift 1.2 has a handy new feature that lets you combine multiple `if let` statements into a single line, like so:
>
> ```
> if error == nil && url != nil, let data = NSData(contentsOfURL: url),
>                        let image = UIImage(data: data) {
>
>   dispatch_async(. . .)
> }
> ```
>
> I find that having everything inside a single if-statement is easier to read than many nested if-statements spread over several lines. Try it out for yourself!

➤ Switch to **SearchResultCell.swift** and add the following lines to the bottom of `configureForSearchResult()`:

```
artworkImageView.image = UIImage(named: "Placeholder")
if let url = NSURL(string: searchResult.artworkURL60) {
  downloadTask = artworkImageView.loadImageWithURL(url)
}
```

This tells the `UIImageView` to load the image from `artworkURL60` and to place it in the cell's image view. While the real artwork is downloading the image view displays a placeholder image (this is the same one from the nib for this cell).

The NSURLSessionDownloadTask object returned by loadImageWithURL() is placed in a new instance variable, downloadTask. You still need to add this instance variable:

```
var downloadTask: NSURLSessionDownloadTask?
```

➤ Run the app and look at those icons!

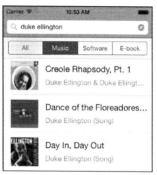

The app now downloads the album artwork

How was that for easy? You're not quite done yet. Remember that table view cells can be reused, so it's theoretically possible that you're scrolling through the table and some cell is about to be reused while its previous image is still loading.

You no longer need that image so you should really cancel the pending download. Table view cells have a special method named prepareForReuse() that is ideal for this.

➤ Add the following method to **SearchResultCell.swift**:

```
override func prepareForReuse() {
  super.prepareForReuse()

  downloadTask?.cancel()
  downloadTask = nil

  nameLabel.text = nil
  artistNameLabel.text = nil
  artworkImageView.image = nil
}
```

Here you cancel any image download that is still in progress. For good measure you also clear out the text from the labels. It's always a good idea to play nice.

Exercise. Put a println() in the prepareForReuse() method and see if you can trigger it. ∎

On a decent Wi-Fi connection, loading the images is very fast. You almost cannot see that it happens, even if you scroll quickly. It probably helps that the image files are small (only 60 by 60 pixels) and that the iTunes servers are fast.

That is key to having a snappy app: don't download more data than you need to.

Caching

Depending on what you searched for, you may have noticed that many of the images were the same. For example, my search for Duke Ellington's music had many identical album covers in the search results.

NSURLSession is smart enough not to download identical images – or at least images with identical URLs – twice. That principle is called **caching** and it's very important on mobile devices.

Mobile developers are always trying to optimize their apps to do as little as possible. If you can download something once and then use it over and over, that's a lot more efficient than re-downloading it all the time.

There's more than just images that you can cache. You can also cache the results of big computations, for example. Or views, as you have been doing in the previous tutorials, probably without even realizing it – when you use the principle of lazy loading, you delay the creation of an object until you need it and then you cache it for the next time.

Cached data does not stick around forever. When your app gets a memory warning, it's a good idea to remove any cached data that you don't need right away. That means you will have to reload that data when you need it again later but that's the price you have to pay. (For NSURLSession this is completely automatic, so that takes another burden off your shoulders.)

Some caches are in-memory only where the cached data stays in the computer's working memory, but it is also possible to cache the data in files on the disk. Your app even has a special directory for it, Library/Caches.

The caching policy used by StoreSearch is very simple – it uses the default settings. But you can configure NSURLSession to be much more advanced. Look into NSURLSessionConfiguration and NSURLCache to learn more.

Merging the branch

This concludes the section on talking to the web service and downloading images. Later on you'll tweak the web service requests a bit more (to include the user's language and country) but for now you're done with this feature.

I hope you got a good glimpse of what is possible with web services and how easy it is to build this into your apps with a great library such as NSURLSession.

➤ Commit these latest changes to the repository.

Now that you've completed a feature, you can merge this temporary branch back into the master branch. To do that, you first have to return to the master branch.

Merging is possible to do in Xcode but it's not always the best experience. I will first explain how to merge the branch using Xcode. If it doesn't work and Xcode keeps messing up your files, then skip ahead to the command line instructions. (It may be a good idea to make a backup copy of your project folder first.)

➤ Open the **Source Control** menu. Go to the **StoreSearch – NSURLSession** submenu and choose **Switch to Branch**.

This opens up dialog that lets you pick the branch to switch to. There's only one branch in here, **master**, so select that and click **Switch**:

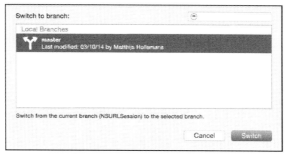

Choosing the branch to switch to

It is possible that you got this message instead:

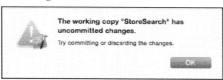

The message that appears when you have uncommitted changes

That means changes were made to the source code, the storyboard, or any other files that are being tracked by Git since your last commit. You may have done that yourself – often just opening a storyboard causes it to be modified – but sometimes Xcode itself decides to change things like the .xcodeproj file.

If that happens you have two choices:

1. Commit those changes. Simply do a new commit from the Source Control menu.

2. Discard the changes. Choose **Source Control** → **Discard All Changes**.

Then try **Switch to Branch** again.

After a few moments, Xcode will have switched back to the master branch. Verify this in the **Source Control** menu: it should now say **StoreSearch – master**. In the **History** window you should see only the commits until "networking is now asynchronous", but none of the NSURLSession stuff.

➤ To merge the NSURLSession branch into the master branch, go to **Source Control** → **StoreSearch – master** → **Merge from Branch**.

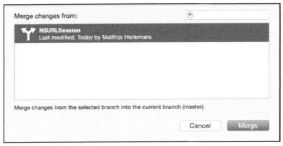

Choosing the branch to merge from

Pick the **NSURLSession** branch and click **Merge**. This brings up a preview pane that lets you review the changes that will be made. Click Merge again.

Now the master branch is up-to-date with the networking changes. If you want to, you can remove the NSURLSession branch or you can keep it and do more work on it later.

Just in case Xcode didn't want to cooperate, here is how you'd do it from the command line.

➤ First close Xcode. You don't want to do any of this while Xcode still has the project open. That's just asking for trouble.

➤ Open a Terminal, cd to the StoreSearch folder and type the following commands:

```
git stash
```

This moves any unsaved files out of the way (it doesn't have anything to do with facial hair). This is similar to doing Discard All Changes from the Xcode menu, although stashed changes are preserved in a temporary location, not thrown away.

```
git checkout master
```

This switches the current branch back to the master branch.

```
git merge NSURLSession
```

This merges the changes from the "NSURLSession" branch back into the master branch. If you get an error message at this point, then simply do git stash again and repeat the merge command.

(By the way, you don't really need to keep those stashed files around, so if you want to remove them from your repository, you can do git stash drop. If you stashed twice, you also need to drop twice.)

➤ Open the project again in Xcode. Now you're back at the master branch and it also has the latest networking changes.

➤ Build and run to see if everything still works.

Git is a pretty awesome tool but it takes a while to get familiar with. Unfortunately, Xcode's support for things like merges is still spotty and you're better off using the command line for the more advanced commands. It's well worth learning!

You can find the files for the app up to this point under **05 - NSURLSession** in the tutorial's Source Code folder.

Note: Even though NSURLSession is pretty easy to use and quite capable, many developers prefer to use third-party networking libraries that are often even more convenient and powerful.

The most popular library at this point is AFNetworking, an Objective-C library (github.com/AFNetworking/AFNetworking). There is also a new native Swift networking library, Alamofire (github.com/Alamofire/Alamofire), from the same creator as AFNetworking, so it's bound to be good.

I suggest you check them out and see how you like them. Networking is such an important feature of mobile apps that it's worth being familiar with the different possible approaches to send data up and down the 'net.

The Detail pop-up

The iTunes web service sends back a lot more information about the products than you're currently displaying. Let's add a "details" screen to the app that pops up when the user taps a row in the table:

The app shows a pop-up when you tap a search result

The table and search bar are still visible in the background, but they have been darkened.

You will place this Detail pop-up on top of the existing screen using the new *presentation controller* API, use *Dynamic Type* to change the fonts based on the user's preferences, draw your own gradients with Core Graphics, and learn to make cool *keyframe* animations. Fun times ahead!

The to-do list for this section is:

• Design the Detail screen in the storyboard.

• Show this screen when the user taps on a row in the table.

• Put the data from the SearchResult into the screen. This includes the item's price, formatted in the proper currency.

• Make the Detail screen appear with a cool animation.

A new screen means a new view controller, so let's start with that.

➤ Add a new **Cocoa Touch Class** file to the project. Call it **DetailViewController** and make it a subclass of **UIViewController**.

You're first going to do the absolute minimum to show this new screen and to dismiss it. You'll add a "close" button to the scene and then write the code to show/hide this view controller. Once that works you will put in the rest of the controls.

➤ Open the storyboard and drag a new **UIViewController** into the canvas. Change its **Class** to **DetailViewController**.

➤ Set the **Background** color of the main view to black, 50% opaque. That makes it easier to see what is going on in the next steps.

➤ Drag a new **View** into the scene. Using the **Size inspector**, make it 240 points wide and 240 high. Center the view in the window.

➤ In the **Attributes inspector**, change the **Background** color of this new view to white, 95% opaque. This makes it appear slightly translucent, just like navigation bars.

➤ With this new view still selected, go to the **Identity inspector**. In the field where it says "Xcode Specific Label", type **Pop-up View**. You can use this field to give your views names, so they are easier to distinguish inside Interface Builder.

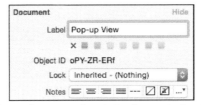

Giving the view a description for use in Xcode

➤ Drag a **Button** into the scene and place it somewhere on the Pop-up View. In the **Attributes inspector**, change **Image** to **CloseButton** (you already added this image to the asset catalog earlier).

➤ Remove the button's text. Choose **Editor → Size to Fit Content** to resize the button and place it in the top-left corner of the Pop-up View (at X = 3 and Y = 0).

➤ If the button's **Type** now says Custom, change it back to **System**. That will make the image turn blue (because the default tint color is blue).

➤ Set the Xcode Specific Label for the Button to **Close Button**. Remember that this only changes what the button is called inside Interface Builder; the user will never see that text.

The design should look as follows:

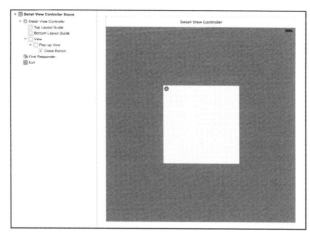

The Detail screen has a white square and a close button on a dark background

Let's write the code to show and hide this new screen.

➤ In **DetailViewController.swift**, add the following action method:

```
@IBAction func close() {
  dismissViewControllerAnimated(true, completion: nil)
}
```

There is no need to create a delegate protocol because there's nothing to communicate back to the SearchViewController.

➤ Connect this action method to the **X** button's Touch Up Inside event in Interface Builder. (As before, Ctrl-drag from the button to the view controller and pick from Sent Events.)

➤ Ctrl-drag from Search View Controller to Detail View Controller to make a **present modally** segue. Give it the identifier **ShowDetail**.

Because the table view doesn't use prototype cells you had to put the segue on the view controller itself. That means you need to trigger the segue manually when the user taps a row.

➤ Open **SearchViewController.swift** and change didSelectRowAtIndexPath to the following:

```
func tableView(tableView: UITableView, didSelectRowAtIndexPath indexPath: NSIndexPath) {
  tableView.deselectRowAtIndexPath(indexPath, animated: true)
  performSegueWithIdentifier("ShowDetail", sender: indexPath)
}
```

You're sending along the index-path of the selected row as the sender parameter. This will come in useful later when you're putting the SearchResult object into the Detail pop-up.

Let's see how well this works.

➤ Run the app and tap on a search result. Hmm, that doesn't look too good.

Even though you set its main view to be half transparent, the Detail screen still has a solid black background. Only during the animation is it see-through:

What happens when you present the Detail screen modally

In addition, the pop-up isn't neatly centered, as it ought to be.

Clearly, presenting this new screen with a regular modal segue isn't going to achieve the effect we're after.

There are three possible solutions:

1. Don't have a `DetailViewController`. You can load the view for the detail pop-up from a nib and add it as a subview of `SearchViewController`, and put all the logic for this screen in `SearchViewController` as well. This is not a very good solution because it makes `SearchViewController` more complex and the logic for a new screen should really go into its own view controller.

2. Use the *view controller containment* APIs to embed the `DetailViewController` "inside" the `SearchViewController`. This is a better solution but still more work than necessary. (You'll see an example of view controller containment in the next section when you're adding a special landscape mode to the app.)

3. Use a *presentation controller*. This is a new feature of iOS 8 that lets you customize how modal segues present their view controllers on the screen. You can even have custom animations to show and hide the view controllers.

Let's go for #3. Transitioning from one screen to another in an iOS app involves a complex web of objects that take care of all the details concerning presentations, transitions, and animations. Normally, that all happens behind the scenes and you can safely ignore it. But if you want to customize how some of this works, you'll have to dive into the excitingly strange world of presentation controllers and transitioning delegates.

➤ Add a new **Swift File** to the project, named **DimmingPresentationController**.

➤ Replace the contents of this new file with the following:

```swift
import UIKit

class DimmingPresentationController: UIPresentationController {
  override func shouldRemovePresentersView() -> Bool {
    return false
  }
}
```

The standard `UIPresentationController` class contains all the logic for presenting new view controllers. You're providing your own version that overrides some of this behavior, in particular telling UIKit to leave the `SearchViewController` visible. That's necessary to get the see-through effect.

In a short while you'll also add a light-to-dark gradient background view to this presentation controller; that's where the "dimming" in its name comes from.

> **Note:** It's called a presentation controller, but it is not a *view* controller. The use of the word controller may be a bit confusing here but not all controllers are for managing screens in your app (only those with "view" in their name).
>
> A presentation controller is an object that "controls" the presentation of something, just like a view controller is an object that controls a view and everything in it. Soon you'll also see an animation controller, which controls –you guessed it – an animation.
>
> There are quite a few different kinds of controller objects in the various iOS frameworks. Just remember that there's a difference between a view controller and other types of controllers.

Now you need to tell the app that you want to use your own presentation controller to show the Detail pop-up.

➤ In **DetailViewController.swift**, add the following extension at the very bottom of the file:

```
extension DetailViewController: UIViewControllerTransitioningDelegate {
  func presentationControllerForPresentedViewController(
        presented: UIViewController, presentingViewController presenting: UIViewController!,
        sourceViewController source: UIViewController) -> UIPresentationController? {

    return DimmingPresentationController(presentedViewController: presented,
                                 presentingViewController: presenting)
  }
}
```

The methods from this delegate protocol tell UIKit what objects it should use to perform the transition to the Detail View Controller. It will now use your new `DimmingPresentationController` class instead of the standard presentation controller.

➤ Also add the `init(coder)` method to class `DetailViewController`:

```
required init(coder aDecoder: NSCoder) {
  super.init(coder: aDecoder)
  modalPresentationStyle = .Custom
  transitioningDelegate = self
}
```

Recall that `init(coder)` is invoked to load the view controller from the storyboard. Here you tell UIKit that this view controller uses a custom presentation and you set the delegate that will call the method you just implemented.

➤ Run the app again and tap a row to bring up the detail pop-up. That looks better already – now the list of search results remains visible:

The Detail pop-up background is see-through

Also verify that the close button works to dismiss the pop-up.

The standard presentation controller removed the underlying view from the screen, making it appear as if the Detail pop-up had a solid black background. Removing the view makes sense most of the time when you present a modal screen, as the user won't be able to see the previous screen anyway (not having to redraw this view saves battery power too).

However, in our case the modal segue leads to a view controller that only partially covers the previous screen. You want to keep the underlying view to get the see-through effect. That's why you needed to supply your own presentation controller object.

Later on you'll add custom animations to this transition and for that you need to tweak the presentation controller some more and also provide your own animation controller objects. But first there are some issues to fix…

Exercise. What do you need to do to center the Detail pop-up? ■

Answer: Add some Auto Layout constraints, of course! The design of the Detail screen is currently for the device-independent square canvas. When this square gets resized to the actual device dimensions, UIKit doesn't know yet that it should keep the pop-up view centered.

➤ In the storyboard, select the **Pop-up View**. Click the **Align** button at the bottom of the canvas and put checkmarks in front of **Horizontal Center in Container** and **Vertical Center in Container**.

Adding constraints to align the Pop-up View

➤ Press **Add 2 Constraints** to finish. This adds two new constraints to the Pop-up View that keep it centered, represented by the orange lines that cross the scene:

The Pop-up View with alignment constraints

One small hiccup: these lines are supposed to be blue, not orange. Whenever you see orange lines, Auto Layout has a problem.

The number one rule for using Auto Layout is this: For each view you always need enough constraints to determine both its position and size.

Before you added your own constraints, Xcode gave automatic constraints to the Pop-up View, based on where you placed that view in Interface Builder. But as soon as you add a single constraint of your own, you no longer get these automatic constraints.

The Pop-up View has two constraints that determine the view's position – it is always centered horizontally and vertically in the window – but there are no constraints yet for its size.

Xcode is helpful enough to point this out in the **Issue navigator**:

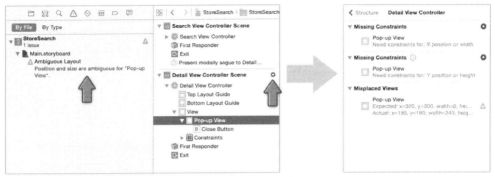

Xcode shows Auto Layout errors in the Issue navigator

➤ Tap the small red arrow in the outline pane to get a more detailed explanation of the errors. It's obvious that something's missing. You know it's not the position – the two alignment constraints are enough to determine that – so it must be the size.

The easiest way to fix these errors is to give the Pop-up View fixed width and height constraints.

➤ Select the Pop-up View and click the **Pin** button. Put checkmarks in front of **Width** and **Height**. Click **Add 2 Constraints** to finish.

Pinning the width and height of the Pop-up View

Now the lines turn blue and Auto Layout is happy.

Note: If your lines do not turn blue and the design looks something like the following, then your constraints and the view's frame do not match up.

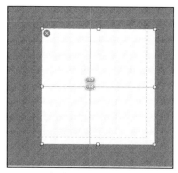

Auto Layout believes the view is misplaced

In other words, Auto Layout thinks that the Pop-up view should be placed where the orange dotted box is but you've put it somewhere else. To fix this, click the **Resolve Auto Layout Issues** button at the bottom (to the right of the Pin button) and choose **Update Frames**:

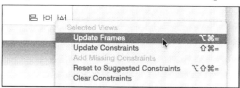

The Resolve Auto Layout Issues menu

➤ Run the app on the different Simulators and verify that the pop-up now always shows up in the exact center of the screen:

The Detail pop-up is now centered in the screen

Adding the rest of the controls

Let's finish the design of the Detail screen. You will add a few labels, an image view for the artwork and a button that opens the product in the actual iTunes store. The design will look like this:

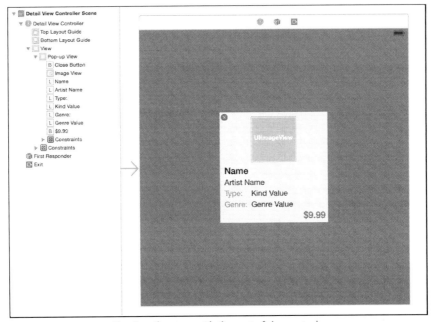

The Detail screen with the rest of the controls

> Drag a new **Image View**, six **Labels**, and a **Button** into the canvas and build a layout like the one from the picture.

Some suggestions for the dimensions:

Control	X	Y	Width	Height
Image View	70	9	100	100
Name label	10	115	220	24
Artist Name label	10	142	220	21
Type: label	10	166	41	21
Kind Value label	70	166	160	21
Genre: label	10	190	52	21
Genre Value label	70	190	160	21
$9.99 button	176	212	60	24

> The **Name** label's font is **System Bold 20.0**. Set **Autoshrink** to **Minimum Font Scale** so the font can become smaller if necessary to fit as much text as possible.

➤ The font for the **$9.99** button is also **System Bold 20.0**. In a moment you will also give this button a background image.

➤ You shouldn't have to change the font for the other labels; they use the default value of System 17.0.

➤ Set the **Color** for the **Type:** and **Genre:** labels to 50% opaque black.

These new controls are pretty useless without outlet properties, so add the following lines to **DetailViewController.swift**:

```
@IBOutlet weak var popupView: UIView!
@IBOutlet weak var artworkImageView: UIImageView!
@IBOutlet weak var nameLabel: UILabel!
@IBOutlet weak var artistNameLabel: UILabel!
@IBOutlet weak var kindLabel: UILabel!
@IBOutlet weak var genreLabel: UILabel!
@IBOutlet weak var priceButton: UIButton!
```

➤ Connect the outlets to the views in the storyboard. Ctrl-drag from Detail View Controller to each of the views and pick the corresponding outlet. (The Type: and Genre: labels and the X button do not get an outlet.)

➤ Run the app to see if everything still works.

The new controls in the Detail pop-up

The reason you did not put a background image on the price button yet is that I want to tell you about **stretchable images**. When you put background images on a button in Interface Builder, they always have to fit the button exactly. That works fine in many cases, but it's more flexible to use an image that can stretch to any size.

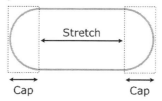

The caps are not stretched but the inner part of the image is

When an image view is wider than the image, it will automatically stretch the image to fit. In the case of a button, however, you don't want to stretch the ends (or "caps") of the button, only the middle part. That's what a stretchable image lets you do.

In the Bull's Eye tutorial you used `resizableImageWithCapInsets()` to cut the images for the slider track into stretchable parts. You can also do this in the asset catalog without having to write any code.

> Open **Images.xcassets** and select the **PriceButton** image set.

The PriceButton image

If you take a detailed look at this image you will see that it is only 11 points wide. That means it has a 5-point cap on the left, a 5-point cap on the right, and a 1- point body that will be stretched out.

Click **Show Slicing** at the bottom.

The Start Slicing button

Now all you have to do is click **Start Slicing** on each of the three images, followed by the **Slice Horizontally** button:

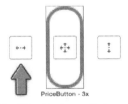

The Slice Horizontally button

You should end up with something like this for each of the button sizes:

After slicing

Each image is cut into three parts: the caps on the end and a one-pixel area in the middle that is the stretchable part. Now when you put this image onto a button or inside a `UIImageView`, it will automatically stretch itself to whatever size it needs to be.

➤ Go back to the storyboard. For the $9.99 button, change **Background** to **PriceButton**.

If you see the image repeating, make sure that the button is only 24 points high, the same as the image height.

➤ Run the app and check out that button. Here's a close-up of what it looks like:

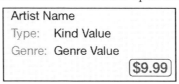

The price button with the stretchable background image

The main reason you're using a stretchable image here is that the text on the button may vary in size so you don't know in advance how big the button needs to be. If your app has a lot of custom buttons, it's worth making their images stretchable. That way you won't have to re-do the images whenever you're tweaking the sizes of the buttons.

The button could still look a little better, though – a black frame around dark green text doesn't particularly please the eye. You could go into Photoshop and change the color of the image to match the text color, but there's an easier method.

The color of the button text comes from the global tint color. UIImage makes it very easy to make images appear in the same tint color.

➤ In the asset catalog, select the **PriceButton** set again and go to the **Attribute inspector**. Change **Render As** to **Template Image**.

When you set the "template" rendering mode on an image, UIKit removes the original colors from the image and paints the whole thing in the tint color.

I like the dark green tint color in the rest of the app but for this pop-up it's a bit too dark. You can change the tint color on a per-view basis; if that view has subviews the new tint color also applies to these subviews.

➤ In **DetailViewController.swift**, add the line that sets the tintColor to viewDidLoad():

```
override func viewDidLoad() {
  super.viewDidLoad()
  view.tintColor = UIColor(red: 20/255, green: 160/255, blue: 160/255, alpha: 1)
}
```

Note that you're setting the new tintColor on view, not just on priceButton. That will apply the lighter tint color to the close button as well:

The buttons appear in the new tint color

Much better, but there is still more to tweak. In the screenshot I showed you at the start of this section, the pop-up view had rounded corners. You can use an image to make it look like that but instead I'll show you a little trick.

UIViews do their drawing using a so-called CALayer object. The CA prefix stands for Core Animation, which is the awesome framework that makes animations so easy on the iPhone. You don't need to know much about those "layers", except that each view has one, and that layers have some handy properties.

> Add the following line to viewDidLoad():

```
popupView.layer.cornerRadius = 10
```

You ask the Pop-up View for its layer and then set the corner radius of that layer to 10 points. And that's all you need to do!

> Run the app. There's your rounded corners:

The pop-up now has rounded corners

The close button is pretty small, about 15 by 15 points. From the Simulator it is easy to click because you're using a precision pointing device (the mouse). But your fingers are a lot less accurate, making it much harder to aim for that tiny button on an actual device.

That's one reason why you should always test your apps on real devices and not just on the Simulator. (Apple recommends that buttons always have a tap area of at least 44×44 points.)

To make the app more user-friendly, you'll also allow users to dismiss the pop-up by tapping anywhere outside it. The ideal tool for this job is a **gesture recognizer**.

➤ Add a new extension to **DetailViewController.swift**:

```
extension DetailViewController: UIGestureRecognizerDelegate {
  func gestureRecognizer(gestureRecognizer: UIGestureRecognizer,
                         shouldReceiveTouch touch: UITouch) -> Bool {
    return (touch.view === view)
  }
}
```

You only want to close the Detail screen when the user taps outside the pop-up, i.e. on the background. Any other taps should be ignored. That's what this delegate method is for. It only returns true when the touch was on the background view but false if it was inside the Pop-up View.

Note that you're using the identity operator === to compare touch.view with view. You want to know whether both variables refer to the same object. This is different from using the == equality operator. That would check whether both variables refer to objects that are considered equal, even if they aren't the same object. (Using == here would have worked too, but only because UIView treats == and === the same. But not all objects do, so be careful!)

➤ Add the following lines to viewDidLoad():

```
let gestureRecognizer = UITapGestureRecognizer(target: self, action: Selector("close"))
gestureRecognizer.cancelsTouchesInView = false
gestureRecognizer.delegate = self
view.addGestureRecognizer(gestureRecognizer)
```

This creates the new gesture recognizer that listens to taps anywhere in this view controller and calls the close() method in response.

➤ Try it out. You can now dismiss the pop-up by tapping anywhere outside the white pop-up area. That's a common thing that users expect to be able to do, and it was easy enough to add to the app. Win-win!

> **Note:** To create the gesture recognizer you could also have written:
>
> ```
> let gestureRecognizer = UITapGestureRecognizer(target: self, action: "close")
> ```
>
> It's OK to leave out Selector() and just write "close". Swift is clever enough to realize that the string "close" really means a selector with the same name and automatically turns it into a Selector object. Personally, I prefer to write out the full thing, just to make it more obvious that it's really a selector, i.e. the name of a method.

Putting the data into the Detail pop-up

Now that the app can show this pop-up after a tap on a search result, you should put the name, genre and price from the selected product in the pop-up.

Exercise. Try to do this by yourself. It's not any different from what you've done in the past tutorials! ∎

There is more than one way to pull this off, but I like to do it by putting the SearchResult object in a property on the DetailViewController.

➤ Add this property to **DetailViewController.swift**:

```
var searchResult: SearchResult!
```

As usual, this is an implicitly-unwrapped optional because you won't know what its value will be until the segue is performed. It is `nil` in the mean time.

➤ Also add a new method, `updateUI()`:

```
func updateUI() {
  nameLabel.text = searchResult.name

  if searchResult.artistName.isEmpty {
    artistNameLabel.text = "Unknown"
  } else {
    artistNameLabel.text = searchResult.artistName
  }

  kindLabel.text = searchResult.kind
  genreLabel.text = searchResult.genre
}
```

That looks very similar to what you did in `SearchResultCell`.

➤ Call this new method from `viewDidLoad()`:

```
override func viewDidLoad() {
  super.viewDidLoad()
  . . .

  if searchResult != nil {
    updateUI()
  }
}
```

The logic for setting the text on the labels has its own method, `updateUI()`, because that is cleaner than stuffing everything into `viewDidLoad()`.

The `if != nil` check is a defensive measure, just in case the developer forgets to fill in `searchResult` on the segue.

The Detail pop-up is launched with a segue triggered from `SearchViewController`'s `tableView(didSelectRowAtIndexPath)`. You'll have to add a `prepareForSegue(sender)` method to configure the `DetailViewController` when the segue happens.

➤ Add this method to **SearchViewController.swift**:

```
override func prepareForSegue(segue: UIStoryboardSegue, sender: AnyObject?) {
  if segue.identifier == "ShowDetail" {
    let detailViewController = segue.destinationViewController as! DetailViewController
    let indexPath = sender as! NSIndexPath
    let searchResult = searchResults[indexPath.row]
    detailViewController.searchResult = searchResult
  }
}
```

This should hold no big surprises for you. "`didSelectRowAtIndexPath`" sent along the index-path of the selected row, which lets you find the `SearchResult` object and put it in `DetailViewController`'s property.

➤ Try it out. All right, that's starting to look like something:

The pop-up with filled-in data

One thing you did in SearchResultCell was translating the kind value from an internal identifier to something that looks a bit better to humans. That logic, in the form of the kindForDisplay() method, sits in SearchResultCell, but now I'd like to use it in DetailViewController as well. Problem: the DetailViewController doesn't have anything to do with SearchResultCell.

You could simply copy-paste the kindForDisplay() method but then you have identical code in two different places in the app.

What if you decide to support another type of product, then you'd have to remember to update this method in two places as well. That sort of thing becomes a maintenance nightmare and is best avoided. Instead, you should look for a better place to put that method.

Exercise: Where would you put it? ∎

Answer: kind is a property on the SearchResult object. It makes sense that you can also ask the SearchResult for a nicer version of that value, so let's move the entire kindForDisplay() method into the SearchResult class.

➤ Cut the kindForDisplay() method out of the SearchResultCell source code and put it in **SearchResult.swift**, inside class SearchResult.

Because SearchResult already has a kind property, you don't have to pass that value as a parameter to this method.

➤ Change the method signature to:

```
func kindForDisplay() -> String {
```

Of course, **SearchResultCell.swift**'s configureForSearchResult() now tries to call a method that no longer exists.

➤ Fix the following line in configureForSearchResult():

```
artistNameLabel.text = String(format: "%@ (%@)", searchResult.artistName,
                                   searchResult.kindForDisplay())
```

Let's also call this new method in **DetailViewController.swift**.

➤ Change the line in updateUI() that sets the "kind" label to:

```
kindLabel.text = searchResult.kindForDisplay()
```

Cool, you refactored the code to make it cleaner and more powerful. I often start out by putting all my code in the view controllers but as the app evolves, more and more gets moved into their own classes where it really belongs.

In retrospect, the kindForDisplay() method really returns a property of SearchResult in a slightly different form, so it is functionality that logically goes with the SearchResult object, not with its cell or the view controller.

It's OK to start out with your code being a bit of a mess – that's what it often is for me! – but whenever you see an opportunity to clean things up and simplify it, you should take it.

As your source code evolves, it will become clearer what the best internal structure is for that particular program. But you have to be willing to revise the code when you realize it can be improved in some way!

➤ Run the app. The "Type" label in the pop-up should now have the same polished text as the list of search results.

There are three more things to do on this screen:

1. Show the price, in the proper currency.

2. Make the price button open the product page in the iTunes store.

3. Download and show the artwork image. This image is slightly larger than the one from the table view cell.

These are all fairly small features so you should be able to do them quite quickly. The price goes first.

➤ Add the following code to updateUI():

```
let formatter = NSNumberFormatter()
formatter.numberStyle = .CurrencyStyle
formatter.currencyCode = searchResult.currency

var priceText: String
if searchResult.price == 0 {
  priceText = "Free"
} else if let text = formatter.stringFromNumber(searchResult.price) {
  priceText = text
} else {
  priceText = ""
}

priceButton.setTitle(priceText, forState: .Normal)
```

You've used NSDateFormatter in previous tutorials to turn an NSDate object into human-readable text. Here you use NSNumberFormatter to do the same thing for numbers.

In the past tutorials you've turned numbers into text using string interpolation \(…) and String(format:) with the %f or %d format specifier. However, in this case you're not dealing with regular numbers but with money in a certain currency.

There are different rules for displaying various currencies, especially if you take the user's language and country settings into consideration. You could program all of these rules yourself, which is a lot of effort, or choose to ignore them. Fortunately, you don't have to make that tradeoff because you have NSNumberFormatter to do all the hard work.

You simply tell the NSNumberFormatter that you want to display a currency value and what the currency code is. That currency code comes from the web service and is something like "USD" or "EUR". NSNumberFormatter will insert the proper symbol, such as $ or € or ¥, and formats the monetary amount according to the user's regional settings.

There's one caveat: if you're not feeding NSNumberFormatter an actual number, it cannot do the conversion. That's why stringFromNumber() returns an optional that you need to unwrap.

➤ Run the app and see if you can find some good deals. ☺

Occasionally you might see this:

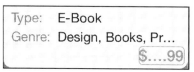

The price doesn't fit into the button

When you designed the storyboard you made this button 60 points wide. You didn't put any constraints on it, so Xcode gave it an automatic constraint that always forces the button to be 60 points wide, no more, no less.

But buttons, like labels, are perfectly able to determine what their ideal size is based on the amount of text they contain. That's called the **intrinsic content size**.

➤ Open the storyboard and select the price button. **Choose Editor → Size to Fit Content** from the menu bar (or press ⌘=). This resizes the button to its ideal size, based on the current text.

That alone is not enough. You also need to add at least one constraint to the button or Xcode will still apply the automatic constraints.

➤ With the price button selected, click the **Pin** button. Add two spacing constraints, one on the right and one on the bottom, both 6 points in size. Also add a 24-point Height constraint:

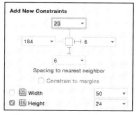

Pinning the price button

Don't worry if your storyboard now looks something like this:

Orange bars indicate the button is misplaced

The orange lines simply mean that the current position and/or size of the button in the storyboard does not correspond to the position and size that Auto Layout calculated from the constraints. This is easily fixed:

➤ Select the button and from the menu bar choose **Editor** → **Resolve Auto Layout Issues** → **Update Frames**. Now the lines should all turn blue.

To recap, you have set the following constraints on the button:

• Fixed height of 24 points. That is necessary because the background image is 24 points tall.

• Pinned to the right edge of the pop-up with a distance of 6 points. When the button needs to grow to accommodate larger prices, it will extend towards the left. Its right edge always stays aligned with the right edge of the pop-up.

• Pinned to the bottom of the pop-up, also with a distance of 6 points.

• There is no constraint for the width. That means the button will use its intrinsic width – the larger the text, the wider the button. And that's exactly what you want to happen here.

➤ Run the app again and pick an expensive product (something with a price over $9.99; e-books are a good category for this).

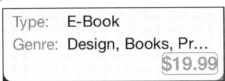

The button is a little cramped

That's better but the text now runs into the border from the background image. You can fix this by setting the "content edge insets" for the button.

➤ Go to the **Attributes inspector** and find where it says **Edge: Content**. Change **Left** and **Right** to 5.

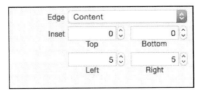

Changing the content edge insets of the button

This adds 5 points of padding on the left and right sides of the button. Of course, this causes the button's frame to be misplaced again because it is now 10 points wider.

➤ Once again, choose **Update Frames** from the **Resolve Auto Layout Issues** menu.

➤ Run the app; now the price button should finally look good:

```
Type:   E-Book
Genre:  Design, Books, Pr...
                    $19.99
```

That price looks so good you almost want to tap it!

Tapping the button should take the user to the selected product's page on the iTunes store.

➤ Add the following method to **DetailViewController.swift**:

```
@IBAction func openInStore() {
  if let url = NSURL(string: searchResult.storeURL) {
    UIApplication.sharedApplication().openURL(url)
  }
}
```

➤ And connect the openInStore action to the button's Touch Up Inside event (in the storyboard).

That's all you have to do. The web service returned a URL to the product page. You simply tell the UIApplication object to open this URL. iOS will now figure out what sort of URL it is and launch the proper app in response – iTunes Store, App Store, or Mobile Safari. (On the Simulator you'll probably receive an error message that the URL could not be opened. Try it on your device instead.)

Finally, to load the artwork image you'll use your old friend again, the handy UIImageView extension.

➤ First add a new instance variable to **DetailViewController.swift**. This is necessary to be able to cancel the download task:

```
var downloadTask: NSURLSessionDownloadTask?
```

➤ Then add the following line to updateUI():

```
if let url = NSURL(string: searchResult.artworkURL100) {
  downloadTask = artworkImageView.loadImageWithURL(url)
}
```

This is the same thing you did in SearchResultCell, except that you use the other artwork URL (100×100 pixels) and no placeholder image.

It's a good idea to cancel the image download if the user closes the pop-up before the image has been downloaded completely.

➤ Add a deinit method:

```
deinit {
  println("deinit \(self)")
  downloadTask?.cancel()
}
```

Remember that deinit is called whenever the object instance is deallocated and its memory is reclaimed. That happens after the user closes the DetailViewController and the animation to remove it from the screen has completed. If the download task is still busy by then, you cancel it.

Exercise. Why did you write `downloadTask?.cancel()` with a question mark? ■

Answer: Because `downloadTask` is an optional you need to unwrap it somehow before you can use it. When you just need to call a method on the object, it's easiest to use optional chaining like you did here. If `downloadTask` is `nil`, there is nothing to cancel and Swift will simply ignore the call to `cancel()`.

➤ Try it out!

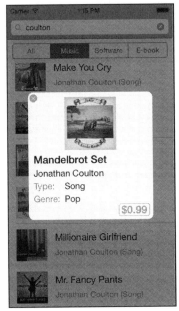

The pop-up now shows the artwork image

Did you see the `println()` from `deinit` after closing the pop-up? It's always a good idea to log a message when you're first trying out a new `deinit` method, to see if it really works. (If you don't see that `println()`, it means `deinit` is never called, and you may have an ownership cycle somewhere keeping your object alive longer than intended.)

➤ This is a good time to commit the changes.

Dynamic Type

The iOS Settings app has an accessibility menu that allows users to choose larger or smaller text. This is especially helpful for people who don't have 20/20 vision – probably most of the population – and for whom the thin default font is too hard to read. Nobody likes squinting at their device!

You can find these settings under **General** → **Accessibility** → **Larger Text** on your device and also in the Simulator:

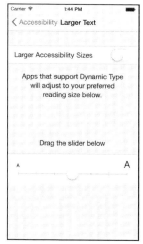

The Larger Text accessibility settings

Apps have to opt-in to use this "Dynamic Type" feature. Instead of choosing a specific font for the text labels, you use one of the built-in dynamic text styles.

Just to get some feel for how this works, you'll change the Detail pop-up to use Dynamic Type for its labels.

➤ Open the storyboard and go to the Detail View Controller scene. Change the font of the **Name** label to **Headline**:

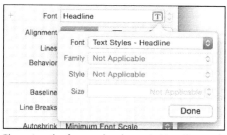

Changing the font to the dynamic Headline style

You can't pick a size for this font. That is up to the user, based on their Larger Text settings.

➤ Choose **Editor → Size to Fit Content** to resize the label.

➤ Set the **Lines** attribute to 0. This allows the Name label to fit more than one line of text.

Of course, if you don't know beforehand how large the label's font will be, you also won't know how large the label will end up being, especially if it sometimes may have more than one line of text. You won't be surprised to hear that Auto Layout and Dynamic Type go hand-in-hand.

You want to make the name label resizable so that it can hold any amount of text at any possible font size, but it cannot go outside the bounds of the pop-up, nor overlap the labels below.

The trick is to capture these requirements in Auto Layout constraints.

Previously you've used the Pin button to make constraints, but that may not always give you the constraints you want. With this menu pins are expressed as the amount of "spacing to nearest neighbor". But what exactly is the nearest neighbor?

If you use the Pin button on the Name label, Interface Builder may decide to pin it to the bottom of the close button, which is weird. It makes more sense to pin the Name label to the image view instead. That's why you're going to use a different way to make constraints.

➤ Select the **Name** label. Now **Ctrl-drag** to the **Image View** and let go of the mouse button.

Ctrl-drag to make a new constraint between two views

From the pop-up that appears, choose **Vertical Spacing**:

The possible constraint types

This puts a vertical spacing constraint between the label and the image view:

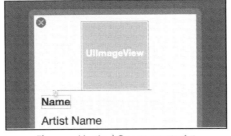

The new Vertical Space constraint

Of course, you'll also get some orange lines because the label still needs additional constraints. I'd like this vertical space to be 8-points.

➤ Select the T-bar (either by carefully clicking it with the mouse or by selecting it from the outline pane), then go to the **Size inspector** and change **Constant** to 8. The Name label may not actually move down yet when you do this, because there are not enough constraints yet.

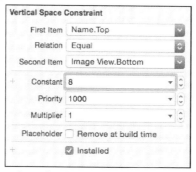

Attributes for the Vertical Space constraint

Note that the inspector clearly describes what sort of constraint this is: Name.Top is connected to Image View.Bottom with a distance (Constant) of 8 points.

➤ Select the **Name** label again and **Ctrl-drag** to the left. From the pop-up choose **Leading Space to Container**:

The pop-up shows different constraint types

This adds a blue T-bar on the left. Notice how the pop-up offered different options this time? The constraints that you can make depend on the direction that you're dragging.

➤ Repeat but this time Ctrl-drag to the right. Now choose **Trailing Space to Container**.

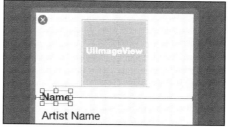

The T-bars for the Name label

The Name label is now connected to the left edge of the Pop-up View and to its right edge – enough to determine its X-position and width – and to the bottom of the image view, for its Y-position. There is no constraint for the label's height, allowing it to grow as tall as it needs to (using the intrinsic content size).

Shouldn't these constraints be enough to uniquely determine the label's position and size? If so, why is there still an orange box?

Simple: the image view now has a constraint attached to it, and therefore no longer gets automatic constraints. You also have to add constraints that give the image view its position and size.

➤ Select the **Image View, Ctrl-drag** up, and choose **Top Space to Container**. That takes care of the Y-position.

➤ Repeat but now choose **Center Horizontally in Container**. That center-aligns the image view to take care of the X-position. (If you don't see this option, then make sure you're not dragging outside the Pop-up View.)

➤ Ctrl-drag again, but this time let the mouse button go while you're still inside the image view. Hold down **Shift** and put checkmarks in front of both **Width** and **Height**, then press **enter**. (If you don't see both options, Ctrl-drag diagonally instead of straight up.)

Adding multiple constraints at once

Now the image view and the Name label have all blue T-bars. If the Name label is misplaced – orange box – then select it and choose Update Frames from the Resolve Auto Layout Issues menu.

There's one more thing you need to fix. Look again at that blue bar on the right of the Name label. This forces the label to be always about 44 points wide. That's not what you want; instead, the label should be able to grow until it reaches the edge of the Pop-up View.

➤ Click that blue bar to select it and go to the Size inspector. Change **Relation** to **Greater Than or Equal**, and **Constant** to **10**.

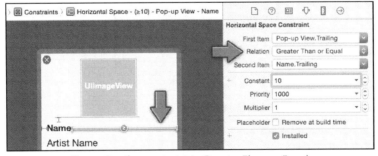

Converting the constraint to Greater Than or Equal

Now this constraint can resize to allow the label to grow, but it can never become smaller than 10 points. This ensures there is at least a 10-point margin between the label and the edge of the Detail pop-up.

By the way, notice how this constraint is between Pop-up View.Trailing and Name.Trailing? In Auto Layout terminology, trailing means "on the right", while leading means "on the left".

Why didn't they just call this left and right? Well, not everyone writes in the same direction. With right-to-left languages such as Hebrew or Arabic, the meaning of trailing and leading is reversed. That allows your layouts to work without changes on these exotic languages.

➤ Run the app to try it out:

The text overlaps the artist name label

Well, the word-wrapping seems to work but the text does overlap the label below it. Let's add some more constraints so that the other labels get pushed down instead.

➤ Select the **Artist Name** label and change its font to **Subhead**. Give the label its ideal size with **Size to Fit Content**.

➤ Change the font of the other four labels to **Caption 1**, and **Size to Fit Content** them too. (You can do this in a single go if you multiple-select these labels by holding down the ⌘ key.)

Let's pin the **Artist Name** label. Again you do this by Ctrl-dragging.

• Pin it to the left with a Leading Space to Container.

• Pin it to the right with a Trailing Space to Container. Just like before, change this constraint's Relation to Greater Than or Equal and Constant to 10.

• Pin it to the Name label with a Vertical Spacing. Change this to size 4.

Repeat for the **Type:** label:

• Pin it to the left with a Leading Space to Container.

• On the right, pin it to the Kind Value label with a Horizontal Spacing. This should be a 20-point distance. You may get an orange label here if the original distance was larger or smaller. You'll fix that in a second.

• Pin it to the Artist Name label with a Vertical Spacing, size 8.

The **Kind Value** label is slightly different:

- Pin it to the right with a Trailing Space to Container. Change this constraint's Relation to Greater Than or Equal and Constant to 10.

- Ctrl-drag from Kind Value to Type and choose Baseline. This aligns the bottom of the text of both labels. This alignment constraint determines the Kind Value's Y-position so you don't have to make a separate constraint for that.

- With the Kind Value label selected, choose **Resolve Auto Layout Issues** → **Update Frames**. This fixes any orange thingies.

Two more labels to go. For the **Genre:** label:

- Pin it to the left with a Leading Space to Container.

- Pin it to the Type: label with a Vertical Spacing, size 4.

And finally, the **Genre Value** label:

- Pin it to the right with a Trailing Space to Container, Greater Than or Equal 10.

- Make a Baseline alignment between Genre Value and Genre:.

- Make a Left alignment between Genre Value and Kind Value. This keeps these two labels neatly positioned below each other.

- Resolve any Auto Layout issues. You may need to set the Constant of the alignment constraints to 0 if things don't line up properly.

That's quite a few constraints but using Ctrl-drag to make them is quite fast. With some experience you'll be able to whip together complex Auto Layout designs in no time.

There is one last thing to do. The last row of labels needs to be pinned to the price button. That way there are constraints going all the way from the top of the Pop-up View to the bottom. The heights of the labels plus the sizes of the Vertical Spacing constraints between them will now determine the height of the Detail pop-up.

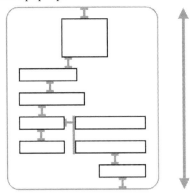

The height of the pop-up view is determined by the constraints

➤ Ctrl-drag from the **$9.99** button up to **Genre Value**. Choose **Vertical Spacing**. In the Size inspector, set **Constant** to **10**.

Whoops. This messes up your carefully constructed layout and some of the constraints turn orange.

Exercise. Can you explain why this happens? ■

Answer: The Pop-up View still has a Height constraint that forces it to be 240 points high. But the labels and the vertical space constraints don't add up to 240.

➤ You no longer need this Height constraint, so select it – **Height (240)** in the outline pane – and press **delete** to get rid of it.

➤ From the **Editor** → **Resolve Auto Layout Issues** menu, choose **Update Frames** (from the "All Views" section).

Now all your constraints turn blue and everything fits snugly together.

Whoops (again!). The close button has disappeared. That happened because you did Update Frames while the button didn't have any constraints yet. For some reason Interface Builder moves such views outside the visible portion of the screen. Better give that button some constraints too.

➤ Select the **Close Button** (from the outline pane) and use the **Pin** button to pin it to the **left** (3 points) and **top** (3 points). Also select **Width** and **Height** and set both to 15. If you set Update Frames to **Items of New Constraints,** then the button should magically reappear in its old position.

(If the button has an orange box around it, use **Size to Fit Content** to fix that.)

➤ Run the app to try it out.

The text properly wraps without overlapping

You now have an automatically resizing Detail pop-up that uses Dynamic Type for its labels.

➤ Close the app and open the Settings app. Go to **General** → **Accessibility** → **Larger Text**. Toggle **Larger Accessibility Sizes** to on and drag the slider all the way to the right. That gives you the maximum font size (it's huge!).

Now go back to StoreSearch and open a new pop-up. The text is a lot bigger:

Changing the text size results in a bigger font

For fun, change the font of the Name label to Body. Bazinga, that's some big text!

When you're done playing, put the Name label font back to Headline, and turn off the Larger Text setting (this slider goes in the middle).

Dynamic Type is an important feature to add to your apps. This was only a short introduction but I hope the principle is clear: instead of a font with a fixed size you use one of the Text Styles: Body, Headline, Caption, and so on. Then you set up Auto Layout constraints to make your views resizable and looking good no matter how large or small the font.

➤ This is a good time to commit the changes.

Exercise. Put Dynamic Type on the cells from the table view. There's a catch: when the user returns from changing the text size settings, the app should refresh the screen without needing a restart. You can do this by reloading the table view when the app receives a `UIContentSizeCategoryDidChangeNotification` (see the previous tutorial for how to handle notifications). Good luck! Check the forums at raywenderlich.com/forums for solutions from other readers. ■

Gradients in the background

As you can see in the previous screenshots, the table view in the background is dimmed by the view of the `DetailViewController`, which is 50% transparent black. That allows the pop-up to stand out more.

It works well, but on the other hand, a plain black overlay is a bit dull. Let's turn it into a circular gradient instead.

You could use Photoshop to draw such a gradient and place an image view behind the pop-up, but why use an image when you can also draw using Core Graphics? To pull this off, you will create your own `UIView` subclass.

➤ Add a new file to the project, **Cocoa Touch Class** template. Name it **GradientView** and make it a subclass of **UIView**.

This will be a very simple view. It simply draws a black circular gradient that goes from a mostly opaque in the corners to mostly transparent in the center. It's a similar dimmed background that you used to see behind alert views on iOS 6 and earlier. Placed on a white background, it looks like this:

What the GradientView looks like by itself

➤ Replace the contents of **GradientView.swift** by:

```swift
import UIKit

class GradientView: UIView {

  override init(frame: CGRect) {
    super.init(frame: frame)
    backgroundColor = UIColor.clearColor()
  }

  required init(coder aDecoder: NSCoder) {
    super.init(coder: aDecoder)
    backgroundColor = UIColor.clearColor()
  }

  override func drawRect(rect: CGRect) {
    // 1
    let components: [CGFloat] = [ 0, 0, 0, 0.3, 0, 0, 0, 0.7 ]
    let locations: [CGFloat] = [ 0, 1 ]
    // 2
    let colorSpace = CGColorSpaceCreateDeviceRGB()
    let gradient = CGGradientCreateWithColorComponents(colorSpace, components, locations, 2)
    // 3
    let x = CGRectGetMidX(bounds)
    let y = CGRectGetMidY(bounds)
    let point = CGPoint(x: x, y : y)
    let radius = max(x, y)
    // 4
    let context = UIGraphicsGetCurrentContext()
    CGContextDrawRadialGradient(context, gradient, point, 0, point, radius,
                    CGGradientDrawingOptions(kCGGradientDrawsAfterEndLocation))
  }
}
```

In the init(frame) and init(coder) methods you simply set the background color to fully transparent (the "clear" color). Then in drawRect() you draw the gradient on top of that transparent background, so that it blends with whatever is below.

The drawing code uses the Core Graphics framework (also known as Quartz 2D). It may look a little scary but this is what it does:

1. First you create two arrays that contain the "color stops" for the gradient. The first color (0, 0, 0, 0.3) is a black color that is mostly transparent. It sits at location 0 in the gradient, which represents the center of the screen because you'll be drawing a circular gradient.

   The second color (0, 0, 0, 0.7) is also black but much less transparent and sits at location 1, which represents the circumference of the gradient's circle. Remember that in UIKit and also in Core Graphics, colors and opacity values don't go from 0 to 255 but are fractional values between 0 and 1. The 0 and 1 from the locations array represent percentages: 0% and 100%, respectively.

2. With those color stops you can create the gradient. This gives you a new CGGradient object. This is not an traditional object, so you cannot send it messages by doing gradient.methodName(). But it's still some kind of data structure that lives in memory, and the gradient constant refers to it. (Such objects are called "opaque" types, or "handles". They are relics from iOS frameworks that are written in the C language, such as Core Graphics.)

3. Now that you have the gradient object, you have to figure out how big you need to draw it. The CGRectGetMidX() and CGRectGetMidY() functions return the center point of a rectangle. That rectangle is given by bounds, a CGRect object that describes the dimensions of the view.

   If I can avoid it, I prefer not to hard-code any dimensions such as "320 by 480 points". By asking bounds, you can use this view anywhere you want to, no matter how big a space it should fill. You can use it without problems on any screen size from the smallest iPhone to the biggest iPad.

   The point constant contains the coordinates for the center point of the view and radius contains the larger of the x and y values; max() is a handy function that you can use to determine which of two values is the biggest.

4. With all those preliminaries done, you can finally draw the thing. Core Graphics drawing always takes places in a so-called graphics context. We're not going to worry about exactly what that is, just know that you need to obtain a reference to the current context and then you can do your drawing.

   The CGContextDrawRadialGradient() function finally draws the gradient according to your specifications.

It generally speaking isn't optimal to create new objects inside your drawRect() method, such as gradients, especially if drawRect() is called often. In that case it is better to create the objects the first time you need them and to reuse the same instance over and over (lazy loading!).

You don't really have to do that here because this drawRect() method will be called just once – when the DetailViewController gets loaded – so you can get away with being less than optimal.

> **Note:** If you've programmed in Objective-C with Core Graphics you may wonder why you're not releasing the gradient and colorSpace objects once you're dong with them. You'll be pleased to know that Swift automatically takes care of the memory management of Core Graphics objects. It is no longer necessary to call `CGGradientRelease()`.

By the way, you'll only use `init(frame)` to create the `GradientView` instance; the other init method, `init(coder)`, is never used in this app. However, `UIView` demands that all subclasses implement `init(coder)` – that is why it is marked as `required`. (Try it out: if you remove this method, Xcode will give an error.)

Putting this new `GradientView` class into action is pretty easy. You'll add it to your own presentation controller object. That way the `DetailViewController` doesn't need to know anything about it. Dimming the background is really a side effect of doing a presentation, so it belongs in the presentation controller.

➤ Open **DimmingPresentationController.swift** and add the following code inside the class:

```
lazy var dimmingView = GradientView(frame: CGRect.zeroRect)

override func presentationTransitionWillBegin() {
  dimmingView.frame = containerView.bounds
  containerView.insertSubview(dimmingView, atIndex: 0)
}
```

The `presentationTransitionWillBegin()` method is invoked when the new view controller is about to be shown on the screen. Here you create the `GradientView` object, make it as big as the `containerView`, and insert it behind everything else in this "container view".

The container view is a new view that is placed on top of the `SearchViewController`, and it contains the views from the `DetailViewController`. So this piece of logic places the `GradientView` in between those two screens.

There's one more thing to do: because the `DetailViewController`'s background color is still 50% black, this color gets multiplied with the colors inside the gradient view, making the gradient look extra dark. It's better to set the background color to 100% transparent, but that makes it harder to see and edit the pop-up inside the storyboard. So let's do that in code instead.

➤ Add the following line to **DetailViewController.swift**'s `viewDidLoad()`:

```
view.backgroundColor = UIColor.clearColor()
```

➤ Run the app and see what happens.

The background behind the pop-up now has a gradient

Nice, that looks a lot smarter.

Animation!

The pop-up itself looks good already, but the way it enters the screen – Poof! It's suddenly there – is a bit unsettling. iOS is supposed to be the king of animation, so let's make good on that.

You've used Core Animation and UIView animations before. This time you'll use a so-called **keyframe animation** to make the pop-up bounce into view.

To animate the transition between two screens, you use an animation controller object. The purpose of this object is to animate a screen while it's being presented or dismissed, nothing more.

Now let's add some liveliness to this pop-up!

➤ Add a new **Swift File** to the project, named **BounceAnimationController**.

➤ Replace the contents of this new file with:

```
import UIKit

class BounceAnimationController: NSObject, UIViewControllerAnimatedTransitioning {

  func transitionDuration(transitionContext: UIViewControllerContextTransitioning)
                        -> NSTimeInterval {
    return 0.4
  }

  func animateTransition(transitionContext: UIViewControllerContextTransitioning) {
    if let toViewController = transitionContext.viewControllerForKey(
                                  UITransitionContextToViewControllerKey) {
      if let toView = transitionContext.viewForKey(UITransitionContextToViewKey) {
        toView.frame = transitionContext.finalFrameForViewController(toViewController)

        let containerView = transitionContext.containerView()
```

```
      containerView.addSubview(toView)

      toView.transform = CGAffineTransformMakeScale(0.7, 0.7)

      UIView.animateKeyframesWithDuration(transitionDuration(transitionContext),
                            delay: 0.0, options: .CalculationModeCubic, animations: {
        UIView.addKeyframeWithRelativeStartTime(0.0, relativeDuration: 0.334,
                                                     animations: {
          toView.transform = CGAffineTransformMakeScale(1.2, 1.2)
        })
        UIView.addKeyframeWithRelativeStartTime(0.334, relativeDuration: 0.333,
                                                     animations: {
          toView.transform = CGAffineTransformMakeScale(0.9, 0.9)
        })
        UIView.addKeyframeWithRelativeStartTime(0.666, relativeDuration: 0.333,
                                                     animations: {
          toView.transform = CGAffineTransformMakeScale(1.0, 1.0)
        })
      }, completion: { finished in transitionContext.completeTransition(finished) })
    }
  }
 }
}
```

To become an animation controller, the object needs to extend NSObject and also implement the UIViewControllerAnimatedTransitioning protocol – quite a mouthful! The important methods from this protocol are:

- transitionDuration() – This determines how long the animation is. You're making the pop-in animation last for only 0.4 seconds but that's long enough. Animations are fun but they shouldn't keep the user waiting.

- animateTransition() – This performs the actual animation.

To find out what to animate, you look at the transitionContext parameter. This gives you a reference to new view controller and lets you know how big it should be.

The actual animation starts at the line UIView.animateKeyframesWithDuration(). This works like all UIView-based animation: you set the initial state before the animation block; UIKit will automatically animate any properties that get changed inside the closure. The difference with before is that a keyframe animation lets you animate the view in several distinct stages.

The property you're animating is the transform. If you've ever taken any matrix math you'll be pleased – or terrified! – to hear that this is an affine transformation matrix. It allows you to do all sorts of funky stuff with the view, such as rotating or shearing it, but the most common use of the transform is for scaling.

The animation consists of several **keyframes**. It will smoothly proceed from one keyframe to the next over a certain amount of time. Because you're animating the view's scale, the different toView.transform values represent how much bigger or smaller the view will be over time.

The animation starts with the view scaled down to 70% (scale 0.7). The next keyframe inflates it to 120% its normal size. After that, it will scale the view down a bit again but not as much as before (only 90% of its original size). The final keyframe ends up with a scale of 1.0, which restores the view to an undistorted shape.

By quickly changing the view size from small to big to small to normal, you create a bounce effect.

You also specify the duration between the successive keyframes. In this case, each transition from one keyframe to the next takes 1/3rd of the total animation time. These times are not in seconds but in fractions of the animation's total duration (0.4 seconds).

Feel free to mess around with the animation code. No doubt you can make it much more spectacular!

To make this animation happen you have to tell the app to use the new animation controller when presenting the Detail pop-up. That happens in the transitioning delegate inside **DetailViewController.swift**.

➤ Inside the `UIViewControllerTransitioningDelegate` extension, add the following method:

```
func animationControllerForPresentedController(
      presented: UIViewController, presentingController presenting: UIViewController,
      sourceController source: UIViewController) -> UIViewControllerAnimatedTransitioning? {
  return BounceAnimationController()
}
```

And that's all you need to do.

➤ Run the app and get ready for some bouncing action!

The pop-up animates

The pop-up looks a lot spiffier with the bounce animation but there are two things that could be better: the `GradientView` still appears abruptly in the background, and the animation on dismissal of the pop-up is very plain.

There's no reason why you cannot have two things animating at the same time, so let's make the `GradientView` fade in while the pop-up bounces into view. That is a job for the presentation controller, because that's what provides the gradient view.

➤ Go to **DimmingPresentationController.swift** and add the following to the bottom of `presentationTransitionWillBegin()`:

```
dimmingView.alpha = 0

if let transitionCoordinator = presentedViewController.transitionCoordinator() {
  transitionCoordinator.animateAlongsideTransition({ _ in
    self.dimmingView.alpha = 1
  }, completion: nil)
}
```

You set the alpha value of the gradient view to 0 to make it completely transparent and then animate it back to 1 (or 100%) and fully visible, resulting in a simple fade-in. That's a bit more subtle than making the gradient appear so abruptly.

The special thing here is the `transitionCoordinator` stuff. This is the UIKit traffic cop in charge of coordinating the presentation controller and animation controllers and everything else that happens when a new view controller is presented.

The important thing to know about the `transitionCoordinator` is that any of your animations should be done in a closure passed to `animateAlongsideTransition()` to keep the transition smooth. If your users wanted choppy animations, they would have bought Android phones!

➤ Also add the method `dismissalTransitionWillBegin()`, which is used to animate the gradient view out of sight when the Detail pop-up is dismissed:

```
override func dismissalTransitionWillBegin()  {
  if let transitionCoordinator = presentedViewController.transitionCoordinator() {
    transitionCoordinator.animateAlongsideTransition({ _ in
      self.dimmingView.alpha = 0
    }, completion: nil)
  }
}
```

This does the inverse: it animates the alpha value back to 0% to make the gradient view fade out.

➤ Run the app. The dimming gradient now appears almost without you even noticing it. Slick!

Let's add one more quick animation because this stuff is just too much fun. ☺

After tapping the Close button the pop-up slides off the screen, like modal screens always do. Let's make this a bit more exciting and make it slide up instead of down. For that you need another animation controller.

➤ Add a new **Swift File** to the project, named **SlideOutAnimationController**.

➤ Replace the new file with:

```
import UIKit

class SlideOutAnimationController: NSObject, UIViewControllerAnimatedTransitioning {
  func transitionDuration(transitionContext: UIViewControllerContextTransitioning)
                        -> NSTimeInterval {
    return 0.3
  }

  func animateTransition(transitionContext: UIViewControllerContextTransitioning) {
    if let fromView = transitionContext.viewForKey(UITransitionContextFromViewKey) {
      let duration = transitionDuration(transitionContext)
      let containerView = transitionContext.containerView()

      UIView.animateWithDuration(duration, animations: {
        fromView.center.y -= containerView.bounds.size.height
        fromView.transform = CGAffineTransformMakeScale(0.5, 0.5)
      }, completion: { finished in
        transitionContext.completeTransition(finished)
      })
    }
  }
}
```

This is pretty much the same as the other animation controller, except that the animation itself is different. Inside the animation block you subtract the height of the screen from the view's center position while simultaneously zooming it out to 50% of its original size, making the Detail screen fly up-up-and-away.

> In **DetailViewController.swift,** add the following method to the
UIViewControllerTransitioningDelegate extension:

```
func animationControllerForDismissedController(dismissed: UIViewController)
                                  -> UIViewControllerAnimatedTransitioning? {
  return SlideOutAnimationController()
}
```

> Run the app and try it out. That looks pretty sweet if you ask me!

> If you're happy with the way the animation looks, then commit your changes.

You can find the project files for the app up to this point under **06 - Detail Pop-up** in the tutorial's Source Code folder.

Exercise. Create some exciting new animations. I'm sure you can improve on mine. Hint: use the transform matrix to add some rotation into the mix. ∎

Fun with landscape

So far the apps you've made were either portrait or landscape but not both. Let's change the app so that it shows a completely different user interface when you flip the device over. When you're done, the app will look like this:

The app looks completely different in landscape orientation

The landscape screen shows just the artwork for the search results. Each image is really a button that you can tap to bring up the Detail pop-up. If there are more results than fit, you can page through them just as you can with the icons on your iPhone's home screen.

The to-do list for this section is:

• Create a new view controller and show that when the device is rotated. Hide this view controller when the device returns to the portrait orientation.

• Put some fake buttons in a UIScrollView, in order to learn how to use scroll views.

• Add the paging control (the dots at the bottom) so you can page through the contents of the scroll view.

• Put the artwork images on the buttons. You will have to download these images from the iTunes server.

• When the user taps a button, show the Detail pop-up.

Let's begin by creating a very simple view controller that shows just a text label.

➤ Add a new file to the project using the **Cocoa Touch Class** template. Name it **LandscapeViewController** and make it a subclass of **UIViewController**.

➤ In Interface Builder, drag a new **View Controller** into the canvas; put it below the Search View Controller.

Even though this view controller will only be used in landscape orientation, you'll still design for the square canvas. If you wanted to, you could change the size and orientation of this view controller under Simulated Metrics, but it wouldn't make any difference to how the view controller behaves at runtime.

➤ In the Identity inspector, change the **Class** to **LandscapeViewController**. Also type this into the **Storyboard ID** field.

Giving the view controller an ID

There will be no segue to this view controller. You'll instantiate this view controller programmatically when you detect a device rotation, and for that it needs to have an ID so you can look it up in the storyboard.

➤ Change the **Background** of the view to **Black Color**.

➤ Drag a new **Label** into the scene and give it some text. You're just using this label to verify that the new view controller shows up in the correct orientation.

➤ Use the Align menu to make horizontal and vertical centering constraints for the label.

Your design should look something like the following image:

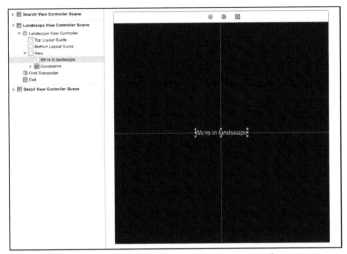

Initial design for the landscape view controller

As you know by now, view controllers have a bunch of methods that are invoked by UIKit at given times, such as viewDidLoad(), viewWillAppear(), and so on. There is also a method that is invoked when the device is flipped over. You can override this method to show (and hide) the new LandscapeViewController.

➤ Add the following method to **SearchViewController.swift**:

```
override func willTransitionToTraitCollection(newCollection: UITraitCollection,
            withTransitionCoordinator coordinator: UIViewControllerTransitionCoordinator) {
  super.willTransitionToTraitCollection(newCollection,
                                    withTransitionCoordinator: coordinator)

  switch newCollection.verticalSizeClass {
  case .Compact:
    showLandscapeViewWithCoordinator(coordinator)
  case .Regular, .Unspecified:
    hideLandscapeViewWithCoordinator(coordinator)
  }
}
```

This method isn't just invoked on device rotations but any time the **trait collection** for the view controller changes. So what is a trait collection? It is, um, a collection of **traits,** where a trait can be:

• the horizontal size class

• the vertical size class

• the display scale (is this a Retina screen or not?)

• the user interface idiom (is this an iPhone or iPad?)

Whenever one or more of these traits change, for whatever reason, UIKit calls willTransitionToTraitCollection(withTransitionCoordinator) to give the view controller a chance to adapt to the new traits.

I mentioned that size classes allow you to design a single storyboard that can be used on both the iPhone and iPad, but what exactly are size classes? Well, there's two of them, a horizontal one and a vertical one, and each can have two values: Compact or Regular.

The combination of these four things creates the following possibilities:

Horizontal and vertical size classes

When an iPhone app is in portrait orientation, the horizontal size class is Compact and the vertical size class is Regular.

Upon a rotation to landscape, the vertical size class changes to Compact.

What you may not have expected is that the horizontal size class doesn't change and stays Compact in both portrait and landscape orientations – except on the iPhone 6 Plus, that is.

In landscape, the horizontal size class on the 6 Plus is Regular. That's because the larger dimensions of the iPhone 6 Plus can fit a split screen in landscape mode, like the iPad (something you'll see later on).

What this boils down to is that to detect an iPhone rotation, you just have to look at how the vertical size class changed. That's exactly what the switch statement does:

```
switch newCollection.verticalSizeClass {
case .Compact:
  showLandscapeViewWithCoordinator(coordinator)
case .Regular, .Unspecified:
  hideLandscapeViewWithCoordinator(coordinator)
}
```

If the new vertical size class is .Compact the device got flipped to landscape and you show the LandscapeViewController. But if the new size class is .Regular, the app is back in portrait and you hide the landscape view again.

The reason the second case statement also checks .Unspecified is because switch statements must always be exhaustive and have cases for all the possible values; .Unspecified shouldn't happen but just in case it does, you also hide the landscape view. This is another example of defensive programming.

Just to keep things readable, the actual showing and hiding happens in methods of their own. You will add these next.

> **Note:** Prior to iOS 8, you'd detect device rotations by overriding the method `willRotateToInterfaceOrientation(duration)`. That method is now *deprecated* and will not be called anymore by iOS. From now on you're supposed to use the new trait collection stuff instead.

In the early years of iOS it was tricky to put more than one view controller on the same screen. The motto used to be: one screen, one view controller. However, on devices with larger screens such as the iPad that became inconvenient – you often want one area of the screen to be controlled by one view controller and a second area by its own view controller – so now view controllers are allowed to be part of other view controllers if you follow a few rules.

This is called *view controller containment*. These APIs are not limited to just the iPad; you can take advantage of them on the iPhone as well. These days a view controller is no longer expected to manage a screenful of content, but manages a "self-contained presentation unit", whatever that may be for your app.

You're going to use view controller containment for the `LandscapeViewController`.

It would be perfectly possible to make a modal segue to this scene and use your own presentation and animation controllers for the transition. But you've already done that and it's more fun to play with something new. Besides, it's useful to learn about containment and child view controllers.

➤ Add an instance variable to **SearchViewController.swift**:

```
var landscapeViewController: LandscapeViewController?
```

This is an optional because there will only be an active `LandscapeViewController` instance if the phone is in landscape orientation. In portrait this will be `nil`.

➤ Add the following method:

```
func showLandscapeViewWithCoordinator(coordinator: UIViewControllerTransitionCoordinator) {
  // 1
  precondition(landscapeViewController == nil)
  // 2
  landscapeViewController = storyboard!.instantiateViewControllerWithIdentifier(
                            "LandscapeViewController") as? LandscapeViewController
  if let controller = landscapeViewController {
    // 3
    controller.view.frame = view.bounds
    // 4
    view.addSubview(controller.view)
    addChildViewController(controller)
    controller.didMoveToParentViewController(self)
  }
}
```

You don't call `presentViewController(animated, completion)` to show the new `LandscapeViewController` as a modal screen, nor did you make a segue. Instead, you add it as a *child* view controller of `SearchViewController`.

Here's how it works, step-by-step:

1. It should never happen that the app instantiates a second landscape view when you're already looking at one. The *pre-condition* that `landscapeViewController` is still `nil` codifies this

requirement and drops the app into the debugger if it turns out that this condition doesn't hold.

If the assumptions that your code makes aren't valid, you definitely want to find out about them during testing; precondition() and assert() are how you document and test for these assumptions. (The difference is that asserts are disabled in the final App Store build of the app but preconditions aren't.)

2. Find the scene with the ID "LandscapeViewController" in the storyboard and instantiate it. Because you don't have a segue you need to do this manually.

The landscapeViewController instance variable is an optional so you need to unwrap it before you can continue.

3. Set the size and position of the new view controller. This makes the landscape view just as big as the SearchViewController, covering the entire screen.

The frame is the rectangle that describes the view's position and size in terms of its superview. To move a view to its final position and size you usually set its frame. The bounds is also a rectangle but seen from the inside of the view.

Because SearchViewController's view is the superview here, the frame of the landscape view must be made equal to the SearchViewController's bounds.

4. These are the minimum required steps to add the contents of one view controller to another, in this order:

   a. First, add the landscape controller's view as a subview. This places it on top of the table view, search bar and segmented control.

   b. Then tell the SearchViewController that the LandscapeViewController is now managing that part of the screen, using addChildViewController(). If you forget this step then the new view controller may not always work correctly.

   c. Tell the new view controller that it now has a parent view controller with didMoveToParentViewController().

In this new arrangement, SearchViewController is the "parent" view controller, and LandscapeViewController is the "child". In other words, the Landscape screen is embedded inside the SearchViewController.

Note: Even though it appears on top, the Landscape screen is not presented modally. It is "contained" in its parent view controller, and therefore owned and managed by it, not independent like a modal screen. This is an important distinction.

View controller containment is also used for navigation and tab bar controllers where the UINavigationController and UITabBarController "wrap around" their child view controllers.

Usually when you want to show a view controller that takes over the whole screen you'd use a modal segue. But when you want just a portion of the screen to be managed by its own view controller you'd make it a child view controller.

One of the reasons you're not using a modal segue for the Landscape screen in this app, even though it is a full-screen view controller, is that the Detail pop-up already is modally presented and this could potentially cause conflicts. Besides, I wanted to show you a fun alternative to modal segues.

➤ To get the app to compile, add an empty implementation of the "hide" method:

```
func hideLandscapeViewWithCoordinator(coordinator: UIViewControllerTransitionCoordinator) {
}
```

By the way, the transition coordinator parameter is needed for doing animations, which you'll add soon.

➤ Try it out! Run the app, do a search and flip over your iPhone or the Simulator to landscape.

We're in landscape

The Simulator after flipping to landscape

Remember: to rotate the Simulator, press ⌘ and the arrow keys. It's possible that the Simulator won't flip over right away – it can be buggy like that. When that happens, press ⌘+**arrow key** a few more times.

This is not doing any animation yet. As always, first get it to work and only then make it look pretty.

If you don't do a search first before rotating to landscape, the keyboard remains visible. You'll fix that shortly. In the mean time you can press ⌘+K to hide the keyboard manually.

Note: It is possible to trip the precondition and break into the debugger by rotating from landscape to portrait and back to landscape. Run the app and flip to landscape with ⌘-Left. Then press ⌘-Right to return to portrait. Now press ⌘-Left again. Whoops. This problem will go away once you've added the code to hide the landscape view.

Flipping back to portrait doesn't work yet but that's easily fixed.

➤ Implement the method that will hide the landscape view controller:

```
func hideLandscapeViewWithCoordinator(coordinator: UIViewControllerTransitionCoordinator) {
  if let controller = landscapeViewController {
    controller.willMoveToParentViewController(nil)
    controller.view.removeFromSuperview()
    controller.removeFromParentViewController()
    landscapeViewController = nil
  }
}
```

This is essentially the inverse of what you did to embed the view controller.

First you call `willMoveToParentViewController()` to tell the view controller that it is leaving the view controller hierarchy (it no longer has a parent), then you remove its view from the screen, and finally you call `removeFromParentViewController()` to truly dispose of the view controller.

You also set the instance variable to `nil` in order to remove the last strong reference to the `LandscapeViewController` object now that you're done with it.

➤ Run the app. Flipping back to portrait should remove the black landscape view again.

Whenever I write a new view controller, I like to put an `println()` in its `deinit` method just to make sure the object is properly deallocated when the screen closes.

➤ Add a `deinit` method to **LandscapeViewController.swift**:

```
deinit {
  println("deinit \(self)")
}
```

➤ Run the app and verify that `deinit` method is indeed being called after rotating back to portrait.

The transition to the landscape view is a bit abrupt. I don't want to go overboard with animations here as the screen is already doing a rotating animation. A simple crossfade will be sufficient.

➤ Change the `showLandscapeViewWithCoordinator()` method to:

```
func showLandscapeViewWithCoordinator(coordinator: UIViewControllerTransitionCoordinator) {
  precondition(landscapeViewController == nil)

  landscapeViewController = . . .
  if let controller = landscapeViewController {
    controller.view.frame = view.bounds
    controller.view.alpha = 0

    view.addSubview(controller.view)
    addChildViewController(controller)

    coordinator.animateAlongsideTransition({ _ in
      controller.view.alpha = 1
    }, completion: { _ in
      controller.didMoveToParentViewController(self)
    })
  }
}
```

You're still doing the same things as before, except now the landscape view starts out completely see-through (`alpha = 0`) and slowly fades in while the rotation takes place until it's fully visible (`alpha = 1`).

Now you see why the `UIViewControllerTransitionCoordinator` object is needed, so your animation can be performed alongside the rest of the transition from the old traits to the new. This ensures the animations run as smoothly as possible.

The call to `animateAlongsideTransition()` takes two closures: the first is for the animation itself, the second is a "completion handler" that gets called after the animation finishes. The completion handler gives you a chance to delay the call to `didMoveToParentViewController()` until the animation is over.

Both closures take a "transition coordinator context" parameter (the same context that animation controllers get) but it's not very interesting here and you use the _ wildcard to ignore it.

> **Note:** You don't have to write `self.controller` inside these closures because `controller` is not an instance variable. It is a local constant that is valid only inside the `if let` statement. `self` is used to refer to instance variables and methods, or the view controller object itself, but is never used for locals.

➤ Make likewise changes to `hideLandscapeViewWithCoordinator()`:

```
func hideLandscapeViewWithCoordinator(coordinator: UIViewControllerTransitionCoordinator) {
  if let controller = landscapeViewController {
    controller.willMoveToParentViewController(nil)

    coordinator.animateAlongsideTransition({ _ in
      controller.view.alpha = 0
    }, completion: { _ in
      controller.view.removeFromSuperview()
      controller.removeFromParentViewController()
      self.landscapeViewController = nil
    })
  }
}
```

This time you fade out the view (back to `alpha` = 0). You don't remove the view and the controller until the animation is completely done.

➤ Try it out. The transition between the portrait and landscape views should be a lot smoother now.

The transition from portrait to landscape

Tip: To see the transition animation in slow motion, select **Debug → Toggle Slow Animations in Frontmost App** from the Simulator menu bar.

> **Note:** The order of operations for removing a child view controller is exactly the other way around from adding a child view controller, except for the calls to `willMove-` and `didMoveToParentViewController()`.
>
> The rules for view controller containment say that when adding a child view controller, the last step is to call `didMoveToParentViewController()`. UIKit does not know when to call this method, as that needs to happen after any of your animations. You are responsible for sending the "did move to parent" message to the child view controller once the animation completes.
>
> There is also a `willMoveToParentViewController()` but that gets called on your behalf by `addChildViewController()` already, so you're not supposed to do that yourself.

The rules are opposite when removing the child controller. First you should call `willMoveToParentViewController(nil)` to let the child view controller know that it's about to be removed from its parent. The child view controller shouldn't actually be removed until the animation completes, at which point you call `removeFromParentViewController()`. That method will then take care of sending the "did move to parent" message.

You can find these rules in the API documentation for `UIViewController`.

Hiding the keyboard and pop-up

There are two more small tweaks to make. Maybe you already noticed that when rotating the app while the keyboard is showing, the keyboard doesn't go away.

The keyboard is still showing in landscape mode

Exercise. See if you can fix that yourself. ∎

Answer: You've done something similar already after the user taps the Search button. The code is exactly the same here.

➤ Add the following line to `showLandscapeViewWithCoordinator()`:

```
func showLandscapeViewWithCoordinator(coordinator: UIViewControllerTransitionCoordinator) {
    . . .
    coordinator.animateAlongsideTransition({ _ in
        controller.view.alpha = 1
        self.searchBar.resignFirstResponder()
    }, completion: { _ in
        . . .
    })
  }
}
```

Now the keyboard disappears as soon as you flip the device. I found it looks best if you call `resignFirstResponder()` inside the animate-alongside-transition closure. After all, hiding the keyboard also happens with an animation.

Speaking of things that stay visible, what happens when you tap a row in the table view and then rotate to landscape? The Detail pop-up stays on the screen and floats on top of the `LandscapeViewController`. I find that a little strange. It would be better if the app dismissed the pop-up before rotating.

Exercise. See if you can fix that one. ∎

Answer: The Detail pop-up is presented modally with a segue, so you can call `dismissViewControllerAnimated(completion)` to dismiss it, just like you do in the `close()` action method.

There's a complication: you should only dismiss the Detail screen when it is actually visible. For that you can look at the `presentedViewController` property. This returns a reference to the current modal view controller, if any. If `presentedViewController` is `nil` there isn't anything to dismiss.

➤ Add the following code inside the `animateAlongsideTransition()` closure in `showLandscapeViewWithCoordinator()`:

```
if self.presentedViewController != nil {
  self.dismissViewControllerAnimated(true, completion: nil)
}
```

➤ Run the app and tap on a search result, then flip to landscape. The pop-up should now fly off the screen. When you return to portrait, the pop-up is nowhere to be seen.

If you look really carefully while the screen rotates, you can see a glitch at the right side of the screen. The gradient view doesn't appear to stretch to fill up the extra space:

There is a gap next to the gradient view

(Press ⌘+T to turn on slow animations in the Simulator so you can clearly see this happening.)

It's only a small detail but we can't have such imperfections in our apps!

The solution is to pin the `GradientView` to the edges of the window so that it will always stretch along with it. But you didn't create `GradientView` in Interface Builder… so how do you give it constraints?

It is possible to create constraints in code, using the `NSLayoutConstraint` class, but there is an easier solution: you can simply change the `GradientView`'s **autoresizing** behavior.

Autoresizing is what iOS developers used before Auto Layout existed. It's simpler to use but also less powerful. You've already used autoresizing in the MyLocations app where you enabled or disabled the different "springs and struts" for your views in Interface Builder. It's very easy to do the same thing from code.

Using the `autoresizingMask` property you can tell a view what it should do when its superview changes size. You have a variety of options, such as: do nothing, stick to a certain edge of the superview, or change in size proportionally.

The possibilities are much more limited than what you can do with Auto Layout, but for many scenarios autoresizing is good enough.

The easiest place to set this autoresizing mask is in `GradientView`'s init methods.

➤ Add the following line to `init(frame)` and `init(coder)` in **GradientView.swift**:

```
autoresizingMask = .FlexibleWidth | .FlexibleHeight
```

This tells the view that it should change both its width and its height proportionally when the superview it belongs to resizes (due to being rotated or otherwise).

In practice this means the `GradientView` will always cover the same area that its superview covers and there should be no more gaps, even if the device gets rotated.

➤ Try it out! The gradient now always covers the whole screen.

Option sets and bitmasks

When setting the `autoresizingMask` property you combined two values, `.FlexibleWidth` and `.FlexibleHeight`. The notation for that is the `|` operator. This is also known as a **bitwise or** (as opposed to a "logical or", which uses two `||`'s).

The symbols `.FlexibleWidth` and `.FlexibleHeight` are part of an **option set** named `UIViewAutoresizing`. An option set is similar to an enum but serves a slightly different purpose.

Recall that an enum is a list of possible values. Instead of using the numeric values 1, 2, 3, 4 and so on you give these numbers symbolic names. Option sets work the same way, except they are really `struct`s, not enums.

With an enum you always choose just one of the values, but with an option set you can combine multiple values using the `|` operator.

The items from an option set also have numbers: `.FlexibleWidth` is 2 and `.FlexibleHeight` is 16. Each of these represents one bit out of a larger 32- or 64-bit word that can be on (true) or off (false).

That's why option sets are also known as *bitmasks*. They are a very efficient way to store multiple boolean values – one per bit – in a single variable. This used to be a big deal when computers were small and slow, but these days bitmasks are going out of fashion as they can be cumbersome to use.

You can think of using the `|` operator as adding two numbers. For example, `.FlexibleWidth | .FlexibleHeight` equals 2 + 16 = 18. I don't know about you, but "autoresizing mask 18" doesn't mean much to me, so I'd rather use the symbolic names.

A better "hide" animation

The animation of the Detail pop-up flying up and out the screen looks a little weird in combination with the rotation animation. There's too much happening on the screen at once, to my taste. Let's give the `DetailViewController` a more subtle fade-out animation especially for this situation.

When you tap the X button to dismiss the pop-up, you'll still make it fly out of the screen. But when it is automatically dismissed upon rotation, the pop-up will fade out with the rest of the table view instead.

Let's give `DetailViewController` a property that that specifies how it will animate the pop-up's dismissal. You can use an enum for this.

➤ Add the following to **DetailViewController.swift**, inside the class:

```swift
enum AnimationStyle {
  case Slide
  case Fade
}

var dismissAnimationStyle = AnimationStyle.Fade
```

This defines a new enum named `AnimationStyle`. It has two values, `Slide` and `Fade`. Those are the animations the Detail pop-up can perform when dismissed.

The `dismissAnimationStyle` variable determines which animation is chosen. This variable is of type `AnimationStyle`, so it can only contain one of the values from that enum. By default it is `.Fade`, the animation used when rotating to landscape.

> **Note:** The full name of the enum is `DetailViewController.AnimationStyle` because it sits inside the `DetailViewController` class.
>
> It's a good idea to keep the things that are closely related to a particular class, such as this enum, inside the definition for that class. That puts them inside the class's *namespace*.
>
> Doing this allows you to also add a completely different `AnimationStyle` enum to one of the other view controllers, without running into naming conflicts.

➤ In the `close()` method set the animation style to `.Slide`, so that this keeps using the animation you're already familiar with:

```swift
@IBAction func close() {
  dismissAnimationStyle = .Slide
  dismissViewControllerAnimated(true, completion: nil)
}
```

➤ In the extension for the transitioning delegate, change the method that vends the animation controller for dismissing the pop-up to the following:

```swift
func animationControllerForDismissedController(dismissed: UIViewController)
                              -> UIViewControllerAnimatedTransitioning? {
  switch dismissAnimationStyle {
  case .Slide:
    return SlideOutAnimationController()
  case .Fade:
    return FadeOutAnimationController()
  }
}
```

Instead of always returning a new `SlideOutAnimationController` instance, it now looks at the value from `dismissAnimationStyle`. If it is `.Fade`, then it returns a new `FadeOutAnimationController` object. You still have to write that class.

➤ Add a new **Swift File** to the project, named **FadeOutAnimationController**.

➤ Replace the source code of that new file with:

```swift
import UIKit

class FadeOutAnimationController: NSObject, UIViewControllerAnimatedTransitioning {
  func transitionDuration(transitionContext: UIViewControllerContextTransitioning)
                          -> NSTimeInterval {
    return 0.4
  }

  func animateTransition(transitionContext: UIViewControllerContextTransitioning) {
    if let fromView = transitionContext.viewForKey(UITransitionContextFromViewKey) {
      let duration = transitionDuration(transitionContext)
      UIView.animateWithDuration(duration, animations: {
        fromView.alpha = 0
      }, completion: { finished in
        transitionContext.completeTransition(finished)
      })
    }
  }
}
```

This is mostly the same as the other animation controllers. The actual animation simply sets the view's alpha value to 0 in order to fade it out.

➤ Run the app, bring up the Detail pop-up and rotate to landscape. The pop-up should now fade out while the landscape view fades in. (Enable slow animations to clearly see what is going on.)

The pop-up fades out instead of flying away

And that does it. If you wanted to create more animations that can be used on dismissal, you only have to add a new value to the AnimationStyle enum and check for it in the animationControllerForDismissedController() method. And build a new animation controller, of course.

That concludes the first version of the landscape screen. It doesn't do much yet, but it's already well integrated with the rest of the app. That's worthy of a commit, methinks.

Adding the scroll view

If an app has more to show than can fit on the screen, you can use a **scroll view**, which allows the user to drag the content up and down or left and right.

You've already been working with scroll views all this time without knowing it: the UITableView object extends from UIScrollView.

In this section you're going to use a scroll view of your own, in combination with a **paging control,** so you can show the artwork for all the search results even if there are more images than fit on the screen at once.

> Open the storyboard and delete the label from the Landscape View Controller.

> Now drag a new **Scroll View** into the scene. Make it as big as the screen (600 by 600 points).

> Drag a new **Page Control** object into the scene (make sure you pick Page Control and *not* Page View Controller).

This gives you a small view with three white dots. Place it bottom center. The exact location doesn't matter because you'll move it to the right position later.

Important: Do not place the Page Control *inside* the Scroll View. They should be at the same level in the view hierarchy:

The Page Control should be a "sibling" of the Scroll View, not a child

If you did drop your Page Control inside the Scroll View instead of on top, then you can rearrange them inside the document pane.

That concludes the design of the landscape screen. The rest you will do in code, not in Interface Builder.

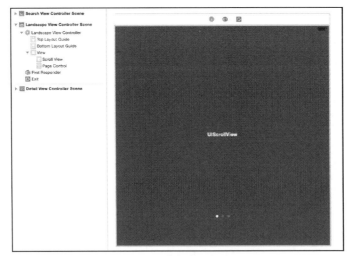

The final design of the landscape scene

The other view controllers all employ Auto Layout to resize them to the dimensions of the user's device, but here you're going to take a different approach. Instead of pinning the Scroll View to the sides of the scene, you'll disable Auto Layout for this view controller and do the entire layout programmatically. So you don't need to pin anything in the storyboard.

You do need to hook up these controls to outlets, of course.

> Add these outlets to **LandscapeViewController.swift**, and connect them in Interface Builder:

```
@IBOutlet weak var scrollView: UIScrollView!
@IBOutlet weak var pageControl: UIPageControl!
```

Next up you'll disable Auto Layout for this view controller. The storyboard has a "Use Auto Layout" checkbox but you cannot use that. It would turn off Auto Layout for *all* the view controllers, not just this one.

> Replace **LandscapeViewController.swift**'s viewDidLoad() method with:

```
override func viewDidLoad() {
  super.viewDidLoad()

  view.removeConstraints(view.constraints())
  view.setTranslatesAutoresizingMaskIntoConstraints(true)

  pageControl.removeConstraints(pageControl.constraints())
  pageControl.setTranslatesAutoresizingMaskIntoConstraints(true)

  scrollView.removeConstraints(scrollView.constraints())
  scrollView.setTranslatesAutoresizingMaskIntoConstraints(true)
}
```

Remember how, if you don't add make constraints of your own, Interface Builder will give the views automatic constraints? Well, those automatic constraints get in the way if you're going to do your own layout. That's why you need to remove these unwanted constraints from the main view, pageControl, and scrollView first.

You also call setTranslatesAutoresizingMaskIntoConstraints(true). That allows you to position and size your views manually by changing their frame property.

When Auto Layout is enabled, you're not supposed to change the frame yourself – you can only indirectly move views into position by creating constraints. Modifying the frame by hand will cause conflicts with the existing constraints and bring all sorts of trouble (you don't want to make Auto Layout angry!).

For this view controller it's much more convenient to manipulate the frame property directly than it is making constraints (especially when you're placing the buttons for the search results), which is why you're disabling Auto Layout.

> **Note:** Auto Layout doesn't really get disabled, but with the "translates autoresizing mask" option set to true, UIKit will convert your manual layout code into the proper constraints behind the scenes. That's also why you removed the automatic constraints because they will conflict with the new ones, causing your app to crash.

Now that Auto Layout is out of the way, you can do your own layout. That happens in the method viewWillLayoutSubviews().

➤ Add this new method:

```
override func viewWillLayoutSubviews() {
  super.viewWillLayoutSubviews()

  scrollView.frame = view.bounds

  pageControl.frame = CGRect(x: 0, y: view.frame.size.height - pageControl.frame.size.height,
                   width: view.frame.size.width, height: pageControl.frame.size.height)
}
```

The scroll view should always be as large as the entire screen, so you make its frame equal to the main view's bounds.

The page control is located at the bottom of the screen, and spans the width of the screen. If this calculation doesn't make any sense to you, then try to sketch what happens on a piece of paper. It's what I usually do when writing my own layout code.

> **Note:** Remember that the bounds describe the rectangle that makes up the inside of a view, while the frame describes the outside of the view.
>
> The scroll view's frame is the rectangle seen from the perspective of the main view, while the scroll view's bounds is the same rectangle from the perspective of the scroll view itself.
>
> Because the scroll view and page control are both children of the main view, their frames sit in the same *coordinate space* as the bounds of the main view.

➤ Run the app and flip to landscape. Nothing much happens yet: the screen has the page control at the bottom (the dots) but it still mostly black.

For the scroll view to do anything you have to add some content to it.

➤ Add the following lines to viewDidLoad():

```
scrollView.backgroundColor = UIColor(patternImage: UIImage(named: "LandscapeBackground")!)
```

This puts an image on the scroll view's background so you can actually see something happening when you scroll through it.

An image? But you're setting the backgroundColor property, which is a UIColor, not a UIImage?! Yup, that's true, but UIColor has a cool trick that lets you use a tile-able image for a color.

If you take a peek at the **LandscapeBackground** image in the asset catalog you'll see that it is a small square. By setting this image as a pattern image on the background you get a repeatable image that fills the whole screen. You can use tile-able images anywhere you can use a UIColor.

Exercise: Why is the ! needed behind the call to UIImage(named: ...)? ■

Answer: UIImage(named) is a failable initializer and therefore returns an optional. Before you can use it as an actual UIImage object you need to unwrap it somehow. Here you know that the image will always exist so you can force unwrap with !.

➤ Also add the following line to viewDidLoad():

```
scrollView.contentSize = CGSize(width: 1000, height: 1000)
```

It is very important when dealing with scroll views that you set the contentSize property. This tells the scroll view how big its insides are. You don't change the frame (or bounds) of the scroll view if you want its insides to be bigger, you set the contentSize property instead.

People often forget this step and then they wonder why their scroll view doesn't scroll. Unfortunately, you cannot set contentSize from Interface Builder, so it must be done from code.

➤ Run the app and try some scrolling:

The scroll view now has a background image and it can scroll

If the dots at the bottom also move while scrolling, then you placed the page control inside the scroll view. Open the storyboard and in the outline pane drag Page Control below Scroll View instead.

The page control itself doesn't do anything yet. Before you can make that work, you first have to add some content to the scroll view.

Adding buttons for the search results

The idea is to show the search results in a grid:

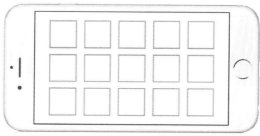

Each of these results is really a button. Before you can place these buttons on the screen, you need to calculate how many will fit on the screen at once. Easier said than done, because different iPhone models have different screen sizes.

Time for some math! Let's assume the app runs on a 3.5-inch device. In that case the scroll view is 480 points wide by 320 points tall. It can fit 3 rows of 5 columns if you put each search result in a rectangle of 96 by 88 points.

That comes to 3×5 = 15 search results on the screen at once. A search may return up to 200 results, so obviously there is not enough room for everything and you will have to spread out the results over several pages.

One page contains 15 buttons. For the maximum number of results you will need 200 / 15 = 13.3333 pages, which rounds up to 14 pages. That last page will only be filled for one-third with results.

The arithmetic for a 4-inch device is similar. Because the screen is wider – 568 instead of 480 points – it has room for an extra column, but only if you shrink each rectangle to 94 points instead of 96. That also leaves 568 – 94×6 = 4 points to spare.

The 4.7-inch iPhone 6 has room for 7 columns plus some leftover vertical space, and the 5.5-inch iPhone 6 Plus can fit yet another column plus an extra row.

That's a lot of different possibilities!

You need to put all of this into an algorithm in LandscapeViewController so it can calculate how big the scroll view's contentSize has to be. It will also need to add a UIButton object for each search result.

Once you have that working, you can put the artwork image inside that UIButton.

Of course, this means the app first needs to give the array of search results to LandscapeViewController so it can use them for its calculations.

> Let's add a property for this, in **LandscapeViewController.swift**:

```
var searchResults = [SearchResult]()
```

Initially this has an empty array. SearchViewController gives it the real array upon rotation to landscape.

> Assign the array to the new property in **SearchViewController.swift**:

```
func showLandscapeViewWithCoordinator(coordinator: UIViewControllerTransitionCoordinator) {
  precondition(landscapeViewController == nil)

  landscapeViewController = . . .
  if let controller = landscapeViewController {
    controller.searchResults = searchResults
    controller.view.frame = view.bounds
    . . .
```

You have to be sure to fill up searchResults before you access the view property from the LandscapeViewController, because that will trigger the view to be loaded and performs viewDidLoad().

The view controller will be reading from the searchResults array in viewDidLoad() to build up the contents of its scroll view. But if you access controller.view before setting searchResults, this property will still be nil and there is nothing to make buttons for. The order in which you do things matters!

> Switch back to **LandscapeViewController.swift**. From viewDidLoad() remove the line that sets scrollView.contentSize. That was just for testing.

Now let's go make those buttons.

➤ Add a new instance variable:

```
private var firstTime = true
```

The purpose for this variable will become clear in a moment. You need to initialize it with the value `true`.

> **Private parts**
>
> You are declaring this instance variable as `private`. `firstTime` is an internal piece of state that only `LandscapeViewController` cares about. It should not be visible to other objects.
>
> You don't want the other objects in your app to know about the existence of `firstTime`, or worse, actually try to use this variable. Strange things are bound to happen if some other view controller changes the value of `firstTime` while `LandscapeViewController` doesn't expect that.
>
> We haven't talked much about the distinction between *interface* and *implementation* yet, but what an object shows on the outside is different from what it has on the inside. That's done on purpose because its internals – the so-called implementation details – are not interesting to anyone else, and are often even dangerous to expose (as in, messing around with them can crash the app).
>
> It is considered good programming practice to hide as much as possible inside the object and only show a few things on the outside. The `firstTime` variable is only important to the insides of `LandscapeViewController`. Therefore it should not be part of its public interface, i.e. what other objects see when they look at `LandscapeViewController`.
>
> To make certain variables and methods visible only inside your own class, you declare them to be `private`. That removes them from the object's interface.
>
> **Exercise:** Find other variables and methods in the app that can be made `private`. ∎

➤ Add the following lines to the bottom of `viewWillLayoutSubviews()`:

```
if firstTime {
  firstTime = false
  tileButtons(searchResults)
}
```

This calls a new method, `tileButtons()`, that performs the math and places the buttons on the screen in neat rows and columns. This needs to happen just once, when the `LandscapeViewController` is added to the screen.

You may think that `viewDidLoad()` would be a good place for that, but at the point in the view controller's lifecycle when `viewDidLoad()` is called, the view is not added into the view hierarchy yet. At this time it doesn't know how large it should be. Only after `viewDidLoad()` is done does the view get resized to fit the actual screen.

The only safe place to perform calculations based on the final size of the view – any calculations that use the view's frame or bounds – is in `viewWillLayoutSubviews()`.

However, that method may be invoked more than once; for example, when the landscape view gets removed from the screen again. You use the `firstTime` variable to make sure you only place the buttons once.

➤ Add the new `tileButtons()` method. It's a whopper, so we'll take it piece-by-piece.

```
private func tileButtons(searchResults: [SearchResult]) {
  var columnsPerPage = 5
  var rowsPerPage = 3
  var itemWidth: CGFloat = 96
  var itemHeight: CGFloat = 88
  var marginX: CGFloat = 0
  var marginY: CGFloat = 20

  let scrollViewWidth = scrollView.bounds.size.width

  switch scrollViewWidth {
  case 568:
    columnsPerPage = 6
    itemWidth = 94
    marginX = 2

  case 667:
    columnsPerPage = 7
    itemWidth = 95
    itemHeight = 98
    marginX = 1
    marginY = 29

  case 736:
    columnsPerPage = 8
    rowsPerPage = 4
    itemWidth = 92

  default:
    break
  }

  // TODO: more to come here
}
```

First, the method must decide on how big the grid squares will be and how many squares you need to fill up each page. There are four cases to consider, based on the width of the screen:

- **480 points**, 3.5-inch device (iPhone 4S). A single page fits 3 rows (`rowsPerPage`) of 5 columns (`columnsPerPage`). Each grid square is 96 by 88 points (`itemWidth` and `itemHeight`). The first row starts at Y = 20 (`marginY`).

- **568 points**, 4-inch device (all iPhone 5 models). This has 3 rows of 6 columns. To make it fit, each grid square is now only 94 points wide. Because 568 doesn't evenly divide by 6, the `marginX` variable is used to adjust for the 4 points that are left over (2 on each side of the page).

- **667 points**, 4.7-inch device (iPhone 6). This still has 3 rows but 7 columns. Because there's some extra vertical space, the rows are higher (98 points) and there is a larger margin at the top.

- **736 points**, 5.5-inch device (iPhone 6 Plus). This device is huge and can house 4 rows of 8 columns.

The variables at the top of the method keep track of all these measurements.

> **Note:** Wouldn't it be possible to come up with some formula that calculates all this stuff for you, rather than *hard-coding* these sizes and margin values? Probably, but it won't be easy.

There are two things you want to optimize for: getting the maximum number of rows and columns on the screen, but at the same time not making the grid squares too small. Give it a shot if you think you can solve this puzzle! (Let me know if you do – I might put your solution in the next book update.)

➤ Add the following lines to the method:

```
let buttonWidth: CGFloat = 82
let buttonHeight: CGFloat = 82
let paddingHorz = (itemWidth - buttonWidth)/2
let paddingVert = (itemHeight - buttonHeight)/2
```

You already determined that each search result gets a grid square of give-or-take 96 by 88 points (depending on the device), but that doesn't mean you need to make the buttons that big as well.

The image you'll put on the buttons is 60×60 pixels, so that leaves quite a gap around the image. After playing with the design a bit, I decided that the buttons will be 82×82 points (buttonWidth and buttonHeight), leaving a small amount of padding between each button and its neighbors (paddingHorz and paddingVert).

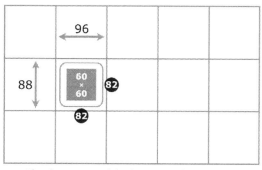

The dimensions of the buttons in the 5x3 grid

Now you can loop through the array of search results and make a new button for each SearchResult object.

➤ Add the following lines:

```
var row = 0
var column = 0
var x = marginX
// 1
for (index, searchResult) in enumerate(searchResults) {
  // 2
  let button = UIButton.buttonWithType(.System) as! UIButton
  button.backgroundColor = UIColor.whiteColor()
  button.setTitle("\(index)", forState: .Normal)
  // 3
  button.frame = CGRect(x: x + paddingHorz,
                        y: marginY + CGFloat(row)*itemHeight + paddingVert,
                        width: buttonWidth, height: buttonHeight)
  // 4
  scrollView.addSubview(button)
  // 5
  ++row
  if row == rowsPerPage {
    row = 0
```

```
    ++column
    x += itemWidth

    if column == columnsPerPage {
      column = 0
      x += marginX * 2
    }
  }
}
```

Here is how this works:

1. The `for in` loop steps through the `SearchResult` objects from the array, but with a twist. By doing `for in enumerate(…)`, you get a *tuple* containing not only the next `SearchResult` object but also its index in the array. Recall that a tuple is nothing more than a temporary list with two or more items in it. This is a neat trick to loop through an array and get both the objects and their indices.

2. Create the `UIButton` object. For debugging purposes you give each button a title with the array index. If there are 200 results in the search, you also should end up with 200 buttons. Setting the index on the button will help to verify this.

3. When you make a button by hand you always have to set its `frame`. Using the measurements you figured out earlier, you determine the position and size of the button. Notice that `CGRect`'s fields all have the `CGFloat` type but `row` is an `Int`. You need to convert `row` to a `CGFloat` before you can use it in the calculation.

4. You add the new button object as a subview to the `UIScrollView`. After the first 18 or so buttons (depending on the screen size) this places any subsequent button out of the visible range of the scroll view, but that's the whole point. As long as you set the scroll view's `contentSize` accordingly, the user can scroll to get to those other buttons.

5. You use the `x` and `row` variables to position the buttons, going from top to bottom (by increasing `row`). When you've reached the bottom (`row` equals `rowsPerPage`), you go up again to row 0 and skip to the next column (by increasing the `column` variable).

   When the column reaches the end of the screen (equals `columnsPerPage`), you reset it to 0 and add any leftover space to `x` (twice the X-margin). This only has an effect on 4-inch and 4.7-inch screens; for the others `marginX` is 0.

If this sounds like hocus pocus to you, I suggest you play around a bit with these calculations to gain insight into how they work. It's not rocket science but it does require some mental gymnastics. Tip: Sketching the process on paper can help!

➤ Finally, add the last part of this very long method:

```
let buttonsPerPage = columnsPerPage * rowsPerPage
let numPages = 1 + (searchResults.count - 1) / buttonsPerPage

scrollView.contentSize = CGSize(width: CGFloat(numPages)*scrollViewWidth,
                                height: scrollView.bounds.size.height)

println("Number of pages: \(numPages)")
```

At the end of the method you calculate the `contentSize` for the scroll view based on how many buttons fit on a page and the number of `SearchResult` objects.

You want the user to be able to "page" through these results, rather than simply scroll (a feature that you'll enable shortly) so you should always make the content width a multiple of the screen width (480, 568, 667 or 736 points).

With a simple formula you can then determine how many pages you need.

> **Note:** Dividing an integer value by an integer always results in an integer. If buttonsPerPage is 18 (3 rows × 6 columns) and there are fewer than 18 search results, searchResults.count / buttonsPerPage is 0.
>
> It's important to realize that numPages will never have a fractional value because all the variables involved in the calculation are Ints, which makes numPages an Int too.
>
> That's why the formula is 1 + (searchResults.count − 1) / buttonsPerPage.
>
> If there are 18 results, exactly enough to fill a single page, numPages = 1 + 17/18 = 1 + 0 = 1. But if there are 19 results, the 19th result needs to go on the second page, and numPages = 1 + 18/18 = 1 + 1 = 2. Plug in some other values for yourself to prove this formula is correct.

I also threw in an println() for good measure, so you can verify that you really end up with the right amount of pages.

➤ Run the app, do a search, and flip to landscape. You should now see a whole bunch of buttons:

The landscape view has buttons

Scroll all the way to the right and it looks like this (on the iPhone 5s):

The last page of the search results

That is 200 buttons indeed (you started counting at 0, remember?).

Just to make sure that this logic works properly you should test a few different scenarios. What happens when there are fewer results than 18 (the amount that fit on a single page on the iPhone 5)? What happens when there are exactly 18 search results? How about 19, one more than can go on a single page?

The easiest way to create this situation is to change the &limit parameter in the search URL.

Exercise. Try these situations for yourself and see what happens. ∎

> Also test when there are no search results. The landscape view should now be empty. In a short while you'll add a "Nothing Found" label to this screen as well.

Paging

So far the Page Control at the bottom of the screen has always shown three dots. And there wasn't much paging to be done on the scroll view either.

In case you're wondering what "paging" means: if the user has dragged the scroll view a certain amount, it should snap to a new page.

With paging enabled, you can quickly flick through the contents of a scroll view, without having to drag it all the way. You're no doubt familiar with this effect because it is what the iPhone uses on its springboard. Many other apps use the effect too, such as the Weather app that uses paging to flip between the cards for different cities.

> Go to the **LandscapeViewController** in the storyboard and check the **Paging Enabled** option for the scroll view (in the Attributes inspector).

There, that was easy. Now run the app and the scroll view will let you page rather than scroll. That's cool but you also need to do something with the page control at the bottom.

> Add this line to viewDidLoad():

```
pageControl.numberOfPages = 0
```

This effectively hides the page control, which is what you want to do when there are no search results (yet).

> Add the following lines to the bottom of tileButtons():

```
pageControl.numberOfPages = numPages
pageControl.currentPage = 0
```

This sets the number of dots that the page control displays to the number of pages that you calculated.

The active dot (the white one) still isn't synchronized with the active page in the scroll view; it never changes unless you tap in the page control and even then it has no effect on the scroll view.

You'll have to make the page control talk to the scroll view, and vice versa.

You're going to make the view controller the delegate of the scroll view so it will be notified when the user is flicking through the pages.

> Add the following to the very bottom of **LandscapeViewController.swift**:

```
extension LandscapeViewController: UIScrollViewDelegate {
```

```
func scrollViewDidScroll(scrollView: UIScrollView) {
    let width = scrollView.bounds.size.width
    let currentPage = Int((scrollView.contentOffset.x + width/2) / width)
    pageControl.currentPage = currentPage
  }
}
```

This is one of the UIScrollViewDelegate methods. You figure out what the index of the current page is by looking at the contentOffset property of the scroll view. This property determines how far the scroll view has been scrolled and is updated while you're dragging the scroll view.

Unfortunately, the scroll view doesn't simply tell us, "The user has flipped to page X", and so you have to calculate this yourself. If the content offset gets beyond halfway on the page (width/2), the scroll view will flick to the next page. In that case, you update the pageControl's active page number.

You also need to know when the user taps on the Page Control so you can update the scroll view. There is no delegate for this but you can use a regular @IBAction method.

➤ Add the action method:

```
@IBAction func pageChanged(sender: UIPageControl) {
    scrollView.contentOffset = CGPoint(
      x: scrollView.bounds.size.width * CGFloat(sender.currentPage), y: 0)
}
```

This works the other way around: when the user taps in the Page Control, its currentPage property gets updated. You use that to calculate a new contentOffset for the scroll view.

➤ In the storyboard, **Ctrl-drag** from the Scroll View to Landscape View Controller and select **delegate**.

➤ Also **Ctrl-drag** from the Page Control to the Landscape View Controller and select **pageChanged:** under Sent Events.

➤ Try it out, the page control and the scroll view should now be in sync.

The transition from one page to another after tapping in the page control is still a little abrupt, though. An animation would help here.

Exercise. See if you can animate what happens in pageChanged(). ∎

Answer: You can simply put the above code in an animation block:

```
@IBAction func pageChanged(sender: UIPageControl) {
  UIView.animateWithDuration(0.3, delay: 0, options: .CurveEaseInOut, animations: {
    self.scrollView.contentOffset = CGPoint(
              x: self.scrollView.bounds.size.width * CGFloat(sender.currentPage), y: 0)
  }, completion: nil)
}
```

You're using a version of the UIView animation method that allows you to specify options because the "Ease In, Ease Out" timing (.CurveEaseInOut) looks good here.

We've got paging!

➤ This is a good time to commit.

Downloading artwork on the buttons

First let's give the buttons a nicer look.

➤ Replace the button creation code in `tileButtons()` with:

```
let button = UIButton.buttonWithType(.Custom) as! UIButton
button.setBackgroundImage(UIImage(named: "LandscapeButton"), forState: .Normal)
```

Instead of a regular button you're now making a `.Custom` one, and you're giving it a background image instead of a title.

If you run the app, it will look like this:

The buttons now have a custom background image

Now you will have to download the artwork images (if they haven't been already downloaded and cached yet by the table view) and put them on the buttons.

Problem: You're dealing with UIButtons here, not UIImageViews, so you cannot simply use that handy extension from earlier. Fortunately, the code is very similar!

➤ Add a new method to **LandscapeViewController.swift**:

```
private func downloadImageForSearchResult(searchResult: SearchResult,
                            andPlaceOnButton button: UIButton) {
  if let url = NSURL(string: searchResult.artworkURL60) {
    let session = NSURLSession.sharedSession()
    let downloadTask = session.downloadTaskWithURL(url, completionHandler: {
    [weak button] url, response, error in
```

```
    if error == nil && url != nil {
      if let data = NSData(contentsOfURL: url) {
        if let image = UIImage(data: data) {
          dispatch_async(dispatch_get_main_queue()) {
            if let button = button {
              button.setImage(image, forState: .Normal)
            }
          }
        }
      }
    }
  })
  downloadTask.resume()
  }
}
```

This looks very much like what you did in the UIImageView extension.

First you get an NSURL object with the URL to the 60×60-pixel artwork, and then create a download task. Inside the completion handler you put the downloaded file into a UIImage, and if all that succeeds, use dispatch_async() to place the image on the button.

➤ Add the following line to tileButtons() to call this new method, right after where you create the button:

```
downloadImageForSearchResult(searchResult, andPlaceOnButton: button)
```

And that should do it. Run the app and you'll get some cool-looking buttons:

Showing the artwork on the buttons

It's always a good idea to clean up after yourself, also in programming. Imagine this: what would happen if the app is still downloading images and the user flips back to portrait mode?

The LandscapeViewController is deallocated but the image downloads keep going. That is exactly the sort of situation that can crash your app if you don't handle it properly.

To avoid ownership cycles, you already capture the button with a weak reference. When LandscapeViewController is deallocated, so are the buttons, and the completion handler's captured button reference automatically becomes nil. The if let inside the dispatch_async block will now safely skip button.setImage(forState). No harm done.

However, to conserve resources the app should really stop downloading these images because they end up nowhere. Otherwise it's just wasting bandwidth and battery life, and users don't take too kindly to apps that do.

> Add a new instance variable to LandscapeViewController:

```
private var downloadTasks = [NSURLSessionDownloadTask]()
```

This array keeps track of all the active NSURLSessionDownloadTask objects.

> Add the following line to the bottom of downloadImageForSearchResult(), right after where you resume the download task:

```
downloadTasks.append(downloadTask)
```

> And finally, tell deinit to cancel any operations that are still on the way:

```
deinit {
  println("deinit \(self)")

  for task in downloadTasks {
    task.cancel()
  }
}
```

This will stop the download for any button whose image was still pending or in transit. Good job, partner!

> Commit your changes.

Exercise. Despite what the iTunes web service promises, not all of the artwork is truly 60×60 pixels. Some of it is bigger, some is not even square, and so it might not always fit nicely in the button. Your challenge is to use the image sizing code from MyLocations to always resize the image to 60×60 points before you put it on the button. Note that we're talking points here, not pixels – on Retina devices the image should actually end up being 120×120 or even 180×180 pixels big. ∎

You can find the project files for the app up to this point under **07 - Landscape** in the tutorial's Source Code folder.

> **Note:** In this section you learned how to create a grid-like view using a UIScrollView. iOS comes with a versatile class, UICollectionView, that lets you do the same thing – and much more! – without having to resort to the sort of math you did in tileButtons().
>
> To learn more about UICollectionView, check out the book *iOS 6 by Tutorials* at: www.raywenderlich.com/store

Refactoring the search

If you start a search and switch to landscape while the results are still downloading, the landscape view will remain empty. It would be nice to also show an activity spinner on that screen while the search is taking place. You can reproduce this situation by artificially slowing down your network connection using the Network Link Conditioner tool.

So how can LandscapeViewController tell what state the search is in? Its searchResults array will be empty if no search was done yet, and have zero or more SearchResult objects after a successful search.

Just by looking at the array object you cannot determine whether the search is still going, or whether it has finished but nothing was found. In both cases, the searchResults array will have a count of 0.

You need a way to determine whether the search is still busy. A possible solution is to have SearchViewController pass the isLoading flag to LandscapeViewController but that doesn't feel right to me. This is known as a "code smell", a hint at a deeper problem with the design of the program.

Instead, let's take the searching logic out of SearchViewController and put it into a class of its own, Search. Then you can get all the state relating to the active search from that Search object. Time for some more refactoring!

➤ If you want, create a new branch for this in Git.

This is a pretty invasive change in the code and there is always a risk that it doesn't work as well as you hoped. By making the changes in a new branch, you can commit every once in a while without messing up the master branch. Making new branches in Git is quick and easy, so it's good to get into the habit.

➤ Create a new file using the **Swift File** template. Name it **Search**.

➤ Change the contents of **Search.swift** to:

```swift
import Foundation

class Search {
  var searchResults = [SearchResult]()
  var hasSearched = false
  var isLoading = false

  private var dataTask: NSURLSessionDataTask? = nil

  func performSearchForText(text: String, category: Int) {
    println("Searching...")
  }
}
```

You've given this class three public properties, one private property, and a method. This stuff should look familiar because it comes straight from SearchViewController. You'll be removing code from that class and putting it into this new Search class.

The performSearchForText(category) method doesn't do much yet but that's OK. First I want to make SearchViewController work with this new Search object and when that compiles without errors, you will move all the logic over. Small steps!

Let's make the changes to **SearchViewController.swift**. Xcode will probably give a bunch of errors and warnings while you're making these changes, but it will all work out in the end.

➤ In **SearchViewController.swift**, remove the declarations for the following instance variables:

```swift
var searchResults = [SearchResult]()
var hasSearched = false
var isLoading = false
var dataTask: NSURLSessionDataTask?
```

and replace them with the following one:

```
let search = Search()
```

The new `Search` object not only describes the state and results of the search, it also will have all the logic for talking to the iTunes web service. You can now remove a lot of code from the view controller.

➤ Cut the following methods and paste them into **Search.swift**:

- `urlWithSearchText(category)`
- `parseJSON()`
- `parseDictionary()`
- `parseTrack()`
- `parseAudioBook()`
- `parseSoftware()`
- `parseEBook()`

➤ Make these methods `private`. They are only important to `Search` itself, not to any other classes from the app, so it's good to "hide" them.

➤ Back in **SearchViewController.swift**, replace the `performSearch()` method with:

```
func performSearch() {
  search.performSearchForText(searchBar.text,
                     category: segmentedControl.selectedSegmentIndex)
  tableView.reloadData()
  searchBar.resignFirstResponder()
}
```

This simply makes the `Search` object do all the work. Of course it still reloads the table view (to show the activity spinner) and hides the keyboard.

There are a few places in the code that still use the old `searchResults` array even though that no longer exists. You should change them to use the `searchResults` property from the `Search` object instead. Likewise for `hasSearched` and `isLoading`.

➤ For example, change `tableView(numberOfRowsInSection)` to:

```
func tableView(tableView: UITableView, numberOfRowsInSection section: Int) -> Int {
  if search.isLoading {
    return 1  // Loading...
  } else if !search.hasSearched {
    return 0  // Not searched yet
  } else if search.searchResults.count == 0 {
    return 1  // Nothing Found
  } else {
    return search.searchResults.count
  }
}
```

➤ In `showLandscapeViewWithCoordinator()`, change the line that sets the `searchResults` property on the new view controller to:

```
controller.search = search
```

This line still gives an error even after you've changed it but you'll fix that soon.

➤ Anywhere else in the code that says `isLoading` or `searchResults`, replace that with `search.isLoading` and `search.searchResults`.

The LandscapeViewController still has a property for a searchResults array so you have to change that to use the Search object as well.

> In **LandscapeViewController.swift**, remove the searchResults instance variable and replace it with:

```
var search: Search!
```

> In viewWillLayoutSubviews(), change the call to tileButtons() into:

```
tileButtons(search.searchResults)
```

OK, that's the first round of changes. Build the app to make sure there are no compiler errors.

The app itself doesn't do much anymore because you removed all the searching logic. So let's put that back in.

> In **Search.swift,** replace performSearchForText(category) with:

```
func performSearchForText(text: String, category: Int) {
  if !text.isEmpty {
    dataTask?.cancel()

    isLoading = true
    hasSearched = true
    searchResults = [SearchResult]()

    let url = urlWithSearchText(text, category: category)

    let session = NSURLSession.sharedSession()
    dataTask = session.dataTaskWithURL(url, completionHandler: { data, response, error in

      if let error = error {
        if error.code == -999 { return }  // Search was cancelled

      } else if let httpResponse = response as? NSHTTPURLResponse {
        if httpResponse.statusCode == 200 {
          if let dictionary = self.parseJSON(data) {
            self.searchResults = self.parseDictionary(dictionary)
            self.searchResults.sort(<)

            println("Success! ")
            self.isLoading = false
            return
          }
        }
      }

      println("Failure! \(response)")
      self.hasSearched = false
      self.isLoading = false
    })

    dataTask?.resume()
  }
}
```

This is basically the same thing you did before, except all the user interface logic has been removed. The purpose of Search is just to perform a search, it should not do any UI stuff. That's the job of the view controller.

➤ Run the app and search for something. When the search finishes, the debug pane shows a "Success!" message but the table view does not reload and the spinner keeps spinning in eternity.

The Search object currently has no way to tell the SearchViewController that it is done. You could solve this by making SearchViewController a delegate of the Search object, but for situations like these closures are much more convenient.

So let's create your own closure!

➤ Add the following line to **Search.swift**, above the class line:

```
typealias SearchComplete = (Bool) -> Void
```

The typealias statement allows you to create a more convenient name for a data type, in order to save some keystrokes and to make the code more readable.

Here you're declaring a type for your own closure, named SearchComplete. This is a closure that returns no value (it is Void) and takes one parameter, a Bool. If you think this syntax is weird, then I'm right there with you, but that's the way it is.

From now on you can use the name SearchComplete to refer to a closure that takes one Bool parameter and returns no value.

> **Note:** Whenever you see a -> in a type definition, the type is intended for a closure, function, or method.
>
> Swift treats these three things as mostly interchangeable; closures, functions, and methods are all blocks of source code that possibly take parameters and return a value. The difference is that a function is really just a closure with a name, and a method is a function that lives inside an object.
>
> Some examples of closure types:
>
> () -> () is a closure that takes no parameters and returns no value.
>
> Void -> Void is the same as the previous example. Void and () mean the same thing.
>
> (Int) -> Bool is a closure that takes one parameter, an Int, and returns a Bool.
>
> Int -> Bool is this is the same as above. If there is only one parameter, you can leave out the parentheses.
>
> (Int, String) -> Bool is a closure taking two parameters, an Int and a String, and returning a Bool.
>
> (Int, String) -> Bool? is as above but now returns an optional Bool value.
>
> (Int) -> (Int) -> Int is a closure that returns another closure that returns an Int. Freaky! Swift treats closures like any other type of object, so you can also pass them as parameters and return them from functions.

➤ Make the following changes to performSearchForText(category):

```
func performSearchForText(text: String, category: Int, completion: SearchComplete) {
  if !text.isEmpty {
    . . .

    dataTask = session.dataTaskWithURL(url, completionHandler: { data, response, error in
```

```
      var success = false

      if let error = error {
        . . .
      } else if let httpResponse = response as? NSHTTPURLResponse {
        if httpResponse.statusCode == 200 {
          if let dictionary = self.parseJSON(data) {
            . . .
            self.isLoading = false
            success = true
          }
        }
      }

      if !success {
        self.hasSearched = false
        self.isLoading = false
      }

      dispatch_async(dispatch_get_main_queue()) {
        completion(success)
      }
    })

    dataTask?.resume()
  }
}
```

You've added a third parameter named `completion` that is of type `SearchComplete`. Whoever calls `performSearchForText(category, completion)` can now supply their own closure, and the method will execute the code that is inside that closure when the search completes.

Instead of returning early from the closure upon success, you now set the `success` variable to `true` (this replaces the `return` statement). The value of `success` is used for the `Bool` parameter of the `completion` closure, as you can see inside the call to `dispatch_async()` at the bottom.

To perform the code from the closure, you simply call it as you'd call any function or method: `closureName(parameters)`. You call `completion(true)` upon success and `completion(false)` upon failure.

This is done so that the `SearchViewController` can reload its table view or, in the case of an error, show an alert view.

➤ In **SearchViewController.swift**, replace `performSearch()` with:

```
func performSearch() {
  search.performSearchForText(searchBar.text,
              category: segmentedControl.selectedSegmentIndex, completion: { success in
    if !success {
      self.showNetworkError()
    }

    self.tableView.reloadData()
  })

  tableView.reloadData()
  searchBar.resignFirstResponder()
}
```

You now pass a closure to `performSearchForText(category, completion)`. The code in this closure gets called after the search completes, with the `success` parameter being either `true` or `false`. A lot simpler than making a delegate, no? The closure is always called on the main thread, so it's safe to use UI code here.

➤ Run the app. You should be able to search again.

That's the first part of this refactoring complete. You've extracted the relevant code for searching out of the SearchViewController and placed it into its own object, Search. The view controller now only does view-related things, which is exactly what it is supposed to do and no more.

➤ You've made quite a few extensive changes, so it's a good idea to commit.

Improving the categories

The idea behind Swift's strong typing is that the data type of a variable should be as descriptive as possible. Right now the category to search for is represented by a number, 0 to 3, but is that the best way to describe a category to your program?

If you see the number 3 does that mean "e-book" to you? It could be anything… And what if you use 4 or 99 or -1, what would that mean? These are all valid values for an Int but not for a category. The only reason the category is currently an Int is because segmentedControl.selectedSegmentIndex is an Int.

There are only four possible search categories, so this sounds like an excellent job for an enum.

➤ Add the following to **Search.swift**, inside the class brackets:

```
enum Category: Int {
  case All = 0
  case Music = 1
  case Software = 2
  case EBook = 3
}
```

This creates a new enumeration type named Category with four possible items. Each of these has a numeric value associated with it, called the **raw** value.

Contrast this with the AnimationStyle enum you made before:

```
enum AnimationStyle {
  case Slide
  case Fade
}
```

This enum does not give numbers to its values (it also doesn't say ": Int" behind the enum name).

For AnimationStyle it doesn't matter that Slide is really number 0 and Fade is number 1, or whatever the values might be. All you care about is that a variable of type AnimationStyle can either be .Slide or .Fade; a numeric value is not important.

For the Category enum, however, you want to connect its four items to the four possible indices of the Segmented Control. If segment 3 is selected, you want this to correspond to .EBook. That's why the items from the Category enum do have numbers.

➤ Change the method signature of performSearchForText(category, completion) to use this new type:

```
func performSearchForText(text: String, category: Category, completion: SearchComplete) {
```

The category parameter is no longer an Int. It is not possible anymore to pass it the value 4 or 99 or -1. It must always be one of the values from the Category enum. This reduces a potential source of bugs and it has made the program more expressive. Whenever you have a limited list of possible values that can be turned into an enum, it's worth doing!

➤ Also change urlWithSearchText(category) because that also assumed category would be an Int:

```
private func urlWithSearchText(searchText: String, category: Category) -> NSURL {
  var entityName: String
  switch category {
  case .All: entityName = ""
  case .Music: entityName = "musicTrack"
  case .Software: entityName = "software"
  case .EBook: entityName = "ebook"
  }

  let escapedSearchText = . . .
```

The switch now looks at the various cases from the Category enum instead of the numbers 0 to 3.

This works, but to be honest I'm not entirely happy with it. I've said before that any logic that is related to an object should be an integral part of that object – in other words, an object should do as much as it can itself.

Converting the category into an "entity name" string that goes into the iTunes URL is a good example – that sounds like something the Category enum itself could do.

Swift enums can have their own methods and properties, so let's take advantage of that and improve the code even more.

➤ Add the entityName property to the Category enum:

```
enum Category: Int {
  case All = 0
  case Music = 1
  case Software = 2
  case EBook = 3

  var entityName: String {
    switch self {
    case .All: return ""
    case .Music: return "musicTrack"
    case .Software: return "software"
    case .EBook: return "ebook"
    }
  }
}
```

Swift enums cannot have instance variables, only computed properties. entityName has the exact same switch statement that you just saw, except that it switches on self, the current value of the enumeration object.

➤ In urlWithSearchText(category) you can now simply write:

```
private func urlWithSearchText(searchText: String, category: Category) -> NSURL {
  let entityName = category.entityName
  let escapedSearchText = . . .
```

That's a lot cleaner. Everything that has to do with categories now lives inside its own enum, Category.

You still need to tell SearchViewController about this, because it needs to convert the selected segment index into a proper Category value.

> In **SearchViewController.swift**, change the first part of performSearch() to:

```
func performSearch() {
  if let category = Search.Category(rawValue: segmentedControl.selectedSegmentIndex) {
    search.performSearchForText(searchBar.text, category: category, completion: {
      . . .
    })

    tableView.reloadData()
    searchBar.resignFirstResponder()
  }
}
```

To convert the Int value from selectedSegmentIndex to an item from the Category enum you use the built-in init(rawValue) method. This may fail, for example when you pass in a number that isn't covered by one of Category's cases, i.e. anything that is outside the range 0 to 3. That's why init(rawValue) returns an optional that needs to be unwrapped before you can use it.

> **Note:** Because you placed the Category enum inside the Search class, its full name is Search.Category. In other words, Category lives inside the Search *namespace*. It makes sense to bundle up these two things because they are so closely related.

> Build and run to see if the different categories still work. Nice!

Enums with associated values

Enums are pretty useful to restrict something to a limited range of possibilities, like what you did with the search categories. But they are even more powerful than you might have expected, as you'll find out in this section...

Like all objects, the Search object has a certain amount of *state*. For Search this is determined by its isLoading, hasSearched, and searchResults variables.

These three variables describe four possible states:

State	hasSearched	isLoading	searchResults
No search has been performed yet (this is also the state after an error)	false	false	Empty array
The search is in progress	true	true	Empty array
No results were found	true	false	Empty array
There are search results	true	false	Contains at least one SearchResult object

The Search object is in only one of these states at a time, and when it changes from one state to another there is a corresponding change in the app's UI. For example, upon a change from "searching" to "have results", the app hides the activity spinner and loads the results into the table view.

The problem is that this state is scattered across three different variables. It's tricky to see what the current state is just by looking at these variables (you may have to refer to the above table).

You can do better than that by giving Search an explicit state variable. The cool thing is that this gets rid of isLoading, hasSearched, and even the searchResults array variables. Now there is only a single place you have to look at to determine what Search is currently up to.

➤ In **Search.swift,** remove the following instance variables:

```
var searchResults = [SearchResult]()
var hasSearched = false
var isLoading = false
```

➤ In their place, add the following enum (this goes inside the class again):

```
enum State {
  case NotSearchedYet
  case Loading
  case NoResults
  case Results([SearchResult])
}
```

This enumeration has a case for each of the four states listed above. It does not need raw values so the cases don't have numbers.

The .Results case is special: it has a so-called **associated value**, which is an array of SearchResult objects.

This array is only important when the search was successful. In all the other cases, there are no search results and the array was empty anyway (see the table).

By making it an associated value, you'll only have access to this array when Search is in the .Results state. In the other states, it simply does not exist.

Let's see how this works.

➤ First add a new instance variable:

```
private(set) var state: State = .NotSearchedYet
```

This keeps track of Search's current state. Its initial value is .NotSearchedYet —obviously no search has happened yet when the Search object is first constructed.

This variable is private, but only half. It's not unreasonable for other objects to want to ask Search what its current state is. In fact, the app won't work unless you allow this.

But you don't want those other objects to be able to *change* the value of state, only read it. With private(set) you tell Swift that reading is OK for other objects, but assigning new values to this variable may only happen inside the Search class.

➤ Change performSearchForText(category, completion) to use this new state variable:

```
func performSearchForText(text: String, category: Category, completion: SearchComplete) {
  if !text.isEmpty {
    dataTask?.cancel()
```

```
    state = .Loading

    let url = urlWithSearchText(text, category: category)
    let session = NSURLSession.sharedSession()
    dataTask = session.dataTaskWithURL(url, completionHandler: { data, response, error in
      self.state = .NotSearchedYet
      var success = false

      if let error = error {
        if error.code == -999 { return }  // Search was cancelled

      } else if let httpResponse = response as? NSHTTPURLResponse {
        if httpResponse.statusCode == 200 {
          if let dictionary = self.parseJSON(data) {
            var searchResults = self.parseDictionary(dictionary)
            if searchResults.isEmpty {
              self.state = .NoResults
            } else {
              searchResults.sort(<)
              self.state = .Results(searchResults)
            }
            success = true
          }
        }
      }
      dispatch_async(dispatch_get_main_queue()) {
        completion(success)
      }
    })
    dataTask?.resume()
  }
}
```

Instead of the old variables isLoading, hasSearched, and searchResults, this now only changes state.

There is a lot that can go wrong between performing the network request and parsing the JSON. By setting self.state to .NotSearchedYet at the start of the completion handler you assume the worst – always a good idea when doing network programming – unless there is evidence otherwise. (That is also why success is initially false.)

That evidence comes when the app was able to successfully parse the JSON and create an array of SearchResult objects. If the array is empty, state becomes .NoResults.

The interesting thing happens when the array is *not* empty. After sorting it like before, you do self.state = .Results(searchResults). This gives state the value .Results and also associates the array of SearchResult objects with it.

You no longer need a separate instance variable to keep track of the array; the array object is intrinsically attached to the value of state.

That completes the changes in **Search.swift**, but there are quite a few other places in the code that still try to use Search's old instance variables.

➤ In **SearchViewController.swift**, change tableView(numberOfRowsInSection) to:

```
func tableView(tableView: UITableView, numberOfRowsInSection section: Int) -> Int {
  switch search.state {
  case .NotSearchedYet:
    return 0
  case .Loading:
```

```
      return 1
  case .NoResults:
    return 1
  case .Results(let list):
    return list.count
  }
}
```

This is pretty straightforward. Instead of trying to make sense out of the separate isLoading, hasSearched, and searchResults variables, this simply looks at the value from state. The switch statement is ideal for situations like this.

The .Results case requires more explanation. Because .Results has an array of SearchResult objects associated with it, you can *bind* this array to a temporary variable, list, and then use that variable inside the case to read how many items are in the array. That's how you make use of the associated value.

This pattern, using a switch statement to look at state, is going to become very common in your code.

➤ Change tableView(cellForRowAtIndexPath) to the following:

```
func tableView(tableView: UITableView,
            cellForRowAtIndexPath indexPath: NSIndexPath) -> UITableViewCell {
  switch search.state {
  case .NotSearchedYet:
    fatalError("Should never get here")

  case .Loading:
    let cell = tableView.dequeueReusableCellWithIdentifier(
          TableViewCellIdentifiers.loadingCell, forIndexPath:indexPath) as! UITableViewCell

    let spinner = cell.viewWithTag(100) as! UIActivityIndicatorView
    spinner.startAnimating()
    return cell

  case .NoResults:
    return tableView.dequeueReusableCellWithIdentifier(
      TableViewCellIdentifiers.nothingFoundCell, forIndexPath: indexPath) as! UITableViewCell

  case .Results(let list):
    let cell = tableView.dequeueReusableCellWithIdentifier(
                    TableViewCellIdentifiers.searchResultCell, forIndexPath: indexPath)
                    as! SearchResultCell

    let searchResult = list[indexPath.row]
    cell.configureForSearchResult(searchResult)

    return cell
  }
}
```

The same thing happened here. The various if statements have been replaced by a switch.

Note that numberOfRowsInSection returns 0 for .NotSearchedYet and no cells will ever be asked for. But because a switch must always be exhaustive you also have to include a case for .NotSearchedYet in cellForRowAtIndexPath. Considering that it's a bug when the code gets there you can use the built-in fatalError() function to help catch such mistakes.

➤ Next up is tableView(willSelectRowAtIndexPath):

```
func tableView(tableView: UITableView,
                willSelectRowAtIndexPath indexPath: NSIndexPath) -> NSIndexPath? {
  switch search.state {
  case .NotSearchedYet, .Loading, .NoResults:
    return nil
  case .Results:
    return indexPath
  }
}
```

It's only possible to tap on rows when the state is .Results, so in all other cases this method returns nil. (You don't need to bind the results array because you're not using it for anything.)

> And finally, prepareForSegue(sender). Change it to:

```
override func prepareForSegue(segue: UIStoryboardSegue, sender: AnyObject?) {
  if segue.identifier == "ShowDetail" {
    switch search.state {
    case .Results(let list):
      let detailViewController = segue.destinationViewController as! DetailViewController
      let indexPath = sender as! NSIndexPath
      let searchResult = list[indexPath.row]
      detailViewController.searchResult = searchResult
    default:
      break
    }
  }
}
```

The one downside of using enums is that you must always use a switch statement to read the associated value. Here you only care about the .Results case but you must still include a default case to stop the compiler from complaining. Oh well, it's a small price to pay for such a cool feature.

There is one more change to make, in **LandscapeViewController.swift**.

> Change the if firstTime section in viewWillLayoutSubviews() to:

```
if firstTime {
  firstTime = false

  switch search.state {
  case .NotSearchedYet:
    break
  case .Loading:
    break
  case .NoResults:
    break
  case .Results(let list):
    tileButtons(list)
  }
}
```

This uses the same pattern as before. If the state is .Results, it binds the array of SearchResult objects to the temporary constant list and passes it along to tileButtons(). Soon you'll add additional code to the other cases.

> Build and run to see if the app still works. (It should!)

I think enums with associated values are one of the most exciting features of Swift. Here you used them to simplify the way the Search state is expressed. No doubt you'll find many other great uses for them in your own apps!

➤ This is a good time to commit your changes.

Spin me right round

If you flip to landscape while the search is still taking place, the app really ought to show an animated spinner to let the user know something is happening.

You're already checking in viewWillLayoutSubviews() what the state of the active Search object is, so that's an easy fix.

➤ In **LandscapeViewController.swift**, change viewWillLayoutSubviews() to:

```
override func viewWillLayoutSubviews() {
  . . .

  if firstTime {
    firstTime = false

    switch search.state {
    case .NotSearchedYet:
      break
    case .Loading:
      showSpinner()
    case .NoResults:
      break
    case .Results(let list):
      tileButtons(list)
    }
  }
}
```

If the Search object is in the .Loading state, you need to show the activity spinner.

➤ Also add the new showSpinner() method:

```
private func showSpinner() {
  let spinner = UIActivityIndicatorView(activityIndicatorStyle: .WhiteLarge)
  spinner.center = CGPoint(x: CGRectGetMidX(scrollView.bounds) + 0.5,
                           y: CGRectGetMidY(scrollView.bounds) + 0.5)
  spinner.tag = 1000
  view.addSubview(spinner)
  spinner.startAnimating()
}
```

This programmatically creates a new UIActivityIndicatorView object (a big white one this time), puts it in the center of the screen, and starts animating it.

You give the spinner the tag 1000, so you can easily remove it from the screen once the search is done.

➤ Run the app. After starting a search, quickly flip the phone to landscape. You should now see a spinner:

A spinner indicates a search is still taking place

Note: You added `0.5` to the spinner's center position. This kind of spinner is 37 points wide and high, which is not an even number. If you were to place the center of this view at the exact center of the screen at (284, 160) then it would extend 18.5 points to either end. The top-left corner of that spinner is at coordinates (265.5, 141.5), making it look all blurry.

It's best to avoid placing objects at fractional coordinates. By adding 0.5 to both the X and Y position, the spinner is placed at (266, 142) and everything looks sharp. Pay attention to this when working with the `center` property and objects that have odd widths or heights.

This is all great, but the spinner doesn't disappear when the actual search results are received. The app never notifies the `LandscapeViewController` of this.

There is a variety of ways you can choose to tell the `LandscapeViewController` that the search results have come in, but let's keep it simple.

➤ In **LandscapeViewController.swift**, add these two new methods:

```
func searchResultsReceived() {
  hideSpinner()

  switch search.state {
  case .NotSearchedYet, .Loading, .NoResults:
    break
  case .Results(let list):
    tileButtons(list)
  }
}

private func hideSpinner() {
  view.viewWithTag(1000)?.removeFromSuperview()
}
```

The private `hideSpinner()` method looks for the view with tag 1000 – the activity spinner – and then tells that view to remove itself from the screen.

You could have kept a reference to the spinner in an instance variable but for a simple situation such as this you might as well use a tag.

Because no one else has any strong references to the `UIActivityIndicatorView`, this instance will be deallocated. Note that you have to use optional chaining because `viewWithTag()` can potentially return `nil`.

The `searchResultsReceived()` method should be called from somewhere, of course, and that somewhere is the `SearchViewController`.

➤ In **SearchViewController.swift**'s `performSearch()` method, add the following lines into the closure:

```
if let controller = self.landscapeViewController {
  controller.searchResultsReceived()
}
```

The sequence of events here is quite interesting. When the search begins there is no `LandscapeViewController` object yet because the only way to start a search is from portrait mode.

But by the time the closure is invoked, the device may have rotated and if that happened `self.landscapeViewController` will contain a valid reference.

Upon rotation you also gave the new `LandscapeViewController` a reference to the active `Search` object. Now you just have to tell it that search results are available so it can create the buttons and fill them up with images.

Of course, if you're still in portrait mode by the time the search completes then `self.landscapeViewController` is `nil` and the call to `searchResultsReceived()` will simply be ignored.

➤ Try it out. That works pretty well, eh?

Exercise. Verify that network errors are also handled correctly when the app is in landscape orientation. Find a way to create – or fake! – a network error and see what happens in landscape mode. Hint: the `sleep(5)` function will put your app to sleep for 5 seconds. Put that in the completion handler to give yourself some time to flip the device around. ∎

Speaking of spinners, you've probably noticed that your iPhone's status bar shows a small, animated spinner when network activity is taking place. This isn't automatic – the app needs to explicitly turn this animation on or off. Fortunately, it's only a single line of code.

➤ In **Search.swift**, first import UIKit (all the way at the top of the file):

```
import UIKit
```

➤ Add the following line to `performSearchForText(category, completion)`, just before starting the search:

```
func performSearchForText(text: String, category: Category, completion: SearchComplete) {
  if !text.isEmpty {
    dataTask?.cancel()

    UIApplication.sharedApplication().networkActivityIndicatorVisible = true
    . . .
```

This makes the animated spinner visible in the app's status bar. To turn it off again, change the code in `dispatch_async()` to the following:

```
dispatch_async(dispatch_get_main_queue()) {
  UIApplication.sharedApplication().networkActivityIndicatorVisible = false
  completion(success)
}
```

➤ Try it out. The app now also shows a spinning animation in the status bar while the search is taking place:

The network activity indicator

Nothing found

You're not done yet. If there are no matches found, you should also tell the user about this if they're in landscape mode.

➤ Change the switch-statement in viewWillLayoutSubviews() to the following:

```
switch search.state {
case .NotSearchedYet:
  break
case .Loading:
  showSpinner()
case .NoResults:
  showNothingFoundLabel()
case .Results(let list):
  tileButtons(list)
}
```

You've changed the .NoResults case: if there are no search results, you'll call the new showNothingFoundLabel() method.

➤ Here is that method:

```
private func showNothingFoundLabel() {
  let label = UILabel(frame: CGRect.zeroRect)
  label.text = "Nothing Found"
  label.backgroundColor = UIColor.clearColor()
  label.textColor = UIColor.whiteColor()

  label.sizeToFit()

  var rect = label.frame
  rect.size.width = ceil(rect.size.width/2) * 2    // make even
  rect.size.height = ceil(rect.size.height/2) * 2  // make even
  label.frame = rect

  label.center = CGPoint(x: CGRectGetMidX(scrollView.bounds),
                         y: CGRectGetMidY(scrollView.bounds))
  view.addSubview(label)
}
```

Here you first create a UILabel object and give it text and color. To make the label see-through the backgroundColor property is set to UIColor.clearColor().

The call to sizeToFit() tells the label to resize itself to the optimal size. You could have given the label a frame that was big enough to begin with, but I find this just as easy. (It also helps when you're translating the app to a different language, in which case you may not know beforehand how large the label needs to be.)

The only trouble is that you want to center the label in the view and as you saw before that gets tricky when the width or height are odd (something you don't necessarily know in advance). So here you use a little trick to always force the dimensions of the label to be even numbers:

```
width = ceil(width/2) * 2
```

If you divide a number such as 11 by 2 you get 5.5. The ceil() function rounds up 5.5 to make 6, and then you multiply by 2 to get a final value of 12. This formula always gives you the next even number if the original is odd. (You only need to do this because these values have type CGFloat. If they were integers, you wouldn't have to worry about fractional parts.)

> **Note:** Because you're not using a hardcoded number such as 480 or 568 but scrollView.bounds to determine the width of the screen, the code to center the label works correctly on all iPhone models.

➤ Run the app and search for something ridiculous (**ewdasuq3sadf843** will do). When the search is done, flip to landscape.

Yup, nothing found here either

It doesn't work properly yet when you flip to landscape while the search is taking place. Of course you also need to put some logic in searchResultsReceived().

➤ Change the switch-statement in that method to:

```
switch search.state {
case .NotSearchedYet, .Loading:
  break
case .NoResults:
  showNothingFoundLabel()
case .Results(let list):
  tileButtons(list)
}
```

Now you should have all your bases covered.

The Detail pop-up

These landscape search results are not buttons for nothing. The app should show the Detail pop-up when you tap them, like the following image:

The pop-up in landscape mode

This is fairly easy to achieve. When adding the buttons you can give them a **target-action**, i.e. a method to call when the Touch Up Inside event is received. Just like in Interface Builder, except now you hook up the event to the action method programmatically.

➤ Add the following two lines to the button creation code in `tileButtons()`:

```
button.tag = 2000 + index
button.addTarget(self, action: Selector("buttonPressed:"), forControlEvents: .TouchUpInside)
```

First you give the button a tag, so you know to which index in the `.Results` array this button corresponds. That's needed in order to pass the correct `SearchResult` object to the Detail pop-up.

Tip: You added 2000 to the index because tag 0 is used on all views by default so asking for a view with tag 0 might actually return a view that you didn't expect. To avoid this kind of confusion, you simply start counting from 2000.

You also tell the button it should call the new `buttonPressed()` method when it gets tapped. This method takes a parameter, so the selector name `buttonPressed:` ends with a colon.

➤ Add the `buttonPressed()` method:

```
func buttonPressed(sender: UIButton) {
  performSegueWithIdentifier("ShowDetail", sender: sender)
}
```

Even though this is an action method you didn't declare it as @`IBAction`. That is only necessary when you want to connect the method to something in Interface Builder. Here you made the connection programmatically, so you can skip the @`IBAction` annotation.

Pressing the button triggers a segue, which means you need a `prepareForSegue` to do all the work:

➤ Add the `prepareForSegue(sender)` method:

```
override func prepareForSegue(segue: UIStoryboardSegue, sender: AnyObject?) {
  if segue.identifier == "ShowDetail" {
    switch search.state {
    case .Results(let list):
      let detailViewController = segue.destinationViewController as! DetailViewController
      let searchResult = list[sender!.tag - 2000]
      detailViewController.searchResult = searchResult
    default:
      break
    }
  }
}
```

This is almost word-for-word identical to SearchViewController's prepareForSegue, except now you don't get the index of the SearchResult object from an index-path but from the button's tag (minus 2000).

Of course, none of this will work unless you actually make a segue in the storyboard first.

➤ Go to the Landscape View Controller in the storyboard and Ctrl-drag to the Detail View Controller.

Make it a **present modally** segue and give it the identifier **ShowDetail**.

The storyboard looks like this now:

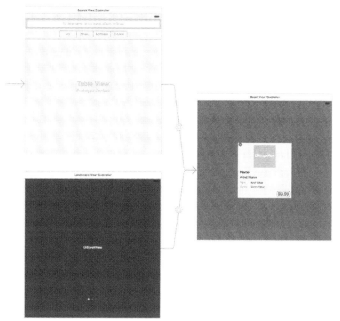

The storyboard after connecting the Landscape view to the Detail pop-up

➤ Run the app and check it out.

Cool. But what happens when you rotate back to portrait with a Detail pop-up showing? Unfortunately, it sticks around. You still need to tell the Detail screen to close.

➤ In **SearchViewController.swift**, in hideLandscapeViewWithCoordinator(), add the following lines to the animateAlongsideTransition animation closure:

```
if self.presentedViewController != nil {
  self.dismissViewControllerAnimated(true, completion: nil)
}
```

In the debug pane output you should see that the DetailViewController is properly deallocated when you rotate back to portrait.

➤ If you're happy with the way it works, then let's commit it. If you also made a branch, then merge it back into the master branch.

You can find the project files for the app under **08 - Refactored Search** in the tutorial's Source Code folder.

Internationalization

So far the apps you've made in this tutorial series have all been in English. No doubt the United States is the single biggest market for apps, followed closely by Asia. But even if you add up all the smaller countries where English isn't the primary language, you still end up with quite a sizable market that you might be missing out on.

Fortunately, iOS makes it very easy to add support for other languages to your apps, a process known as **internationalization**. This is often abbreviated as "i18n" because that's a lot shorter to write; the 18 stands for the number of letters between the i and the n. You'll also often hear the word **localization**, which basically means the same thing.

In this section you'll add support for Dutch, which is my native language. You'll also make the web service query return results that are optimized for the user's regional settings.

The structure of your source code folder probably looks something like this:

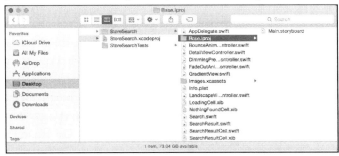

The files in the source code folder

There is a subfolder named **Base.lproj** that contains one file, **Main.storyboard**. The Base.lproj folder is for files that can be localized. So far that's only the storyboard but you'll add more files to this folder soon.

When you add support for another language, a new **XX.lproj** folder is created with XX being the two-letter code for that new language (**en** for English, **nl** for Dutch).

Let's begin by localizing a simple file, the **NothingFoundCell.xib**. Often nib files contain text that needs to be translated. You can simply make a new copy of the existing nib file for a specific language and put it in the right .lproj folder. When the iPhone is using that language, it will automatically load the translated nib.

> Select **NothingFoundCell.xib** in the Project navigator. Switch to the **File inspector** pane (on the right of the Xcode window).

Because the NothingFoundCell.xib file isn't in any XX.lproj folders, it does not have any localizations yet.

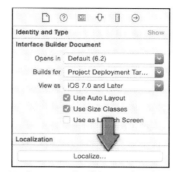

The NothingFoundCell has no localizations

➤ Click the **Localize…** button in the Localization section.

Xcode asks for confirmation because this involves moving the file to a new folder:

Xcode asks whether it's OK to move the file

➤ Choose **English** (not Base) and click **Localize** to continue.

Look in Finder and you will see there is a new **en.lproj** folder (for English) and NothingFoundCell.xib has moved into that folder:

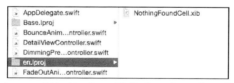

Xcode moved NothingFoundCell.xib to the en.lproj folder

Select **NothingFoundCell.xib** again in the Project navigator and you'll see that the **File inspector** now lists English as one of the localizations.

The Localization section now contains an entry for English

To add a new language you have to switch to the **Project Settings** screen.

➤ Click on **StoreSearch** at the top of the Project navigator to open the settings page.

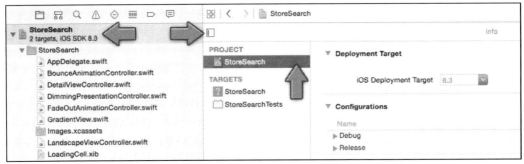

The Project Settings

> From the sidebar, choose StoreSearch under **PROJECT** (not under TARGETS). If the sidebar isn't visible click the small icon at the top to open it.

> In the **Info** tab, under the **Localizations** section press the + button:

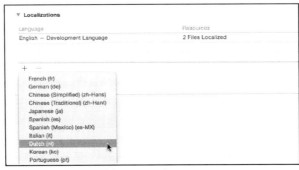

Adding a new language

> From the pop-up menu choose **Dutch (nl)**.

Xcode now asks which resources you want to localize. Uncheck everything except for **NothingFoundCell.xib** and click **Finish**.

Choosing the files to localize

If you look in Finder again you'll notice that a new subfolder has been added, **nl.lproj,** and that it contains another copy of NothingFoundCell.xib.

That means there are now two nib files for `NothingFoundCell`. You can also see this in the Project navigator:

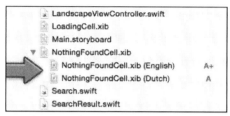

NothingFoundCell.xib has two localizations

Let's edit the new Dutch version of this nib.

➤ Click on **NothingFoundCell.xib (Dutch)** to open it in Interface Builder.

➤ Change the label text to **Niets gevonden** and center the label again in the view (if necessary, use the Resolve Auto Layout Issues menu).

That's how you say it in Dutch

It is perfectly all right to resize or move around items in a translated nib. You could make the whole nib look completely different if you wanted to (but that's probably a bad idea). Some languages, such as German, have very long words and in those cases you may have to tweak label sizes and fonts to get everything to fit.

If you run the app now, nothing will have changed. You have to switch the Simulator to use the Dutch language first. However, before you do that you really should remove the app from the simulator, clean the project, and do a fresh build.

The reason for this is that the nibs were previously not localized. If you were to switch the simulator's language now, the app would still keep using the old, non-localized versions of the nibs.

Note: For this reason it's a good idea to already put all your nib files and storyboards in the **en.lproj** folder when you create them (or in **Base.lproj**, which we'll discuss shortly), even if you don't intend to internationalize your app any time soon, just so users won't run into the same problem. You don't want to ask your users to uninstall the app – and lose their data – in order to be able to switch languages.

➤ Remove the app from the Simulator. Do a clean (**Product → Clean** or **Shift-⌘-K**) and re-build the app.

➤ Open the **Settings** app in the Simulator and go to **General → Language & Region → iPhone Language**. From the list pick **Nederlands (Dutch)**.

Switching languages in the Simulator

The Simulator will take a moment to switch between languages. This terminates the app if it was still running.

➤ Search for some nonsense text and the app will now respond in Dutch:

I'd be surprised if that did turn up a match

Pretty cool. Just by placing some files in the **en.lproj** and **nl.lproj** folders, you have internationalized the app. You're going to keep the Simulator in Dutch for a while because the other nibs need translating too.

> **Note:** If the app crashes for you at this point, then the following might help. Quit Xcode. Reset the Simulator and then quit it. In Finder go to your **Library** folder, **Developer**, **Xcode** and throw away the entire **DerivedData** folder. Empty your trashcan. Then open the StoreSearch project again and give it another try. (Don't forget to switch the Simulator back to **Nederlands**.)

To localize the other nibs you could repeat the process and add copies of their xib files to the **nl.lproj** folder. That isn't too bad for this app but if you have an app with really complicated screens then having multiple copies of the same nib can become a maintenance nightmare.

Whenever you need to change something to that screen you need to update all of the nibs. There's a risk that you forget one nib and they go out-of-sync. That's just asking for bugs – in languages that you probably don't speak!

To prevent this from happening you can use **base internationalization**. With this feature enabled you don't copy the entire nib, but only the text strings. This is what the **Base.lproj** folder is for.

Let's translate the other nibs.

➤ Open **LoadingCell.xib** in Interface Builder. In the **File inspector** press the **Localize...** button. This time use **Base** as the language:

Choosing the Base localization as the destination

Verify with Finder that LoadingCell.xib got moved into the **Base.lproj** folder.

➤ Select **LoadingCell.xib** again in the Project navigator. The Localization section in the **File inspector** now contains three options: Base (with a checkmark), English, and Dutch. Put a checkmark in front of **Dutch**:

Adding a Dutch localization

In Finder you can see that **nl.proj** doesn't get a copy of the nib, but a new type of file: **LoadingCell.strings**.

➤ Click the arrow in front of **LoadingCell.xib** to expand it in the Project navigator and open the **LoadingCell.strings (Dutch)** file.

You should see something like the following:

The Dutch localization is a strings file

There is still only one nib, the one from the Base localization. The Dutch translation consists of a "strings" file with just the texts from the labels, buttons, and other controls.

The contents of this particular strings file are:

```
/* Class = "IBUILabel"; text = "Loading..."; ObjectID = "6T7-DE-Wuc"; */
"6T7-DE-Wuc.text" = "Loading...";
```

The green bit is a comment, just like in Swift. The second line says that the **text** property of the object with ID "6T7-DE-Wuc" contains the text **Loading…**

That ID is an internal identifier that Xcode uses to keep track of the objects in your nibs; your own nib probably has a different code than mine.

➤ Change the text **Loading…** into **Zoeken…**

Tip: You can use the Assistant editor in Interface Builder to get a preview of your localized nib. Go to **LoadingCell.xib (Base)** and open the Assistant editor. From the Jump bar, choose **Preview**. In the bottom-right corner it says English. Click this to switch to a Dutch preview.

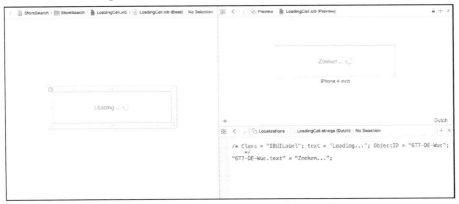

The Assistant editor shows a preview of the translation

If you open a second assistant pane (with the +) and set that to **Localizations**, you can edit the translations and see what they look like at the same time. Very handy!

➤ Do a **Product → Clean** and run the app again.

The localized loading text

> **Note:** If you don't see the "Zoeken…" text then do the same dance again: quit Xcode, throw away the DerivedData folder, reset the Simulator.

➤ Repeat the steps to add a Dutch localization for **Main.storyboard**. It already has a Base localization so you simply have to put a check in front of **Dutch** in the File inspector.

For the Search View Controller screen two things need to change: the placeholder text in the Search Bar and the labels on the Segmented Control.

➤ In **Main.strings (Dutch)** change the placeholder text to **Naam van artiest, nummer, album**.

```
"2gB-Cc-lwJ.placeholder" = "Naam van artiest, album";
```

The segment labels will become: **Alles, Muziek, Software**, and **E-boeken**.

```
"mRd-gb-Otl.segmentTitles[0]" = "Alles";
"mRd-gb-Otl.segmentTitles[1]" = "Muziek";
"mRd-gb-Otl.segmentTitles[2]" = "Software";
"mRd-gb-Otl.segmentTitles[3]" = "E-boeken";
```

(Of course your object IDs will be different.)

The localized SearchViewController

➤ For the Detail pop-up you only need to change the **Type:** label to say **Soort:**

```
"hCI-ga-T99.text" = "Soort:";
```

You don't need to change these:

```
"Mn8-GZ-kAm.text" = "Genre:";
"Wga-hk-bp5.text" = "Kind Value";
"reI-1b-hMI.text" = "Artist Name";
"xVY-g8-jS4.text" = "Name";
"KV2-4b-M2g.text" = "Genre Value";
"x97-RR-LLC.normalTitle" = "$9.99";
```

These labels can remain the same because you will replace them with values from the SearchResult object anyway. ("Genre" is the same in both languages.)

> **Note:** If you wanted to, you could even remove the texts that don't need localization from the strings file. If a localized version for a specific resource is missing for the user's language, iOS will fall back to the one from the Base localization.

The app in Dutch

Thanks to Auto Layout, the labels automatically resize to fit the translated text. A common issue with localization is that English words tend to be shorter than words in many other languages so you have to make sure your labels are big enough. With Auto Layout that is a piece of cake.

The Landscape View Controller doesn't have any text to translate.

➤ There is no need to give **SearchResultCell.xib** a Dutch localization (there is no on-screen text in the nib itself) but do give it a Base localization. This prepares the app for the future, should you need to localize this nib at some point.

When you're done there should be no more **xib** files outside the **.lproj** folders.

That's it for the nibs and the storyboard. Not so bad, was it? I'd say all these changes are commit-worthy.

> **Tip:** You can also test localizations by changing the settings for the active scheme. Click on **StoreSearch** in the Xcode toolbar (next to the Simulator name) and choose **Edit Scheme**.
>
> In the **Options** tab you can change the **Application Language** and **Region** settings. That's a lot quicker than restarting the Simulator.

Localizing on-screen texts

Even though the nibs and storyboard have been translated, not all of the text is. For example, in the image above the text from the `kind` property is still "Song".

While in this case you could get away with it – probably everyone in the world knows what the word "Song" means – not all of the texts from the `kindForDisplay()` method will be understood by non-English speaking users.

To localize texts that are not in a nib or storyboard, you have to use another approach.

➤ In **SearchResult.swift**, replace the `kindForDisplay()` method with:

```swift
func kindForDisplay() -> String {
  switch kind {
  case "album":
    return NSLocalizedString("Album", comment: "Localized kind: Album")
  case "audiobook":
    return NSLocalizedString("Audio Book", comment: "Localized kind: Audio Book")
  case "book":
    return NSLocalizedString("Book", comment: "Localized kind: Book")
  case "ebook":
    return NSLocalizedString("E-Book", comment: "Localized kind: E-Book")
  case "feature-movie":
    return NSLocalizedString("Movie", comment: "Localized kind: Feature Movie")
  case "music-video":
    return NSLocalizedString("Music Video", comment: "Localized kind: Music Video")
  case "podcast":
    return NSLocalizedString("Podcast", comment: "Localized kind: Podcast")
  case "software":
    return NSLocalizedString("App", comment: "Localized kind: Software")
  case "song":
    return NSLocalizedString("Song", comment: "Localized kind: Song")
  case "tv-episode":
    return NSLocalizedString("TV Episode", comment: "Localized kind: TV Episode")
  default:
    return kind
  }
}
```

Tip: Rather than typing in the above you can use Xcode's powerful Regular Expression Replace feature to make those changes in just a few seconds.

Go to the **Search inspector** and change its mode from Find to **Replace > Regular Expression**.

In the search box type:
   return "(.+)"

In the replacement box type:
   return NSLocalizedString("$1", comment: "Localized kind: $1")

Press **enter** to search. This looks for any lines that match the pattern *return "something"*. Whatever that *something* is will be put in the $1 placeholder of the replacement text.

Click **Preview**. Make sure only **SearchResult.swift** is selected – you don't want to make this change in any of the other files! Click **Replace** to finish.

Thanks to Scott Gardner for the tip!

The structure of `kindForDisplay()` is still the same as before, but instead of doing,

```
return "Album"
```

it now does:

```
return NSLocalizedString("Album", comment: "Localized kind: Album")
```

Slightly more complicated but also a lot more flexible.

`NSLocalizedString()` takes two parameters: the text to return, `"Album"`, and a comment, `"Localized kind: Album"`.

Here is the cool thing: if your app includes a file named **Localizable.strings** for the user's language, then `NSLocalizedString()` will look up the text (`"Album"`) and returns the translation as specified in Localizable.strings.

If no translation for that text is present, or there is no Localizable.strings file, then `NSLocalizedString()` simply returns the text as-is.

➤ Run the app again. The "Type:" field in the pop-up (or "Soort:" in Dutch) should still show the same kind of texts as before because you haven't translated anything yet.

To create the **Localizable.strings** file, you will use a command line tool named **genstrings**. This requires a trip to the Terminal.

➤ Open a Terminal, `cd` to the folder that contains the StoreSearch project. You want to go into the folder that contains the actual source files. On my system that is:

```
cd ~/Desktop/StoreSearch/StoreSearch
```

Then type the following command:

```
genstrings *.swift -o en.lproj
```

This looks at all your source files (***.swift**) and writes a new file called **Localizable.strings** in the **en.lproj** folder.

➤ Add this **Localizable.strings** file to the project in Xcode. I like to put it under the **Supporting Files** group. (To be safe, disable **Copy items if needed**. You want to add the file from en.lproj, not make a copy.)

If you open the Localizable.strings file, this is what it currently contains:

```
/* Localized kind: Album */
"Album" = "Album";

/* Localized kind: Software */
"App" = "App";

/* Localized kind: Audio Book */
"Audio Book" = "Audio Book";

/* Localized kind: Book */
"Book" = "Book";

/* Localized kind: E-Book */
"E-Book" = "E-Book";
```

```
/* Localized kind: Feature Movie */
"Movie" = "Movie";

/* Localized kind: Music Video */
"Music Video" = "Music Video";

/* Localized kind: Podcast */
"Podcast" = "Podcast";

/* Localized kind: Song */
"Song" = "Song";

/* Localized kind: TV Episode */
"TV Episode" = "TV Episode";
```

The things between the /* and */ symbols are the comments you specified as the second parameter of NSLocalizedString(). They give the translator some context about where the string is supposed to be used in the app.

> **Tip:** It's a good idea to make these comments as detailed as you can. In the words of fellow tutorial author Scott Gardner:
>
> "The comment to the translator should be as detailed as necessary to not only state the words to be transcribed, but also the perspective, intention, gender frame of reference, etc. Many languages have different words based on these considerations. I translated an app into Chinese Simplified once and it took multiple passes to get it right because my original comments were not detailed enough."

➤ Change the "Song" line to:

```
"Song" = "SUPER HIT!";
```

➤ Now run the app again and search for music. For any search result that is a song, it will now say "SUPER HIT!" instead.

Where it used to say Song it now says SUPER HIT!

Of course, changing the texts in the English localization doesn't make much sense, so put Song back to what it was and then we'll do it properly.

➤ In the **File inspector**, add a Dutch localization for this file. This creates a copy of Localizable.strings in the **nl.lproj** folder.

➤ Change the translations in the Dutch version of **Localizable.strings** to:

```
"Album" = "Album";
"App" = "App";
"Audio Book" = "Audioboek";
"Book" = "Boek";
"E-Book" = "E-Boek";
"Movie" = "Film";
"Music Video" = "Videoclip";
"Podcast" = "Podcast";
"Song" = "Liedje";
"TV Episode" = "TV serie";
```

If you run the app again, the product types will all be in Dutch. Nice!

Always use NSLocalizedString() from the beginning

There are a whole bunch of other strings in the app that need translation as well. You can search for anything that begins with " but it would have been a lot easier if you had used NSLocalizedString() from the start. Then all you had to do was run the **genstrings** tool and you'd get all the strings.

Now you have to comb through the source code and add NSLocalizedString() everywhere there is text that will be shown to the user.

You should really get into the habit of always using NSLocalizedString() for strings that you want to display to the user, even if you don't care about internationalization right away.

Adding support for other languages is a great way for your apps to become more popular, and going back through your code to add NSLocalizedString() is not much fun. It's better to do it right from the start!

Here are the other strings I found that need to be NSLocalizedString-ified:

```
// DetailViewController, updateUI()
artistNameLabel.text = "Unknown"
priceText = "Free"

// SearchResultCell, configureForSearchResult()
artistNameLabel.text = "Unknown"

// LandscapeViewController, showNothingFoundLabel()
label.text = "Nothing Found"

// SearchViewController, showNetworkError()
title: "Whoops...",
message: "There was an error reading from the iTunes Store. Please try again.",
title: "OK"
```

➤ Add NSLocalizedString() around these texts.

For example, when instantiating the UIAlertController in showNetworkError(), you could write:

```
let alert = UIAlertController(
  title: NSLocalizedString("Whoops...", comment: "Error alert: title"),
  message: NSLocalizedString("There was an error reading from the iTunes Store.
                      Please try again.", comment: "Error alert: message"),
  preferredStyle: .Alert)
```

Note: You don't need to use NSLocalizedString() with your println()'s. Debug output is really intended only for you, the developer, so it's best if it is in English (or your native language).

➤ Run the **genstrings** tool again. Give it the same arguments as before. It will put a clean file with all the new strings in the **en.lproj** folder.

Unfortunately, there really isn't a good way to make genstrings merge new strings into existing translations. It will overwrite your entire file and throw away any changes that you made. There is a way to make the tool append its output to an existing file but then you end up with a lot of duplicate strings.

> **Tip:** Always regenerate only the file in en.lproj and then copy over the missing strings to your other Localizable.strings files. You can use a tool such as FileMerge or Kaleidoscope to compare the two to see where the new strings are. There are also several third-party tools on the Mac App Store that are a bit friendlier to use than genstrings.

➤ Add these new translations to the Dutch **Localizable.strings**:

```
"Nothing Found" = "Niets gevonden";

"There was an error reading from the iTunes Store. Please try again." = "Er ging iets fout
bij het communiceren met de iTunes winkel. Probeer het nog eens.";

"Unknown" = "Onbekend";

"Whoops..." = "Foutje...";
```

It may seem a little odd that such as long string as "There was an error reading from the iTunes Store. Please try again." would be used as the lookup key for a translated string, but there really isn't anything wrong with it.

(By the way, the semicolons at the end of each line are not optional. If you forget a semicolon, the Localizable.strings file cannot be compiled and the build will fail.)

Some people write code like this:

```
let s = NSLocalizedString("ERROR_MESSAGE23", comment: "Error message on screen X")
```

The Localizable.strings file would then look like:

```
/* Error message on screen X */
"ERROR_MESSAGE23" = "Does not compute!";
```

This works but I find it harder to read. It requires that you always have an English Localizable.strings as well. In any case, you will see both styles used in practice.

Note also that the text "Unknown" occurred only once in Localizable.strings even though it shows up in two different places in the source code. Each piece of text only needs to be translated once.

If your app builds strings dynamically, then you can also localize these texts. For example in SearchResultCell, configureForSearchResult() you do:

```
artistNameLabel.text = String(format: "%@ (%@)", searchResult.artistName,
                              searchResult.kindForDisplay())
```

You could internationalize this as follows:

```
artistNameLabel.text = String(format: NSLocalizedString("%@ (%@)",
                        comment: "Format for artist name label"),
                        searchResult.artistName, searchResult.kindForDisplay())
```

This shows up in Localizable.strings as:

```
/* Format for artist name label */
"%@ (%@)" = "%1$@ (%2$@)";
```

If you wanted to, you could change the order of these parameters in the translated file. For example:

```
"%@ (%@)" = "%2$@ van %1$@";
```

It will turn the artist name label into something like this:

There are a lot of songs named Happy

In this circumstance I would advocate the use of a special key rather than the literal string to find the translation. It's thinkable that your app will employ the format string "%@ (%@)" in some other place and you may want to translate that completely differently there.

I'd call it something like "ARTIST_NAME_LABEL_FORMAT" instead (this goes in the Dutch Localizable.strings):

```
/* Format for artist name label */
"ARTIST_NAME_LABEL_FORMAT" = "%2$@ van %1$@";
```

You also need to add this key to the English version of Localizable.strings:

```
/* Format for artist name label */
"ARTIST_NAME_LABEL_FORMAT" = "%1$@ (%2$@)";
```

Don't forget to change the code as well:

```
artistNameLabel.text = String(format:
    NSLocalizedString("ARTIST_NAME_LABEL_FORMAT", comment: "Format for artist name label"),
    searchResult.artistName, searchResult.kindForDisplay())
```

There is one more thing I'd like to improve. Remember how in **SearchResult.swift** the kindForDisplay() method is this enormous switch statement? That's "smelly" to me. The problem is that any new products require you to add need another case to the switch.

For situations like these it's better to use a *data-driven* approach. Here that means you place the product types and their human-readable names in a data structure, a dictionary, rather than a code structure.

> Add the following dictionary to **SearchResult.swift**:

```
private let displayNamesForKind = [
   "album": NSLocalizedString("Album", comment: "Localized kind: Album"),
   "audiobook": NSLocalizedString("Audio Book", comment: "Localized kind: Audio Book"),
   "book": NSLocalizedString("Book", comment: "Localized kind: Book"),
   "ebook": NSLocalizedString("E-Book", comment: "Localized kind: E-Book"),
   "feature-movie": NSLocalizedString("Movie", comment: "Localized kind: Feature Movie"),
   "music-video": NSLocalizedString("Music Video", comment: "Localized kind: Music Video"),
   "podcast": NSLocalizedString("Podcast", comment: "Localized kind: Podcast"),
   "software": NSLocalizedString("App", comment: "Localized kind: Software"),
   "song": NSLocalizedString("Song", comment: "Localized kind: Song"),
   "tv-episode": NSLocalizedString("TV Episode", comment: "Localized kind: TV Episode"),
]
```

Now the code for `kindForDisplay()` becomes really short:

```
func kindForDisplay() -> String {
   return displayNamesForKind[kind] ?? kind
}
```

It's nothing more than a simply dictionary lookup.

The `??` is the **nil coalescing** operator. Remember that dictionary lookups always return an optional, just in case the key you're looking for – `kind` – does not exist in the dictionary. That could happen if the iTunes web service added new product types.

If the dictionary gives you `nil`, the `??` operator simply returns the original value of `kind`. It's equivalent to writing,

```
if let name = displayNamesForKind[kind] {
   return name
} else {
   return kind
}
```

but shorter!

InfoPlist.strings

The apps can also have a different name depending on the user's language. The name that is displayed on the iPhone's home screen comes from the **Bundle name** setting in **Info.plist** or if present, the **Bundle display name** setting.

To localize the texts from Info.plist you need a file named **InfoPlist.strings**. Previous versions of Xcode included this file in the project templates but as of Xcode 6 you have to make your own.

> Add a new file to the project. From the **Resource** group, choose **Strings File**. Name it **InfoPlist.strings** (the capitalization matters!).

Adding a new Strings file to the project

➤ Open **InfoPlist.strings** and press the **Localize...** button from the File inspector. Choose the **Base** localization.

➤ Also add a Dutch localization for this file.

➤ Open the Dutch version and add the following line:

```
CFBundleDisplayName = "StoreZoeker";
```

The key for the "Bundle display name" setting is CFBundleDisplayName.

(Dutch readers, sorry for the stupid name. This is the best I could come up with.)

➤ Run the app and close it so you can see its icon. The Simulator's stringboard should now show the translated app name:

Even the app's name is localized!

If you switch the Simulator back to English, the app name is StoreSearch again (and of course, all the other text is back in English as well).

Regional settings

I don't know if you noticed in some of the earlier screenshots, but even though you switched the language to Dutch, the prices of the products still show up in US dollars. That has two reasons:

1. The language settings are independent of the regional settings. How currencies and numbers are displayed depends on the region settings, not the language.

2. The app does not specify anything about country or language when it sends the requests to the iTunes store, so the web service always returns prices in US Dollars.

First you'll fix the app so that it sends information about the user's language and regional settings to the iTunes store. The method that you are going to change is **Search.swift**'s urlWithSearchText(category) because that's where you construct the parameters that get sent to the web service.

➤ Change the urlWithSearchText(category) method to the following:

```
private func urlWithSearchText(searchText: String, category: Category) -> NSURL {
  let entityName = category.entityName
  let locale = NSLocale.autoupdatingCurrentLocale()
  let language = locale.localeIdentifier
  let countryCode = locale.objectForKey(NSLocaleCountryCode) as! String

  let escapedSearchText = searchText.stringByAddingPercentEscapesUsingEncoding(
                                          NSUTF8StringEncoding)!

  let urlString = String(format:
          "http://itunes.apple.com/search?term=%@&limit=200&entity=%@&lang=%@&country=%@",
          escapedSearchText, entityName, language, countryCode)

  let url = NSURL(string: urlString)
  println("URL: \(url!)")
  return url!
}
```

The regional settings are also referred to as the user's **locale** and of course there is an object for it, NSLocale. You get a reference to the autoupdatingCurrentLocale.

This locale object is called "autoupdating" because it always reflects the current state of the user's locale settings. In other words, if the user changes her regional information while the app is running, the app will automatically use these new settings the next time it does something with that NSLocale object.

From the locale object you get the language and the country code. You then put these two values into the URL using the &lang= and &country= parameters.

The println() lets you see what exactly the URL will be.

➤ Run the app and do a search. Xcode should output the following:

```
http://itunes.apple.com/search?term=bird&limit=200&entity=&lang=en_US&country=US
```

It added "en_US" as the language identifier and just "US" as the country. For products that have descriptions (such as apps) the iTunes web service will return the English version of the description. The prices of all items will have USD as the currency.

➤ While keeping the app running, switch to the **Settings** app to change the regional settings. Go to **General** → **Language & Region** → **Region**. Select **Netherlands**.

If the Simulator is still in Dutch, then it is under **Algemeen** → **Taal en Regio** → **Regio**. Change it to **Nederland**.

➤ Switch back to StoreSearch and repeat the search.

Xcode now says:

```
http://itunes.apple.com/search?term=bird&limit=200&entity=&lang=nl_NL&country=NL
```

The language and country have both been changed to NL (for the Netherlands). If you tap on a search result you'll see that the price is now in Euros:

The price according to the user's region settings

Of course, you have to thank `NSNumberFormatter` for this. It now knows the region settings are from the Netherlands so it uses a comma for the decimal point.

And because the web service now returns `"EUR"` as the currency code, the number formatter puts the Euro symbol in front of the amount. You can get a lot of functionality for free if you know which classes to use!

That's it as far as internationalization goes. It will take only a small bit of effort that definitely pays back. (You can put the Simulator back to English now.)

➤ It's time to commit because you're going to make some big changes in the next section.

If you've also been tagging the code, you can call this v0.9, as you're rapidly approaching the 1.0 version that is ready for release.

The project files for the app up to this point are under **09 - Internationalization** in the tutorial's Source Code folder.

The iPad / Distributing the App

But wait, there is more! I promised that you'd learn how to make this app work on the iPad, and how to submit the app to the App Store. Unfortunately, we couldn't fit everything into a single printed volume, so these chapters are available as an additional download.

You can download the extra chapters for free here:

http://www.raywenderlich.com/store/ios-apprentice/bonus-chapters

Enjoy these extra 50 pages!

Credits for this tutorial: The shopping cart from the app icon is based on a design from the Noun Project (thenounproject.com).

Conclusion

Awesome, you've done it! You made it all the way through *The iOS Apprentice*. It's been a long journey but I hope you have learned a lot about iPhone and iPad programming, and software development in general. I had a lot of fun writing these tutorials and I hope you had a lot of fun reading them!

Because these tutorials are packed with tips and information you may want to go through them again in a few weeks, just to make sure you've picked up on everything!

The world of mobile apps now lies at your fingertips. There is a lot more to be learned about iOS and I encourage you to read the official documentation – it's pretty easy to follow once you understand the basics – and to play around with the myriad of APIs that the iOS SDK has to offer.

Most importantly, go write some apps of your own!

Want to learn more?

There are many great videos and books out there to learn more about iOS development. Here are some suggestions for you to start with:

- The iOS Developer Library. You can find this on the iOS Dev Center.
  https://developer.apple.com/devcenter/ios/

- iOS Technology Overview
  https://developer.apple.com/library/ios/documentation/Miscellaneous/Conceptual/iPhoneOS
  TechOverview/Introduction/Introduction.html

- Mobile Human Interface Guidelines (the "HIG"):
  https://developer.apple.com/library/ios/documentation/userexperience/conceptual/mobilehig/i
  ndex.html

- iOS App Programming Guide
  https://developer.apple.com/library/ios/documentation/iphone/conceptual/iphoneosprogramm
  ingguide/Introduction/Introduction.html

- View Controller Programming Guide for iOS
  https://developer.apple.com/library/ios/featuredarticles/ViewControllerPGforiPhoneOS/Introduction/Introduction.html

- The WWDC videos. WWDC is Apple's yearly developer conference and the videos of the presentations can be watched online at developer.apple.com/videos/. It's really worth it!

- Myself and the rest of the raywenderlich.com team also have several other books for sale, including more advanced tutorials on iOS development and books about game programming on iOS. If you'd like to check these out, visit our store here:
  http://www.raywenderlich.com/store

Stuck?

If you get stuck, ask for help. Sites such as Stack Overflow (stackoverflow.com) and iPhoneDevSDK (www.iphonedevsdk.com/forum/) are great, and let's not forget our own Ray Wenderlich forums (www.raywenderlich.com/forums).

I often go on Stack Overflow to figure out how to write some code. I usually more-or-less know what I need to do – for example, resize a UIImage – and I could spend a few hours figuring out how to do it on my own, but chances are someone else already wrote a blog post about it. Stack Overflow has tons of great tips on almost anything you can do with iOS development.

However, don't post questions like this:

> "i am having very small problem i just want to hide load more data option in tableview after finished loading problem is i am having 23 object in json and i am parsing 5 obj on each time at the end i just want to display three object without load more option."

This is an actual question that I copy-pasted from a forum. That guy isn't going to get any help because a) his question is unreadable; b) he isn't really making it easy for others to help him.

Here are some pointers on how to ask effective questions:

- Getting Answers http://www.mikeash.com/getting_answers.html

- What Have You Tried? http://mattgemmell.com/what-have-you-tried/

- How to Ask Questions the Smart Way http://www.catb.org/~esr/faqs/smart-questions.html

And that's a wrap!

Again, I hope you learned a lot through the *iOS Apprentice*, and that you take what you've learned and go forth and make some great apps of your own.

Above all, *have fun programming*, and let me know about your creations!

— Matthijs Hollemans

Made in the USA
Charleston, SC
20 May 2015